HARCOURT HORIZONS

HARCOURT HORIZONS

The Pledge of Allegiance

I pledge allegiance to the Flag

of the United States of America,

and to the Republic

for which it stands,

one Nation under God, indivisible,

with liberty and justice for all.

HARCOURT HORIZONS

The World

Harcourt

Orlando   Austin   Chicago   New York   Toronto   London   San Diego

Visit *The Learning Site!*
www.harcourtschool.com

HARCOURT HORIZONS 2003 Edition Copyright © Harcourt, Inc.

All rights reserved. No part of this publication may be reproduced or transmitted in any form or by any means, electronic or mechanical, including photocopy, recording, or any information storage and retrieval system, without permission in writing from the publisher.

Requests for permission to make copies of any part of the work should be addressed to School Permissions and Copyrights, Harcourt, Inc., 6277 Sea Harbor Drive, Orlando, Florida 32887-6777. Fax: 407-345-2418.

HARCOURT and the Harcourt Logo are trademarks of Harcourt, Inc., registered in the United States of America and/or other jurisdictions.

Printed in the United States of America

ISBN 0-15-335786-X

4 5 6 7 8 9 10 048 10 09 08 07 06 05 04

Contents

25,000-year-old sculpture

Hammurabi

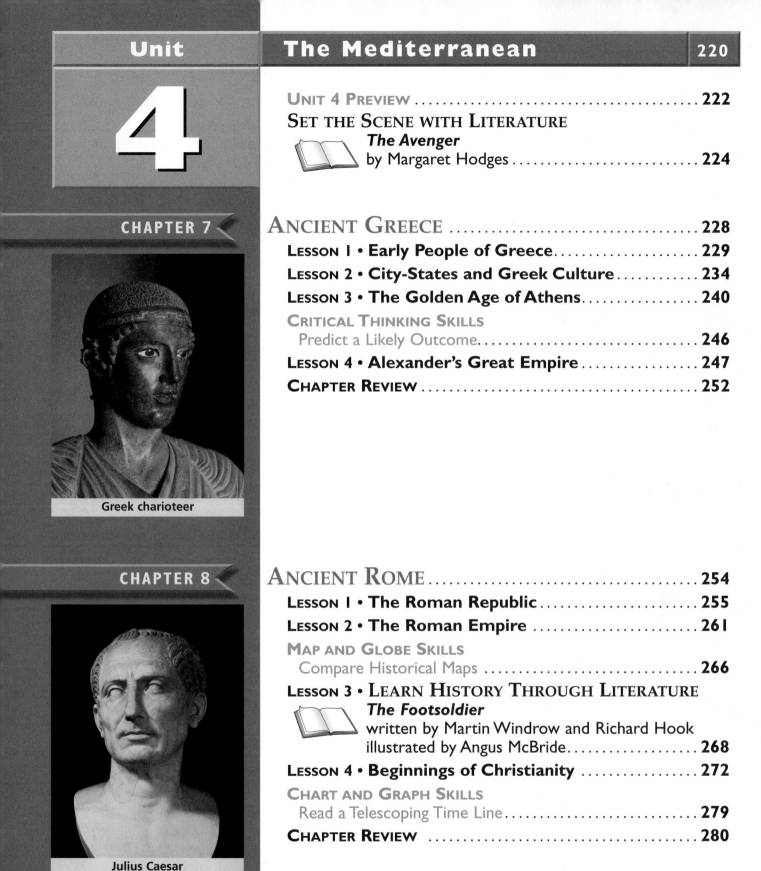

Ming dynasty empress

José de San Martín

Faces of the Great Depression

United States marine in Vietnam

10

Woman from Peru

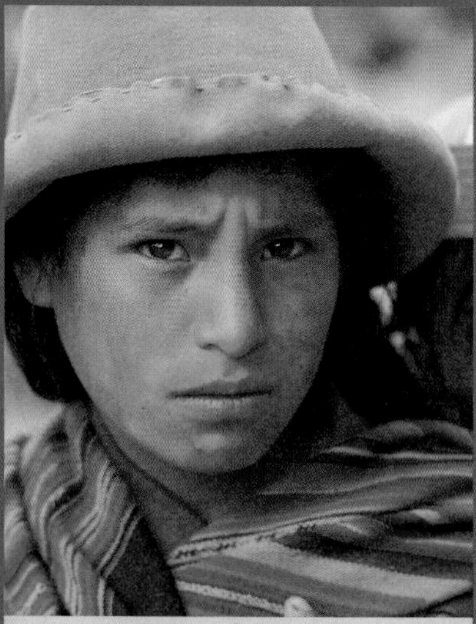

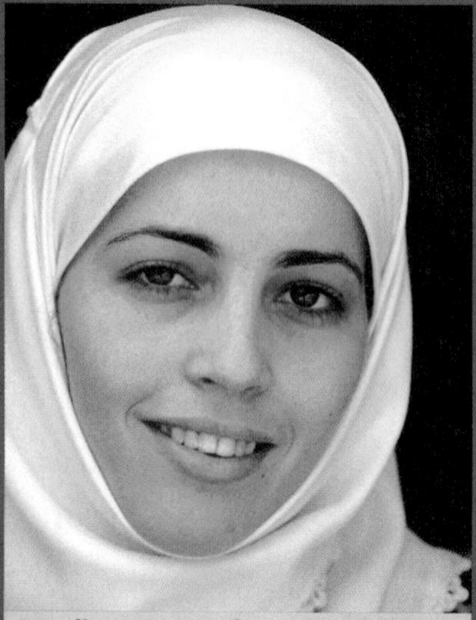

Muslim woman from North Africa

Young girl from Senegal

CHAPTER 23

For Your Reference | R1

Library of Congress, Washington, D.C.

F.Y.I.

xvi

Building Citizenship

Features

Maps

F.Y.I.

Time Lines

Charts, Graphs, Diagrams, and Tables

F.Y.I.

Atlas

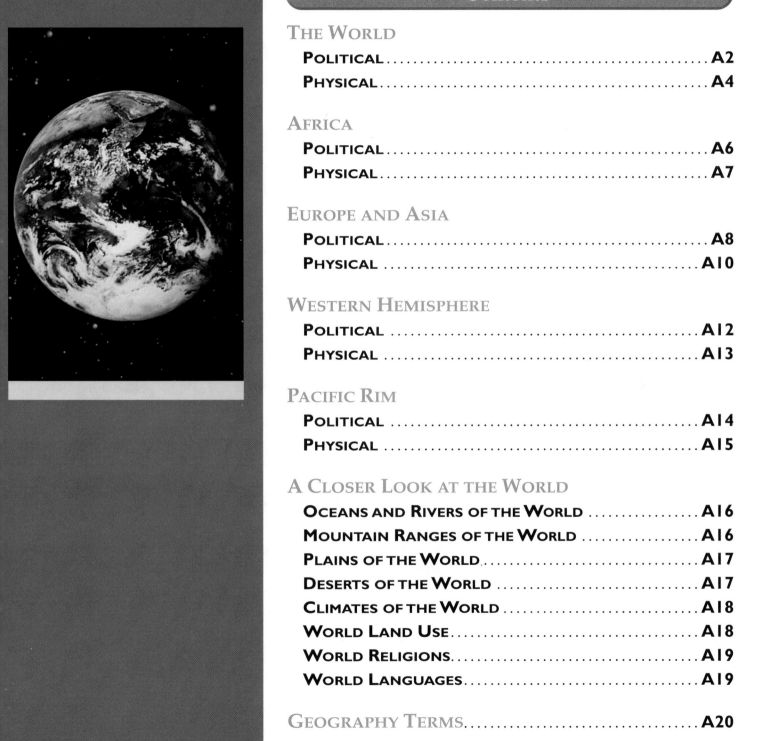

Contents

Atlas

The World: Political

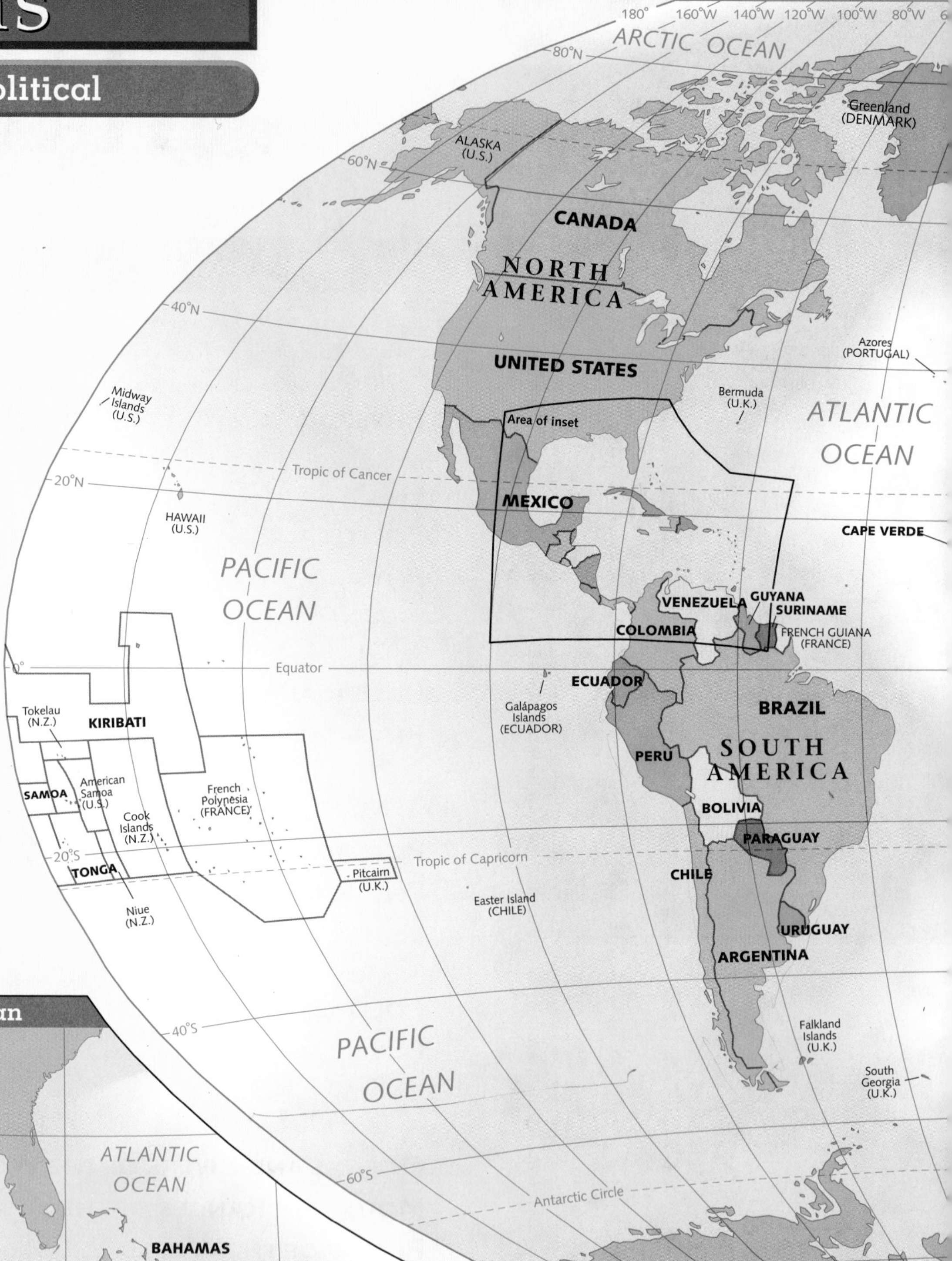

ARCTIC OCEAN

80°N

ALASKA (U.S.)

60°N

Greenland (DENMARK)

CANADA

NORTH AMERICA

40°N

UNITED STATES

Azores (PORTUGAL)

ATLANTIC OCEAN

Midway Islands (U.S.)

20°N — Tropic of Cancer

Bermuda (U.K.)

Area of inset

MEXICO

HAWAII (U.S.)

CAPE VERDE

PACIFIC OCEAN

VENEZUELA GUYANA SURINAME

COLOMBIA FRENCH GUIANA (FRANCE)

Galápagos Islands (ECUADOR)

ECUADOR

— Equator

Tokelau (N.Z.)

KIRIBATI

PERU

BRAZIL

SOUTH AMERICA

SAMOA

American Samoa (U.S.)

French Polynesia (FRANCE)

BOLIVIA

PARAGUAY

Cook Islands (N.Z.)

20°S

TONGA

Pitcairn (U.K.)

Tropic of Capricorn

CHILE

Niue (N.Z.)

Easter Island (CHILE)

URUGUAY

ARGENTINA

40°S

PACIFIC OCEAN

Falkland Islands (U.K.)

South Georgia (U.K.)

ATLANTIC OCEAN

60°S

Antarctic Circle

80°S

180° 160°W 140°W 120°W 100°W 80°W

Central America and the Caribbean

30°N

Gulf of Mexico

N W E S

ATLANTIC OCEAN

100°W

20°N

BAHAMAS

Tropic of Cancer

Turks and Caicos (U.K.)

CUBA

HAITI **DOMINICAN REPUBLIC**

Puerto Rico (U.S.)

Anguilla (U.K.)

St. Martin (FRANCE AND NETH.)

Cayman Islands (U.K.)

JAMAICA

Virgin Islands (U.S. AND U.K.)

ANTIGUA AND BARBUDA

Montserrat (U.K.)

Guadeloupe (FRANCE)

ST. KITTS AND NEVIS

DOMINICA

Martinique (FRANCE)

BELIZE

Caribbean Sea

ST. LUCIA

BARBADOS

GUATEMALA HONDURAS

EL SALVADOR NICARAGUA

Aruba (NETH.)

Netherlands Antilles (NETH.)

ST. VINCENT AND THE GRENADINES

GRENADA

TRINIDAD AND TOBAGO

PACIFIC OCEAN

10°N

A2

Panama Canal

0   200   400 Miles

0   200   400 Kilometers

Azimuthal Equal-Area Projection

COSTA RICA

PANAMA

90°W 80°W 70°W 60°W

	National border

ARCTIC OCEAN

80°N

Arctic Circle

60°N

ICELAND   Area of inset

RUSSIA

ASIA

EUROPE

KAZAKHSTAN   MONGOLIA

40°N

UZBEKISTAN   KYRGYZSTAN   NORTH
GEORGIA   KOREA   JAPAN
ARMENIA AZERBAIJAN   SOUTH
TURKEY   TURKMENISTAN TAJIKISTAN   CHINA   KOREA
CYPRUS SYRIA   PACIFIC
LEBANON IRAQ   IRAN AFGHANISTAN   OCEAN
ISRAEL JORDAN   PAKISTAN NEPAL BHUTAN
Canary Is. MOROCCO   KUWAIT   TAIWAN
(SPAIN) TUNISIA   BAHRAIN QATAR   20°N
ALGERIA   LIBYA   EGYPT   SAUDI U.A.E.   BANGLADESH   Northern
WESTERN   ARABIA   BURMA LAOS   Mariana Islands
SAHARA   OMAN   INDIA   (MYANMAR)   (U.S.)
(MOROCCO)   Guam (U.S.)   MARSHALL
MAURITANIA MALI NIGER CHAD SUDAN ERITREA YEMEN   THAILAND VIETNAM PHILIPPINES   ISLANDS
SENEGAL   DJIBOUTI   CAMBODIA
BURKINA   FEDERATED
GUINEA FASO   NIGERIA CENTRAL   ETHIOPIA   BRUNEI   STATES OF
SIERRA CÔTE BENIN   AFRICAN REPUBLIC   SRI   PALAU   MICRONESIA
LEONE D'IVOIRE EQU. CAMEROON   SOMALIA MALDIVES LANKA   MALAYSIA   0°
LIBERIA   GUINEA   UGANDA   SINGAPORE   NAURU
GUINEA- GHANA   RWANDA KENYA   INDONESIA   PAPUA KIRIBATI
BISSAU   TOGO GABON REP.   BURUNDI   SEYCHELLES   INDIAN   NEW GUINEA TUVALU
THE   SÃO TOMÉ CONGO DEM. REP.   SOLOMON
GAMBIA   AND PRÍNCIPE   CONGO TANZANIA   OCEAN   ISLANDS
CABINDA   COMOROS   VANUATU   FIJI
(ANGOLA)   ANGOLA MALAWI   20°S
NAMIBIA ZAMBIA MOZAMBIQUE MADAGASCAR   MAURITIUS   New
ZIMBABWE   Reunion   AUSTRALIA   Caledonia
BOTSWANA   (FRANCE)   (FRANCE)
ATLANTIC   SWAZILAND
OCEAN   SOUTH LESOTHO
AFRICA

N
W   E
S

1,000   2,000 Miles
0
1,000   2,000 Kilometers
Scale accurate at equator
Winkle Projection

Kerguelen
Islands
(FRANCE)

NEW
ZEALAND   40°S

60°S

80°S

ANTARCTICA

60°W 40°W 20°W 0° 20°E 40°E 60°E 80°E 100°E 120°E 140°E 160°E 180°

Abbreviations

DEM. REP. CONGO	DEMOCRATIC REPUBLIC OF THE CONGO
EQU. GUINEA	EQUATORIAL GUINEA
NETH.	NETHERLANDS
N.Z.	NEW ZEALAND
REP. CONGO	REPUBLIC OF THE CONGO
U.A.E.	UNITED ARAB EMIRATES
U.K.	UNITED KINGDOM
U.S.	UNITED STATES

Europe

Arctic Circle

FINLAND

NORWAY

ESTONIA

SWEDEN   LATVIA   RUSSIA

60°N

North   LITHUANIA
Sea   DENMARK   KALININGRAD
UNITED   (RUSSIA)
KINGDOM   BELARUS

IRELAND   NETHERLANDS   POLAND
BELGIUM GERMANY   UKRAINE
ATLANTIC   50°N
OCEAN   LUXEMBOURG   CZECH
REPUBLIC   SLOVAKIA MOLDOVA
LIECHTENSTEIN   AUSTRIA HUNGARY ROMANIA
SWITZERLAND SLOVENIA
FRANCE   CROATIA
SAN   BOSNIA AND YUGOSLAVIA BULGARIA
MARINO   HERZEGOVINA   MACEDONIA
ANDORRA MONACO   ITALY   ALBANIA   TURKEY
(FRANCE)   40°N
Corsica VATICAN
(FRANCE) CITY   GREECE
PORTUGAL   Balearic Islands Sardinia
SPAIN   (SPAIN)   (ITALY)
Mediterranean Sea Sicily   Crete
GIBRALTAR (ITALY)   MALTA   (GREECE)
10°W 0°   10°E   20°E

N
W   E
S

200   400 Miles
0
200 400 Kilometers
Azimuthal Equal-Area Projection

Atlas

The World: Physical

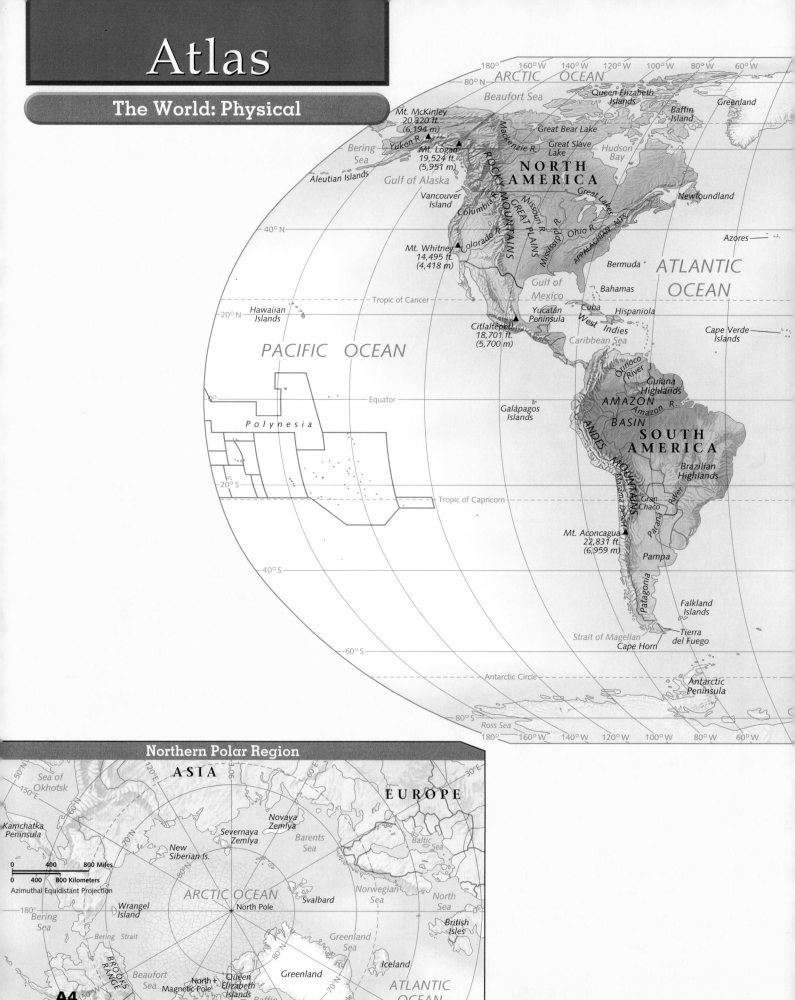

180° **160° W** **140° W** **120° W** **100° W** **80° W** **60° W**

80° N

ARCTIC OCEAN

Beaufort Sea

Queen Elizabeth Islands

Greenland

Baffin Island

Great Bear Lake

Mt. McKinley
20,320 ft.
(6,194 m)

Bering Sea

Yukon R.

Mackenzie R.

Great Slave Lake

Hudson Bay

Mt. Logan
19,524 ft.
(5,951 m)

ROCKY MOUNTAINS

NORTH AMERICA

Aleutian Islands

Gulf of Alaska

40° N

Vancouver Island

Columbia R.

GREAT PLAINS

Missouri R.

Great Lakes

Newfoundland

Mt. Whitney
14,495 ft.
(4,418 m)

Colorado R.

Mississippi R.

Ohio R.

APPALACHIAN MTS.

Azores

Bermuda

ATLANTIC OCEAN

Tropic of Cancer

Gulf of Mexico

Bahamas

Cuba

Hispaniola

Hawaiian Islands

20° N

Citlaltépetl
18,701 ft.
(5,700 m)

Yucatán Peninsula

West Indies

Caribbean Sea

Cape Verde Islands

PACIFIC OCEAN

Galápagos Islands

Orinoco River

Guiana Highlands

Equator

Polynesia

AMAZON BASIN

Amazon R.

SOUTH AMERICA

Brazilian Highlands

ANDES MOUNTAINS

20° S

Atacama Desert

Gran Chaco

Paraná River

Tropic of Capricorn

Mt. Aconcagua
22,831 ft.
(6,959 m)

Pampa

40° S

Patagonia

Falkland Islands

60° S

Strait of Magellan

Tierra del Fuego

Cape Horn

Antarctic Circle

Antarctic Peninsula

80° S

Ross Sea

180° **160° W** **140° W** **120° W** **100° W** **80° W** **60° W**

Northern Polar Region

ASIA

EUROPE

Sea of Okhotsk

Novaya Zemlya

Severnaya Zemlya

Barents Sea

Baltic Sea

Kamchatka Peninsula

New Siberian Is.

0   400   800 Miles
0   400   800 Kilometers
Azimuthal Equidistant Projection

Wrangel Island

ARCTIC OCEAN

North Pole

Svalbard

Norwegian Sea

North Sea

British Isles

Bering Sea

Bering Strait

Greenland Sea

Iceland

ATLANTIC OCEAN

BROOKS RANGE

Beaufort Sea

North Magnetic Pole

Queen Elizabeth Islands

Greenland

Baffin Bay

Arctic Circle

A4

PACIFIC OCEAN

NORTH AMERICA

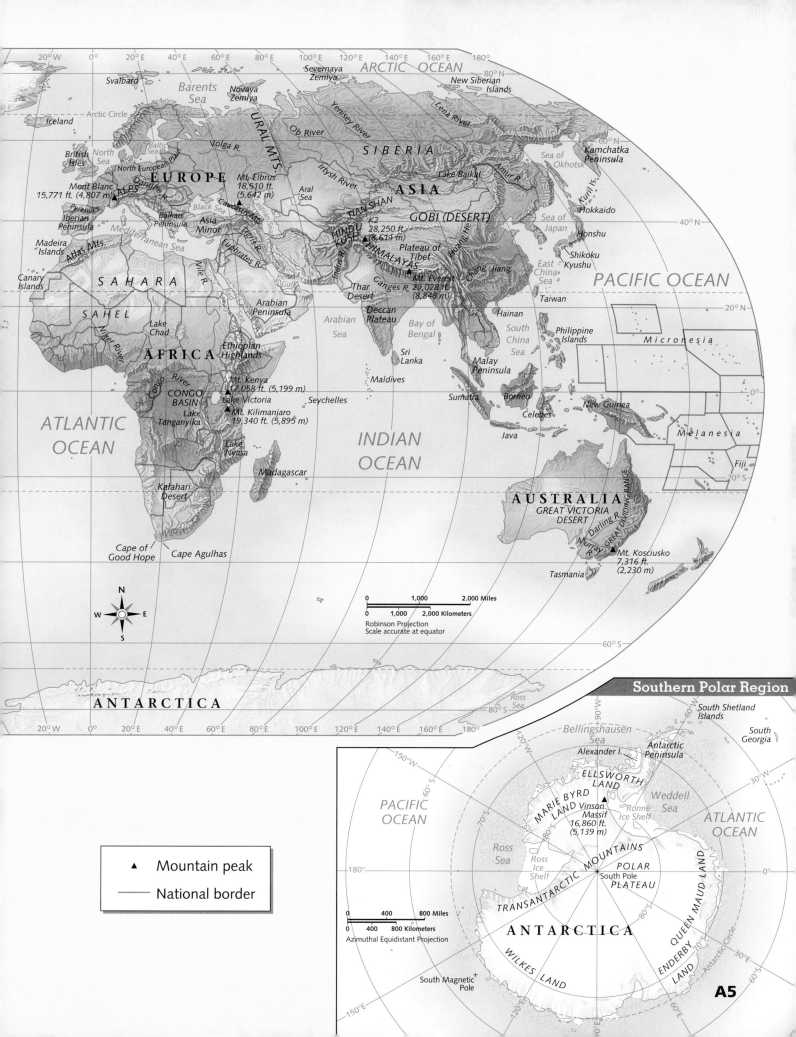

ARCTIC OCEAN

Svalbard
Barents Sea
Novaya Zemlya
Severnaya Zemlya
New Siberian Islands
Iceland
Arctic Circle
British Isles
North Sea
Baltic Sea
North European Plain
URAL MTS.
Ob River
Yenisey River
Lena River
Kamchatka Peninsula
Sea of Okhotsk
EUROPE
Volga R.
Danube R.
Mont Blanc 15,771 ft. (4,807 m)
ALPS
Pyrenees
Iberian Peninsula
Balkan Peninsula
Black Sea
Caucasus Mts.
Mt. Elbrus 18,510 ft. (5,642 m)
Irtysh River
Aral Sea
SIBERIA
ASIA
Lake Baikal
Amur R.
Kuril Is.
Hokkaido
Honshu
Sea of Japan
TIAN SHAN
K2 28,250 ft. (8,611 m)
GOBI (DESERT)
HINDU KUSH
HIMALAYAS
Plateau of Tibet
Huang He
Chang Jiang
Shikoku
Kyushu
East China Sea
PACIFIC OCEAN
Madeira Islands
Atlas Mts.
Mediterranean Sea
Asia Minor
Tigris R.
Euphrates R.
Nile R.
Red Sea
Persian Gulf
Indus R.
Ganges R.
Mt. Everest 29,028 ft. (8,848 m)
Thar Desert
Deccan Plateau
Taiwan
Canary Islands
SAHARA
SAHEL
Arabian Peninsula
Arabian Sea
Bay of Bengal
Sri Lanka
Maldives
Hainan
South China Sea
Philippine Islands
Micronesia
AFRICA
Lake Chad
Niger River
Ethiopian Highlands
Mt. Kenya 17,058 ft. (5,199 m)
CONGO BASIN
Congo River
Lake Victoria
Mt. Kilimanjaro 19,340 ft. (5,895 m)
Lake Tanganyika
Seychelles
Malay Peninsula
Sumatra
Borneo
Celebes
New Guinea
Java
Melanesia
Lake Nyasa
INDIAN OCEAN
ATLANTIC OCEAN
Madagascar
Fiji
Kalahari Desert
AUSTRALIA
GREAT VICTORIA DESERT
Darling R.
GREAT DIVIDING RANGE
Murray R.
Cape of Good Hope
Cape Agulhas
Mt. Kosciusko 7,316 ft. (2,230 m)
Tasmania

N
W   E
S

0   1,000   2,000 Miles
0   1,000   2,000 Kilometers
Robinson Projection
Scale accurate at equator

ANTARCTICA
Ross Sea

▲ Mountain peak
— National border

Southern Polar Region

PACIFIC OCEAN
Bellingshausen Sea
South Shetland Islands
South Georgia
Alexander I.
Antarctic Peninsula
ELLSWORTH LAND
MARIE BYRD LAND
Vinson Massif 16,860 ft. (5,139 m)
Ronne Ice Shelf
Weddell Sea
ATLANTIC OCEAN
Ross Sea
Ross Ice Shelf
TRANSANTARCTIC MOUNTAINS
South Pole
POLAR PLATEAU
QUEEN MAUD LAND
ENDERBY LAND
ANTARCTICA
WILKES LAND
South Magnetic Pole
Antarctic Circle

0   400   800 Miles
0   400   800 Kilometers
Azimuthal Equidistant Projection

A5

Atlas

Africa: Political

EUROPE

ASIA

ATLANTIC OCEAN

Madeira Islands (PORTUGAL)

Ceuta (SPAIN)
Tangier
Rabat
Casablanca
Marrakech
Fès
Melilla (SPAIN)
Oran
Algiers
Constantine
Tunis
Sfax
Tripoli
Banghazi

TUNISIA

Mediterranean Sea

Alexandria
Tanta
Al Jizah
Port Said
Suez Canal
Suez
Cairo

MOROCCO

Canary Islands (SPAIN)

WESTERN SAHARA
(Occupied by Morocco)
El Aaiún

ALGERIA

LIBYA

EGYPT

Aswan

Tropic of Cancer

MAURITANIA
Nouakchott

NIGER

CHAD

Port Sudan

Red Sea

Timbuktu
Gao
MALI

Omdurman
Khartoum

ERITREA
Asmara

Gulf of Aden

Dakar
SENEGAL
GAMBIA
Banjul
GUINEA-BISSAU
Bissau
GUINEA
Conakry
Freetown
SIERRA LEONE

Niamey
BURKINA FASO
Ouagadougou
Kano
BENIN
TOGO
NIGERIA
N'Djamena

SUDAN

DJIBOUTI
Djibouti

Bamako

Addis Ababa
Dire Dawa
ETHIOPIA

CÔTE D'IVOIRE
GHANA
Yamoussoukro
Monrovia
LIBERIA
Abidjan
Lomé
Accra
Porto-Novo
Ibadan
Ogbomosho
Lagos
Abuja

CENTRAL AFRICAN REPUBLIC

SOMALIA
Mogadishu

CAMEROON
Malabo
Douala
Yaoundé
Bangui

UGANDA
Kampala
KENYA
Kisumu
Nairobi
Kismaayo

EQUATORIAL GUINEA
SÃO TOMÉ AND PRÍNCIPE
São Tomé
Libreville
GABON
REPUBLIC OF THE CONGO

Kisangani

Lake Victoria
RWANDA
Kigali
BURUNDI
Bujumbura
Mwanza
Mombasa

Equator

Annobón (EQUATORIAL GUINEA)

Brazzaville
Kinshasa
DEMOCRATIC REPUBLIC OF THE CONGO
Kananga
Mbuji-Mayi

Dodoma
TANZANIA
Dar es Salaam

INDIAN OCEAN

Ascension (UNITED KINGDOM)

CABINDA (ANGOLA)
Luanda

Lake Tanganyika

ATLANTIC OCEAN

Lobito
Huambo
ANGOLA
Kolwezi
Lubumbashi
Kitwe
ZAMBIA
Lusaka

Lake Malawi
MALAWI
Lilongwe
Blantyre

COMOROS
Moroni

St. Helena (UNITED KINGDOM)

Harare
ZIMBABWE
Bulawayo
Beira
MOZAMBIQUE

Mozambique Channel

Antananarivo

NAMIBIA
Windhoek
BOTSWANA

MADAGASCAR

Tropic of Capricorn

Gaborone
Johannesburg
Kimberley
Pretoria
Mbabane
Maputo
SWAZILAND

Bloemfontein
Maseru
LESOTHO
Durban

SOUTH AFRICA

N
W   E
S

Cape Town
Port Elizabeth

Legend:
— National border
⊛ National capital
• Major city

0   500   1,000 Miles
0   500   1,000 Kilometers
Azimuthal Equal-Area Projection

A6

Atlas

Africa: Physical

EUROPE

ASIA

ATLANTIC OCEAN

Strait of Gibraltar

Madeira Islands

Canary Islands

Atlas Mountains

Mediterranean Sea

Nile Delta

Qattara Depression

Suez Canal

Sinai Peninsula

Gulf of Suez

SAHARA

Ahaggar Mountains

Libyan Desert

Nile River

Lake Nasser

Tropic of Cancer

Tibesti Mountains

Air Massif

Nubian Desert

Red Sea

Senegal River

SAHEL

Cape Verde

Niger River

Black Volta R.

White Volta

Fouta Djallon

Lake Chad

Chari River

Athara River

White Nile

Blue Nile

Lake Tana

Bab el Mandeb

Gulf of Aden

Lake Assal 509 ft. (-155 m)

Niger River

Benue River

Ethiopian Highlands

Lake Volta

Cape Palmas

Gulf of Guinea

Mt. Cameroon 13,353 ft. (4,070 m)

Bioko

Bahr el Jabal

White Nile

Great Rift Valley

Lake Turkana

Príncipe

São Tomé

Sangha River

Bomu River

Uele River

Ubangi River

Mt. Kenya 17,058 ft. (5,199 m)

Equator

Annobón

Congo River

Congo Basin

Margherita Peak 16,762 ft. (5,109 m)

Lake Albert

Lake Victoria

Mt. Kilimanjaro 19,340 ft. (5,895 m)

INDIAN OCEAN

Kasai River

Lualaba River

Mitumba Mts.

Serengeti Plain

Pemba Island

Zanzibar Island

Ascencion

ATLANTIC OCEAN

Katanga Plateau

Great Rift Valley

Lake Tanganyika

Bié Plateau

Lake Malawi

Comoro Islands

St. Helena

Victoria Falls

Zambezi River

Kariba Lake

Madagascar

Mozambique Channel

Namib Desert

Limpopo River

Tropic of Capricorn

Kalahari Desert

Tropic of Capricorn

Vaal River

N
W E
S

Orange River

Drakensberg Escarpment

	National border
▲	Mountain peak
▼	Below sea level
	Canal
	Falls

Cape of Good Hope

Cape Agulhas

0   500   1,000 Miles

0   500   1,000 Kilometers

Azimuthal Equal-Area Projection

A7

Atlas

Europe and Asia: Political

Legend:

— National border
- - - Disputed border
⊛ National capital
• Major city

Abbreviations

AUST.	AUSTRIA
BELG.	BELGIUM
BOS. & HERZ.	BOSNIA AND HERZEGOVINA
CRO.	CROATIA
CZECH REP.	CZECH REPUBLIC
LIECHT.	LIECHTENSTEIN
LUX.	LUXEMBOURG
MAC.	MACEDONIA
NETH.	NETHERLANDS
SLOV.	SLOVENIA
SWITZ.	SWITZERLAND
U.K.	UNITED KINGDOM
U.S.	UNITED STATES
YUGO.	YUGOSLAVIA

Robinson Projection

0   500   1,000 Miles
0   500   1,000 Kilometers

ARCTIC OCEAN

Severnaya Zemlya

Laptev Sea

New Siberian Islands

75°N

East Siberian Sea

Wrangel I.

ALASKA (U.S.)

165°W

180°

165°E

150°E

135°E

120°E

105°E

90°E

- Arctic Circle -

Bering Strait

RUSSIA

Lena River

Magadan

60°N

Bering Sea

Yenisey River

Angara River

• Novosibirsk

• Krasnoyarsk

• Irkutsk

Lake Baikal

Petropavlovsk-Kamchatskiy

Sea of Okhotsk

Sakhalin

Khabarovsk

MONGOLIA

⊛ Ulaanbaatar

45°N

Harbin •

Kuril Islands

• Ürümqi

Changchun

Vladivostok •

Sapporo

Shenyang •

NORTH KOREA

Sea of Japan

Beijing ⊛

JAPAN

Tianjin •

P'yongyang ⊛

Taiyuan •

Seoul ⊛

Nagoya

⊛ Tokyo

CHINA

Xian •

Huang He

SOUTH KOREA

Pusan •

Osaka

Yokohama

Lhasa •

• Chengdu

Nanjing •

Yellow Sea

30°N

Kathmandu •

Chongqing •

Wuhan •

Shanghai •

PACIFIC OCEAN

⊛ Thimphu

NEPAL

BHUTAN

Chang Jiang

East China Sea

BANGLADESH

⊛ Dhaka

Kunming •

Mekong R.

Taipei ⊛

Ryukyu Islands

Okinawa

- Tropic of Cancer -

• Calcutta

Chittagong •

Guangzhou •

TAIWAN

Ganges River

BURMA (MYANMAR)

Hanoi •

Macao (PORT.)

Hong Kong •

LAOS

⊛ Vientiane

Hainan

Bay of Bengal

Chiang Mai •

• Hue

South China Sea

Philippine Sea

Rangoon (Yangon) ⊛

THAILAND

Bangkok ⊛

VIETNAM

Manila •

Quezon City

15°N

Andaman Islands (INDIA)

CAMBODIA

Phnom Penh ⊛

• Ho Chi Minh City

PHILIPPINES

Nicobar Islands (INDIA)

Sulu Sea

Davao •

Kuala Lumpur •

Bandar Seri Begawan ⊛

• Medan

BRUNEI

Celebes Sea

MALAYSIA

⊛ **SINGAPORE**

Singapore •

Borneo

Halmahera

0° Equator

Sumatra

Java Sea

Celebes

INDONESIA

Banda Sea

New Guinea

Jakarta ⊛

Bandung •

Java

Surabaya •

Timor

Arafura Sea

Timor Sea

15°S

AUSTRALIA

A9

90°E

105°E

120°E

135°E

150°E

165°E

Atlas

Europe and Asia: Physical

Kara Sea

Novaya Zemlya

Arctic Circle

Norwegian Sea

Iceland

Faeroe Islands

Kjølen Mountains

Lapland

Kola Peninsula

White Sea

Mt. Narodnaya 6,214 ft. (1,894 m) ▲

Gulf of Ob

Scandinavian Peninsula

Galdhøpiggen 8,100 ft. (2,469 m) ▲

Gulf of Bothnia

Lake Onega

Lake Ladoga

Volga River

UREAL MOUNTAINS

Ob River

West Siberian Plain

ATLANTIC OCEAN

Highlands

British Isles

Ireland

Great Britain

North Sea

Jutland

Baltic Sea

Gulf of Finland

Central Russian Upland

Kama River

Ural River

Irtysh River

NORTHERN EUROPEAN PLAIN

Oka-Don Lowland

Kazakh Upland

Celtic Sea

English Channel

Rhine R.

Volga Upland

Donets Basin

Don River

Caspian Lowland

The Steppes

Lake Balkhash

Bay of Biscay

Mt. Blanc 15,771 ft. (4,807 m) ▲

ALPS

Massif Central (Plateau)

Carpathian Mountains

Danube River

Dinaric Alps

Apennines

Adriatic Sea

Sea of Azov

Crimea

El'brus 18,510 ft. (5,642 m)

Caucasus Mts.

Caspian Sea -92 ft. (-28 m) ▽

Aral Sea

Turan Lowland

Kyzyl Kum (Desert)

Syr Darya

Amu Darya

TIAN SHAN

Takla Maka (Desert)

Pyrenees

Iberian Peninsula

Corsica

Sardinia

Balearic Islands

Tyrrhenian Sea

Balkan Peninsula

Balkan Mts.

Pindus Mts.

Aegean Sea

Bosporus

Dardanelles

Pontic Mountains

Plateau of Anatolia

Black Sea

Mt. Ararat 16,946 ft. (5,165 m) ▲

Elburz Mts.

Mt. Damavand 18,934 ft. (5,771 m) ▲

Kara Kum (Desert)

Dasht-e Kavir (Desert)

Plateau of Iran

Pamirs

HINDU KUSH

K2 28,250 ft. (8,611 m) ▲

Kunlu

HIMALAYAS

Strait of Gibraltar

Mediterranean Sea

Sicily

Ionian Sea

Crete

Cyprus

Taurus Mts.

Tigris River

Mesopotamia

Euphrates R.

Zagros Mountains

Syrian Desert

Dead Sea -1,319 ft. (-402 m) ▽

Sinai Peninsula

Strait of Hormuz

Indus River

Thar Desert

Tropic of Cancer

Red Sea

Persian Gulf

Gulf of Oman

Narmada River

AFRICA

Arabian Peninsula

Rub' al Khali

Arabian Sea

Deccan

Godavari River

Plateau

Western Ghats

Eastern Ghats

Gulf of Aden

Socotra

Palk Strait

Sri Lanka

INDIAN OCEAN

	Legend
——	National border
----	Disputed border
▲	Mountain peak
▽	Point below sea level

N
W E
S

0   500   1,000 Miles

0   500   1,000 Kilometers

Robinson Projection

Atlas

Western Hemisphere: Political

ARCTIC OCEAN

Beaufort Sea

Viscount Melville Sound

Baffin Bay

Greenland (DENMARK)

Bering Strait

Davis Strait

Arctic Circle

ALASKA (U.S.)

Fairbanks

Yukon River

Great Bear Lake

Foxe Basin

Anchorage

Whitehorse

Mackenzie River

Yellowknife

Great Slave Lake

CANADA

Hudson Strait

Juneau

Gulf of Alaska

Liard River

Peace River

Lake Athabasca

James Bay

Hudson Bay

Labrador Sea

60° N

Bering Sea

Edmonton

Athabasca R.

Saskatoon

Saskatchewan R.

Lake Winnipeg

St. John's

Calgary

Regina

Winnipeg

Thunder Bay

Gulf of St. Lawrence

Vancouver

UNITED STATES

Great Lakes

St. Lawrence River

Quebec

St. John

Puget Sound

Seattle

Ottawa

Montreal

Halifax

Portland

Columbia R.

Snake R.

Boise

Salt Lake City

Great Salt Lake

Toronto

Detroit

Cleveland

Albany

Boston

New York City

Reno

Chicago

Philadelphia

Washington, D.C.

San Francisco

Denver

St. Louis

Indianapolis

Richmond

Norfolk

Las Vegas

Colorado R.

Missouri R.

Memphis

Atlanta

Raleigh

Charleston

Los Angeles

Phoenix

Dallas

Savannah

San Diego

Tucson

El Paso

Houston

New Orleans

Jacksonville

ATLANTIC OCEAN

30° N

Hermosillo

Rio Grande

San Antonio

Tampa

Miami

BAHAMAS

Tropic of Cancer

Chihuahua

Gulf of Mexico

Nassau

Durango

MEXICO

Monterrey

Havana

CUBA

HAITI

HAWAII (U.S.)

Honolulu

León

Tampico

Port-au-Prince

Santo Domingo

PUERTO RICO (U.S.)

Guadalajara

Mexico City

JAMAICA

Puebla

Veracruz

BELIZE

Kingston

DOMINICAN REPUBLIC

PACIFIC OCEAN

Acapulco

GUATEMALA

Belmopan

Guatemala City

HONDURAS

San Salvador

Tegucigalpa

Caribbean Sea

EL SALVADOR

Managua

San José

NICARAGUA

Maracaibo

COSTA RICA

Panama City

Caracas

GUYANA

PANAMA

VENEZUELA

SURINAME

Medellín

Georgetown

Paramaribo

Cayenne

Cali

Bogotá

FRENCH GUIANA (FRANCE)

COLOMBIA

Rio Negro

Quito

Amazon R.

Galápagos Islands (ECUADOR)

Guayaquil

Manaus

Belém

Equator

ECUADOR

Iquitos

Fortaleza

0°

Trujillo

Tapajós River

Xingu R.

Tocantins R.

Recife

PERU

São Francisco R.

BRAZIL

Lima

Cuzco

Salvador

FRENCH POLYNESIA (FRANCE)

Lake Titicaca

La Paz

Brasília

Papeete

Arequipa

BOLIVIA

Goiânia

Belo Horizonte

Sucre

Campo Grande

Rio de Janeiro

Tropic of Capricorn

Antofagasta

PARAGUAY

São Paulo

Salta

Asunción

Curitiba

0   1,000   2,000 Miles

San Miguel de Tucumán

Pôrto Alegre

0   1,000   2,000 Kilometers

CHILE

Córdoba

Miller Cylindrical Projection

30° S

Valparaíso

Rosario

URUGUAY

Santiago

Buenos Aires

Montevideo

Concepción

La Plata

Rio de la Plata

Mar del Plata

Valdivia

Bahia Blanca

N

---- National border

W   E

⊛ National capital

ARGENTINA

• City

S

A12

Falkland Islands (U.K.)

South Georgia (U.K.)

Punta Arenas

150° W   120° W   90° W   60° W   30° W

Atlas

Western Hemisphere: Physical

North Magnetic Pole

Queen Elizabeth Islands

Ellesmere Island

Melville Island

Devon Island

Banks Island

Viscount Melville Sound

Baffin Bay

Greenland

Beaufort Sea

Point Barrow

Victoria Island

Baffin Island

Davis Strait

Arctic Circle

Brooks Range

Mt. McKinley 20,320 ft. (6,194 m)

Yukon

Yukon River

Alaska Range

Plateau

Mackenzie Mts

Great Bear Lake

Mackenzie River

Great Slave Lake

River

Foxe Basin

Hudson Strait

60° N

Cape Farewell

Mt. Logan 19,524 ft. (5,951 m)

Liard R.

Peace

Athabasca R.

Lake Athabasca

Hudson Bay

James Bay

Labrador

Labrador Sea

Gulf of Alaska

Kodiak Island

Alaska Peninsula

Aleutian Islands

Queen Charlotte Islands

Vancouver Island

Puget Sound

Coast Mountains

Saskatchewan River

Lake Winnipeg

CANADIAN

SHIELD

ROCKY

GREAT

NORTH AMERICA

Great Lakes

St. Lawrence R.

Gulf of St. Lawrence

Newfoundland

Nova Scotia

Cascade Range

Coast Ranges

Snake R.

Black Hills

Missouri R.

Mississippi R.

Ohio R.

APPALACHIAN MTS.

Cape Cod

Long Island

Great Salt Lake

GREAT BASIN

Sierra Nevada

MOUNTAINS

Platte

Arkansas

Ozark Plateau R.

Cape Hatteras

Mt. Whitney 14,495 ft. (4,418 m)

Colorado R.

COASTAL PLAIN

River

ATLANTIC OCEAN

30° N

Death Valley (lowest point in N.A.) -282 ft. (-86 m)

Sonoran Desert

Rio

Grande

Baja California

Sierra Madre Occidental

Gulf of California

Sierra Madre Oriental

Gulf of Mexico

Bahamas

Cuba

Greater Antilles

Hispaniola

Puerto Rico

Lesser Antilles

Tropic of Cancer

Hawaiian Islands

Citlaltépetl 18,701 ft (5,700 m)

Yucatán Peninsula

Caribbean Sea

PACIFIC OCEAN

Lake Nicaragua

Isthmus of Panama

Lake Maracaibo

Orinoco R.

Llanos

Guiana Highlands

Line Islands

Galápagos Islands

Chimborazo 20,561 ft. (6,267 m)

Rio Negro

Amazon R.

Cape São Roque

Equator

AMAZON

BASIN

ANDES

Tapajós River

Xingu River

Tocantins R.

São Francisco River

Marquesas Islands

Huascarán 22,205 ft. (6,768 m)

Mato Grosso Plateau

Brazilian

Cook Islands

Tuamotu Archipelago

Society Islands

Lake Titicaca

Altiplano

Paraguay R.

Highlands

SOUTH AMERICA

Tropic of Capricorn

Atacama Desert

MOUNTAINS

Gran Chaco

Paraná

Uruguay R.

Iguazú Falls

30° S

Mt. Aconcagua 22,831 ft. (6,959 m)

Pampa

Rio de la Plata

▲ Mountain peak

▼ Point below sea level

— National border

≈ Waterfall

N

W   E

S

Patagonia

Valdés Peninsula (lowest point in S.A.) -131 ft. (-40 m)

Falkland Islands

A13

South Georgia

Strait of Magellan

Tierra del Fuego

Cape Horn

150° W   120° W   90° W   60° W   30° W

0   1,000   2,000 Miles

0   1,000   2,000 Kilometers

Miller Cylindrical Projection

Atlas

Pacific Rim: Political

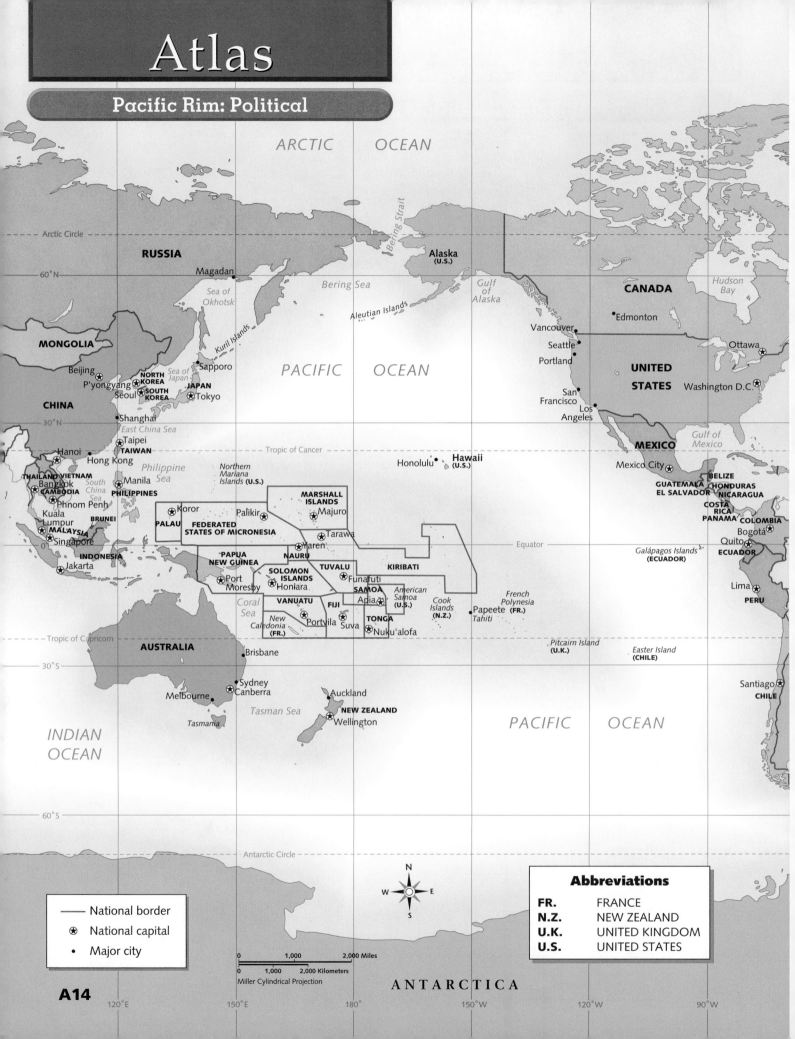

ARCTIC OCEAN

Arctic Circle

RUSSIA

60°N

Magadan

Alaska (U.S.)

Bering Strait

Bering Sea

Gulf of Alaska

Hudson Bay

CANADA

Edmonton

Sea of Okhotsk

Vancouver

Seattle

Portland

Ottawa

MONGOLIA

Aleutian Islands

PACIFIC OCEAN

Kuril Islands

Beijing

Sapporo

NORTH KOREA

Sea of Japan

JAPAN

UNITED STATES

P'yongyang

SOUTH KOREA

Seoul

Tokyo

Washington D.C.

CHINA

San Francisco

Los Angeles

30°N

Shanghai

East China Sea

Gulf of Mexico

Hanoi

Taipei

Tropic of Cancer

Honolulu

Hawaii (U.S.)

MEXICO

Mexico City

Hong Kong

TAIWAN

Philippine Sea

Northern Mariana Islands (U.S.)

BELIZE

GUATEMALA

HONDURAS

THAILAND VIETNAM

Bangkok

South China Sea

Manila

MARSHALL ISLANDS

EL SALVADOR

NICARAGUA

COSTA RICA

CAMBODIA

PHILIPPINES

Koror

Palikir

Majuro

PANAMA COLOMBIA

Phnom Penh

PALAU

FEDERATED STATES OF MICRONESIA

Tarawa

Bogotá

Kuala Lumpur

BRUNEI

Quito

Singapore

MALAYSIA

Yaren

Equator

Galápagos Islands (ECUADOR)

ECUADOR

0°

INDONESIA

PAPUA NEW GUINEA

NAURU

TUVALU

KIRIBATI

Jakarta

SOLOMON ISLANDS

Funafuti

Lima

Port Moresby

Honiara

SAMOA

American Samoa (U.S.)

Cook Islands (N.Z.)

French Polynesia (FR.)

PERU

Coral Sea

VANUATU

FIJI

Apia

Papeete

Tahiti

Tropic of Capricorn

New Caledonia (FR.)

Portvila

Suva

TONGA

Nuku'alofa

Pitcairn Island (U.K.)

Easter Island (CHILE)

AUSTRALIA

Brisbane

30°S

Sydney

Santiago

Melbourne

Canberra

Auckland

CHILE

Tasman Sea

NEW ZEALAND

PACIFIC OCEAN

Tasmania

Wellington

INDIAN OCEAN

60°S

Antarctic Circle

N
W   E
S

Legend

——	National border
⊛	National capital
•	Major city

120°E   150°E   180°   150°W   120°W   90°W

0   1,000   2,000 Miles
0   1,000   2,000 Kilometers
Miller Cylindrical Projection

ANTARCTICA

Abbreviations

FR.	FRANCE
N.Z.	NEW ZEALAND
U.K.	UNITED KINGDOM
U.S.	UNITED STATES

Atlas

Pacific Rim: Physical

Severnaya Zemlya

ARCTIC OCEAN

Laptev Sea

New Siberian Islands

East Siberian Sea

Taymyr Peninsula

Wrangel Island

Chukchi Sea

Chukchi Peninsula

Bering Strait

Beaufort Sea

Banks Island

Melville Island

Victoria Island

Ellesmere Island

Baffin Island

Melville Peninsula

S I B E R I A

Kolyma Lowland

Kolyma R.

Chukchi Range

Arctic Circle

Brooks Range

Amundsen Gulf

Great Bear Lake

Lena River

Kolyma Range

Korya Range

Yukon River

Mackenzie River

Great Slave Lake

Ungava Peninsula

60°N

Mt. McKinley 20,320 ft. (6,194 m) ▲

Mt. Logan 19,524 ft. 5,951 m) ▲

Peace R.

ASIA

Lake Baikal

Sea of Okhotsk

Central Range

Kamchatka Peninsula

Bering Sea

Aleutian Islands

Alaska Peninsula

Gulf of Alaska

Hudson Bay

Amur R.

Greater Khingan Range

Sikhote Alin Range

Sakhalin

Manchurian Plain

Kuril Islands

Gobi (Desert)

Hokkaido

Vancouver Island

Columbia R.

Coast Ranges

Saskatchewan R.

NORTH AMERICA

Huang He

Sea of Japan

Honshu

PACIFIC OCEAN

Great Lakes

Chiang Jiang

North China Plain

Yellow Sea

Mt. Fuji 12,388 ft. (3,776 m) ▲

Shikoku

Kyushu

ROCKY MOUNTAINS

GREAT PLAINS

Missouri R.

Mississippi R.

APPALACHIAN MTS.

East China Sea

30°N

Mt. Whitney 14,495 ft. (4,418 m) ▲

Colorado R.

Taiwan

Tropic of Cancer

Baja California

Sierra Madre

Gulf of Mexico

Indochina Peninsula

South China Sea

PHILIPPINE IS.

Philippine Sea

Northern Mariana Islands

MARSHALL ISLANDS

Hawaiian Islands

Yucatán Peninsula

Greater Antilles

Cuba

Malay Peninsula

Mt. Kinabalu 13,455 ft. (4,101 m) ▲

CAROLINE ISLANDS

M I C R O N E S I A

Caribbean Sea

Sumatra

Celebes Sea

INDONESIA

Greater Sunda Islands

Java

New Guinea

0°

M E L A N E S I A

P O L Y N E S I A

Equator

Galápagos Islands

SOUTH AMERICA

Timor

Great Barrier Reef

Coral Sea

American Samoa

Cook Islands

TUAMOTU ARCHIPELAGO

French Polynesia

Huascarán 22,206 ft. (6,768 m) ▲

GREAT SANDY DESERT

New Caledonia

Tahiti

GREAT VICTORIA DESERT

AUSTRALIA

Great Dividing Range

Tropic of Capricorn

Pitcairn Island

Easter Island

ANDES

Darling R.

30°S

Aconcagua 22,831 ft. (6,959 m) ▲

Mt. Kosciusko 7,310 ft. (2,228 m) ▲

Tasman Sea

Mt. Cook 12,349 ft. (3,764 m) ▲

New Zealand

PACIFIC OCEAN

Tasmania

INDIAN OCEAN

Cape Horn

60°S

Antarctic Circle

Alexander Island

Thurston Island

Bellingshausen Sea

Amundsen Sea

N

W E

S

Ross Sea

National border
▲ Mountain Peak

0   1,000   2,000 Miles
0   1,000   2,000 Kilometers
Miller Cylindrical Projection

ANTARCTICA

A15

120°E   150°E   180°   150°W   120°W   90°W

Atlas

Oceans and Rivers of the World

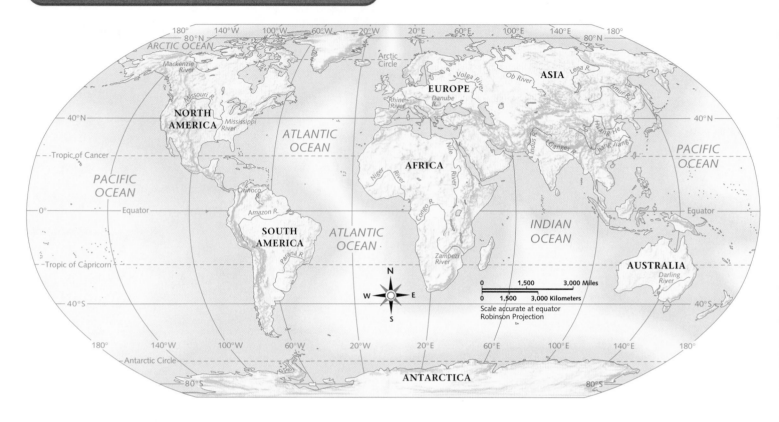

Mountain Ranges of the World

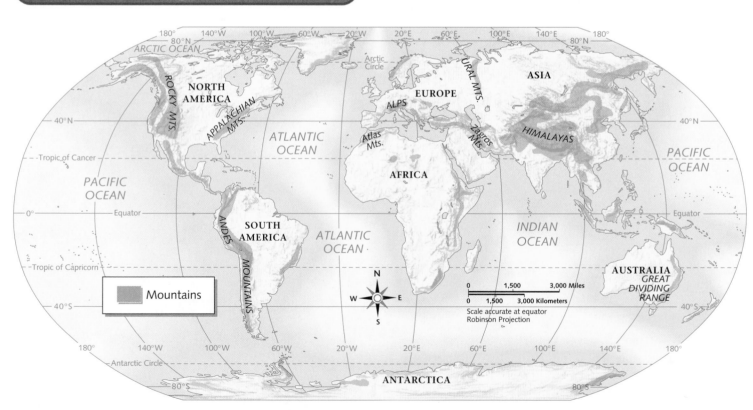

Mountains

Atlas

Plains of the World

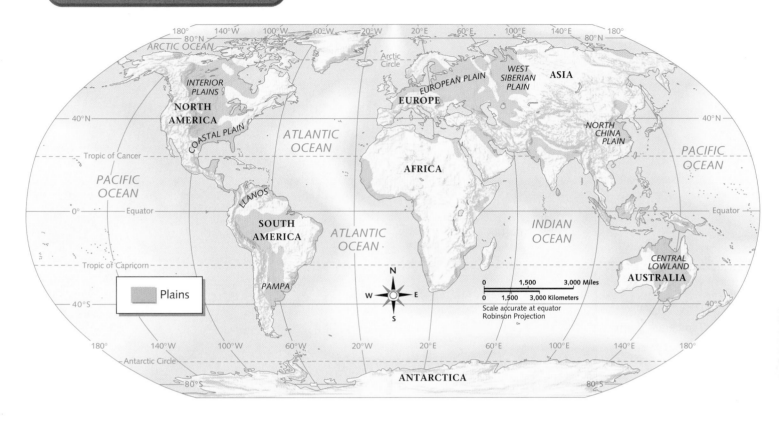

Deserts of the World

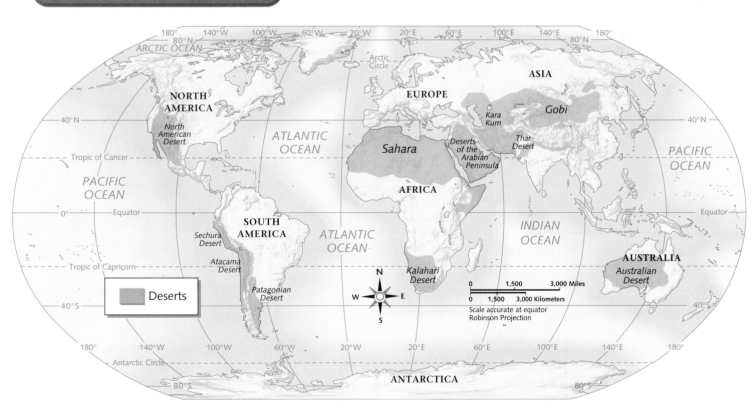

Atlas

Climates of the World

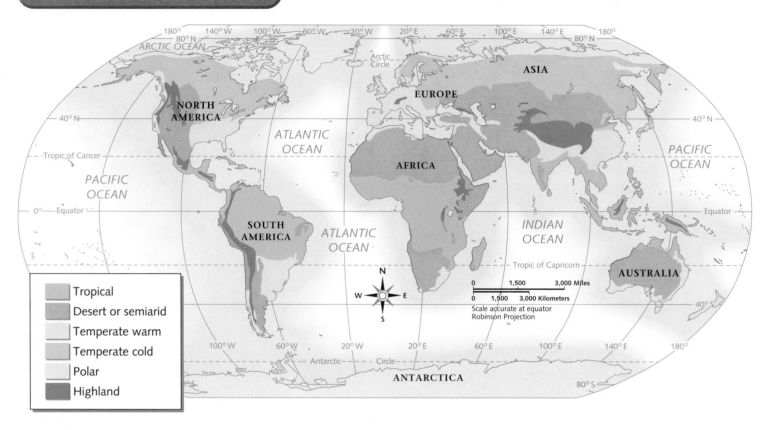

Legend:
- Tropical
- Desert or semiarid
- Temperate warm
- Temperate cold
- Polar
- Highland

World Land Use

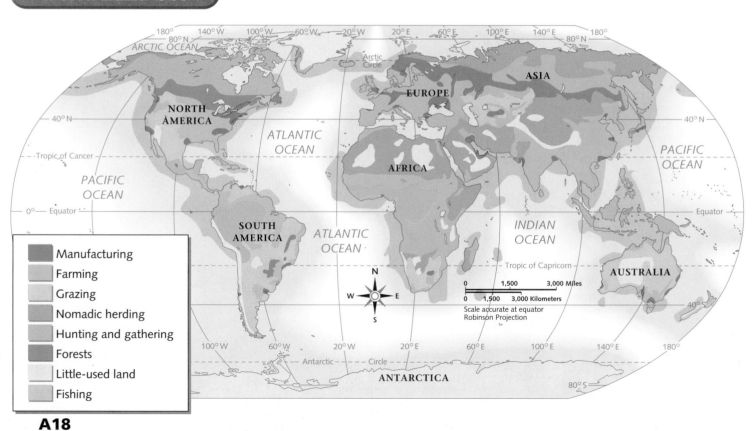

Legend:
- Manufacturing
- Farming
- Grazing
- Nomadic herding
- Hunting and gathering
- Forests
- Little-used land
- Fishing

Atlas

World Religions

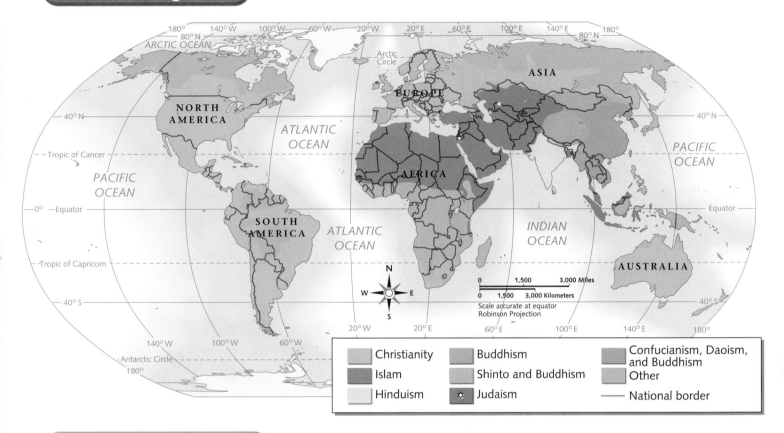

Christianity
Islam
Hinduism
Buddhism
Shinto and Buddhism
Judaism
Confucianism, Daoism, and Buddhism
Other
National border

World Languages

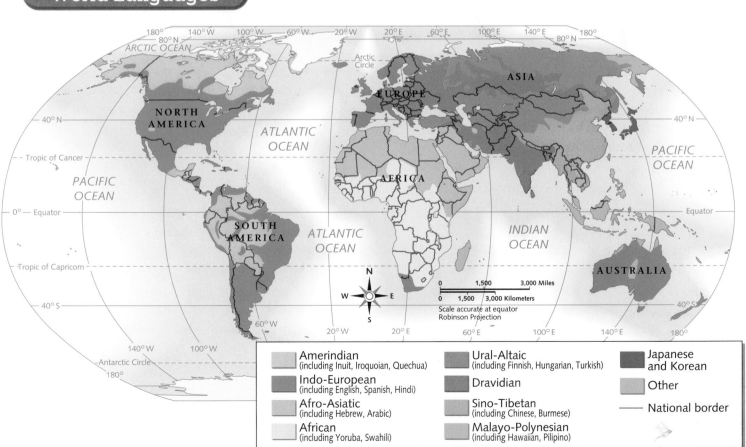

Amerindian (including Inuit, Iroquoian, Quechua)
Indo-European (including English, Spanish, Hindi)
Afro-Asiatic (including Hebrew, Arabic)
African (including Yoruba, Swahili)
Ural-Altaic (including Finnish, Hungarian, Turkish)
Dravidian
Sino-Tibetan (including Chinese, Burmese)
Malayo-Polynesian (including Hawaiian, Pilipino)
Japanese and Korean
Other
National border

Atlas

Geography Terms

Timberline

Slope

MOUNTAIN RANGE

Sea level

Glacier

VALLEY

Inlet

PLATEAU

Canyon

Mesa

PLAIN

COASTAL PLAIN

Coast

Sea level

Mouth of river

Lake

Lagoon

Channel

Isthmus

Peninsula

Cape

OCEAN

---

basin bowl-shaped area of land surrounded by higher land

bay body of water that is part of a sea or ocean and is partly enclosed by land

bluff high, steep face of rock or earth

canyon deep, narrow valley with steep sides

cape point of land that extends into water

cataract place where water runs fast over rocks

channel deepest part of a body of water

cliff high, steep face of rock or earth

coast land along a sea or ocean

coastal plain area of flat land along a sea or ocean

delta triangle-shaped land at a river's mouth

desert dry land with few plants

dune hill of sand piled up by the wind

fall line area along which rivers form waterfalls or rapids as the rivers drop to lower land

floodplain flat land that is near the edges of a river and is formed by the silt deposited by floods

foothills hilly area at the base of a mountain

glacier large ice mass that moves slowly down a mountain or across land

gulf body of water that is partly enclosed by land but is larger than a bay

hill land that rises above the land around it

inlet narrow strip of water leading into the land from a larger body of water

island land that has water on all sides

isthmus narrow strip of land connecting two larger areas of land

lagoon small body of water in the middle of a coral reef

lake body of water with land on all sides

marsh lowland with moist soil and tall grasses

A20

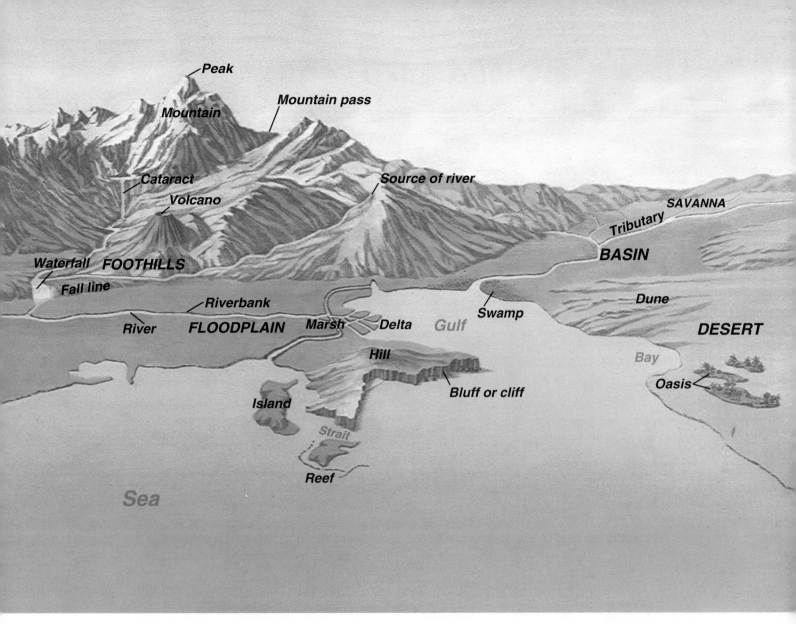

Peak

Mountain

Mountain pass

Cataract

Source of river

SAVANNA

Volcano

Tributary

BASIN

Waterfall FOOTHILLS

Dune

Fall line

Riverbank

Swamp

DESERT

River FLOODPLAIN

Marsh Delta

Gulf

Bay

Hill

Oasis

Bluff or cliff

Island

Strait

Reef

Sea

mesa flat-topped mountain with steep sides

mountain highest kind of land

mountain pass gap between mountains

mountain range row of mountains

mouth of river place where a river empties into another body of water

oasis area of water and fertile land in a desert

ocean body of salt water larger than a sea

peak top of a mountain

peninsula land that is almost completely surrounded by water

plain flat land

plateau area of high, flat land with steep sides

reef ridge of sand, rock, or coral that lies at or near the surface of a sea or ocean

river large stream of water that flows across the land

riverbank land along a river

savanna grassy plain

sea body of salt water smaller than an ocean

sea level level even with the surface of an ocean or a sea

slope side of a hill or mountain

source of river place where a river begins

strait narrow channel of water connecting two larger bodies of water

swamp area of low, wet land with trees

timberline line on a mountain above which it is too cold for trees to grow

tributary stream or river that empties into a larger river

valley low land between hills or mountains

volcano opening in the Earth, often raised, through which lava, rock, ashes, and gases are forced out

waterfall steep drop in a stream or river

A21

WHY STUDY SOCIAL STUDIES?

"Every one of you already holds the important office of citizen. Over time you will become more and more involved in your community. You will need to know more about what being a citizen means. Social studies will help you learn about citizenship. That is why social studies is important in your life."

The authors of
Harcourt Brace
Social Studies

The Themes of Social Studies

Think about the many groups of which you are a part. Your family, your class, and your community are different kinds of groups, and you are a member of each one. You are also a member—or **citizen**—of your town or city, your state, and your country. Citizens work to improve the many groups to which they belong and to make their world a better place.

To help you think, feel, and act as a citizen, *Harcourt Brace Social Studies* begins every lesson with a question. That question connects the lesson to one or more of five themes, or key topics, of social studies. Citizens need to understand these themes in order to make decisions. Each question also links you to the lesson's story, helping you see how the story relates to your own life. The lesson helps you learn about being a citizen by letting you see how people from many places and times have thought, felt, and acted. Each lesson will help you organize your thinking around one or more of the following five themes of social studies.

In this painting the Roman orator Cicero delivers a speech in the Roman senate. By taking part in government, Cicero and the Roman senators were carrying out the office of citizen.

Commonality and Diversity

In some ways people everywhere are alike. We all have the same basic needs for things such as food, clothing, and shelter. We all laugh, get angry, and have our feelings hurt. These are a few examples of our commonality (kah•muh•NAL•uh•tee), or what we all share. At the same time, we need to understand that each person is different from everyone else. We each have our own ways of thinking, feeling, and acting. That is our diversity (duh•VER•suh•tee). Learning about commonality and diversity can help you see that every person is unique and deserves understanding and respect.

All people are alike in some ways, but each person has different ways of thinking, feeling, and acting.

Conflict and Cooperation

Because people are different from one another, they sometimes have conflicts, or disagreements. People can often settle their conflicts by cooperating, or working together. In social studies you will learn about the disagreements people have had in the past and about many of the ways people have found to settle their disagreements. You will also learn ways to cooperate and to settle conflicts in your own life.

Continuity and Change

While some things change over time, other things stay the same. Many things have stayed the same for years and will probably stay the same in the future. This means that they have continuity (kahn•tuhn•OO•uh•tee). Understanding continuity and change can help you see how things in the world came to be as they are. You will learn how a past event, or something that has happened, may have helped shape your life. You will also learn how present events can help you make better decisions about the future.

Individualism and Interdependence

Citizens can act by themselves to make a difference in the world. Their actions as individuals (in•duh•VIJ•wuhlz) may be helpful or harmful to other citizens. Much of the time, however, people do not act alone. They depend on others for help, and others depend on them. People depend on one another in families, schools, religious groups, government groups, and other groups and organizations. Such interdependence (in•ter•dih•PEN•duhns) connects citizens with one another.

When you take part in a student government meeting (top), vote for class officers (center), or campaign in a school election (bottom), you are carrying out the office of citizen. Understanding each of the powerful ideas will help you make decisions as a citizen.

Interaction Within Different Environments

People's actions affect other people. People's actions also affect their environment (in•VY•ruhn•muhnt), or surroundings. This is true of their physical environment, their home environment, their school environment, and any other environments of which they may be a part. Their environments affect them, too.

Understanding such interactions is important to understanding why things happened in the past and why things happen today. Understanding interaction is important for understanding social studies. The subjects that make up social studies are all related. You will learn, for example, that history—the study of people's past—is related to geography—the study of the Earth's surface and the way people use it. Civics and government, or the study of how people live together in a community, is related to economics, or the study of how people use resources. And all of these subjects are related to the study of culture.

Culture is a people's way of life, including customs, ideas, and practices. These subjects interact with one another to tell a story. Together they tell how people have lived over time and how they have made contributions as citizens. Understanding this story will help you learn how to hold the office of citizen.

REVIEW *What are the five themes of social studies?*

Read Social Studies

1. Why Learn This Skill?

Social studies is made up of stories about people, places, and events. Sometimes you read these stories in library books. At other times you read them in textbooks like this one. Knowing how to read social studies can make it easier to study and do your homework. It can help you find important ideas and learn about people, places, and events.

2. Getting Started

Your book is divided into ten units. At the beginning of each unit, you will find several pages that will help you preview the unit and predict what it will be about.

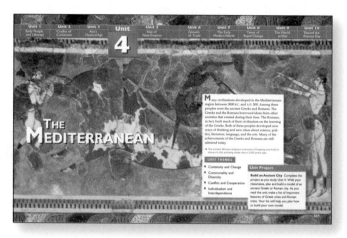

▲
Each unit begins with a short overview of the unit and a list of the social studies themes it teaches. You will also read about a project you can complete as you study the unit.

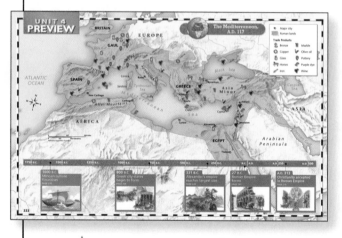

▲
The Unit Preview has a map that shows where some of the important events you will read about took place. It also has a time line that shows the order in which the events happened. There may be a story line that shows some of the people, places, or events.

▲
Each unit has at least one literature selection that helps you understand the time and place you are studying.

3. The Parts of a Lesson

Each unit has two or more chapters, and each chapter is divided into lessons. The beginning and the end of a lesson are shown below.

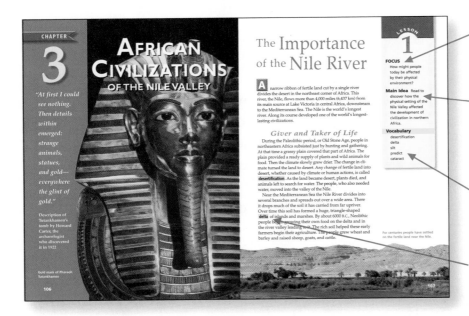

This question helps you see how the lesson relates to life today.

This statement gives you the lesson's main idea. It tells you what to look for as you read the lesson.

These are the new terms you will learn in the lesson.

The first time a vocabulary term appears in the lesson, it is highlighted in yellow.

Each lesson, like each chapter and each unit, ends with a review. The review questions and activities help you check your understanding and show what you know.

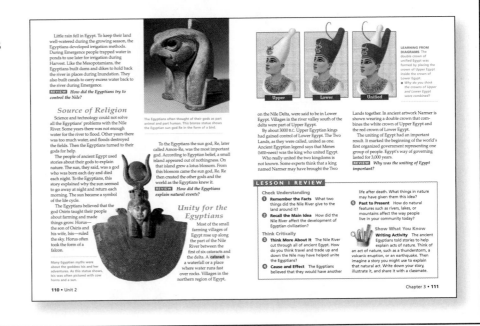

4. Understand the Process

You can follow these steps to read any lesson in this book.

1 Preview the whole lesson.

- Look at the title and the headings to find out what the lesson is about.

- Look at the pictures, the captions, and the questions to get an idea of what is most important in the lesson.

- Read the Focus question at the beginning of the lesson to see how the lesson relates to life today.

- Read the Main Idea statement to find out the main idea of the lesson.

- Look at the Vocabulary list to see what new terms you will learn.

2 Read the lesson to learn more about the main idea. As you read, you will come to a number of questions with the label **REVIEW**. Be sure to answer these questions before you continue reading the lesson.

3 When you finish reading the lesson, say in your own words what you have learned.

4 Look back over the lesson. Then answer the Lesson Review questions from memory. These questions will help you check your understanding of the lesson. The activity at the end of the review will help you show what you know.

5. Some Other Parts of Your Book

Your textbook has many other features to help you learn. Some of them are shown below.

The feature called Making Social Studies Relevant helps you see how social studies is connected to your life and the lives of other people.

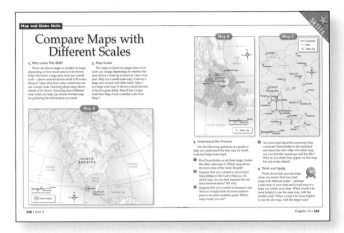

Skill lessons help you build basic study skills. They also help you build citizenship skills as you work with others.

At the back of your book is a section called *For Your Reference*. It includes the following reference tools.

- How to Gather and Report Information
- Almanac
- Biographical Dictionary
- Gazetteer
- Glossary
- Index

6. Think and Apply

Use the four steps in Understand the Process each time you read a lesson in *Harcourt Brace Social Studies*.

The Counterpoints pages help you understand the different points of view people may have about certain issues.

History

History helps you see the links between the past and the present. It also helps you understand how things that happen today can affect the future. History is about what happened last month and last year as well as in the ancient past.

As you read about the people, places, and events of the past, ask yourself the four questions below. They will help you think more like a historian, a person who studies the past.

- What happened?
- Who took part in it?
- When did it happen?
- How and why did it happen?

What Happened?

To find out what really happened in the past, you need proof. You can find proof by studying two kinds of sources—primary sources and secondary sources. Historians use these kinds of sources in writing history.

Primary sources are the records made by people who saw or took part in an event. They may have written down their thoughts in a journal. They may have told their story in a letter or a poem. They may have taken a photograph, made a film, or painted a picture. Each of these records is a primary source, giving the people of today a direct link to a past event.

Hourglass (top), ancient writing from southwestern Asia (center), Egyptian wall painting (bottom)

A **secondary source** is not a direct link to an event. It is a record of the event written by someone who was not there at the time. A magazine article, newspaper story, or book written at a later time by someone who only heard or read about an event is a secondary source. A newspaper may include both primary sources and secondary sources.

When there are no written records of an event, historians gather proof with the help of archaeologists. Archaeologists study buildings, tools, and other objects people make or use. Based on their studies of these things, archaeologists form opinions about people and places in the past.

In this book, you will read many kinds of primary and secondary sources. The stories told in each lesson contain primary sources—the words and photographs of people in the past—as well as secondary sources written by historians. Maps, graphs, literature, pictures, and diagrams also help tell the stories you will read.

Archaeologists study items made or used by peoples of the past. This archaeologist is looking at a tomb of the ancient Mayas in what is today Mexico.

People of the past often depended on the spoken word rather than the written word to tell of their past. Below left is a nineteenth-century painting of a Native American storyteller. Below right a present-day storyteller holds students' interest with a tale about the past.

Who Took Part in It?

To understand the stories of the past, you need to know something about the people who took part in them and about the times and places in which they lived. This will help you understand their actions and feelings. Understanding of how people acted and felt long ago is called **historical empathy**. Historical empathy helps make the past seem alive.

By reading the words of people of the past, you can come to understand their **perspective**, or point of view. A person's perspective will depend on whether that person is old or young, a man or a woman, and rich or poor. Perspective is also shaped by a person's culture and race. Your understanding of history will grow as you study the many perspectives of the people who took part in a story. You will see that all people, even those living in other places and times, are a lot like you.

History puts scenes of the past at your fingertips.

When Did It Happen?

One way to tell or write a story of the past is to put the events in the order in which they happened. This presents the story's **chronology** (kruh•NAH•luh•gee), or time order. As you read this book, you will notice that it is organized by chronology. The events described at the beginning of the book happened before the events described at the end of the book.

You will see many time lines in this book. They will help you understand each story's chronology. A time line is a diagram that shows the events that took place during a certain period of time in the order in which they happened. Time lines may show a period of a month or a year. They may show a period of 10 years, 100 years, or 1,000 years. Time lines can help you understand how one event may have led to another.

How and Why Did It Happen?

Many events in history are linked to other events. To find the links between events, you will need to identify causes and effects. A **cause** is any action that makes something happen. What happens because of that action is an **effect**. Historians have found that most events have many causes and many effects.

To understand an event, you need to analyze its causes and effects. When you **analyze** something, you break it into its parts and look closely at how those parts connect with one another. Once you have analyzed an event, you can summarize it or draw a conclusion about how or why it happened.

REVIEW *What questions should you ask yourself when you read about the past?*

Three Hundred Years Ago

Two Hundred Years Ago

One Hundred Years Ago

The Present

Time lines help you understand *when* in the past something happened.

Work Together in Groups

1. Why Learn This Skill?

Many of the projects you do in social studies will be easier if you work with a partner or in a group. Each of you can work on part of the project. For a group project to succeed, each member needs to cooperate with the others. Knowing how to work together is an important skill for students and for all citizens.

2. Understand the Process

Suppose your group were asked to do a project, such as presenting a short play about everyday life long ago. You might find it helpful to follow a set of steps.

1 Organize and plan together.
- Set your goal as a group.
- Share your ideas.
- Cooperate with others to plan your work.
- Make sure everyone has a job.

2 Act on your plan together.
- Take responsibility for your work.
- Help one another.
- If there are conflicts, talk about them until they are settled.
- Show your group's finished work to the class.

3 Talk about your work.
- Discuss what you learned by working together.
- Discuss what could have been done differently to improve how your group worked together.

3. Think and Apply

Follow the steps above for working together as you take part in the activities in *Harcourt Brace Social Studies.*

These students are preparing for a class play about life in ancient Egypt.

Geography

The stories you will read in this book all have a setting. The setting of a story includes the place where it happened. Knowing about places is an important part of **geography**—the study of the Earth's surface and the way people use it. **Geographers**, people whose work is to study geography, think about the following five topics and questions when they study a place.

- **Location**
  Where is it?

- **Place**
  What is it like there?

- **Human-environment interactions**
  How does this place affect the lives of people living there? How do people living there affect this place?

- **Movement**
  How and why do people, ideas, and goods move to and from this place?

- **Regions**
  How is this place like other places? How is it different?

Thinking about these topics and questions will help you understand the setting of a story. These five topics are so important that people call them the five themes of geography.

Location

Everything on the Earth has its own location. Knowing your location helps you tell other people where you are. It also helps you know more about the world around you.

To tell exactly where you live in your town or city, you can use the names and numbers of your home address. To find your **absolute location**, or exact location, on the Earth, you can use the numbers of your "global address." These numbers appear on a pattern of imaginary lines drawn around the Earth.

The location of a place can also be described in relation to the location of other places. You describe the **relative location** of a place when you say what it is near. You might say that the city of Rome is south of the city of Amsterdam.

Place

Every location on the Earth has a place identity made up of unique features that make it different from all other locations. A place can be described by its **physical features**—landforms, bodies of water, climate, soil, plant and animal life, and other natural resources. Many places also have **human features**—buildings, bridges, farms, roads, and the people themselves. People's culture, or way of life, also helps form a place's identity.

The physical and human features of a place can be seen in this photograph of Bergen, Norway.

Human-Environment Interactions

Humans and the environment interact, or behave in ways that affect each other. People interact with their environment in different ways. Sometimes they change it. They clear land to grow crops. They build cities and towns. Sometimes people pollute the environment. The environment can also cause people to change the way they act. People who live in cold places wear warm clothing. Sometimes things that happen in nature, such as hurricanes, tornadoes, and earthquakes, cause great changes in people's lives.

Humans and the environment they live in affect one another in many ways. In this photograph people cope with the effects of the flooding of the Red River in Vietnam.

Movement

Each day, people in different parts of the country and different parts of the world interact with one another. People, products, and ideas move from place to place by transportation and communication. Geography helps you understand the causes and effects of this movement. It also helps you understand how people came to live where they do.

Immigrants from other countries celebrate becoming citizens of the United States.

Regions

Areas on the Earth with features that make them different from other areas are called **regions**. A region can be described by the physical features, such as mountains or a dry climate, that exist there. A region can also be described by its human features, such as the language spoken there or the kind of government. Sometimes a region is described by its political, cultural, or economic features.

Regions are sometimes divided into smaller regions that are easier to compare. Some geographers who study the Earth's surface and its people divide large areas of land into regions named for their relative locations. The huge continent of Asia is often divided into these regions—northern Asia, central Asia, southern Asia, southwestern Asia, southeastern Asia, and eastern Asia. The countries in each region are alike in many ways. They are all in the same part of Asia. They may have the same kind of landforms, climate, and natural resources.

REVIEW *What are the five themes of geography?*

LEARNING FROM DIAGRAMS
The continent of Asia can be separated into six geographic regions.
■ *Which country is a part of two regions?*

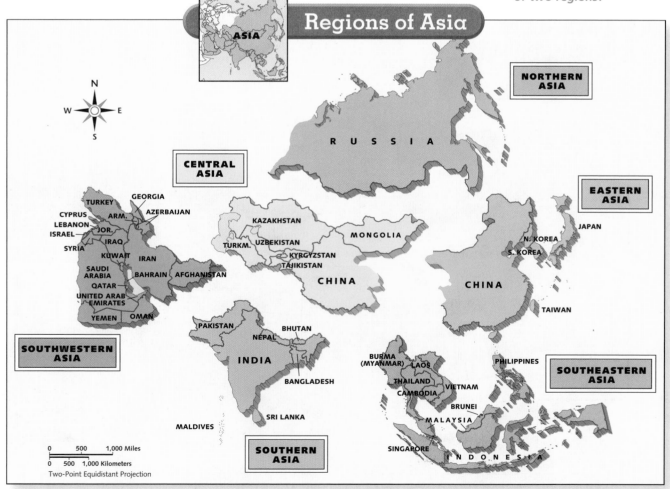

Regions of Asia

ASIA

NORTHERN ASIA

CENTRAL ASIA

EASTERN ASIA

SOUTHWESTERN ASIA

SOUTHEASTERN ASIA

SOUTHERN ASIA

RUSSIA

GEORGIA
TURKEY
AZERBAIJAN
CYPRUS
ARM.
LEBANON
ISRAEL
JOR.
SYRIA
IRAQ
KUWAIT
IRAN
SAUDI ARABIA
BAHRAIN
AFGHANISTAN
QATAR
UNITED ARAB EMIRATES
YEMEN
OMAN

KAZAKHSTAN
TURKM.
UZBEKISTAN
KYRGYZSTAN
TAJIKISTAN
MONGOLIA
CHINA

N. KOREA
S. KOREA
JAPAN
CHINA
TAIWAN

PAKISTAN
BHUTAN
NEPAL
INDIA
BANGLADESH
BURMA (MYANMAR)
LAOS
THAILAND
CAMBODIA
VIETNAM
PHILIPPINES
BRUNEI
MALAYSIA
SRI LANKA
MALDIVES
SINGAPORE
INDONESIA

0   500   1,000 Miles
0   500   1,000 Kilometers
Two-Point Equidistant Projection

Introduction • 37

Read a Map

1. Why Learn This Skill?

To answer questions about the world around you, you need information. One way you can get this information is by studying maps. Maps tell you about the world by using one or more of the five themes of geography. Knowing how to read and understand maps is an important skill both for learning social studies and for taking action as a citizen.

2. The Parts of a Map

Maps are drawings that show the Earth or part of the Earth on a flat surface. To help you read maps, mapmakers add certain features to most maps they draw. These are a title, a map key, a compass rose, a locator, a map scale, and an inset map. Mapmakers may also show a grid of numbered lines on maps to help people locate places more easily.

The United States

National capital
State capital
National border
State border

The **map title** tells the subject of the map. What is the title of the map shown on page 38? A map title may also help you understand what kind of map it is. Physical maps show landforms and bodies of water. Sometimes, shading is used to help you see where the hills and mountains are located. Political maps show cities and national boundaries, or borders. Many of the maps in this book are historical maps that show parts of the world as they were in the past. Historical maps often have dates in their titles. When you look at any map, look for information in the title to find out what the map is about.

The **map key**, sometimes called a map legend, explains what the symbols on the map stand for. Symbols may be colors, patterns, lines, or other special marks, such as circles, triangles, or squares. According to the map key for the map on page 38, stars are used to show state capitals. What symbol is used to show the national capital?

The **compass rose**, or direction marker, shows the **cardinal directions**, or main directions—north, south, east, and west. A compass rose also helps you find the **intermediate directions**, which are between the cardinal directions. Intermediate directions are northeast, northwest, southeast, and southwest.

The **locator** is a small map or picture of a globe. It shows where the area shown on the main map is located in a state, in a country, on a continent, or in the world. The locator on the map of the United States on page 38 is a globe that shows the continent of North America. The United States is shown in red.

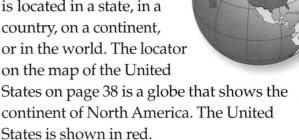

The **map scale** compares a distance on a map to a distance in the real world. A map scale helps you find the real distance between places on a map. Each map in this book has a scale that shows both miles and kilometers.

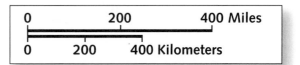

Map scales are different, depending on the size of the area the map shows. Look at the map of the United States on page 38. On that map are two smaller maps—one of Alaska and one of Hawaii. A small map within a larger map is called an **inset map**. The boxes around Alaska and Hawaii show that they are inset maps. Inset maps have their own scales. Inset maps make it possible to show places in greater detail or to show places that are beyond the area shown on the main map.

The north-south and east-west lines on a map cross each other to form a pattern of squares called a **grid**. The east-west lines are **lines of latitude**. The north-south lines are **lines of longitude**. This grid helps you find the absolute location, or global address, of a place.

3. Understand the Process

Use the map of Venezuela on this page to answer the following questions.

1 What is the title of the map?

2 What three countries share a border with Venezuela?

3 In which direction would you travel if you went from Valencia to Canaima?

4 Find the map key. What symbol is used to show a national capital?

5 What line of latitude is closest to Barcelona?

6 Find the locator map. How is the location of Venezuela shown?

7 Find the map scale. How long is the line that stands for 200 miles?

8 Find the inset map. What area is shown in the inset map?

4. Think and Apply

Look again at the map below. Find the different parts of the map, and discuss with a partner what information the map gives you about Venezuela.

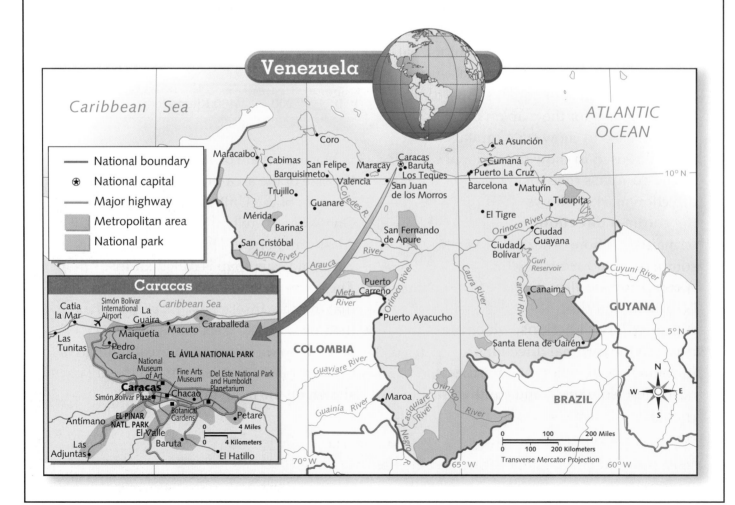

Civics and Government

Civics and government is the study of citizenship and the ways in which citizens govern themselves. A government is a system of leaders and laws that helps people live together in their community, state, or country.

In *The World* you will learn about the different kinds of government in the world today. You will learn about the people and events that shaped governments in the past. You will also learn about citizenship and the rights and responsibilities of citizens in governments in both the past and the present.

Economics

The **economy** of a country is the way its people use its resources to meet their needs. The study of how people do this is called economics. In this book you will read about how people in the past made, bought, sold, and traded goods to get what they needed or wanted. You will learn about different kinds of economies—from the simple ones of the ancient past to the more complex ones of today—and how they came to be.

Culture

In this book you will learn about the people of the past who shaped the present. You will learn who these people were, what they looked like, and how they spoke and acted. You will explore their customs and beliefs and their ways of thinking and expressing ideas. You will look at their families and communities. All these things make up their culture. Each human group, or **society**, has a culture. This book will help you discover the many cultures that are part of our world's story, both past and present.

REVIEW *What kinds of things do you learn when you study civics and government, economics, and culture?*

Unit 1

Unit 2	Unit 3	Unit 4	Unit 5
Cradles of Civilization	Asia's Classical Age	The Mediterranean	Rise of New Empires

EARLY PEOPLE AND LIFEWAYS

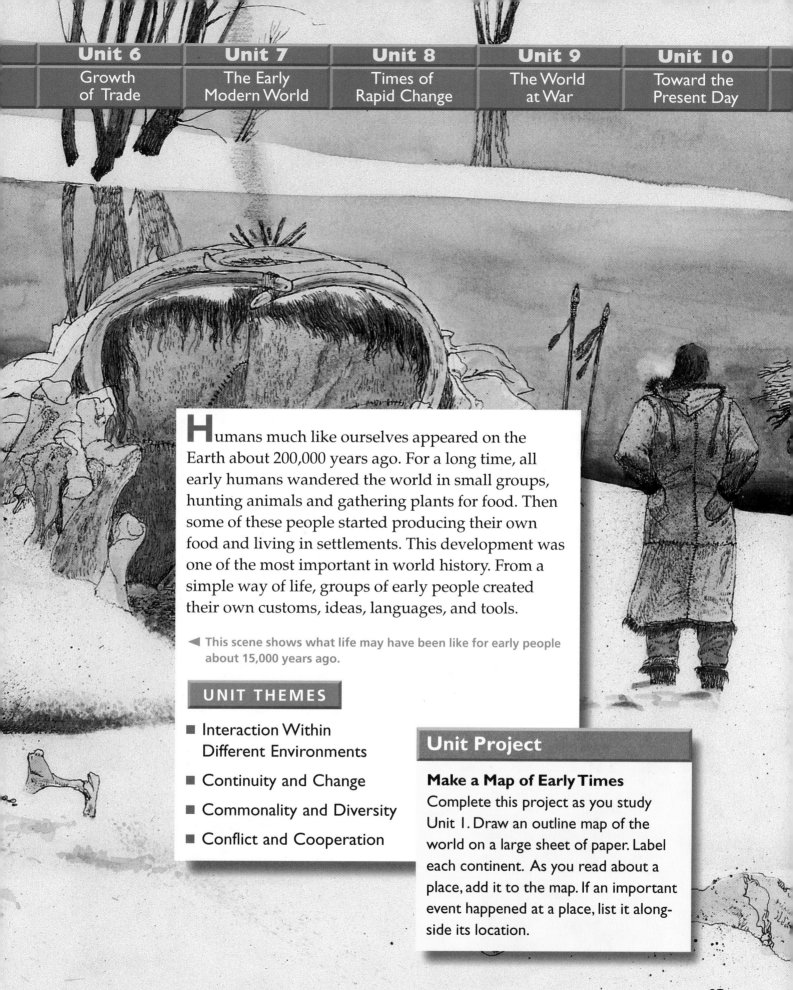

Humans much like ourselves appeared on the Earth about 200,000 years ago. For a long time, all early humans wandered the world in small groups, hunting animals and gathering plants for food. Then some of these people started producing their own food and living in settlements. This development was one of the most important in world history. From a simple way of life, groups of early people created their own customs, ideas, languages, and tools.

◄ This scene shows what life may have been like for early people about 15,000 years ago.

UNIT THEMES

- Interaction Within Different Environments
- Continuity and Change
- Commonality and Diversity
- Conflict and Cooperation

Unit Project

Make a Map of Early Times
Complete this project as you study Unit 1. Draw an outline map of the world on a large sheet of paper. Label each continent. As you read about a place, add it to the map. If an important event happened at a place, list it along-side its location.

43

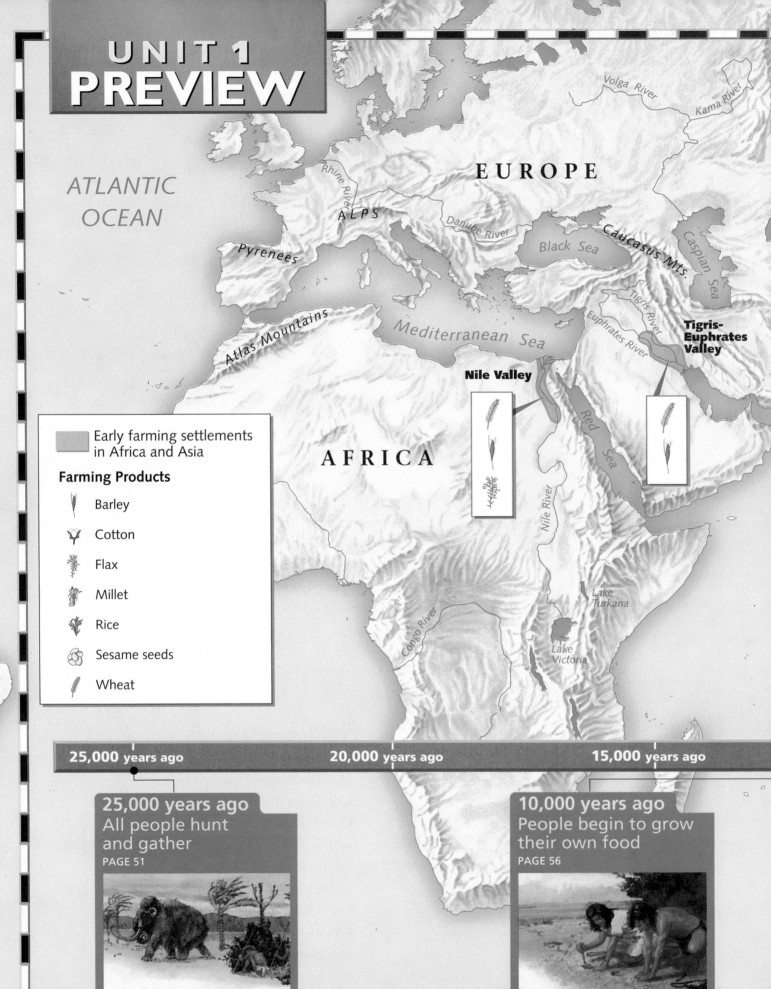

ATLANTIC OCEAN

EUROPE

Volga River

Kama River

Rhine River

ALPS

Danube River

Pyrenees

Black Sea

Caucasus Mts.

Caspian Sea

Atlas Mountains

Mediterranean Sea

Euphrates River

Tigris River

Tigris-Euphrates Valley

Nile Valley

AFRICA

Red Sea

Nile River

Congo River

Lake Turkana

Lake Victoria

Early farming settlements in Africa and Asia

Farming Products

- Barley
- Cotton
- Flax
- Millet
- Rice
- Sesame seeds
- Wheat

25,000 years ago   **20,000** years ago   **15,000** years ago

25,000 years ago
All people hunt and gather
PAGE 51

10,000 years ago
People begin to grow their own food
PAGE 56

Ancient Africa, Europe, and Asia

ASIA

Ob River

Irtysh River

Sea of Okhotsk

Amur River

Huang He

Huang He Valley

Sea of Japan

Chang Jiang

East China Sea

Indus River

Sutlej River

HIMALAYAS

Mekong River

Indus Valley

Ganges River

Bay of Bengal

South China Sea

PACIFIC OCEAN

N
W   E
S

INDIAN OCEAN

0   800   1,600 Miles
0   800   1,600 Kilometers
Miller Cylindrical Projection

10,000 years ago   5,000 years ago   **Present**

5,500 years ago
Earliest cities form
PAGE 73

4,000 years ago
Time of invention in Mesopotamia
PAGE 73

2,600 years ago
First coined money
PAGE 88

Boy of the Painted Cave

by Justin Denzel

From rocky cliffs in Africa to caves in Europe, Australia, and the Americas, early people left behind clear images of life thousands of years ago. The world's earliest artists covered the cave walls and rocks with beautiful paintings. Some of the earliest paintings are patterns of handprints. Other paintings show magnificent scenes of the animals the early people hunted for food.

No one knows for sure why the early people of the world began painting. Perhaps they painted as part of their religious beliefs. Perhaps they wanted to tell about how they lived and what they did.

The following story is set more than 30,000 years ago in the Stone Age, a time when people made tools and weapons from stone. The main characters are Tao and Graybeard. Tao is a young boy who is fascinated by the wild animals that his people depend on to meet their needs. Young Tao dreams of becoming a cave painter like Graybeard. Read now about Stone Age people who counted on the natural resources around them for all their needs.

Ancient artists used their own handprints to create this cave painting found in the South American country of Argentina.

Tao winced as he saw the worn face, the pinched cheekbones. He was worried, but he knew the old man would not want him to show concern. "The cave is ready," Tao said. "But first you must rest and eat." He took some dried meat and fish from his leather pouch and they sat with their backs against an old red oak and ate their meal. Tao wondered if Graybeard remembered his promise.

When they were finished, they started across the valley. Graybeard stopped many times, poking around the streambeds and gravel banks with the shaft of his spear, searching. Then he found what he was looking for. He picked up a stick and dug out a handful of bright red earth.

"Here," he said, as he poured it into an empty leather sack. "This will make good red paint. Now we must find yellows and whites."

Ancient artists used tools similar to these. On a grindstone rest two rocks used for sculpting, pieces of manganese and ocher for painting, and a paint scraper.

"I have yellow clay," said Tao. The old man did remember.

"Good. We can dig up some limestone powder near the foot of the cliffs. That will mix well for the lighter colors."

When they had all the red, white and yellow earth they needed, they went up to the top of the cliff, using the easy path that Graybeard had found. They reached the tunnel to the Hidden Cave and removed the cover of branches to let in the sunlight.

In the cave Graybeard sat on the ground and Tao squatted beside him. The old man poured some of the red earth into one of the saucer-shaped rocks that Tao had collected. Then, using a smooth, round stone, he began grinding it into a fine powder. When it was to his liking, he added some of Tao's fish oil, mixing it into a dark red paint. He poured a small amount of this into three other shallow stone dishes. In the first one he added a lump of yellow clay, in the second he sprinkled limestone powder and in the third he added charcoal dust. Using a small, clean stick for each, he mixed them well, ending with three different colors: a bright orange, a salmon pink and a dark brown.

Tao was amazed. He sat quietly, watching. This too was magic, he thought. Graybeard spread out more saucers and began blending shades of yellows, browns, grays and blacks. Some he mixed with honey, and some with the boiled fat and clotted blood from the boar.

"Next we must make our brushes," he said. He took a handful of twigs from his pouch and began mashing the ends with a stone until they were soft and ragged. He held one up in the shaft of sunlight beaming through the cave entrance. He turned it around for Tao to see. "These are small," he said, "for painting eyes and fine lines of hair and fur."

He made larger brushes by tying feathers and boar bristles around the ends of long sticks with strings of vegetable fiber.

Cave painting from South America, near Perito Moreno, Argentina

When all the paints and brushes were made, the old man got to his feet. "Now," he said, "we are ready to paint."

Tao held out the shoulder blade of the horse, while Graybeard poured spots of the colored paints onto its broad white surface. He handed the boy one of the large brushes and pointed to Tao's pictures of the rhinos, bison and mammoths.

The boy held his breath. He had never had a brush in his hand before. "Which one will I paint?"

Horses seem to come alive in this ancient cave painting from Lascaux, France.

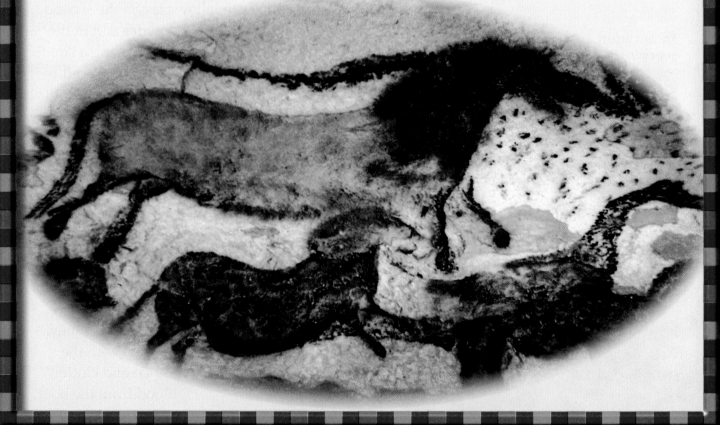

Graybeard smiled. "You are the image maker. Paint the one you like the best."

"The mountain-that-walks," said Tao.

Graybeard nodded. "Then begin."

Tao hesitated, glancing at the paints on the shoulder blade, uncertain.

"You saw the mammoths," said Graybeard. "What color were they?"

"Reddish-brown."

"Good," said the old man. "Then mix a little black with the red until you have the color you wish."

Tao dipped his brush into the spot of black, then mixed it with the red. He lifted his hand and touched it to the drawing. It was still too light, so he dipped in another dab of black. Again his brush touched the drawing. He smiled. It was a deep reddish-brown, the color he wanted. He continued to dip and touch.

Graybeard watched as Tao repeated the motion again and again. He reached out and stopped the boy's hand. "You are not painting on an antler or a seashell," he said. "You are painting on a wall. Do not dab. Swing the brush with your whole arm."

Graybeard took the brush and began sweeping it across the drawing, following the lines of the mammoth's body.

Tao saw the old man's face brighten as he worked, laying on great swaths of color. He felt the excitement as the picture came alive.

"Do not be afraid," said Graybeard, his eyes glowing. "You can always go over what you do not like."

He gave the brush back to Tao and the boy tried again. This time he let his arm go free, swinging the brush across the wall. He mixed gray with yellow to fill in the light

North American rock carving, found in Monument Valley, Utah

areas around the chest and stomach. He painted dark shadows on the shoulders and back to add shading. He saw his mammoth begin to breathe as he filled in the eye and the waving trunk.

When the painting was finished, Graybeard cracked open the duck eggs. He separated the yolks and set them aside. He poured the whites into a clean cockleshell, stirred them with a stick and handed the shell to Tao.

The boy was puzzled. "What is this for?"

"Spread it over your painting and you will see."

With a feather brush Tao washed the egg white over the picture. This time the mammoth came alive with bright new colors. He stared at it in surprise. This had been done by his own hand. He smiled. Never had he felt so happy.

As you read more about early people in this unit, you will discover how people on different continents met their needs and developed unique ways of life.

CHAPTER

1

PEOPLE OF THE STONE AGE

"The sudden emergence of full human creativity among the advanced hunters of this period . . . is surely one of the most astonishing chapters in all our history."

Jacquetta Hawkes,
The Atlas of Early Man

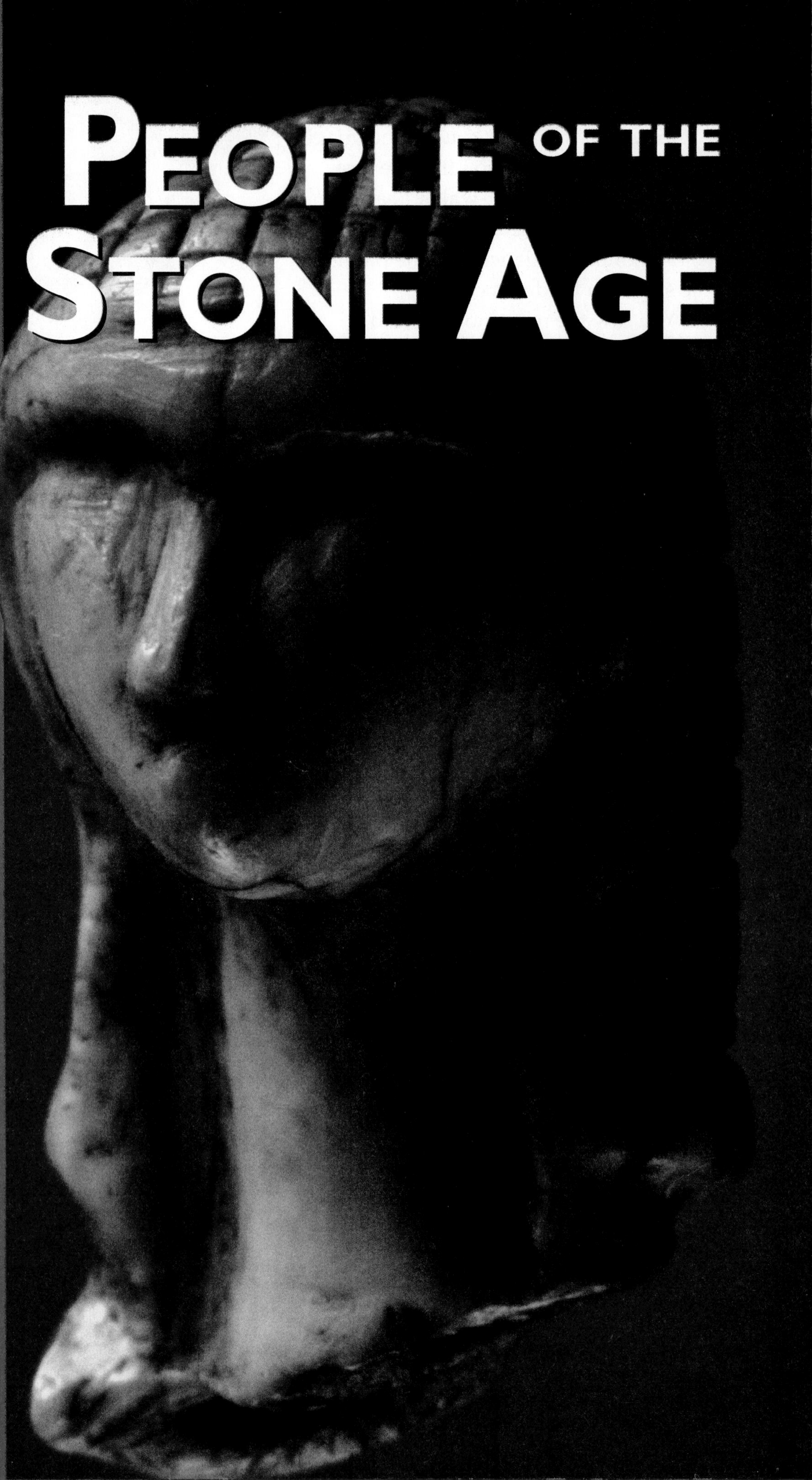

Found in France, this 25,000-year-old sculpture of a woman is one of the earliest images of a human face.

Hunters and Gatherers

FOCUS
Why do people join
groups today?

Main Idea As you
read, look for reasons
early people lived and
worked in groups.

Vocabulary

band
consequence
migration
Ice Age
tundra
culture
artifact
society
division of labor
role

The earliest humans, people like us, probably lived in Africa. Over tens of thousands of years, they slowly spread into Asia, Europe, Australia, and North and South America. Generation after generation of these early people moved in groups, hunting and gathering enough food to survive. As they wandered, they populated much of the Earth. They continued to follow the same way of life wherever they lived.

Getting Food

Most of the earliest people united in **bands**, groups of related families brought together for a common purpose. At first, no more than 20 people lived and worked together in a band. Members of a band cooperated to meet their basic needs for food, clothing, and shelter.

Band members spent their days roaming the land, collecting wild fruits, nuts, roots, and seeds for the group to eat. Occasionally they captured fish, turtles, birds, or small rodents. Experience taught them which plants and animals could be eaten without causing unwelcome **consequences**, or effects, such as illness or death from poisoning.

Some bands hunted large animals that are now extinct, such as giant oxen, woolly rhinoceroses, and elephant-like mammoths. Other common prey, such as reindeer and bison, still exist. All these animals provided meat for food, bones for tools, and hides for clothing and shelter.

To kill large animals, early hunters needed special tools. They sharpened stones, animal bones, antlers, or tusks to make spears and knives. Band members also needed special skills and teamwork to hunt large game animals. Some early hunters, for example, killed these creatures by chasing them over a cliff. Others wrapped themselves in animal hides and crept close enough to make a kill.

Because early bands were always on the move to hunt animals and gather wild plants, they had no permanent

These blades from southwestern Asia (left) and this carved rock from northern Africa (far left) are examples of early tools used to hunt and kill prey.

Migrations of Early People

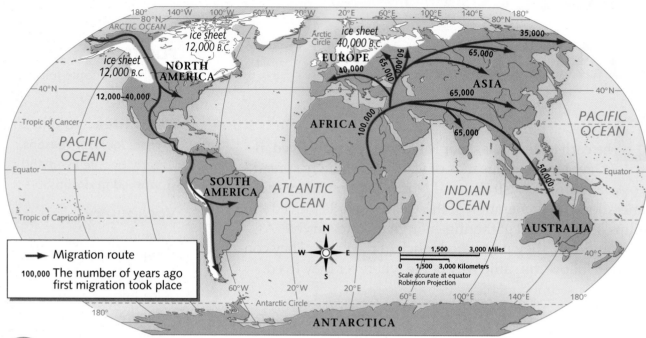

Movement Early people probably began to migrate from Africa about 100,000 years ago.

- On what continents had people arrived by about 60,000 years ago?

year-round settlements. Instead, they set up seasonal camps in caves or rock shelters near places where plants and animals were plentiful. When food became scarce in one place, bands moved to other familiar places. There they knew they would find more food.

Usually bands traveled around a particular area as they searched for food. By following a regular seasonal pattern of **migration**, or movement from one place to the next, bands of hunters and gatherers found enough to eat.

REVIEW *Why was cooperation important for early hunters and gatherers?*

Spreading Through the World

As some bands grew in number, they had to roam farther from their usual hunting and gathering grounds to find enough food. Each new generation expanded the band's

migration pattern. Some experts believe that just 2 or 3 miles (3.2 to 4.8 km) were added every 20 years—the average length of an early person's life. By this very slow process, humans began to spread

LEARNING FROM DIAGRAMS Hunters and gatherers in different regions used the resources in their environments to make clothes, tools, weapons, and shelters. They hunted large animals and gathered any fruits, nuts, and roots they could find.

- Look at the three scenes. What kinds of resources are shown in each scene?

AFRICA

throughout the world. It probably took hundreds of generations tens of thousands of years to accomplish this!

For a long time, early people lived only in Africa. Then about 100,000 years ago, some people crossed from Africa into southwestern Asia. Today this land is a wide desert. Long ago, herds of gazelle and deer ranged over a grassy plain. Following these herds, generation after generation of early people slowly migrated farther in every direction.

Those who moved to the east about 65,000 years ago crossed land barriers of rugged mountains into the green valleys of what is now China. Later generations overcame the ocean barrier and crossed the deep, narrow passage east to what is now Indonesia. From there men, women, and children paddled log rafts across open sea, finally reaching Australia.

About 40,000 years ago some groups of people spread into Europe. Others migrated to the northeast, following herds of wild animals. They reached what is now Siberia in Russia about 35,000 years ago. This was during the time of the last **Ice Age**, a long cold-weather period when huge sheets of ice covered about one-third of the Earth's surface.

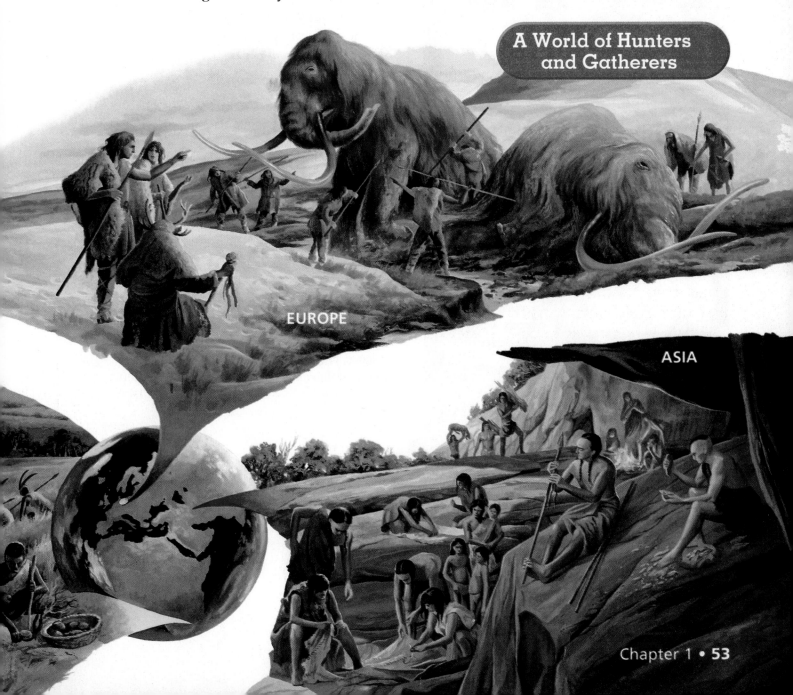

A World of Hunters and Gatherers

EUROPE

ASIA

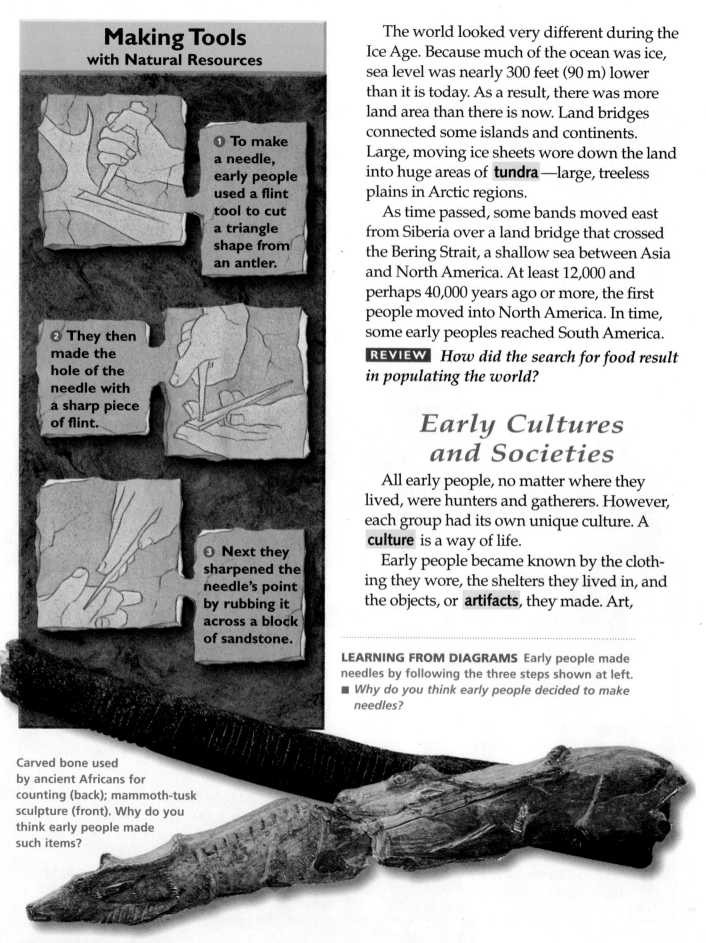

Making Tools
with Natural Resources

1 To make a needle, early people used a flint tool to cut a triangle shape from an antler.

2 They then made the hole of the needle with a sharp piece of flint.

3 Next they sharpened the needle's point by rubbing it across a block of sandstone.

Carved bone used by ancient Africans for counting (back); mammoth-tusk sculpture (front). Why do you think early people made such items?

The world looked very different during the Ice Age. Because much of the ocean was ice, sea level was nearly 300 feet (90 m) lower than it is today. As a result, there was more land area than there is now. Land bridges connected some islands and continents. Large, moving ice sheets wore down the land into huge areas of **tundra**—large, treeless plains in Arctic regions.

As time passed, some bands moved east from Siberia over a land bridge that crossed the Bering Strait, a shallow sea between Asia and North America. At least 12,000 and perhaps 40,000 years ago or more, the first people moved into North America. In time, some early peoples reached South America.

REVIEW *How did the search for food result in populating the world?*

Early Cultures and Societies

All early people, no matter where they lived, were hunters and gatherers. However, each group had its own unique culture. A **culture** is a way of life.

Early people became known by the clothing they wore, the shelters they lived in, and the objects, or **artifacts**, they made. Art,

LEARNING FROM DIAGRAMS Early people made needles by following the three steps shown at left.
■ *Why do you think early people decided to make needles?*

beliefs, customs, and languages also set people apart.

Using spoken language, band members shared their feelings and let each other know their needs. Older members used language to pass on customs and knowledge to younger members. Language helped early people join together to become a society. A **society** is an organized group of people living and working under an established set of rules and traditions.

As bands merged and grew in size, their society changed. In a small band with only 20 members, everyone did similar tasks. For example, they collected plants, hunted, made tools, built shelters, and prepared hides for clothing. In larger bands of 50 to 100 members, a **division of labor** began. Different members did different tasks, based on their abilities and the band's needs.

Each person in these larger bands took on a **role**, a part he or she played to help society. A person good at carving spent most of his or

This horse carved from amber was found in Brandenburg, Germany.

her time making tools for the group. An expert at preparing and sewing hides became the group's clothing maker. Because food gathering and hunting were important to early societies, the group's hunters and gatherers came to be viewed as its leaders.

In some early societies, women who were skilled at gathering plants became leaders. In other societies, men who were successful at hunting were made leaders. With the division of labor, men's and women's roles in some societies most likely became different.

REVIEW *How is a culture different from a society?*

LESSON 1 REVIEW

Check Understanding

1 Remember the Facts How did early people get the food they needed to survive?

2 Recall the Main Idea Why did early people work together?

Think Critically

3 Think More About It For what purposes besides getting food might early people have worked together?

4 Past to Present How do people in our society cooperate today?

5 Explore Viewpoints Leaders may have had different ideas from other group members about how resources should be shared. Why might this have been so?

Show What You Know

Story Activity Imagine that you are a hunter-gatherer. Make up a story about a time when your band worked together to find food. Tell your story to a classmate.

Early Farmers

FOCUS

How does change affect your life today?

Main Idea Consider the effects of change on the early people who became food producers instead of food collectors.

Vocabulary

domesticate
economy
livestock
nomad
agriculture
environment
maize
subsist

As early societies grew, many bands found that they could no longer depend on hunting and gathering for their basic needs. Some early societies began to change from food collecting to food producing—growing crops and raising livestock.

Controlling Nature

About 10,000 years ago some hunter-gatherer societies began to produce some of their food. Instead of simply being part of nature, they began to find ways to control nature. This change meant that people no longer depended just on what they could find or hunt. Instead, people learned to domesticate plants and animals. To **domesticate** living things means to tame them for people's use.

Women probably did most of the food gathering in early societies and may have been the first to domesticate plants. They probably began this process as they cared for wild plants. They learned that seeds from fully grown plants produced new plants. As time passed, they most likely began planting seeds from carefully selected plants. They chose seeds from plants that were plentiful, healthy, fast growing, and good tasting.

Some societies soon came to depend less on wild plants and more on crops grown in small gardens by early farmers. Growing crops, however, meant that the people in those societies had to stay in one place. The process of planting, caring for, and harvesting crops takes many months of constant care. Early farming societies built year-round shelters, formed small villages, and grew crops on the surrounding land. These societies' **economy**, or the way people use resources to meet their needs, became based mainly on their crops.

Even in farming societies animals were still an important resource. Some societies went on hunting wild animals for food, bones, and hides. Others began to domesticate animals as well as plants. Dogs had long been tamed and used for hunting. Now people began to domesticate wild sheep and

As people began to raise their own crops, they needed new kinds of tools. Early people used this tool, called a quern, to grind grain. How do you think early people made this tool?

Early Farming Areas

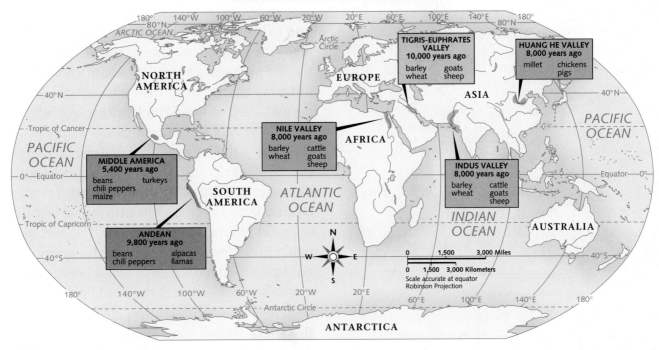

Regions Early farming areas developed in different places around the world. This map shows the most important areas.

■ *What does this map tell you about where early farming areas developed?*

goats as well. These newly domesticated animals provided a ready supply of meat, milk, and wool. Some early people came to depend less on raising crops and more on raising **livestock**, domesticated animals such as cattle, sheep, and pigs.

Many of the early people who cared for livestock were **nomads**. They moved from place to place with their herds of animals to find pasture and water. Like hunting-and-gathering nomads, those who herded livestock did not build villages or other year-round settlements. Instead, they lived in temporary shelters and traveled in bands.

Not all people adopted a new way of life as farmers or herders. Some went on hunting and gathering their food. In fact, a few groups of people still do.

REVIEW *What major change took place in the food supply of early people?*

Effects of Change

Agriculture, the raising of domesticated plants and animals, changed human societies forever. Agriculture provided a reliable food source. Food production increased as people invented tools, such as the plow, and came up with refinements, such as domesticating cattle to pull plows and collecting water for crops.

Agriculture made more food available, but it also made living conditions more difficult in some ways. Instead of finding food only for the band, people also had to raise crops to feed their domesticated animals.

In some places agriculture increased the rate of population growth. Yet there were deaths due to starvation and disease when drought and insect attacks killed crops and livestock. There were also deaths due to wars

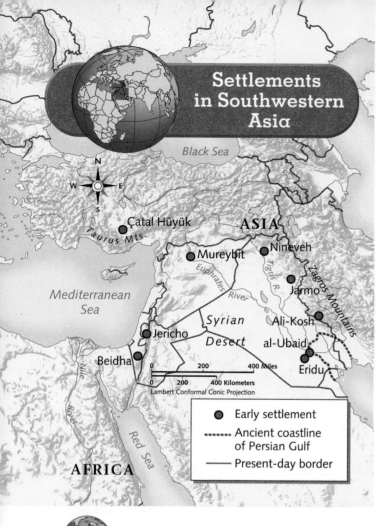

Settlements in Southwestern Asia

Black Sea

ASIA

Çatal Hüyük

Taurus Mts.

Mureybit

Nineveh

Euphrates River

Tigris R.

Zagros Mountains

Jarmo

Mediterranean Sea

Syrian Desert

Ali-Kosh

Jericho

al-Ubaid

Beidha

Eridu

0   200   400 Miles
0   200   400 Kilometers
Lambert Conformal Conic Projection

Nile River

Red Sea

AFRICA

● Early settlement

······· Ancient coastline of Persian Gulf

—— Present-day border

Human-Environment Interactions | Early farming villages rose in southwestern Asia.

■ *Near what type of natural feature did early people often build their farming villages?*

when people fought to protect farmland or to take land away from others.

People began to make weapons for war and to build walls around their farming villages for protection. One of the oldest-known walled villages was built at a site known today as Jericho in southwestern Asia. The people lived in mud-brick huts grouped inside the village's stone walls.

Some of the ways in which early farmers practiced agriculture had consequences for their surroundings, or **environment**. Farmers cleared land for crops by cutting and burning the wild plants that grew there. The ashes made good fertilizer. But the rich variety of wild plants that once supported herds of wild animals was lost when the land began to be used as fields and pastures.

REVIEW *What were some advantages and disadvantages of agriculture?*

Diversity in Early Agriculture

In the different places where agriculture developed, people domesticated a wide variety of plants and animals. Agriculture in the Tigris-Euphrates river valley of

LEARNING FROM GRAPHS The population of the world grew dramatically as a result of the introduction of agriculture.

■ *What was the world's population 12,000 years ago? How many more people were there by 6,000 years ago?*

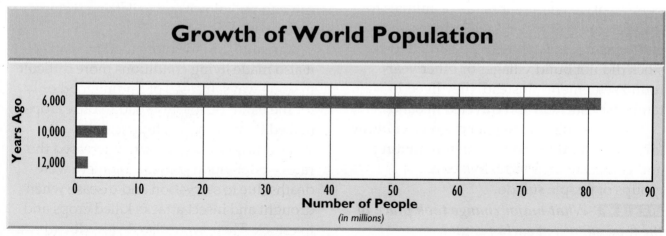

Growth of World Population

Years Ago

6,000
10,000
12,000

0   10   20   30   40   50   60   70   80   90

Number of People
(in millions)

Some cave paintings, like this one from Algeria, Africa, reflect everyday life. In this painting men, women, and children work alongside herds of cattle. At the far left is one main farm product of early people—wheat.

southwestern Asia was based on growing wheat and barley and on raising sheep, goats, and cattle. Throughout the Nile Valley in northern Africa, agriculture produced wheat, barley, flax, sheep, goats, cattle, and pigs. Far to the east, people settling the river valleys of present-day Pakistan and China raised grains such as rice and millet and kept pigs, chickens, and water buffalo.

Meanwhile, in the Americas, early farmers began growing beans and chili peppers in the mountain valleys of what is now Peru and potatoes in what is now Bolivia. Plants later domesticated in the Americas included squash, gourds, guavas, and **maize**, or corn.

At its beginning, agriculture offered another way besides hunting and gathering for people to **subsist**, or survive. In many places agriculture led to year-round villages and more complex societies. People did not always stay in one place, however. Many groups went on migrating, searching for new land for their crops and fresh pastures for their herds.

REVIEW *What is meant by diversity of agriculture?*

LESSON 2 REVIEW

Check Understanding

1. **Remember the Facts** What new way of getting food changed societies?

2. **Recall the Main Idea** How did early people become food producers? What effect did this change have?

Think Critically

3. **Think More About It** Why did farming societies feel a need to control land while hunter-gatherer societies did not?

4. **Past to Present** Clearing forest land today affects the environment just as clearing wild plants did long ago. What were the effects then? What are they now?

Show What You Know

Debate Activity Think about how domesticating plants and animals changed societies. Take the side either of a farmer or of a hunter-gatherer in a debate over the consequences of the change from hunting and gathering to agriculture among early people.

Use a Parallel Time Line

1. Why Learn This Skill?

Just as maps help you understand *where* something happened, time lines help you understand *when* something happened. Time lines let you put events in sequence.

Some time lines are simple to read and understand. Others, such as the one below, are more difficult. It is important to look at complex time lines carefully to be sure you understand them fully.

2. Think About Time Lines

The time line you see on this page is a **parallel time line**. It is really several time lines in one. Parallel time lines are useful if you want to show related events. You could show when the same kind of events happened in different areas. Or you could show events that happened in different places at the same time.

Each section of this parallel time line is divided into spans of 2,000 years, beginning at

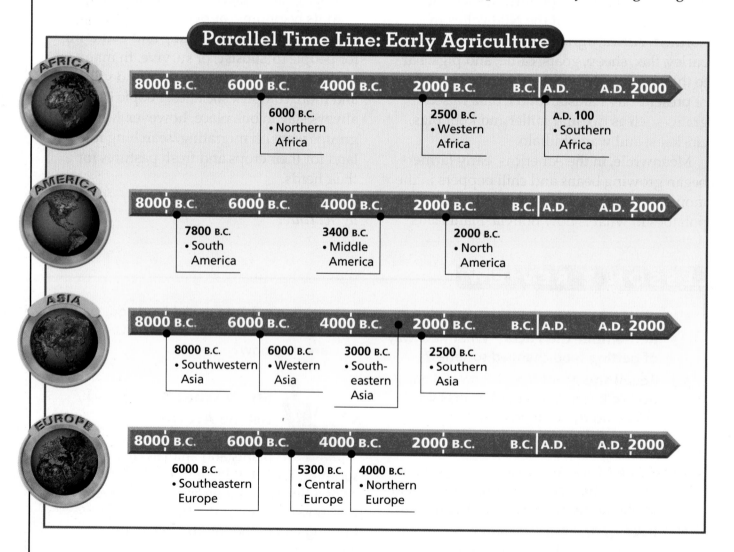

Parallel Time Line: Early Agriculture

AFRICA
8000 B.C.   6000 B.C.   4000 B.C.   2000 B.C.   B.C. | A.D.   A.D. 2000

6000 B.C.
• Northern Africa

2500 B.C.
• Western Africa

A.D. 100
• Southern Africa

AMERICA
8000 B.C.   6000 B.C.   4000 B.C.   2000 B.C.   B.C. | A.D.   A.D. 2000

7800 B.C.
• South America

3400 B.C.
• Middle America

2000 B.C.
• North America

ASIA
8000 B.C.   6000 B.C.   4000 B.C.   2000 B.C.   B.C. | A.D.   A.D. 2000

8000 B.C.
• Southwestern Asia

6000 B.C.
• Western Asia

3000 B.C.
• Southeastern Asia

2500 B.C.
• Southern Asia

EUROPE
8000 B.C.   6000 B.C.   4000 B.C.   2000 B.C.   B.C. | A.D.   A.D. 2000

6000 B.C.
• Southeastern Europe

5300 B.C.
• Central Europe

4000 B.C.
• Northern Europe

8000 B.C. and ending at A.D. 2000. The abbreviation B.C. stands for "before Christ." A.D. stands for *anno Domini,* a Latin phrase meaning "in the year of the Lord." This abbreviation tells how many years have passed since the birth of Jesus Christ. Some time lines are labeled B.C.E. and C.E. rather than B.C. and A.D. The abbreviation B.C.E. stands for "before the Common Era" and C.E. stands for "Common Era." The terms B.C.E. and C.E. refer to the same years as B.C. and A.D.

No one knows exactly when some events of long ago happened. Therefore, a date on a time line sometimes is approximate, or not exact. This usually means that the earliest evidence, or proof, is from about that time. Approximate times are often shown after the Latin term *circa,* or *c.,* its abbreviation. The term *circa* means "about."

The time line on page 60 shows when agriculture developed during the Stone Age in different geographic regions. The Stone Age was a time when early people developed the first societies. The Stone Age is divided into two parts. The Paleolithic period, or Old Stone Age, is the time before 8000 B.C. The Neolithic period, or New Stone Age, is the time from 8000 B.C. to as late as the present day. During the Paleolithic period, all people were hunters and gatherers. During the Neolithic period, people began to domesticate plants and animals. This led to the development of agriculture.

3. Understand the Process

Look down the left-hand side of the time line. Find the top bar, labeled *Africa.* What is the first date that is highlighted on the top bar? If you said 6000 B.C., you are right. Under that date are the words *Northern Africa.* This means that agriculture began in northern Africa in about 6000 B.C.

Now look at the other bars on the time line. In which regions of the world did people develop agriculture at about the same time?

4. Think and Apply

Make a parallel time line comparing important events in your life with events in the lives of family members or friends. Make sure that your time line has a bar for each person and a title. Write three questions for a classmate to answer using your time line.

The following steps will help you make your time line:

- Identify the events you want to show.
- Determine the length of time over which the events took place.
- Make the time line, divide it into equal parts, and mark the years on it.
- Add the events you want to display. It is always a good idea to double-check the dates of events to be sure your information is accurate.
- Give your time line a title that explains its contents.

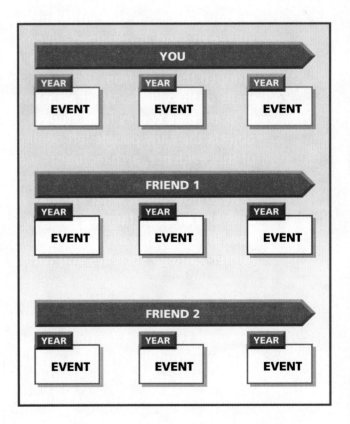

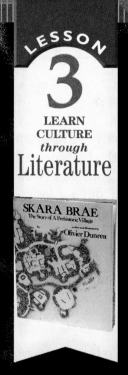

Skara Brae

THE STORY OF A PREHISTORIC VILLAGE

written and illustrated
by Olivier Dunrea

Skara Brae was an early farming village on an island off northern Scotland. Shortly before 2400 B.C. a sudden storm covered the village in sand. It remained covered for more than 4,300 years. Then, in A.D. 1850, a powerful windstorm stripped the sand from the dunes and uncovered the stone walls of the village. What archaeologists know about life in Skara Brae comes from studying the stone huts and the objects the early people left behind. Through careful study of this evidence, archaeologists were able to piece together the story of this village of long ago.

Read now about what life may have been like in Skara Brae and in other farming villages long ago. Think about how life in these early settlements compared with life in hunter-gatherer societies and with our lives today.

By 3500 B.C. farmers and herders had reached a group of islands to the north of Scotland—the Orkneys.

They found the Orkneys an ideal place to live. There were gently rolling hills, open grasslands for their sheep and cattle, and wide, sand-fringed bays. The islands had no predatory animals that would attack their livestock. It was a good area to settle.

Orkney was a strange place to these early settlers. They were accustomed to trees and forests. In Orkney there were far fewer trees.

But though there was very little wood, there was plenty of fuel. Mosses and other plants had decayed in bogs to form peat. The peat could be burned like coal. The settlers could keep warm and cook their meat around a peat fire.

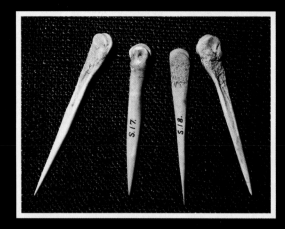

Pins made of bone in Skara Brae around 2500 B.C.

Most of all, there was a great abundance of stone on the islands. Stones were everywhere—on the beaches, on the grasslands, and on the hills. The herders and farmers chose these stones to build their permanent homes and monuments.

In time the Orkneys became more populated. New masses of migrating people reached their shores. Several generations of settlers came and went, and some ventured off to the smaller and less populated islands.

One band of settlers, seeking better grazing land for their animals, moved farther out on the main island. Making their way to the farthest west coast, they explored the land for a suitable place to live.

As they marched northward along the rugged cliffs and inlets, they came to a beautiful wide bay—the Bay of Skaill. There were sand dunes, open grassland, and no other settlers to compete for the land's resources. It was here the band decided to make their new home.

There were twenty people in the group: four small families. Together they owned a flock of sheep, a small herd of cattle, and a few pigs.

After surveying the land around the bay, they chose the southwest corner in which to erect their temporary shelters. The women and older children put up the tents, using wooden poles they had brought with them. These tents made of skins would protect them from rain and wind.

It was the task of the older children to tend the livestock, even though the animals mostly fended for themselves and found food wherever they could.

Orkney Islands

0   5   10 Miles
0   5   10 Kilometers
Lambert Conformal Conic Projection

2°30′W

North Ronaldsay

Westray

ATLANTIC OCEAN

Sanday

Rousay   Eday

North Sea

SKARA BRAE

Stronsay

Shapinsay

59°N   59°N

Mainland
Stromness   Kirkwall

2°30′W

Hoy

South Ronaldsay

UNITED KINGDOM

FRANCE

3°W

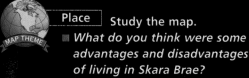

Place   Study the map.
■ What do you think were some advantages and disadvantages of living in Skara Brae?

64 • Unit 1

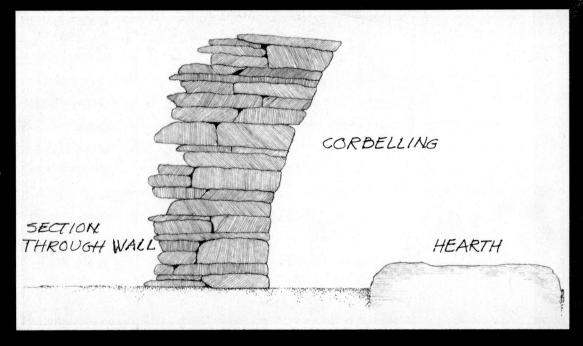

Example of building method used in Skara Brae home

SECTION THROUGH WALL

CORBELLING

HEARTH

During this period, settlers lived off their animals. To their diet of meat and milk they added wild foods foraged[1] from the land and sea—birds and eggs, fish, shellfish such as limpets,[2] and wild grains. The men sometimes brought in the meat of deer and other wild animals as well.

Through the summer, autumn, and winter the band continued to live in their tents. During the winter months they started construction of a new village that would have proper houses for all the families.

While they built the permanent stone houses, everyone worked. The men gathered the larger stones needed for the foundations and walls. The women and children also gathered stones to be used in the construction of the huts.

Everyone worked together on all the houses. One partly completed house was used as a shelter for the cattle, sheep, and pigs. The band continued to live off their animals as well as the land and sea.

There were plenty of stones on the beach around the bay, and collecting them went quickly. The stones could be easily split to make straight, uniform surfaces for building.

The stones were laid one on top of another without the use of mortar.[3] We now call this method of building drywall construction. The settlers might have used curved whalebones washed up on the beach to help support the roofs.

The houses were small when completed, measuring only twelve feet long by six to nine feet wide in the interior. The plan of each house was basically square, with rounded corners. In one of the corners, there was a small, beehive-shaped cell, used either for storage or as a latrine.[4]

The walls were built by piling stone upon stone. A few feet above the floor the stones began to project a little toward the inside of the hut. This overlapping construction is called corbelling.[5]

[1] **foraged:** searched for food
[2] **limpets:** small shellfish

[3] **mortar:** mixture of lime, sand, and water
[4] **latrine:** toilet
[5] **corbelling:** stepping upward and outward

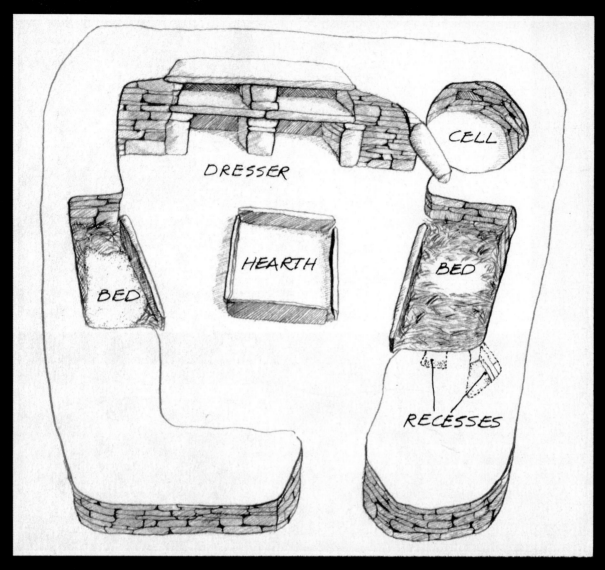

Layout of a typical Skara Brae home

Each hut was big enough to allow room for a central hearth,[6] a stone bed set into the wall on either side of the hearth, and a stone dresser built into the rear wall. The mother and small children slept in the bed to the left of the hearth; the father slept in the bed to the right.

The stone beds were filled with heather[7] and skins, making them comfortable and warm for sleeping. There were one or two small recesses for keeping personal posses- sions in the wall above each bed.

Within a few weeks the little huts were completed. And so began the occupation of the village. It was around 3100 B.C.

As they went about the routine of their daily life, the villagers allowed their refuse to pile up against the outside walls of their huts. Shells, broken bones, fragments of pottery, sand, and everything no longer used was heaped around the structures.

This refuse, called midden, helped to insulate the huts. It kept the cold winds from blowing through the chinks in the

[6] **hearth:** fireplace
[7] **heather:** low evergreen shrub

stones. Over the years these midden heaps mixed with sand and became a claylike covering from which grass grew.

Now the huts looked like the surrounding dunes of the Bay of Skaill. And thus came into existence the village we now call Skara Brae—the village of the hilly dunes.

As the generations came and went, so did the huts. The older huts were sometimes taken down stone by stone to build new huts.

The wind-blown sands constantly shifted around the dunes and the dwellings of Skara Brae. Sometimes one of the huts was overcome by the drifts and disappeared. Another hut was often built on top of it, and life continued as before.

The shifting sands and the ever-increasing midden heaps continually changed the appearance of the village. Other changes also took place. The new huts were built to be larger and more comfortable.

The beds had stone pillars at each corner supporting a canopy made of skins. The stone dresser was now built against the rear wall and was no longer set into it.

Inside, the hearth remained the focal point of the room. The stone beds, however, were no longer built into the walls

Comb made of bone from Skara Brae

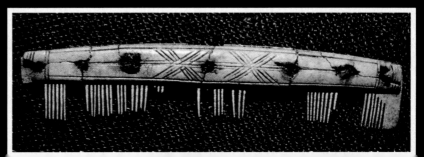

In the floor of the huts the villagers built stone boxes carefully sealed with clay to make them watertight. In these holding tanks they kept their limpets in the water for later use as bait or perhaps as food. Several tanks were built so that there could always be a ready supply of limpets.

At some point in their history the inhabitants of Skara Brae most likely began to cultivate small plots of grain. They remained an isolated group, living a quiet life off the land and sea and their stock of animals.

As the village grew, so did its population. The villagers were bound together by common need, common activity, and the beliefs and ceremonies that characterize all Stone Age peoples.

Evidence of one of these beliefs was found underneath a wall of one of the later huts. Two aged women of the village had died. Their bodies were buried beneath the wall in the hope and belief that their spirits would support the wall and help sustain the life of the village. This was the only time the villagers performed this rite. Henceforth the dead would be buried in communal burial mounds.

When the settlers were first building their perma-

For the Neolithic villagers of Skara Brae, one such activity might have been the construction of a communal burial mound, or cairn.

The construction of the cairn took longer than that of the huts because it was much larger. Once it was completed, it served generation after generation.

The exterior of the cairn was covered with earth, and in time grass grew over it. It looked like a hill in the landscape.

There was also time for the villagers to practice their various crafts. The women made pottery. Sometimes they made engraved or raised designs on their pots. But the people of Skara Brae, unlike many Neolithic peoples, were not especially skilled at this craft.

The men spent hours carving strange, intricate patterns on stone balls.

The teeth and bones from sheep, cattle, and whales were used to make beautiful beads and necklaces.

For a long time the life of Skara Brae continued uninterrupted. Then, around 2400 B.C., when the village had settled into its way of life, a terrible catastrophe occurred that caused it to be abandoned forever.

As the villagers went about their daily tasks of collecting food and tending their

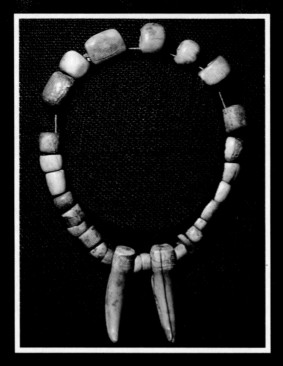

Necklace of bone and teeth made in Skara Brae about 2500 B.C.

The necklace fell to the floor of the passageway, and there it remained.

In another hut an old man was gnawing a choice bit of mutton when the storm took him by surprise. He dropped the bone by his bed and fled the hut in panic.

Then the wind-driven sands quickly filled all the stone huts, burying the necklace and the half-eaten bone for the ages.

The storm raged with a fury the villagers had never experienced before. They fled the village in blind terror.

The sea pounded in the bay, and to the prehistoric people of Skara Brae it must have seemed that the world was coming to an end.

The villagers abandoned their village in the hilly dunes. Several times a small number of them returned and camped under the remaining exposed walls of the huts. And then they never returned again. Over the centuries the sand continued to drift in, until nothing was visible.

Although the name Skara Brae remained, memory of the village itself vanished.

LITERATURE REVIEW

Make a Generalization

1. Why Learn This Skill?

Sometimes the same kind of event happens over and over and over. When this occurs, you can make a general statement about the cause of or the effect of the event. This kind of statement is called a generalization. A generalization is a summary statement made about a group of related ideas. Generalizations explain things that are usually true. By making generalizations, you can describe events or relationships and how they are alike.

Suppose that you stayed up late and were too tired the next day to do your best on a test. Your friend, kept awake by noise, did poorly in math that same day. Another classmate did not sleep much because of a toothache and was too tired to do well on schoolwork.

How are these three examples alike? In each, a student didn't get enough sleep and didn't do his or her best work at school. You could say the following: *People don't do their best work when they haven't had enough sleep.* This is a generalization.

2. Remember What You Have Read

You have read *Skara Brae: The Story of a Prehistoric Village*. Look at the following

questions. Think of a generalization that explains how the people of Skara Brae met their basic needs.

- What materials did the people of Skara Brae use to build houses? Where did they get those materials?
- What did they eat at first? Where did they get that food?
- What did they use as fuel? Where did they get that fuel?

To make a generalization, summarize the events and facts and determine how they are alike. You might say: *People in simple societies met their basic needs by using materials from the environment around them.*

3. Understand the Process

Use the following steps to make a generalization.

1. List the facts or events.
2. Think about how the facts or events are alike.
3. Write a sentence that makes a general statement linking the facts or events.
4. Test your generalization. Make sure it is true for most things that might happen.

4. Think and Apply

How do people in society today meet their basic needs? How do they get housing materials, food, and fuel? Develop a generalization based on these questions. Test your generalization to be sure it is true.

Gathering fuel in Skara Brae

40,000 B.C.   30,000 B.C.

About 40,000 B.C.
• Groups of early people
  have migrated from Africa
  to Asia and Europe

CONNECT MAIN IDEAS

Use this organizer to describe the ways of life of people who lived during the Stone Age. Write three examples for each box. A copy of the organizer appears on page 7 of the Activity Book.

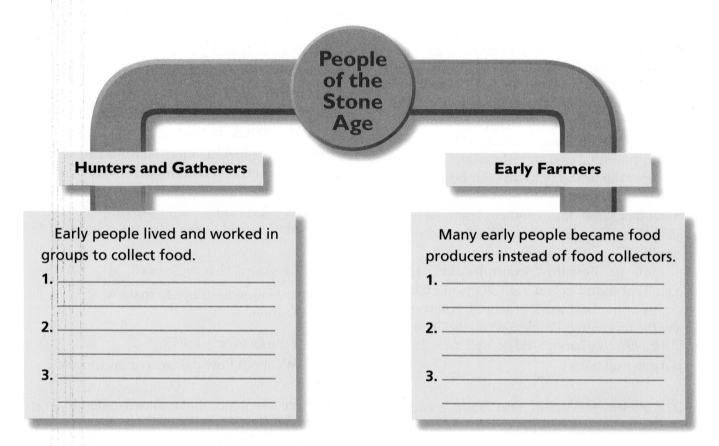

People of the Stone Age

Hunters and Gatherers

Early people lived and worked in groups to collect food.

1. _____
_____
2. _____
_____
3. _____
_____

Early Farmers

Many early people became food producers instead of food collectors.

1. _____
_____
2. _____
_____
3. _____
_____

WRITE MORE ABOUT IT

Write a Diary Entry Imagine that you are a young person who is part of a band of early people. Your band survives by hunting and gathering. Write a diary entry about going on a hunt. Describe the animals you are hunting and the tools you are using. Your entry should also describe what the land and the climate are like where your band hunts.

Write a Magazine Article Describe a home in Skara Brae as if you were writing an article for a magazine about homes. Write as though you are giving a tour from one part of the home to another. Be sure to tell how the home fits into the environment. Your final article should look like it is part of a magazine. You may include your own illustrations.

About 12,000 B.C.
• People have reached the Americas

About 8,000 B.C.
• Early domestication of plants and animals

USE VOCABULARY

Write a term from this list to complete each of the sentences that follow.

agriculture   culture   migration

artifact   domesticate

❶ Movement from one place to another is called ____.

❷ A ____ is a way of life.

❸ An ____ is an object made and used by people.

❹ The raising of plants and animals for the use of people is called ____.

❺ People ____ plants and animals for food and other uses.

CHECK UNDERSTANDING

❻ Why did early people live and work in bands?

❼ What plants and animals did early people domesticate?

❽ What is a society?

❾ Which provided a more steady food supply, hunting and gathering or agriculture? Explain your answer.

❿ Why did the people of Skara Brae build stone houses?

THINK CRITICALLY

⓫ **Personally Speaking** Would you rather have been a hunter-gatherer or an early farmer? Give reasons to support your answer.

⓬ **Past to Present** What are some of the objects, customs, and clothing that identify your culture?

⓭ **Think More About It** How do you think controlling the food supply might have helped leaders of long ago keep order?

APPLY SKILLS

Use a Parallel Time Line After the development of agriculture, societies with governments and social classes formed. Look at the time line on page 60. After which date would you expect to find such a society in South America? in North America? in southeastern Asia?

Make a Generalization Make a generalization about the development of agriculture and the daily work of early people.

READ MORE ABOUT IT

Digging Up the Past: The Story of an Archaeological Adventure by Carollyn James. Franklin Watts. Damien, his mother, and his friend Joe complete an archaeological dig to find out where treasures and junk they have found in their neighborhood came from. Soon they discover the history of their town. As you read, you will find out how to do an archaeological dig from start to finish.

HARCOURT BRACE
Visit the Internet at
http://www.hbschool.com
for additional resources.

2

SOUTHWEST ASIA

*" I am
Hammurabi,
noble king.
I have not
been careless
or negligent
toward
humankind. . . .
I have sought
for them
peaceful places.
I removed
serious
difficulties."*

Hammurabi,
King of Babylon
about 1750 B.C.

Bronze statue of Hammurabi

Civilization in Mesopotamia

FOCUS
Why do people today try new ways of doing things?

Main Idea As you read, think about the new lifeways developed by societies living in ancient Mesopotamia.

Vocabulary

civilization
technology
ziggurat
government
city-state
monarchy
authority
surplus
merchant
social class
scribe
innovation

The Fertile Crescent starts on the eastern shore of the Mediterranean Sea in southwestern Asia. Like the shape of a quarter moon, it curves around the Syrian Desert, reaching south to the Persian Gulf. By about 4000 B.C. many farming villages dotted the rich land of the Fertile Crescent. In the valley of the Tigris and Euphrates rivers at the eastern end of the Fertile Crescent, some farming villages attracted thousands of new settlers. There in the region called Mesopotamia, "the land between the rivers," several villages grew into cities by about 3500 B.C. The earliest cities rose up in a part of Mesopotamia called Sumer. As people began to live and work together in these cities, they formed a complex society, or civilization. A **civilization** is a centralized society with developed forms of religion, ways of governing, and learning. City life brought new problems, however. The need arose to find creative ways to solve them.

New Inventions

Farmers living in the region of Sumer used the Tigris and Euphrates rivers to water their crops. Yet these rivers were unpredictable. At times they flooded the land without warning. They carried away crops and sometimes whole villages. For people who subsisted on agriculture, a flood was the worst possible natural disaster. The loss of crops when farmland was flooded meant starvation.

To control the water on which they depended, farmers in Sumer built dikes and dug canals. Dikes held the flooding rivers within their banks. Canals carried extra water back to the rivers after floods. Building dikes and canals took special knowledge of making and using tools. The skills and knowledge to make products or meet

Clay tablet containing ancient Sumerian writing

73

goals is called **technology**. The early settlers of Sumer developed the technology to carry out successful agriculture and to build cities.

The technology of Sumer was greatly advanced by the invention of the wheel. Farmers in Sumer made wheels by attaching boards together and rounding them off. Later they covered the rims with pieces of copper.

Wheel technology made possible other inventions, including the wheeled cart. With a wheeled cart, a domesticated animal such as an ox or a donkey could pull a heavy load. Wheeled carts were important in moving construction materials for houses and other buildings in Sumer's growing cities.

REVIEW *What two inventions helped early farmers deal with flooding?*

Architecture and Religious Beliefs

The largest building in most Sumerian cities was a huge mud-brick temple called a **ziggurat** (ZIH•guh•rat). Some ziggurats stood as tall as a seven-story building. They towered above the houses like skyscrapers.

Builders constructed a ziggurat in layers, each one smaller than the one below. On the highest level of each ziggurat stood a shrine to the city's special god.

The religious beliefs of the Sumerian people showed the importance of agriculture in their lives. They believed that by pleasing their gods, they would get large harvests in return. Floods and other natural disasters, they thought, were signs that the gods were

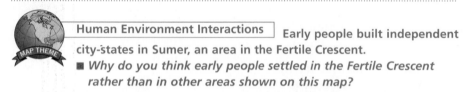

Human Environment Interactions Early people built independent city-states in Sumer, an area in the Fertile Crescent.

■ *Why do you think early people settled in the Fertile Crescent rather than in other areas shown on this map?*

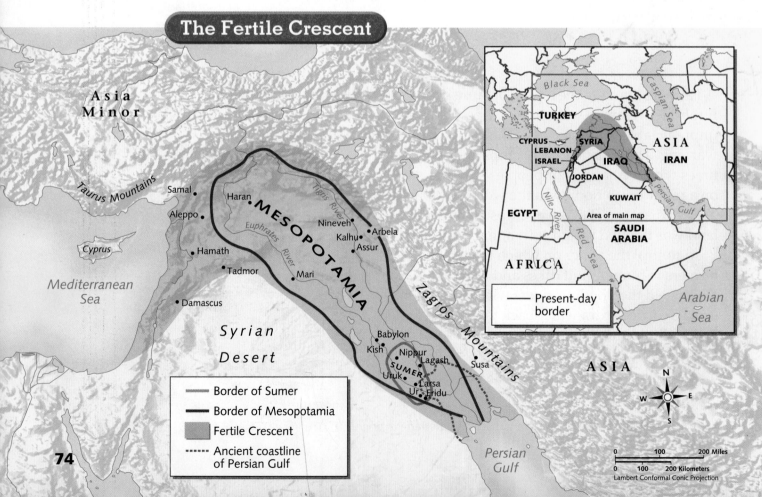

The Fertile Crescent

Asia Minor

Taurus Mountains

Samal
Haran
MESOPOTAMIA
Aleppo
Nineveh
Arbela
Kalhu
Assur
Euphrates River
Tigris River

Cyprus
Hamath

Mediterranean Sea

Tadmor
Mari

Damascus

Syrian Desert

Babylon
Kish
Nippur
Lagash
SUMER
Uruk
Larsa
Susa
Ur
Eridu

Zagros Mountains

Persian Gulf

ASIA

Border of Sumer
Border of Mesopotamia
Fertile Crescent
Ancient coastline of Persian Gulf

Black Sea
Caspian Sea
TURKEY
CYPRUS
SYRIA
ASIA
LEBANON
ISRAEL
IRAQ
IRAN
JORDAN
KUWAIT
EGYPT
Nile River
Area of main map
SAUDI ARABIA
Red Sea
Persian Gulf
AFRICA
Arabian Sea

Present-day border

0   100   200 Miles
0   100   200 Kilometers
Lambert Conformal Conic Projection

N
W   E
S

A Ziggurat

angry at them. Chief among the gods of Sumer were Enlil, the god of winds, storm, and rain, and Ea, the god of the waters and wisdom.

In time, a ziggurat became more than a shrine for a god. The people in Sumer built smaller buildings around the base of the ziggurat. Some of these buildings had different kinds of workshops where craftworkers, or skilled workers, made clothing and metal goods. Others were temples in which priests performed religious ceremonies. The ziggurat with all its buildings, enclosed within great walls, was the center of activity in each city.

REVIEW *How did religion in Sumer reflect the importance of agriculture?*

The Role of Government

Constructing dikes, canals, ziggurats, and other city buildings took large numbers of people. When large numbers of people live and work together, laws are needed to keep order. In societies as large as those in Sumer, this could be done only with a government. A **government** is an organized system that groups use to make laws and decisions.

Sumer was made up of several independent city-states. A **city-state** included a city or village and the farmlands around it. Each city-state had its own leaders and its own government. In early days each government was run by a small group of leaders and a

Gilgamesh

Gilgamesh was probably a real king who ruled over the Sumerian city-state of Uruk sometime between 2700 B.C. and 2500 B.C. Over time King Gilgamesh became a figure of legend. People began to think of Gilgamesh as one-third man and two-thirds god. Stories of Gilgamesh and his adventures were passed on as oral tradition for centuries before being recorded in writing. Scribes in Mesopotamia put the stories of Gilgamesh into their most complete form by 1300 B.C.

Statue of Gilgamesh, made of terra cotta

complete **authority**, or right, to rule in peacetime and to lead soldiers in time of war.

Sumerians called the rulers of their city-states "big men," or kings. They were concerned with every part of Sumerian life. Because of the king's importance, the Sumerians believed their kings were almost like gods. One of the oldest stories in the world is a story-poem from Sumerian times. It tells the adventures of Gilgamesh, a Sumerian "big man." The story praises Gilgamesh as "he who knew everything."

REVIEW *What kind of government did Sumerian city-states form to provide stronger leadership?*

Changing Economy

By about 3000 B.C. some Sumerian city-states had large populations, while others remained small. The city-state of Uruk may have grown to have as many as 60,000 people. Such population growth was possible only because of the success of agriculture. Sumerian farms produced enough food to create a **surplus**, or extra supply, to feed the people who came to settle in Sumer.

Having a surplus meant that some people could spend their working hours doing things other than growing or finding food. As a result, a complex division of labor occurred. Some people became craftworkers in stone, clay, wool, leather, or metals such as copper. Others became managers, skilled at directing the work of others. Some became **merchants**, people who bought and sold goods for a living.

Sumerian merchants traded with merchants throughout the Fertile Crescent as far away as the Mediterranean Sea. The Sumerians traded what they had in surplus—wheat, barley, and copper tools such as plowheads. In return, they got what they wanted—wood, salt, precious stones, and raw copper.

REVIEW *What effect did a surplus of food have on life in Sumer?*

chief leader chosen by that group. Together they made laws and decided what work had to be done.

The city-states of Sumer often waged wars to enlarge their farmland or to protect it from others who wanted to take it. In times of peril, the group of leaders could not always agree on what to do. To provide stronger leadership, each Sumerian city-state formed a new government. The new government was a **monarchy**, in which one person had

Divisions in Society

Because the work of some people came to be valued more than the work of others, Sumerian society became divided. This division created **social classes**, or groups with different levels of importance.

The most important or highest social class in Sumer was made up of nobles—the king, priests, and other important leaders and their families. Nobles owned much of the land and were regarded as the privileged class. They had the most wealth and honor.

Next came the class of merchants, craftworkers, and managers. This middle class included carpenters, potters, bricklayers, doctors, and scribes. A **scribe** was a person who wrote things for others. Writing was a valuable skill in Sumer, where most people—including kings and nobles—could neither read nor write. Scribes kept records, wrote letters for other people, and copied down stories and songs. Scribes and others in the middle social class of Sumer exchanged their services or the goods they made for the services and goods they needed.

Laborers, or unskilled workers, and slaves made up the lowest class in Sumerian society. Most slaves were prisoners of war. Others were enslaved as punishment for crimes or to pay off debts. Slaves in Sumerian society were not enslaved for life. For example, those who owed a debt could gain their freedom when the debt was paid.

In each Sumerian social class, a division existed between men and women. Men owned most of the property and held most leadership roles. Laws in Sumer allowed women to own property. However, most women did not. Women sometimes held positions of leadership, especially as priests. In fact, the female high priest at Ur was second in power only to the king. Ancient Sumerian records also refer to women scribes and doctors.

REVIEW *What were Sumer's social classes?*

These gypsum statues (left) show how one early artist pictured the Sumerians. Below is a model of a Sumerian house. What social class do you think the owners of this house belonged to?

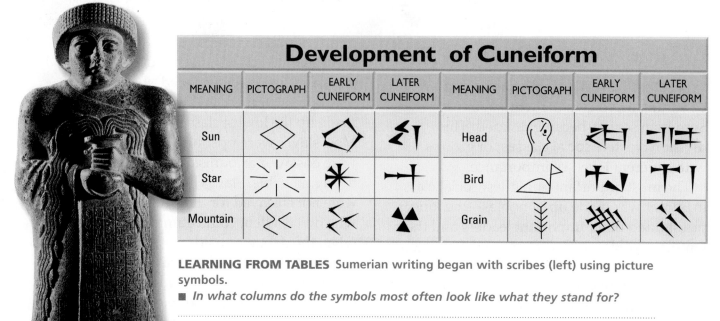

Development of Cuneiform

MEANING	PICTOGRAPH	EARLY CUNEIFORM	LATER CUNEIFORM	MEANING	PICTOGRAPH	EARLY CUNEIFORM	LATER CUNEIFORM
Sun				Head			
Star				Bird			
Mountain				Grain			

LEARNING FROM TABLES Sumerian writing began with scribes (left) using picture symbols.

■ *In what columns do the symbols most often look like what they stand for?*

Innovations

The needs of a large complex society led to further **innovations**, or new ways of doing things. The need in Sumer to mark boundaries for farming led to a unit of land measurement the Sumerians called the *iku*. Today we call it the *acre*.

The need to measure the wheat and barley harvests established the quart as a basic unit of measurement. The need to carry trade goods up the river led people to build cargo boats with sails. The need to keep a record of ownership and trade led to one of the Sumerians' greatest innovations—writing.

Scribes in Sumer marked picture symbols in pieces of wet clay. They attached these pieces to baskets as tags to identify the contents and the owner. By about 2000 B.C. the Sumerians had developed their symbols into a complete writing system. This system was based on *cuneiform*, (kyoo•NEE•uh•fawrm), or wedge-shaped symbols.

To make the cuneiform marks in soft clay tablets, Sumerian scribes used a pointed reed, or stylus. The clay tablets were then baked to harden them. Cuneiform tablets that have been found give a record of Sumer's growing economic activity, way of life, and history.

REVIEW *What innovations did the Sumerians develop?*

LESSON 1 REVIEW

Check Understanding

1 Remember the Facts What kind of government formed in Mesopotamia?

2 Recall the Main Idea How did the need for organization affect the development of city-states in Sumer?

Think Critically

3 Cause and Effect How did a crop surplus affect Sumerian civilization?

4 Past to Present What problems faced by people in Sumer are similar to problems in the United States today?

Show What You Know

News-Writing Activity Prepare a news story that describes an important event that might have happened in Sumer when an innovation was introduced.

Conquests and Empires

FOCUS

Why are laws important today?

Main Idea As you read, look for ways in which early civilizations protected themselves and kept order within their societies.

Vocabulary

conquer
empire
emperor
taxation
Code of Hammurabi
equal justice

As city-states all over Mesopotamia kept growing in area and population, conflict among them increased. City-states competed with one another to control fertile land and water sources. Soon people were fighting wars to **conquer**, or take over, the land of others.

Causes and Effects of Conflict

Most wars among early agricultural societies such as those in Mesopotamia were fought to protect farmland and water rights. A Sumerian saying warned of how unsure ownership was: "You can go and carry off the enemy's land; the enemy comes and carries off your land."

The land between the Tigris and Euphrates rivers was flat. No natural boundaries such as mountains separated one city-state from another. Without natural boundaries, city-states put up pillars to mark their borders. When one city-state moved or destroyed another city-state's pillars, it "violated both the decree of the gods, and the word given by man to man." Such acts often led to war.

As more disagreements about land and water arose, more wars were fought. The need for weapons resulted in new technology. Craftworkers used metalworking and wheel-making skills to create such innovations as war chariots. A war chariot was a light, two-wheeled cart pulled by horses. From a fast-moving war chariot, a soldier could speed by and throw spears or shoot arrows at an enemy who was on foot. With new technology for war, of course, more people died in battle.

REVIEW *What was the major cause of wars among the people of Mesopotamia?*

This Sumerian helmet was hammered from a single sheet of gold. About 4,500 years old, the helmet was uncovered in the royal cemetery of the ancient city of Ur.

As this ancient stone artwork (above) shows, war was often a part of day-to-day living for the ancient Mesopotamians. The scene is part of the famed *Standard of Ur.*

Mesopotamian ruler, possibly Sargon

Sargon the Conqueror

The first known conqueror in the region of Mesopotamia was a warrior named Sargon. He lived in the city-state of Kish. As a young man he served as an official in the king's government. Sargon later killed the king and took control of Kish. Gathering an army, Sargon then marched through Mesopotamia, establishing a vast empire. An **empire** is a conquered land of many people and places governed by one ruler. Sargon became the region's first **emperor**, or ruler of the empire.

In the middle of his empire, Sargon built a capital city called Akkad (AH•kahd). His empire and its people came to be known as Akkadian. As a sign of his conquest over the huge area, Sargon ordered every boundary pillar and city wall torn down.

For the next 55 years, Sargon of Akkad ruled over his empire. He maintained his rule both by force and by good organization. Sargon was the first king in the region of Mesopotamia to set up a standing army. Before this time people became soldiers only in time of war. Sargon also appointed loyal nobles as governors to maintain control of conquered cities. Sargon organized his empire so well that it lasted long after his death. By about 2300 B.C. the Akkadian Empire stretched from what is now Iran westward to the Mediterranean Sea.

The Akkadian Empire eventually weakened. When the Akkadian Empire ended, the Mesopotamian city-states found themselves caught between two strong centers of power—Assyria (us•SIR•ee•uh) and Babylonia (ba•buh•LOH•nyuh).

REVIEW *Why did Sargon tear down boundary pillars and city walls?*

Hammurabi the Lawgiver

Between 1790 and 1750 B.C. Hammurabi, king of the city-state of Babylon, conquered and reunited most of Mesopotamia and the upper valley of the Tigris and Euphrates rivers. Like Sargon, Hammurabi was more than a military leader. He improved each city-state under his rule by promoting trade and by building and keeping up dikes and canals.

One of Hammurabi's most important achievements was his reorganization of Mesopotamia's system of **taxation**. Under a system of taxation, people are required to pay taxes to support the government. Hammurabi made changes to the tax system to ensure that all the people of Mesopotamia paid their share. Tax collectors traveled throughout the region, collecting tax money. The money collected paid for all of Hammurabi's improvements.

Perhaps Hammurabi is best remembered for the work he did with the laws of his land. Each city-state had long had its own set of laws, or rules. Hammurabi collected all these laws, sorted through them, and came up with one complete listing of laws. The collection of laws compiled by the Babylonian leader is known as the **Code of Hammurabi**.

Hammurabi's collection consisted of 282 laws that dealt with almost every part of daily life. The laws covered such topics as marriage, divorce, adoption, slaves, murder, stealing, military service, land, business, loans, prices, and wages. Almost no area was overlooked.

The old laws were complicated and often unfair. The Code of

On this stela, or stone marker, Hammurabi stands before the Babylonian sun god. Hammurabi's laws are carved at the base of the stela.

Hammurabi explained the laws in clear statements and set standard punishments.

Some of the laws within the Code of Hammurabi followed the idea of "an eye for an eye." These laws explained that whoever caused an injury should be punished with that same injury. This means that a person who broke someone's arm in a fight would be punished by having his or her own arm broken.

Not all Hammurabi's laws offered "an eye for an eye" punishment. Some laws outlined specific fines for crimes. Others imposed a penalty of death.

In describing the purpose of his code, Hammurabi explained that he wrote it

66 To cause justice to prevail . . .
To destroy the wicked . . .
To enlighten the land and to further
the welfare of the people. 99

In addition to putting together a code of laws, Hammurabi introduced the idea of **equal justice**, or fair treatment under the law. His equal justice, however, was limited to equality within each social class. Under the Code of Hammurabi, leaders, priests, and the wealthy were often favored over other people.

Hammurabi's code lasted over the years, but the leader's empire did not. By 1600 B.C. the Babylonians, too, had been conquered.

REVIEW *What is an "eye for an eye" law?*

Events in Mesopotamia

2500 B.C.	2000 B.C.	1500 B.C.	1000 B.C.	500 B.C.
About 2350 B.C. • Sargon establishes the Akkadian Empire	**About 1790 B.C.** • Hammurabi becomes king of Babylon	**By 1750 B.C.** • Hammurabi conquers and reunites most of Mesopotamia	**721 B.C.** • Assyria conquers the kingdom of Israel	

LEARNING FROM TIME LINES Many rulers fought for control of ancient Mesopotamia between 2500 B.C. and 500 B.C.

■ *Which of these rulers reigned longest ago?*

The Assyrians in Mesopotamia

After the collapse of Hammurabi's empire, Mesopotamia was ruled by several different peoples. Around 1600 B.C. the Kassites, from what is now the country of Iran, claimed the region. The Kassites ruled Mesopotamia for more than 400 years. Eventually the Assyrian Empire gained control of the region. This empire included lands that lay outside of Mesopotamia, such as parts of present-day Turkey, Egypt, and the Persian Gulf.

Assyria was a region of rolling hills between the Tigris River and the Zagros Mountains in northern Mesopotamia. Most Assyrians lived in cities, of which the most important were Assur, Kalhu, and Nineveh. Surrounding each city were many small farming villages.

The Assyrians had a great desire to control trade routes in southwestern Asia. By conquering neighboring lands, they could better meet this goal. Advancing in war chariots,

the Assyrians began conquering their neighbors so they could gain this fertile land. They went on taking land until their empire covered much of southwestern Asia.

After completing their conquest, the Assyrians worked to bring the people of their many lands together. They began building a system of roads throughout their empire.

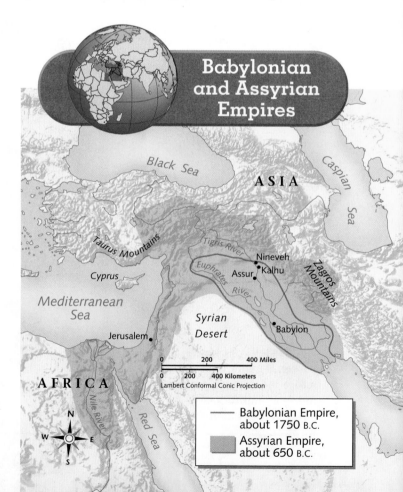

Babylonian and Assyrian Empires

— Babylonian Empire, about 1750 B.C.

▢ Assyrian Empire, about 650 B.C.

Location Several empires rose and fell in southwestern Asia during ancient times.
■ *What empire was Assur a part of in 1750 B.C? in 650 B.C?*

During this time, the Assyrians made many improvements to their city of Nineveh. Throughout the city many new buildings rose, including a magnificent palace. Nineveh's new buildings dazzled the eye with stone carvings.

In time the mighty Assyrian Empire was brought down by other people. In 612 B.C. the Medes attacked Nineveh and killed its king. A writer who may have lived near Nineveh described the fall of the city. The description shows how violent the age of conquest was.

> 66 Woe to the bloody city! . . .
> The noise of a whip and the
>   noise of rattling wheels,
> And of the prancing horses,
>   and of leaping chariots.
> The horseman lifts up the
>   bright sword and glittering spear,
> And there is a multitude
>   slain. . . . 99

REVIEW *Why did the Assyrians seek more land?*

This stela shows Assyrian warriors riding a chariot into battle.

LESSON 2 REVIEW

Check Understanding

1 Remember the Facts What collection of "an eye for an eye" laws was developed in Babylon?

2 Recall the Main Idea How did the people of Mesopotamia maintain order and protect themselves from outsiders?

Think Critically

3 Think More About It Most people living today would consider some of Hammurabi's punishments to be cruel. Why do you think that the Code of Hammurabi was so well accepted by people living long ago?

4 Past to Present What kinds of laws in your community do you consider the most important? Why?

Show What You Know

Brainstorming Activity Hammurabi wrote a code of laws that seemed fair for his time. In a group, write a short code of rules for the students in your school with consequences that seem fair for your time. Discuss your rules with other groups.

FOCUS

What changes have individuals and groups brought about in your community?

Main Idea As you read, look for ways in which Israelites, Phoenicians, and Lydians contributed to change long ago.

Vocabulary

monotheism
covenant
Ten Commandments
Judaism
Torah
colony
cultural diffusion
barter
money economy

Israelites, Phoenicians, and Lydians

The groups of people who lived in or near the western end of the Fertile Crescent did not create large empires. Yet they contributed to world history in important ways. Between about 2000 B.C. and 500 B.C., the Israelites, the Phoenicians, and the Lydians made important contributions in religion, language, and economics.

Abraham

Many people all over the world trace their identity as a people to a man named Abram. Abram was born in the Sumerian city of Ur and lived most of his life in the city of Haran in northern Mesopotamia. The Mesopotamians, like most early people, worshipped many gods. They prayed to one god for water, another god for good harvests, and still another god for both love and war. The Mesopotamians also thought of the sun, the moon, and the wind as gods.

Unlike their neighbors, Abram and his family worshipped one God. Belief in one God is called **monotheism**. God, Abram believed, was all-powerful. According to Abram, God spoke to him one day, saying, "Leave your country, your people, and your father's house and go to the land I will show you."

Abram obeyed God without question. He soon left

Jewish people today read from the Torah, just as their ancestors, the ancient Israelites, did.

Mesopotamia and traveled west with his wife Sarah and other family members. By about 2000 B.C. they came to a region of hills, valleys, and coastal plains along the Mediterranean Sea. This region was known as Canaan.

Abram and his family journeyed through Canaan until they reached Shechem (SHEH•kuhm). It was there, according to the Bible, that Abram heard God say, "I will give this land to your children." Abram made a **covenant**, or special agreement, with God. The covenant promised that in return for Abram's being faithful, God would give Abram's descendants the land of Canaan as a home country. As a sign of his promise, Abram changed his name to Abraham. The name means "father of many nations." Abraham became known as the father of the Jewish people through his son Isaac and the father of the Arab people through his son Ishmael.

REVIEW *How did Abraham's religious beliefs differ from the beliefs of other people of Mesopotamia?*

The Ten Commandments

Abraham's son Isaac had a son who was named Jacob. Later, Jacob also became known as Israel, and his descendants were called Israelites. When famine came to Canaan, many Israelites left for Egypt. The Israelites who left Canaan found food and work during their early years in Egypt. Later, however, they were enslaved by Egyptian rulers.

In about 1225 B.C. Moses, a leader of the Israelites, led his people back toward Canaan. The journey, which was filled with hardships, took many years. The Bible says that on a mountain in the Sinai desert, God gave Moses the **Ten Commandments**, a set of laws for responsible behavior.

THE TEN COMMANDMENTS

According to the Bible, God spoke to Moses, and these were his words:

1. I am the Lord your God, who brought you out of Egypt, out of the land of slavery. You shall have no other gods before me.

2. You shall not make for yourself an idol in the form of anything in heaven above or on the earth beneath or in the waters below. . . .

3. You shall not misuse the name of the Lord your God, for the Lord will not hold anyone guiltless who misuses his name.

4. Remember the Sabbath day by keeping it holy. Six days you shall labor and do all your work, but the seventh day is a Sabbath to the Lord your God. On that day you shall not do any work. . . .

5. Honor your father and your mother. . . .

6. You shall not murder.

7. You shall not commit adultery.

8. You shall not steal.

9. You shall not give false testimony against your neighbor.

10. You shall not covet your neighbor's house . . . or anything that belongs to your neighbor.

Exodus 20:2-17
(Source: The New International Version of the Bible)

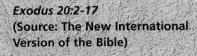

The Ten Commandments (above) are just one part of the Torah, writings holy to the Jewish religion. The Torah cover at left was made during the eighteenth century.

The Ten Commandments became an important part of **Judaism**—the religion of the Jewish people—and later of Christianity and of Islam. Judaism teaches belief in a God who cannot be pictured and whose qualities must be imitated. For example, God is fair, and people must deal fairly with their neighbors.

After their return to Canaan, the Israelites set up their own country, which they called Israel. The first king of Israel was Saul. Saul was followed as king by David, who built up the capital city at Jerusalem. David's son, Solomon, became one of Israel's most famous kings, known for his ability to make good decisions. "Solomon's wisdom excelled the wisdom of all the children of the east country," says the Bible.

The stories of the Israelites are in the first five books of the Bible, or the Five Books of Moses. Jewish people refer to these five books as the **Torah**.

BIOGRAPHY

Moses

According to the Bible, Moses was born in Egypt to Jewish parents who were enslaved there. At that time the Egyptian leader, the pharaoh, had ordered that all the sons of Jews be killed. Moses' mother placed her baby son in a basket at the edge of the Nile River. The pharaoh's daughter found the basket and decided to raise Moses as her own son. Moses' mother became his nurse and told him of his true identity. Moses never forgot that he was a Jew. Later, as the Bible recounts, he obeyed God's call to lead the enslaved Jewish people out of Egypt to Canaan, the Promised Land.

Israel and Judah

□ Israel at the beginning of Solomon's rule

■ Kingdom of Israel

■ Kingdom of Judah

0   25   50 Miles
0   25   50 Kilometers
Transverse Cylindrical Projection

PHOENICIA

Sea of Galilee

Jordan River

Nazareth

Samaria

Joppa

Mediterranean Sea

PHILISTIA

Bethel
Jericho
Jerusalem

Gaza

Hebron

(Dead Sea)

Beersheba

N
W   E
S

After Solomon's rule the Land of Israel was divided into two parts—the kingdom of Israel and the kingdom of Judah. The kingdom of Israel lasted until about 721 B.C., when it was conquered by the Assyrians. Judah lasted until about 586 B.C., when it was captured by the Babylonians. Much later the region of Judah became known as Judaea under the control of a people called the Romans. Around A.D. 70 the Jews were forced to leave Judaea. The Romans changed the region's name to Palestine to remove all connection of the land to the Jews.

REVIEW *What set of rules became an important part of three major religions?*

MAP THEME

Place   The land of Israel was divided into two parts.
■ *Which part was more likely to be invaded by sea?*

The Alphabet

While Israel occupied the southern section of the narrow strip of the Fertile Crescent along the Mediterranean Sea, Phoenicia occupied the northern section. Phoenicia consisted of a loose union of city-states, each governed by a king. Phoenicia had little land to farm and few important natural resources. The nearby Lebanon Mountains did have cedar trees, however. So the people of Phoenicia traded cedar trees to get the food and materials they needed.

For hundreds of years the Phoenicians sailed the waters of the Mediterranean Sea in search of metals, ivory, and other goods they could not find at home. In the process, they developed the most advanced sailing technology among the ancient peoples.

Between 1000 B.C. and 700 B.C., the Phoenicians started colonies all over the Mediterranean region. A **colony** is a settlement separate from, but under the control of, a home country. Phoenician colonies throughout the Mediterranean served as rest stops for sailors on long voyages and as trade links with other civilizations in Africa and Europe.

The Phoenicians modeled their civilization after those of the many peoples with whom they came into contact. They borrowed ideas from the Egyptians, the Babylonians, and other trading partners. Basing their work on the writing systems of the Egyptians and others, the Phoenicians developed an early alphabet.

LEARNING FROM TABLES The Phoenician alphabet was an important step in the development of many present-day alphabets.
- *Which Phoenician letters look most like letters in our alphabet today?*

CULTURE

Phoenician Purple

The Phoenicians are remembered not only for their alphabet but also for a color. In the coastal waters of Phoenicia lived a certain kind of mollusk, a sea animal with a hard shell. The early Phoenicians used this mollusk to make a purple dye called Tyrian purple. Kings often wore clothes dyed this beautiful color. Soon Tyrian purple came to be thought of as a royal color. Some leaders even ruled that only they could wear it. The Phoenicians' sea trade grew as more and more rulers demanded Tyrian purple. Over time the dye became very closely connected with the land where it was made. In fact, the name Phoenician comes from a Greek word for reddish-purple.

Development of the Alphabet

EGYPTIAN (About 3000 B.C.)	PHOENICIAN (About 1000 B.C.)	GREEK (About 600 B.C.)	PRESENT-DAY
			A
			B
			D
			I, J
			L
			M
			P
			T
			Y
			Z

The Phoenician alphabet made writing easier. Earlier written language used wedge shapes, as in cuneiform, or pictures to stand for syllables in words. The Phoenician alphabet was made up of written symbols that stood for single sounds.

The Phoenicians used their alphabet in their businesses to record trade agreements and to draw up bills. Phoenician colonies made it possible for knowledge of the alphabet to spread quickly among the Phoenicians' contacts. The spreading of new ideas to other places is called **cultural diffusion**.

REVIEW *How did the Phoenician people spread the use of their alphabet?*

Coined Money

The Lydians lived in a region northwest of the Fertile Crescent, along the eastern Mediterranean. Like the Phoenicians, the Lydians made a major contribution to ancient life. Theirs, too, was related to trade. In 600 B.C. the Lydians became the first people to use coined money put out by their government.

Lydian coins, made around 600 B.C.

As people around the Mediterranean and all over the Fertile Crescent began to trade with one another, they needed a kind of money. Its value had to be accepted, and it had to be light enough to be carried on ships without sinking them. The first coins were the size of beans. They were made of a mixture of gold and silver. Each coin was stamped with the personal mark of the king of Lydia.

Before the innovation of coined money, traders relied on **barter**, the exchange of one good or service for another. The trouble with barter was that two people could make a deal only if each had a good or a service that the other wanted.

The use of money allowed traders to set prices for various kinds of goods and services. Societies could then develop a **money economy**, an economic system based on the use of money rather than on barter.

Lydia remained an independent kingdom until 545 B.C. Though it never regained its independence, it has long been remembered for its early coins.

REVIEW *How did the use of coined money change trade?*

Statue of the Phoenician god Baal

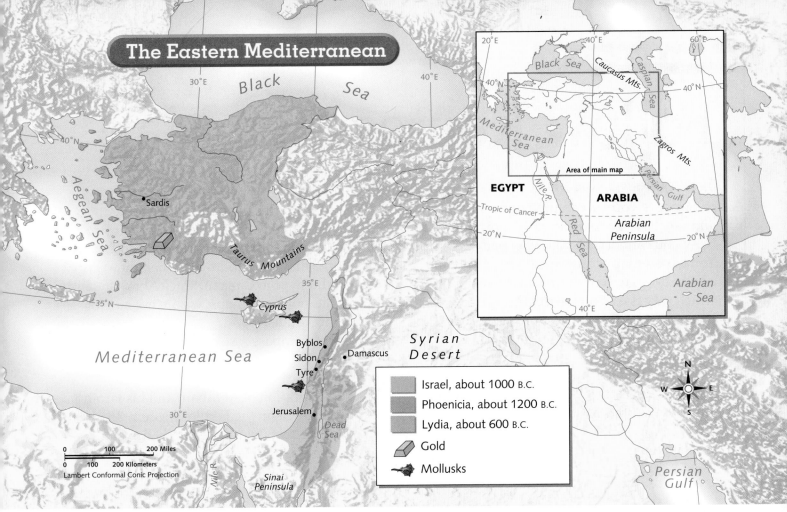

The Eastern Mediterranean

Black Sea

30°E 40°E

40°N

Aegean Sea

•Sardis

Taurus Mountains

35°E

Cyprus

35°N

Mediterranean Sea

Byblos
Sidon •Damascus
Tyre

30°E Jerusalem•

Dead Sea

Syrian Desert

Nile R.

Sinai Peninsula

0   100   200 Miles
0   100   200 Kilometers
Lambert Conformal Conic Projection

Inset map

20°E   40°E   60°E

Black Sea   Caucasus Mts.   Caspian Sea

40°N   40°N

Mediterranean Sea   Zagros Mts.

Area of main map

EGYPT   Nile R.   ARABIA   Persian Gulf

Tropic of Cancer

Arabian Peninsula

20°N   Red Sea   20°N

40°E

Arabian Sea

N
W   E
S

Persian Gulf

Legend

Israel, about 1000 B.C.

Phoenicia, about 1200 B.C.

Lydia, about 600 B.C.

Gold

Mollusks

Movement   The ideas of the Israelites, Phoenicians, and Lydians influenced the peoples around them.
■ *Why do you think ideas traveled freely among people of the eastern Mediterranean?*

MAP THEME

LESSON 3 REVIEW

Check Understanding

1 Remember the Facts What did the Israelites, the Phoenicians, and the Lydians each give to the civilization of the Fertile Crescent?

2 Recall the Main Idea How were the contributions of the Israelites, the Phoenicians, and the Lydians helpful to the people of ancient times?

Think Critically

3 Think More About It What were some of the advantages and the disadvantages of the use of a written alphabet and the use of coined money?

4 Past to Present How do the contributions made by the Israelites, the Phoenicians, and the Lydians affect our lives today?

Show What You Know

Speech Activity With a partner, prepare a speech to persuade a person who has never heard of it to adopt either the Phoenician alphabet or Lydian coined money. Be sure to explain how the innovation will improve that person's way of life. If time allows, present your speech to one or more of your classmates.

Follow Routes on a Map

1. Why Learn This Skill?

Suppose you are camping with your family and you have gone on an early morning walk. Now you cannot find your way back to camp. You have a map with you, however, and you also know that the sun rises in the east. But which way is east on the map? If you knew, you would be able to find your way back to camp easily. Luckily, your map has a compass rose.

A compass rose is a symbol that shows directions on a map. The directions it shows are north, south, east, west, and points in between. The compass rose makes it possible to relate the map to the real world.

2. Understand the Process

The map on this page shows the route that Abraham may have followed from Ur to Canaan. It also shows the route that Moses and his people may have followed when they traveled from Egypt to Canaan. Since Abraham and Moses did not leave maps, we are not sure of their exact routes.

Use the compass rose on the map to help you answer the questions:

1 The migration of Abraham and his family began at Ur, in the Fertile Crescent. In which direction did the family travel to get from Ur to Haran?

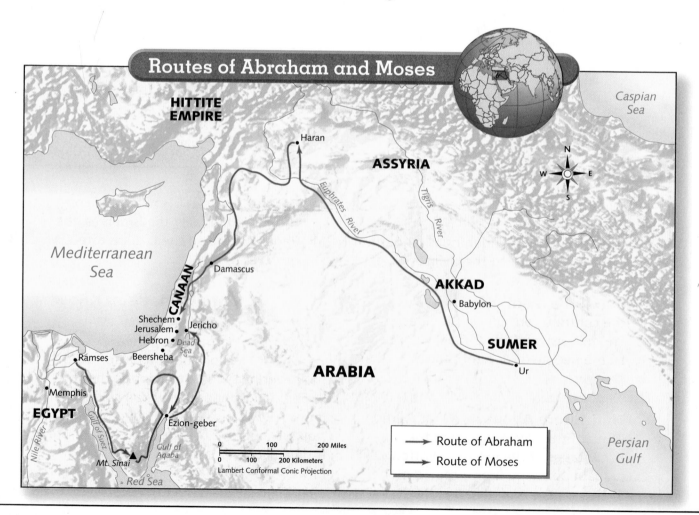

Routes of Abraham and Moses

2 Abraham and his family then moved to the land of Canaan. In what direction did the family travel on the way from Haran to Canaan?

3 When Moses and the Israelites fled from Egypt, they left from Ramses. Find that city on the map. In which direction did they travel from Ramses to Mount Sinai?

4 From Mount Sinai, Moses and his followers traveled to Ezion-geber, at the north end of the Gulf of Aqaba. From Mount Sinai to Ezion-geber, the route curves and turns. If the Israelites had traveled in a straight line from Mount Sinai to Ezion-geber, in what direction would they have gone?

5 On the last part of their journey, Moses and the ancient Israelites traveled from the Gulf of Aqaba to the Dead Sea and on to Jericho. In what direction did they turn when they left Ezion-geber?

6 If an ancient traveler had gone in a straight line from Hebron to Ur, in what direction would he or she have gone?

7 If an ancient traveler had traveled from Ur to Ezion-geber to Jericho in the straightest way possible, in what directions would he or she have gone?

3. Think and Apply

Think about someone you would like to visit who lives in another city. Look at the map below to learn the best route to get to that city. Then draw your own map that shows the route you would take to get to the city you have chosen. Put a compass rose on your map. In which general direction would you travel to the place you have chosen? Does your route change directions along the way? Why or why not? About how many miles is it from your home to the city selected?

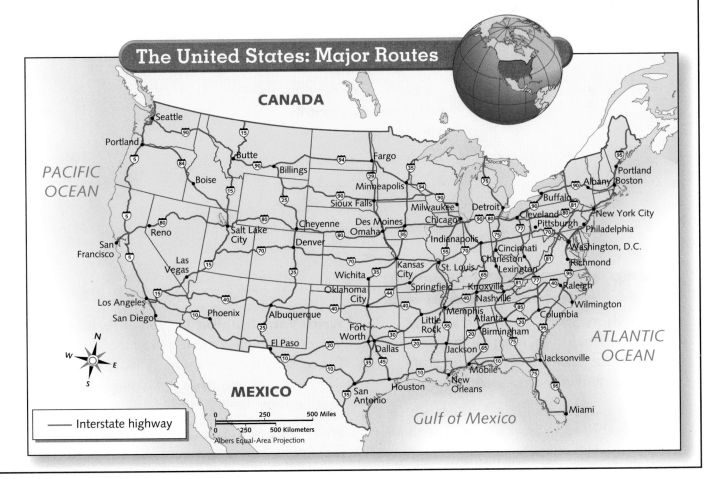

The United States: Major Routes

— Interstate highway

0   250   500 Miles

0   250   500 Kilometers

Albers Equal-Area Projection

CHAPTER 2 REVIEW

3500 B.C. | 3000 B.C. | 2500 B.C.

About 3500 B.C.
- Sumerian city-states form

CONNECT MAIN IDEAS

Use this organizer to tell about the achievements of the early people of southwestern Asia. Write three details to support each main idea. A copy of the organizer appears on page 14 of the Activity Book.

Southwest Asia

Civilization in Mesopotamia
The people of ancient Sumer developed new ways of doing things.
1. ______________
2. ______________
3. ______________

Conquests and Empires
Early civilizations protected themselves and kept order within their societies.
1. ______________
2. ______________
3. ______________

Israelites, Phoenicians, and Lydians
Cultures in or near the Fertile Crescent contributed to change.
1. ______________
2. ______________
3. ______________

WRITE MORE ABOUT IT

Write a Short Story To understand the importance of writing, imagine that you are a scribe in Sumer. Write a very short story telling how and why writing was invented.

Write a Report Explain the importance of agriculture by telling how a surplus of food affected life in Sumer.

Write Your Opinion Do you think that inventions always change life for the better? List reasons for your opinion. Use examples from the past and from today to see how much or how little things have changed.

Write a Commercial Design an advertisement for a new invention—the wheel.

About 2000 B.C.
• Development of cuneiform

About 1225 B.C.
• Moses leads revolt against Egyptians

About 586 B.C.
• Judah is conquered by Babylonians

USE VOCABULARY

Use each term in a sentence that will help explain its meaning.

1. city-state
2. empire
3. equal justice
4. innovation
5. scribe
6. technology

CHECK UNDERSTANDING

7. What were some needs that led to innovations in Sumer? What were the innovations?
8. What was the main purpose of the Sumerian ziggurats?
9. What were some of the causes of war in Mesopotamia?
10. Why was Hammurabi's code so important?
11. How was the worship of one God different from the beliefs of other religions in the area of southwestern Asia?
12. Why was the development of a written alphabet important?

THINK CRITICALLY

13. **Think More About It** What do you think was the most important achievement of the Sumerians?
14. **Cause and Effect** How did the waging of wars affect the government of Sumer?
15. **Personally Speaking** Do you think that Hammurabi's idea of equal justice within classes was fair or unfair for its time? Explain your answer.

16. **Past to Present** How many things can you think of in today's world that would not work without the wheel? What would life be like without it? Can you think of an innovation of our time that seems as important as the invention of the wheel?

APPLY SKILLS

Follow Routes on a Map Look at the map on page 90. Then answer these questions.

17. In what direction was Abraham traveling when he entered Canaan? In what direction were the followers of Moses traveling when they entered Canaan?
18. When Moses and his followers traveled from Egypt to Jericho, in what main direction or directions did they go?

READ MORE ABOUT IT

Gilgamesh the King by Ludmila Zeman. Tundra Books. This ancient tale, retold from stone tablets over 5,000 years old, is about the stern ruler Gilgamesh, who is taught to be kind to his people by the wild man Inkidu.

Visit the Internet at **http://www.hbschool.com** for additional resources.

Chapter 2 • 93

Will There Be Enough Food?

From the distant past to the present day, agriculture has made it possible for civilizations to feed their many people. Today, however, people wonder whether agriculture can produce enough food for a world population that grows by 90 million people each year.

Already, more than 700 million people are at risk of starving to death every day. Right here in the United States, 30 million people—12 million of them children—do not get enough food to stay in good health.

New technology is helping farmers grow more food. On large commercial farms, machines plant, care for, and harvest crops faster and better than people can. New ways of breeding produce larger and healthier plants and animals. Modern chemicals improve the soil, fight plant diseases, and kill pests. New methods also protect the soil for future crops.

Yet even with these new and better ways of farming, many people in the world go to bed hungry every night. In some cases political disorder and poor leadership prevent food from getting to hungry people. Technology alone will not solve the problem of hunger.

Hydroponic farming, or raising plants without soil, in Japan

Carrot harvesting in the United States

Think and Apply

Think about ways you might help people who do not get enough to eat each day. One way might be to collect food in your school for a community food bank. Make a list of ideas, and share your list with the class.

HARCOURT BRACE

Visit the Internet at
http://www.hbschool.com
for additional resources.

CNN
Turner
Le(@)rning

Check your media center or classroom video library for the Making Social Studies Relevant videotape of this feature.

A young child in India

Soybean harvesting in Zambia

UNIT 1 REVIEW

Summarize the Main Ideas
Study the pictures and captions to help you review the events you read about in Unit 1.

Interpreting Pictures
Look closely at the scenes in the visual summary. In a group, discuss how people's lives differed during the time periods illustrated.

1 Early people lived in groups and cooperated to hunt animals and gather plants.

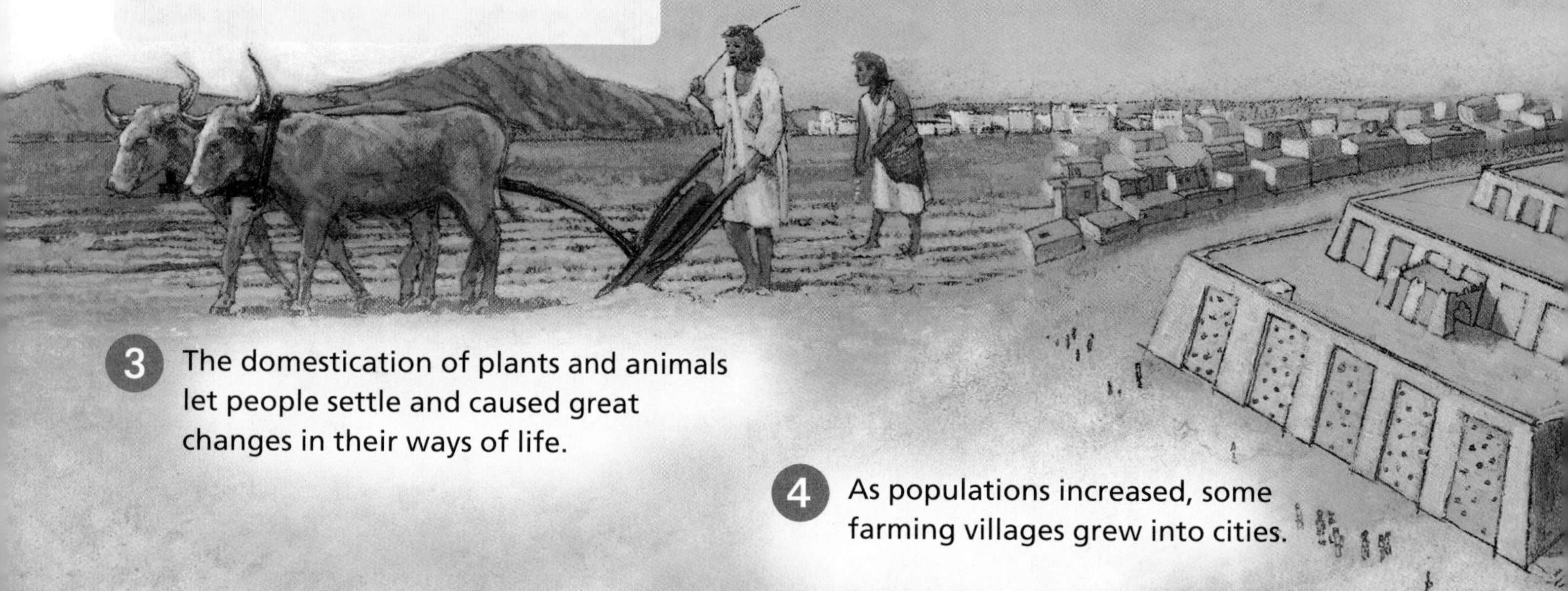

3 The domestication of plants and animals let people settle and caused great changes in their ways of life.

4 As populations increased, some farming villages grew into cities.

6 Unlike many other early cultures, the ancient Israelites believed in one God. They lived by the teachings of the Ten Commandments.

2 Early people learned to domesticate plants and animals.

5 The ancient Sumerians developed creative ways to solve the problems of city life.

7 The Phoenician alphabet and the Lydians' use of coined money brought about great changes.

UNIT 1
REVIEW

USE VOCABULARY

To show that you know what these words mean, use each pair in a sentence.

1. band, migration
2. agriculture, domesticate
3. civilization, government
4. technology, innovation
5. city-state, monarchy

CHECK UNDERSTANDING

6. What were advantages of living in bands?
7. How did migration change the population of the world?
8. How did agriculture change the world's early societies?
9. How did food surpluses lead to a division of labor in Sumer?
10. Why did early societies need governments?

THINK CRITICALLY

11. **Cause and Effect** Agriculture changed society forever. In what ways were the effects of agriculture positive? In what ways were the effects negative?
12. **Explore Viewpoints** Why might some people dislike using new technology or inventions?
13. **Past to Present** How did the Israelites, the Phoenicians, and the Lydians change society?
14. **Think More About It** How would life be different today if we bartered instead of using money? What would a trip to a store be like?

APPLY SKILLS

Follow Routes on a Map
The map below shows the routes used by different armies as they conquered areas in Mesopotamia. Use the map to answer the questions.

15. In what direction did Hammurabi travel to get from Babylon to
    a. Larsa?
    b. Eshnunna?
    c. Mari?

16. From what direction did the Kassites come to conquer Babylon?

17. From what direction did the Assyrians come to conquer Babylon?

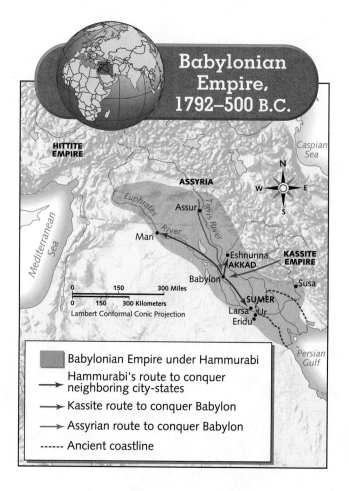

Babylonian Empire, 1792–500 B.C.

HITTITE EMPIRE

Caspian Sea

ASSYRIA

Euphrates River

Assur

Tigris River

Mediterranean Sea

Mari

Eshnunna

AKKAD

KASSITE EMPIRE

Babylon

Susa

0   150   300 Miles
0   150   300 Kilometers
Lambert Conformal Conic Projection

SUMER

Larsa Ur

Eridu

Persian Gulf

Babylonian Empire under Hammurabi
→ Hammurabi's route to conquer neighboring city-states
→ Kassite route to conquer Babylon
→ Assyrian route to conquer Babylon
------ Ancient coastline

REMEMBER

- Share your ideas.
- Cooperate with others to plan your work.
- Take responsibility for your work.
- Help one another.
- Show your group's work to the class.
- Discuss what you learned by working together.

 Present a ## Play

Work with a group to write and act out a brief play about the advances of early people. The first scene should show life as hunters and gatherers. The second scene should show the settled life of farmers. The third scene should show early city life.

 Make a ## Classroom Midden

One way in which archaeologists learned about Skara Brae was by studying its middens, or garbage piles. To see how people can learn from garbage, make a classroom "midden." At home, choose some items that you will probably throw away or recycle. Make sure that what you choose is clean and safe. At school, work with a group to make a "midden" by placing everything collected in a pile. Change places with another group and examine that group's midden. What do the things found in the midden tell about the group that made it?

 Draw Plans for a ## Model Home

Work with several classmates to draw a picture of the outside of a home at Skara Brae. Then, draw the inside of the home. Show your drawings to the class, and explain how the environment helped determine the way the home looked.

Unit Project Wrap-Up

Make a Map of Early Times Work in a group to finish the Unit Project on page 43. First, double-check that you have added all places correctly. Next, review the unit to find out where different crops were grown long ago. Use symbols on your map to show locations of crops. Identify your symbols and explain any other important information on a map key. If you wish, add illustrations to the map.

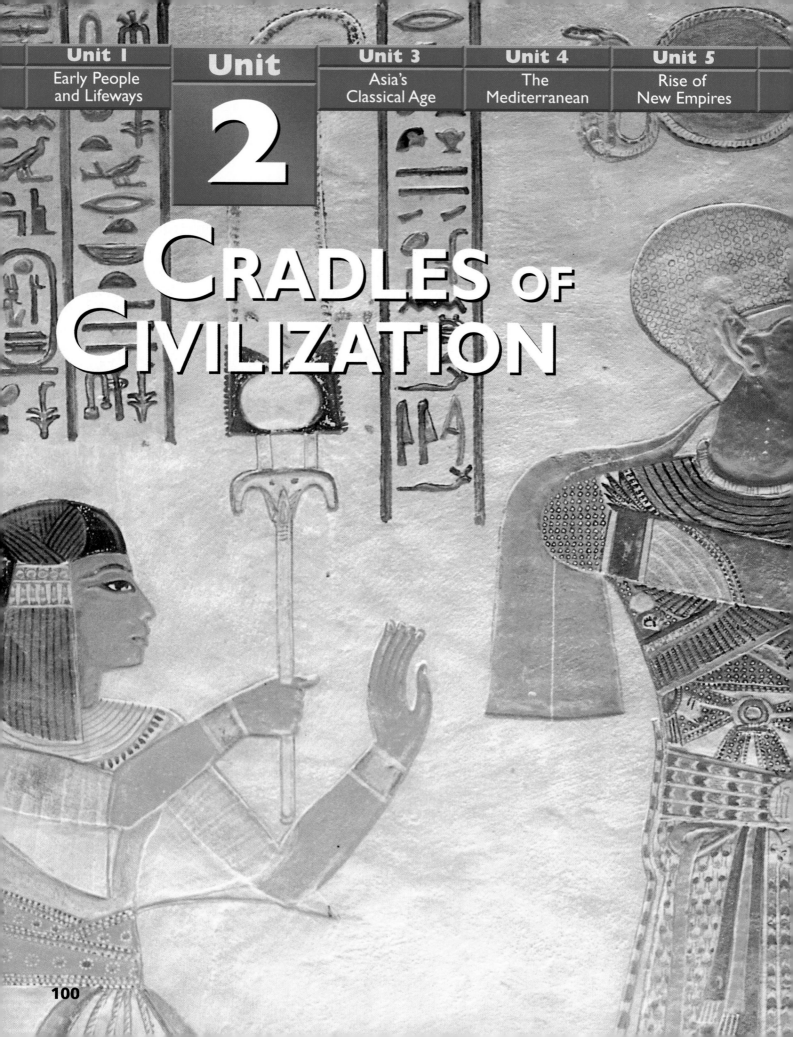

Unit 2

CRADLES OF CIVILIZATION

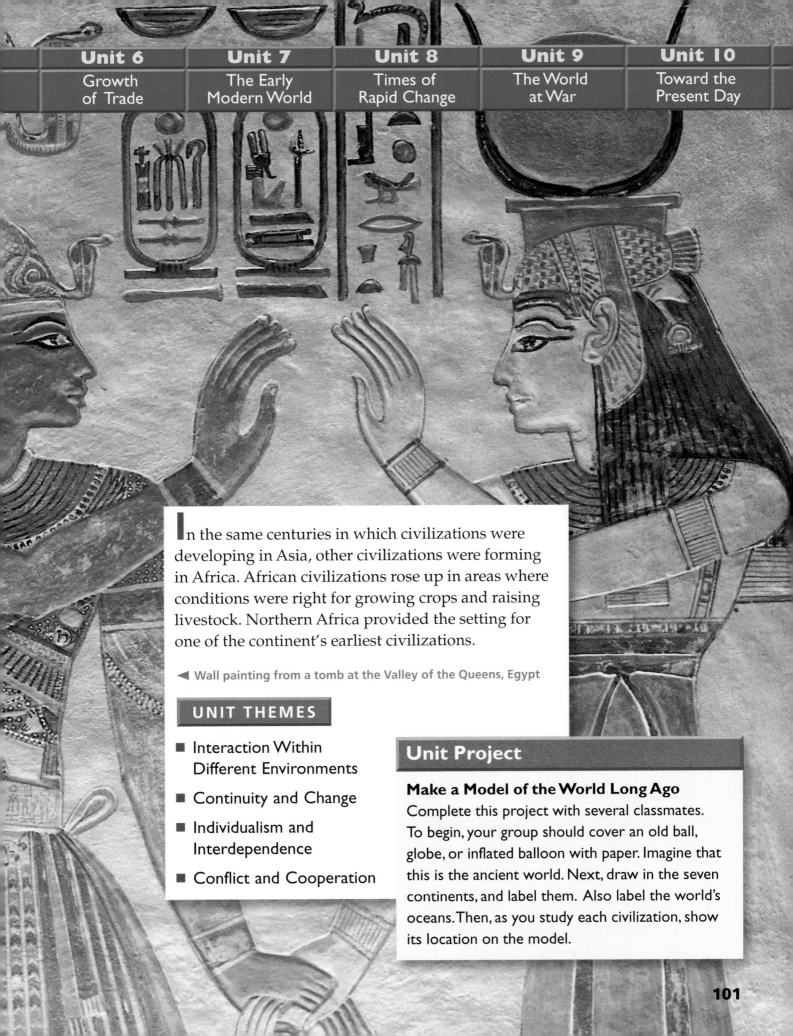

In the same centuries in which civilizations were developing in Asia, other civilizations were forming in Africa. African civilizations rose up in areas where conditions were right for growing crops and raising livestock. Northern Africa provided the setting for one of the continent's earliest civilizations.

◄ Wall painting from a tomb at the Valley of the Queens, Egypt

UNIT THEMES

- Interaction Within Different Environments
- Continuity and Change
- Individualism and Interdependence
- Conflict and Cooperation

Unit Project

Make a Model of the World Long Ago
Complete this project with several classmates. To begin, your group should cover an old ball, globe, or inflated balloon with paper. Imagine that this is the ancient world. Next, draw in the seven continents, and label them. Also label the world's oceans. Then, as you study each civilization, show its location on the model.

101

NORTH AMERICA

Mississippi River

ATLANTIC
OCEAN

N
W — E
S

Olmec
1200 B.C.–400 B.C.

Maya
500 B.C.–A.D. 1450

Amazon River

SOUTH
AMERICA

PACIFIC
OCEAN

0   750   1,500 Miles
0   750   1,500 Kilometers
Miller Cylindrical Projection

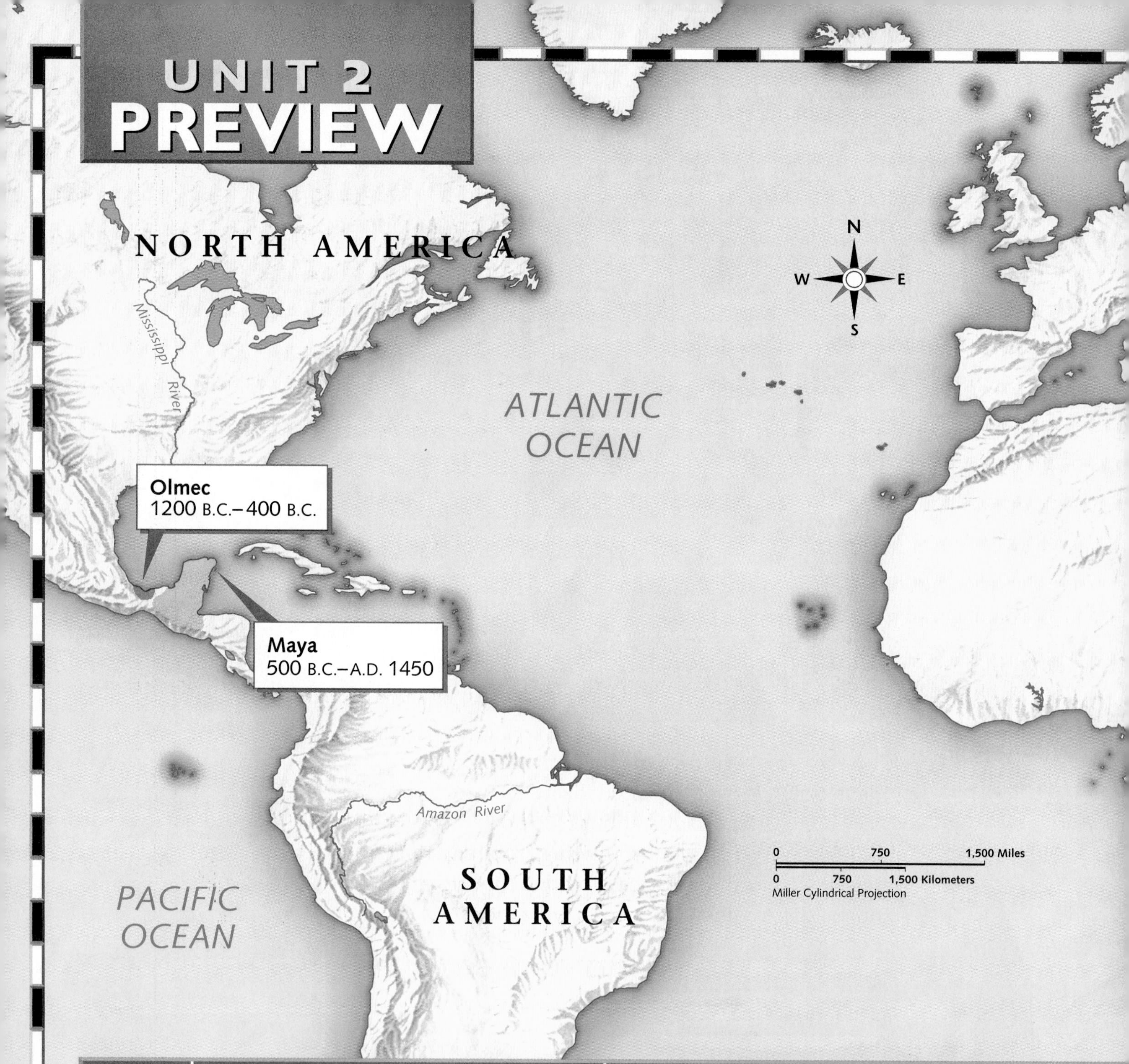

3500 B.C.   3000 B.C.   2500 B.C.

3000 B.C.
Ancient Egypt creates
a united government
PAGE 111

2500 B.C.
Harappan civilization
begins in India
PAGE 136

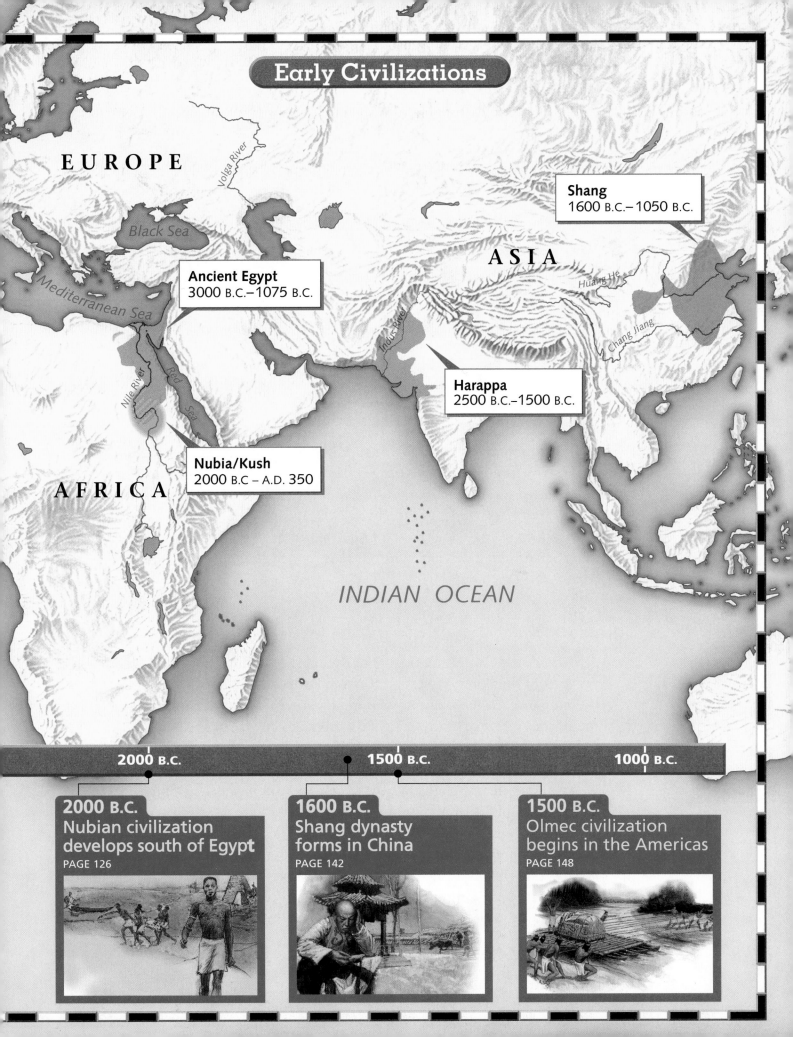

Early Civilizations

EUROPE

Volga River

Black Sea

ASIA

Shang
1600 B.C.–1050 B.C.

Mediterranean Sea

Ancient Egypt
3000 B.C.–1075 B.C.

Huang He

Indus River

Chang Jiang

Nile River

Red Sea

Harappa
2500 B.C.–1500 B.C.

Nubia/Kush
2000 B.C – A.D. 350

AFRICA

INDIAN OCEAN

2000 B.C.   1500 B.C.   1000 B.C.

2000 B.C.
Nubian civilization
develops south of Egypt
PAGE 126

1600 B.C.
Shang dynasty
forms in China
PAGE 142

1500 B.C.
Olmec civilization
begins in the Americas
PAGE 148

E·G·Y·P·T·I·A·N STORIES

retold by Robert Hull

People in ancient civilizations looked for ways to explain the world and their place in it. For many people religion was a way to do this. The ancient Egyptians worshipped many gods. The Egyptians thought that one of these gods, Osiris, gave life to the Earth. Ancient Egyptian stories told of the adventures of Osiris and other gods. This retelling of one ancient story describes how Osiris helped the ancient Egyptians survive on Earth.

Osiris taught the people of the world when to expect the gentle wind from the north. He taught them how to make buildings and raise them up toward the stars, how to make words, how to write down memories with marks on stone, how to make laws. Osiris spoke a law to keep people from killing and eating each other.

Osiris wondered what else he could give to the people. One day, he was walking near the Nile, among the high barley grasses. A breeze swept through the grass, and Osiris watched the ripe grains being blown through the air and rolling along the earth. Then his sharp eyes noticed that though most of the ripe grains blew away in the wind, some of the heavier ones fell alongside the plant, and stayed there, undisturbed. "Next year," he thought, "those seeds will grow again here, in the same place. Most grains will be scattered and lost, but if a few fall where they have grown, men can gather the grains and keep them. In that way men can make barley grow always in the same place."

Agriculture was an important part of the lives of the ancient Egyptians. This painting from ancient times shows farmers planting seeds.

Osiris kept the grain that hadn't blown away and buried it in the earth. Next year, in the same place, the barley grass grew. He had found the way to make barley stay in one place. He told men to scrape at the earth with sticks and make a safe place to put the heavy barley grain, the grain that fell where it had grown.

Osiris had given the people fields.

Then Osiris saw something else. When the Nile came, and the soft wind blew from the north and the world shone with water, the barley grew more thickly. He told men and women to dig small channels to the fields and guide the waters out along these channels. So, with the guidance of the great god-king Osiris, the people learned to lead the waters to the barley and spread the waters there.

Gradually the people had learned to till and sow the earth and guide water to it from the Nile, and to gather the crops that grew from the fields. Osiris had taught them to be farmers. He had given them the harvest.

As you read this unit, you will learn more about the ancient Egyptians and their lifeways. You will also learn about other civilizations around the world.

3

AFRICAN CIVILIZATIONS
OF THE NILE VALLEY

"At first I could see nothing. Then details within emerged: strange animals, statues, and gold— everywhere the glint of gold."

Description of Tutankhamen's tomb by Howard Carter, the archaeologist who discovered it in 1922

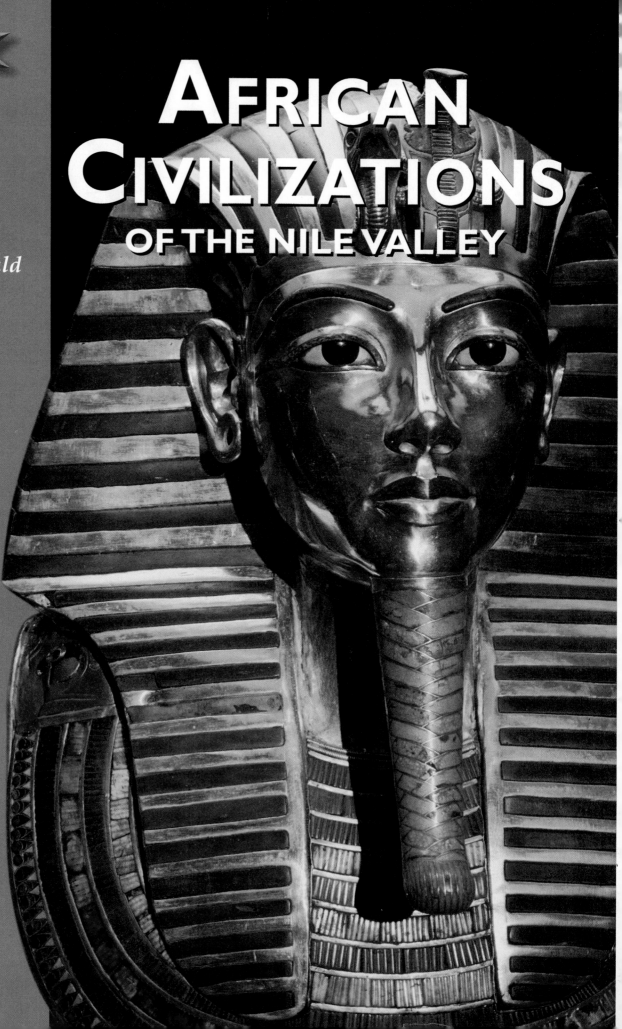

Gold mask of Pharaoh Tutankhamen

The Importance of the Nile River

FOCUS
How might people today be affected by their physical environment?

Main Idea Read to discover how the physical setting of the Nile Valley affected the development of civilization in northern Africa.

Vocabulary
desertification
delta
silt
predict
cataract

A narrow ribbon of fertile land cut by a single river divides the desert in the northeast corner of Africa. This river, the Nile, flows more than 4,000 miles (6,437 km) from its main source at Lake Victoria in central Africa, downstream to the Mediterranean Sea. The Nile is the world's longest river. Along its course developed one of the world's longest-lasting civilizations.

Giver and Taker of Life

During the Paleolithic period, or Old Stone Age, people in northeastern Africa subsisted just by hunting and gathering. At that time a grassy plain covered that part of Africa. The plain provided a ready supply of plants and wild animals for food. Then the climate slowly grew drier. The change in climate turned the land to desert. Any change of fertile land into desert, whether caused by climate or human actions, is called **desertification**. As the land became desert, plants died, and animals left to search for water. The people, who also needed water, moved into the valley of the Nile.

Near the Mediterranean Sea the Nile River divides into several branches and spreads out over a wide area. There it drops much of the soil it has carried from far upriver. Over time this soil has formed a huge, triangle-shaped **delta** of islands and marshes. By about 6000 B.C., Neolithic people began growing their own food on the delta and in the river valley leading to it. The rich soil helped these early farmers begin their agriculture. The people grew wheat and barley and raised sheep, goats, and cattle.

For centuries people have settled on the fertile land near the Nile.

107

Ancient Egypt and Nubia

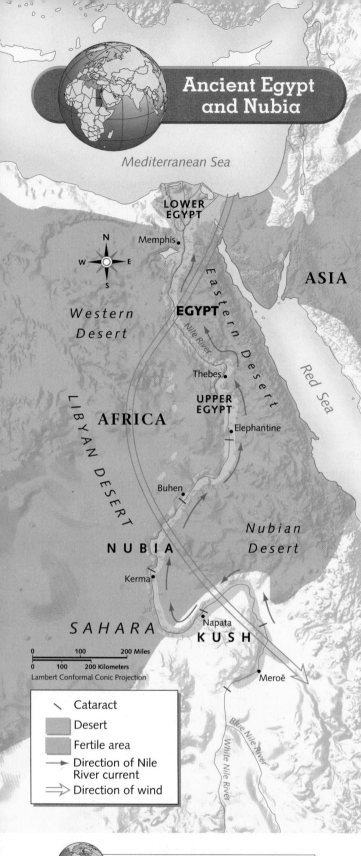

Mediterranean Sea

LOWER EGYPT

Memphis

ASIA

Western Desert

EGYPT

Eastern Desert

Nile River

Red Sea

Thebes

UPPER EGYPT

AFRICA

Elephantine

LIBYAN DESERT

Buhen

Nubian Desert

NUBIA

Kerma

SAHARA

Napata

KUSH

Meroë

Blue Nile River

White Nile River

0   100   200 Miles
0   100   200 Kilometers
Lambert Conformal Conic Projection

\ Cataract
☐ Desert
☐ Fertile area
→ Direction of Nile River current
⇒ Direction of wind

Human-Environment Interactions This map of ancient Egypt and Nubia shows the flow of the Nile River and the direction of wind.

■ *Why do you think the land to the north was called Lower Egypt and the land farther south was called Upper Egypt?*

The Egyptians understood how important the Nile River was to their survival. Because of this the Nile played a role in their religion, their writing, and their art. This painting shows a ruler and his wife traveling to a life after death.

By 5000 B.C. small villages had grown up on the delta and along the valley. The people called this place Kemet, or the Black Land, because of the rich, dark mud found along the banks of the Nile. They called the dried-out desert that surrounded Kemet the Red Land. Kemet of ancient times is known today as ancient Egypt. *Egypt* was the name given to Kemet by the ancient Greeks.

"Hail to you, O Nile, that flows from the Earth and keeps Egypt alive!" an Egyptian prayer begins. Just as the Sumerians depended on the waters of the Tigris and Euphrates rivers, the early Egyptians depended on the Nile.

The great river gave not only water but also good farmland. When the Nile flowed over its banks each year, it spread **silt**, fine bits of rock and soil. After the river returned to its banks, early farmers plowed their fields and sprinkled seeds in the fertile silt. Then they led cattle and sheep through the fields to walk over the seeds and push them into the ground. The sunny weather did the rest. Crops grew quickly, sometimes producing two or three harvests a year. "It is to be a beautiful year, free from want and rich in all herbs," an Egyptian farmer said in a year of plentiful crops. The Nile, it was said, was a "giver of life."

Some years the Nile took life away. When rains fell too lightly upriver, the Nile did not overflow. The land lay baked by the sun and crops dried up. Without a harvest, people starved. When too much rain fell, the Nile flooded wildly. It washed away crops and drowned people and animals. For a long time, the people could not **predict**, or tell ahead of time, what the river might do.

REVIEW *How did the Nile help the ancient Egyptians?*

Source of Innovation

Over the centuries, the Egyptians worked out ways to predict when the Nile would flood. By studying the skies, they began to understand the weather and learned to predict times of heavy rain and the floods that followed. They kept track of the pattern of flooding by using a calendar with a 365-day year. This calendar is the oldest known calendar based on the sun.

The Egyptian calendar divided a year into three parts: Inundation, Emergence, and Harvest. Each part lasted several months, and its name told what was happening to the land along the Nile.

Egyptians celebrated during the late spring when the floods began. The rising water spilled onto the land along the river. The Egyptians called this time Inundation. In late summer the waters reached their peak and then began to leave the fields. This time of returning waters became known as Emergence. At this time of the year, farmers plowed their fields and planted crops. Emergence lasted until the middle of winter and was followed by the dry time of Harvest. At this time, farmers cared for and harvested their crops.

The season of Emergence was a time of great activity for Egyptian farmers. In this wooden model from about 2000 B.C., an Egyptian farmer plows the land after it is no longer flooded.

Little rain fell in Egypt. To keep their land well-watered during the growing season, the Egyptians developed irrigation methods. During Emergence people trapped water in ponds to use later for irrigation during Harvest. Like the Mesopotamians, the Egyptians built dams and dikes to hold back the river in places during Inundation. They also built canals to carry excess water back to the river during Emergence.

REVIEW *How did the Egyptians try to control the Nile?*

Source of Religion

Science and technology could not solve all the Egyptians' problems with the Nile River. Some years there was not enough water for the river to flood. Other years there was too much water, and floods destroyed the fields. Then the Egyptians turned to their gods for help.

The people of ancient Egypt used stories about their gods to explain nature. The sun, they said, was a god who was born each day and died each night. To the Egyptians, this story explained why the sun seemed to go away at night and return each morning. The sun became a symbol of the life cycle.

The Egyptians believed that the god Osiris taught their people about farming and made things grow. Horus— the son of Osiris and his wife, Isis—ruled the sky. Horus often took the form of a falcon.

The Egyptians often thought of their gods as part animal and part human. This bronze statue shows the Egyptian sun god Re in the form of a bird.

Many Egyptian myths were about the goddess Isis and her adventures. As this statue shows, Isis was often pictured with cow horns and a sun.

To the Egyptians the sun god, Re, later called Amon-Re, was the most important god. According to Egyptian belief, a small island appeared out of nothingness. On that island grew a lotus blossom. From this blossom came the sun god, Re. Re then created the other gods and the world as the Egyptians knew it.

REVIEW *How did the Egyptians explain natural events?*

Unity for the Egyptians

Most of the small farming villages of Egypt rose up along the part of the Nile River between the first of six cataracts and the delta. A **cataract** is a waterfall or a place where water runs fast over rocks. Villages in the northern region of Egypt,

Upper

Lower

Unified

LEARNING FROM DIAGRAMS The double crown of unified Egypt was formed by placing the crown of Upper Egypt inside the crown of Lower Egypt.
■ *Why do you think the crowns of Upper and Lower Egypt were combined?*

on the Nile Delta, were said to be in Lower Egypt. Villages in the river valley south of the delta were part of Upper Egypt.

By about 3000 B.C. Upper Egyptian kings had gained control of Lower Egypt. The Two Lands, as they were called, united as one. Ancient Egyptian legend says that Menes (MEE•neez) was the king who united Egypt.

Who really united the two kingdoms is not known. Some experts think that a king named Narmer may have brought the Two Lands together. In ancient artwork Narmer is shown wearing a double crown that combines the white crown of Upper Egypt and the red crown of Lower Egypt.

The uniting of Egypt had an important result. It marked the beginning of the world's first organized government representing one group of people. Egypt's way of governing lasted for 3,000 years.

REVIEW *Why was the uniting of Egypt important?*

LESSON 1 REVIEW

Check Understanding

1 **Remember the Facts** What two things did the Nile River give to the land around it?

2 **Recall the Main Idea** How did the Nile River affect the development of Egyptian civilization?

Think Critically

3 **Think More About It** The Nile River cut through all of ancient Egypt. How do you think travel and trade up and down the Nile may have helped unite the Egyptians?

4 **Cause and Effect** The Egyptians believed that they would have another life after death. What things in nature may have given them this idea?

5 **Past to Present** How do natural features such as rivers, lakes, or mountains affect the way people live in your community today?

Show What You Know

Writing Activity The ancient Egyptians told stories to help explain acts of nature. Think of an act of nature, such as a thunderstorm, a volcanic eruption, or an earthquake. Then imagine a story you might use to explain that natural act. Write down your story, illustrate it, and share it with a classmate.

FOCUS

What causes some societies to change over time and others to stay the same?

Main Idea Read to find out how the ancient Egyptian people maintained their civilization for so long while making some changes.

Vocabulary

dynasty
pharaoh
edict
hieroglyphics
papyrus
pyramid
mummy
peasant

The Dynasties of Egypt

Modern experts trace the beginning of Egyptian civilization to the rule of King Narmer. When Narmer died, rule of Egypt passed on to a family member. This continued for several generations, creating Egypt's first **dynasty**, or series of rulers from the same family. About 33 dynasties ruled Egypt over the next 3,000 years, making the Egyptian civilization one of the longest-lasting in world history.

The Early Period

The kings of Dynasties 1 and 2 went by names that showed a relationship with the gods. Later, Egyptians began to call their king **pharaoh**. The word means "great house" and referred to the ruler's magnificent palace.

Egyptians believed that their pharaoh was a god in human form. They honored the ruler as the son of Re, the sun god. As a god in human form, the pharaoh held total authority over both the people and the land.

The strong rule of the pharaoh helped the Egyptians keep their civilization going for thousands of years. The pharaoh decided almost everything about the people's lives and made sure that Egyptian lifeways and government did not change much over the years.

Many nobles and officials helped the pharaoh govern Egypt. These people collected taxes, planned building projects, and made sure the laws were obeyed. One of the most important government officials was the vizier (vuh•ZIR), or adviser. The vizier carried out the pharaoh's **edicts**, or commands, and took care of the day-to-day running of the government.

We know about Egypt's earliest pharaohs and their governments because the Egyptians left written records. They developed a system of writing known as

The ancient Egyptians left behind many examples of fine artwork and jewelry. This ring, made from solid gold, was worn by Pharaoh Ramses II.

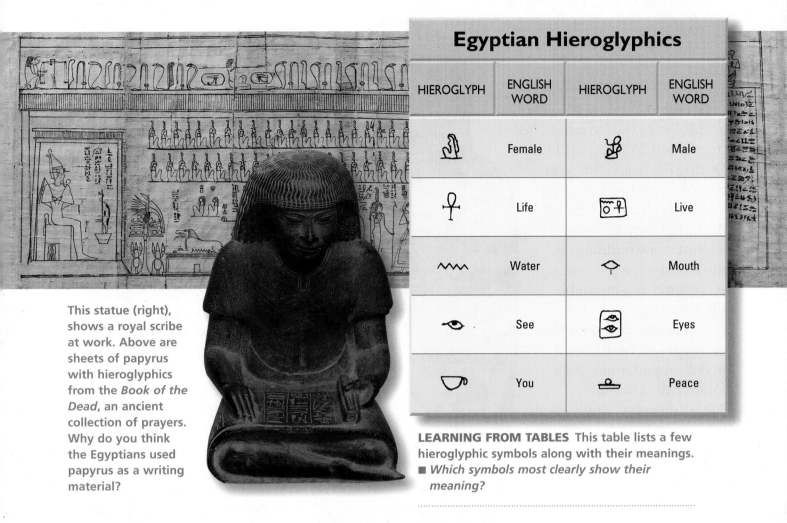

This statue (right), shows a royal scribe at work. Above are sheets of papyrus with hieroglyphics from the *Book of the Dead*, an ancient collection of prayers. Why do you think the Egyptians used papyrus as a writing material?

Egyptian Hieroglyphics

HIEROGLYPH	ENGLISH WORD	HIEROGLYPH	ENGLISH WORD
	Female		Male
	Life		Live
	Water		Mouth
	See		Eyes
	You		Peace

LEARNING FROM TABLES This table lists a few hieroglyphic symbols along with their meanings.
■ *Which symbols most clearly show their meaning?*

hieroglyphics (hy•ruh•GLIH•fiks). Egyptian hieroglyphic writing used more than 700 different symbols. Most hieroglyphic symbols stood for sounds, though some stood for whole words or ideas.

The Egyptians wrote on stone, on walls, and on a paperlike material called **papyrus** (puh•PY•ruhs). Our word *paper* comes from *papyrus*. Papyrus, one of the great innovations of the Egyptians, helped make Egypt's central government possible. The Egyptians used papyrus for keeping all the important written records of their society.

To make this kind of paper, the Egyptians cut strips of the stalk of the papyrus plant, a reed that grows in the marshes of the Nile Delta. They laid the strips close together, with the edges touching. Across the top of these strips, they placed another layer.

Then they pressed the layers of papyrus with stones until the layers became a single sheet. To write, the Egyptian scribes sharpened other reeds to use as pens. The scribes then dipped the reeds into ink made of soot, ground-up plants, and water.

For the Egyptians a "book" was a scroll— a roll made of sheets of papyrus joined end to end. Some rolls were more than 100 feet (30 m) long. On these rolls, or scrolls, scribes recorded the history of Egypt. This history is usually divided into three parts: the Old Kingdom, the Middle Kingdom, and the New Kingdom. In the times between these kingdoms, competing dynasties ruled parts of Egypt and sometimes fought with each other. These periods are called intermediate periods.

REVIEW *Who controlled the land and people of ancient Egypt?*

The Old Kingdom

The Old Kingdom, also known as the Age of the Pyramids, lasted from about 2625 B.C. to 2130 B.C. During the nearly 500-year rule of Dynasties 4 through 8, the Egyptians developed the technology to create the biggest stone buildings in the world—the pyramids. A **pyramid** is a burial place for the dead.

Before this time the kings of Egypt had been buried in flat-topped, mud-brick tombs called mastabas (MAS•tuh•buhz). The mastabas were built far from the Nile's banks so the floods would not wash them away. Egyptians built these strong tombs because they believed they would need their bodies in another life after death. For this reason also, the Egyptians developed ways to preserve dead bodies. They removed all the body organs except the heart. Then they rubbed the body with special oils and wrapped it in linen cloth. This process took about 70 days. Only then was the preserved body, or **mummy**, ready to be placed in its tomb.

All the things a person might need in the afterlife were also placed in the tomb. Clothing, jewelry, furniture, and even games were included. Tomb walls were covered with painted scenes of the person's life. Prayers from the *Book of the Dead* were also carved into tomb walls. The Egyptians thought that these practices would help the soul in the afterlife.

The Egyptians believed that the soul of a dead person appeared before a group of judges. The judges placed the dead person's heart on one side of a scale. They placed a feather, the symbol of truth, on the other side. If the two balanced, the soul earned life forever. If not, the soul was eaten by an animal that was part crocodile, part lion, and part hippopotamus.

Thoughts about the afterlife caused rulers to care deeply about their tombs. Sometime about 2650 B.C., King Zoser's architect, Imhotep, decided to build the pharaoh's tomb of stone, not mud brick. Imhotep started a stone tomb that looked much like a mastaba. Then he changed his mind. He had more mastabas built on top of the first one, each smaller than the one below. The result was a pyramid of mastabas, looking somewhat like a Sumerian ziggurat. This early pyramid looked so much like a set of steps that people today call it a step pyramid.

At about that time, a new idea came about in the Egyptian religion. The Egyptians began to believe that after death the pharaoh went to live with Amon-Re, the sun god. One of their religious writings said, "A staircase to heaven is laid for

This mummy case was prepared for Paankhenamun, an Egyptian who lived sometime between 900 B.C. and 700 B.C.

him [the pharaoh] so that he may climb to heaven." This may have been the reason that Imhotep built a step pyramid.

Around 2600 B.C. pyramid builders tried still another idea. They made pyramids with slanting sides and a pointed peak instead of steps. This, too, may have had to do with the sun god. Possibly the slanting sides of the pyramids stood for the rays of the sun.

The best known of Egypt's pyramids is the Great Pyramid built at Giza (GEE•zuh). The Pharaoh Khufu ordered this pyramid built for himself. He wanted his tomb to be the largest pyramid ever built. Workers may have spent 20 years building the Great Pyramid. During the times of Inundation, when no one was able to farm, the pharaoh ordered as many as 100,000 farmers to work on the Great Pyramid.

The workers cut and moved more than 2 million blocks of stone. Most blocks weighed about 5,000 pounds (about 2,300 kg). No one knows exactly how the Egyptians solved the problem of moving the large blocks from the ground to the top of the pyramid. Most archaeologists believe the Egyptians built ramps to move the blocks. Whatever solution they chose worked. When completed, the Great Pyramid stood about 480 feet (about 146 m) high and covered 13 acres. Its tip was covered with gold to reflect the sun's rays. It was the largest and most spectacular pyramid built in Egypt.

REVIEW *How are pyramids and mastabas alike yet different?*

The Middle Kingdom

The year 1980 B.C. marks the beginning of the Middle Kingdom. The rule of Dynasty 12, which started about 1938 B.C., is considered the high point of the Middle Kingdom. It began when Amenemhet (AHM•uhn•em•HET), a vizier in Lower Egypt, took over as pharaoh. He and those who ruled after him made Egypt an empire. They conquered

Egyptian workers built more than 80 pyramids at Giza during the time of the Old Kingdom. Some of these pyramids still stand. These huge stone structures are proof of the Egyptians' understanding of mathematics, engineering, and architecture.

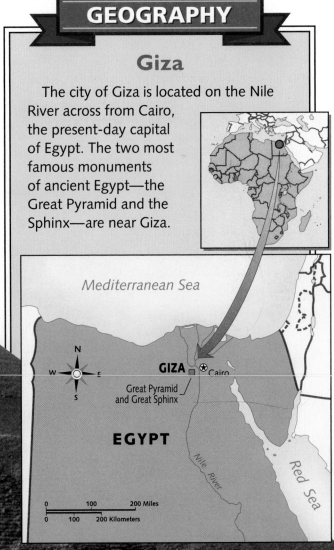

GEOGRAPHY

Giza

The city of Giza is located on the Nile River across from Cairo, the present-day capital of Egypt. The two most famous monuments of ancient Egypt—the Great Pyramid and the Sphinx—are near Giza.

Mediterranean Sea

N W E S

GIZA ⊡ ⊛ Cairo
Great Pyramid
and Great Sphinx

EGYPT

Nile River

Red Sea

0   100   200 Miles
0   100   200 Kilometers

much of Nubia, a land to the south, and led armies into the Fertile Crescent to protect trade routes.

Prisoners of war from both places were taken as slaves to Thebes and other large Egyptian cities. Unlike slaves in some societies, Egyptian slaves had some rights. They were allowed to own personal items and even hold government jobs. They were also allowed to earn their freedom.

During the Middle Kingdom, Egyptian society saw the rise of a middle class. Before this time, Egyptian society had been made up of two social classes—nobles, who governed the people, and **peasants**, who farmed the land. The new middle class was made up of craftworkers, merchants, scribes, and people who had jobs in the pharaoh's government.

During the Middle Kingdom, the middle class gained the right to own land—a right that once only pharaohs had.

Beginning with Dynasty 13 strong rule began to give way to disorder. Egypt's prosperity came to an end by about 1630 B.C. when the Hyksos (HIK•sahs) gained control of Lower Egypt and part of Upper Egypt. The Hyksos had come to Egypt from western Europe. Hyksos kings ruled over Egypt for about 100 years as Dynasty 15. During their rule the Hyksos introduced the Egyptians to many important military innovations. These included the horse-drawn chariot and a stronger kind of bow called a composite bow.

REVIEW *How did Egypt's social classes change during the Middle Kingdom?*

LEARNING FROM CHARTS This pyramid-shaped chart shows the different classes of Egyptian society.
■ *What people owned most of the farmland?*

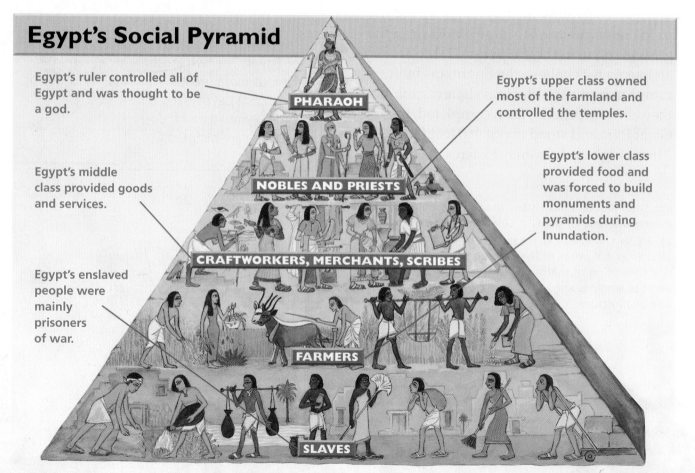

Egypt's Social Pyramid

Egypt's ruler controlled all of Egypt and was thought to be a god.

Egypt's upper class owned most of the farmland and controlled the temples.

Egypt's middle class provided goods and services.

Egypt's lower class provided food and was forced to build monuments and pyramids during Inundation.

Egypt's enslaved people were mainly prisoners of war.

PHARAOH

NOBLES AND PRIESTS

CRAFTWORKERS, MERCHANTS, SCRIBES

FARMERS

SLAVES

Expansion of Egypt

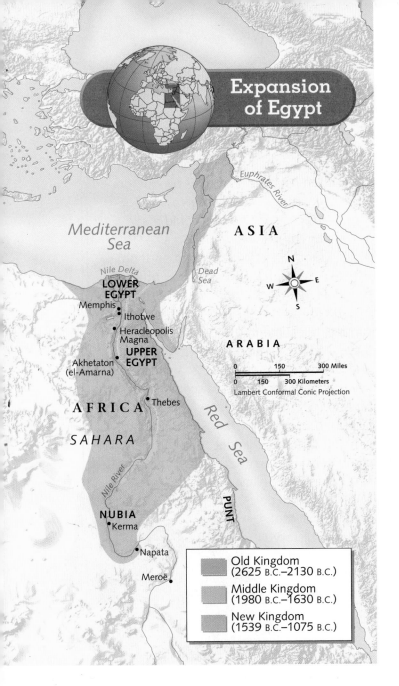

Mediterranean
Sea

Euphrates River

ASIA

Nile Delta
**LOWER
EGYPT**
Memphis
Ithotwe
Heracleopolis
Magna
**UPPER
EGYPT**
Akhetaton
(el-Amarna)

Dead
Sea

ARABIA

N
W   E
S

0   150   300 Miles
0   150   300 Kilometers
Lambert Conformal Conic Projection

AFRICA   •Thebes

SAHARA

Red Sea

Nile River

PUNT

NUBIA
•Kerma

•Napata

Meroë•

■	Old Kingdom (2625 B.C.–2130 B.C.)
■	Middle Kingdom (1980 B.C.–1630 B.C.)
■	New Kingdom (1539 B.C.–1075 B.C.)

Human-Environment Interactions This map shows the borders of ancient Egypt during the different kingdoms.

■ *How may improved ways of agriculture have affected the growth of Egypt?*

sent armies into the western part of the Fertile Crescent and pushed trade routes farther south in Africa. Thutmose III continued Egypt's conquests by invading both Nubia and the Fertile Crescent. By 1450 B.C. Egypt controlled lands from Syria to Nubia.

Amenhotep IV (ah•muhn•HOH•tep) came to the throne in 1353 B.C. The new ruler brought change to the empire. Amenhotep and his wife Nefertiti (nef•er•TEET•ee) urged the Egyptian people to worship only one god, the Aton. Amenhotep was so devoted to the Aton that he changed his own name to Akhenaton (ahk•NAHT•uhn), or "servant of

Akhenaton and the royal family offer gifts to the Egyptian god, the Aton, shown here as a sun disk.

The New Kingdom

In 1539 B.C., after about 100 years of Hyksos rule, the Egyptians took back their country. They were able to do this because they learned to use war chariots and other new weapons. To be safe from other wars, Dynasty 18 rulers formed Egypt's first full-time army. Pharaohs then sent armies to conquer lands beyond the Nile Valley.

Pharaoh Thutmose I led armies as far north as the Euphrates River. His son, Thutmose II, continued to expand Egypt. After Thutmose II died, his wife, Hatshepsut, (hat•SHEP•soot) became pharaoh. Hatshepsut

the Aton." The Egyptians feared that such a change would bring an end to their civilization.

The attack on Amon-Re and the other gods of Egypt's long-established religion angered the priests. When Akhenaton died, they picked a new pharaoh whom they could control. They chose a 9-year-old boy of the royal house and changed the young leader's name from Tutankhaton to Tutankhamen (too•tahng•KAH•muhn). Tutankhamen ruled Egypt for only nine years. During that time his ministers brought back the old gods. Tutankhamen died at age 18 and was buried in a solid-gold coffin in a tomb filled with gold and jewelry. It was a very visible display of Egypt's great wealth.

Following Tutankhamen's death, Egypt's wealth began to slip away. By 1075 B.C., the New Kingdom had ended. For the next 700 years, ten dynasties ruled the Egyptian people. Most of them were formed by conquerors from outside Egypt.

Rule by outsiders caused Egyptian civilization to weaken. However, the achievements of the ancient Egyptians were not forgotten.

REVIEW *What was a source of conflict between Akhenaton and the people he ruled?*

HISTORY

The Rosetta Stone

After the Egyptians were conquered, the written languages of their conquerors were used rather than hieroglyphics. For thousands of years, no one could read ancient Egyptian writings. Then, in A.D. 1798, European armies invaded northern Africa. A year later a French army officer found a large black stone near the city of Rosetta in the Nile Delta. On the stone's surface, the same message appears in three kinds of writing—two Egyptian and one Greek. The Greek gave scholars the key to one of the Egyptian scripts. The other script, Egyptian hieroglyphics, remained a mystery. Then, in 1822, Jean-François Champollion decoded the hiero-glyphics using the other forms of writing as a guide. The ability to read hieroglyphics unlocked all the recorded history of the ancient Egyptians for today's world.

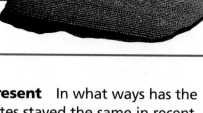

LESSON 2 REVIEW

Check Understanding

1 **Remember the Facts** Into what three periods is Egyptian history usually divided?

2 **Recall the Main Idea** What stayed the same about Egypt's government, religion, and way of life throughout the years? What changed?

Think Critically

3 **Think More About It** In what ways did the pharaohs keep Egyptian civilization the same and change it?

4 **Past to Present** In what ways has the United States stayed the same in recent years? How has it changed?

Show What You Know

Art Activity In the style of the ancient Egyptians, draw pictures of one or more events from each of these periods: the Old Kingdom, the Middle Kingdom, and the New Kingdom. You may want to draw your pictures on shelf paper that can be rolled to look like an Egyptian scroll.

Solve a Problem

1. Why Learn This Skill?

You have to solve problems every day. Some problems are bigger than others, but most are easier to solve if you follow a set of steps. Knowing the steps to use will help you solve problems throughout your life.

2. Remember What You Have Read

The builders of the Great Pyramid at Giza had a *big* problem. The pharaoh Khufu had ordered the largest pyramid ever made to be built in ancient Egypt. It was to cover 13 acres and rise as high as a 36-story building of today. Mud bricks would not be strong enough, so the Great Pyramid was to be built of huge blocks cut from limestone. The builders of the Great Pyramid had to figure out a way to move the huge limestone blocks without pulleys or wheels, which were still unknown to the ancient Egyptians during this time.

3. Understand the Process

No one knows what steps the Egyptian builders used to solve their problem. The fact that the Great Pyramid still stands proves that they did find a solution. Listed below are some steps you can use to solve problems, large or small. After each step is a brief description of how archaeologists think the Egyptian builders may have solved their problem.

1 **Identify the problem.** The builders had to raise huge blocks of stone to the top of the pyramid without pulleys or wheels.

2 **Think of possible solutions.**
  a. Workers could lift the stone blocks up each step of the pyramid.
  b. Workers could pull the blocks up a ramp built on the side of the pyramid.

3 **Compare the solutions, and choose the best one.**
  a. Many workers would be needed to lift each block up one step at a time. This would be hard to do and would take much time.
  b. Fewer workers would be needed to move the stones up a ramp. They could do this more easily and in less time.

4 **Plan a way to carry out the solution.** Temporary ramps could be built on each side of the pyramid. With four ramps, workers could move stones into place faster.

5 **Try your solution, and think about how well it solves the problem.** The Great Pyramid at Giza is still standing after 4,500 years.

4. Think and Apply

What if the Great Pyramid had to be built today? How would you solve the problem the Egyptian builders faced? With a partner, brainstorm ways builders today might solve the problem. Use the steps you just learned, and share your solution with your class.

His Majesty

Queen Hatshepsut

by Dorothy Sharp Carter

Women in ancient Egyptian society shared with men the right to own property and businesses. Some women in ancient Egypt became government officials and trusted advisers to pharaohs. Historians believe that Queen Tiye, wife of Pharaoh Amenhotep III, ruled alongside her husband, making many important decisions. Few women, however, became pharaohs.

Queen Hatshepsut also ruled with her husband, Thutmose II. Hatshepsut had married her half-brother, a common custom among Egyptian royalty. After the death of her husband, Hatshepsut refused to give up her rule to young Thutmose III, the son of Thutmose II and another of his wives. Because he was male, Thutmose III stood next in line to the throne. However, Hatshepsut believed she deserved to rule because she was the daughter of Thutmose I.

Hatshepsut succeeded in her quest to rule as pharaoh. In doing so, she became the first important woman ruler in world history. Advised by her vizier, Hatshepsut ruled Egypt during the period of the New Kingdom. As pharaoh she helped bring strength and wealth to Egypt. Hatshepsut is remembered for her expansion of trade routes to the land of Punt.

You will now read a story about Hatshepsut's coronation, or crowning, as pharaoh. As you read, think about what it might be like for a person to take on a new role in a society.

nd so arrangements for my coronation go forward. The sooner it takes place, the better. For plots of defiance to hatch, time is essential. We will dispense with time.

Throughout the Two Lands and abroad, the edict of my ascension to the throne is sent, only a few weeks before the ceremony. By tradition the event takes place on a major religious holiday, in this case the Feast of Opet. Hapusoneb insists this is a bit hurried but perfectly proper. But then anything Pharaoh-to-be decides is proper.

The edict reads:

> *A letter of the King to cause thee to know that My Majesty is risen as King on the throne of Horus, without equal forever. My titles are: for my Horus name, Usert-Kau, mighty in kas; for Vulture-Cobra, Uadjit-Renpet, fresh in years; for Golden Horus, Netert-khau, divine in apparitions[1]; my royal and birth names, Makare Hatshepsut.*
>
> *Cause thou that worship of the gods be made at the desire of the King of Upper and Lower Egypt, Hatshepsut. Cause thou that all oaths be taken in the*

---

[1] **apparitions:** religious spirits

name of My Majesty, born of the royal mother Ahmose. This is written that thou mayest bow thy head in obedience and knowest that the royal house is firm and strong.

The third year, third month of Inundation, day 7. Day of Coronation.

I worry over my dress. As ceremony demands that the king wear the royal braided beard strapped to his chin (no matter whether he has a beard of his own or not), I shall certainly do so. Ought I, then, to wear

This painted sandstone sculpture captures the beauty of Queen Hatshepsut. Hatshepsut ruled Egypt as pharaoh from 1479 B.C. to 1458 B.C.

the long dress of a queen or the short kilt of a king? With a question Hapusoneb supplies the answer.

He is preoccupied, poor man, at having to oversee so many elaborate arrangements in such a short period of time. At each succeeding audience with me he appears more harried, more bent with care, until his back curves like a strung bow.

"One of the problems, Majesty, is that the titles and coronation ceremonies are designed for men. How are we to change them?"

The solution strikes me, clear as Hapusoneb's harassed face.

"There is no need to change anything, Vizier. I mean to rule as a king, with the full powers of a king. And I shall dress as a king. The rituals, the titles, will remain the same as those initiated by Narmer, first King of the Two Lands."

Hapusoneb appears dubious, then relieved. After all, he can scarcely overrule Pharaoh-to-be, no matter what his misgivings.

And as I am resolved to be as resolute, as forceful as any king, I will begin by donning full regalia[2] for my coronation. Around my waist, over the short kilt, I fasten a broad belt adorned with a metal buckle in the form of my

In this statue Queen Hatshepsut wears the traditional pharaoh's beard.

personal cartouche.[3] Tied to it in front is an apron of beads, in back a bull's tail. A girl attaches the beard to my chin. Over my wig is fitted the *nems*, the leather headcloth with the two striped lappets falling forward over my shoulders.

For the ceremony I have ordered a dazzling gold-and-jeweled pectoral[4] suspended from a double gold chain. On each of my arms a girl clasps a pair of wide bracelets, another on each wrist, a third pair on my ankles. On my fingers rings are strung like chunks of beef on skewers. Surely I must weigh twice as much as usual.

As I take a final peek in my silver mirror, I gasp to Henut,[5] "But I look a mummy! One can hardly see the flesh for the gold."

"Very appropriate, Highness." Henut nods approvingly. "Egypt is wealthy beyond measure. You are the symbol of that wealth."

Perhaps so, but wealth, I find, does not always signal comfort.

The ceremony goes off with fanfare. Although the coronation of my husband occurred fifteen years before, the rites are still clear in my memory.

I sit on a light throne borne by six slaves from the Great House to the royal barge, which carries us down the river. From the shore to the temple the procession is headed by heralds crying, "Earth, beware! Your god comes!" Rows of soldiers

---

[2] **regalia:** symbols of royalty

[3] **cartouche** (kar•TOOSH): an Egyptian decoration with the name of a ruler written in hieroglyphics
[4] **pectoral:** an object worn on the chest
[5] **Henut** (HEN•uht): Hatshepsut's servant

Pectoral, or chest plate, worn by a pharaoh of Dynasty 19

pace before and behind my carrying chair, and in back of them hundreds of priests.

Behind my chair a servant supports a long-handled sunshade to provide me some relief from the sun, and beside me two young pages wave fans of ostrich plumes. (Vizier has promised boys with endurance and dedication enough not to whack off my headpiece.) The tail of the procession—a very long tail—is made up of government dignitaries,[6] the nobility, and foreign envoys.[7]

Most of the spectators sink to their knees, heads in the dust, although a few bewildered country folk stand gaping in amazement. A guard motions them sternly to bow, or even strikes one or two with his spear. As Hapusoneb says, "Manners grow more and more out of fashion." Still, the atmosphere is a happy mixture of reverence and rejoicing.

In the main hall of the temple my litter is lowered and I walk, accompanied by the High Priest, to the gleaming gilded throne set on a dais.[8] After prayers and hymns to Amon, the Priest makes an address in which he repeats my father's words uttered in the dream: "I have appointed her to be my successor upon my throne. She it is, assuredly, who shall sit upon my glorious throne; she shall order all matters for the people in every department of the state; she it is who shall lead you."

Finally he pronounces me Lord of the Two Lands, seated on the Horus-throne, and living forever and ever. Into my hands he puts the two scepters, emblems of Osiris: the golden crook, and the golden flail with its handle carved in the form of a lotus flower. And on my head he places one symbolic crown after another, ending with the double crown, combining the white crown of Upper Egypt and the red of Lower Egypt, with the golden uraeus, or cobra, attached to the front. The cobra has the reputation of spitting poisonous fire at anyone venturing too near to Pharaoh. (Someday for amusement I must persuade Vizier to test this.) The whole contraption is so heavy that my neck soon aches with the weight.

During the crowning I notice my daughter and the Prince standing beside each other. As Nefrure refused to ride in a carrying chair for fear of falling, the two march (when Nefrure is not being carried by a guard) in the procession, close behind my litter. Nefrure beams at me, proud and excited, while Thutmose's gaze is as blank as when he viewed the gems and vases at

---

[6] **dignitaries:** persons holding high office
[7] **envoys:** persons sent to another place or country as representatives

[8] **dais** (DAY•uhs): a raised platform

the reception of ambassadors. Lost in his own world (perhaps a world where his stepmother is either feeble or dead), he seems oblivious of all movement about him.

The return journey to the palace is agonizing, so that I have to grit my teeth and lock my neck in position. What if suddenly my neck were to bend—or break—and the unwieldy crown bounce off onto the pavement and into the crowd? King Hatshepsut would have to fabricate a glib story; else all of Egypt would believe that Amon had sent a warning that I was unfit to be Pharaoh. I shudder and lock my neck even more tightly.

Finally it is over. I am home in my suite, resting, my head and neck painful but still intact. The reception and banquet lie ahead, but those I can manage easily. In the distance I hear the celebration of the people, with their eating and drinking, their singing and dancing, their roars of amusement at the acrobats and jugglers

and clowns provided for their entertainment. Egypt's treasury will sink this day like the Nile during harvest, but then coronations do not happen every day, that of a queen practically never.

I, Makare Hatshepsut, am Pharaoh of all of Egypt! The thought is too stupendous to fit into my head just yet. First I must view it from all sides . . . and stroke it . . . and shape it . . . till it can slip naturally into place.

LITERATURE REVIEW

❶ In what ways did Hatshepsut both keep to and change Egyptian tradition by taking on the role of ruler?

❷ What do you think caused Hatshepsut to challenge tradition and seek to become pharaoh?

❸ Use what you have learned about Hatshepsut to write a character sketch of the female pharaoh. Be sure to mention any leadership qualities you think she showed.

Thutmose III, who followed Hatshepsut as pharaoh, destroyed many statues of her. This statue of Hatshepsut in the form of a sphinx—a creature half-human and half-animal—remained untouched.

Kush: Egypt's Rival

FOCUS
How can contact between neighboring groups lead to both cooperation and conflict?

Main Idea Look for ways that the people of Nubia and the people of Egypt influenced each other.

Vocabulary
obelisk
annex
independence
trading network

Near the Temple of Karnak stands a large stone pillar called an **obelisk** (OH•buh•lisk), an ancient monument, honoring Hatshepsut and her glorious reign. The single piece of granite rises almost 100 feet (about 30 m). Hieroglyphics on each side describe gold, emeralds, ostrich feathers, and panthers. The obelisk tells of the sources of these prized goods—lands south of Egypt in Africa. One of these lands was Nubia.

Early People in Nubia

The land of Nubia extended along the Nile River from Egypt's southern border almost to where the city of Khartoum, Sudan, stands today. Some of the earliest settlers in Nubia built villages and farmed the Nile floodplain. Others lived as nomads, herding cattle in the nearby desert and hills.

The people of Nubia lived just as the Egyptians had lived before the dynasties. In fact, some experts believe that the ancient Nubians provided some of the basic ideas of Egyptian culture. For example, some Egyptian gods may have been first worshipped in Nubia. Nubian culture almost certainly began at least 8,000 years ago.

As in Egypt, the band was the basic social unit. Each band lived independently of the others. No single king was powerful enough to unite the bands. There were no cities and probably few specialized craftworkers. Almost everyone either farmed crops or herded livestock.

Exactly when a civilization, or complex society, began to develop in Nubia is not known. Based on evidence of irrigation canals,

The people of Nubia will long be remembered for their many achievements. Ancient artifacts such as these show the Nubians' skill as craftworkers. These finely made pieces of pottery date from around 2000 B.C. (detail from a photo grouping).

While under the rule of the Egyptians, ancient Nubians were often required to offer tribute to the Egyptian pharaoh. This wall painting shows a Nubian princess riding in a chariot and four Nubian princes on foot. The group is on its way to offer gold to the pharaoh.

archaeologists believe it may have been about 2000 B.C. The early people of Nubia must have developed an advanced technology to have been able to build canals there.

During the Middle Kingdom some Nubians came into contact with neighboring Egyptians. Egyptian merchants traded their goods for gold, hardwoods, animal tusks, and even huge blocks of granite from Nubian cliffs. The granite was used to build temples and obelisks in Egypt.

Coming to depend on Nubia's natural resources, the Egyptians built trading centers there. Then, during the Middle Kingdom, Egyptian pharaohs moved to **annex**, or take over, northern Nubia, making it a part of Egypt. The Egyptians named the northern region Wawat. The southern region of Nubia became known as Kush.

REVIEW *Why did the Egyptians build trading centers in Nubia?*

Kush

By the time the Hyksos took over Egypt at the end of the Middle Kingdom, Nubia had regained its **independence**, or complete freedom, from Egypt. During this time the city of Kerma was the capital of Kushite government. Kerma also served as an important trading center for central and southern Africa. Goods such as gold, salt, ivory, rhinoceros horns, and spices moved through Kerma to markets throughout Africa and across the Red Sea. Human beings were also offered there as slaves in exchange for trade goods. Kerma eventually became the center for the Kushite civilization. This civilization was known for its beautifully crafted pottery and its use of metals.

In the 1500s B.C. the empire-building pharaohs of the New Kingdom invaded Nubia, taking back their control over its people. The Egyptians introduced their way of life into the Kushite way of life. Because they wanted to keep a government apart from Egypt, Kushite leaders fled Kerma and set up a new capital at Napata, farther south along the Nile River. Over the next centuries, Kush became an independent kingdom. The only ties it kept with Egypt were for trade.

REVIEW *How did the Kushites maintain their civilization after being conquered?*

Conquest of Egypt

Several weak dynasties brought the Egyptian Empire into a time of disorder. King Kashta (KASH•tuh) of Kush saw this weakness and invaded Egypt. By about 750 B.C. Kashta's armies had taken over Upper Egypt. Twenty years later his son Piye (PEE•yeh), also known as Piankhi (PYANG•kee), followed his father's successes and conquered Lower Egypt. After Piye's death his brother Shabaka (SHA•buh•kuh) claimed the pharaoh's throne

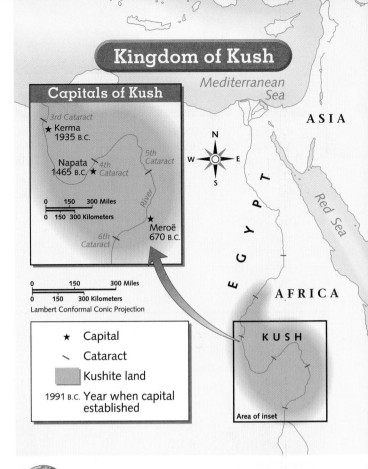

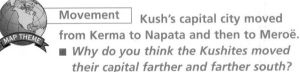
Kush's capital city moved from Kerma to Napata and then to Meroë.
■ *Why do you think the Kushites moved their capital farther and farther south?*

Below is an army of wooden Nubian soldiers, complete with bows and arrows, made about 2100 B.C.

Chapter 3 • **127**

Egypt and Nubia: Conflicts and Conquests

2100 B.C.	1850 B.C.	1600 B.C.	1350 B.C.	1100 B.C.	850 B.C.	600 B.C.

About 1935 B.C.
• Pharaoh Amenemhet conquers Nubia
• Independent Kush establishes capital at Kerma

About 1650 B.C.
• Nubia regains independence

About 1465 B.C.
• Egypt claims Nubia
• Independent Kush establishes capital at Napata

750 B.C.
• King Kashta conquers Upper Egypt

730 B.C.
• King Piye conquers Lower Egypt

671 B.C.
• Kushite rule in Egypt ends
• Independent kingdom of Kush continues

LEARNING FROM TIME LINES This time line shows that Egypt and Nubia often were in conflict with one another.

■ *According to the time line, during what years was Kush in control of Egypt?*

in Thebes, beginning a new dynasty in Egypt. Dynasty 25 is known as the Kushite dynasty.

The Kushite pharaohs ruled less than 100 years. During that time they made Egypt stronger by setting up trade links with other peoples again. They rebuilt many temples that had been destroyed by earlier invasions of Egypt and built many new ones. They also created lasting records of their conquests on stone obelisks.

The writing on one stone column repeats Piye's orders to his soldiers in their final victory over Egypt:

66 Delay not, day or night . . .
Fight at sight . . .
Yoke the war-horse!
Draw up the line of
    battle! 99

Piye had conquered a world power. In conquering Egypt, he made Kush a world power.

REVIEW *What two Kushite rulers conquered Egypt?*

Early Ironworkers

Kushite rule of Egypt ended about 671 B.C., when invaders from the Fertile Crescent gained control of the Nile Valley. Chased but not defeated, Kushite leaders moved their capital south to Meroë (MAIR•oh•wee), where Kushite civilization grew once again.

Free from Egyptian influence, the Kushite people built temples to their own gods and pyramids for their own leaders. They returned to their own customs and developed their own innovations. The Kushites invented their own writing, using an alphabet of 23 letters. They used their writing system to keep records of trade.

In Meroë, Kushite merchants once again set up their old **trading network**, or group of buyers and sellers. Traders from the Fertile Crescent and from all

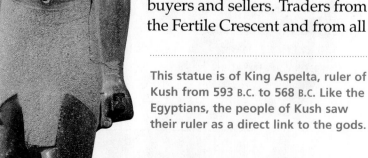

This statue is of King Aspelta, ruler of Kush from 593 B.C. to 568 B.C. Like the Egyptians, the people of Kush saw their ruler as a direct link to the gods.

parts of Africa came to Meroë. Along with gold and spices, the Kushites began to offer well-made iron products, including spears, plows, and wheel rims.

The people of Kush discovered that under their new land lay much iron ore. In mining pits near Meroë, Kushite workers dug up pieces of the iron ore from beneath the rock and sand. Ironworkers melted the metal, removing the minerals and other materials that could not be used. The metal was then hauled to the city, where craftworkers used it to make iron tools and weapons.

Meroë was one of the earliest centers for ironworking in Africa. Today huge heaps of slag, the waste from melting iron ore, are evidence of this important economic activity of long ago.

Meroë grew weaker as traders began to use new trade routes that bypassed the city. Then, around A.D. 350, the African kingdom of Axum defeated the Kushites. "I burned their towns, both those built of bricks and those built of reeds," the leader of Axum boasted.

REVIEW *What changes came about once the Kushites were free of Egyptian control?*

Many experts believe that women often held positions of authority in Nubia. This silver and gold mask shows Queen Malaqaye of Kush. The mask was made about 2,500 years ago.

LESSON 4 REVIEW

Check Understanding

1. **Remember the Facts** How did the people of Egypt and the people of Nubia come into close contact with each other?

2. **Recall the Main Idea** How did the people of Egypt and the people of Nubia influence each other?

Think Critically

3. **Explore Viewpoints** As a Nubian farmer, how might you have felt about Egypt's conquest of Nubia? As an Egyptian soldier in Nubia, how might you have felt about the conquest?

4. **Past to Present** How has United States society been affected by other societies? How has the United States kept its own way of life?

Show What You Know

Brainstorming Activity
In a group, brainstorm ways your community has cooperated with other communities. You may want to look in the newspaper for ideas. List all your ideas on a sheet of paper. Then, with your group, write several paragraphs about how cooperation with others has affected your community.

Which Civilization Came First: Nubia or Egypt?

For many years archaeologists and other scholars knew little about either the Egyptians or the Nubians. Then, in 1822, Jean-François Champollion used the Rosetta Stone to decode the language of the ancient Egyptians. His work gave the world the key to understanding their written records. These writings, however, gave only the Egyptians' view of the Nubians. For nearly 150 years, scholars believed that the Nubians were of little importance.

It was not until the 1960s that archaeologists and scholars began to learn more about ancient Nubia. They have uncovered and studied artifacts and monuments that show that Nubia had a highly developed civilization.

Now some scholars wonder which civilization, the Nubian or the Egyptian, affected the other more. One topic of the debate centers on which civilization was the first to have a unified government ruled by a single king. The opinions of two scholars follow on page 131.

At near right is an incense burner. This artifact was found among the remains of ancient Nubia. The sketch below shows a portion of the incense burner that has an image of a falcon and a king.

Bruce Williams

Bruce Williams, an archaeologist at the University of Chicago, believes that Nubian artifacts from 3300 B.C. show the world's earliest representations of kings. One of the artifacts Williams has studied is a stone incense burner that shows a falcon and a human figure.

66 The falcon means a god. . . . That [figure] is definitely a representation of a king, and he's wearing a crown. . . . The burner is definitely a typical Nubian, not an Egyptian, object. 99

David O'Connor

David O'Connor of the University of Pennsylvania believes that the Nubians copied many Egyptian ideas, including that of having a united government ruled by a king.

66 I think there may well have been an elite group in Nubia at the time, in charge of a complex chiefdom. But the artifacts Williams's argument depends on are almost certainly Egyptian, not Nubian—traded to Nubia in early . . . times. The kings he sees were Egyptian kings. 99

Nubian pyramids are generally much steeper and smaller than Egyptian pyramids.

Compare Viewpoints

1. Why does Bruce Williams believe that Nubia was the first civilization to have kings?

2. Why does David O'Connor disagree with Bruce Williams?

3. How might knowing which culture made the incense burner help archaeologists settle this disagreement?

Think and Apply

People often use evidence to support their views. However, people do not always agree on what the evidence means. What situations today deal with the meaning of evidence? Does everyone agree on what that evidence means?

REVIEW

CONNECT MAIN IDEAS

Use this organizer to describe the ancient civilizations of Egypt and Kush. Write three details to support each main idea. A copy of the organizer appears on page 22 of the Activity Book.

The Importance of the Nile River

The physical setting of the Nile Valley affected the development of civilization in northern Africa.

1. _____
2. _____
3. _____

The Dynasties of Egypt

The ancient Egyptian people maintained their civilization for centuries while making some changes.

1. _____
2. _____
3. _____

Kush: Egypt's Rival

The people of Nubia and the people of Egypt influenced each other.

1. _____
2. _____
3. _____

African Civilizations of the Nile Valley

WRITE MORE ABOUT IT

Write a Description Imagine that you are the son or daughter of an Egyptian farmer. You are living alongside the Nile in about the year 2000 B.C. Describe what your life is like. Use these questions to help you plan what you will write: How does the Nile River affect you? What do you do each day? What is important to you and your family? What are your plans for the future?

Write a News Report Think about how the environment has affected people's lives. Then imagine that you are a reporter for the *Ancient Egyptian Times* and the Nile River is flooding. Write a news article about what is happening in your area. Describe both the good and the bad results of the flooding. Answer these questions: Who? What? Why? Where? When? and How?

3000 B.C.		2000 B.C.		1000 B.C.		B.C.	A.D.

About 3000 B.C.
• Egypt is united

2625 B.C.
• Old Kingdom begins

1980 B.C.
• Middle Kingdom begins

1539 B.C.
• New Kingdom begins

USE VOCABULARY

For each group of terms, write at least one sentence that shows how the terms are related.

1 delta, cataract

2 dynasty, pharaoh, edict

3 papyrus, hieroglyphics

4 pyramid, mummy

5 annex, independence

CHECK UNDERSTANDING

6 What is silt? Why was it important to early Egyptian farmers?

7 How did nature affect the religion of the ancient Egyptians?

8 In what ways did the pharaohs of Egypt give continuity to Egyptian life?

9 How did the Egyptian religion cause changes in the building of tombs of the pharaohs?

10 In what way did the social classes of ancient Egypt change during the Middle Kingdom?

11 Why was the reign of the Pharaoh Hatshepsut important?

12 How was King Kashta able to take control of Upper Egypt in 750 B.C.?

13 What was the result of the nearly 100 years of Kushite rule of Egypt?

14 What important activity was centered in the Kushite capital of Meroë?

THINK CRITICALLY

15 **Cause and Effect** What is the Rosetta Stone, and how did its discovery help our understanding of ancient Egyptian history?

16 **Think More About It** Why was the new religion of Akhenaton not popular among the Egyptian people?

17 **Past to Present** What might archaeologists find 2,000 years from now that would give them clues about our culture?

APPLY SKILLS

Solve a Problem Ask an adult family member about a problem he or she has had to solve. What steps did that person take? Compare those steps with the ones listed on page 119.

READ MORE ABOUT IT

Pepi and the Secret Names by Jill Paton Walsh. Lothrop, Lee & Shepard. An Egyptian boy uses his knowledge of Egyptian animals to help his father paint a prince's tomb.

Visit the Internet at **http://www.hbschool.com** for additional resources.

Chapter 3 • **133**

EARLY CIVILIZATIONS IN ASIA AND THE AMERICAS

"Only a century ago, the Olmecs were entirely unknown, yet today they are regarded as the creators of the first civilization of America."

Henri Stierlin
The World's Last Mysteries

Wood and jade mask from the time of the Olmec culture of the Americas

Civilization
in the
Indus Valley

FOCUS

Why do some civilizations last a long time, while others do not?

Main Idea As you read, consider how the physical setting of the Indus Valley civilization affected its development and survival.

Vocabulary

subcontinent
tributary
inscription

The present-day countries of Pakistan, Bangladesh, and India are located on a large peninsula that juts out from southern Asia. Geographers call the peninsula a **subcontinent** because of its size and its isolation from the rest of the continent of Asia. A long wall of rocky, snowy mountain peaks separates the subcontinent from the rest of Asia. High in these mountains, called the Himalayas (hih•muh•LAY•uhz), a river begins. That river is the Indus. In its valley the subcontinent's earliest civilization developed.

Settling the Indus Valley

Fed by melting snows, the Indus River tumbles down from the high mountains, carrying rocks, gravel, and silt. It flows west and south onto a hot, dry plain in present-day Pakistan. Four **tributaries**, or smaller rivers that feed into a larger river, join the Indus as it flows over the low plain and out to the Arabian Sea.

Each spring, when the snow melts, the Indus swells and spills over its banks. Muddy water spreads across the floodplain, and old soil is made fertile by a new layer of silt.

Early farmers in the Indus Valley grew barley and other grains in the rich soil. These grains supplemented, or added to, the food people got by hunting animals and gathering wild plants.

The plain where the four tributaries flow into the Indus offered the best conditions for early agriculture. People settled there, piling mud and stones into large mounds so that they could live safely above the flooded land. People built small villages on the mounds and

Children of the ancient Indus Valley played with toys like this pottery ram on wheels.

Indian Subcontinent

IRAN

AFGHANISTAN

HINDU KUSH

PAKISTAN

Indus River

CHINA

HIMALAYAS

NEPAL

BHUTAN

Ganges River

BANGLADESH

OMAN

Tropic of Cancer

20°N

Arabian Sea

Vindhya Range

INDIA

Western Ghats

Godavari River

Krishna River

Eastern Ghats

Ghats

20°N

Bay of Bengal

BURMA (MYANMAR)

THAILAND

INDIAN OCEAN

Andaman Islands

10°N

Nicobar Islands

10°N

60°E

70°E

SRI LANKA

90°E

100°E

0   200   400 Miles
0   200   400 Kilometers
Two-Point Equidistant Projection

Place | This map shows present-day India and Pakistan.
■ *Where are most of the mountains located in India?*

farmed the surrounding land. By about 2500 B.C., not long after people in the Fertile Crescent and in the Nile Valley had developed civilizations, the early people of the Indus Valley had built cities and formed a civilization of their own.

Two of the largest and most important cities in the Indus Valley of long ago were Harappa (huh•RA•puh) and Mohenjo-Daro (moh•HEN•joh•DAR•oh). Harappa became so important that this early civilization is often called the Harappan civilization. However, the remains of Mohenjo-Daro provide more complete evidence of city life in the early Indus Valley.

REVIEW *Why did early people in the Indus Valley build cities where they did?*

The City of Mohenjo-Daro

In its time, Mohenjo-Daro was a model of city planning. Straight, wide streets, some as wide as 30 feet (about 9 m), crisscrossed the city. These streets were carefully laid out to form rectangular blocks for houses and other buildings.

On a hill at the end of the city nearest the Indus River, a walled fortress was built on a platform of bricks. The thick walls protected government buildings, a bathhouse, and a huge storage shed. The shed stood 30 feet (about 9 m) tall and was 1,200 feet (about 366 m) long. It held more than enough grain to feed the city's population, which by 1500 B.C. was about 45,000.

Most of the buildings in Mohenjo-Daro, including the huge grain shed, were made of bricks. Instead of sun-drying their bricks, as people in the Fertile Crescent and in the Nile Valley did, people of the Indus Valley baked their bricks in ovens. These baked bricks became harder and lasted longer than sun-dried bricks.

Most people in the Indus Valley lived in small huts in villages surrounding Mohenjo-Daro. Only the civilization's wealthiest families lived in the city. Some city houses were two stories high and were large enough to have a courtyard and rooms for servants. The doors of most city houses opened onto alleys rather than onto the busy main streets. The fronts of the houses, which had no windows, looked much alike.

Even the smallest city houses had inside walls to make separate rooms for cooking, sleeping, and bathing. Almost every house in Mohenjo-Daro had a bathroom. Family members showered by pouring fresh water over themselves with jugs. The runoff water then flowed through brick pipes into a city drain system running along the main streets. Each house also had a chute through which trash could be emptied into a bin in the street. The garbage would then be collected by city workers.

Within Mohenjo-Daro's fortress was a large bathhouse. The main tank was 40 feet (12 m)

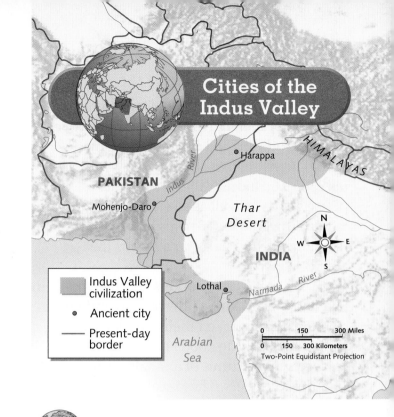

Cities of the Indus Valley

Regions Excavations have revealed that three ancient cities shown on this map—Mohenjo-Daro, Harappa, and Lothal—looked almost identical.

■ *Why is it interesting that these ancient cities had many similarities?*

long and 8 feet (2 m) deep. The bathhouse may have been used by the people in the practice of their religion. It may also have been a gathering place where people exchanged news and conducted business.

REVIEW *What were the streets like in Mohenjo-Daro?*

In what is today Pakistan, archaeologists are unearthing the remains of the ancient city of Mohenjo-Daro.

City People

Most people in Mohenjo-Daro were craftworkers or merchants. Craftworkers wove cotton cloth, shaped clay pots, and made metal items such as silver jewelry. As early as 2300 B.C., Indus Valley merchants traded these goods as well as surplus grain for turquoise, gold, copper, and food from settlements in Asia as far away as the Fertile Crescent.

Many of the craftworkers and merchants in Mohenjo-Daro knew how to read and write. Picture signs marked their clay pots and other items. Trade goods had stone seals carved with pictures of animals such as elephants and tigers. These seals showed who owned the items.

Many seals also had an **inscription**, or written message. By putting a string through a hole at the back, a person could tie the seal to bales of grain and other trade goods.

An interesting fact about Harappan cities is that they were all very much alike. People in each city used the same standard weights and measures. Their street layouts were similar. So were their beads, jewelry, and copper and bronze tools.

REVIEW *What are some ways Harappan cities were alike?*

The Mystery of Mohenjo-Daro

No one has lived in Mohenjo-Daro for more than 3,000 years. How the city and all the rest of Harappan civilization ended is still a mystery. We do know that the end came quickly, probably around 1500 B.C.

Looking for evidence of ancient life in the city of Mohenjo-Daro, archaeologists found signs of sudden death. They discovered many unburied human skeletons. The poses of the skeletons suggested that the people had been running from something. Houses and other buildings appear to have been abandoned suddenly. Perhaps the people of Mohenjo-Daro were the victims of an earthquake or a flood.

To identify goods and crafts, Indus Valley merchants marked their property with seals. The seals were either stamped onto goods or tied to them with string. The seal on the left shows an elephant. The seal on the right shows the Sumerian ruler Gilgamesh.

ECONOMICS

Trade Beyond the Indus Valley

Indus Valley seals have been uncovered in Ur and other Mesopotamian cities. Seals from Mesopotamia have also been found in the ruins of the Indus Valley port city of Lothal. Seagoing Indus Valley traders may have made use of the strong monsoon winds to cross the Arabian Sea from Lothal. Their ships probably carried gems, sesame oil, and cotton. The Sumerians most likely sailed to Lothal with barley, wool, and silver.

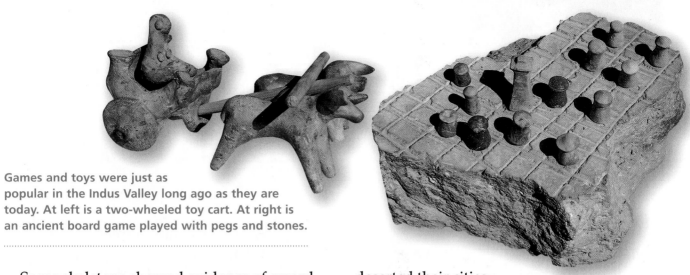

Games and toys were just as popular in the Indus Valley long ago as they are today. At left is a two-wheeled toy cart. At right is an ancient board game played with pegs and stones.

Some skeletons showed evidence of sword cuts, however. This suggests that Mohenjo-Daro was attacked by invaders. No one knows exactly who the invaders might have been. If such an attack did come, perhaps the people were already weak. Floods had become more frequent, and this may have caused the people to suffer. There is also evidence that underground water in the Indus Valley had become salty, making the farmland salty too. If so, farmers would have had a hard time growing crops. Without food many people would have starved. The rest of the people of the Indus Valley probably deserted their cities and moved somewhere else. In time they may have become part of other cultures.

What we know today about Mohenjo-Daro, the Harappan people, and their lifeways comes from bits of evidence archaeologists have pieced together. Only parts of buildings and small artifacts—human-made objects such as pots, jewelry, and toys—remain as proof of a civilization that no longer exists.

REVIEW *What are some possible reasons to explain why the Harappan civilization came to an end?*

LESSON 1 REVIEW

Check Understanding

1 **Remember the Facts** Why is the early Indus Valley civilization called Harappan?

2 **Recall the Main Idea** In what ways did the physical setting of the Indus Valley civilization affect its development and its ability to survive?

Think Critically

3 **Think More About It** What does the similarity among the Indus Valley cities tell you about the ancient Harappan civilization?

4 **Past to Present** Why might large groups of people today leave their homelands and move elsewhere?

5 **Explore Viewpoints** What are some concerns that people have about the environment today? Why do people disagree about the nature of these problems?

Show What You Know

Diary Activity Imagine that you are an archaeologist who is exploring the ruins of the ancient Indus Valley civilization. Write diary entries that record your work for one week. Describe the artifacts you find and what you are learning about how the early people of the Indus Valley made use of natural resources.

FOCUS

How can people's beliefs affect the way a civilization forms and changes?

Main Idea Read to find out how the beliefs of the ancient Chinese people affected the development and growth of their civilization.

Vocabulary

legend
ancestor
oracle
pictograph

Early Chinese Civilization

Chinese civilization has a long and complex history. Over the years, historians have kept an almost complete record of rulers, cultures, and events. Today the chain of Chinese history directly links present-day China with China's earliest civilizations. Two of the most important early civilizations were located in river valleys. One was in the valley of the Huang He. The other was in the valley of the Chang Jiang.

Legends and Facts About China's Origins

Like many other people, the Chinese have often used **legends**, or stories handed down from earlier times, to explain the distant past. One Chinese legend tells that the goddess Nugua (NOO•GWAY) made the first humans out of clay. Another story tells that her husband, Fuxi (FOO•SHEE), invented writing by studying the scratches of birds and other animals.

The story of Yu the Great and the Great Flood may be the most famous Chinese legend of all. This legend tells of a time when floods covered much of China. To save China, Yu the Great dug deep rivers to hold the extra water. Yu worked for 13 years to remove floodwaters from the land. When his work was done, the farmers could once again plant their crops. Even today Chinese students say, "If it were not for Yu the Great, we would all be fishes."

Historians may never know if Yu the Great helped farmers control floods. There is no proof that he even existed. Still, the ancient legend tells us a lot about the early Chinese. It helps show the importance that they placed on agriculture.

As early as 5000 B.C., farmers were growing crops in both northern and southern China. There is also evidence that dogs and pigs were domesticated at this time. In northern China early farmers grew grains such as millet, as well as

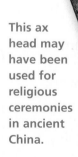

This ax head may have been used for religious ceremonies in ancient China.

China

RUSSIA

KAZAKHSTAN

Altai Mountains

MONGOLIA

GOBI (DESERT)

KYRGYZSTAN

TIAN SHAN

Takla Makan
(Desert)

KUNLUN SHAN

Plateau of
Tibet

HIMALAYAS

NEPAL

BHUTAN

BANGLADESH

INDIA

Bay of
Bengal

BURMA
(MYANMAR)

LAOS

VIETNAM

CHINA

Huang He

Chang Jiang

Xi Jiang

NORTH
KOREA

SOUTH
KOREA

Yellow
Sea

East China
Sea

TAIWAN

South
China Sea

Sea of
Japan

JAPAN

PACIFIC
OCEAN

Tropic of Cancer

0   250   500 Miles
0   250   500 Kilometers
Two-Point Equidistant Projection

Place China has many different regions.
■ *Why do you think early Chinese civilization developed in the eastern part of what is now China rather than in the western part?*

fruits and vegetables. At the same time, farmers in southern China were growing rice. By 3000 B.C. cattle were being raised in northern and southern China.

The Chinese people soon built settlements and developed technology for irrigation and flood control. In doing so, they started a civilization not long after civilizations had begun in the Fertile Crescent, in the Nile Valley, and in the Indus Valley.

The early Chinese traded and exchanged ideas with other peoples living in lands that are now part of China and Thailand. Unlike people in the Indus Valley, the Chinese did not trade with Sumer or other distant civilizations. Surrounded by mountains and deserts

and located far from these other peoples, China had no contact with these civilizations. Because they did not come into contact with people of other cultures, the ancient Chinese came to have a strong feeling of their importance in the world.

REVIEW *What caused the ancient Chinese to have a strong sense of their importance in the world?*

The Xia and Shang Dynasties

By about 2000 B.C. there were hundreds of settlements in ancient China. As in other civilizations, some settlements grew into towns. Later these towns developed into powerful city-states ruled by kings. The city-states fought each other for farmland. One king, perhaps Yu the Great, gained control of a number of villages and city-states. His family members continued to rule after his death, starting the Xia (SYAH) dynasty.

In 1600 B.C. a different city-state came to be the most powerful. Its king established a new ruling dynasty, the Shang. Many different families would rule China, but the idea of dynasty—rule passed down through the generations of one family—continued for more than 3,500 years.

The Shang established their rule by conquering more than 1,800 city-states and villages in northern and central China. Shang warriors used war chariots and strong metal weapons to seize control by force.

To keep control of their lands, the Shang created a simple form of government. The Shang king gave land to his most important followers. In return the followers promised loyalty, performed services, and paid fees

This pot was used for cooking food during the Shang dynasty. Its shape allowed it to stand easily over a small fire.

and taxes. A strong army helped the Shang gain more land. Shang rulers kept their control of China until about 1050 B.C.

REVIEW *What were the first and second dynasties of China?*

Oracle Bones

Most people of the Shang period lived in small farming villages. The farmers grew millet, kept chickens and pigs, and raised silkworms for silk cloth. Craftworkers used bronze—a metal made by combining copper and tin—to form tools, weapons, and beautiful vessels.

The people asked their ancestors and their gods for advice and for answers to

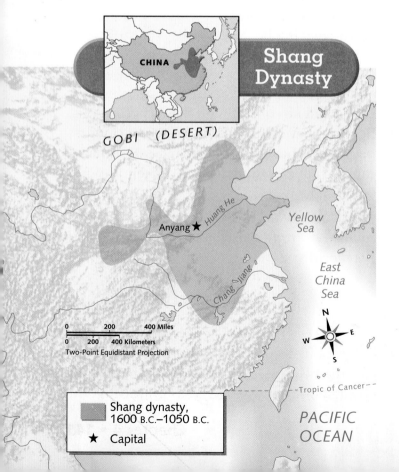

CHINA

Shang Dynasty

GOBI (DESERT)

Huang He

Anyang ★

Yellow Sea

Chang Jiang

East China Sea

N
W E
S

0   200   400 Miles
0   200   400 Kilometers
Two-Point Equidistant Projection

Shang dynasty,
1600 B.C.–1050 B.C.

★ Capital

-Tropic of Cancer--

PACIFIC OCEAN

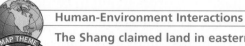

Human-Environment Interactions

The Shang claimed land in eastern Asia.
■ *Why do you think other groups may have wanted the land that was controlled by the Shang?*

Loess

The enriched sandy soil of the Huang He Valley is called loess (LOH·uhs). Loess is different from other soils because it never stops collecting and then shifting in the howling winds. Loess can build up in the Huang He, causing the river to flood. Mounds of loess in the river can even cause the river to change course, drowning people and destroying homes. Since the earliest days, people have had good reason to call the Huang He "The River of Sorrows." However, the same destructive floods also deposit loess alongside the Huang He. This has enriched the soil there, making it perfect for growing crops. In this way, "The River of Sorrows" makes agriculture possible in the area.

Loess colors the water of the Huang He yellow. The name Huang He means "Yellow River." The loess collected in the river has caused the Huang He to change its course many times.

their questions. They believed that their **ancestors**—dead relatives further back than grandparents—were wise and that they guided the lives of the living.

The ancient Shang thought that their ancestors could communicate with the gods. Ancestors were asked to encourage the powerful gods of nature to be kind to humankind. The Shang feared that angry gods might bring disasters, diseases, or enemy attacks.

The ancient Chinese looked to oracle bones for the answers to major and everyday problems. What sources do people today turn to for help in solving problems?

Shang kings would often ask their ancestors for advice on a wide variety of subjects. To learn the answers to his questions, the king needed the help of a diviner. A diviner was a person who, it was believed, could communicate with the spirits of the dead.

The diviner would lay out animal bones or turtle shells. Then the diviner would touch the bones or shells with hot metal sticks. The heat caused cracks to form on the bones and shells. The diviner then gave the bones and shells to the king. The Shang king "read" the cracks to find out the answers to his questions. After the Shang king received answers from his ancestors, a scribe wrote the answers on the bones or shells.

About 100 years ago farmers near Anyang began to find the animal bones and turtle shells the Shang had used long ago. The farmers could not read the writing on them. They mistakenly believed the bones were dragon bones. They sold these "dragon bones" to local drugstores, where they were used to make medicines.

In time, archaeologists heard about the farmers' discoveries. Only then were the "dragon bones" correctly identified. The world learned that the bones show answers to questions that the ancient Shang kings asked their ancestors. Today scholars who study ancient China call the shells and bones oracle bones. An **oracle** is a person who gives wise advice.

Oracle bones give important clues to the way of life of the Shang people. They help give an idea of the problems the Shang people faced and how they sought solutions to their problems. Oracle bones also show what daily life was like in ancient China.

REVIEW *How did the Shang people use oracle bones?*

Shang Writing

Ancient drawings on bones, bronze, and pottery formed the basis of the written language of the Shang period. The drawings, called **pictographs**, were combined to make thousands of words.

The people of the Shang period used writing to keep tax records and to record building plans. The Shang government sent its armies written orders and made written treaties with its enemies. At Shang funerals people carried silk banners with writing that told the name of the dead person and the details of his or her life. Legend says that people of the Shang period wrote in books of bamboo and wood, but none of these books have ever been found.

Writing had an important effect on the development of China's social classes. To read and write, a person had to learn as many as 5,000 different pictographs. Only

HISTORY

The Legend of Silk

Silk has long been used in China to weave beautiful clothing, fine ribbons, and colorful decorations. A legend tells that the Chinese discovered silk in 2700 B.C. when Xilingshi (SEE•LING•SHIR), a ruler's wife, noticed worms eating a prized mulberry tree. She took a cocoon spun by a worm, dropped it into hot water, and watched the thread unwind. Xilingshi then used the thread to weave a beautiful piece of cloth. No one knows whether this story is true or false, but silk has been produced throughout the Huang He Valley since the time of the Shang and probably earlier.

Silk cloth has long been a prized product of China. Eighteenth-century Chinese craftworkers weave silk on a large loom (right).

the wealthy had the time to learn to read and write. Since all government officials had to be able to read and write, most farmers and laborers were unable to get these jobs. As a result, wealthy, educated Chinese were the ones in charge of the government. As government officials they passed laws to protect their wealth and to set themselves above other people. Social classes became separate and clearly defined over time.

Chinese writing has changed over the years. In some cases, new ways of writing characters have developed. However, present-day Chinese writing has strong roots in the characters used long ago in the Shang dynasty.

REVIEW *What were the advantages of being wealthy in ancient China?*

LEARNING FROM TABLES This table shows the development of the Chinese language from ancient times to the present day.
■ *What similarities can you see between the characters of the past and those of the present?*

Chinese Writing

WRITING FROM SHANG PERIOD	ENGLISH WORD	CURRENT CHINESE WRITING
⊙	Sun	日
☽	Moon	月
ⵣ	Tree	木
⋔	Rain	雨
⩛	Mountain	山
〣	Water	水

LESSON 2 REVIEW

Check Understanding

1 Remember the Facts When did farmers begin raising crops in China?

2 Recall the Main Idea How did the beliefs of the ancient Chinese affect the growth of their civilization?

Think Critically

3 Think More About It How might modern Chinese civilization be different if the early Chinese had traded with people in Sumer or the Indus Valley?

4 Past to Present Oracle bones provide a source for learning about the types of problems the early Chinese faced. What sources might give clues to the everyday problems people experience today?

Show What You Know

Role-Play Activity With a partner, plan and act out two dramatic scenes about people finding oracle bones. First, act out a scene between two farmers who are amazed to find "dragon bones" in their fields. Then, act out a scene in which two archaeologists uncover oracle bones while on a dig. After you have acted out the scenes, think about how the two scenes were alike and different. Compare and contrast the differing views each group had about the oracle bones.

Use Elevation Maps

1. Why Learn This Skill?

Different kinds of maps provide different kinds of information. A road map, for example, shows which routes go from one place to another and how far it is between places. Sometimes, however, people need information that is not given on a road map. If you wanted to know how high or low the land is, you would need an elevation (eh•luh•VAY•shuhn) map. **Elevation** is the height of the land. Elevation maps help city planners decide where to lay water pipes or build a shopping center. Elevation maps can also help you choose a good place for skateboarding or riding your bike.

2. Contour Lines and Color

To find out how tall you are, you must measure the distance from your base (the bottom of your feet) to your top (the top of your head). Land is also measured from the base to the top. The base for all landforms is sea level, or 0 feet (0 m). Find sea level on Drawing A.

The lines on this drawing of a hill are contour lines. A **contour line** connects all points of equal elevation. Find the 400-foot (122-m) contour line on Drawing A. This line connects all the points that are exactly 400 feet above sea level.

Imagine that you are flying in an airplane over the hill shown in the drawing. Picture the drawing as a rising hill. As you look down on it from above, you can see the contour lines as loops. If you flew over the hill in Drawing B, you would see each contour line labeled with its elevation. You would see that the contour lines are not evenly spaced. On the steeper side of the hill, the contour lines are closer together. On the gently sloping side, the contour lines are farther apart.

On some elevation maps, such as Drawing C, color is added between the contour lines. A key is used instead of labels. The key shows that everything green is between sea level and 100 feet (30 m). The line between green and

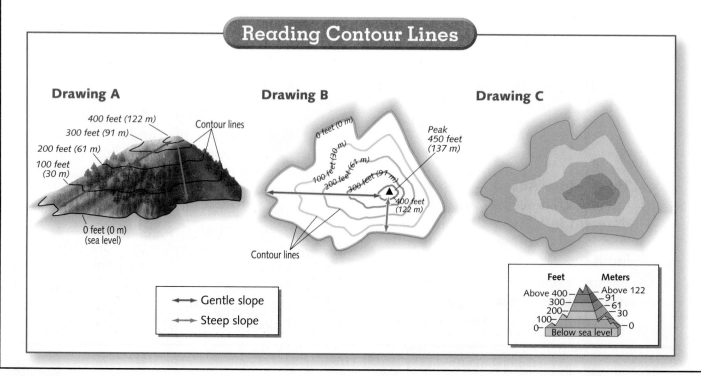

Reading Contour Lines

Drawing A

400 feet (122 m)
300 feet (91 m)
200 feet (61 m)
100 feet (30 m)
Contour lines
0 feet (0 m) (sea level)

Drawing B

0 feet (0 m)
100 feet (30 m)
200 feet (61 m)
300 feet (91 m)
400 feet (122 m)
Peak 450 feet (137 m)
Contour lines

← → Gentle slope
←→ Steep slope

Drawing C

Feet   Meters
Above 400 — Above 122
300 — 91
200 — 61
100 — 30
0 — 0
Below sea level

Elevation Map: Southeast Asia

CHINA

BURMA
(MYANMAR)

Irrawaddy River

Hanoi ⊛

LAOS

*Gulf
of
Tonkin*

⊛ Vientiane

INDIAN
OCEAN

Rangoon
(Yangon) ⊛

THAILAND

VIETNAM

*Chao
Phraya*

*Andaman
Sea*

⊛ Bangkok

CAMBODIA

Phnom
Penh ⊛

*South
China
Sea*

*Gulf
of
Thailand*

⊛ National capital

— Present-day border

Feet   **Meters**
Above 13,120 — Above 4,000
6,560 — 2,000
1,640 — 500
655 — 200
0 — 0
Below sea level

0   150   300 Miles
0   150   300 Kilometers
Two-Point Equidistant Projection

---

yellow on the map is a 100-foot (30-m) contour line. The lines bordering the other colors are also contour lines.

Most elevation maps use a few important contour lines with colors added between the lines. Look at the elevation map of southeastern Asia. The map key shows the range of elevation that each color stands for. Land that is 13,120 feet (4,000 m) above sea level or higher is shown in purple. Green is used for the land in the range between sea level and 655 feet (200 m). When you study the map, you cannot tell whether land in the green areas is at sea level, at 655 feet (200 m) above sea level, or at some elevation in between.

3. Understand the Process

Use these questions as a guide to better understand elevation maps.

❶ What is the difference between what a contour line and an area of color shows?

❷ To find the exact elevation of a place, should you look for a contour line or a band of color? Why?

❸ How high are the highest areas of Burma? How can you tell?

❹ Where are the lowest areas in Vietnam? How can you tell?

❺ Is most of the land in Cambodia high or low? Explain your answer.

4. Think and Apply

Around 2000 B.C. people living in northeastern and central Thailand began making bronze objects. They made tools and weapons, ornaments, and drums. They traded these objects with people in nearby settlements. Imagine that you are a Thai trader traveling from central Thailand to the coast of the South China Sea. Use your finger to trace the route. Describe the land you pass along the way.

FOCUS

What advantages are there to building on the achievements of past societies?

Main Idea As you read, think about how the Mayas both built on the achievements of the Olmec civilization and contributed their own.

Vocabulary

Middle America
protein
intercropping
reclaim

Ancient Civilizations of the Americas

The earliest known civilization in the Americas was the Olmec (AHL•mek) civilization, which developed along the southern coast of the Gulf of Mexico. Later civilizations that developed in Middle America used many of the Olmecs' ideas. Middle America, also called Mesoamerica, is the region of North America where southern Mexico, Belize, Guatemala, Honduras, El Salvador, Nicaragua, Costa Rica, and Panama are today. The Olmec civilization is often called the "mother civilization" of the Mayas and other Middle American groups that arose in later centuries.

Early Olmec Farmers

The Olmec people first settled along the coast of the Gulf of Mexico in what are now the Mexican states of Veracruz and Tabasco. By the early 1500s B.C. the Olmecs were living along coastal rivers in clusters of small houses made of reed and straw. The people fished in the rivers and farmed land made fertile by river flooding.

Olmec farmers grew beans, squash, and maize, or corn. These three crops fed most early agricultural societies in Middle America as well as in other parts of North America and in South America. Eaten together, beans, squash, and maize provided a diet rich in protein. Protein is a substance in food that helps build the body and keep it healthy.

Farmers planted these important crops together in the same mound. The stalk, or stiff stem, of the maize was used as a pole to support the bean vines. The squash vines spread out on the ground between the stalks.

By such intercropping, or planting different crops together, Olmec farmers made the best possible use of the small amount of fertile soil they had.

Olmec clay figure crafted around 100 B.C.

Like other agricultural societies the Olmecs came to depend on seasonal flooding to water their crops and make the soil rich. And like many early peoples in other parts of the world, the Olmecs developed a calendar to keep track of the flood season. The Olmecs also used hieroglyphic writing to keep a record of events.

Also like early civilizations elsewhere, the Olmecs based their religion on the forces of nature that affected the growing of crops. The people worshipped many different gods, but the most important was the jaguar, the cat god, who they believed brought rain.

Olmec cities were centers of religion. In the middle of each city were great stone temples. Looking out over the city were huge faces of carved stone, some more than 9 feet (2.7 m) tall and weighing 20 tons. Each face

This large head and others carved by the Olmecs long ago still amaze visitors to Mexico today. Olmec artists used simple stone tools to create the stone heads.

HERITAGE

The Oldest Ball Game in the Americas

The word *Olmec* means "rubber people." The name was given to these people by later Middle American civilizations because the Olmecs found so many uses for the rubber they got from trees in the rain forest. For example, the Olmecs made a ball out of rubber and played a game in which two teams competed on a special court. A version of the game is still played today in Mexico. In the game, players cannot hit the ball with their hands or feet. Instead, they use other parts of their body, such as their hips. Because the ball is very hard and travels at high speeds, all players must wear heavy clothing to protect them.

An ancient ballplayer

may have been carved to look like Olmec rulers and priests. No one knows exactly how the Olmec builders moved the giant stones. Their technology did not include the wheel. The Olmecs probably moved the stones downriver on balsa rafts. Some of these stones may have been moved from more than 50 miles (about 80 km) away!

No one knows how or why the Olmec civilization came to an end. The last of its cities were left empty or destroyed about 400 B.C. Perhaps, like the Indus Valley civilization, the Olmec civilization ended with an enemy attack, with a natural disaster, or with crop failure. But the ideas of the Olmecs lived on in the cultures of later civilizations.

REVIEW *What ideas might the Olmecs have passed on to later peoples?*

The Mayas

At about the same time the Olmecs were building religious centers in Mexico, the Mayas had a simple farming culture. The people lived along the edges of the Middle American rain forests. By about 500 B.C. Mayan civilization began to take shape. Borrowing many Olmec ways, the Mayas cleared the forest to farm more land and to build cities. They built more than 100 cities in what is now Guatemala, Mexico, Belize, and Honduras. Chichén Itzá (chee•CHAYN it•SAH), Tikal, and Mayapán were just some of the many cities built by the Mayas.

Each city had its own ruler and its own government. Like the Olmecs, the Mayas never united to form a central government. Yet from time to time, a powerful ruler may have ruled many cities.

The largest Mayan city was Tikal, with a population of as many as 100,000 people. In the heart of Tikal, located in what is now Guatemala, six large temples surrounded the city center. Each was made of huge blocks of limestone and shaped like a pyramid. On top of the pyramids were roof combs,

decorations that looked like a crown or the crest of a bird. A jaguar with sharp, curving claws is carved on one of the beams of Tikal's largest temple. This is the one sometimes called the Temple of the Giant Jaguar. It honors the rain god whom the Mayas borrowed from the Olmecs.

Religion was important in the lives of the Mayas, just as it was for the Olmecs. The Mayas had as many as 160 different gods. Each was believed to have control over some part of their daily lives.

As in other agricultural civilizations, the Mayas' innovations were based on farming needs. The Mayas had two calendars. One calendar had a 365-day year, used to keep track of planting, harvesting, and seasonal flooding. The Mayas also developed a number system based on the number 20 to keep track of their stored crops. Unlike other numbering systems, the Mayan system had a symbol for zero. Mathematicians today say that the zero is one of the greatest innovations of all time.

Below are the ruins of the Mayan city Tikal, deep in the jungle of Guatemala. The illustration at right shows Tikal as it may have looked during the time of Mayan civilization.

Middle America

Feet · Meters
Above 13,120 — Above 4,000
6,560 — 2,000
1,640 — 500
655 — 200
0 — Below sea level — 0

PACIFIC OCEAN

MEXICO

Gulf of Mexico

VALLEY OF MEXICO

SIERRA MADRE OCCIDENTAL

SIERRA MADRE DEL SUR

MIDDLE AMERICA

Gulf of Tehuantepec

Yucatán Peninsula

Caribbean Sea

BELIZE

GUATEMALA

110°W · 90°W
Tropic of Cancer
20°N · 20°N

N W E S

0 — 150 — 300 Miles
0 — 150 — 300 Kilometers
Albers Equal-Area Projection

—— Olmec homeland • Olmec site —— Present-day border
—— Mayan homeland • Mayan site

Regions This map of Middle America shows where the ancient Olmecs and Mayas lived.
■ *How were the lands of the Olmecs and the Mayas alike and different?*

In addition to a number system, the Mayas created a system of hieroglyphic writing. They carved and painted picture messages on pillars, on bowls, and on walls. The Mayas also wrote in books. But archaeologists can read only a few Mayan pictographs, so they do not know what all the writing means.

Archaeologists do know that the great Mayan civilization lasted for more than 600 years. After A.D. 900, however, some of the Mayan cities were left empty and **reclaimed**, or taken back, by the surrounding rain forests. The knowledge and skills of the Mayas, like those of the Olmecs, would become part of the culture of later civilizations in the Americas.

REVIEW *What ideas might the Mayas have passed on to later peoples?*

LESSON 3 REVIEW

Check Understanding

1 Remember the Facts What did the Olmecs do to make the most of their limited soil?

2 Recall the Main Idea How did the Mayas build on the Olmecs' achievements? What were their own innovations?

Think Critically

3 Cause and Effect What influence did the Olmec civilization have on the later development of Mayan civilization?

4 Past to Present Why do archaeologists want to find out more about the Mayas? What else would you like to learn about the Mayas?

Show What You Know

Poster Activity Think about ways the Olmecs and the Mayas were similar to each other and to civilizations in other parts of the world. Make a poster that shows what these cultures had in common. Display your poster in your classroom.

Chapter 4 • **151**

Learn from Artifacts

1. Why Learn This Skill?

Artifacts are objects people make and use. You have seen pictures of artifacts made by people who lived long ago in different places. You know that artifacts can be large, like the Olmec head on page 149, or small, like the Indus Valley toy cart on page 139. Tools, weapons, coins, and cooking pots are all artifacts. The artifacts of a society of long ago can tell us much about how its people lived and worked and what they may have thought was important.

Artifacts do not have to be ancient. Televisions, computers, automobiles, watches, and telephones are artifacts, too. These are all things that people living today make and use. The things we make and use today may tell future generations what our time was like.

2. Understand the Process

Although early civilizations around the world were different from one another, they often had things in common. Most early societies depended on agriculture. They also built cities, set up governments, and practiced religions. Many used some form of money for exchange.

Some societies produced artifacts that were very similar to those of other societies. People in both the Nile Valley and the Americas built pyramids. What does this tell you about the two cultures?

Three artifacts are shown on pages 152–153. One was made in Egypt, one in the Americas, and one in China. They look different, yet they are alike in important ways. Study the pictures and their captions. Then use the

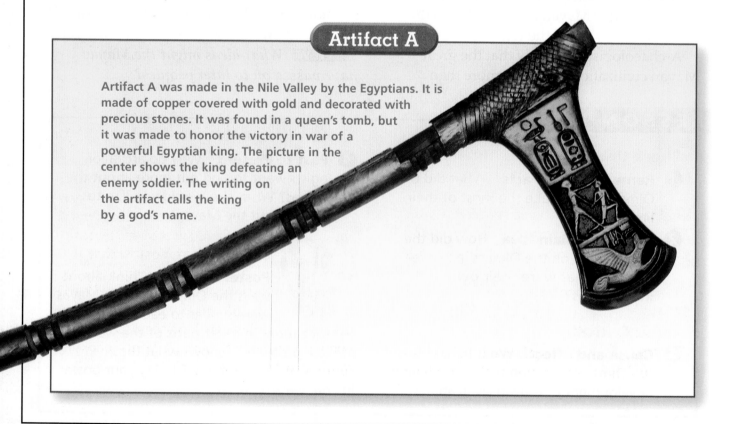

Artifact A

Artifact A was made in the Nile Valley by the Egyptians. It is made of copper covered with gold and decorated with precious stones. It was found in a queen's tomb, but it was made to honor the victory in war of a powerful Egyptian king. The picture in the center shows the king defeating an enemy soldier. The writing on the artifact calls the king by a god's name.

Artifact B

Artifact B was made in Middle America by the Olmecs. It is made of jade, a stone the Olmecs valued more than gold. The artifact is shaped like a creature part human and part jaguar. Such objects have been found in the tombs of kings and other leaders. The jaguar may have been a symbol of authority for the Olmecs.

Artifact C

Artifact C is from the Shang dynasty in China. It is made of bronze, a metal with which the Shang formed objects used in public ceremonies. This artifact was found in the tomb of a Shang lord or king. To the Shang, it may have been a symbol of political strength.

questions as a guide in comparing these early civilizations.

1. How do you know what each artifact is?

2. How was each artifact used by the people who made it?

3. What tells you that each artifact was important to the people who made it?

4. How are the three artifacts alike? In what ways do you think the societies that made them may have been alike?

5. Why do you think the artifacts do not look exactly alike?

6. What do the materials used to make the artifacts say about each of the societies?

3. Think and Apply

The Egyptian artifact gives information in hieroglyphics and pictures. The information provided by the writing and the pictures lets us know that a powerful king most likely owned the object. Look back at the illustrations in Chapter 3 and Chapter 4 of this unit. Find other ancient artifacts that are shown in these chapters. Remember that ancient artifacts are items that people of long ago made and used. With a partner, make a list of the different artifacts you have found. Then describe what these artifacts seem to tell you about the societies that made them. Share your findings with the class.

5000 B.C.   4000 B.C.   3000 B.C.

About 5000 B.C.
• Agriculture begins in China

CONNECT MAIN IDEAS

Use this organizer to tell about ancient civilizations in the Indus Valley, China, and the Americas. Write two details to support each main idea. A copy of the organizer appears on page 29 of the Activity Book.

Early Civilizations in Asia and the Americas

Civilization in the Indus Valley

The physical setting of the Indus Valley civilization affected its development and survival.

1. _____
2. _____

Early Chinese Civilization

The beliefs of the ancient Chinese people affected the development and the growth of their civilization.

1. _____
2. _____

Ancient Civilizations of the Americas

The Mayas built on earlier achievements of the Olmec civilization and contributed their own.

1. _____
2. _____

WRITE MORE ABOUT IT

Write to Compare The ancient civilizations of the Indus Valley, the Huang He Valley, and the Nile Valley all depended on rivers for their survival. Think about how the different peoples made use of rivers. Then write a paragraph that compares the effects of the rivers on these people.

Write an Inscription Imagine that you are a worker making an object for a time capsule that will be opened 1,000 years from now. To give the people of that time an understanding of how life has changed and how it has remained the same, write an inscription describing yourself and your culture.

About 2500 B.C.
• Harappan civilization begins

About 1600 B.C.
• Shang dynasty begins

About 1500 B.C.
• Olmecs develop early agriculture

About 500 B.C.
• Mayan civilization begins

USE VOCABULARY

Write a word from this list to complete each of the sentences that follow.

intercropping   protein   pictographs
oracle   tributary

① A person who gives wise advice is called an _____.

② _____ is a substance in food that helps build the body.

③ A _____ is a small river that flows into a larger river.

④ Planting combined crops, as the Olmecs did, is called _____.

⑤ Shang writing used drawings, or _____, to make words.

CHECK UNDERSTANDING

⑥ What was life like in ancient Indus Valley cities?

⑦ What caused the fall of the ancient city of Mohenjo-Daro?

⑧ What proof do archaeologists have that Indus Valley civilizations existed?

⑨ How did the Shang establish their rule?

⑩ How did the Shang people use pictographs?

⑪ The Olmec civilization developed in Middle America. What present-day countries are in Middle America?

⑫ Why did the Olmecs and the Mayas develop calendars?

⑬ What important ideas of the Mayas have been passed on to other cultures?

THINK CRITICALLY

⑭ **Think More About It** How was the city of Mohenjo-Daro similar to a small city of today?

⑮ **Cause and Effect** How did flooding affect the development of early cultures in the Indus Valley and in China?

APPLY SKILLS

Use an Elevation Map Use the map of Middle America on page 151 to answer the questions.

⑯ Where in Mexico are the highest elevations?

⑰ What generalization can you make about the relationship between elevations and the locations of Olmec sites?

Learn from Artifacts Imagine that you are an archaeologist in the year A.D. 2999. You have just discovered an automobile that was used in the last years of the twentieth century. What information does this artifact give you about the society that used it?

READ MORE ABOUT IT

Ancient China by Brian Williams. Viking. History, rulers, cities, and inventions are some of the topics included in this book.

HARCOURT BRACE

Visit the Internet at
http://www.hbschool.com
for additional resources.

Why Preserve the Past?

To some people in the United States, building a shopping mall on a Civil War battle site or knocking down an old school to put in a parking lot is making progress. To others, it is destroying a memory from a community's past.

Ancient buildings, monuments, and other structures link the world of today with history. They are reminders that people who lived long ago achieved important things. As long as the structures that they built remain, those people will not be forgotten.

One of the most remarkable of the world's monuments is the Great Sphinx of Egypt. It reminds people of the powerful Egyptian pharaohs who ruled more than 4,000 years ago. These pharaohs ordered thousands of workers to labor for years to build huge structures such as the pyramids and the Sphinx.

In recent years the Sphinx has shown much damage from pollution, weather, and age. The present-day Egyptian people might have lost this link with their past. To keep this from happening, they began a costly project to save the Sphinx. Adam Henein, an artist, explained his reason for giving long hours to restore and protect the Sphinx. "To me," said Henein, "[the Sphinx] is the soul of Egypt."

Think and Apply

BUILDING CITIZENSHIP

Think about why it is important to preserve the memories of our past. What objects would you leave behind so that people in the future could remember what you achieved? Work with your class to prepare a time capsule that contains these objects. Find a safe place to keep the capsule so that it can be opened by students in your school many years from now.

HARCOURT BRACE

Visit the Internet at **http://www.hbschool.com** for additional resources.

CNN
Turner
Le@rning

Check your media center or classroom video library for the Making Social Studies Relevant videotape of this feature.

Scaffolds help workers restore the Great Sphinx (top). Workers are also trying to preserve Kushite pyramids (bottom).

UNIT 2 REVIEW

Summarize the Main Ideas
Study the pictures and captions to help you review the events you read about in Unit 2.

Write Creatively
Imagine that you could visit one of the civilizations shown in this visual summary. Now imagine meeting a person from that civilization. Write about that meeting.

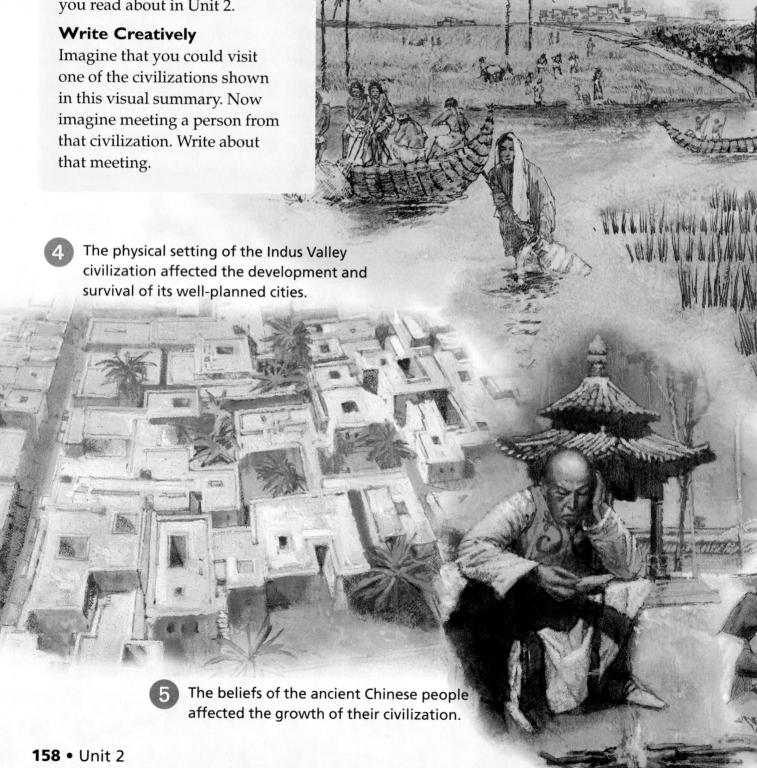

1 The early Egyptians lived in villages along the Nile River. The Nile shaped life, farming, trade, and religion in Egypt.

4 The physical setting of the Indus Valley civilization affected the development and survival of its well-planned cities.

5 The beliefs of the ancient Chinese people affected the growth of their civilization.

3 Nubian culture developed south of Egypt, in what is today Sudan. Nubian and Egyptian culture influenced each other.

2 Huge building projects were completed during Egypt's Old Kingdom. Hieroglyphic writing also developed at this time. The Old Kingdom was followed by the Middle Kingdom and the New Kingdom.

6 In the Americas the Mayas built on the achievements of the Olmec civilization and developed their own ideas.

UNIT 2
REVIEW

USE VOCABULARY

Write the term that matches each meaning.

dynasty	legend	predict
intercropping	obelisk	

1 to tell what will happen in the future

2 planting different crops together

3 a story handed down from earlier times to explain the past

4 a series of rulers from the same family

5 a stone column often used to honor important people or events

CHECK UNDERSTANDING

6 Why did Egyptians call the Nile River the "giver of life"? How was the Nile also a taker of life?

7 How did the pharaohs help continue Egyptian civilization throughout the centuries?

8 How did Kush's conquest of Egypt affect both Kush and Egypt?

9 How were Indus Valley settlers able to live safely on the floodplain at the place where the four tributaries flowed into the Indus River?

10 Why did the ancient Chinese not trade with outsiders?

11 How do we know that religion played an important part in Mayan culture?

THINK CRITICALLY

12 **Cause and Effect** How did the problems caused by the Nile River lead to the development of Egyptian technology?

13 **Personally Speaking** If you had been young Thutmose III, what would you have thought of Hatshepsut's becoming the first female pharaoh of Egypt?

14 **Past to Present** Why do archaeologists want to learn the meaning of Mayan hieroglyphics?

APPLY SKILLS

Read Elevation Maps Use the map shown below to answer the questions.

15 What country shown on the map has the highest areas?

16 Where are the highest areas of Egypt?

17 How would you describe Sudan's elevation?

18 Can you use this map to find the exact height of land? Explain your answer.

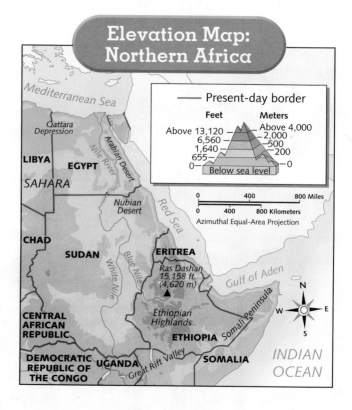

Elevation Map: Northern Africa

Present-day border

Feet	Meters
Above 13,120	Above 4,000
6,560	2,000
1,640	500
655	200
0	0
Below sea level	

Mediterranean Sea

Qattara Depression

LIBYA   EGYPT   Arabian Desert   Nile River

SAHARA

Nubian Desert   Red Sea

CHAD

SUDAN   White Nile   Blue Nile   ERITREA

Ras Dashan 15,158 ft. (4,620 m)   Gulf of Aden

CENTRAL AFRICAN REPUBLIC   Ethiopian Highlands   Somali Peninsula

DEMOCRATIC REPUBLIC OF THE CONGO   UGANDA   Great Rift Valley   ETHIOPIA   SOMALIA   INDIAN OCEAN

0   400   800 Miles
0   400   800 Kilometers
Azimuthal Equal-Area Projection

REMEMBER

- Share your ideas.
- Cooperate with others to plan your work.
- Take responsibility for your work.
- Help one another.
- Show your group's work to the class.
- Discuss what you learned by working together.

ACTIVITY

Make a
Model

In a group, think about the monuments and structures built by early civilizations in the Americas. Then choose one to build as a model. You and your group might make an Olmec head or a Mayan temple. Whatever you build, include a human figure to show the scale. Display your finished model in the classroom.

ACTIVITY

Make a
Poster

Work with two classmates to create a poster that shows the seasons of the ancient Egyptian calendar. Draw a large circle divided into three equal parts. Label each part with the name of a season and illustrate it.

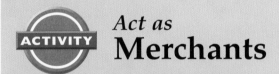

ACTIVITY

Act as
Merchants

Your class will divide into two groups. One group will be Nubian traders traveling to Egypt. The other group will be Egyptian merchants. Each group should create a list of goods that it will have to trade and then write each item on a separate index card. The traders will then meet to exchange goods. The goal for each group is to come away pleased with the trade it has made.

Unit Project Wrap-Up

Make a Model of the World Long Ago
All the world's early civilizations should be shown on your model of the world. Now it is time to complete the model. It is up to you and the other members of your group to decide how to finish it. For example, you might color it to show elevation and add longitude and latitude lines. You might also include a brief description of each civilization.

ASIA'S CLASSICAL AGE

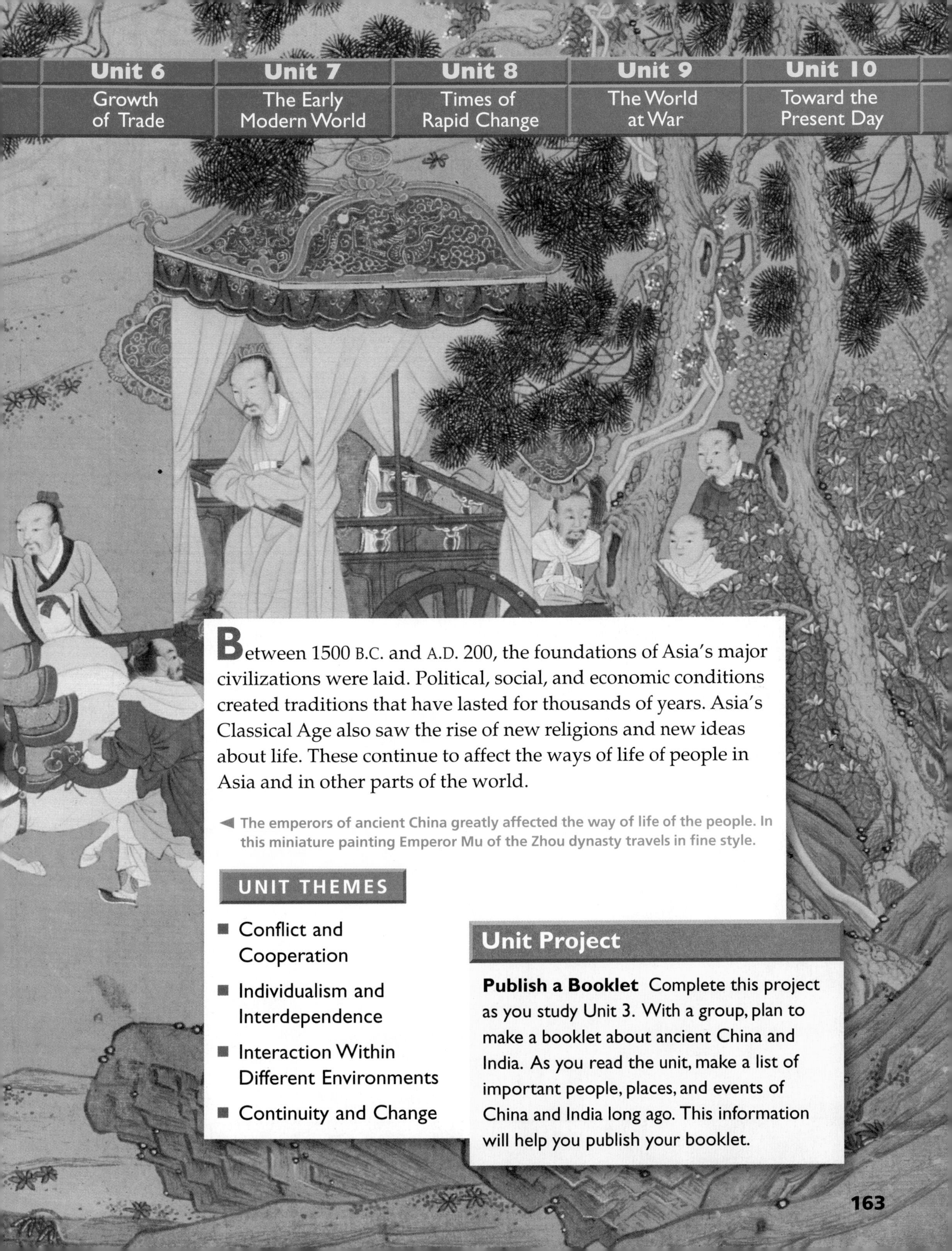

Between 1500 B.C. and A.D. 200, the foundations of Asia's major civilizations were laid. Political, social, and economic conditions created traditions that have lasted for thousands of years. Asia's Classical Age also saw the rise of new religions and new ideas about life. These continue to affect the ways of life of people in Asia and in other parts of the world.

◀ The emperors of ancient China greatly affected the way of life of the people. In this miniature painting Emperor Mu of the Zhou dynasty travels in fine style.

UNIT THEMES

- Conflict and Cooperation
- Individualism and Interdependence
- Interaction Within Different Environments
- Continuity and Change

Unit Project

Publish a Booklet Complete this project as you study Unit 3. With a group, plan to make a booklet about ancient China and India. As you read the unit, make a list of important people, places, and events of China and India long ago. This information will help you publish your booklet.

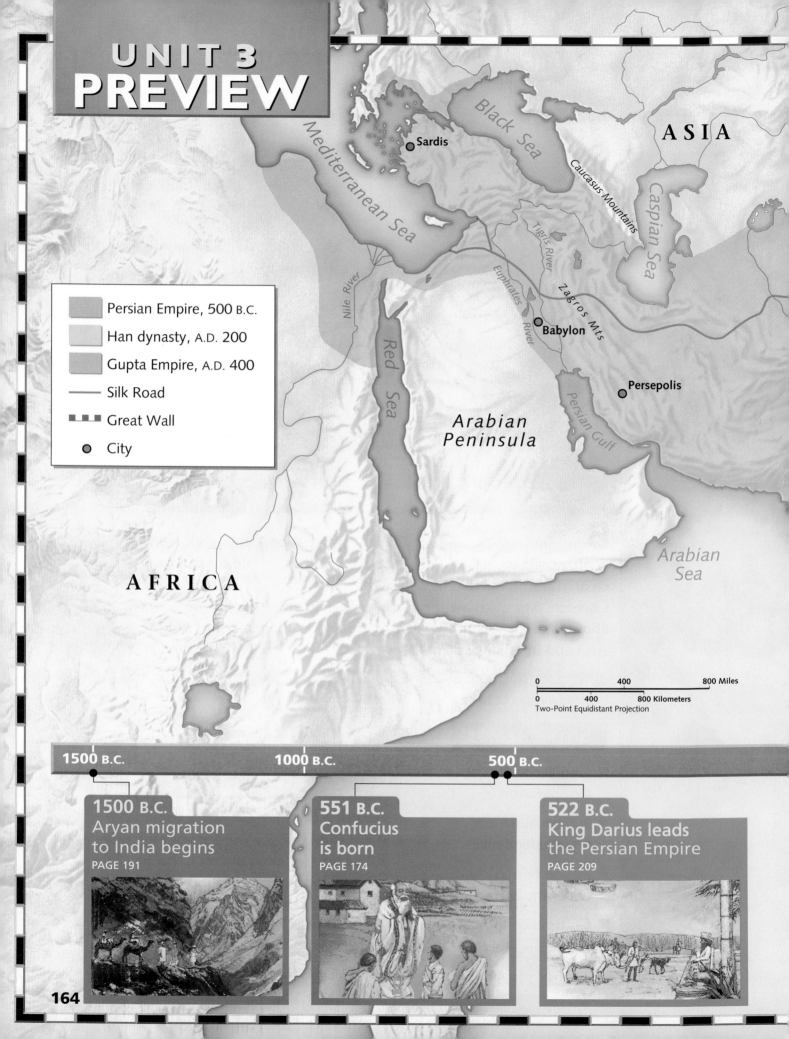

UNIT 3 PREVIEW

Legend

- Persian Empire, 500 B.C.
- Han dynasty, A.D. 200
- Gupta Empire, A.D. 400
- —— Silk Road
- ▬▬ Great Wall
- ● City

ASIA

AFRICA

Mediterranean Sea

Black Sea

Caucasus Mountains

Caspian Sea

Sardis

Nile River

Tigris River

Euphrates River

Zagros Mts

Babylon

Persepolis

Red Sea

Arabian Peninsula

Persian Gulf

Arabian Sea

```
0          400        800 Miles
0     400      800 Kilometers
Two-Point Equidistant Projection
```

Timeline

1500 B.C.   1000 B.C.   500 B.C.

1500 B.C.
Aryan migration
to India begins
PAGE 191

551 B.C.
Confucius
is born
PAGE 174

522 B.C.
King Darius leads
the Persian Empire
PAGE 209

164

Empires of Ancient China and India

ASIA

GOBI (DESERT)

Beijing

PACIFIC OCEAN

HINDU KUSH

H I M A L A Y A S

Huang He

Chang'an

CHINA

Hangzhou

Indus River

Delhi

Ajodha

Ganges River

Chang Jiang

Changsha

Ujjain

Guangzhou

INDIA

South China Sea

INDIAN OCEAN

N
W   E
S

| B.C. | A.D. | | A.D. 500 | | A.D. 1000 |

206 B.C.
Han dynasty rules China
PAGE 182

A.D. 320
Gupta Empire begins in India
PAGE 205

165

Discovery and Excavation of Shi Huangdi's Tomb

from *Calliope* magazine
written by Helen Wieman Bledsoe
illustrated by Higgins Bond

Qin Shi Huangdi, China's first emperor, united China in 221 B.C. His rule became known as a time of great cruelty by later historians. It is known that Shi Huangdi forced peasant farmers to complete large construction projects such as the Great Wall, roads, canals, and several new palaces. Shi Huangdi also made many enemies during his rule. He was almost assassinated three times.

After Shi Huangdi survived the assassination attempts, he became determined to find a way to live forever. For example, he sent groups of men and women out to sea to look for a land where people did not die. Knowing that he really might not live forever, Shi Huangdi continued with his plans for an elaborate tomb to hold his body after his death. Read now to find out why his tomb, the ruins of which were discovered in 1974, has fascinated people around the world.

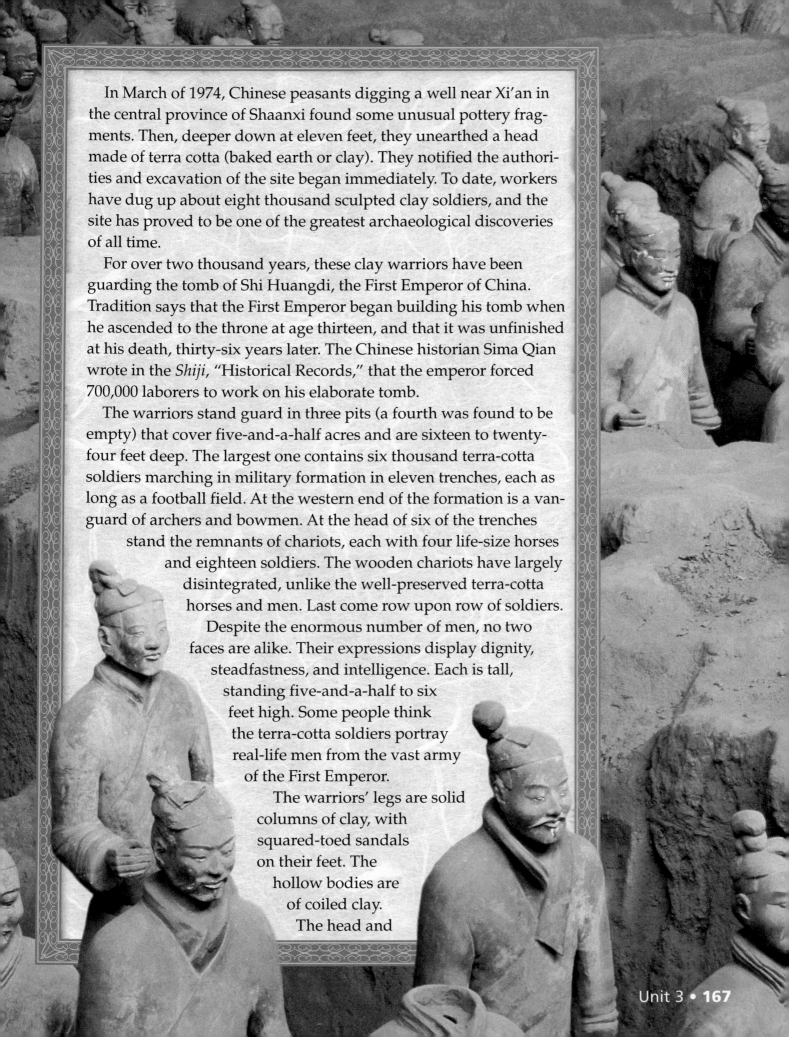

In March of 1974, Chinese peasants digging a well near Xi'an in the central province of Shaanxi found some unusual pottery fragments. Then, deeper down at eleven feet, they unearthed a head made of terra cotta (baked earth or clay). They notified the authorities and excavation of the site began immediately. To date, workers have dug up about eight thousand sculpted clay soldiers, and the site has proved to be one of the greatest archaeological discoveries of all time.

For over two thousand years, these clay warriors have been guarding the tomb of Shi Huangdi, the First Emperor of China. Tradition says that the First Emperor began building his tomb when he ascended to the throne at age thirteen, and that it was unfinished at his death, thirty-six years later. The Chinese historian Sima Qian wrote in the *Shiji*, "Historical Records," that the emperor forced 700,000 laborers to work on his elaborate tomb.

The warriors stand guard in three pits (a fourth was found to be empty) that cover five-and-a-half acres and are sixteen to twenty-four feet deep. The largest one contains six thousand terra-cotta soldiers marching in military formation in eleven trenches, each as long as a football field. At the western end of the formation is a vanguard of archers and bowmen. At the head of six of the trenches stand the remnants of chariots, each with four life-size horses and eighteen soldiers. The wooden chariots have largely disintegrated, unlike the well-preserved terra-cotta horses and men. Last come row upon row of soldiers. Despite the enormous number of men, no two faces are alike. Their expressions display dignity, steadfastness, and intelligence. Each is tall, standing five-and-a-half to six feet high. Some people think the terra-cotta soldiers portray real-life men from the vast army of the First Emperor.

The warriors' legs are solid columns of clay, with squared-toed sandals on their feet. The hollow bodies are of coiled clay. The head and hands of each soldier were carefully molded and attached to the body in assembly-line fashion. Traces of pink, yellow, purple, blue, orange, green, brown, and black pigment show that the figures were once brightly painted. The horses were roan (reddish-brown, brown, or black) with pink mouths.

The warriors' hair styles and topknots, and the tassels trimming their garments, denote their military rank. Many do not wear helmets or carry shields, a mark of bravery in battle. Their armor was probably of lacquered leather; some pieces look like baseball catchers' pads. The soldiers' hands are positioned to hold weapons, but most of the weapons have disappeared. Very likely they were stolen when the pits were looted after the fall of the Qin dynasty (the dynasty founded by Shi Huangdi). Even so, bronze spears, halberds (a combination spear and battle-ax), swords, daggers, and about fourteen hundred arrowheads remain. Some of the blades are still very sharp.

A second pit, only partially excavated, contains about fourteen hundred more soldiers. While the first pit holds mostly infantry, the second has a more mobile attack force of horses and chariots. A third pit is thought to hold the high command of the army. The chariot of the Commander-in-Chief survives, with men surrounding it in protective formation.

Covered by a wooden roof and ten feet of earth, these figures were not intended to be seen. When the pits were looted and burned, the roof fell in and damaged most of the sculptures. Reconstruction is a slow, delicate task. Today, a visitor to the site can walk on long wooden platforms sixteen feet above the pits and gaze down with astonishment at the thousands of sculptured soldiers below.

Approximately a mile away from the pits is a gently sloping, rounded mountain covered with trees—the burial mound of the First Emperor. The four-sided, rammed-earth mound covers three quarters of a square mile and is one hundred fifty-six feet high. It once stood at four hundred feet. Of the two great walls that enclosed the funerary park only rubble remains. The perimeter of the outer wall is almost four miles. Set into the strong thick walls were four gates and four corner towers. Inside the walls were gardens, pavilions, and a sacrificial palace, in addition to the burial mound. The burial chamber itself is still untouched, its contents as yet unknown.

Tradition based on the *Shiji* says that the emperor's body was buried in a suit of small jade pieces sewed together with gold thread and covered with a pearl and jade shroud. Also in the burial mound were bronze models of Shi Huangdi's palaces and government offices. The replicas featured such details as pearls to represent the sun and moon, and pools of mercury to recreate rivers and seas.

According to the ancient Chinese, the soul of the dead continued living and therefore required all of life's necessities within the tomb. Kings especially needed many luxuries and that is why their tombs are treasure houses of jewels, gold, silver, and bronze.

The *Shiji* states that in order to prevent people from robbing the tomb, "Craftsmen built internal devices that would set off arrows should anyone pass through the tunnels." Because Sima Qian wrote his history a century after the death of the First Emperor, the accuracy of his statements is questionable. In fact, grave robbers did enter and loot Shi Huangdi's tomb for thirty years after the fall of the Qin dynasty (four years after the Emperor's death). During this time, many precious relics most likely were stolen.

In 1980, additional smaller pits were discovered. One contains pottery coffins with bones of exotic birds and animals, probably from the royal zoo. Another has vessels inscribed with the words, "Belonging to the Officials in Charge of Food at Mount Li," and must be where food and sacrifices were offered to the dead emperor. Uncovered in the nearby Hall of Slumber were clothes and everyday objects for use by the soul of the Emperor.

As the excavations continue, each find serves to remind us of the tremendous energy and genius of Shi Huangdi and his people.

As you read this unit, you will find out more about the history, beliefs, and ways of life of ancient Asian peoples.

5

CHINA

Life-size statue of a
Chinese soldier, carved
about 210 B.C.

"*Eastward goes the great river,
its waves have swept away
a thousand years of gallant men.*"

Chinese poet Su Shi,
1037–1101

The Zhou Dynasty

LESSON

1

T he Classical Age in China began with the conquest of the Huang He Valley in 1050 B.C. by the Zhou (JOH) dynasty. Under the Zhou and the dynasties that followed, China became large and powerful. These dynasties left a heritage that has lasted for thousands of years. A **heritage** is a set of ideas that has been passed down from one generation to another.

FOCUS

How do ideas and values affect societies today?

Main Idea As you read, think about the ideas that first arose during the Zhou dynasty and still define Chinese civilization.

Vocabulary

heritage
virtue
Mandate of Heaven
public works
philosopher
responsibility
filial piety
Confucianism

Winning the Mandate of Heaven

The beginnings of the Zhou are not entirely clear. Even experts in Chinese history are not sure how different the Zhou were from the Shang. One difference is clear, however. The Zhou worshipped a god they called Tian (TYEN), or "Heaven." This god seems to have been unknown to the Shang people.

The ancestors of the Zhou dynasty may have lived in the Wei River Valley as herders. In time, they learned to farm and settled in villages. According to legend, the founder of the Zhou, Hou Ji (HOH•JEE), discovered agriculture when he was a child.

Gradually, the Zhou began to move farther east in the Wei River Valley. As they moved, they came into contact with the Shang. Around the year 1150 B.C., the Zhou attacked the Shang. In about 1050 B.C. the Zhou ruler, King Wu, claimed victory over the Shang.

According to the Zhou, Heaven ordered King Wu to conquer the Shang and begin a new dynasty. The early Zhou kings believed that the god Heaven disapproved of the Shang king. They thought that the Shang did not have the **virtues**, or good qualities, needed to lead the people.

The *Book of Documents*, an early Chinese text, calls Heaven's order to claim rule over China the **Mandate of Heaven**. The Zhou kings believed that they would be able to keep the mandate as long as they continued to show virtues.

REVIEW *What was the Mandate of Heaven?*

The sacred *bi*, or ring of heaven, was a symbol of the bond between the Chinese gods and the leaders chosen to carry out Heaven's commands.

Division of Classes

To help control the large kingdom, the Zhou created a new social structure. The king was at the top of Zhou society. Noble families were in the middle. Peasant farmers were at the bottom.

Everyone owed loyalty to the king. The king gave land to the nobles in return for military service. The nobles ruled their land as separate states, governing in whatever way they wanted. The king used the nobles' powerful armies to protect the whole kingdom.

The peasants lived on the land owned by the nobles and farmed it. In return for the right to farm a noble's land, the peasants had to serve in the noble's army.

The life of a peasant was filled with hardships. This poem from the *Book of Songs*, written sometime after 1000 B.C., offers a personal view of a peasant's life:

66 What plant is not faded?
What day do we not march?
What man is not taken
To defend the four bounds?
What plant is not wilting?
What man is not taken from his wife?
Alas for us soldiers,
Treated as though we were not
fellow men! 99

Peasant farmers supplied the king with an almost endless number of workers. They constructed many huge public works. **Public works** are structures built by the government for everyone's use.

Under the Zhou kings China's civilization grew. By the 700s B.C. more people lived in China than anywhere else in the world.

REVIEW *What were the advantages and disadvantages of China's government?*

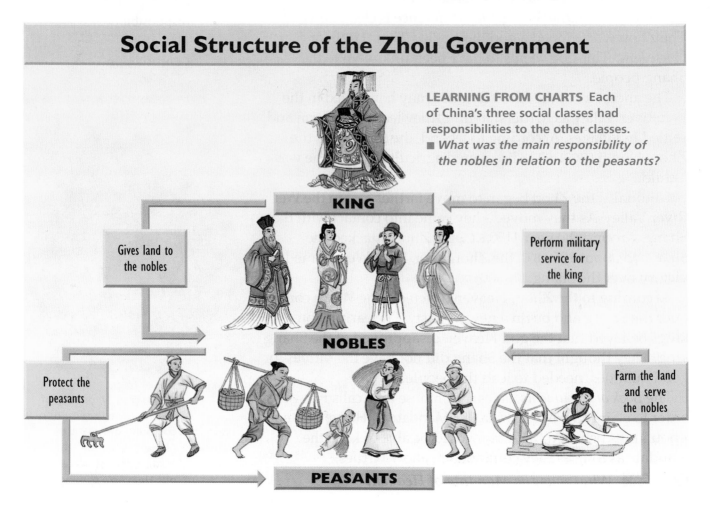

Social Structure of the Zhou Government

LEARNING FROM CHARTS Each of China's three social classes had responsibilities to the other classes.
■ *What was the main responsibility of the nobles in relation to the peasants?*

KING

Gives land to the nobles

Perform military service for the king

NOBLES

Protect the peasants

Farm the land and serve the nobles

PEASANTS

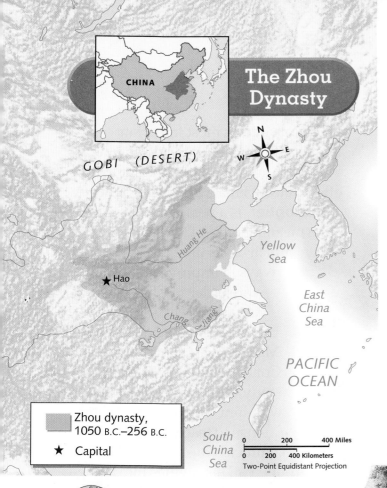

The Zhou Dynasty

GOBI (DESERT)

Huang He

★ Hao

Chang Jiang

Yellow Sea

East China Sea

PACIFIC OCEAN

South China Sea

| Zhou dynasty, 1050 B.C.–256 B.C. |
| ★ Capital |

0   200   400 Miles
0   200   400 Kilometers
Two-Point Equidistant Projection

Regions Land held by the Zhou dynasty stretched about 1,000 miles (1,609 km) inland from the coast of the Yellow Sea.
■ *What major rivers flowed through the land of the Zhou?*

The Decline of the Zhou

King Wu and the kings who followed him were all strong rulers. The *Book of Documents* says that the Zhou governed carefully because they feared losing the Mandate of Heaven. The power and good standing of the Zhou kings, however, eventually weakened. Soon, people to the north and to the west of the Zhou kingdom invaded the valley of the Wei River.

In 771 B.C. the people of the Zhou capital city of Hao (HOW) got ready for an attack by the invaders. A legend tells that the Zhou leader, King You (YOO), ordered fires lighted on hills around the capital when an attack seemed likely. However, several times he lit the fires when there was no invasion. He just wanted to see if the nobles would come. Finally, there really was an attack. King You ordered the fires to be lit, in hopes of bringing the nobles' armies. The nobles thought this was another false alarm and did not send their armies to help the king.

King You died in the attack, and the invaders captured the Wei River Valley. As a result, the next Zhou king was forced to move his capital city east to the North China Plain. After the move, the power of the Zhou kings weakened. At the same time, the power of the nobles increased. Many nobles made their fiefs—lands given to them by the king—independent. Some nobles even began to call themselves king.

The collapse of the Zhou brought China into a time of warfare. For this reason the last few centuries of the Zhou dynasty are sometimes called the Warring Kingdoms Period, or the Warring States Period. During this time people in China were often at war with one another. Yet this time of war also brought the development of new forms of government to bring back law and order. For example, in 535 B.C. the king of Zheng (ZHENG), a small kingdom in northern China, wrote down a set of laws. These were the earliest written laws in China.

REVIEW *What was the Warring Kingdoms Period?*

A Chinese artist may have been thinking of the legend of King You when making this statue of a man holding a lamp.

Confucius 551–479 B.C.

Confucius is believed to have been born in 551 B.C. The name *Confucius* is a Latin form of the philosopher's name—Kong Fuzi (KOONG FOO•zuh), which means Master Kong. Confucius' father was a government official. By the time Confucius was 25 years old, he also worked in the Lu government. Perhaps because he had offended powerful noble families, Confucius was exiled from Lu. According to legend, Confucius wandered for 25 years. During this time, he formed his ideas about government and society. Many of his ideas are still respected and used today.

No one knows for sure what Confucius looked like. A portrait of him from A.D. 1734 (above) and an ivory statue from about A.D. 1000 (above right) provide very different views.

The Ideas of Confucius

One of China's most important thinkers, Confucius, lived during the Warring Kingdoms Period. Confucius is often called China's first philosopher. A **philosopher** is a person who studies the meaning of life. Confucius spent much of his time thinking about ways to improve society and restore order in China.

Confucius is also remembered as China's first teacher. Many people sought out Confucius so that they could study the ancient traditions with him. Often he used short sayings to teach his ideas. After Confucius died, his students grouped all his sayings into a huge collection. Many later followers argued that some of the sayings were not really from Confucius. A book was then made containing the sayings most people agreed were really spoken by Confucius. This book is called *Lunyu* (LUN•YOO) in Chinese and the *Analects* in English. The Chinese word *lunyu* means "discussions."

The *Analects* tell much about the philosopher's ideas. Confucius thought that the use of written laws and punishments was not the best way to bring back order. Instead, Confucius supported the old Zhou dynasty idea that a ruler should set a good example for his people. He believed that rulers should be both kind and caring.

Confucius believed that a good society is like a family in which all members know their place and their **responsibilities**, or duties. Many of Confucius' thoughts about government seem to be based on his views about families. In ancient China, children were expected to treat their parents with

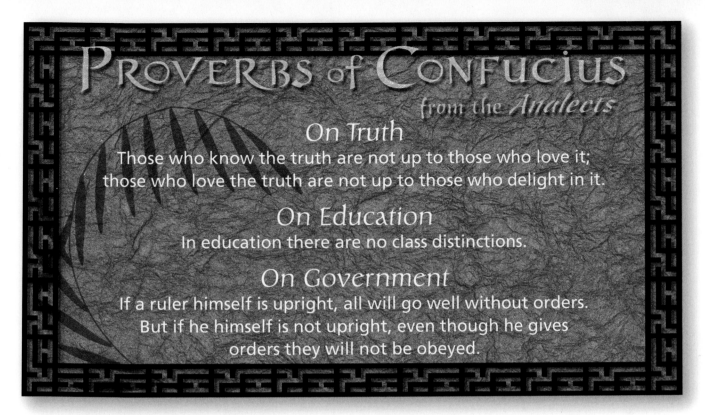

PROVERBS of CONFUCIUS
from the *Analects*

On Truth
Those who know the truth are not up to those who love it;
those who love the truth are not up to those who delight in it.

On Education
In education there are no class distinctions.

On Government
If a ruler himself is upright, all will go well without orders.
But if he himself is not upright, even though he gives
orders they will not be obeyed.

great honor and respect. The ancient Chinese called this kind of treatment of parents *xiao* (SHOW), or **filial piety** (FIH•lee•uhl PY•uh•tee). Confucius told his followers that by studying filial piety they could learn how to become loyal subjects. Confucius also taught that rulers could gain loyalty only by treating their subjects with the same love that parents show to their children. He called such love *ren*, or kindness.

For the most part, the teachings of Confucius were ignored during his lifetime. In time, however, his ideas, which came to be called **Confucianism**, spread throughout eastern Asia.

REVIEW *What qualities did Confucius believe that rulers should have?*

LESSON 1 REVIEW

Check Understanding

1 Remember the Facts What Chinese philosopher developed an important system of ideas and values?

2 Recall the Main Idea How did the Chinese people's shared belief in a set of ideas strengthen their civilization?

Think Critically

3 Personally Speaking Zhou society was divided into three classes, each with different responsibilities. In your opinion, would such a system be more likely to lead to cooperation or to conflict? Explain.

4 Think More About It In what ways did Confucianism support the idea of the Mandate of Heaven?

Show What You Know

Creative Writing Activity Confucius often presented his ideas about society as proverbs, or short sayings. Some examples can be found in the Proverbs of Confucius from the *Analects,* on this page. Using these examples as models, write several of your own proverbs about the need for order and cooperation in your school or community.

Skills

Identify Causes and Effects

1. Why Learn This Skill?

To find links between different events in history, you need to understand causes and their effects. A cause is something that makes something else happen. What happens is an effect. Knowing about causes and effects is important not only for understanding history but also for making personal decisions. It can help you think about the consequences of your actions. In that way you can make more thoughtful decisions.

2. Remember What You Have Read

Before the decline of the Zhou, their society was divided into three levels. The king was at the top, nobles were in the middle, and peasants were at the bottom. For the structure to work, the king had to be virtuous. In return, the nobles expected to remain loyal to the king, and the peasants had to obey the nobles. You read the legend of King You. His story gives an example of what happened when a king was not thought to be virtuous.

3. Understand the Process

Many events in history have more than one cause and more than one effect. Follow the arrows on the chart in the next column to help you understand the causes and effects of the fall of the Zhou dynasty.

1. What caused King You to send signals to the nobles? What was the effect?
2. Why did the nobles not respond when the Zhou capital was invaded?
3. What happened as a result of the nobles failing to respond?
4. What were the effects of the fall of the Zhou dynasty?

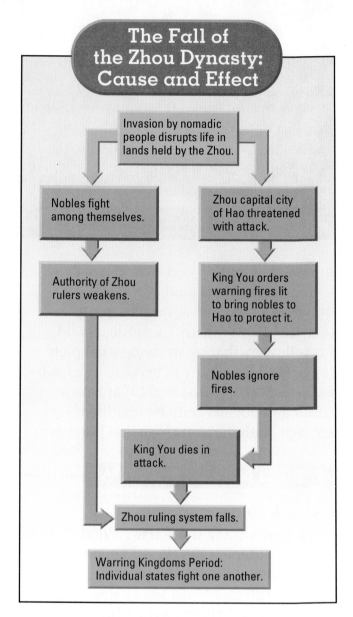

The Fall of the Zhou Dynasty: Cause and Effect

Invasion by nomadic people disrupts life in lands held by the Zhou.

Nobles fight among themselves.

Zhou capital city of Hao threatened with attack.

Authority of Zhou rulers weakens.

King You orders warning fires lit to bring nobles to Hao to protect it.

Nobles ignore fires.

King You dies in attack.

Zhou ruling system falls.

Warring Kingdoms Period: Individual states fight one another.

4. Think and Apply

Identify an event that took place in your community or one that was reported in the news. Perhaps there was a bad storm or a community cleanup day. Link the event's causes and effects on a chart like the one on this page. Use your chart to explain the event to a classmate or a family member.

The Qin Dynasty

LESSON

2

FOCUS

How can people with different backgrounds be united today?

Main Idea   Read about the ways the ruler of the Qin united people and created the first Chinese empire.

Vocabulary

Legalism
standardization
bureaucracy
civil war

During the 300s B.C., large kingdoms in China began to conquer smaller ones. The last Zhou kingdom met its end in 256 B.C., bringing the Zhou dynasty to a close. Three independent kingdoms remained in China—the Qi, Chu, and Qin (CHIN). These kingdoms fought each other for control of China. The Qin eventually won and united China under their rule.

Rule of Qin Shi Huangdi

The Qin king established the Qin Empire in 221 B.C. He named himself Qin Shi Huangdi (CHIN SHIR HWAHNG•DEE), or "First Emperor of the Qin." The uniting of China by the Qin dynasty is one of the most important events in all Chinese history. The importance of the Qin dynasty is reflected in the fact that the name *China* comes from the word *Qin*.

Shi Huangdi was born about 259 B.C. He became the king of Qin in 246 B.C., when he was just 13 years old. At first, he depended on advisors, who told him to adopt the teachings of Confucius. When he reached the age of 20 in 239 B.C., the young king decided to reject the teachings of Confucius. He appointed new advisors who taught him other ideas about governing. These other ideas included the strict following of laws.

The most powerful of Shi Huangdi's new advisors was Li Si (LEE SUH). Shi Huangdi made Li Si his prime minister in 237 B.C. Some Chinese scholars believe that Li Si deserves much of the credit for uniting China.

The Qin dynasty used their army to conquer the other kingdoms in what is now China.

Later Chinese historians often described the Qin government as cruel and uncaring. According to these historians, all those who were foolish enough to challenge Shi Huangdi were killed along with their families to warn others to obey.

REVIEW *Why is the Qin dynasty remembered today?*

Legalism

To help him rule his empire, Shi Huangdi used both written laws and a powerful government. The strict following of laws to govern is known as **Legalism**. Legalism taught that people obeyed their rulers out of fear, not out of respect. Under a system of Legalism, people who obey receive rewards. Those who do not obey are punished.

Shi Huangdi ordered books not approved by the Qin to be burnt. Books during this time were made of strips of wood or bambo. This painting by Hung Wu, an artist from a later period, shows one of the book burnings.

Qin Dynasty

CHINA

0   200   400 Miles
0   200   400 Kilometers
Two-Point Equidistant Projection

GOBI (DESERT)

YAN

ZHAO

QIN   WEI   QI   Yellow Sea
★Xianyang
HAN

CHU

South China Sea

N W E S

Xi Jiang

Qin dynasty, 221 B.C.–206 B.C.   ····· Existing walls
★ Capital city   QI Warring state

The most well-thought-out writings about Legalism were done by Master Han Fei (HAHN FAY). Han Fei's ideas were different from those of Confucius. Han Fei believed that a government based on virtues and respect would not work. Instead, he urged rulers to rely on laws and on the "two handles" of reward and punishment. Eventually, Han Fei introduced Shi Huangdi to his thoughts on Legalism.

REVIEW *What were the "two handles" Han Fei thought rulers should use?*

Human-Environment Interactions
Several independent warring kingdoms were united under the Qin dynasty.
■ *In what directions would the Qin most likely have traveled to expand their empire?*

The Great Wall

The First Emperor not only united China, but also extended the borders of the Qin Empire. As the empire grew, communication and travel became more difficult. To solve this problem, Shi Huangdi used prisoners as workers to build new roads and canals. These workers built more than 4,000 miles (6,437 km) of roads. This construction linked even the distant parts of the empire to the center of the Qin government at Xianyang (shee•AHN•yang).

LEARNING FROM DIAGRAMS This diagram shows a cross-section of the Great Wall.
■ *Why do you think builders used a variety of materials to build different parts of the wall?*

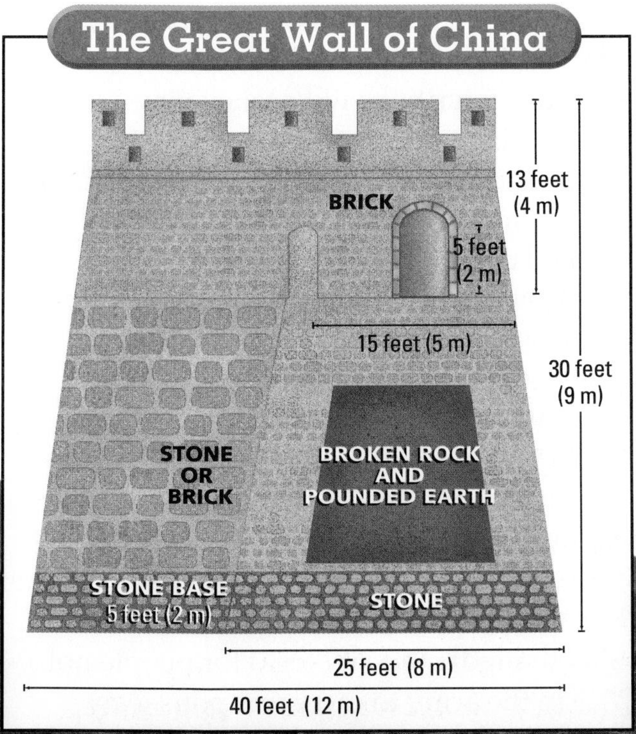

The Great Wall of China

BRICK

13 feet (4 m)

5 feet (2 m)

15 feet (5 m)

30 feet (9 m)

STONE OR BRICK

BROKEN ROCK AND POUNDED EARTH

STONE BASE 5 feet (2 m)

STONE

25 feet (8 m)

40 feet (12 m)

Shi Huangdi found that protecting his large empire was not easy. To the north of the empire lived large tribes of fierce warriors who rode horses. In earlier times, the people of the northern kingdoms of China had built walls of rammed earth to protect their borders from these people. But these walls did not keep the invaders away for long. Shi Huangdi ordered his workers to link together the existing walls. Using this forced labor, the Qin created a single long wall—a Great Wall.

The Great Wall stood 30 feet (9 m) high, with 40-foot (12-m) towers. The long wall twisted and turned through mountains, valleys, and deserts for more than 1,500 miles (2,414 km). Yet in spite of its size, Shi Huangdi's wall was built in just seven years.

The Great Wall not only kept invaders out of China, it warned people when invasions were taking place. Soldiers on the Great Wall communicated with each other by using signals. Smoke was used as a signal during the day, while fire was used as a signal at night. Signals would travel from tower to tower along the Great Wall, until they reached the Qin capital.

The Great Wall of China as it appears today. Much of the wall that stands today was built in the 1300s.

The Great Wall Today

Today visitors to China marvel at the Great Wall. The Great Wall seen today is a result of construction started in 1368 by the Ming dynasty. This construction lasted for 200 years and extended the wall. The Great Wall now runs for more than 3,700 miles (5,954 km), over twice its original size. The original wall was not maintained after the Qin dynasty. The Ming dynasty found it necessary to rebuild the wall to defend themselves from invaders known as the Mongols.

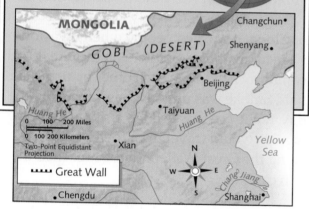

MONGOLIA

Changchun•

GOBI (DESERT)

Shenyang•

•Beijing

•Taiyuan

Huang He

Huang He

0   100   200 Miles

0 100 200 Kilometers

Two-Point Equidistant Projection

•Xian

Yellow Sea

▪▪▪▪ Great Wall

N W E S

Chang Jiang

•Chengdu

Shanghai•

The cost of building the wall was high in terms of human life. Some estimates say that more than 500,000 workers died during the building of the wall. Some were buried between its stones.

REVIEW *Why did the Qin build the Great Wall?*

A Program of Standardization

Walls, canals, and roads helped unite China. So, too, did Shi Huangdi's program of standardization. **Standardization** means making all things of a certain type

alike. The use of standardized coins, weights, and writing helped make trade and communication easier throughout China. Use of the same standards also helped the many peoples of the empire think of themselves as one.

Writing was also standardized in China during the time of the Qin. There were two official kinds of Chinese writing. One kind of writing was used for stone carvings and official documents. Another kind was used for everyday writing.

Education became another focus of standardization. Shi Huangdi wanted tight control of all the books used to teach. Li Si complained that too many books praised the Zhou and questioned the ideas of the Qin. In 213 B.C. Shi Huangdi ordered the burning of certain books. Many of the books destroyed were about Confucianism. Legends say that teachers who refused to give up their Confucian writings were taken prisoner and buried alive.

As part of his program of standardization, Shi Huangdi also did away with the fiefs created during the Zhou dynasty. The smaller ones became counties. The larger ones became provinces. Provinces are political regions of a country, similar to the states of the United States.

Shi Huangdi ordered the noble families who had owned the fiefs to move to Xianyang, the Qin Empire's capital. This forced move helped end any loyalty peasants had felt toward their nobles. In addition, Shi Huangdi made it illegal for people not in the army to carry weapons. Any weapons that did not belong to the army were collected and melted down.

The introduction of standardized coins during the Qin dynasty made buying and selling easier. The hole in the middle of the coins allowed them to be strung together.

During the Time of the Qin

While Shi Huangdi was bringing standardization to China, other civilizations around the world were changing as well. The long-lasting Egyptian Empire in northern Africa had lost its independence. The kingdom of Kush, however, was growing because of a successful ironmaking industry. Europe had recently seen a time of empire building. Now it was in the midst of a time of scientific and mathematical advances. In the Americas, the Mayas were creating new hieroglyphics and experimenting with new ways of building.

Standard weights, like the one shown here, helped the Chinese measure like goods, such as pieces of jade, the same way. Why was it important that like goods be measured the same way?

To oversee his huge empire, Shi Huangdi created a bureaucracy. A **bureaucracy** is a network of appointed government officials. To support this bureaucracy, the people of China were required to pay heavy taxes.

The Qin government was designed to place all power in the hands of the emperor. The emperor had to be strong, however, to maintain rule over China. Many people in China were unhappy with the Qin but were too afraid of Shi Huangdi to rebel.

Shi Huangdi, the First Emperor, died in 210 B.C. His favorite son became the Second Emperor, but he proved to be a weak ruler. Soon civil war broke out. In a **civil war**, different groups of people from the same place or country fight one another. By 206 B.C., the Qin had collapsed. After four more years of civil war, the king of the Han, Liu Bang, defeated all other rival powers in 202 B.C.

REVIEW *What was an important result of standardization and the creation of a bureaucracy?*

LESSON 2 REVIEW

Check Understanding

1 Remember the Facts Did the Qin dynasty use Legalism or Confucianism to unite and rule China?

2 Recall the Main Idea What were some of the ideas and projects that helped unite China under the Qin?

Think Critically

3 Cause and Effect What do you think happened when the Qin government took fiefs away from nobles?

4 Past to Present What are some ways leaders today bring together the people they govern?

Show What You Know

Poster Activity Divide a sheet of posterboard into two columns. In one column, list the ideas used by the Zhou dynasty when they governed. In the other column, list the ideas the Qin used in place of those of the Zhou.

FOCUS

Why are some periods in history remembered as times of achievement?

Main Idea Think about the achievements that made the years of Han rule an outstanding time in Chinese history.

Vocabulary

ambassador
civil service
Daoism
import
export
Silk Road
profit
caravan

The Han Dynasty

L iu Bang, the founder of the Han dynasty, came from a peasant background. Unlike the nobles of the time, Liu Bang wanted the kingdoms of China to be united under one government. As the first ruler of the Han dynasty, he achieved this goal and more. The dynasty he founded lasted for more than 400 years, from 206 B.C. until A.D. 220.

The Han View of Government

After claiming control of China, Liu Bang took the name of Han Gaozu (GOW•ZOO), or "High Ancestor." He located his capital city at Chang'an (CHANG•AHN) in the valley of the Wei River, not far from the old Qin capital of Xianyang. Gaozu made sure that his government differed from that of Shi Huangdi. He feared that the Chinese people would turn against him if he set up a Legalist government. In place of Legalism, Gaozu turned to Confucianism.

Gaozu knew the importance of having the support of those he ruled. "The prince is the boat; the common people are the water. The water can support the boat, or the water can capsize the boat," he said. He thought out each of his decisions so that his ship of state—China—would stay afloat.

Gaozu won the support of the nobles by giving them land and by allowing them to rule their lands as they wished. He won over the peasant farmers by lowering taxes. The leaders of the Qin dynasty had taxed the peasants heavily to pay for the Great Wall and other public works. The peasants welcomed Gaozu's new policy of lower taxes.

As emperor, Gaozu was as respected as Shi Huangdi had been feared. But just when Gaozu had ended problems within China, trouble appeared on its borders. Invaders

Woman in traditional clothing of the Han period

from the north attacked. One attack brought them to the city walls of Chang'an, the Han capital. Gaozu was wounded while defending his city. He died from his wounds in 195 B.C.

Later Han dynasty emperors took back the kingdoms Gaozu had given to the nobles and appointed government officials to rule them. The officials reported only to the emperor.

Han government began to use both Confucian and Legalist ideas. While Han leaders believed that ruler should set an example for the people, they also saw a need for strong central government and an all-powerful leader.

REVIEW *What type of leader did Gaozu think should rule China?*

Wu Di and the Civil Service System

In 140 B.C. Wu Di (WOO DEE) came to the Han throne. The name *Wu Di* means "Warlike Emperor." Wu Di created armies, some with as many as 300,000 soldiers, to conquer new lands. These armies pushed the borders of the empire north, south, and west.

To guard against attacks by nomads, Wu Di extended the Great Wall. Wu Di also took other actions. In some cases he paid nomads—with silk, rice, or money—not to attack. These payments gave outsiders their first taste of the riches of China.

Wu Di also sent out **ambassadors**, or representatives of the Chinese government,

Regions Ancient China grew under the various dynasties. Compare the size during the Shang dynasty to its size during the Han dynasty.

■ *In what directions did the empire expand during the Han dynasty?*

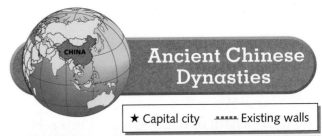

Ancient Chinese Dynasties

★ Capital city ····· Existing walls

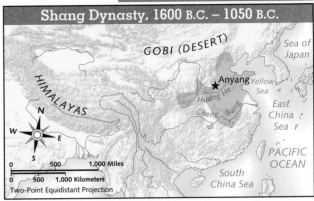

Shang Dynasty, 1600 B.C. – 1050 B.C.

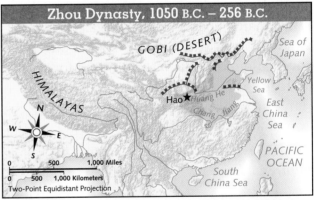

Zhou Dynasty, 1050 B.C. – 256 B.C.

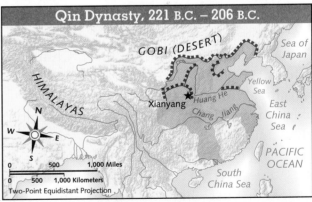

Qin Dynasty, 221 B.C. – 206 B.C.

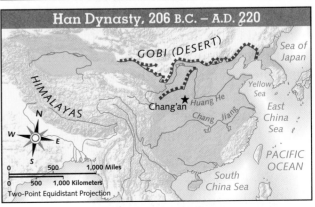

Han Dynasty, 206 B.C. – A.D. 220

to make peace with his enemies. Wu Di's peacekeeping efforts helped bring about what historians later called the *Pax Sinica,* or "Chinese Peace."

Wu Di's changes in government brought peace within his empire. Wu Di set up China's first civil service system. A **civil service** oversees the day-to-day business of running a government.

In the bureaucracy created under the Qin, jobs were given to people as a reward for loyalty. In contrast, some Han civil service officials earned their jobs by scoring well on tests. Many of these tests were open to people of all classes. Only those who made the highest grades earned government jobs. While many jobs were still given as rewards for loyalty, the examination system for government officials was also used for centuries. The civil servants who ran the Han Empire so well were proof that the examination system worked.

REVIEW *How did Wu Di protect his empire and run it?*

A Golden Age

Under Wu Di's "Chinese Peace," China entered a Golden Age in both the arts and learning. Without the fear of war, the study of language, history, philosophy, and religion blossomed.

During Han rule, scholars improved the Chinese writing system. One scholar created the first Chinese dictionary, in 100 B.C. Other scholars, such as Sima Qian (SOO•MAH CHIH•YIN), recorded China's history. Sima's review of China's past from the earliest dynasties to the Han was not just a listing of dates and events. He connected causes and effects. This made it easier for people to understand *why* things happened.

Confucianism became the official teaching of the Han Empire. Wu Di and later Han rulers also supported the study of such teachings as **Daoism** (DOW•ih•zuhm). Daoism teaches that the key to long life and happiness is to accept life as it is.

The Han Golden Age also brought new ideas in technology. A Han general, for example, developed the wheelbarrow. This invention was of great use to the army

LEARNING FROM TIME LINES The ancient Chinese made many advances in technology from prehistoric times to A.D. 220.

■ *Which was invented first, an instrument for detecting earthquakes or the wheelbarrow?*

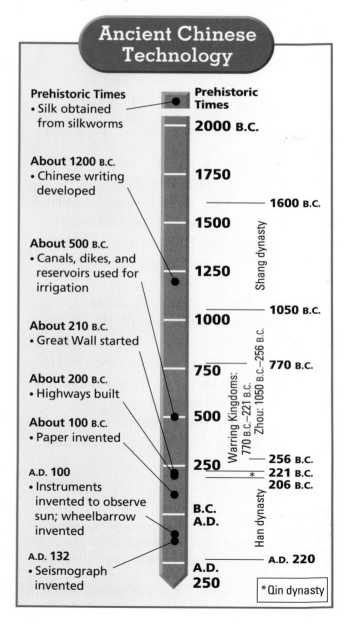

Ancient Chinese Technology

Prehistoric Times
- Silk obtained from silkworms

About 1200 B.C.
- Chinese writing developed

About 500 B.C.
- Canals, dikes, and reservoirs used for irrigation

About 210 B.C.
- Great Wall started

About 200 B.C.
- Highways built

About 100 B.C.
- Paper invented

A.D. 100
- Instruments invented to observe sun; wheelbarrow invented

A.D. 132
- Seismograph invented

Prehistoric Times
2000 B.C.
1750
1600 B.C.
1500
1250
1050 B.C.
1000
770 B.C.
750
500
256 B.C.
221 B.C.
206 B.C.
250
B.C.
A.D.
A.D. 220
A.D. 250

Shang dynasty

Zhou: 1050 B.C.–256 B.C.

Warring Kingdoms: 770 B.C.–221 B.C.

Han dynasty

*Qin dynasty

184 • Unit 3

TECHNOLOGY

Seismograph

About A.D. 132 Chang Heng invented China's first seismograph. A modern seismograph tells the location and strength of earthquakes. The early seismograph worked in much the same way. A rod inside the seismograph fell toward the dragon nearest the earthquake, making a loud noise. A ball then dropped from the dragon's mouth into a bronze frog below. The noise let the Chinese emperor know that there had been an earthquake in his empire. The direction in which the ball fell told him the general location of the earthquake.

Chang Heng's seismograph not only worked well but also was beautifully crafted.

---

because one soldier alone could now move more than 330 pounds (150 kg) of equipment. In A.D. 132 a Han inventor created an instrument to detect earthquakes.

The most important innovation of the Han dynasty was paper. The first paper was probably made about 100 B.C. in western China. Paper proved to be an ideal material for recording information. The use of paper led to advances in printing. Han workers soon began printing on paper by using designs etched on stone.

REVIEW *What was the most important innovation of the Han dynasty?*

Trade on the Silk Road

Even before the Han dynasty, Chinese traders **imported**, or brought in, goods for sale from other lands. They also **exported**, or sent out, their own goods for sale in other places. However, during the time of the Han dynasty, trade with the outside world grew dramatically.

In 139 B.C. Wu Di sent an ambassador to talk to enemies of the Xiongnu (shee•UNG•noo), a nomadic

Wealthy Chinese during the Han dynasty lived in large houses like this. The poor usually lived in small, one-story houses.

people from the north. The Xiongnu made raids into China. Wu Di wanted to find allies to help China fight the Xiongnu. The ambassador, Zhang Qian (JAHNG CHIH•yin), did not find any allies. However, he did learn about some of the civilizations to the west of China. Zhang Qian came back with tales of resources unknown to the people of China. The Chinese people were especially interested in stories of magnificent horses. The stories led Chinese traders to travel in search of these horses and other foreign goods.

Most of China's trade was done by land. The trade route used the most began near the Han capital of Chang'an. It continued through the deserts and high plains of central Asia. The route finally ended at the shores of the Mediterranean Sea.

The Chinese product most in demand was silk. In fact, it was silk that gave the trade route its nickname—the **Silk Road**. Traders traveled west with products made from silk. They returned with lumber, horses, and other products that the Chinese people needed.

The journey on the Silk Road was sometimes dangerous. Thieves often robbed traders of their money and goods. However, the **profits**, or money gained, more than made up for the risks. Camel **caravans**, or groups of traders, became common sights on the Silk Road.

Chinese traders easily found buyers for their silk. Those who bought silk directly from the Chinese traded it to others farther west. Chinese traders did not go all the way to Africa and Europe, but their goods did.

REVIEW *What was the Silk Road?*

This wooden model of a servant girl, placed in a tomb over 2,000 years ago, wears silk clothing that has been little damaged by time.

LESSON 3 REVIEW

Check Understanding

1 **Remember the Facts** What were the major achievements of Gaozu and Wu Di?

2 **Recall the Main Idea** What ideas did later Han emperors combine in order to create a strong government?

Think Critically

3 **Think More About It** Why was the Silk Road important?

4 **Personally Speaking** For centuries the Chinese people have proudly called themselves children of Han. Why do you think they feel this way?

5 **Past to Present** In what ways does the government of your community blend ideas?

Show What You Know

Collage Activity Some people say that the twentieth century was a century of innovations. Using pictures and headlines from newspapers and magazines, create a collage that illustrates this idea. Show recent inventions and discoveries in your collage.

Use a Table to Classify Information

1. Why Learn This Skill?

Imagine looking through a pile of papers on your desk. Your math homework, book reports, and other assignments are mixed together in a big jumble. You cannot quickly find what you need. In the same way, it can be hard to search through jumbled information. Like a pile of papers, information is easier to use if it is classified, or sorted. Knowing how to classify information can make it easier to find.

2. Remember What You Have Read

When you read about the dynasties of the Classical Age in China, you were given a lot of information. You learned when the Zhou, Qin, and Han dynasties ruled China, when the Warring Kingdoms Period occurred, who the important leaders were, and what contributions each dynasty made to Chinese civilization. These and other facts can be classified by using a table. A **table** is a chart that lists information in categories.

3. Understand the Process

In the table on this page, China's early history is classified according to its dynasties and its Warring Kingdoms Period. The years for each period appear in the first column. The earliest periods are listed first.

Each row gives facts about a single period in Chinese history. Suppose you want to find information about the Qin dynasty. Move your finger down the second column, labeled *Name*, until you find *Qin dynasty*. Then, move your finger across the row to the column labeled *Contributions*. What was a contribution of the Qin dynasty? Now go to the next column to find out who led the Qin.

4. Think and Apply

Make your own table to show information about the Classical Age in China. Use the information in the table on this page, but classify it differently. Share your table with a partner as you review the chapter.

China's Early History

YEARS	NAME	CONTRIBUTIONS	IMPORTANT LEADERS
1600 B.C. to 1050 B.C.	Shang dynasty	Writing Use of bronze	
1050 B.C. to 256 B.C.	Zhou dynasty	Idea of Mandate of Heaven Improved ways of farming	Wu
770 B.C. to 221 B.C.	Warring Kingdoms Period	New forms of government	
221 B.C. to 206 B.C.	Qin dynasty	Building of Great Wall Standardization of weights and measures Creation of road system	Shi Huangdi
206 B.C. to A.D. 220	Han dynasty	Civil service examinations Invention of paper Invention of seismograph Beginning of trade on the Silk Road	Gaozu Wu Di

1250 B.C.   1000 B.C.   750 B.C.

About 1050 B.C.
• Zhou dynasty defeats the Shang dynasty

About 770 B.C.
• Warring Kingdoms Period begins

CONNECT MAIN IDEAS

Use this organizer to show that you understand the beginnings of Chinese civilization. Write a sentence or two that describes each topic listed below. A copy of the organizer appears on page 36 of the Activity Book.

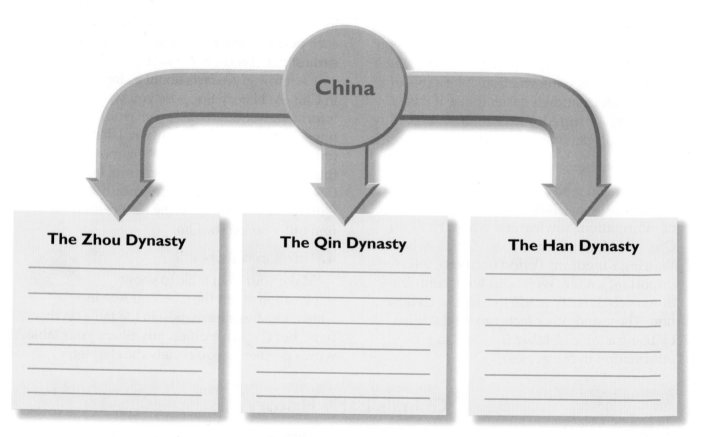

China

The Zhou Dynasty

The Qin Dynasty

The Han Dynasty

WRITE MORE ABOUT IT

Write Your Opinion Zhou rulers ordered peasant farmers to build public works and serve as soldiers. Why did the farmers agree to this? Do you think the arrangement between the rulers and farmers was fair? Explain.

Write a Proverb Write your own proverb about government, truth, or education.

Write a Short Report Compare and contrast the ruling methods of Shi Huangdi and Gaozu. How did their different styles of leadership affect the Chinese people?

Write a Description Write your own description of the Great Wall. You may wish to use additional references.

| 500 B.C. | 250 B.C. | B.C. | A.D. | A.D. 250 |

551 B.C.
• Confucius is born

221 B.C.
• Qin Shi Huangdi establishes Qin Empire

206 B.C.
• Han dynasty begins

USE VOCABULARY

Write the term that correctly matches each definition. Then use each term in a complete sentence.

bureaucracy   philosopher

export   standardization

import   virtue

1 a person who studies the meaning of life

2 making all things of a certain kind alike

3 a good quality

4 to send out goods for sale in other countries

5 to bring in goods from other countries

6 a network of appointed government officials

CHECK UNDERSTANDING

7 How did the Zhou kings explain their conquest of the Shang in 1050 B.C.?

8 What did Confucius say a ruler must do to be successful?

9 What was Legalism?

10 For what is Shi Huangdi of the Qin dynasty most remembered?

11 Why was standardization important to China?

12 How did Wu Di achieve the *Pax Sinica*, or the "Chinese Peace"?

13 What was the most important innovation of the Han dynasty? Why?

14 Why was the Silk Road important to people long ago?

THINK CRITICALLY

15 **Past to Present** Confucius said that a good society is like a family in which each member knows his or her place. Would Confucius think our society is a good society? Explain your answer.

16 **Think More About It** How did Wu Di's civil service program differ from Shi Huangdi's bureaucracy?

17 **Cause and Effect** What effect did Wu Di's Chinese Peace have on Chinese arts and sciences?

APPLY SKILLS

Identify Causes and Effects Look at a newspaper or magazine article. List at least one cause in the article and the effect or effects of that cause.

Use a Table to Classify Information Interview several classmates about the following: favorite foods, songs, books, and subjects in school. Then make a chart that classifies this information.

READ MORE ABOUT IT

The Great Wall by Elizabeth Mann. Mikaya. This book discusses how and why the Great Wall of China was built.

HARCOURT BRACE

Visit the Internet at
http://www.hbschool.com
for additional resources.

INDIA
AND
PERSIA

"An age like this one, which is golden while it lasts and proves a culture's greatness forever after, is never a sudden or rootless event."

Lucille Schulberg,
Historic India

Young girl from Chennai (Madras), India, in traditional dress

Aryans
Bring Changes to India

FOCUS
How does the movement of people into an area affect those already living there?

Main Idea As you read, consider how the arrival of the Aryans changed life for the people of India.

Vocabulary
Aryan
Sanskrit
Vedas
Hinduism
reincarnation
caste
untouchable
Buddhism

Around 1500 B.C. large numbers of people began to migrate into India. These migrations lasted for more than 3,000 years. They were important because they brought together people with different customs and ideas. The earliest immigrants called themselves **Aryans** (AIR•ee•uhnz). The Aryans were warriors and herders who came from eastern Europe and western Asia. Their arrival marked the beginning of the Classical Age in India.

Aryan Immigrants

The earliest Aryan migrations took place over hundreds of years. They were part of a larger southward movement of people called Indo-Europeans. Why the Aryans and others left their homeland is not known. Drought, famine, or disease may have forced them to leave their homes. Perhaps invaders drove them out.

Some Aryans moved west. Others pushed south. The Aryans who moved south crossed through the mountain passes of the Hindu Kush, the wall of mountains between the Indian subcontinent and the rest of Asia. These Aryans moved to the region of the Indus Valley now known as Pakistan. In time, however, the Aryans occupied much of the northern parts of India.

Each wave of migration brought more Aryans into the subcontinent. Soon the Aryans competed with the native people of India for farmland. The Aryans had one advantage in the fight for land: they had horses. Until the Aryans arrived, there were no horses in India.

Before coming to India the Aryans had lived as herders. They raised cattle, goats, horses, and sheep. In India they

The Aryan migrations brought the first horses to India. The clay horses shown here were made by the ancient Aryans sometime after 1500 B.C.

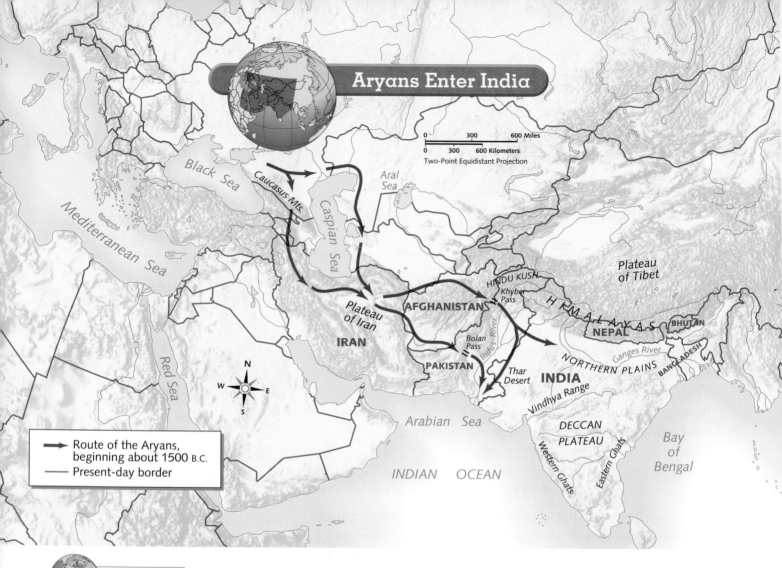

Aryans Enter India

Route of the Aryans, beginning about 1500 B.C.
Present-day border

Movement This map shows Aryan migration into India beginning about 1500 B.C.

■ *Why do you suppose the Aryans stopped and settled in northern India?*

became farmers. Small villages rose up in the countryside. In the following centuries Indian life and work came to center on the villages. Even today, although India has huge cities, it remains a nation of villages.

REVIEW *Why did the Aryans leave their homeland?*

Hinduism

The ideas of the Aryans can be seen in present-day Indian culture and beliefs. For example, the Aryans brought their language, **Sanskrit**, to India. Many Indian languages of today are based on Sanskrit.

The Aryans believed that Sanskrit was a holy language, the language spoken by the gods. The Aryans' holiest books, the **Vedas** (VAY•duhz), are written in Sanskrit. These four books of sacred writings describe the Aryan religion.

The Aryan religion developed into the religion of Hinduism. **Hinduism** is one of the oldest religions still practiced today. Believers in Hinduism worship three main gods—Brahma the Creator, Vishnu the Preserver, and Shiva the Destroyer. Below these gods are many other lesser gods.

Hinduism teaches that people live many lives until they reach spiritual perfection. Hindus believe that the soul lives on after death and returns to life in a new body. This rebirth is called **reincarnation**. According to Hinduism, those who obey their religious teachings and lead good lives will be reborn into higher social positions. Those who do not will return as lower lifeforms. Hindus also believe that animals have souls and that cows are holy. For this reason, many do not eat beef.

REVIEW *What religion of today comes from the religion of the Aryans?*

The Caste System

For hundreds of years Aryan priests used the Vedas and the belief in reincarnation to give order to their society. Following the teachings of the Vedas, the Aryans divided their society into social classes: priests, warriors, farmers and merchants, and common people. In India the Aryans added a lower group for the conquered Indians.

The Aryan social classes led to India's caste system. A **caste** is a group within a social class. A person born into one caste could never change caste or mix with members of other castes. Caste members lived, married, and worked within their own group.

To the Indian people the caste system was like the human body. The Brahmans (BRAH•muhnz), the priests and scholars, made up the head. The Kshatriyas (KSHAH•tree•uhz), the rulers and warriors, made up the arms. The Vaisyas (VYSH•yuhz), the farmers and merchants, made up the legs. The Sudras (SOO•druhz), the laborers, craftworkers, and servants, made up the feet.

The Hindu god Shiva

Below all the castes were the **untouchables**. These people did all the unpleasant jobs in Indian society. They picked up garbage, cleaned stables, and handled the dead. Untouchables were thought to be impure. They had to avoid all contact with the rest of society. An untouchable could not even let his or her shadow fall on a person of a higher caste.

Hinduism required people to accept the caste into which they were born. Each person had a place in society and a job to do. Life might be hard, but if people did the work of their caste, there was hope that the next life would be better.

Around the sixth century B.C., a new religion appeared in India. This new religion challenged the rituals and caste system of Hinduism.

REVIEW *What was the ancient Indian caste system?*

This statue (far left) made in the A.D. 100s shows a servant from the Sudra caste. At near left are two Brahmans, or priests. Brahmans are often shown with the right hand raised as a sign of understanding.

The Origins of Buddhism

An Indian story tells that a traveling Brahman met a stranger one day. The Brahman asked the stranger's name and received this answer:

66 Although born in the world, grown up in the world, having overcome the world, I abide unsoiled by the world. Take it that I am Buddha. 99

We know little of this man who called himself Buddha, or "the Enlightened One." What we do know comes from information written many years after his death. These writings tell us that his given name was Siddhartha Gautama (sih•DAR•tuh GOW•tuh•muh). Born in northern India in 563 B.C., Gautama lived a comfortable life as the son of an Indian prince. His father gave him everything he wanted and kept him from seeing the suffering of the common people.

At about age 30, Gautama went outside the walls of his palace for the first time. Outside the walls, he saw an old man bent over with age. Then, he came upon a man too sick to care for himself. Finally, he saw a dead body. Gautama asked a servant to explain what he had seen. The servant said that age, sickness, and death come to us all. This answer was not enough for Gautama. Why, he asked, was there so much suffering? How might this suffering be ended? Gautama decided to spend the rest of his life finding the answers

Buddha has been pictured in many ways by artists from many cultures. The cave wall painting showing Buddha seated on a lotus flower (left) and the carving of a seated Buddha (below) were found in the Ajanta Caves in Hyderabad, India.

to his questions. He left his father's palace and lived the life of a wandering beggar.

For a few years Gautama studied with Brahman priests. Then he continued his search for knowledge by praying and fasting. Nothing helped him find answers. One day Gautama sat down to rest under a tree. He began once again to think about the problem. After hours of deep thought, Gautama suddenly felt that he understood the meaning of life. He decided that people should seek love, truth, the joy of knowledge, and a calm mind. At that moment he became Buddha, the Enlightened One.

Gautama spent the rest of his life carrying his message to all who would listen. After his death his followers told of his teachings. **Buddhism**, the religion based on those teachings, eventually spread across Asia.

Neither Buddha nor his followers organized a central church. They did not write holy books like the Vedas. Their aim was to set an example for others. They did so through unselfish and peaceful behavior.

REVIEW *Why did Gautama begin a search for truth?*

Path of Buddhism

Practicing proper concentration

Knowledge of the truth

Controlling feelings and thoughts

Deciding to resist evil

Nirvana

Striving to free one's mind of evil

Saying nothing to hurt others

Holding a job that does not hurt others

Respecting life and property

LEARNING FROM CHARTS Buddhists follow these eight points, called the Noble Eightfold Path, in their search for nirvana—a feeling of happiness, peace, and complete understanding.

■ *Why would practicing proper concentration be important?*

LESSON 1 REVIEW

Check Understanding

1 Remember the Facts Where did the Aryans come from? Where did they migrate to?

2 Recall the Main Idea How did the Aryan migrations affect civilization in India?

Think Critically

3 Past to Present Today India is an industrialized country. What effect do you think the development of industry has had on the caste system?

4 Explore Viewpoints If you had been a Brahman in early Indian society, how might you have felt about the teachings of Buddha? How might you have felt about the teachings if you had been an untouchable?

Show What You Know

Research Activity Use information from this textbook and from encyclopedias and almanacs to create a chart comparing Indian civilization before and after the arrival of the Aryans. Topics you might present include how people lived, where people lived, what religions people practiced, and what the social classes were.

Use a Cultural Map

1. Why Learn This Skill?

Symbols on road signs give people information without using words. They show information in a way that lets people understand it quickly. If you see a road sign showing a picture of a leaping deer, for example, you know that deer cross the road there. On maps, too, symbols show information in a way that lets people understand it quickly. For example, map symbols may show you where certain products are made or where battles were fought.

Like other kinds of maps, cultural maps can give you a general picture of a region of the world. Cultural maps may use symbols that show places where most of the people speak a certain language or follow a certain religion. These maps can help you understand more about the people and cultures in those places.

2. Think About Map Symbols

This map of the present-day Indian subcontinent has two map keys. The key on the left uses colors as symbols. The colors divide the subcontinent into regions based on language. The color key shows that there are five major language groups on the Indian subcontinent.

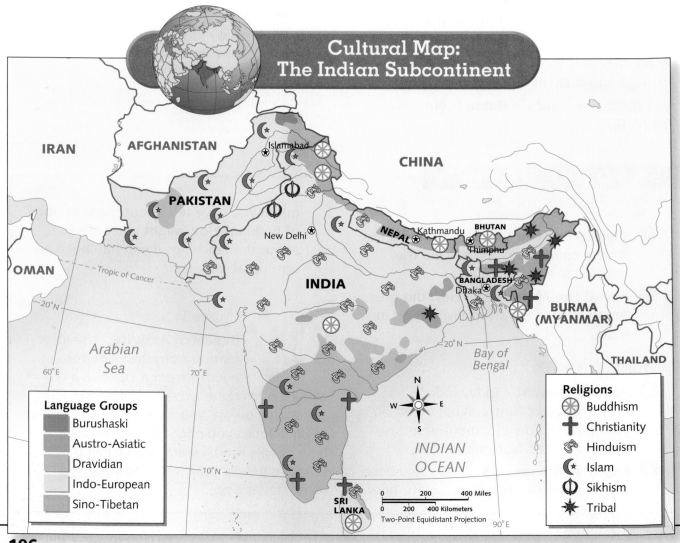

Cultural Map: The Indian Subcontinent

Language Groups
- Burushaski
- Austro-Asiatic
- Dravidian
- Indo-European
- Sino-Tibetan

Religions
- Buddhism
- Christianity
- Hinduism
- Islam
- Sikhism
- Tribal

IRAN
AFGHANISTAN
Islamabad
CHINA
PAKISTAN
New Delhi
NEPAL Kathmandu BHUTAN
Thimphu
OMAN
Tropic of Cancer
INDIA
BANGLADESH
Dhaka
20°N
BURMA (MYANMAR)
Arabian Sea
60°E 70°E
20°N Bay of Bengal
THAILAND
INDIAN OCEAN
10°N
SRI LANKA
0 200 400 Miles
0 200 400 Kilometers
Two-Point Equidistant Projection
90°E

One of these is the Indo-European group. One language within the Indo-European group is Hindi, the official language of India today. Other Indo-European languages, including English, are also spoken in India.

The map key on the right of the map uses pictures as symbols. Each picture symbol stands for a major religion and is shown in the middle of an area where that religion is practiced. Look at the symbol for Hinduism. It is the written form of *om*, a sacred Hindu word. The symbol for Buddhism is the Wheel of the Law. The spokes of the wheel stand for parts of the Noble Eightfold Path in Buddhist teachings.

3. Understand the Process

Now that you know about the symbols in the map keys, use these questions as a guide for making generalizations about the present-day cultures of the Indian subcontinent.

1 Identify the color that covers most of the northern half of India. What generalizations can you make about the language of the people who live there?

2 What is the main language group in southern India?

3 What is the main language group in Pakistan?

4 What do the symbols in Pakistan tell you?

5 In what country do most of the people follow Buddhism?

6 How is Sri Lanka divided according to language groups?

7 Do all the people in Bangladesh follow the same religion? Explain your answer.

8 Make a generalization about language and religion in each of these countries: Bangladesh, Bhutan, India, and Pakistan.

4. Think and Apply

Draw a cultural map of all of Asia. Then use an encyclopedia, atlas, or almanac to gather the information you will need. Use colors to show different language groups, and use picture symbols to show where different religions are practiced. Be sure to label the countries. What language groups and religions will appear on your map that do not appear on the map on page 196? Have a classmate use your map to make some generalizations about the cultures of present-day Asia.

MAP SKILLS

Sikh "Golden Temple" at Amritsar, India, near the India-Pakistan border

Two Fables

from Jataka Tales

edited by Nancy DeRoin

illustrated by Navin Patel

When Buddha taught, he spoke in a way that all people could understand. Sometimes he used folktales to get his message across. A number of these folktales were fables, short stories that have animal characters and that teach a special lesson. Buddha's followers believed that he remembered these fables from past lives, when his soul was in the bodies of various animals. Many years after Buddha's death, some of these fables were collected and written down in a book called the **Jataka Tales,** *or "Birth Stories." Although animals speak the words, the messages they have for humans are very clear.*

The Wonders of Palace Life

Once upon a time when Brahmadatta ruled Benares, a young monkey lived with a troop of monkeys near the Himalaya

Mountains. A woodsman caught him and gave him to the king as a present.

During the winter months, the monkey lived as a palace pet. He charmed the king and the royal family with his ways. The monkey was allowed to run freely in the palace, and he learned a great deal about the ways of men.

When summer came, the king and his court prepared to move to the summer palace. The king called for the woodsman and said, "I have been very pleased with this little monkey. He has amused us very much. Here is a reward for you." And he gave the woodsman a sack of gold coins.

"Now, as a reward for this monkey, I want you to return him to the place where you captured him and set him free."

The woodsman was pleased to do as the king wished. The monkey, once free, returned to the Himalayas, and the monkey troop all gathered on a large rock to hear about his adventures.

"Friend," they asked, "where have you been all this time?"

"In the king's palace at Benares."

"How did you get free?"

"I amused the king and his court so well that the king felt kindly toward me and set me free."

"You must know all about palace life. How grand it must be! We would like to live in that grand style. Will you teach us the ways of men?"

At first the monkey refused. "No, you would not like to live that way."

But the monkeys insisted that he teach them the ways of men.

The monkey was allowed to run freely in the palace, and he learned a great deal about the ways of men.

said, "Now, you are king. You must sit on this rock and order all the monkeys to bring you fruit."

The king monkey did as he was told. Each monkey brought him fruit.

"But I cannot eat all this fruit," the king monkey said.

"The fruit," said the monkey who had lived at the palace, "is not for you to eat. It is for you to keep in a big pile. To be king, you must be rich. To be rich, you must have a big pile of fruit."

So the monkeys, wishing to live like men, piled a mountain of fruit behind the king monkey.

"What next?" they all asked.

"Now all of you must approach the king and compliment him." The monkeys gladly agreed.

"Oh, King," one said, "your fur is very thick and shiny."

"Oh, King," said another, "your eyes are very bold and bright."

"Oh, King," said a third, "you are wise and very strong." And this went on until all the monkeys had spoken the king's praise.

"Now," said the monkey who had lived in the palace, "all you monkeys

So the monkeys stood behind the king monkey and said in turn:

"His fur is thin. I think he must be getting bald."

"His eyes are dull. I don't think his eyesight is what it used to be."

"He is as weak as a worm and almost as stupid."

Finally, the king monkey became so angry that he left his throne and started chasing the monkeys who were insulting him. When he returned, all his fruit was gone.

"My fruit! My fruit! Someone has taken all my fruit!"

"Now," said the monkey who lived in the palace, "you must find the guilty monkey and put him to death."

"To death?" the king monkey cried. "Oh, what are you saying?" And he covered his ears with his hands and buried his head between his knees.

"Stop! Stop!" all the monkeys cried, covering their ears. "Teach us no more about palace life." And they ran away, crying:

Flattering, lying, stealing, killing,
The ways of men are really chilling!
If in a palace men do these,
We're safer here among our trees.

Friends and Neighbors

One day while hunting deer, a big lion slipped down a steep hill and landed in a swamp. Due to his great weight,

he sank into the mud up to his neck. Try as he might, he could not get out. As soon as he lifted one foot, the other three sank in deeper. Finally, afraid to struggle any more for fear of sinking in above his head, he stood as still as a stone with only his huge head sticking out of the mud.

He stood there for seven days, his feet sunk like posts in the mud, without a bite to eat or a drop to drink.

Toward the end of the seventh day, a jackal, who was hunting for food, came upon him. Seeing a lion's head sticking out of the mud, the jackal ran away yelping in terror. But the lion called after him:

"I say, jackal, Stop! Don't run away. Here am I, caught fast in the mud. Please save me!"

The jackal came back slowly, looked at the lion, and said, "I could get you out I think, but I am afraid that once free you would eat me."

"Do not fear," the lion said. "If you save me, I will be your friend for life."

The jackal decided to trust him. He dug a hole around each of the lion's four feet. From these holes, he dug trenches out to the nearby pond. Water from the pond filled the trenches and ran into the holes at the lion's feet. It made the mud very soft, indeed. Then the jackal said:

"Now, make one great effort!"

The weakened lion strained every nerve, every muscle, every bone in his body. At last his feet broke loose from the mud with a loud slurp! The lion crawled onto dry land.

After washing the mud from his golden body, the great lion killed a buffalo and said to the jackal, "Help

he saved part of the meat.

"Why do you not eat your fill?" the lion asked.

"I am saving some to take to my mate," the jackal replied.

"I, too, have a mate," said the lion. "I will go with you."

When they neared the jackal's den, his mate almost died of fright to see a huge lion heading straight toward her cave. But the jackal called out:

"Fear nothing. This lion is my friend." And the lion said to her, "Now, my lady, from this day on I am going to share my life with you and your family." He led the jackals to the place where he lived, and they moved into a cave next to his own.

After that, the jackal and the lion would go hunting together, leaving their mates at home. Soon, cubs were born to both families, and as they grew, they played together.

But one day, quite suddenly, the lioness thought, "My mate seems very fond of those jackals. It does not seem mind, and she could think of nothing else. "We are lions and they are jackals," she thought. "I must get rid of them."

So, whenever the lion and the jackal were away on the hunt, the lioness began to frighten her neighbor. The lioness would spring from hiding and snarl, "Why do you stay where you are not wanted?" Or she would creep up on the sleeping jackal and hiss in her ear, "Do you not know when your life is in danger?" Then again, she would say under her breath, "Such darling little jackal cubs. Too bad their mother does not care about their safety."

Finally, the mother jackal told her mate all that had been happening. "It is clear," she said, "that the lion must have told his wife to do this. We have been here a long time, and he is tired of us. Let us leave, or those lions will be the death of us."

Hearing this, the jackal went to the lion and said:

"Friend lion, in this world the strong will always have their way. But, I must say, even if one does not like a neighbor, it is cruel to frighten his wife and children half to death."

"Why, what are you talking about?" the lion asked in surprise.

Then the jackal told him how the lioness had been scaring his wife and cubs. The lion listened very carefully; then he called his wife before him. In front of everyone he said:

"Wife, do you remember long ago when I was out hunting and did not come back for a week? After that, I brought this jackal and his wife back with me."

"Yes, I remember very well," the lioness replied.

"Do you know why I was gone for a week?"

"No, I do not," she answered.

"I was ashamed to tell you then," the lion said, "but I will now. I was trying to catch a deer, and I jumped too far, slipped down a hill, and got stuck fast in the mud. There I stayed for a week without food or water. Then along came this jackal and saved my life. This jackal is my friend."

From that day on, the lions and jackals lived in peace and friendship. Furthermore, after their parents died, the cubs did not part. They, too, lived together in friendship, always remembering the words of the great lion:

A friend who truly acts like one,
Whoever he may be,
Is my comrade and my kin,
He is flesh and blood to me.

LITERATURE REVIEW

1. What lessons do you think people today might learn from these fables?

2. What message is Buddha teaching in the fable of the monkeys? in the fable of the lion and the jackal?

3. Consider a quality that is important to you—responsibility, honesty, friendship, cooperation, or respect for others, for example. Write your own fable that teaches a message about that quality. Be sure to end your fable with a verse, as in the *Jataka Tales.*

United Rule in India

FOCUS
What forces create and maintain unity among people?

Main Idea As you read, think about the methods used by Maurya and Gupta rulers to unite India.

Vocabulary
rajah
assassination
turning point
missionary
Arabic numeral
inoculation

During the time of Buddha, India was a divided land. Princes called **rajahs** ruled over large city-states rich in foods, jewels, and metals. This wealth attracted invaders such as the Persians from Asia and then the Greeks from Europe. For more than 200 years after the death of Buddha, parts of the Indian subcontinent were held by outsiders. Finally, a young Indian emperor drove the invaders out of India and conquered all the rajahs.

India's First Empire

Around 320 B.C. the young emperor, Chandragupta Maurya (chuhn•druh•GUP•tuh MOW•ree•uh), united India and formed the Maurya Empire. Chandragupta Maurya ruled the new empire harshly. He made peasants work as slaves to chop down forests, drain swamps, and farm the newly cleared land. He then taxed the crops that were grown.

Chandragupta's cruelty made him many enemies in the empire. He feared for his own safety. He had servants taste all his food before he ate it. To protect himself from assassination, Chandragupta slept in a different room every night. An **assassination** (uh•sa•suh•NAY•shun) is murder for a political reason. No attack came, however. In 297 B.C. Chandragupta quietly gave up the throne to his son.

Chandragupta and his son governed the empire according to ideas in a book called the *Arthashastra* (ar•thuh•SHAH•struh). The *Arthashastra* said that rulers

Arthashastra, both Chandragupta and his son expanded the Maurya Empire to include what is today western Pakistan and southern India.

REVIEW *What kind of ruler was Chandragupta?*

This Mauryan artwork is part of a series of tablets that describe ancient emperors.

The Reign of Ashoka

Chandragupta's grandson, Ashoka (uh•SHOH•kuh), became Maurya emperor about 273 B.C. The new emperor ruled as firmly as his father and grandfather had. "Any power superior in might to another should launch into war," Ashoka believed.

About 265 B.C. Ashoka's army marched into the kingdom of Kalinga on the empire's southern border. In a vicious war Maurya forces crushed the Kalingans. Ashoka recorded that "150,000 people were deported, 100,000 were killed, and many times that number died."

The invasion of Kalinga was a turning point in Ashoka's life. A **turning point** is a

During the time of the Mauryas, Buddhists built large stupas, or religious shrines. The Great Stupa (below) at Sanchi, India, still stands today. This stupa, like most, is filled with ancient drawings and carvings (left).

time of important change. The bloody invasion of Kalinga turned Ashoka against violence. He began to follow the teachings of Buddha. He refused to eat meat or to hunt and kill animals. His change led many of his people to adopt peaceful ways, too.

To spread the message of Buddhism, Ashoka issued a number of edicts. He had these edicts carved on rocks and stone pillars along main roads, where people might easily read them. One of Ashoka's edicts called on people to show "obedience to mother and father." Ashoka also sent **missionaries**, or religious teachers, to carry the ideas of Buddhism to other parts of Asia.

Ashoka used his power to make the lives of his people better. At his command, people began to place less importance on the caste system.

So fair was Ashoka that he is known in history as "the greatest and noblest ruler India has known." Yet not long after his death in 232 B.C., his good works were forgotten for a time. The caste system returned. The ideas of Buddhism faded away in India. Today, however, the people of India again honor Ashoka. The lion and the wheel, two designs Ashoka used to decorate his edicts, are symbols of present-day India.

REVIEW *What principles guided*

vasion of Kalinga?

This sculpture of an armed soldier can be found on the Stupa of Babrut, in India.

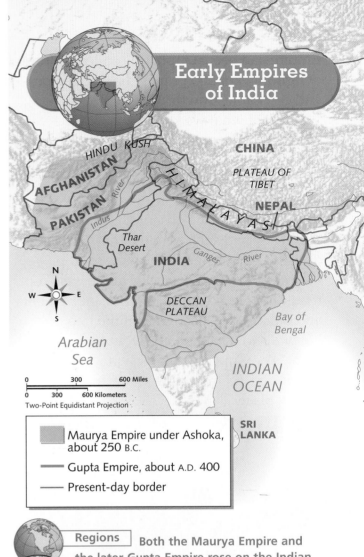

Early Empires of India

Regions Both the Maurya Empire and the later Gupta Empire rose on the Indian subcontinent of Asia.

■ *Why do you think neither empire expanded northeast into what is today China?*

The Guptas Come to Power

Only 50 years after Ashoka's death, the Maurya Empire broke up into quarreling city-states. About 500 years passed before another great empire, the Gupta Empire,

of a small kingdom in the Ganges Valley. Chandragupta I soon controlled much of the valley. His son Samudra (suh•MUH•druh) Gupta and grandson Chandragupta II enlarged the empire. Even so, the Gupta Empire never grew as large as the Maurya

Empire had been. Gupta rule ended centuries of fighting. For 200 years India enjoyed peace and economic growth.

Much of what we know about Gupta society comes from the writings of Faxian (FAH•SHYUHN), a Chinese Buddhist monk. Around A.D. 400 Faxian traveled through India and wrote down what he saw. The people, he observed, "are very well off." They had such freedom that "if they desire to go, they go; if they like to stop, they stop." Faxian marveled at the well-kept roads and the beautiful temples, monuments, and palaces. He also wrote of the free hospitals to which people went for treatment. The Gupta Empire, Faxian concluded, seemed to be a safe and happy place.

REVIEW *What was life like during Gupta times?*

The Golden Age of India

Faxian visited India during the rule of Chandragupta II. Historians call this period India's Golden Age. It was a time of peace, growth, and progress.

During the Golden Age, Chandragupta II supported many artists and writers. Perhaps the most famous of these was Kalidasa (kah•lih•DAH•suh), an author known for his poems and plays. Unknown writers collected and wrote down a series of folktales called the *Panchatantra* (pahn•chah•TAHN•truh). Over the centuries these popular tales traveled throughout the world. You may know some of the stories, such as "Sinbad the Sailor" and "Jack the Giant-Killer."

Many important advances were made in mathematics and medicine. Indian

This coin (at right) shows Chandragupta II, who led ancient India during its Golden Age. The rulers of ancient India understood the importance of learning. These rulers began universities to help the Indian people gain knowledge. Below are the ruins of an ancient Buddhist university in what is now Nalanda, India.

The Ajanta Caves, in India, are actually Buddhist temples that were carved from solid rock sometime between 200 B.C. and A.D. 600. These caves have given much information about the ancient cultures of India.

mathematicians developed the base-ten number system: 1 through 9 and the zero. These so-called **Arabic numerals** were used in India as early as A.D. 595 before they were borrowed by Arab traders.

During the Golden Age, Indian doctors discovered ways to set broken bones and to help women give birth. Like surgeons today, they used skin from other parts of the body to mend ears and noses. Understanding the need for cleanliness in surgery, they sterilized their cutting tools. Indian doctors also used the technique of **inoculation**, giving a person a mild form of a disease so that he or she would not get sick with a more serious form. European and American doctors did not use inoculation until the 1700s.

Many of the ideas of India were carried to other lands by traders. Arab merchants took Indian spices, cloth, carpets, and jewelry west to the Mediterranean region. They carried Indian books and ideas to Europe and Africa. News of India's innovations reached many parts of the world.

REVIEW *What important advances took place during Gupta times?*

LESSON 3 REVIEW

Check Understanding

1 **Remember the Facts** Who created India's first empire? What ruler suddenly turned against violent ways?

2 **Recall the Main Idea** What methods

similar? How were they different?

Think Critically

3 **Personally Speaking** Who was more suited to be a leader, Chandragupta Maurya or Ashoka? Why?

4 **Think More About It** Why do historians refer to the period of the Gupta kings as India's Golden Age?

by following Buddhist teachings. Imagine that you are a visitor to the India of Ashoka's time. In your own words, describe the effect of Ashoka's actions on the Indian people.

LESSON 4

The Persian Empire

FOCUS

How do powerful leaders create change?

Main Idea As you read, think about the ways strong leaders played a role in the development of the Persian Empire and its civilization.

Vocabulary

plateau
cavalry
tribute
courier
prophet
Zoroastrianism

Some Aryans migrated to lands west of India and settled in what is now the country of Iran around 900 B.C. The name *Iran* may come from the word *Aryan*. The Aryan people of Iran came to be known as Persians.

Cyrus, the Empire Builder

The Persians of long ago lived on the Plateau of Iran, a large area stretching from India to the Zagros Mountains. From the **plateau**, a high, flat area of land, the Persians spread out in all directions. They began by conquering the Babylonians in the Fertile Crescent in 539 B.C. and the Egyptians in 525 B.C. Over the years, they formed the largest empire the world had seen.

The Persian army was huge. Its size and advanced war technology overwhelmed its enemies. Persian footsoldiers wore bronze helmets and carried shields. This protection often made them the winners in hand-to-hand combat.

The Persians used **cavalry**, soldiers who rode horses and camels, to make swift attacks. In addition, they fought in war chariots with sharp knives attached to the wheels. The Persians fought well not only on land but also at sea. Within 20 years the Persian army had conquered lands all the way from northern India to northern Africa.

The leader who built the Persian Empire was Cyrus the Great. The only battle Cyrus lost was his last. In that battle he led his army to fight people who lived near the Caspian Sea. Their ruler was Queen Tomyris (tuh•MY•ruhs). Angered at the Persian invasion of her land, Queen Tomyris led her smaller army

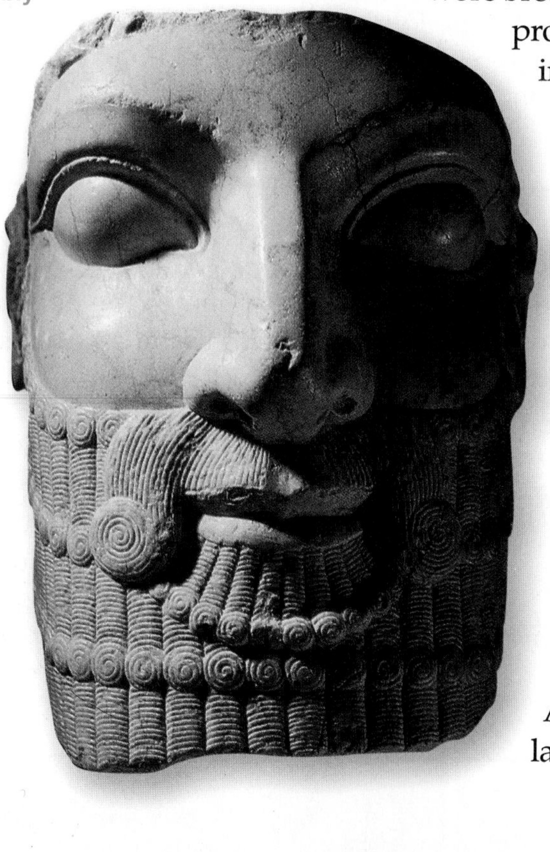

The subject of this sculpture is possibly Cyrus the Great, who built the ancient Persian Empire.

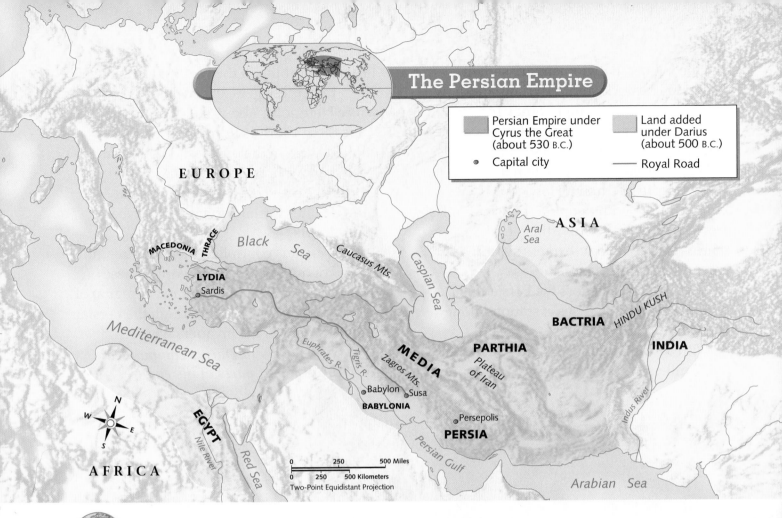

Persian Empire under Cyrus the Great (about 530 B.C.)
Land added under Darius (about 500 B.C.)
● Capital city
— Royal Road

Movement The Persian Empire gained most of its land under Cyrus the Great.

■ *On what continents did Darius add new territories?*

against Cyrus's fighting force. One historian, Herodotus (hih•RAH•duh•tuhs) of Greece, later offered the following description of the battle:

66 First the two armies stood apart and shot their arrows at each other. Then, when their quivers were empty, they closed and fought hand-to-hand with
~~lances and daggers. And thus they~~
~~neither choosing to give ground~~ . . .

In the end most of the Persians were killed, including Cyrus the Great. Persia's time of great growth had ended.

REVIEW *What leader created the Persian Empire?*

Darius, the Organizer

Darius (duh•RY•uhs), a later Persian emperor, faced the task of organizing the large empire. Darius was a successful organizer. He let the different peoples in the empire keep their own customs and chose local leaders to rule. Darius also completed many projects to improve travel
Nile River.

The people conquered by the Persians were expected to send **tribute**, or yearly payments, to the emperor. At Persepolis (per•SEH•puh•luhs), the capital built by Darius, artists left a record in stone of people

Chapter 6 • **209**

paying tribute. Babylonians are shown bringing livestock, and Assyrians are shown bringing hides of tanned leather. Indians carry containers of gold dust. Other people offer fine cloth, pottery, horses, and camels.

Darius faced a great problem in ruling his widespread empire. How could he communicate with people a thousand miles from his capital? To solve this problem, Darius started a pony-express system for delivering messages. Riders called **couriers** galloped across the Persian Empire, changing horses at stations along the way.

With couriers, information could travel 1,677 miles (2,699 km) in seven days.

"There is nothing in the world that travels faster than these Persian couriers," wrote Herodotus about 440 B.C. "Nothing stops these couriers from covering their allotted stage in the quickest possible time—neither snow, rain, heat, nor darkness." Words like these are used today by the United States Postal Service to describe its mail carriers.

The Persians controlled their empire until it was conquered by other people. These invaders came from the west in the region of the Mediterranean Sea. Although the Persian army was larger, the invaders were stronger.

REVIEW *How did Darius communicate with the different parts of his empire?*

In the wall carving (left), people under Persian control offer tribute to Darius, the Persian ruler from 522 B.C. to 486 B.C. Below are the ruins of Darius's palace in Persepolis. Today Persepolis is part of Iran.

Zarathustra the Prophet

The earliest Persians worshipped many gods. But a prophet named Zarathustra (zar•uh•THOOS•trah) changed that. A **prophet** is a person who others believe speaks or writes with a divine message. Zarathustra began a religion called **Zoroastrianism** (zohr•uh•WASS•tree•uh•nih•zuhm), which taught a belief in two gods.

One god was the good and kind Ahura Mazda, or "Wise Lord." Ahura Mazda stood for truth. The other god, Ahriman, was his enemy. Zoroastrians believed that good and evil fought each other but that one day good would win. "The Earth is a battleground, a struggle between forces of light and forces of darkness," said Zarathustra. People who followed Zoroastrianism believed that they would live in a paradise after they died.

As the Persians built their empire, they spread the customs of their culture. As their empire declined, they had to fight

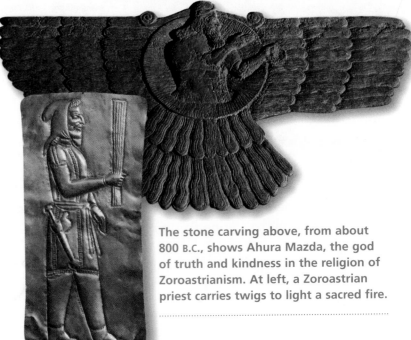

The stone carving above, from about 800 B.C., shows Ahura Mazda, the god of truth and kindness in the religion of Zoroastrianism. At left, a Zoroastrian priest carries twigs to light a sacred fire.

their conquerors to hold on to their Persian heritage. First they fought the Greeks and later the Byzantines. The fight continued until about A.D. 750. At that time the Arabs conquered the region. They brought their culture and the religion of Islam to the area.

REVIEW *What is Zoroastrianism?*

LESSON 4 REVIEW

Check Understanding

1 **Remember the Facts** Who expanded the Persian Empire to its largest size?

2 **Recall the Main Idea** What was one accomplishment of each of these people: Cyrus, Darius, and Zarathustra?

important for messages to reach all parts of the Persian Empire quickly?

4 **Cause and Effect** What might have happened if Cyrus had won his battle against Queen Tomyris?

Show What You Know

Simulation Activity
Congratulations! You have been elected president of your class. Prepare an acceptance speech in which you describe the changes you plan to make as a strong but fair

If a tape recorder is available, you may want to record your speech and play it back to see how it sounds. Present your speech to your family or to your classmates.

1500 B.C.   1000 B.C.

About 1500 B.C.
• Aryan migrations
  to India begin

563 B.C.
• Buddha
  is born

CONNECT MAIN IDEAS

Use this organizer to describe the cultures of ancient India and Persia. List three details to express each main idea listed below. A copy of the organizer appears on page 44 of the Activity Book.

India and Persia

Aryans Bring Changes to India

The arrival of the Aryans changed life for the early people of India.

1. _____
2. _____
3. _____

United Rule in India

Maurya and Gupta rulers used different methods to unite India.

1. _____
2. _____
3. _____

The Persian Empire

Strong leaders played an important role in the development of the Persian Empire and its civilization.

1. _____
2. _____
3. _____

WRITE MORE ABOUT IT

Write Questions Write five questions you would like to ask someone who practices the religion of Hinduism today.

Write to Compare and Contrast Write several paragraphs that tell ways the religions of Hinduism and Buddhism are similar and ways they are different.

Write a Description This quotation from the *Arthashastra* describes how some rulers govern: "Government is the science of punishment." Do you agree that punishing citizens is a good way for rulers to govern? Why or why not? Write your own brief description of a good government.

500 B.C.   B.C. | A.D.   A.D. 500   A.D. 1000

About 320 B.C.
• Maurya Empire begins

A.D. 320
• Gupta Empire begins

About A.D. 750
• Arabs conquer the Persian Empire

USE VOCABULARY

For each group of terms, write a sentence or two that explain how the terms are related.

1. Sanskrit, Vedas
2. Hinduism, caste, untouchable
3. Arabic numeral, inoculation
4. prophet, Zoroastrianism

CHECK UNDERSTANDING

5. What advantage did the Aryans have over the native people of India in the competition for farmland?

6. What were some of the things the Aryans brought to India?

7. Who are the three main gods of the Hindu religion?

8. How did the caste system affect early Indian society?

9. What caused Siddhartha Gautama to begin his search for knowledge?

10. What was the turning point of Ashoka's life?

11. What important contributions were made during India's Golden Age?

12. How did Darius's pony-express system affect Persia?

13. **Think More About It** How might a belief in reincarnation help people who live in the Indian subcontinent and are part of the Hindu caste system?

14. **Explore Viewpoints** How would a Hindu priest probably view the Hindu caste system? How might an untouchable feel about it?

15. **Past to Present** Buddhism has spread to many countries with very different cultures. Why do you think Buddhism is followed in so many different places?

16. **Personally Speaking** Imagine that you are a member of the Sudra class. Do you plan to willingly accept your place in society? Explain why or why not.

APPLY SKILLS

Use a Cultural Map Select a present-day country anywhere in the world. Use an encyclopedia to find out which religions and languages are most common in different parts of the country. Make a map that shows this information. Show different religions and different languages through the use of colors and symbols. Then exchange maps with a classmate. Write a paragraph that describes the information shown on your classmate's map.

READ MORE ABOUT IT

Come with Me to India by Sudha Koul. Cashmir. This book covers many subjects, including the government

HARCOURT BRACE

Visit the Internet at
http://www.hbschool.com
for additional resources.

RELIGION in the WORLD TODAY

Religion has always played an important part in people's lives. Religion connects people who share beliefs. Many countries have a national religion or have one religion that most of its people follow. More than 80 percent of the people in India today are Hindus. In Japan most people are Buddhists or Shintoists.

Unlike other countries in the world, the United States was founded on the idea of religious freedom. The Bill of Rights of the United States Constitution gives citizens the freedom to follow their own religious beliefs, whatever they may be. Members of religions that have been followed for many centuries— Christianity, Islam, Hinduism, Buddhism, and Judaism—live together in the United States today. Followers of many newer religions live here, too. In fact, there are more than 1,000 different religious groups in our country!

BUILDING CITIZENSHIP

Read a number of news sources to learn how differences in religious beliefs are affecting people's lives today—in schools, government, and other parts of society. Look for examples from our country and from other countries. Then, with a partner, make a visual display of your information and share it with classmates.

HARCOURT BRACE

Visit the Internet at **http://www.hbschool.com** for additional resources.

CNN Turner Le@rning

Check your media center or classroom video library for the Making Social Studies Relevant videotape of this feature.

VISUAL SUMMARY

Summarize the Main Ideas
Study the pictures and captions to help you review the events you read about in Unit 3.

Examine the Scenes
Look closely at each scene. What details are shown for each period illustrated? After you have looked at every scene, write your own description for each.

1 The Chinese philosopher Confucius lived during a time of disorder known as the Warring Kingdoms Period.

4 The movement of Aryans into the Indian subcontinent caused many changes there.

5 The religions of Hinduism and Buddhism began in ancient India.

2 The emperor Shi Huangdi united many independent states to create China's first empire. Shi Huangdi is remembered for his Great Wall and for bringing standardization to China.

3 The Han dynasty was a time of great achievement for the Chinese in government, the arts, the recording of history, and trade.

6 The Gupta Empire in India brought about a time of growth in the arts, writing, mathematics, and medicine.

Persian Empire grow.

USE VOCABULARY

For each group of terms, write at least one sentence that shows how the terms are different from each other.

1 Legalism, bureaucracy

2 import, export

3 Silk road, caravan

4 Buddhism, reincarnation

5 cavalry, courier

CHECK UNDERSTANDING

6 What caused the breakdown of China's ruling system in the 700s B.C.?

7 What Chinese philosopher compared society to a family?

8 What were some of the innovations of the Han dynasty?

9 Who were the untouchables?

10 Who was Zarathustra?

THINK CRITICALLY

11 **Personally Speaking** What do you think it would have been like to live during the time of the Zhou? the Qin? the Han?

12 **Past to Present** The arrival of Aryan immigrants changed the culture of ancient India. How does the arrival of immigrants in the United States change lives today?

13 **Cause and Effect** What effect did the conflicts of China's Warring Kingdoms Period have on Chinese society?

14 **Think More About It** In what ways were ancient India and ancient China alike? How were they different?

APPLY SKILLS

Use a Cultural Map The labels on the map below show the location of cultural groups in China. The colors show languages spoken. Use the map to answer the questions.

15 In what parts of China are languages other than Chinese spoken?

16 Why do you think different cultural groups live mainly on the edges of China?

17 Which groups live along the western and southern borders of China?

18 What language is spoken most often in China?

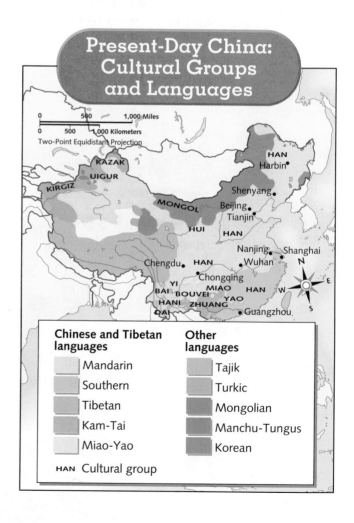

Present-Day China: Cultural Groups and Languages

Chinese and Tibetan languages
- Mandarin
- Southern
- Tibetan
- Kam-Tai
- Miao-Yao

Other languages
- Tajik
- Turkic
- Mongolian
- Manchu-Tungus
- Korean

HAN Cultural group

REMEMBER

- Share your ideas.
- Cooperate with others to plan your work.
- Take responsibility for your work.
- Help one another.
- Show your group's work to the class.
- Discuss what you learned by working together.

Make a Class Collage

ACTIVITY

As a class, make a collage that illustrates some of the ideas of Confucianism. Cut out magazine and newspaper pictures of people doing things that show each idea. Place pictures showing the same idea near each other in the collage. Then label each idea. Display the collage outside your classroom.

Tell a Fable

ACTIVITY

With three or four classmates, think of a message you would like to give to the world. Then, with your group, write a fable that tells the message in an interesting way. Present your fable orally to the class.

Make a Travel Plan

ACTIVITY

Imagine that you have a chance to visit China. Make a list of the ancient Chinese sites you would most like to visit. Beside each entry, explain why you would want to visit that site. Describe each site in detail and tell why it is important in Chinese history. Compare your list with those of your classmates.

Unit Project Wrap-Up

Publish a Booklet Now you are ready to make your booklet about ancient India and China. To complete your booklet, you will work in a small group. First write an outline. Each group member should have a different job. One member could be the researcher, another member should review the writing and illustrations and proofread the completed booklet. When you finish, pass your booklet around the classroom.

THE MEDITERRANEAN

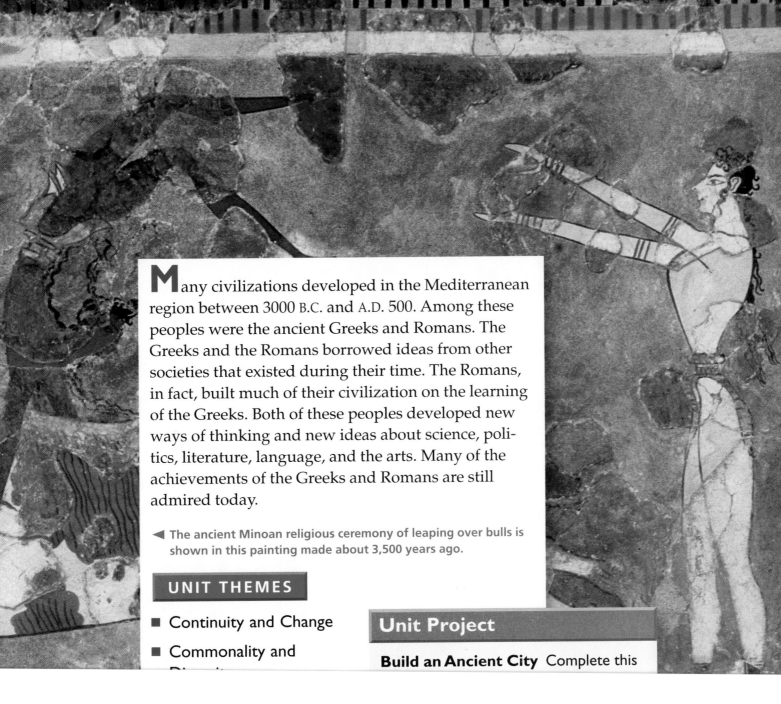

Many civilizations developed in the Mediterranean region between 3000 B.C. and A.D. 500. Among these peoples were the ancient Greeks and Romans. The Greeks and the Romans borrowed ideas from other societies that existed during their time. The Romans, in fact, built much of their civilization on the learning of the Greeks. Both of these peoples developed new ways of thinking and new ideas about science, politics, literature, language, and the arts. Many of the achievements of the Greeks and Romans are still admired today.

◄ The ancient Minoan religious ceremony of leaping over bulls is shown in this painting made about 3,500 years ago.

UNIT THEMES

- Continuity and Change
- Commonality and Diversity
- Individualism and Interdependence

Unit Project

Build an Ancient City Complete this ancient Greek or Roman city. As you read the unit, make a list of important features of Greek cities and Roman cities. Your list will help you plan how to build your own model.

221

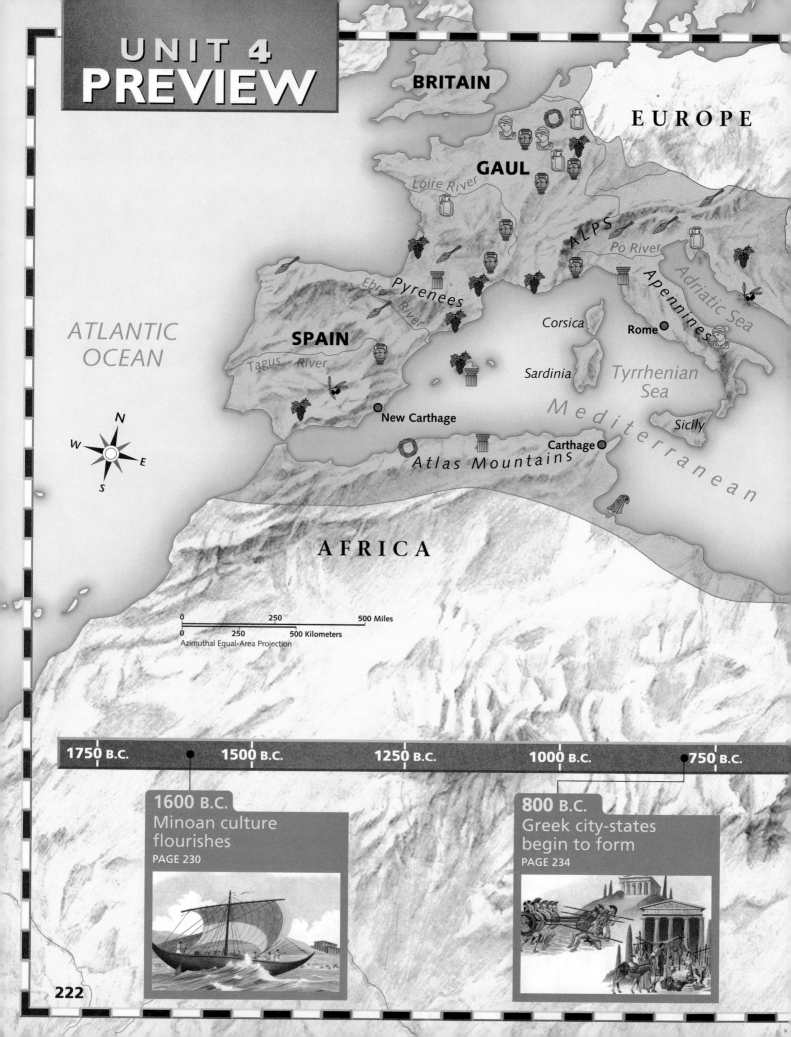

BRITAIN

EUROPE

GAUL

Loire River

ALPS

Po River

Adriatic Sea

Pyrenees

Ebro River

Apennines

ATLANTIC
OCEAN

Corsica

Rome

SPAIN

Tagus River

Sardinia

Tyrrhenian Sea

N
W   E
S

New Carthage

Sicily

Atlas Mountains

Carthage

Mediterranean

AFRICA

0   250   500 Miles
0   250   500 Kilometers
Azimuthal Equal-Area Projection

1750 B.C.   1500 B.C.   1250 B.C.   1000 B.C.   750 B.C.

1600 B.C.
Minoan culture
flourishes
PAGE 230

800 B.C.
Greek city-states
begin to form
PAGE 234

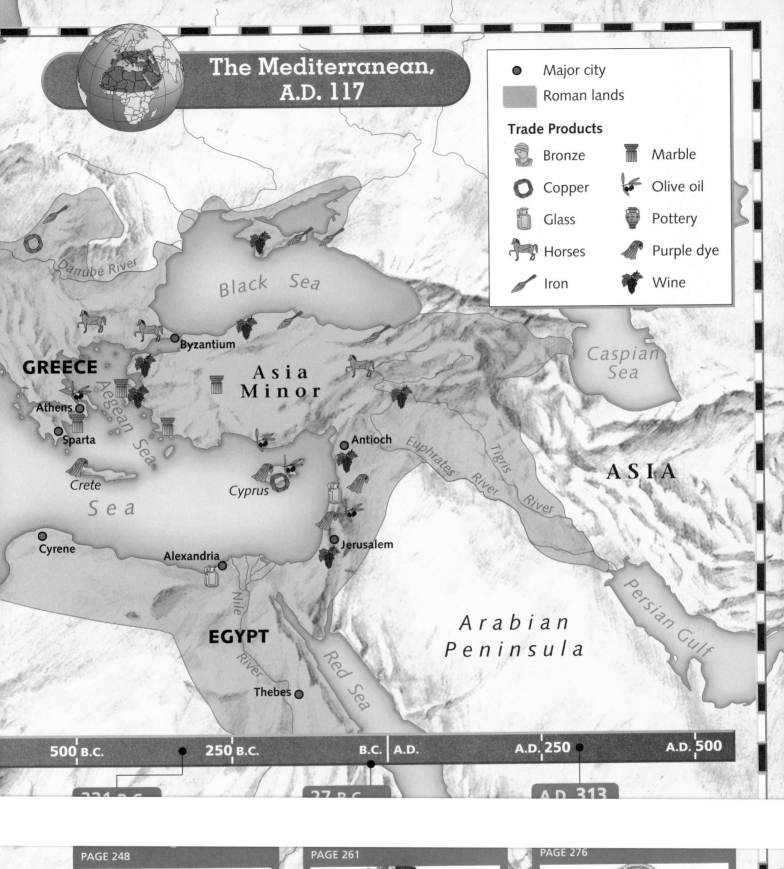

The Mediterranean, A.D. 117

Legend
- Major city
- Roman lands

Trade Products
- Bronze
- Copper
- Glass
- Horses
- Iron
- Marble
- Olive oil
- Pottery
- Purple dye
- Wine

Danube River

Black Sea

Caspian Sea

GREECE

Byzantium

Asia Minor

ASIA

Athens

Aegean Sea

Sparta

Antioch

Euphrates River

Tigris River

Crete

Cyprus

Sea

Cyrene

Jerusalem

Alexandria

Nile River

EGYPT

Arabian Peninsula

Persian Gulf

Red Sea

Thebes

Timeline

| 500 B.C. | 250 B.C. | B.C. | A.D. | A.D. 250 | A.D. 500 |

221 B.C.   27 B.C.   A.D. 313

PAGE 248

PAGE 261

PAGE 276

THE AVENGER

BY MARGARET HODGES

INTRODUCING THE CHARACTERS:

Alexis: *a young athlete from Asini* **Niki:** *Alexis's sister*

Lampis: *a rival athlete from Sparta* **Aristes:** *Alexis's father*

Dion: *Alexis's brother* **Telamon:** *Alexis's trainer*

Like many people living today, the people of the ancient Mediterranean civilizations enjoyed sports. They believed in "a sound mind in a sound body." The ancient Greeks, for example, included athletic contests in their religious festivals. The most famous contests in Greece were the Olympic Games.

The Greeks held the Olympic Games every four years to honor Zeus, who was believed to be the most powerful of the Greek gods. Cities and towns sent their finest young athletes to take part in the games. They came from such places as Athens, Sparta, Elis, and Delphi to run, throw, and wrestle. Like Olympic athletes today, they competed for the honor of their hometowns, their families, and themselves.

Read now about a 15-year-old athlete named Alexis, who competed in the Olympic Games in 492 B.C. for his hometown of Asini in Greece. As you read, imagine the sights, sounds, and feelings you would have experienced while watching or taking part in the Olympic Games long ago.

In the first light the athletes came again to the Altis[1] and gathered around the altar of Zeus at the center of the sacred olive grove. It towered high, filled with the ashes of sacrifices offered for more years than any living man could remember or even guess. A priest moved through the crowd, carrying a torch from the eternal fire that burned on the altar of Hestia, goddess of the hearth. He climbed the steps to the top of the altar of Zeus and set fire to the wood piled there. The smell of blazing poplar and of incense filled the grove. Then the Olympic flame burst through the smoke and the crowd gave a sigh like the sound of a wave breaking on a long beach. Officials were coming with this year's sacrifices for the Games, baskets of meat cut from the thighs of a hundred cattle that had been brought to the slaughter with their horns gilded[2] and with wreaths of flowers about their necks. At last the fire died down and was quenched with water from the Alpheus.[3] When the ashes were cold, they would be hard and smooth, and the altar of Zeus would have mounted even closer to heaven; earth, air, fire, and water mingled[4] to praise him who ruled all things. On the last night of the Games, after the gods were satisfied, the crowds would feast.

Alexis remembered what followed as if it had been a dream. Somehow he got to the stadium for the boys' race. The slopes were

lot. Luckily, he was to run in the first heat[6] and would have time to rest while four other heats were run, supposing that he survived to run in the finals. There were fifteen boys in the first heat, but Lampis was not among them.

He remembered very little from the moment he toed the starting line and heard the trumpet until he reached the finish. He only knew that another runner had been ahead of him almost to the end. Then, with the blood beating in his ears and his lungs bursting, he had somehow closed the gap. But he did not know that he had won until he fell into the crowd at the finish line and felt himself being pounded on the back to shouts of "Asini! Asini has won the first heat! Alexis of Asini!"

His mouth was dry, his head throbbing. Then his father and Dion were breaking a

basin where he took a long drink and sank

---

[1]**Altis:** name for the sacred olive grove
[2]**gilded:** coated with gold
[3]**Alpheus:** a river in Greece
[4]**mingled:** mixed together
[5]**revelers:** party-goers

---

[6]**heat:** a round or part of a contest

225

down on the grass. He could not believe that he had won. His legs were numb. Could he run again? He needed time, and it would not take much time to run off four more heats.

Telamon was rubbing him down and gently kneading the muscles of his legs. "There will be time enough. The managers will be announcing the name and town of each contestant, you know, and the umpires usually argue about who has won, and there may be some false starts. It all takes time. You will be ready."

It was as Telamon had predicted. Twice the heats were delayed when runners made false starts and were punished by sharp blows from officials with long forked sticks. But Lampis won his heat easily, and all too soon they were announcing the final race for boys.

Aristes and Dion embraced Alexis. Above the noise of the crowd he could not hear what they were saying—something about Lampis, something about Asini—but he knew what

they meant, and nodded as he went to the starting line.

"Eucles of Athens . . ." All over the stadium Athenians shouted encouragement to their runner. "Sotades of Elis . . . Lampis of Sparta . . . Alexis of Asini . . . Troilus of Delphi . . ." Each name was followed by cheers from some parts of the stadium and silence from others whose own champions had been beaten by one of the finalists or whose own city had been at war with one of these cities.

Alexis stared down the length of the stadium to the finish line. Lampis was the one to beat and he had to do it for Asini. But Lampis always went into the lead from the very start. If Alexis held himself back this time, tired as he was, he would never be able to close the gap at the end. He must start fast and stay even with Lampis all the way, then do even better in the last stretch. He drew a deep breath, let it out, and leaned forward, his toes gripping the starting stone. The trumpet blared and the runners shot forward.

Out of the corner of his eye Alexis saw to his left Lampis and the boy from Elis, running smoothly. On his right, no one. Athens and Delphi were somewhere behind. Another glance showed him that Lampis was going into the lead. Alexis felt his lungs and his legs laboring painfully. Then suddenly he heard, as if the words were spoken, "I belong to Zeus." He saw in his mind the beach at Asini, and he felt his breath coming easily and powerfully. His leg muscles were obeying his will and he was overtaking, passing Lampis. The crowd at the finish line loomed up and overwhelmed him.

It was over. Alexis had won. Sprays of flowers and olive branches flicked his shoulders. Arms pummeled him. And then, while faces were still a blur, he saw one familiar face that made him think he had gone mad. It happened in a flash. Slender arms were around his neck and a girl's voice spoke into his ear. "You won and I saw you win! Oh, you are excellent!"

It was Niki. Niki where no girl was allowed to be on pain of death, Niki with her hair cropped so like a boy's and wearing one of his old tunics that she must have brought from home, planning this trick all along. No one seemed to be giving her even a second glance, but his blood froze.

"You fool!" he said under his breath. "Quick! Leave, before it's too late. You know the penalty."

"I don't believe in the penalty." She gave him a flashing smile and slipped away into the crowd.

Telamon was wiping the sweat from Alexis's face, his father and brother lifted him shoulder-high, and his townsmen put a crown of flowers on his head. They tied a ribbon on his arm, another on his thigh, and so carried him to the stone seat of the judges to receive the palm branch that would serve as a token of victory until the final night when victors were crowned with wild olive. As Alexis looked down, dazed and smiling, from his high perch, he saw Lampis, his cheeks white and tear-stained, leaving the crowd, followed by his grim-faced trainer. Again, in the midst of his own triumph, Alexis felt pity. It was a weakness, one he must try to overcome. He did not allow himself to picture the arrival of Lampis in Sparta.

As you read more about the ancient people of the Mediterranean, you will discover why Alexis felt pity for Lampis, the runner from Sparta. You also will learn that the ancient Greeks are remembered today for more than the Olympic Games.

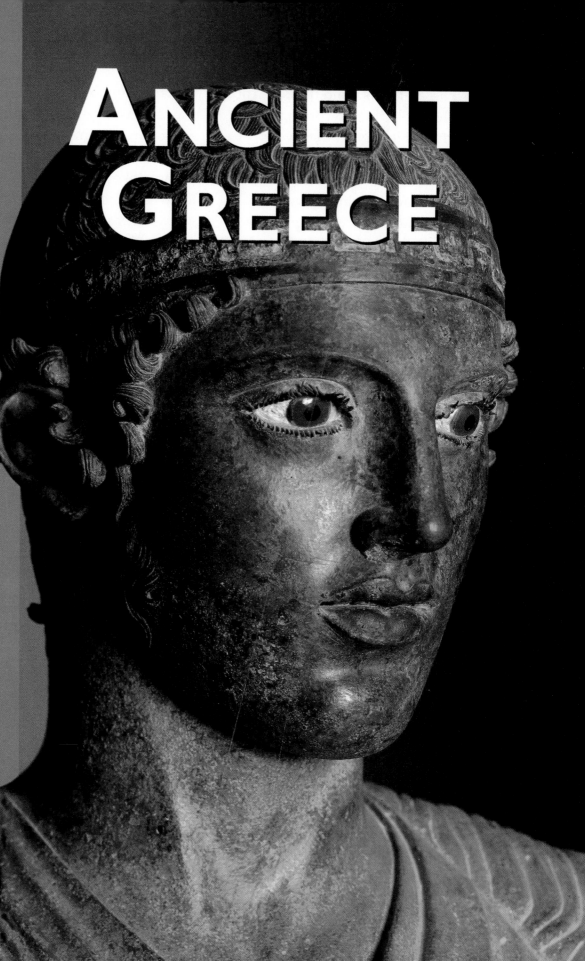

ANCIENT GREECE

"Here each individual is interested not only in his own affairs, but in the affairs of state as well."

Pericles, leader of Athens, 430 B.C.

Statue of a young Greek charioteer, made about 470 B.C.

Early People of Greece

FOCUS
What could cause a culture to lose or gain control of an area?

Main Idea As you read, think about how different cultures came to control Greece as time passed.

Vocabulary
isthmus
cultural borrowing
epic

Over the centuries peoples of several cultures settled on the land now known as Greece. Directly or indirectly, each culture formed part of what would become the Greek civilization.

Mountains and the Sea

Present-day Greece occupies a large peninsula on the southern edge of eastern Europe. This peninsula—the Balkan Peninsula—curves south and east into the Mediterranean Sea toward a part of the Asian continent called Asia Minor, or "Little Asia." Today the country of Turkey fills Asia Minor. Turkey and Greece are separated by an island-dotted arm of the Mediterranean called the Aegean (ih•JEE•uhn) Sea.

The surrounding sea reaches far into the southern part of the Balkan Peninsula. In fact, it nearly divides the peninsula in two. The southern part, called the Peloponnesus (peh•luh•puh•NEE•suhs), is connected to the rest of the mainland by a small strip of land, or **isthmus** (IS•muhs).

Mountains cover nearly three-fourths of Greece. In the thin, rocky soil and dry climate, early farmers grew olives, grapes, and grain for food. They also raised sheep, goats, pigs, and cattle to get skins for clothing.

The rugged land made travel hard and trade nearly impossible. The people of each mountain village had to survive on only the food they raised. Since they had no contact with each other, each mountain village formed its own government and became fiercely independent.

The mountainous land of Greece made both travel and trade difficult.

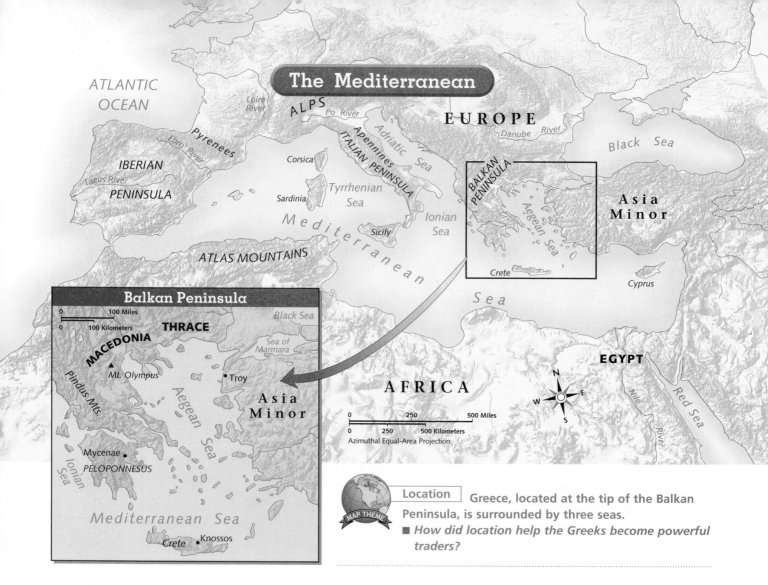

The Mediterranean

ATLANTIC
OCEAN

Loire River

ALPS

Po River

EUROPE

Danube River

Black Sea

Pyrenees

Ebro River

Corsica

Adriatic Sea

Apennines

ITALIAN PENINSULA

BALKAN PENINSULA

Asia Minor

IBERIAN PENINSULA

Tagus River

Sardinia

Tyrrhenian Sea

Aegean Sea

Atlas Mountains

Sicily

Ionian Sea

Mediterranean

Crete

Cyprus

Sea

EGYPT

AFRICA

Nile River

Red River

Balkan Peninsula

0   100 Miles
0   100 Kilometers

Black Sea

THRACE

MACEDONIA

Sea of Marmara

Mt. Olympus

Troy

Pindus Mts.

Aegean Sea

Asia Minor

Mycenae

Ionian Sea

PELOPONNESUS

Mediterranean Sea

Crete   Knossos

0   250   500 Miles
0   250   500 Kilometers
Azimuthal Equal-Area Projection

Location Greece, located at the tip of the Balkan Peninsula, is surrounded by three seas.

MAP THEME

■ *How did location help the Greeks become powerful traders?*

Along the coast the sea connected Greeks with people in Asia and Africa. Greeks living near the Mediterranean became fishers, sailors, and merchants. The fact that Greece had only a few types of natural resources led the Greeks to look to the outside for trade.

Greece's location in the eastern Mediterranean made it a perfect trade center. Traders on the Mediterranean were eager to exchange their goods for Greek olive oil, wool, and wine. Between 3000 B.C. and 1550 B.C., the Mediterranean's first great trading center grew up on the island of Crete, to the south of Greece.

REVIEW *How did geography affect the way early people lived in ancient Greece?*

The Minoans

The island of Crete lies 60 miles (97 km) south of the Peloponnesus. The Greek poet Homer described Crete as "a rich and lovely land, washed by the waves on every side."

Around 1900 B.C. the people of Crete began building huge buildings called palaces. These palaces were like small cities. Some were several stories tall. They were centers for managing the government and may have been religious centers.

The Minoans will long be remembered for their beautiful wall paintings.

Archaeologists have uncovered the remains of four palaces. The largest, Knossos (NAHS•uhs), stood at least three stories high. Knossos and two other palaces had large central courtyards and areas for storing food. Beautiful paintings showing peaceful scenes decorated the palace walls.

The people who built Knossos and the other cities of Crete are called Minoans (muh•NOH•uhnz). They were named for the legendary King Minos (MY•nuhs). If Minos existed, he probably ruled Crete in the years of its greatest success, sometime between 1750 B.C. and 1550 B.C.

The Minoans were seafaring traders. They traded with people in ancient Africa, Asia, and Europe. Egypt and Syria were just two of their many trading partners. Minoan trading ships carried olive oil, wine, wool, pottery, and other goods from Crete to overseas ports. The ships returned with such treasures as copper, tin, and gold. The Minoans mixed copper and tin to form the metal bronze. Using bronze they crafted beautiful bowls and other objects.

To keep better records, the Minoans developed a system of writing. Unfortunately,

Dolphins were just one of the subjects of Minoan artists. This wall painting once decorated the Queen's Room in the Palace of Knossos.

some of their writings may have been destroyed by a fire that swept through the Minoan kingdom in about 1370 B.C. Only records written on clay tablets remain. Some historians believe that fire may have brought an end to all Minoan civilization. Others believe a powerful earthquake struck the island. The way in which the Minoan kingdom ended may never be known.

REVIEW *What were Minoan palaces like?*

Parts of the city-like palace of Knossos were restored in the beginning of the twentieth century. What can you tell about the ancient palace from the photograph?

The Mycenaeans

During the last years of their kingdom, Minoan merchants started trading with the city of Mycenae (my•SEE•nee), near the coast of the mountainous Peloponnesus. The Mycenaeans (my•suh•NEE•uhnz) seem to have been a warlike people who measured their wealth by the

many Minoan customs through trade. This **cultural borrowing**

Mycenaean warriors wore bronze armor with helmets made from boars' tusks (top). Mycenaean vases (bottom) often showed warlike scenes.

led the Mycenaeans to adapt Minoan art styles and pottery designs to make them look more warlike. They changed Minoan writing to fit their language and also borrowed some religious beliefs.

In 1450 B.C., after the Minoan kingdom weakened, the Mycenaeans invaded Crete. Mycenae controlled both Crete and much of the Peloponnesus from about 1450 B.C. to 1100 B.C. By 1100 B.C. the Mycenaeans had begun to lose their hold on Greece.

No one knows why Mycenaean control of Greece grew weaker. For years historians believed that warriors called Dorians marched south into the Peloponnesus and burned palaces and villages in their path. Now some experts believe that invaders from the north called the Sea Peoples conquered the Mycenaeans. According to these experts, the

Dorians simply moved into the area after this conquest. Others claim that disagreements among the Mycenaeans themselves weakened their civilization.

Some great change must have caused the Mycenaeans to give up their writing and art and stop trading. During the period from about 1100 B.C. to 800 B.C., much of Minoan and Mycenaean learning was lost. The ancient people of Greece returned to a simpler way of life.

REVIEW *From whom did the Mycenaeans borrow many ideas?*

Ancient Stories and Legends

Much of what we know about the Mycenaeans comes from the stories of Homer. Four centuries after the Mycenaean civilization had lost its strength, Homer created long story-poems, or **epics**, that kept its memory alive. The poems were based on old stories he had heard. Storytellers through the centuries had retold these epics.

BIOGRAPHY

Homer, 700s B.C.

Historians know little about Homer, the author of the *Iliad* and the *Odyssey*. Homer probably grew up in Ionia in Asia Minor sometime between 800 B.C. and 700 B.C. Tradition says that Homer was blind and that he recited from memory the 28,000 verses of his epic poems.

This gold mask, made by a Mycenaean artist, is a reminder of the early cultures that once lived in what is now Greece.

One epic, the *Iliad*, tells about people's actions during a great war. Another epic, the *Odyssey*, describes the adventures of the hero Odysseus (oh•DIH•see•uhs) on his long journey home from the war described in the *Iliad*. During his ten-year journey, Odysseus has many strange adventures, such as a fight with a one-eyed giant. At the same time, his wife, Penelope (puh•NEH•luh•pee), deals with problems caused by his absence.

The war Homer described in the *Iliad* was fought between the Mycenaeans and the people of Troy, a city in what is now north-western Turkey. This war has become known as the Trojan War.

Legend says that the fighting began when

king's brother, Agamemnon, took soldiers to Troy to get Helen back.

The conflict dragged on and on with no end in sight. Then the Mycenaeans came up with a plan to trick the Trojans. They built a huge, hollow wooden horse, dragged it to

the gates of Troy during the night, and left it there.

The curious Trojans pulled the large horse into the city the next morning, just as the Mycenaeans had hoped they would. That night Mycenaean soldiers hiding inside the hollow horse crawled out. Then they opened the city gates to other Mycenaean soldiers waiting outside. By morning the Mycenaeans had rescued Helen and set fire to the city of Troy.

The legend of the Trojan War, Homer's epics, and other stories left a lasting record of the early people of Greece. From this traditional beginning the Greek civilization continued to grow and change.

REVIEW *How did Homer keep alive the memory of Mycenae?*

LESSON 1 REVIEW

Check Understanding

1. **Remember the Facts** Who were the Minoans and the Mycenaeans?

2. **Recall the Main Idea** What may have caused the Minoans to lose their strength? What may have caused the Mycenaeans to lose their strength?

Think Critically

3. **Past to Present** What might cause a culture of today to gain and then lose its strength?

4. **Think More About It** Why did the Mycenaeans change the ideas they borrowed from the Minoans rather

 Art Activity Make a wall painting that shows what you think may have caused the Minoans or the Mycenaeans to lose their power.

FOCUS

What might cause people to develop very different ways of life?

Main Idea As you read, look for reasons the peoples of ancient Greece developed different ways of life.

Vocabulary

polis
acropolis
agora
tyrant
aristocracy
assembly
helot
oligarchy
democracy
majority rule
cultural identity
myth

This figurine, from 375 B.C., shows a scene of everyday life in ancient Greece.

City-States and Greek Culture

Around 800 B.C. the people of Greece again began to build settlements. At first most Greeks lived in small villages. The growth of trade in local products helped villages grow into towns. In time each town joined with nearby villages and farms to form a **polis**, or city-state.

Rise of City-States

To protect themselves from invaders, Greek communities built forts on the tops of hills. Farmers from the countryside moved to these protected areas during enemy attacks. Later the fortress, or **acropolis** (uh•KRAH•puh•luhs), became the center for daily life in many city-states.

Outside the acropolis were houses, temples, and an open-air market and gathering place called an **agora** (A•guh•ruh). People met in the agora to exchange goods and discuss the news of the day.

A king or tyrant ruled each city-state and made all political decisions. In ancient Greece a **tyrant** was someone who took control of a government by force and ruled alone. Today the word *tyrant* refers to a cruel ruler.

As time passed, the people in each city-state developed their own way of governing. In some city-states the richest men shared authority with a king. This wealthy ruling class, or **aristocracy**, was made up of landowners and merchants. In other city-states all free men, rich or poor, took part in government. These men met in an **assembly**, or lawmaking group, to make decisions for the whole community.

Most city-states had fewer than 5,000 people. As the population of a city-state grew, overcrowding forced some people to look for new places to live. Several city-states set up colonies, creating new city-states in Asia Minor, southern Europe, and northern Africa.

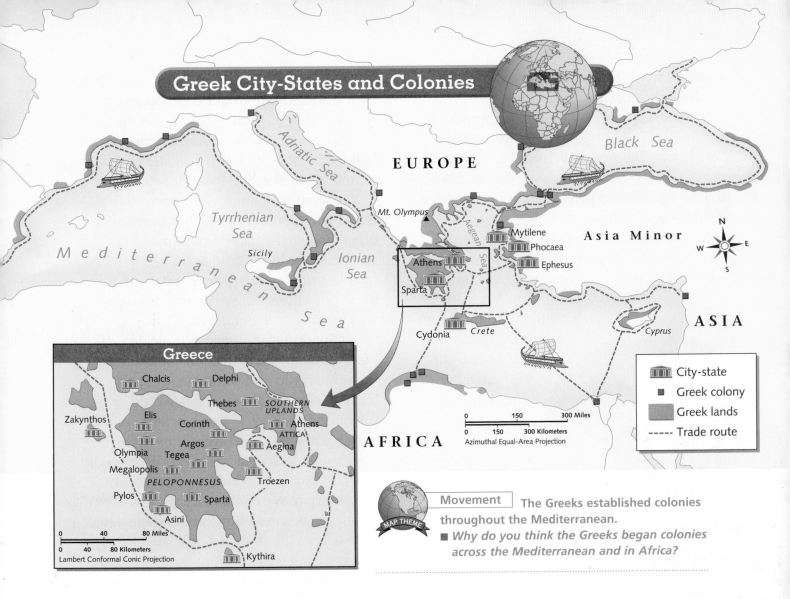

Greek City-States and Colonies

EUROPE

Adriatic Sea

Tyrrhenian Sea

Sicily

Ionian Sea

M e d i t e r r a n e a n   S e a

Mt. Olympus ▲

Aegean Sea

Mytilene

Phocaea

Athens

Ephesus

Sparta

Black Sea

Asia Minor

ASIA

Cydonia   Crete

Cyprus

AFRICA

0   150   300 Miles
0   150   300 Kilometers
Azimuthal Equal-Area Projection

Greece

Chalcis   Delphi

Thebes   SOUTHERN UPLANDS

Zakynthos   Elis   Corinth   Athens
ATTICA

Argos   Aegina

Olympia   Tegea

Megalopolis

PELOPONNESUS   Troezen

Pylos   Sparta

Asini

0   40   80 Miles
0   40   80 Kilometers
Lambert Conformal Conic Projection

Kythira

	City-state
	Greek colony
	Greek lands
-----	Trade route

Movement The Greeks established colonies throughout the Mediterranean.

■ *Why do you think the Greeks began colonies across the Mediterranean and in Africa?*

Besides providing space for more people, the colonies brought the Greeks new natural resources and trade markets. As more and more colonies were set up, Greek ideas and customs spread through the Mediterranean region.

Rivalries grew as the city-states began to compete for land and colonies. The city-states of Sparta and Argos both wanted control of the Peloponnesus. Athens and Thebes fought

became the most powerful city-states. While not rivals at first, Sparta and Athens had strikingly different ways of life.

REVIEW *What features did the city-states share? How were they different from one another?*

Sparta

Sparta was located in the southern Peloponnesus. In this city-state, soldiers marching and young boys and girls exercising were common sights. Spartan citizens led a simple life filled with physical activity.

the earlier people of the

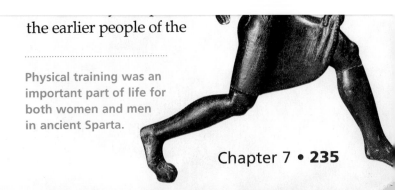

Physical training was an important part of life for both women and men in ancient Sparta.

area and made them **helots**—slaves owned by the state, not by private citizens.

Spartan leaders used military strength to control their city-state. Historians believe that Sparta may have had ten times as many slaves as citizens. Fear that the slaves would rebel led the Spartans to protect themselves with a military way of life.

Spartan children went through long physical-training programs. Boys had to leave their families at age 7 to attend training camps. Girls stayed at home but received gymnastics training. Boys continued training until age 18 and served in the Spartan army until age 30.

Spartan soldiers were fierce and disciplined. This bronze warrior still guards the tomb of King Leonidas, who lived during the 400s B.C.

The army camps taught Spartans to obey their leaders without question. Spartans believed that they must never give up a battle, even when wounded. The Spartans believed that there was no greater honor than to die defending their city-state.

The women of Sparta had fewer rights than men but more rights than women in other Greek city-states. Spartan women managed the household and often handled business matters. However, the main duty of women, according to Spartan leaders, was to raise strong children.

All Spartans followed a simple way of life. By law everyone ate "in common, of the same bread and same meat." Spartan leaders feared that new ideas would bring unwanted changes to their society. For this reason, citizens were rarely allowed to travel outside Sparta and were discouraged from trading with outsiders. This meant that the Spartans could use only their own resources. Because they kept to themselves, their way of life changed little over time.

Sparta had two kings, each from a different royal family. Except in times of war, the kings had little authority. Both kings served as part of a 30-member senate. The other members of the senate—all over the age of 60—were elected by an assembly of citizens. All male Spartans were allowed to be part of the assembly. The assembly elected five landowners called *ephors* (EH•ferz) to handle daily governing.

Only the senate or the ephors could suggest new laws in Sparta. The assembly of citizens voted for or against new laws, but their votes could be ignored by the ephors and the senate. This meant that the ephors and the senators held most of the power in Sparta. Any small ruling group such as this is called an **oligarchy**.

Although strict, Spartan government was among the most admired governments in all of Greece. Many Greeks thought that the

Spartan government's tight control over its citizens made it a strong city-state.

REVIEW *Why did Spartans believe they needed a strong army?*

Athens

Athens was the main city-state in Attica (A•tih•kuh), the ancient name for land in the southern uplands. Unlike Sparta, Athens required its young men to serve in the army only in time of war. Athenian government encouraged the people to take part in community decisions. This civic participation grew into a system of **democracy**, or rule by the people. The Greek historian Thucydides (thoo•SIH•duh•deez) said about Athens, "Its administration favors the many instead of the few."

The Athenian leader Solon had helped bring democracy to Athens about 594 B.C. Under his leadership male Athenians were able to take a greater part in government. About 508 B.C., a leader named Cleisthenes (KLYS•thuh•neez) changed the form of Athenian government to a full democracy. By the year 500 B.C., every free man over age 20 had full political rights.

All citizens took part in the city-state's assembly, called the Ecclesia. Every member of the assembly had one vote. All decisions were made by **majority rule**. In other words, the idea that received the most votes became law.

The reforms of Cleisthenes kept any one person from taking control of Athens.

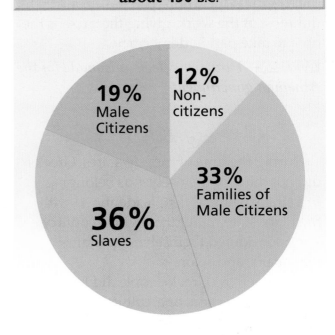

Population of Athens
about 430 B.C.

- 12% Non-citizens
- 19% Male Citizens
- 33% Families of Male Citizens
- 36% Slaves

LEARNING FROM GRAPHS Male citizens with the right to vote made up only a small part of Athens's population.

■ *Athens's population was about 285,000 people. About how many male citizens were there? About how many slaves were there?*

(AHS•truh•kuh). This practice gave us the English word *ostracize*, meaning "to shut out."

The changes made by Cleisthenes let more people take part in government. But Athenian democracy did not include everyone. Women could not take part in government even though they were considered citizens. However, as in Sparta, women managed the family budget and the household.

received the most votes out of 6,000 was forced to leave Athens for ten years. The candidates' names were written on broken pieces of pottery called ostraca

Athenian democracy probably

Paintings on Greek pottery illustrated history and legend, religious ceremonies, or daily life.

helped make that democracy possible. These were the slaves, who made up about one-third of the population. The slaves of Athens did most of the work, giving the citizens the time to take part in democracy.

REVIEW *How were decisions made by the Athenian government?*

Greek Identity

During the time of the city-states, Greeks did not think of themselves as belonging to a single country. People identified with their city-state rather than with a country. They considered themselves Spartans, Athenians, and so on.

However, the Greek people did feel a cultural connection, or a **cultural identity**, with one another. All Greeks called themselves Hellenes because they believed they had a common ancestor, the hero Hellen. A Greek **myth**, or story passed down

HERITAGE

The First Olympics

The first Olympic Games were held in the valley of Olympia near the city-state of Elis in 776 B.C. As many as 40,000 people watched athletes from city-states throughout Greece compete in one event—a footrace. Women were not allowed to enter the stadium at Olympia to compete or even to watch. Later, however, women in Elis held their own footraces to honor the goddess Hera.

Early bronze discus

A boxer who competed in the Olympic Games of long ago. How do the modern Olympics connect different cultures today?

about an ancient god or hero, said that Hellen alone had survived a flood long ago. In addition, their shared religion set the Greeks apart, in their minds, from other peoples who lived alongside the Mediterranean, such as the Phoenicians and the Egyptians.

The Greek cultural identity was seen in various activities. The Olympic Games, for example, brought the city-states together in peace. Beginning about 776 B.C. Greeks met every four years to compete in athletic contests to honor the god Zeus. The Greeks believed that Zeus and their other gods controlled daily events in the world.

A common written language also helped bring the city-states closer together. In the 700s B.C. the Greeks developed an alphabet based on the alphabet of the Phoenicians.

The Greek Alphabet

GREEK LETTER	WRITTEN NAME	ENGLISH SOUND
A	alpha	a
B	beta	b
Γ	gamma	g
Δ	delta	d
E	epsilon	e
Z	zeta	z
H	eta	e
Θ	theta	th
I	iota	i
K	kappa	c, k
Λ	lambda	l
M	mu	m
N	nu	n
Ξ	xi	x
O	omicron	o
Π	pi	p
P	rho	r
Σ	sigma	s
T	tau	t
Y	upsilon	y, u
Φ	phi	ph
X	chi	ch
Ψ	psi	ps
Ω	omega	o

LEARNING FROM TABLES The Greek alphabet borrowed many letters from the Phoenicians but added its own vowels to form a 24-letter alphabet.
■ *In what ways is the ancient Greek alphabet similar to today's English alphabet?*

The painting on this bowl is of Zeus, the chief god of the Greeks. The Greeks believed that many gods ruled both nature and people.

LESSON 2 REVIEW

Check Understanding

❶ **Remember the Facts** Which Greek city-state was centered around its army? What Greek city-state was known for its democracy?

❷ **Recall the Main Idea** What caused the people in different parts of ancient Greece to develop different ways of life?

Think Critically

❸ **Think More About It** Why did the Athenians feel it was important for citizens to take part in government?

❹ **Explore Viewpoints** Why do people around the world have different ideas about governing?

Like the Minoans long before them, the Phoenicians were traders and needed a writing system to keep track of their trade.

In changing this system to fit their needs, the Greeks called the first letter *alpha*. The second letter was *beta*. The English word *alphabet* comes from the names of those Greek letters.

REVIEW *What helped the Greeks feel a cultural identity?*

that you are an observer first in Sparta and then in Athens. Give a speech that describes the differences in the ways of life of the two city-states.

FOCUS

How do times of war and times of peace affect societies today?

Main Idea Look for ways war and peace affected the ways of life of the ancient Greeks.

Vocabulary

league
tragedy
comedy
demagogue

The Golden Age of Athens

For centuries the Greek city-states fought over land and differences in ways of life. Then, beginning in the early fifth century B.C., a common enemy brought the Greek people together.

The Athenian leader Pericles lived from about 495 B.C. to 429 B.C.

The Persian Wars

Beginning about 540 B.C., armies from Persia conquered Babylon, Assyria, Egypt, and other lands around the Mediterranean. They also captured the Greek cities in Asia Minor. Soon Persian armies crossed the Aegean Sea separating Europe from Asia and invaded the Balkan Peninsula. About 500 B.C. the Greeks of Asia Minor rebelled against the Persians. Although the Athenians sent help, the Greeks in Asia Minor could not defeat the Persians.

In 490 B.C. the Persian king, Darius I, turned his soldiers toward Athens because Athens had helped the colonies fight the Persians. The Athenians met the Persians on the plain of Marathon, not far from Athens. Although the Persians had more soldiers, the Athenians managed to defeat them in just one day of fighting. Later, people told a story of a messenger running all the way to Athens from Marathon to report the amazing victory. Athletes in today's Olympic Games re-create this action in the long-distance running event called the marathon.

Darius died in 486 B.C. In 480 B.C. his son Xerxes (ZERK•seez) sent 200,000 soldiers in 800 ships to attack Greece. This time the Persians met Greek forces made up of armies and navies from Athens, Sparta, and other Greek city-states. The Persians still had more soldiers than all the city-states combined. Yet in a sea battle near the island of Salamis (SAL•uh•muhs), the Greeks defeated the Persians.

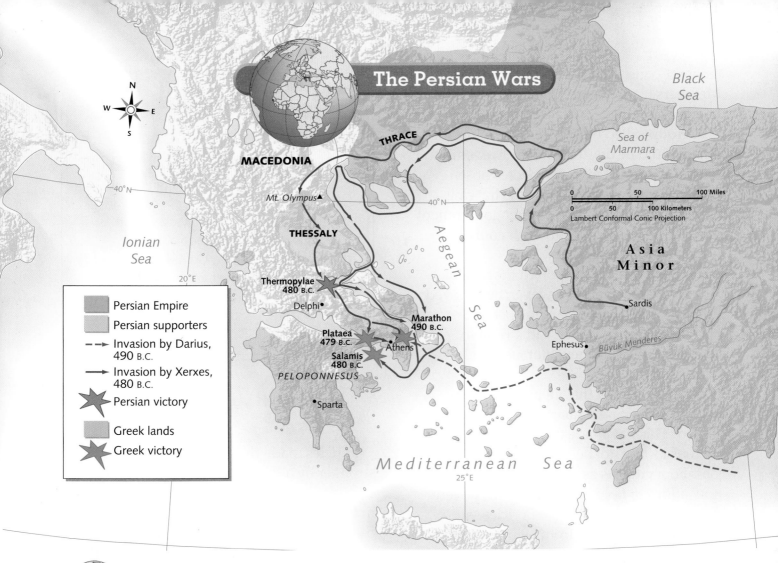

The Persian Wars

Black Sea

Sea of Marmara

THRACE

MACEDONIA

Mt. Olympus▲

THESSALY

Ionian Sea

Thermopylae 480 B.C.

Delphi•

Plataea 479 B.C.

Marathon 490 B.C.

Salamis 480 B.C.

Athens

PELOPONNESUS

•Sparta

Aegean Sea

A s i a M i n o r

•Sardis

Ephesus• Büyük Menderes

Mediterranean Sea

Persian Empire

Persian supporters

- - -▸ Invasion by Darius, 490 B.C.

⟶ Invasion by Xerxes, 480 B.C.

✶ Persian victory

Greek lands

✶ Greek victory

0   50   100 Miles
0   50   100 Kilometers
Lambert Conformal Conic Projection

Human-Environment Interactions The Greeks and Persians met in battle on the Balkan Peninsula.
■ *Who controlled the land on which the Greeks won victories?*

No one knew at the time that the war would have a lasting effect on world history. Because the Greeks won, it was their customs, language, and ideas and not those of the Persians that would shape many other cultures for centuries to come.

After the wars, the Greek city-states feared for protection. Sparta led a group of city-states in the Peloponnesian League. The city-states of Attica formed the Delian League, led by Athens.

REVIEW *What caused the Greek city-states to band together?*

The Golden Age

The Greeks felt great pride after defeating Persia. From about 479 B.C. to 431 B.C., the Athenians turned their pride into a time of achievement that came to be known as the Golden Age.

A member of the aristocracy named who believed in the saying "Nothing to excess," meaning that a person should not overdo anything.

Pericles led Athens with the help of an assembly made up of thousands of male citizens. Any member could speak to the

Chapter 7 • **241**

assembly, and each had the right to vote. Members usually voted by raising their hands.

A group called the Council of 500 decided what would be discussed at each assembly meeting. Council members were chosen from the assembly each year by drawing names from a bowl. Many other government officials, as well as the juries for court cases, were also chosen this way.

Pericles strongly supported the idea of Athenian democracy. However, he believed the democracy could be made better. He felt that every citizen had a right to take part in government, not just wealthy citizens.

Pericles ordered that all public officials and jurors be paid a salary for the days they served. This pay made up for the money citizens lost by not being at their regular jobs. Poor citizens as well as rich ones could now afford to hold office. "With us, poverty does not stand in the way," Pericles said. "No one is prevented from being of service to the city-state."

REVIEW *How did Pericles improve Athenian democracy?*

The most remarkable building of the Golden Age in Athens was the Parthenon, which was built on the city's acropolis. This marble temple celebrated Greek victories in the Persian Wars and honored the Greek goddess Athena. The Parthenon was completed in 432 B.C. Its ruins still stand in the present-day city of Athens, Greece.

Direct Democracy

Unlike the democracy of the United States, ancient Athens had a direct democracy. Each citizen took a direct role in day-to-day government. Most countries today have too many people to have a direct democracy. The United States has a representative democracy. In this type of democracy, large numbers of citizens elect other citizens, or representatives, to make governmental decisions for them.

Achievements of the Golden Age

Pericles made the government of Athens stronger by allowing all citizens to take part. He also made it easier for Athenians to work in the arts and sciences by having the government support them. Pericles wanted Athens to become "the school of Greece." To do this, he hired the best artists and scholars and put them to work.

Architects and builders set about making Athens more beautiful. Architects designed new temples, gymnasiums, theaters, and other public buildings. Artists then decorated the buildings with murals, or wall paintings, showing scenes from Athens's glorious history.

Writers also recorded Athens's past. Herodotus, whom some consider the first historian and one of the earliest geographers, wrote about the Persian Wars. Herodotus explained that he wrote this history to put on record "the astonishing achievements of our own and of other peoples." Even today many people read his works.

Other great writers also contributed to the achievements of the Golden Age. Sophocles (SAH•fuh•kleez) wrote **tragedies**, or serious plays, in which the main character comes to an unhappy end. Aristophanes (air•uh•STAH•fuh•neez) wrote **comedies**, or humorous plays. His comedies usually made fun of political leaders or traditional ideas.

Pericles and the Athenian government also paid scholars to study nature and human life. Their findings changed forever the way people saw their world. One of the greatest scientists of the Golden Age was Hippocrates (hih•PAH•kruh•teez). Hippocrates and his followers showed that illnesses came from natural causes. They were not punishment from the gods, as most people had believed.

To stay healthy, Hippocrates told the Athenians, "wheaten bread is to be preferred to barley cake, and roasted to boiled meats." While many of his suggestions made good sense, he also thought "vegetables should be reduced to a minimum." Hippocrates is perhaps best remembered for writing a code of conduct that doctors still follow today.

REVIEW *What kinds of people worked in Athens during the Golden Age?*

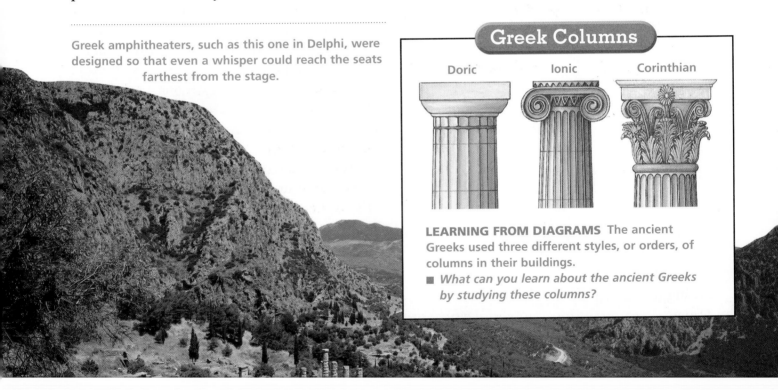

Greek amphitheaters, such as this one in Delphi, were designed so that even a whisper could reach the seats farthest from the stage.

Greek Columns

Doric Ionic Corinthian

LEARNING FROM DIAGRAMS The ancient Greeks used three different styles, or orders, of columns in their buildings.

■ *What can you learn about the ancient Greeks by studying these columns?*

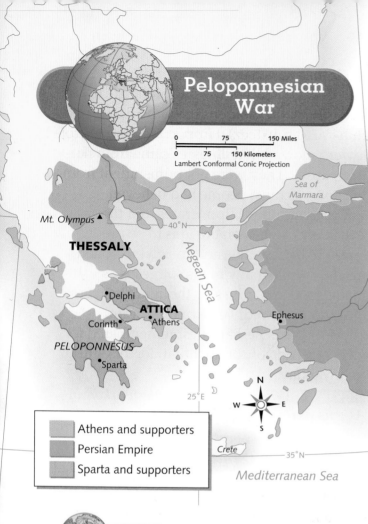

Peloponnesian War

0 75 150 Miles
0 75 150 Kilometers
Lambert Conformal Conic Projection

Sea of Marmara

Mt. Olympus ▲

40°N

THESSALY

Aegean Sea

•Delphi

ATTICA

Corinth• •Athens

Ephesus

PELOPONNESUS

•Sparta

25°E

N W E S

Athens and supporters
Persian Empire
Sparta and supporters

Crete

35°N

Mediterranean Sea

Place The Peloponnesian War resulted from ongoing conflicts between Sparta and Athens.

■ *During the war, which do you think had control of the Aegean Sea, Sparta or Athens?*

The End of the Golden Age

During the time of the Golden Age, Athens and Sparta became the most powerful city-states in Greece. Yet neither was satisfied. Athens wanted more land. Sparta wanted to weaken the influence of Athens. The city-states of the Peloponnesian League supported Sparta, while those of the Delian League supported Athens. In 431 B.C. the Peloponnesian War broke out. The war lasted 27 years.

After Sparta attacked Attica, many people from the countryside moved into Athens. Because of the crowding, diseases swept

through the city-state. One-fourth of the Athenian army died from diseases. Pericles also died at this time.

Without the wise leadership of Pericles, the members of the assembly began to follow bad leaders called **demagogues** (DEH•muh•gahgz). The demagogues made promises they could not keep and led the assembly into making poor decisions. Faced with ruin, Athens surrendered to Sparta in 404 B.C. Sparta quickly replaced the Athenian assembly with an oligarchy like its own. However, the Athenians soon rebelled and brought democracy back to Athens.

Great thinkers and teachers lived in Athens after the Peloponnesian War. However, the city-state no longer paid for their work as it had during the Golden Age. One famous teacher was Socrates (SAHK•ruh•teez), who taught by asking questions and making his students think rather than by simply telling them information.

Socrates called himself Athens's "gadfly," after an insect that bites horses and makes them jump. Socrates used criticism to "sting" Athens into returning to its earlier greatness. Such criticism would have been welcome in Pericles' day. In 399 B.C., however, an Athenian court convicted Socrates of teaching dangerous ideas to the city's young people. Socrates was sentenced by the court to end his own life by drinking poison. One of Socrates' students was Plato.

The ideas of Socrates are still studied today.

Aristotle, who lived from 384 B.C. to 322 B.C., loved all knowledge.

Like Socrates, Plato was disappointed in the kinds of leaders who came after Pericles. Plato said that a ruler should be a good person. He felt that philosophers, or "lovers of wisdom," would make the best rulers. In 385 B.C. Plato started a school called the Academy, where philosophers could learn how to govern.

Plato also thought a lot about what it takes to be a good citizen. He pictured a good citizen as someone who thinks and feels and then takes action. Plato believed that every citizen had both the right and the responsibility to take part in public life. He felt it was important for people to be informed, to understand other viewpoints, and to be responsible for their own actions. This idea of citizenship is shared by many people today.

One of Plato's students, Aristotle (AIR•uh•staht•uhl), was more interested

At Plato's Academy, philosophers studied the responsibilities of citizens and leaders.

in how things were rather than in how he would like them to be. Aristotle's wide search for knowledge covered many subjects. Some of the subjects he studied were science, law, economics, astronomy, and sports.

REVIEW *What brought an end to the Golden Age of Athens?*

LESSON 3 REVIEW

Check Understanding

1. **Remember the Facts** What wars did the Athenians fight in the 400s B.C.?

2. **Recall the Main Idea** How did periods of war and peace affect life in Athens?

3. **Past to Present** Do people's ways of life change in time of war? Explain.

4. **Think More About It** How did the Persian Wars help bring the Greeks together? How did the Peloponnesian War tear the Greeks apart?

5. **Personally Speaking** Socrates taught by asking questions. Which is a better way to teach, asking or telling? Why?

Show What You Know

Poster Activity After the in being Greek by creating great works in art and science. Think about the pride you feel in the United States. Make a poster that explains why you feel proud to be a citizen. Display your artwork in your classroom or somewhere else in your school.

Predict a Likely Outcome

1. Why Learn This Skill?

When you make a prediction, you are not just guessing about what will happen in the future. Rather, you are using what you already know along with new information to predict a probable, or likely, outcome.

2. Remember What You Have Read

The Persians fought the Greeks to try to gain more land. Although the Greeks won the Battle of Marathon, the Persians returned. The Persian king, Xerxes, sent 800 ships to attack Greece.

3. Apply New Information

The Greek ships sailed into the narrow strait at Salamis. In the strait they had the chance to rest while they waited. As the Greeks hoped, the 800 Persian ships followed. The Persians had to row for 12 hours before they reached the Greek fleet in the small body of water. Imagine that you are one of the Greek sailors. What do you predict will happen next?

4. Understand the Process

To make a prediction, you can follow these steps:

1. Think about what you already know. *The Persians wanted more land and sent a fleet of ships to attack the Greeks.*
2. Review any new information you have learned. *The Persians rowed their large fleet into a narrow body of water where the rested Greeks were waiting.*
3. Make a prediction.

Here's what happened when the Persian fleet followed the Greeks. After more than 12 hours of rowing, the tired Persian sailors met the Greek fleet. The huge Persian fleet was too large to move around in the narrow strait. The smaller Greek fleet, with its well-rested sailors, was easily able to ram and sink most of the Persian ships.

5. Think and Apply

As you read the next lesson, follow the steps listed above to predict how Greek culture would influence other cultures.

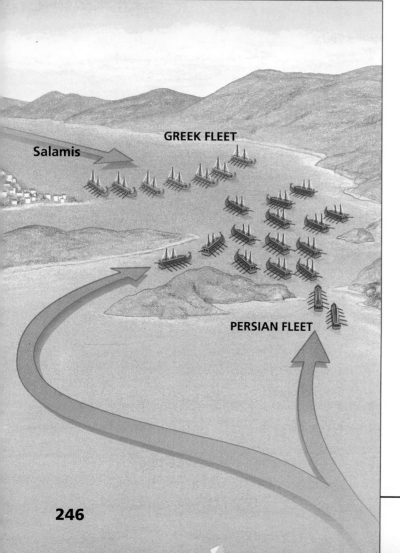

The battle of Salamis

Alexander's Great Empire

FOCUS

How can one person affect the course of history?

Main Idea As you read, look for ways Alexander brought changes to the people of Europe and Asia.

Vocabulary

alliance
Hellenistic
multicultural

Greece needed a leader who could bring together people with different ideas and ways of life. In time such an individual came to power. He controlled lands that stretched from the Greek peninsula to northern India. This leader created the largest empire the world had known.

Conquest of Greece

After the Peloponnesian War, Greece became a land of conflict and distrust. City-states formed **alliances**, or agreements to help each other. Most of these alliances did not last long. A friend in one conflict became an enemy in the next. Each city-state put its own interests above the common good of Greece.

Meanwhile, north of Greece in a land called Macedonia, a strong king named Philip II came to the throne. Philip had brought his own people together under one rule. He planned to do the same for Greece.

Philip had spent part of his boyhood in Greece and greatly admired Greek culture. Philip even hired the Greek philosopher Aristotle to teach his 13-year-old son, Alexander. From Aristotle, young Alexander learned to appreciate the cultures of other peoples. From his father, Alexander learned to be a fearless warrior. Stories say that Alexander slept with a dagger and a copy of Homer's *Iliad* under his pillow.

Even the combined armies of Athens and Thebes could not stop Philip's well-trained

Alexander the Great was only 20 years old when he became king of Macedonia. This marble sculpture is a Roman copy of the original, which was made in 320 B.C.

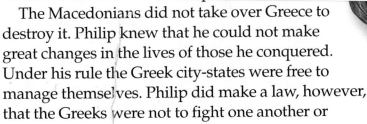

The Macedonians did not take over Greece to destroy it. Philip knew that he could not make great changes in the lives of those he conquered. Under his rule the Greek city-states were free to manage themselves. Philip did make a law, however, that the Greeks were not to fight one another or

247

challenge his rule. Greece was at peace, united not by a Greek but by an outsider.

REVIEW *What ruler united Greece and where was he from?*

Building an Empire

Alexander's mother, Olympias, had tried for years to convince Philip that Alexander should be the one to follow in his footsteps. When Philip died in 336 B.C., her dreams came true and 20-year-old Alexander became king.

Young Alexander wanted to rule not only Greece but all the world. The world known to Alexander was eastern Europe, northern Africa, and western Asia. Alexander began by conquering Greece's old enemy, the Persians.

In 334 B.C. Alexander led more than 35,000 soldiers from Greece to Asia Minor. One by one Alexander seized the region's Greek colonies, which were controlled by Persia.

For the most part, Alexander established democratic rule in the Greek cities he freed. However, this did not mean that they had full independence. The Greek cities were forced to accept Alexander as their new ruler.

Throughout his growing empire Alexander, or Alexander the Great as he came to be called, built new cities. The cities became centers of learning and helped spread Greek culture. Alexander named many of these cities Alexandria, after himself. In time Alexandria, Egypt, rivaled Athens as the center of Greek culture.

The many different peoples throughout Alexander's empire learned to speak the Greek language and began to worship Greek gods. Greek influence became so

This gold crown (left) was worn by Alexander the Great. In this portrait from long ago (below), Alexander charges into battle against the Persians.

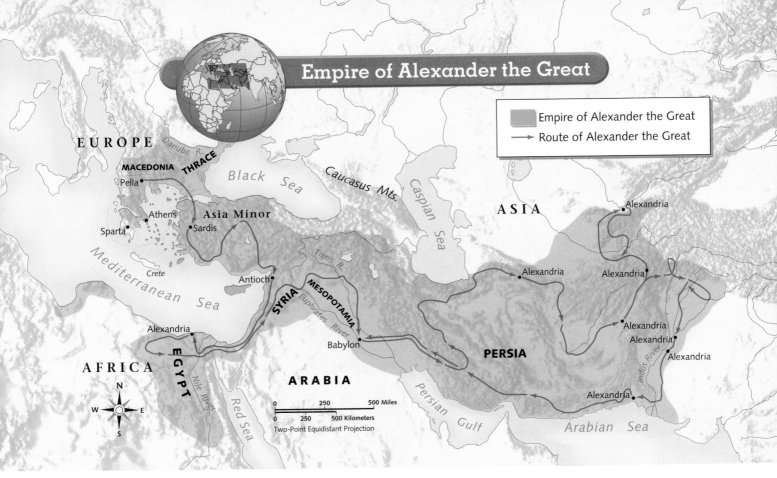

Empire of Alexander the Great

Empire of Alexander the Great
→ Route of Alexander the Great

EUROPE
MACEDONIA
THRACE
Pella
Danube R.
Black Sea
Caucasus Mts.
Caspian Sea
ASIA
Athens
Asia Minor
Sardis
Sparta
Crete
Mediterranean Sea
Antioch
SYRIA
MESOPOTAMIA
Tigris R.
Euphrates River
Alexandria
Alexandria
Alexandria
Babylon
PERSIA
Indus River
Alexandria
Alexandria
Alexandria
AFRICA
EGYPT
Nile River
ARABIA
Red Sea
Persian Gulf
Alexandria
Arabian Sea
N W E S

0   250   500 Miles
0   250   500 Kilometers
Two-Point Equidistant Projection

Regions   In 13 years Alexander conquered much of the world known to him. He ruled over many people and cultures.
■ *How many continents did Alexander's empire reach?*

strong that the period of Alexander's rule and the time shortly after his death became known as the **Hellenistic**, or "Greek-like," Age.

Alexander's conquests made him the ruler of a **multicultural** empire, or an empire of many cultures. As the ruler of many different peoples, Alexander felt it was wise to adopt Greek culture. This helped the Persians and other conquered people accept his rule. By 331 B.C. Alexander's empire stretched from the Danube River in Europe south to the Nile River in Africa and east beyond the Tigris and Euphrates rivers in Asia. Alexander had conquered Asia Minor, Syria, Egypt, Mesopotamia, and the once-mighty Persian Empire—all without losing a single major battle!

REVIEW *In what way did Alexander build his empire?*

The Breakup of the Empire

wanted more lands. Beyond Persia lay India. Alexander led

This silver coin made in Babylon honors Alexander's battle against soldiers on elephants in India.

The scenes on this limestone coffin show Alexander in battle.

his soldiers east from Babylon to the Indus River. He planned to push on from there to the Ganges River. However, his conquest-weary soldiers refused to follow. Bitterly disappointed, Alexander turned back to Babylon in 326 B.C.

Shortly after he returned to Babylon, in 323 B.C., Alexander became ill with a fever. He died a few days later, just months before his thirty-third birthday. Legend says that before Alexander's death a soldier asked, "To whom will rule of the great empire go?" Alexander answered, "To the strongest!"

No one leader proved strong enough to replace Alexander. His empire broke up quickly after his death as his generals fought for control. In time the empire split into many parts. The largest of these parts were Macedonia, Syria, and Egypt. These three kingdoms were often at war with one another. Even so, these Hellenistic kingdoms continued and built upon many of Alexander's ideas.

REVIEW *Why did Alexander's empire break up after his death?*

Alexander's Legacy

The empire may not have lasted, but the Hellenistic culture that started with Alexander did. As in the time of Pericles, great thinkers of the Hellenistic Age shaped later cultures for centuries.

Hellenistic teachers worked out new ideas in mathematics. In Alexandria, Egypt, Euclid (YOO•kluhd) studied lines and angles and began the study of geometry.

This stone artwork from India shows how far Hellenistic influence in art had reached.

Archimedes (ar•kuh•MEE•deez), of Syracuse on the island of Sicily, used mathematics to build many useful machines.

Hellenistic scientists also used mathematics in their thinking about the Earth and the other planets. For example, Aristarchus (air•uh•STAR•kuhs) used mathematics to discover that the Earth and the other planets move around the sun.

Hellenistic scientists built on the knowledge of medicine that Hippocrates had introduced. During the Hellenistic Age, Alexandria, Egypt, became the center for the study of medicine and surgery. Doctors there learned that the brain was the center of the nervous system.

By 146 B.C. another group of people, the Romans, had grown strong enough to gain control of the Mediterranean world. But the knowledge the Greeks had gained was not forgotten. The Romans borrowed from the religion, the art, the architecture, the philosophy, and the language of the Greeks to build their own civilization.

REVIEW *In what subject areas did great thinkers of the Hellenistic Age make discoveries?*

Hellenistic advances in architecture can be seen in these tombs, carved around the year 7 B.C. The tombs were cut out of rock in what is now Turkey.

LESSON 4 REVIEW

Check Understanding

1. **Remember the Facts** Who was Alexander the Great?

2. **Recall the Main Idea** How did Alexander the Great affect the region around the Mediterranean?

Think Critically

empire?

4. **Explore Viewpoints** Alexander believed that by taking up some of the ideas and customs of the people he conquered he could gain support for his rule. Many of his soldiers did not share this view. Why do you think they disagreed on this issue?

5. **Past to Present** Who are some individuals affecting events in the world today?

Show What You Know

in your school, such as student attitudes, clothing, or behavior. Then, for one week, see how much impact your team can have in making changes in that area. When the week ends, make a report to the class.

2000 B.C.   1500 B.C.

1600 B.C.   **1450 B.C.**
• Minoan culture   • Mycenaean
  flourishes   culture
                        gains
                        strength

CONNECT MAIN IDEAS

Use this organizer to describe the history of ancient Greece. Write two examples for each box. A copy of the organizer appears on page 52 of the Activity Book.

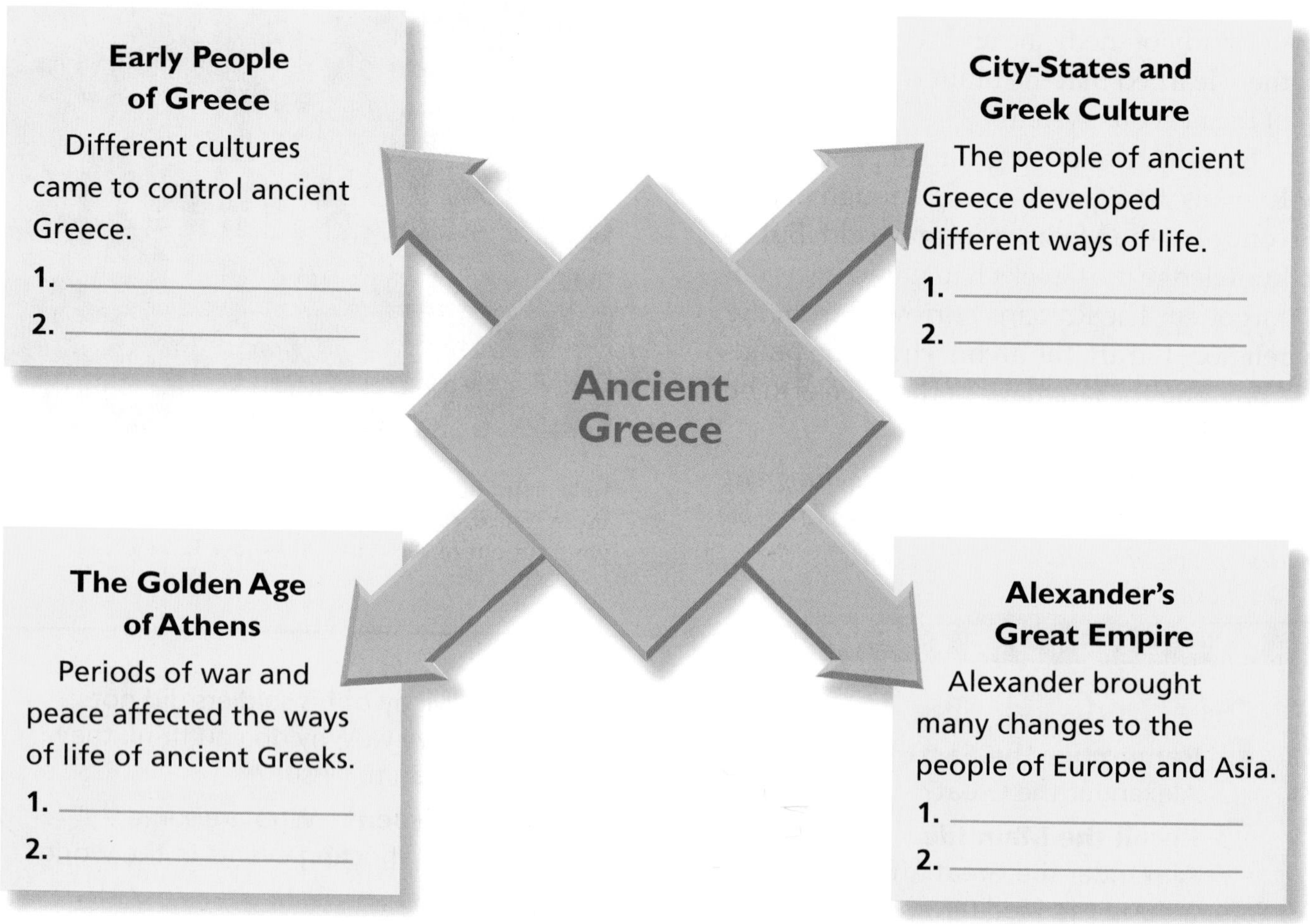

Early People of Greece

Different cultures came to control ancient Greece.

1. _____
2. _____

City-States and Greek Culture

The people of ancient Greece developed different ways of life.

1. _____
2. _____

Ancient Greece

The Golden Age of Athens

Periods of war and peace affected the ways of life of ancient Greeks.

1. _____
2. _____

Alexander's Great Empire

Alexander brought many changes to the people of Europe and Asia.

1. _____
2. _____

WRITE MORE ABOUT IT

Write a Compare-and-Contrast Report
Write a report that compares and contrasts the city-states of Athens and Sparta. Discuss their governments and achievements.

Write a Description The poet Homer described Crete as "a rich and lovely land, washed by the waves on every side." Write your own description of Greek lands.

800 B.C.
• Greek city-states begin to form

479 B.C.
• Golden Age of Athens begins

331 B.C.
• Alexander's empire reaches largest size

USE VOCABULARY

For each pair of terms, write at least one sentence that shows how the terms are different from each other.

1. epic, myth

2. acropolis, agora

3. aristocracy, oligarchy

4. league, alliance

CHECK UNDERSTANDING

5. Why was Greece a good center for trade?

6. Who was Homer?

7. For what did the Minoans use their huge palaces?

8. Why did the Spartans form a military culture?

9. What were three ways in which the people in the different Greek city-states felt a cultural connection with one another?

10. What people were not included in Athenian democracy?

11. How did winning the Persian Wars affect Athens?

12. Why is the period of Alexander's rule known as the Hellenistic Age?

13. What happened to Alexander's empire

THINK CRITICALLY

14. **Past to Present** How is the present-day government of the United States like the Athenian government under Pericles? How is it different?

15. **Personally Speaking** Why do you think Alexander the Great wanted to control a large empire?

16. **Cause and Effect** How did the thinkers of the Hellenistic Age change people's understanding of the world?

APPLY SKILLS

Predict a Likely Outcome During the time of Alexander the Great, Greek culture strongly affected the Mediterranean region. Before you read Chapter 8, predict how the death of Alexander would change this. Be sure to use the three-step process listed on page 246. Write down your prediction. Then, as you read Chapter 8, see whether the information you learn supports your prediction.

READ MORE ABOUT IT

Alexander the Great by Robert Green. Franklin Watts. This biography gives details about the life of the young conqueror, who built a mighty empire in Europe and Asia. The author not only describes Alexander's

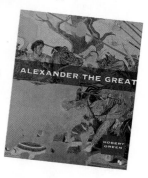

military leader.

Visit the Internet at
http://www.hbschool.com
for additional resources.

ANCIENT ROME

*"Veni, vidi,
vici."*
*(I came,
I saw,
I conquered.)*

Julius Caesar,
after a victory
in battle in 46 B.C.

The Roman Republic

FOCUS
What causes change in government today?

Main Idea As you read, look for changes in the government of Rome and the reasons for these changes.

Vocabulary

republic
consul
dictator
senate
patrician
plebeian
tribune
veto
province

After the death of Alexander in 323 B.C., control of the Mediterranean slowly shifted from Greece to Rome. Beginning as a small village on the peninsula of Italy, Rome grew to control a great empire. As Rome grew larger, its government changed to help meet the changing needs of the Romans.

The Peninsula of Italy

The Italian Peninsula lies just west of the Balkan Peninsula in southern Europe. It looks like a long, high-heeled boot. The "toe" of the boot seems ready to kick away the nearby island of Sicily. Less than 100 miles (161 km) across the Mediterranean Sea lies the northern coast of Africa. Halfway up the peninsula the Tiber River flows east to west. Surrounding Italy in every direction but north are seas—the Adriatic in the east, the Tyrrhenian (tuh•REE•nee•uhn) in the west, and the Mediterranean in the south.

Because the hills and mountains in Italy are less rugged than those in Greece, greater travel, trade, and communication were possible. Also, the peninsula's fertile soil let early farmers raise many different crops to meet their needs. Italy, however, had few good harbors, so overseas travel and trade were difficult. Because of this, the early people of Italy traded more with each other than with

In A.D. 79 the ancient city of Pompeii was covered by ashes and stone from a volcanic eruption of Mount Vesuvius. The ashes and stone helped protect artifacts and artwork, such as this portrait.

rises a snow-capped mountain range called the Alps. Another mountain range, the Apennines (A•puh•nynz), runs along Italy's northeast coast.

REVIEW *How did geography affect early people of the Italian Peninsula?*

The Founding of Rome

People have lived on the peninsula of Italy for thousands of years. Around 1000 B.C. people known as Latins migrated from central Europe to the peninsula. They built villages near the banks of the Tiber River. One of these villages later became the city of Rome.

The rolling land around Rome offered good soil for farming. It also had natural resources such as wood and stone for building. The inland location and hilly country protected the settlers of Rome from enemies. "Not without good reason did gods and men choose this spot as the site of a city," a Roman historian wrote.

The early farmers of Rome told colorful legends to explain the beginnings of their city. One legend says that a cruel uncle left twin baby boys to die on the banks of the Tiber. A mother wolf saved the twins. Romulus and Remus, the twins, grew up to be heroes. In 753 B.C., according to the legend, they founded a city near where they had grown up. Romulus became the first king of the new city. The city was named Rome in his honor. Romulus promised that the small city would rise to greatness. "My Rome shall be the capital of the world," Romulus said.

REVIEW *Why was the area around Rome a good place to settle?*

From Monarchy to Republic

In about 600 B.C. a neighboring people called the Etruscans took control of Rome. The Etruscans, who had frequently traded with the Greek colonies, introduced the Romans to Greek ideas and customs. Etruscan writing, which was based on the Greek alphabet, became the model for the

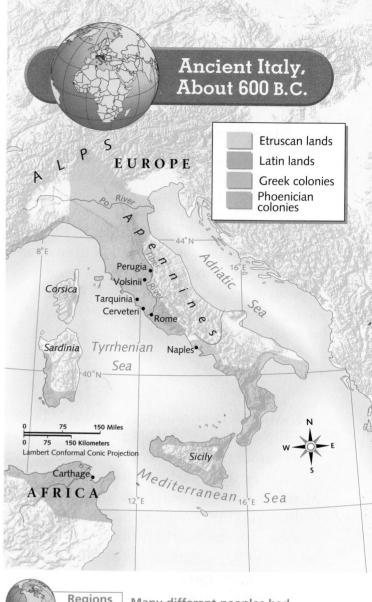

Ancient Italy, About 600 B.C.

- Etruscan lands
- Latin lands
- Greek colonies
- Phoenician colonies

Regions Many different peoples had settled on the peninsula of Italy by 600 B.C. ■ *Why do you think people settled where they did in Italy?*

Latin alphabet. After almost 100 years of Etruscan rule, the Romans rebelled. They ended the monarchy and started a new kind of government. Roman citizens now elected leaders to make all government decisions. They called their new government a **republic**.

As in Athens, free males in the Roman Republic formed an assembly of citizens. But the Roman assembly, unlike the assembly of Athens, did not make government decisions directly. Instead, the Roman assembly passed laws and elected representatives to carry out the business of Roman government.

Each year the Roman assembly elected two chief officials called **consuls**. Having two consuls meant that no one person would gain too much power. The consuls led the armies, served as judges, and acted for the citizens of Rome. In an emergency, Romans could appoint a dictator for a six-month term. A **dictator** is a ruler with complete authority. In Rome a dictator could give orders that even the two consuls had to obey.

The elected consuls were advised by a governing body called the **senate**. Only people of Rome's upper class could become senators. Roman citizens were divided into two classes. **Patricians** (puh•TRIH•shuhnz), who were the descendants of Rome's earliest settlers, formed the upper class. **Plebeians** (plih•BEE•uhnz)—the farmers, merchants, soldiers, and craftworkers—made up the lower class. The patricians controlled Rome's government and considered the plebeians to be less important.

In 494 B.C. the plebeians rebelled. They marched out of Rome to set up their own assembly. They then elected their own special officials called **tribunes**. The patricians realized that Rome's economy would suffer without the plebeians. They agreed to let the plebeians keep their assembly and tribunes. The tribunes could attend meetings of the senate and **veto**, or refuse to agree to, any laws they did not like.

The plebeians also protested Rome's unwritten laws. Only patrician leaders knew exactly what the laws were. In 451 B.C. and 450 B.C., the Roman government began recording its laws on tablets called the Twelve Tables. The laws were posted in Rome's forum, or public square.

Because the laws were now common knowledge, the plebeians knew how their rights differed from those of the patricians. More and more, they began to ask for changes. In time, the rights of plebeians and patricians became more nearly equal.

In all classes, men ruled Roman households. Women did help make household decisions and often gave advice to their

The ancient Etruscans are particularly remembered for their fine art. This stone coffin, with the images of an Etruscan husband and wife, was made about 2,600 years ago.

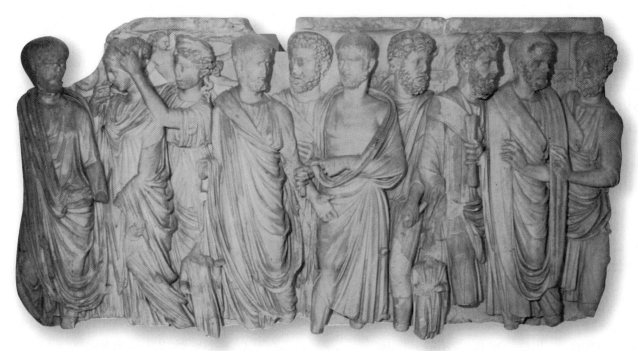

This wall sculpture shows a group of Roman senators and a Roman woman and her servant. While Roman women did enjoy some freedoms, they were not allowed to take part in government.

husbands. They were also allowed to own property. However, women took no direct part in government decision making.

REVIEW *What form of government did the Romans set up after they freed themselves from Etruscan rule?*

The Path of Roman Conquest

Around 500 B.C. the Romans extended their power. The Romans fought many wars to defend themselves from attack. By 272 B.C. the whole Italian Peninsula belonged to Rome.

During this time, a strong rivalry developed between Rome and Carthage, a city-state in northern Africa started by the Phoenicians. Between 264 B.C. and 146 B.C., Rome fought three wars with Carthage. The wars are called the Punic (PYOO•nik) Wars, after the Roman name for Phoenician—*Punicus.*

The wars erupted because both Rome and Carthage wanted to control sea trade in the western Mediterranean. After a long fight

Rome won the first Punic War. In the second Punic War, the city of Rome itself was threatened. Led by a general named Hannibal, Carthage's army marched on Rome. Starting in what is now Spain, Hannibal led his soldiers and war elephants over high, snow-covered mountains into Italy. A Roman historian later wrote about Hannibal,

66 No work could tire his body or his spirit. Heat and cold were the same to him. . . . He was always the first into battle and the last to leave. 99

Although tired, the soldiers of Carthage surprised the Romans with sudden attacks. They fought so fiercely that they nearly defeated Rome. Then a Roman general named Scipio (SIH•pee•oh) made a clever move. He left the Italian Peninsula and attacked lands in northern Africa under Carthage's control. Hannibal was forced to return and defend his home city. In 202 B.C. Hannibal lost an important battle in the town of Zama near Carthage, and Carthage had to give up.

In 146 B.C. the third and final Punic War left Carthage in ruins. The Romans sold many Carthaginians into slavery.

By this time Greece, Macedonia, and parts of southwestern Asia were under Roman control. The Romans divided the land they now ruled into **provinces**, or self-governing regions. A Roman governor ruled each province. The people had to pay taxes to Rome, and many individuals were enslaved. The victory over Carthage provided a steady supply of grain to feed the growing population of the city of Rome.

REVIEW *What lands did Rome conquer between 500 B.C. and 146 B.C.?*

This coin shows Hannibal, whose war methods are still studied today.

From Republic to Dictatorship

The tax money from the provinces made the upper class richer, but the slaves who came made the lower class poorer. Many plebeians lost their jobs to the enslaved workforce. This caused conflicts between patricians and plebeians. Two brothers, Tiberius and Gaius Gracchus, tried to change the laws to help the lower classes. However, the senate rejected these changes. Both brothers were killed for their ideas.

Movement By 44 B.C. Rome controlled lands in Europe and Africa.
■ *What advantages did Rome gain by conquering all the land around Italy?*

Lands Controlled by Rome, to 44 B.C.

ATLANTIC OCEAN

EUROPE

Rhine River
Loire River
ALPS
Po River
Pyrenees
Ebro River
Apennines
Danube River
Black Sea
Byzantium

New Carthage (Cartagena)
Carthage
Zama
Mediterranean Sea
Cyrene
Alexandria
Antioch
Jerusalem
EGYPT
Nile River
Red Sea
AFRICA

Roman lands, about 509 B.C.
New lands by 270 B.C.
New lands by 133 B.C.
New lands by 44 B.C.
→ Hannibal's route, 218–216 B.C.

0   250   500 Miles
0   250   500 Kilometers
Azimuthal Equal-Area Projection

For the next 50 years, many leaders tried to gain control of the republic. In 82 B.C., after a bloody civil war, Lucius Sulla became dictator. He ruled for three years, not for just the six months Roman law allowed. The Romans' acceptance of rule by one rather than rule by many meant that the republic could not last much longer. Sulla retired in 79 B.C., and the office of consul was restored. Such leaders as Pompey and Cicero (SIH•suh•roh) ruled as consuls after Sulla.

In 59 B.C. a Roman general named Julius Caesar was elected as consul. Caesar put together a careful plan. His first move was to form an army and capture Gaul (what is now France). His success in winning Gaul for the Romans proved his military genius. As governor of the new province of Gaul, Caesar kept close watch on Rome.

In 49 B.C. Caesar prepared to return to Rome. By this time the senate feared that he would try to take over the Roman government. The senate warned Caesar not to bring his soldiers past the Rubicon River, the border between Gaul and Italy. "The die is cast," Caesar said as he crossed the Rubicon with his army and declared war on his enemies in Rome. Civil war broke out as Caesar fought his enemies for power.

In 46 B.C. Julius Caesar was declared dictator for ten years. In 44 B.C. Caesar became

HISTORY

Roman Calendar

July, the seventh month of our modern calendar year, is named for Julius Caesar. Before Caesar's time, the calendar was not long enough to match the 365-day solar year. To solve this problem, Caesar added 67 days to the calendar. Then Caesar made the first year of the new calendar very long to get the new calendar on track. The year 46 B.C. had 445 days! The Romans called this unusual year "the year of confusion."

Julius Caesar

dictator for life. The republic had become a dictatorship. Caesar proved to be a strong leader. He immediately made changes, such as creating laws to help the poor. He also gave citizenship to more people.

Caesar's time of glory was short. He was stabbed to death in 44 B.C. on March 15, the Ides of March on the Roman calendar. Caesar's death led to a time of civil war.

REVIEW *What kind of ruler was Julius Caesar?*

LESSON I REVIEW

Check Understanding

1 **Remember the Facts** What three forms of government did Rome have between 600 B.C. and 44 B.C.?

2 **Recall the Main Idea** What caused each change in Rome's government?

Think Critically

3 **Past to Present** Has our country ever changed its form of government? If so, describe the changes.

4 **Explore Viewpoints** At first, only patricians could become Roman senators. How might a patrician have felt differently than a plebeian about this?

Show What You Know

Writing Activity Imagine that you are a Roman politician trying to get people to vote for you. Write a speech promising good government for Rome.

The Roman Empire

FOCUS
What factors help unite many different peoples under one government today?

Main Idea As you read, look for reasons that many peoples united under the Roman Empire.

Vocabulary

forum	basilica
policy	gladiator
census	acid rain
legion	aqueduct

After Julius Caesar's death a new leader rose up to rule the Roman lands. This new leader brought many different peoples into the Roman culture. Over the next few hundred years, more than 75 million people came to call themselves Romans.

Rome Becomes an Empire

Julius Caesar's death left Rome without a leader. Crowds gathered daily in Rome's **forum**, or public square. There they listened as people who wished to be leaders spoke for or against the **policies**, or plans, that Julius Caesar had wanted to carry out.

Meanwhile, Octavian (ahk•TAY•vee•uhn), Caesar's grandnephew, and Mark Antony, a general in the army, had gained control of all Roman lands. Octavian claimed the western part of the empire. Antony claimed the eastern part, made up of Asia Minor, Syria, and Egypt. Antony fell in love with the Egyptian queen, Cleopatra. Together they planned to set up their own empire. Octavian declared war on Antony and Cleopatra when he learned of their plan.

In 31 B.C. Octavian and Antony met in a great sea battle near Actium in Greece. Octavian defeated Antony and Cleopatra and gained absolute leadership of all Roman lands.

In 27 B.C. the Roman senate gave Octavian the title *Augustus.* The title means "respected one" or "holy one."

Upon gaining control of Rome, Augustus boasted,

❝ I freed the Roman Republic from the control of those who assassinated Julius Caesar. . . . The Roman senate . . . and all the Roman people have called me 'Father of the Country.' ❞

Julius Caesar's grandnephew, Octavian, later known as Augustus

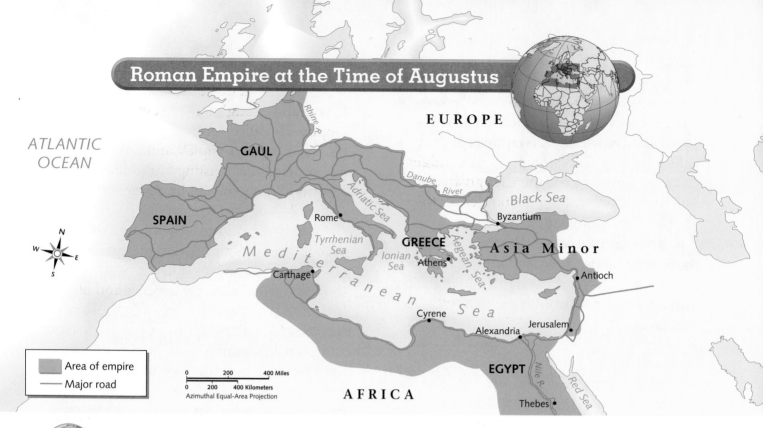

EUROPE

ATLANTIC
OCEAN

GAUL

Rhine R.

SPAIN

Danube
River

Black Sea

Byzantium

Rome

Adriatic Sea

Tyrrhenian
Sea

GREECE

Asia Minor

Mediterranean Sea

Ionian
Sea

Athens

Aegean Sea

Antioch

Carthage

Cyrene

Jerusalem

Alexandria

EGYPT

Nile R.

Red Sea

AFRICA

Thebes

N
W E
S

Area of empire
Major road

0   200   400 Miles
0   200   400 Kilometers
Azimuthal Equal-Area Projection

Place Augustus's empire included lands in Africa, Asia, and Europe.
The Roman Empire stretched for thousands of miles.

MAP THEME

■ *How do you think ancient Romans traveled to Carthage, by land
or by water?*

Augustus was Rome's first true emperor, but he never called himself by this title. The new leader believed that he was continuing the Roman Republic. Yet, unlike in a republic, Augustus ruled year after year after year.

The Roman people cherished the idea of a republic, so Augustus made sure his government seemed to be representative. But his rule signaled the end of the Roman Republic.

REVIEW *Who was Rome's first emperor?*

The Age of Augustus

Augustus turned out to be the strong leader the Romans needed. Under Augustus a *Pax Romana*, or Roman Peace, spread across the empire. This time of peace and unity for the Romans lasted for more than 200 years—from 27 B.C. to A.D. 180, long after Augustus's death. During this time, the

empire grew to about 2 ½ million square miles (about 6 ½ million sq km).

Augustus began his rule by making changes in the Roman government. He carefully chose the people for top government jobs, such as governors for the provinces. Like Julius Caesar, he passed laws that made more men eligible for citizenship. These policies helped create a government that was popular and strong enough to hold the empire together.

Over the years Roman laws were created so that people would be treated more fairly and equally. One law said that a person is innocent until proven guilty. Another law stated that people could not be forced to speak against themselves in a court of law. These and other Roman principles are still important to our legal system today.

The Romans also created the idea of a **census**, or count of a country's people. The census helped the government make sure that all the people paid their taxes.

To help keep peace and unity, Augustus depended on the Roman army. The well-trained army was divided into large groups called **legions** (LEE•juhnz). A legion might have as many as 6,000 men. Augustus had legions stationed along the borders of the empire to keep invaders out.

The roads the army built and traveled on united the Roman people. The Roman road system was built to help legions move quickly from province to province, but traders and travelers used them too. In time the roads connected almost all parts of the empire to Rome. The saying "All roads lead to Rome" came from this time. Roman roads brought together goods and ideas from all over the empire. The movement of ideas led to cultural borrowing between provinces.

REVIEW *How did the army's road system unite the peoples of the Roman Empire?*

Pride in Rome

Augustus felt that the city of Rome did not look grand enough for the center of a great empire. He called for new government offices, libraries, temples, and public baths and ordered that existing buildings be rebuilt. "I found Rome a city of bricks and left it a city of marble," he said.

Around the Palatine (PA•luh•tyn), the hill in the center of Rome, stood huge marble government buildings called **basilicas** (buh•SIL•ih•kuhz). New temples and other buildings rose beside them. In this area merchants sold fresh meats and vegetables, cloth, and pottery. The rich could buy fine things from faraway parts of the empire such as Egypt and Spain. For those who could read, there were papyrus scrolls filled with writing for sale.

The influence of Greek culture could be seen in every new building. Roman builders admired the beauty of Greek architecture. They used the straight Greek columns and

Roman stone roads (left) still cross the land that once was the Roman Empire. Horses and carriages (below) could be rented in large towns for travel on these roads.

beams in their own buildings. Then the Romans added ideas of their own, such as domes. They also used arches, an idea they borrowed from the Etruscans.

The Romans enjoyed entertainment, so some of the new buildings were theaters and sports arenas. The largest arena, the Colosseum (kah•luh•SEE•uhm), was completed in A.D. 80, after Augustus's death. Here as many as 50,000 Romans watched battles between **gladiators**, who were slaves and prisoners forced to fight, often to their death.

The buildings in Rome gave leaders all over the empire the idea of rebuilding their cities in the same way. As far away as Britain and Syria, people built forums in the centers of their cities. Around the forums they built temples, baths, libraries, and arenas.

Some of Rome's ancient buildings still stand today. However, the survival of these buildings is in question. A type of pollution called acid rain is damaging the ancient ruins. **Acid rain** is water mixed with gases caused by the burning of fossil fuels, such as coal and oil. The gases and water form an acid that falls to Earth with the rain.

All over the empire Romans built many aqueducts. An **aqueduct** uses bridges and canals to carry water from place to place. The stone aqueducts of the Roman Empire carried water from far-off rivers to the cities.

REVIEW *What kinds of buildings were put up in Rome?*

Arts, Literature, and Language

Rome was the leader of the Mediterranean region, but Romans often looked to Greece for cultural ideas. Roman artists and sculptors copied Greek art. Roman writers copied Greek writing styles. The ideas of the Greek philosophers Socrates, Plato, and Aristotle also spread to Rome. As the Roman poet Horace said, "Conquered Greece conquered its uncultured conqueror and brought the arts to Rome."

Augustus asked Roman artists and writers to create works that would bring out patriotic feelings among the Roman people. Above all, Augustus wanted an epic to glorify Rome as the *Iliad* and the *Odyssey* had glorified Greece.

The Romans are well known for their skilled building of aqueducts (top left), arenas, and other structures. As many as 50,000 Romans could gather to watch events in the Colosseum, an arena completed in A.D. 80 (below left and right).

Public Baths

The Roman government built many large pools and baths. People not only washed themselves there, but also met their friends or discussed business. Some Roman baths even contained libraries and shops. The Romans built baths all over the lands they had conquered. Ruins of Roman baths can be found in places such as Britain, France, Israel, Syria, Tunisia, and Algeria.

A poet named Virgil (VER•juhl) wrote the *Aeneid* (ih•NEE•uhd), which gives the poet's view of early Roman history. As Augustus had hoped, the *Aeneid* stirred the feelings of Romans everywhere.

Language also helped bring together all parts of the Roman Empire. As Roman soldiers and traders traveled through the provinces, they used the Latin language. Latin came to be used in government and education in all the Roman provinces. Latin became an important part of the Roman way of life that spread across the empire.

REVIEW *In what ways did the arts and literature help unify the Roman Empire?*

The Romans often borrowed the ideas of the Greeks. This statue of the Greek goddess Athena is a Roman copy of a Greek statue.

LESSON 2 REVIEW

Check Understanding

1 **Remember the Facts** What changes in government and the arts were made after Augustus became emperor of Rome?

2 **Recall the Main Idea** What helped

Think Critically

3 **Explore Viewpoints** Why do you think Augustus liked to use peaceful methods to bring together the people of his empire?

4 **Past to Present** Like the Roman Empire, the United States is a land of many cultures. What unites the people of the United States?

Show What You Know

map as a guide, make a model or a relief map of the Roman Empire. Show the borders of the present-day countries that now occupy these lands, and write in their names. Use one color to shade all the lands that made up the Roman Empire.

Compare Historical Maps

1. Why Learn This Skill?

One way to learn about history is to study historical maps. A **historical map** gives information about the past. Some historical maps show where events took place. Others show how the world looked at a certain time in the past. Knowing how to use historical maps can help you learn how boundaries have changed or what different names have been given to the same area at different times.

Map A: Rome in 274 B.C.

Map B: Rome in A.D. 117

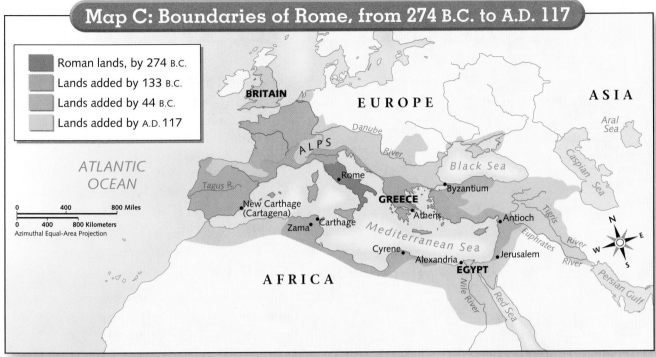

Map C: Boundaries of Rome, from 274 B.C. to A.D. 117

- Roman lands, by 274 B.C.
- Lands added by 133 B.C.
- Lands added by 44 B.C.
- Lands added by A.D. 117

ATLANTIC OCEAN

0   400   800 Miles
0   400   800 Kilometers
Azimuthal Equal-Area Projection

BRITAIN

EUROPE

ASIA

Aral Sea

ALPS

Danube River

Black Sea

Caspian Sea

Rome

Byzantium

GREECE

Athens

Antioch

Tigris River

New Carthage (Cartagena)

Tagus R.

Zama

Carthage

Mediterranean Sea

Cyrene

Alexandria

Jerusalem

Euphrates River

Persian Gulf

AFRICA

EGYPT

Nile River

Red Sea

N E S W

2. Understand the Process

History books and many atlases contain historical maps. Often the title or key of a historical map tells what year or time period is shown on the map.

Map A shows ancient Roman lands in 274 B.C., when Rome controlled the whole Italian Peninsula. The purple area on the map shows lands governed by Rome. The cream-colored areas show lands controlled by other groups.

The Roman Empire grew until it reached its greatest size under the emperor Trajan in A.D. 117. As on Map A, the purple areas on Map B show lands governed by Rome. The cream-colored areas show lands controlled

shows how the boundaries of Rome changed from 274 B.C. to A.D. 117. Look at the map key to learn what each color means. Then use the questions in the next column to help you gather information about the growth of the Roman Empire.

1 What color is the land controlled by Rome in 274 B.C.?

2 What lands did Rome add to its empire by 133 B.C.?

3 By what year did Rome take control of Britain?

4 By what year did Rome take control of Athens?

5 Between what years did Roman lands grow the most? How can you tell?

6 By what year did Rome gain its first land in Africa?

3. Think and Apply

Find a historical map showing the growth of the United States. Study

and when your state became part of the United States. Then, draw your own map to go with your paragraph. Using different colors, show how the United States looked before and after your state joined the Union. Share your paragraph and your map with a partner.

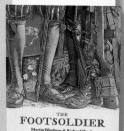

THE
FOOTSOLDIER
Martin Windrow & Richard Hook
OXFORD

THE FOOTSOLDIER

WRITTEN BY
MARTIN WINDROW AND RICHARD HOOK
ILLUSTRATED BY ANGUS MCBRIDE

For centuries Rome's army consisted of volunteers, citizens who served only in times of need. As the Roman Empire grew, leaders decided that the army needed professional soldiers—full-time trained fighters paid by the Roman government. The story that follows tells about the life of professional soldier Sextus Duratius, 2nd Augusta Legion. As you read, think about what makes people willing to lead the life of a soldier.

Roman soldiers protected themselves with body armor similar to the suit shown above.

As a soldier, in what he considered the finest legion in the Empire, Sextus could hope for travel, adventure, and promotion: promotion, perhaps, to the unapproachable godlike status of a senior centurion, commanding a cohort[1] of 500 men. In return for hard knocks and unquestioning obedience he would receive 337½ silver pennies a year, in three installments—less compulsory[2] deductions for rations, boots, replacement of lost kit,[3] burial insurance, and anything else the penny-pinching clerks could think up. He might get handsome[4] bonuses from time to time—if he was in an important victory, or if a new Emperor came to power. Part of his pay would be safely banked for him, and if he survived his term of enlistment he would get a generous lump-sum pension, or a grant of land instead. It was not at all a bad deal—provided you lived to collect it.

Roman helmets (left) protected soldiers in battle. These hob-nailed sandals (below) helped soldiers keep their balance.

During the first months Sextus often doubted that he would survive his first year. He learned the soldier's trade the hard way, harried about the parade ground and practice field by the brazen[5] tongues and vine-wood cudgels[6] of the instructing

---

[1]**cohort:** a part of a legion
[2]**compulsory:** required
[3]**kit:** supplies
[4]**handsome:** generous

[5]**brazen:** bold
[6]**cudgels:** heavy clubs

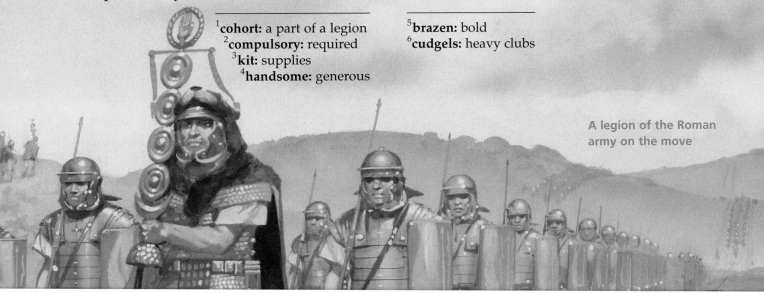

A legion of the Roman army on the move

centurions. He learned how to keep his armor clean and bright, even if it meant sitting up half the night. He learned how to march twenty-five miles a day in full kit, rain or shine, with hob-nailed sandals raising blisters on his blisters. As often as not he reeled back to barracks only to be herded straight off to the practice ground to dig ditches and build ramparts[7]—and to see them filled in again, ready for tomorrow's session. He learned to handle javelin, sword and shield. He suffered more bruises and grazes than he could count from the double-weight wooden swords they practiced with before being trusted with Roman steel in their shaky hands. He learned to recognize the signals for the different battle formations—the "wedge," the "saw," and all the other tricks of combat. And he learned just who, when, and how much to bribe, in order to avoid the frequent appearance of his name on the

---

[7]**ramparts:** walls of earth

centurion's little lists for latrine-cleaning, cookhouse-cleaning, camp-cleaning, and a dozen other traps for the unwary recruit. Before two years had passed he was a thoroughly trained, disciplined, and dangerous professional soldier.

It had been eight years before Sextus and his comrades started their long journey by foot and barge and ship from the familiar surroundings of Strasbourg, with its stone barracks and lively civilian town, to the empty beaches and rolling, forested hills of Britain. In that time he had served on two or three short local expeditions on the German frontier—nothing serious, not much more than tax-gathering trips enlivened by the occasional brisk skirmish.[8] He discovered that his training really worked, and that gave him confidence.

He had needed it, on this rather frightening expedition into the far northern mists. Only the gods knew what horrors awaited a man in these black woods and wind-haunted uplands, to say nothing of the dangers of drowning in the choppy grey seas or dying under the spears of the Britons. They were only savages, of course, but there had been a lot of them in some of the early battles of the invasion. But the magic of Roman arms and discipline worked again, and Sextus soon forgot his doubts and fears.

---

[8]**skirmish:** brief fight

Throughout the Roman Empire, soldiers built forts from which they could defend the land they had conquered.

When the Augusta was detached from the other legions and marched westwards things improved even more. Away from the eyes of the generals and staff officers, the Legate Vespasian proved a fair and decent commander. He expected his legionaries to do their duty, and do it quickly and thoroughly; but he didn't nag at men who were fighting almost every day.

Tonight, for instance, when the battle was over—and to judge from the thickening smoke and the noise from beyond the gateway it wouldn't be long now—Sextus could hope for a good night's rest. Perhaps the auxiliary cohorts which hadn't been in action would be ordered to dig the ramparts and pitch the tents for the men who had fought today? At any rate, Sextus probably wouldn't have to stand guard.

Roman soldiers used daggers and other weapons to win victory over their enemies. Shown above are a Roman dagger (top) and a dagger cover (bottom).

LITERATURE REVIEW

1 What was daily life like for Sextus?

2 Why do you think Sextus joined the army? Why do you think people serve in the armed forces today?

3 Do you think Sextus would want his son to join the army? Make a list of the good points and bad points Sextus might mention about serving as a Roman soldier.

FOCUS

How do religions and societies affect each other today?

Main Idea As you read, look for ways the Christian religion and Roman society affected each other.

Vocabulary

parable
messiah
disciple
crucifixion
Christianity
apostle
persecute
martyr
Gospels
New Testament
Old Testament

Beginnings of Christianity

Parts of the Roman Empire lay far from the city of Rome itself. More than 1,200 miles (1,931 km) from their central city, the Romans claimed the region of Judaea, once known as Judah. Many Jews, the descendants of the Israelites, lived in this distant region. Today, Judaea is remembered by many people around the world as the birthplace of Christianity.

Religion and the Roman Empire

Augustus was not only the ruler of the Roman Empire but also a leader of Rome's religion. As a religious leader, he wanted all citizens to take part in religious ceremonies. He believed that this would help unite the many groups of Romans.

Like most cultures of long ago, the Romans worshipped many gods. Of all their gods, Jupiter was believed to be the most powerful. Other Roman gods included Mars, the god of war, and Ceres, the goddess of the harvest.

Although the Romans had their own religion, they often adopted the gods and the beliefs of the people whom they conquered. The Romans also came to identify some of the gods they already believed in with the gods of other peoples. For example, the Roman goddess Juno, who protected marriage and women, came to be like the Greek goddess Hera. Jupiter, the main Roman god, began to match Zeus, the ruler of the Greek gods. The Roman religion even included myths borrowed from the Greeks.

Belief in the gods was an important part of Roman life. The Romans thought that harm would come to the empire if people did not respect the Roman gods. So Roman law punished those who refused to worship these gods.

The Chi-Rho design (above) was made during the early days of Christianity. Chi and Rho are the first two sounds of the word *Christ* in Greek.

Catacombs (above) were underground tunnels used as burial places for Christians persecuted and killed by the Romans. Many catacombs were decorated with paintings of early Christian scenes (above right) or funeral writings (left).

known as Christians and their religion as **Christianity**.

Among the first to spread the word of Jesus were the **apostles**, a group of twelve men who had been Jesus' closest followers, plus one who joined them later. Peter, the leader of the apostles, was very courageous in spreading the word of Jesus. He talked first to the Jews in Jerusalem and then to both Jews and non-Jews in other parts of the empire.

Paul, a later apostle, was another important teacher of Christianity. Paul was a new believer in Christianity. After he became a convert, he spent the rest of his life explaining the teachings of Jesus to others, converting both Jews and non-Jews to Christianity. Wherever he went in the empire he began Christian communities.

Rome and the New Religion

The spread of Christianity caused concern for Roman leaders. The Romans allowed people to have other religious beliefs as long as they also worshipped the Roman gods. The Roman leaders believed that their gods would become angry because the Christians did not worship them. Therefore, they began to persecute the Christians. To **persecute** someone is to punish him or her for following certain religious beliefs. Often they ordered the death of Christians who would not worship the Roman gods. Christians were killed in cruel ways such as by crucifixion.

Roman persecution did not stop Christianity. In fact, the persecutions who willingly died for their beliefs. Polycarp (A.D. 69–A.D. 155), an 86-year-old bishop from Asia Minor, was one such martyr. A bishop is a leader of a Christian group. When Polycarp was brought before the Roman governor, he was given several chances to give up his beliefs. Polycarp refused, saying he had served Jesus for many years and would not stop. The examples set by Polycarp and other martyrs helped other Christians to remain strong in their beliefs.

Writings by Christians played an important role in the growth of Christianity. Many of the letters that Paul wrote to members of the communities he founded were saved and shared with other Christians. Other Christian writings were grouped to form the **Gospels**, which describe Jesus' life, death, and resurrection. The word *gospel* means "good news." The Gospels are made up of four books: Matthew, Mark, Luke, and John. These and other Christian writings were combined to form the **New Testament**. This part of the Christian Bible tells about the life and teachings of Jesus and about his followers. The first part of the Bible, the **Old Testament**, contains the books of the Hebrew Bible.

REVIEW *How did Roman persecution affect the Christians?*

Constantine Accepts Christianity

As Christianity was growing stronger, the Roman government was growing weaker. The cost of running the empire was very high. The government increased taxes, but even this did not meet the empire's needs. It only caused great hardships for Roman citizens.

At the same time, the Roman Empire faced attack from every side. Outsiders frequently crossed the empire's borders and forced Romans into battle. Invaders from the north attacked Gaul and Spain. The Persians tried to seize Roman lands in Asia. An African people called the Berbers (BER•berz) raided Roman lands in northern Africa.

Today Christianity is practiced throughout the world. The top photograph shows a service in Lewisburg, Pennsylvania. At bottom, Christians worship in Nairobi, Kenya.

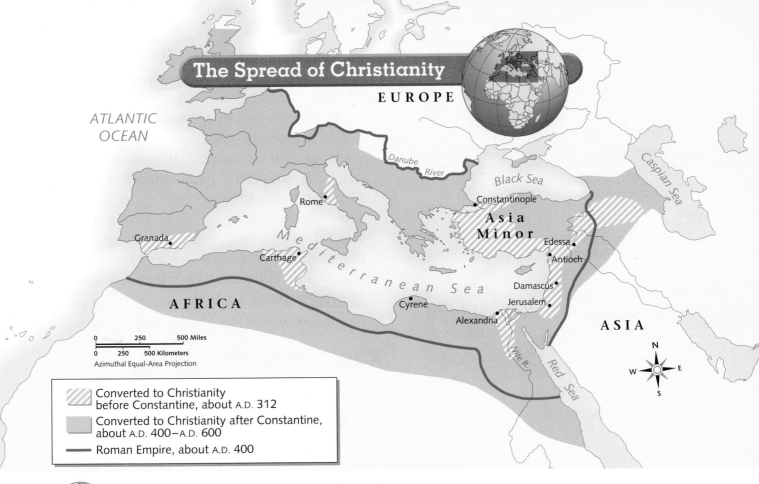

The Spread of Christianity

EUROPE

ATLANTIC OCEAN

Danube River

Black Sea

Constantinople

Asia Minor

Rome

Granada

Carthage

Mediterranean Sea

Edessa

Antioch

Damascus

Jerusalem

Cyrene

Alexandria

AFRICA

ASIA

Caspian Sea

Nile R.

Red Sea

0   250   500 Miles
0   250   500 Kilometers
Azimuthal Equal-Area Projection

N W E S

Converted to Christianity before Constantine, about A.D. 312

Converted to Christianity after Constantine, about A.D. 400–A.D. 600

Roman Empire, about A.D. 400

MAP THEME

Movement Constantine helped Christianity grow by making it the official religion of the Roman Empire.
■ *How many continents had Christianity reached by A.D. 400?*

In addition, many of the Roman emperors between A.D. 180 and A.D. 312 governed badly. They lost the respect of those they ruled. Also, the empire had grown so large that many of its citizens had never been to Rome. They did not care about being a part of the empire. Even the soldiers who fought to keep the empire together felt little loyalty to Rome. Instead, they gave their loyalty to their generals. Wars broke out within the empire as generals fought one another.

In A.D. 312 two Roman generals were both determined to become the next emperor of the Roman Empire. Their armies faced off

changed his life. According to Constantine the Greek letters for the word Christ— *chi rho*— appeared in the sky above him. Over these letters were the Latin words *in hoc signo vinces*, meaning "In this sign you will conquer." So Constantine ordered his soldiers to paint crosses on their shields. The cross was a symbol of Christianity because Jesus had died on a cross.

Constantine won the battle and became emperor. Unlike Roman generals before him, Constantine did not thank the Roman gods. Instead, Constantine began to support Christianity. In A.D. 313 the Edict of Milan made Christianity an accepted religion. Later in that century Christianity became the offi-

but something had just happened that

The Roman Empire Splits in Two, A.D. 395

★ Capital

ATLANTIC OCEAN

EUROPE

WESTERN ROMAN EMPIRE

Black Sea

Rome

Constantinople

Athens

EASTERN ROMAN EMPIRE

Carthage

Mediterranean Sea

Alexandria

AFRICA

0   250   500 Miles
0   250   500 Kilometers
Azimuthal Equal-Area Projection

Place   Fearing that Rome was dangerous, Constantine moved the Roman Empire's capital to Byzantium. Eventually, the empire began to decline and split in two.
■ Which city became the capital of the eastern part?

The Decline of Rome

Constantine did not think Rome was a good place for the capital of the Roman Empire. He felt that Rome was too far from the center of things. He also feared that Rome was unsafe. Constantine chose the city of Byzantium (buh•ZAN•tee•uhm) on the shores of the Black Sea as the new capital. In A.D. 330 Byzantium was renamed Constantinople (kahn•stan•tuhn•OH•puhl), "the city of Constantine."

Rome's power declined after A.D. 330. Since the emperor no longer lived there, many other people left the city of Rome. Then in A.D. 410, Visigoths, led by their king, Alaric (AL•uh•rik), crossed the Alps and attacked the city of Rome.

Few Romans were ready to defend their city. The city of Rome lived on, but it no longer had much power. However, it was still important as the headquarters of the Christian Church.

The Roman Empire split apart. The eastern part of the former empire would keep Roman ways alive for centuries. The western part broke into many small kingdoms. Christianity began to see great growth.

In fact, the message of Jesus spread far beyond the Roman Empire. Christianity has brought together people of many races, languages, and cultures all over the world.

REVIEW *What made the city of Rome lose its importance in the Roman Empire?*

LESSON 4 REVIEW

Check Understanding

1 **Remember the Facts**   Why were Romans concerned about the growth of Christianity?

2 **Recall the Main Idea**   How did the Christian religion and Roman society affect each other?

Think Critically

3 **Think More About It**   Why weren't the Romans successful in stopping Christianity?

4 **Past to Present**   How do religions and societies affect one another today? Why is religious freedom important in the United States?

5 **Cause and Effect**   What do you think caused the Roman Empire to split apart?

Show What You Know

Using a Newspaper
For a week, look for newspaper articles that show how religion affects modern society. Read the articles, and bring the best ones to school to share with your classmates.

Read a Telescoping Time Line

1. Why Learn This Skill?

Think of a time in your life that was very important to you. Maybe it was a vacation you took last summer. Perhaps it was when a favorite relative came for a visit. You probably want to remember every single detail of each day of that special time. In the same way, you may want to remember or take a closer look at a certain time in history. You may want to know more of the details about that time.

One way to look at the details of events in history is with a telescoping time line. Just as a telescope helps you take a closer look at a far-away object, a **telescoping time line** helps you take a closer look at a long-ago time. Knowing how to read a telescoping time line can help you learn the details of events in history.

2. Understand the Process

The time line of early Christianity on this page shows the years between A.D. 1 and A.D. 350. Each date on the main part of the time line marks a period of 50 years.

Many important events happened between the years A.D. 310 and A.D. 330. To show these events more clearly, part of the time line was expanded. The expanded part of the time line gives a "telescope" view of that time period. Each of its dates marks a period of five years.

Use the information on both parts of the time line to answer these questions:

1. Which event took place first, the issuing of the Edict of Milan or the death of Constantine? How do you know?
2. Was the Edict of Milan issued before or after Constantine became emperor? How do you know?
3. Did Constantinople become the capital of the Roman Empire before or after Constantine's death? How do you know?

3. Think and Apply

Use events of your school year to make your own time line. Show one month in detail by including a telescoping section. Share your time line with a family member.

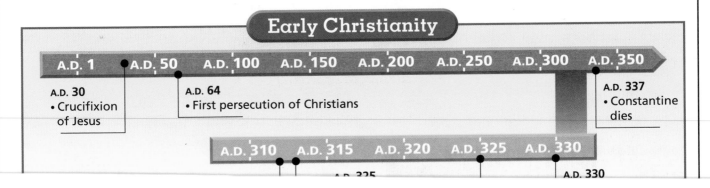

Early Christianity

A.D. 1 · A.D. 50 · A.D. 100 · A.D. 150 · A.D. 200 · A.D. 250 · A.D. 300 · A.D. 350

A.D. 30
• Crucifixion of Jesus

A.D. 64
• First persecution of Christians

A.D. 337
• Constantine dies

A.D. 310 · A.D. 315 · A.D. 320 · A.D. 325 · A.D. 330

A.D. 325

A.D. 330

600 B.C.

500 B.C.
• Roman Republic
begins

400 B.C.

264 B.C.
• First Punic
War starts

CONNECT MAIN IDEAS

Use this organizer to show the growth of the Roman Empire and the changes it faced. Write two details to support each main idea. A copy of the organizer may be found on page 60 of the Activity Book.

Ancient Rome

The Roman Republic
Over the years the government of Rome changed.

1. _____
   _____

2. _____
   _____

The Roman Empire
Many peoples were united under the Roman Empire.

1. _____
   _____

2. _____
   _____

Beginnings of Christianity
The Christian religion and Roman society affected each other.

1. _____
   _____

2. _____
   _____

WRITE MORE ABOUT IT

Write a Speech Write a speech that you, as Roman emperor, will give about why Romans were able to unite many different peoples under one empire.

Write a Diary Entry Imagine that you are a Roman soldier during the time of the Punic Wars. Write a diary entry that describes your thoughts about fighting Hannibal's army.

27 B.C.
• Roman Empire forms

A.D. 30
• Crucifixion of Jesus

A.D. 313
• Christianity becomes an accepted religion in the Roman Empire

A.D. 395
• Roman Empire splits

USE VOCABULARY

For each pair of terms, write at least one sentence that shows how the terms are related.

1. patrician, plebeian

2. tribune, veto

3. republic, consuls

4. Christianity, New Testament

CHECK UNDERSTANDING

5. Who were Romulus and Remus?

6. Why did the Romans set up a republic?

7. How did Julius Caesar plan to rule Rome?

8. Why did Augustus call for new buildings in Rome?

9. Which culture's ideas could be seen in every new Roman building?

10. Why did Roman leaders persecute Christians?

11. What made Constantine begin to support Christianity?

THINK CRITICALLY

12. **Personally Speaking** Do you think that Julius Caesar was right to declare himself dictator of Rome? Explain your answer.

13. **Past to Present** What Roman principles are still important to the United States legal system?

Christians hold on to their beliefs more strongly?

APPLY SKILLS

Compare Historical Maps Use Map C on page 267 and the map on page 277 to answer these questions.

15. Was the Roman Empire larger in A.D. 400 or in A.D. 117?

16. By A.D. 600 had Christianity come to all the lands that had belonged to the Roman Empire in A.D. 117?

Read a Telescoping Time Line Use the information on the time line on page 279 to answer the questions.

17. Did Constantine become emperor nearer to when Jesus was crucified or to when Constantinople became the capital of the Roman Empire? How do you know?

18. About how long after their first persecution did Christians in Rome gain freedom to worship? How do you know?

19. Why is there a telescoping view of the time period between A.D. 310 and A.D. 330?

READ MORE ABOUT IT

Ancient Rome by Simon James. Viking. This fact-filled book explores ancient Roman life, including food and dining, homes, work, and entertainment.

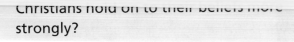

THE GIFTS OF CIVILIZATIONS

You can find many signs of earlier cultures in your life today. Look for the Latin words *e pluribus unum*, "out of many, one," on a coin. You might also find words written in Latin on government buildings. Look at such buildings in your town. They may look like those built by the Greeks and Romans long ago.

The ancient Greek and Roman cultures have affected present-day American life in many ways, especially in government and law. Many of our ideas about democracy came from the Greeks. And law students still study the ideas of Cicero, a Roman lawyer who lived from 106 B.C. to 43 B.C. United States citizens also elect national, state, and local representatives much as the Romans chose representatives during the time of the Roman Republic.

Just as Americans have built on the achievements of Greek and Roman civilizations, the Greeks and Romans built on the achievements of earlier civilizations in Africa and Asia. This cultural borrowing links us with the ancient past and explains how some of our ways of life came to be.

LONG AGO

Think and Apply

With a partner, make an illustrated booklet titled *Cultural Borrowing*. Show some ways in which different cultures from the past and present affect you. Include architecture, holidays, names, ideas, literature, clothing, art, music, and ways of daily life. Share your booklet with the class. Then take it home and discuss it with family members.

BUILDING CITIZENSHIP

HARCOURT BRACE

Visit the Internet at **http://www.hbschool.com** for additional resources.

CNN Turner Le@rning

Check your media center or classroom video library for the Making Social Studies Relevant videotape of this feature.

VISUAL SUMMARY

Summarize the Main Ideas
Study the pictures and captions to help you review the events you read about in Unit 4.

Illustrate the Story
Make your own visual summary for one of the following: 1) the development of democracy in Greece, 2) the growth of Rome, or 3) the beginning and growth of Christianity.

1 The seagoing Minoans and the Mycenaeans were among the earliest people to live in the land now known as Greece.

3 Times of peace in the Greek city-state of Athens led to growth and the development of new ideas.

5 Roman government changed from a monarchy to a republic to an empire.

2 Later, the peoples of ancient Greece developed different ways of life. The Spartans built a military culture. The Athenians developed a democratic government.

4 The conquests of Alexander the Great introduced Greek culture to the peoples of the Mediterranean.

6 Augustus united many groups of people under the Roman Empire.

spread throughout the Roman Empire.

UNIT 4
REVIEW

USE VOCABULARY

Write the term that correctly matches each meaning.

gladiator   isthmus   republic

Hellenistic   martyr

1 a small strip of land that connects two larger pieces of land

2 Greek-like

3 a form of government in which citizens elect leaders to make all government decisions

4 a slave or prisoner forced to fight, often to the death

5 a person who suffers for his or her beliefs

CHECK UNDERSTANDING

6 What do historians think brought an end to Minoan civilization?

7 Who was allowed to take part in Athenian democracy?

8 Why did the early people of Italy trade more with one another than with outsiders?

9 What were the Punic Wars?

10 What effects did the teachings of Jesus have on the Roman Empire?

THINK CRITICALLY

11 **Past to Present** Why might people today be interested in learning how the Minoan and Mycenaean civilizations ended?

12 **Think More About It** Do you think that it is a good idea for people to obey leaders without question, as citizens were taught to do in Sparta? Explain your answer.

APPLY SKILLS

Compare Historical Maps Look closely at the two maps. Then use them to answer the questions.

13 Why are there more colors on the second map than on the first map?

14 What kingdoms formed on the land once ruled by Alexander?

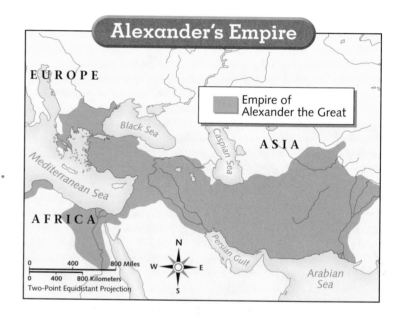

Alexander's Empire

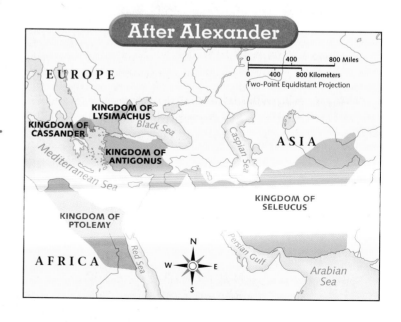

After Alexander

286 • Unit 4

REMEMBER

- Share your ideas.
- Cooperate with others to plan your work.
- Take responsibility for your work.
- Help one another.
- Show your group's work to the class.
- Discuss what you learned by working together.

ACTIVITY

Make a Time Line

With two or three classmates, make a list of important events that you have read about in this unit. For each, write the date and a description of the event at the top of a separate sheet of paper. Below the description, draw a picture to illustrate the event. Then, tape the sheets in the correct time order to create a fold-out time line of Greek and Roman history.

ACTIVITY

Paint a Mural

Work with a group of classmates to paint a mural that shows some of the people and the achievements of the Golden Age of Athens.

ACTIVITY

Plan a Book

Imagine that you have been asked to write a book about ancient civilizations of the Mediterranean. Your publisher says that you may include any topics you like. Work in a group to prepare an outline for the book. Once you have a rough draft, use it to write your outline on a piece of posterboard.

Unit Project Wrap-Up

Build an Ancient City With your classmates, plan and build a model of an ancient Greek or Roman city. Study the notes you made as you read to help you decide what features to include. For example, a Greek city might include an acropolis, an agora, and a theater. A Roman city might include a forum, a temple, a bath, an arena, and aqueducts. To complete this project, the class could divide into several groups. Each group

RISE OF NEW EMPIRES

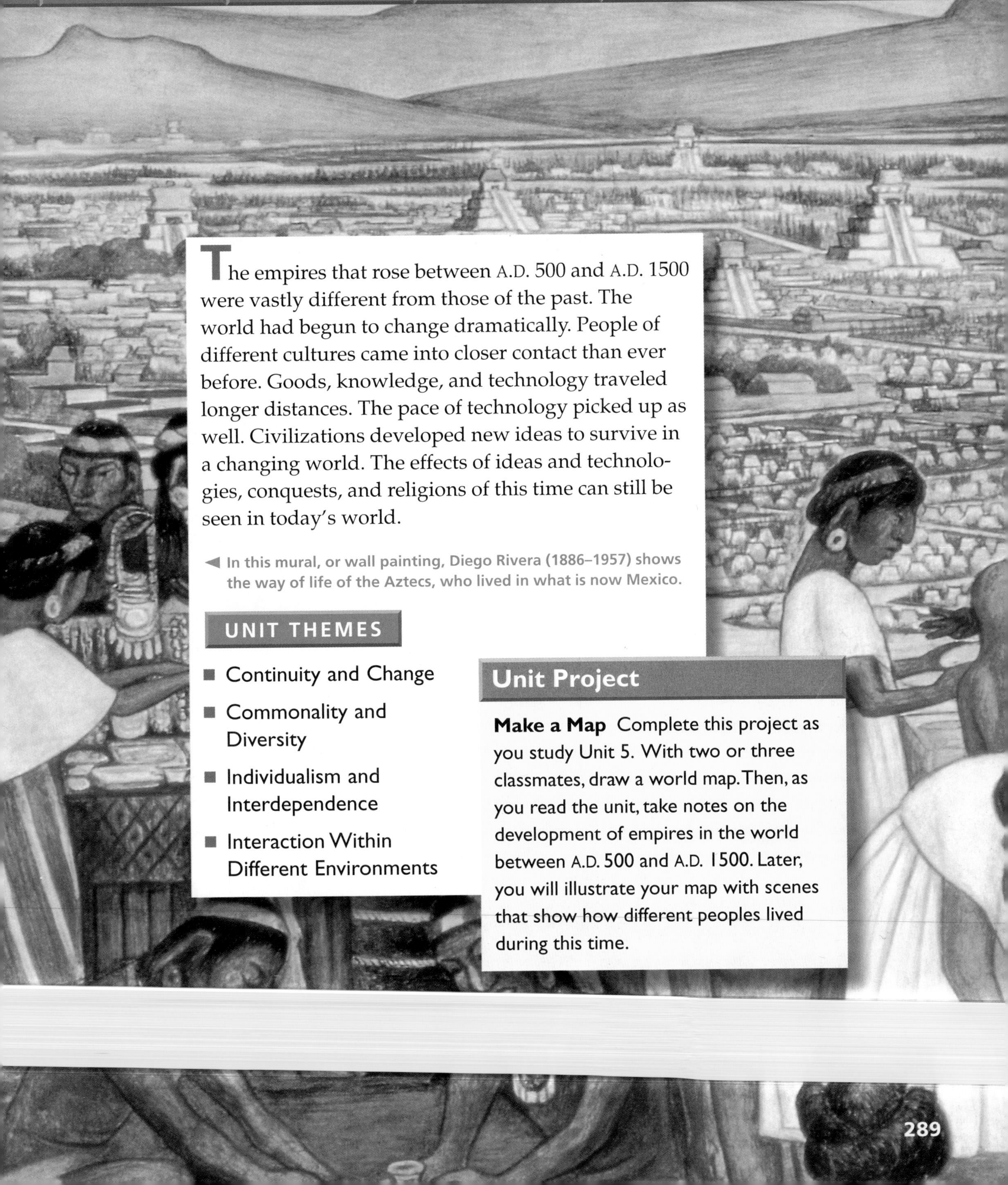

The empires that rose between A.D. 500 and A.D. 1500 were vastly different from those of the past. The world had begun to change dramatically. People of different cultures came into closer contact than ever before. Goods, knowledge, and technology traveled longer distances. The pace of technology picked up as well. Civilizations developed new ideas to survive in a changing world. The effects of ideas and technologies, conquests, and religions of this time can still be seen in today's world.

◄ In this mural, or wall painting, Diego Rivera (1886–1957) shows the way of life of the Aztecs, who lived in what is now Mexico.

UNIT THEMES

- Continuity and Change
- Commonality and Diversity
- Individualism and Interdependence
- Interaction Within Different Environments

Unit Project

Make a Map Complete this project as you study Unit 5. With two or three classmates, draw a world map. Then, as you read the unit, take notes on the development of empires in the world between A.D. 500 and A.D. 1500. Later, you will illustrate your map with scenes that show how different peoples lived during this time.

NORTH AMERICA

PACIFIC OCEAN

ATLANTIC OCEAN

Mississippi River

•Cahokia

Moundville•

Tenochtitlán•

0   1,500   3,000 Miles
0   1,500   3,000 Kilometers
Miller Cylindrical Projection

	Aztec Empire, 1325–1519
	Byzantine Empire, by 565
	Charlemagne's Empire, 814
	Fujiwara, 1200
	Inca Empire, 1438–1532
	Minamoto, 1200
	Mississippian culture, 1250–1400
	Mongol Empire, 1260
	Muslim Empire, 662–750
	Song dynasty, 960–1271
	Tang dynasty, 618–960
•	Major city

SOUTH AMERICA

Amazon River

Machu Picchu• •Cuzco

ANDES MOUNTAINS

N
W   E
S

500   700   900

527
Justinian I becomes
Byzantine emperor
PAGE 297

645
Japan begins to form a
unified government
PAGE 338

750
Muslim Empire
reaches Africa, Asia,
and Europe   PAGE 305

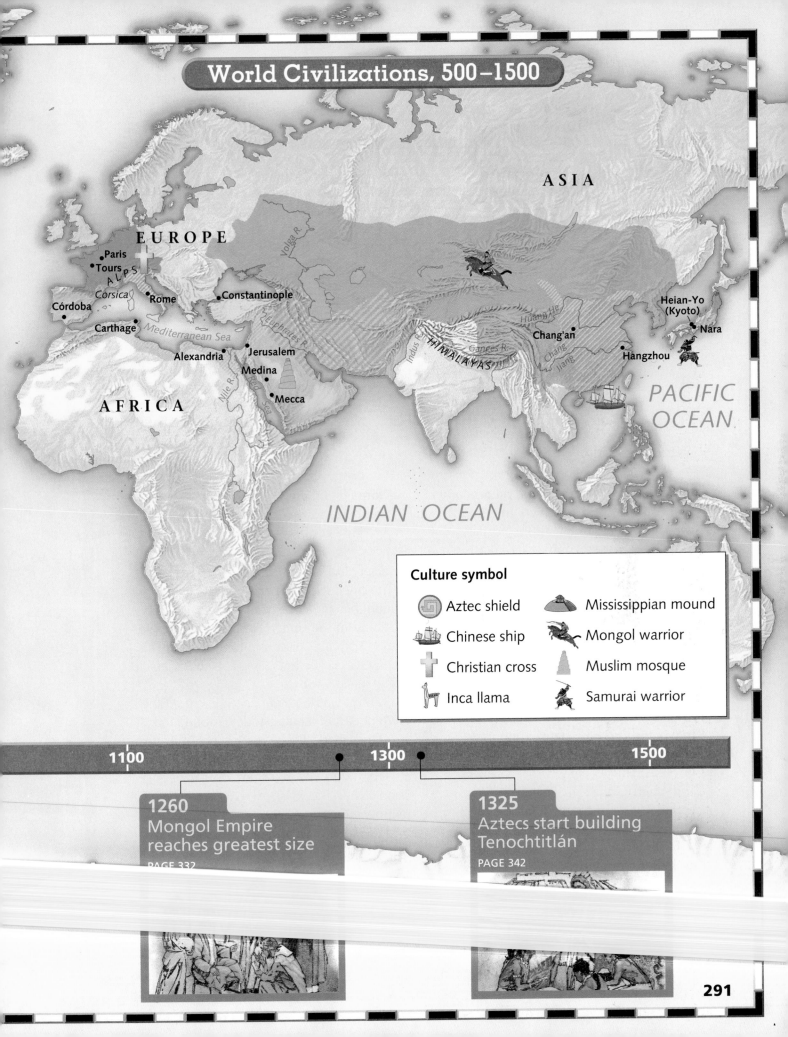

World Civilizations, 500–1500

ASIA

EUROPE

Paris
Tours
ALPS
Corsica
Córdoba
Rome
Constantinople
Carthage
Mediterranean Sea
Alexandria
Jerusalem
Medina
Mecca

Volga R.
Euphrates R.
Nile R.
Red Sea

Indus R.
HIMALAYAS
Ganges R.
Huang He
Chang Jiang

Chang'an

Heian-Yo
(Kyoto)
Nara

Hangzhou

AFRICA

INDIAN OCEAN

PACIFIC
OCEAN

Culture symbol

Aztec shield		Mississippian mound	
Chinese ship		Mongol warrior	
Christian cross		Muslim mosque	
Inca llama		Samurai warrior	

1100   1300   1500

1260
Mongol Empire
reaches greatest size
PAGE 332

1325
Aztecs start building
Tenochtitlán
PAGE 342

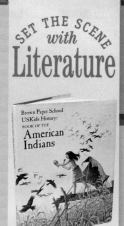

Brown Paper School
USKids History:
BOOK OF THE
American
Indians

THE MOUNDS OF CAHOKIA

written by Marlene Smith-Baranzini & Howard Egger-Bovet
illustrated by George Gaadt

Around the world, unique cultures and empires formed and grew between the years A.D. 500 and A.D. 1500. In Europe the fall of the Roman Empire brought changes in ways of life for the people in both the western and eastern parts of the continent. In southwestern Asia a growing belief in the religion of Islam brought many new ideas to the culture there. In Africa trade brought about strong, wealthy empires. In the Americas a variety of cultures tried out new ideas and new technologies.

One of these cultures was that of the Mississippians in North America. In what is today the state of Illinois arose the largest Mississippian city—Cahokia. The people who lived there and others of the same culture are perhaps best remembered for the huge mounds that they built in their cities.

First read the authors' introduction in the box at right. Then read the story that begins on the next page. The story is about a young man who travels to Cahokia and describes what he sees. Try to picture in your mind the city of Cahokia as it was about 1,000 years ago.

A Society Comes and Goes

The city of Cahokia was part of a larger civilization that stretched from what is now the southeast of the United States, to Oklahoma in the west, and Wisconsin to the north. This society was called the Mississippian Society. It began in A.D. 800.

Cahokia was located near where the Illinois town of East St. Louis is today. Around A.D. 1200 the city declined. The reason is not clear.

Some experts believe the people of Cahokia moved to other nearby cities. Others believe Cahokia became so large it became impossible to grow enough food to feed the city's people. Whatever the reason, the great city of Cahokia was eventually abandoned.

The chief gazed out from his home atop a towering mound of earth. Before him was the city Cahokia with its broad plaza surrounded by many villages.

It was early morning. All across the flat, green land many of the thirty thousand residents had started fires in their homes. The smoke rose up through their dried grass roofs, creating miles of white ribbons in the sky.

By the only entrance to the city, traders, their paid bearers,[1] and city workers lined up waiting to be let in. A guard questioned each

person before allowing him to pass through the small gate shaped like an "L." The city designers created the gate this way to prevent large groups of people from rushing the guard and entering the city.

The wait was long. For those who had traveled to the city by canoe on Cahokia Creek, the wait was an annoyance, a test of their patience. For the bearers paid to carry a trader's supply of stone, it was a test of their strength. These men would get no rest till they reached the city marketplace.

One bearer was not thinking about the dark flintlike rocks he was carrying. He was thinking about Cahokia. As a boy, he had

---

[1] **bearers:** people who carry objects for others

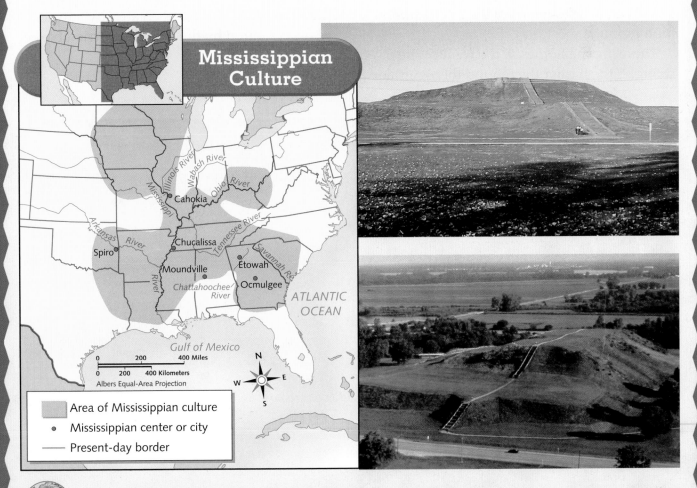

Mississippian Culture

Area of Mississippian culture
• Mississippian center or city
— Present-day border

Place — The Mississippians occupied a large part of what is today the eastern half of the United States. At Cahokia Mounds State Historic Site in Illinois, visitors can see some of the mounds (right) built by the Mississippians.

■ *In which states might you find Mississippian artifacts?*

watched the daily departure of farmers and traders to take their products to the city behind the walls. He had pestered the men, on their return, to tell him of Cahokia. He begged them to hire him as a bearer. They laughed and told him to stop asking and keep growing. He would see Cahokia in time. Now it was his time.

Passing through the gate, the bearer desperately wanted to stop and look around. He had no choice but to follow his trader. The bearer noticed mounds everywhere. He walked by open courts where children played. He passed hundreds of bare-backed men who were carrying baskets of dirt between villages. The bearer saw, among the clay and pole houses of the villages, that certain homes stood above the others upon high mounds.

These are the homes of the wealthy, he thought; the higher the mound the wealthier

the person. He kept moving. Once again, he observed men who carried baskets of dirt.

The bearer stopped, even though his body ached to remove the enormous weight he was carrying. He couldn't believe the size of the mound he was standing next to. He squinted his eyes as he looked up, trying to see the flattened summit[2] 100 feet from the ground. All of Cahokia lived in this mound's shadow. It was the chief's mound, which was 700 feet wide and 1,000 feet long.

The bearer again saw bare-backed men who were carrying baskets of dirt. This time, though, he spotted them dumping the dirt from their baskets onto the ground. A new mound was being formed.

He realized what he had heard was true. These mounds were not created by nature. Workers, hired by the wealthy, carried basket

_____

[2] **summit:** top

after basket of dirt to form the earthworks.[3] He wondered how long it would take to complete the mound. He had no idea that many of the men who were carrying the dirt would never live to see the mound completed. The chief's mound took over two hundred years to build.

The bearer raced to catch up with his trader. Fortunately, the trader hadn't noticed the bearer had been lagging[4] behind. The trader entered the bright, open plaza. It was a maze of traders and craftsmen, all urging the passersby to see their wares that rested beside them on the ground.

The bearer's employer maneuvered[5] his way through the crowd, talking to potential buyers. Craftsmen, who were making arrowheads, baskets, and pottery, discussed business with wealthy men who wanted to buy their goods and sell them many miles away. A jeweler argued with a customer over the worth of his fresh-pearl jewelry.

The trader stopped. He ordered the bearer to put down his merchandise. The bearer released his heavy burden and looked out beyond the people-filled plaza at the burial mounds, and the mounds that held temples. The mounds mesmerized[6] him. Someday, he pondered,[7] I will live in Cahokia, even if I have to carry baskets of dirt.

At the end of this unit, you will learn more about the Mississippians and other peoples of the Americas who lived between A.D. 500 and A.D. 1500. But first, read about the ways of life of others who lived at that time in Europe, Africa, and Asia.

---

[3] **earthworks:** large structures made of earth
[4] **lagging:** moving slowly
[5] **maneuvered:** changed directions for a purpose

[6] **mesmerized:** fascinated
[7] **pondered:** thought

Statue of a Cahokia woman grinding corn (above); one artist's view of how Cahokia looked long ago (left)

HEIRS OF ROME AND PERSIA

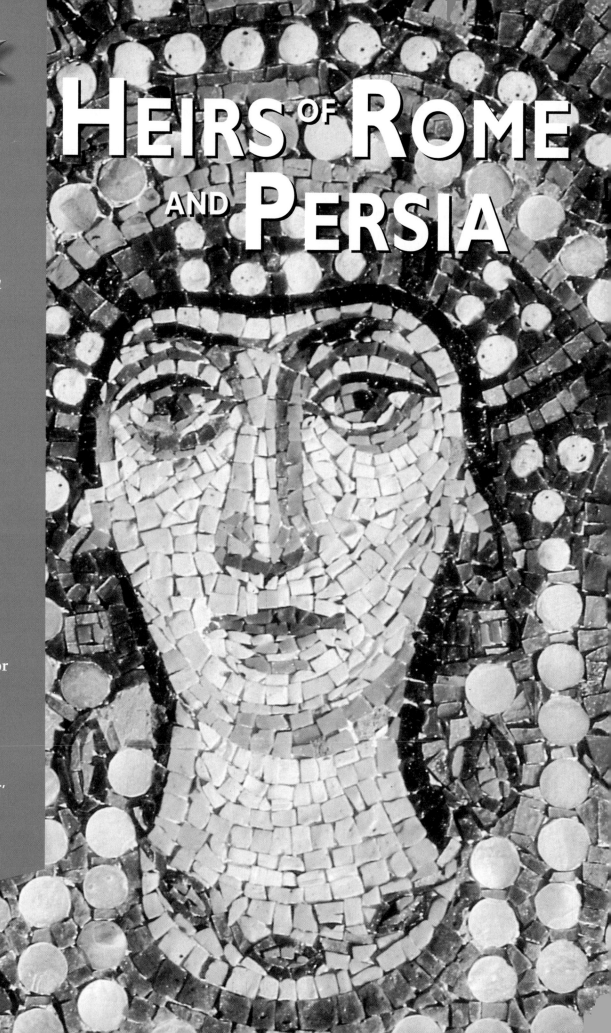

"Our kingdom is only an imitation of yours, a copy of the only true empire on earth."

Theodoric, sixth-century king of the Ostrogoths, in a letter to Byzantine emperor Anastasius I

This artwork, created in the sixth century A.D., shows the empress Theodora. She was the wife of Justinian I, an early emperor of the Byzantine Empire.

The Byzantine Empire

FOCUS

How do people today keep the ways of the past while changing with the times?

Main Idea As you read, look for ways the Byzantine emperors built on their Roman past while making needed changes.

Vocabulary

Justinian Code
monopoly
mosaic
orthodox
icon
patriarch
Catholic

Roman civilization lived on for centuries after invaders attacked the city of Rome. In the 400s Roman ways of life continued in the eastern region of the old empire. This thriving region became known as the Byzantine Empire. With its capital at Constantinople, the Byzantine Empire covered Greece, the Balkans, and Asia Minor (present-day Turkey). The Byzantine Empire lasted almost a thousand years. A strong army, good government, and a rich economy helped give it a long life.

Justinian I Looks to the Past

The people of the Byzantine Empire thought of themselves as Romans. They wanted the greatness of Rome to be remembered. They even built their homes and other buildings to be like those in Rome.

In 527 Emperor Justinian I began to plan ways to make his Byzantine Empire as mighty as the Roman Empire had been. He started conquering many of the lands that Rome had lost. With powerful armies Justinian pushed into northern Africa and western Europe. By 565 much of the land along the Mediterranean Sea belonged to the Byzantine Empire. People thought of the Mediterranean Sea as a "Roman lake." Such cities as Alexandria and Carthage in northern Africa and Athens in Europe were all part of the Byzantine Empire.

Justinian did much more than conquer other lands. Early in his reign he ordered a code of laws written. This new code built on the old Roman codes and added to them. Laws were changed to fit the times and written in language that was easy to understand. As one sixth-century historian said, Justinian "purified" the laws, getting rid of "a mass of quibbles."

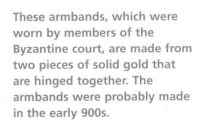

These armbands, which were worn by members of the Byzantine court, are made from two pieces of solid gold that are hinged together. The armbands were probably made in the early 900s.

The Byzantine Empire

British Isles
North Sea
Baltic Sea
RUSSIA
EUROPE
Aral Sea
ATLANTIC OCEAN
Caspian Sea
SPAIN
ITALY
Rome
Adriatic Sea
Danube River
Black Sea
Constantinople
ASIA
Balkan Peninsula
Aegean Sea
Asia Minor
GREECE
AFRICA
Mediterranean Sea
Crete
SYRIA
EGYPT
Red Sea

Legend:
- Byzantine Empire, about 565
- Byzantine Empire, about 1020
- Eastern Orthodox, after 1054
- Roman Catholic, after 1054

0 250 500 Miles
0 250 500 Kilometers
Azimuthal Equal-Area Projection

Regions Justinian's empire grew to include much of the old Roman Empire. By 1020 the Byzantines had lost some of these lands. In 1054 a split in the Christian Church divided the people in the lands shown above into two religions.

■ *Were most of the people who lived in the Byzantine Empire after 1054 Roman Catholic or Eastern Orthodox?*

The new set of laws became known as the **Justinian Code**. It served as the law of the Byzantine Empire for hundreds of years. And it became the basis for many of the legal systems used in Europe today.

Justinian tried to make the Byzantine economy as strong as the Roman Empire's had been. He built up trade by making Constantinople a meeting place for merchants from Europe and Asia. He also developed new industries in Constantinople. For example, Justinian started the Byzantine silk industry by ordering silkworm eggs smuggled out of China, along with mulberry trees

to feed the silkworms. This action ended China's **monopoly**, or complete control, of the world silk trade.

Money from taxes on trade and industry paid for the building program Justinian began in order to make Constantinople a "New Rome." Many new churches, roads, bridges, and aqueducts were built in Constantinople. The greatest of the buildings still stands today—the church of Hagia Sophia (ah•YEE•uh soh•FEE•uh), or "Holy Wisdom." Artists filled it with magnificent paintings and **mosaics**, pictures made from bits of colored stone or glass. The base of the church's dome forms a circle of 40 windows. One visitor of long ago said that the dome seemed to be "suspended from heaven." In Justinian's time Hagia Sophia was the world's largest and most beautiful church.

As in the Roman Empire, the riches of the Byzantine Empire were enjoyed only by government leaders and merchants. Most people worked almost constantly and earned barely enough for food, clothing, and shelter—and for their taxes to the empire.

REVIEW *In what ways did Justinian look to the past to build his empire?*

Theodora, Bringer of Change

Many laws in Justinian's new code showed the point of view of his wife, the empress Theodora. Theodora helped improve the lives of Byzantine women. She encouraged Justinian to make new laws that were fairer to women. One of these laws allowed parents to leave their property to daughters as well as to sons.

Theodora also took part in choosing government leaders. She believed that people should be given jobs because of their abilities, not because they were born into a high social class.

BIOGRAPHY

Theodora
A.D. 500–548

Most empresses of the Mediterranean region came from noble families. They grew up in fine palaces with everything they could want. Theodora's early life, however, was very different from this. Her father trained bears at the Hippodrome, a giant open-air theater in Constantinople. Theodora also became a circus performer. Then, in her early 20s, she left the circus. Not long after that, she met and married Justinian, becoming empress of the Byzantines.

The highest dome of Hagia Sophia (below) stands 200 feet (61 m) high. The inside (far right) is decorated with gold, silver, marble, and ivory.

Theodora suggested that Justinian choose Belisarius (beh•luh•SAR•ee•uhs) to head the Byzantine army. Belisarius was the son of a poor farmer and had little training as a soldier. However, he had shown great skill as a leader during an important battle. Belisarius's strong command of the Byzantine army allowed Justinian to claim much of the lands that were part of the old Roman Empire.

Theodora and Justinian were both Christians. However, they disagreed about religious ways. Justinian wanted all the Byzantine people to follow **orthodox**, or officially accepted, Christianity. Theodora worked to protect people who followed other forms of Christianity. Theodora's actions helped keep these Christians safe as well as loyal to the Byzantine government.

REVIEW *How did Theodora help bring about change in the Byzantine Empire?*

The Christian Church Divides

Religion caused much disagreement throughout the Christian lands. People often quarreled bitterly about their beliefs. Many of their leaders felt that these matters were more important than trade, government, or the military.

One argument centered around **icons**, holy pictures of Jesus and the saints. Some people liked to look at the icons as they prayed at home and in churches. Others felt that using icons in this way was like worshipping idols, which is forbidden in the Ten Commandments.

This argument led to disagreement between Christians in western Europe and Christians in the Byzantine Empire. In western Europe few people could read or write. Church leaders there believed that

Theodora worked to improve the lives of women, such as those shown in this mosaic. How have women in our society tried to improve their lives?

Books for children who are still learning to read have many pictures and few words. Icons were a lot like these books. Icons allowed people who could not read to better understand their religion.

the use of icons was a good way to teach about Christianity. The Byzantine **patriarchs**, or Church leaders, did not want people to use icons. They believed that the use of icons went against God's laws. In 726 the Byzantine emperor Leo ordered that all icons in the empire be destroyed. Later the Byzantine empress Irene, who ruled the empire from 780 to 802, declared that icons could be used as long as people prayed to God and not to the icons.

The quarrel over icons between Christians in western Europe and Christians in the Byzantine Empire helped pull the two groups apart. Over time other religious issues caused more conflict. Finally, in 1054, the Christian Church split. Eventually the Church in the Byzantine Empire became the Eastern Orthodox Church, based in Constantinople.

The Church in western Europe became the Roman Catholic Church, based in Rome. The word **Catholic** means "all-embracing."

Both churches continued to grow strong. However, the Byzantine Empire itself began to weaken. Eventually it lost both its strong army and its organized government. Its economic power weakened as well. In 1453 the Byzantine Empire came to an end.

REVIEW *How did disagreements cause the Christian Church to change?*

LESSON I REVIEW

Check Understanding

1 **Remember the Facts** Who were the leaders who brought change to the Byzantine Empire? What were their successes?

2 **Recall the Main Idea** How did the Byzantine Empire build on the ways of the Roman Empire? In what ways did the Byzantine Empire change with the times?

Think Critically

3 **Think More About It** One historian has called Justinian "the great simplifier." How else could you describe him?

4 **Past to Present** What issues affecting people might Theodora have focused on if she were alive today?

Show What You Know

Art Activity Byzantine mosaics were often displayed on the walls of government buildings and other public places. In this way everyone could see these images of Byzantine life. Make your own mosaic about our society. Where would you want to have your mosaic displayed?

Understand Point of View

1. Why Learn This Skill?

A person's point of view is the set of beliefs he or she holds. It may be shaped by such things as that person's age or gender. Point of view can also be shaped by a person's culture, religion, and race or nationality. Studying the points of view of the different people who took part in an event will help your understanding of history grow.

2. Remember What You Have Read

Theodora helped the emperor Justinian make many decisions. In 532, early in Justinian's reign, a terrible riot broke out. The crowd burned much of Constantinople and prepared to name a new emperor. Justinian and Theodora, hiding in the palace, debated what action they should take. Procopius (pruh•KOH•pee•uhs), a government official, wrote down what Theodora told Justinian:

66 As to the belief that a woman should not be daring among men or assert herself boldly, I consider the present crisis does not allow us to debate that. My opinion is that now is a poor time for flight, even though it bring safety. For any man who has seen the light of day will also die, but one who has been an emperor cannot endure to be a fugitive. If now you wish to go, Emperor, nothing prevents you. There is the sea, there are the steps to the boats. 99

Theodora's words had a great effect on Justinian. After listening to her, Justinian decided to remain in Constantinople and defend his position.

3. Understand the Process

Here are some steps to help you understand a speaker's or writer's point of view:

• Reread the quotation. Identify the person who is speaking or writing. Think about what you know about the person. This can help you see the reasons for his or her statements.
• Think about the situation in which the statements were made. Look for clues to what life was like in the time and place in which the person lived.
• Look for words that help you find a person's point of view. Often statements giving points of view contain words like *think, believe, probably*, and *in my opinion*.

4. Think and Apply

Use the steps above as you answer these questions:

1 What reasons do you think Theodora had for making her statement?

2 What does Theodora's statement tell you about her point of view about women?

3 What words in Theodora's statement tell you that she is expressing her point of view?

Empress Theodora

The Muslim Empire

FOCUS

How can ideas about religion affect governments and their people's ways of life today?

Main Idea Look for ways the religion of Islam affected people living in the lands into which it spread.

Vocabulary

steppe
Islam
Qur'an
Muslim
caliph
mosque
minaret
astrolabe
Sunni
Shiite

At the end of the sixth century, the emperor of Persia wrote to the Byzantine emperor. He praised their two empires as the greatest of their day. The Persians and the Byzantines, he said, "are to the world what . . . two eyes are to a man." The Persian emperor did not know that this would soon change. Within 100 years a new empire—the Muslim Empire—would defeat the Persians and threaten the Byzantines.

Herders and Townspeople

Desert covers more than two-thirds of the peninsula of Arabia. Some parts of the desert are dunes of shifting sand. Other parts are semi-dry plains called **steppes**. Some grasses and plants grow on the steppes, but these provide only enough food for the camels, sheep, and goats of herders. In the 500s many tribes of Arab people lived as nomads on the steppes. A sheikh (SHAYK), or chief, led each tribe.

Towns formed on spots of fertile land with underground water supplies. The people who lived in these towns supported themselves by farming. Often the towns were stops for travelers on desert trading routes. As more and more traders visited, the towns grew.

One of the largest towns in Arabia was Mecca (MEH•kuh). There was no agriculture in the city, but other activities supported its people. Mecca was an important stop on the caravan routes. Goods from Asia and Africa passed through on their way to Syria, Yemen, and the Mediterranean.

The Arabian steppes (below) are part of the Arabian Peninsula. The peninsula includes over 1,000,000 square miles (2,590,000 sq km) of land.

Mecca was also a religious center. Each year Arabs from across the Arabian Peninsula came to worship at a cube-shaped building called the Ka'ba. The Ka'ba contained the statues of the gods that the Arabs had come to believe in. Having the Ka'ba in their town brought influence and income to the people of Mecca.

REVIEW *What activities supported the people of Mecca?*

Muhammad and Islam

In about 570 an Arab boy given the name of Muhammad was born into a poor but important family in Mecca. Muhammad's parents died when he was a child, and relatives cared for him. He grew up to be a man who was well respected by his tribe. Muhammad became a trader and married a wealthy widow named Khadija (kah•DEE•juh).

Muhammad became unhappy about his tribe's idol worship. He often spent time in deep thought in a cave outside the town.

On one of these occasions, Muhammad had a vision—the angel Gabriel told him that he would become a messenger to humankind.

The message confirmed to Muhammad that there is no god but God, or *Allah* in Arabic. Over the next 23 years, Muhammad received more messages. The religion based on these messages is Islam. *Islam* means "submitting to God's will." The messages given to Muhammad make up the Qur'an (kuh•RAN), the holy book of Islam. A Muslim (MUS•lim), or follower of Islam, believes that the Qur'an is God's word. A Muslim lives by following the Qur'an and Muhammad's example.

Muhammad's family and close friends became the first Muslims. As the number of Muslims grew, tribal leaders in Mecca became worried. They believed that they would lose their own religious influence. They also believed that if people accepted Islam, people would no longer come to worship at the Ka'ba. If this happened, Mecca's economy would suffer. The leaders of Mecca tried to force the Muslims to give up their

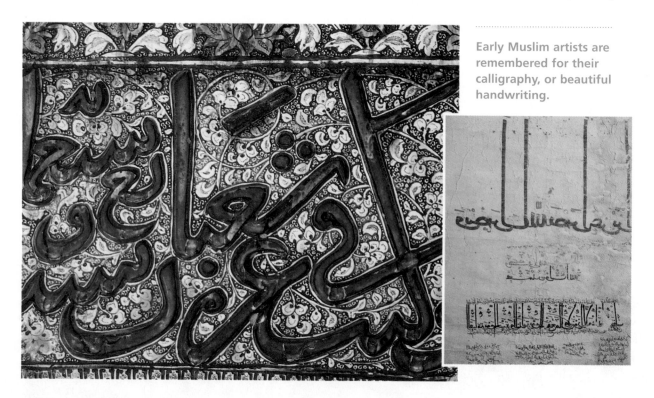

Early Muslim artists are remembered for their calligraphy, or beautiful handwriting.

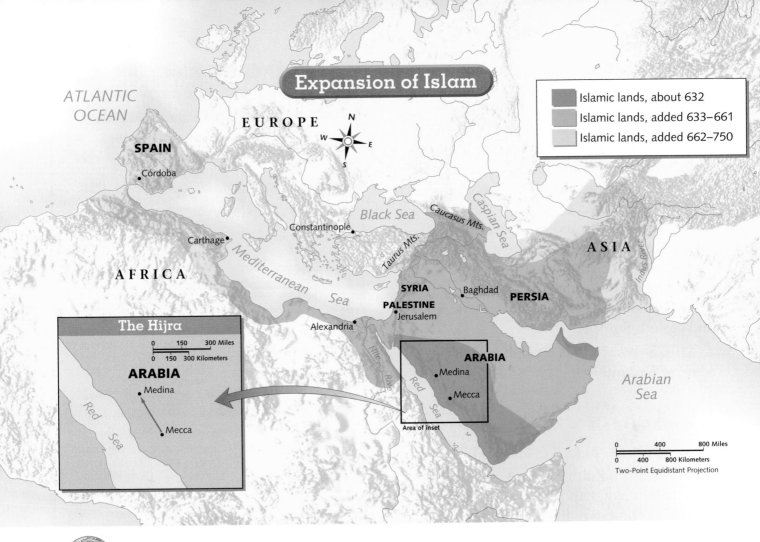

Expansion of Islam

Islamic lands, about 632
Islamic lands, added 633–661
Islamic lands, added 662–750

ATLANTIC OCEAN

EUROPE

SPAIN
• Córdoba

Black Sea

Caucasus Mts.

Caspian Sea

ASIA

Constantinople

Carthage •

AFRICA

Mediterranean Sea

Taurus Mts.

SYRIA
PALESTINE
• Jerusalem

Baghdad

PERSIA

Indus River

Alexandria

Nile River

Red Sea

ARABIA
• Medina

• Mecca

Arabian Sea

The Hijra

0   150   300 Miles
0   150   300 Kilometers

ARABIA

Red Sea

• Medina

• Mecca

Area of inset

0   400   800 Miles
0   400   800 Kilometers
Two-Point Equidistant Projection

Movement Following Muhammad's Hijra, the religion of Islam spread through southwestern Asia and into parts of Europe and Africa.
MAP THEME
■ *About when did much of Spain become part of the Muslim Empire?*

beliefs. After ten years Muhammad left Mecca. His journey, called the Hijra (HIJ•rah), was the sign of a new beginning for Muslims. Its date—622—marks the first year of the Muslim calendar.

Muhammad's journey took him to the town of Medina, where he was welcomed by Muslims already living there. As Islam spread to other Arab tribes, conflict with Mecca grew. Nine years after the Hijra, the Muslims defeated the Meccans. Muhammad destroyed all the idols in the Ka'ba. He then dedicated it to the worship of Allah only. Mecca is still a holy city for Muslims all over the world.

REVIEW *Why were tribal leaders in Mecca worried about the growth of Islam?*

The Muslim Empire Grows

Muhammad saw it as his duty to spread the message of Islam. He did this through teaching and by personal example. He also told his followers to spread the message to others.

After Muhammad's death Muslim leaders chose a **caliph** (KAY•luhf), or "successor" to Muhammad. The caliph's role was to govern the Muslim community according to the Qur'an and Muhammad's example.

Within a few years the first caliphs united Arabia under Muslim rule. Then they carried Islam to the peoples around them. Caliphs led their armies into Mesopotamia, Syria, and

Egypt. The Arabs met little resistance from people such as the Persians and the Byzantines. These peoples welcomed the invaders, believing that they would then be freed from the heavy taxes and religious persecution of their own rulers.

By about 750, less than 200 years after the death of Muhammad, the Muslim Empire reached from Spain and northern Africa through Arabia and Persia into parts of China and the Indus River Valley. Only the Byzantine Empire, much smaller than before, stood between the Muslim lands and eastern Europe.

REVIEW *What lands became part of the Muslim Empire?*

Achievements of Muslim Civilization

The Muslim Empire united people of many languages and cultures. As Muslims grew in number in those lands, they created a civilization that has lasted since the seventh century.

From its beginnings the Muslim civilization took a strong interest in art. Among the most beautiful works of

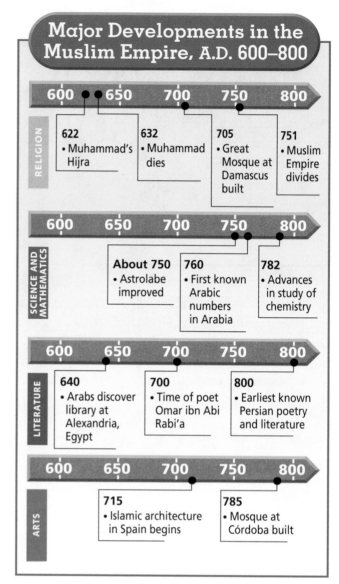

Major Developments in the Muslim Empire, A.D. 600–800

RELIGION

600	650	700	750	800
622 • Muhammad's Hijra	**632** • Muhammad dies	**705** • Great Mosque at Damascus built	**751** • Muslim Empire divides	

SCIENCE AND MATHEMATICS

600	650	700	750	800
		About 750 • Astrolabe improved	**760** • First known Arabic numbers in Arabia	**782** • Advances in study of chemistry

LITERATURE

600	650	700	750	800
640 • Arabs discover library at Alexandria, Egypt		**700** • Time of poet Omar ibn Abi Rabi'a	**800** • Earliest known Persian poetry and literature	

ARTS

600	650	700	750	800
	715 • Islamic architecture in Spain begins		**785** • Mosque at Córdoba built	

LEARNING FROM TIME LINES The years 600 to 800 brought great achievement to the Muslim Empire.
■ *What important events happened between 700 and 750?*

The style of a mosque and its minarets may differ from one region to another. This spiral minaret (left) is from a mosque in Iraq. The tall, slender minaret (far left) is from one in Turkey.

Islamic art are **mosques**, or houses of worship. The basic form of a mosque is simple, and the building has little furniture. A mosque might have one or more towers, called **minarets**, from which the call to prayer is heard five times a day. Mosques are often decorated with rich designs, using geometric shapes and verses from the Qur'an.

Muslims also made advances in science. Muslim scholars charted the movement of stars and planets. From their observations they improved the **astrolabe**, an instrument that helped sailors navigate using the positions of the stars. The astrolabe helped mapmakers prepare better maps.

Muslim scientists made contributions to medicine as well. As early as the 900s, a large teaching hospital was built as part of a mosque in Baghdad, in what is now Iraq. In this and other hospitals, doctors were trained to treat the sick. The work of these doctors became an important source of knowledge about diseases for centuries to come.

Trade within and outside of the empire helped bring Muslims new ideas. From the Chinese the Arabs learned how to make paper. From India, Muslims borrowed a system of numbers made up of nine digits and a zero. The Arabs called these Indian numerals, but we call them Arabic numerals, in honor of the traders who spread their use across the Muslim Empire and into the West. They are the numbers we use today.

REVIEW *What were some achievements of the Muslim culture?*

More than 800 marble columns line the Great Mosque of Córdoba, which was built in the late 700s.

Divisions Within the Muslim Empire

As the Muslim Empire grew, powerful families argued over who should rule it. In 661 a member of the Umayyad (oo•MY•yuhd) family became caliph and moved the Muslim

GEOGRAPHY

Córdoba, Spain

In the ninth and tenth centuries, people from all over Europe and northern Africa went to Córdoba to study such subjects as philosophy, mathematics, medicine, poetry, astronomy, and theology (the study of religion). This center of Muslim learning had a huge library with more than 400,000 books. The city also had a university, more than 60 smaller libraries, and many bookshops. Visitors were amazed by the city's paved and lighted streets. Córdoba, as well as most of what is now Spain, was controlled by the Moors, Muslims who had left northern Africa to settle there.

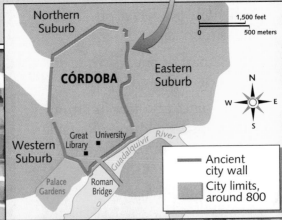

307

capital from Medina to Damascus in Syria. The Umayyads ruled from the new capital until 750. In that year the Abbasid (uh•BA•suhd) family claimed the right to rule. The Abbasids moved their capital east and built the city of Baghdad on the Tigris River.

One member of the Umayyad family escaped the Abbasids and began his own government in Córdoba, Spain. Later, descendants of Muhammad's daughter Fatima formed still another government, with its capital in Cairo, Egypt. Now rival

A dinar, the gold coin issued by the Abbasid government

caliphs ruled different parts of the Muslim Empire.

As time passed, the Muslim community split into several groups. Perhaps the most important of the Muslim groups were the **Sunni** (SOON•nee) Muslims and the **Shiite** (SHEE•yt) Muslims. Shiite Muslims stayed loyal to the descendants of the fourth caliph, Ali. They did not want either the Umayyad or the Abbasid families as rulers. In contrast, Sunni Muslims accepted the changing dynasties. Sunni Muslims and Shiite Muslims still disagree on many issues today.

REVIEW *What caused divisions in Islam and the Muslim Empire?*

The Five Pillars of Islam

The Qur'an says that the Islamic religion is based on five important ideas called the Five Pillars. The pillars help shape the lives of Muslims and their communities.

Believe that there is no god but God, and Muhammad is God's prophet.

Make five prayers at specific times each day.

Give a part of one's savings to take care of the needy.

Fast (do not eat or drink) from dawn to sunset during Ramadan (RAH•muh•dahn), the ninth month in the Muslim calendar.

Make a pilgrimage, or visit for religious reasons, to Mecca during one's lifetime.

LESSON 2 REVIEW

Check Understanding

1. **Remember the Facts**   What did Muhammad and his followers do to bring about the growth of Islam?

2. **Recall the Main Idea**   How did Islam affect the lives of people living in the lands into which it spread?

Think Critically

3. **Personally Speaking**   Do you think some people resisted coming under Arab rule? Explain.

4. **Past to Present**   What is the relationship between religion and government in the United States today?

Show What You Know

Map Activity   Sketch a map of the world showing all the continents. Then do research to find out where Muslims live today. Add this information to your map.

Europe in the Middle Ages

At the time the Muslim Empire began expanding, the continent of Europe was divided into many small kingdoms. The Roman Empire's strong central government, which had once kept Europe together, was gone. In its place were the independent governments of the smaller kingdoms. These small kingdoms were ruled by groups of people the Romans had called barbarians. Historians call the years from about 500 to about 1500 in Europe the medieval period, or **Middle Ages**.

Charlemagne Builds an Empire

During the last years of the Roman Empire, groups of people from northern Europe—in or near what is now Germany—came to control much of western Europe. Together these groups were known as the Germanic tribes. The most powerful of these tribes was the Franks, from whom France got its name. Under their leader Charlemagne (SHAR•luh•mayn), the Franks brought new life to the lands of a dying Roman Empire.

The name Charlemagne means "Charles the Great." Great in size at 6 feet 4 inches (193 cm) tall, Charlemagne was also a great warrior. He led his armies to conquer large parts of Italy, Germany, and central Europe. He also won part of northern Spain. Soon he controlled land from the Pyrenees Mountains in the west to the Danube River in the east.

FOCUS

How can the actions of both individuals and groups change governments today?

Main Idea Read about how individuals and groups affected governments during the Middle Ages in Europe.

Vocabulary

Middle Ages
pope
manor
serf
tenant
vassal
contract
feudal system
Christendom
crusader
bubonic plague
nation-state
Magna Carta

During the early Middle Ages, Europe was a land of small kingdoms. This seventh-century horseman is from the kingdom of the Lombards.

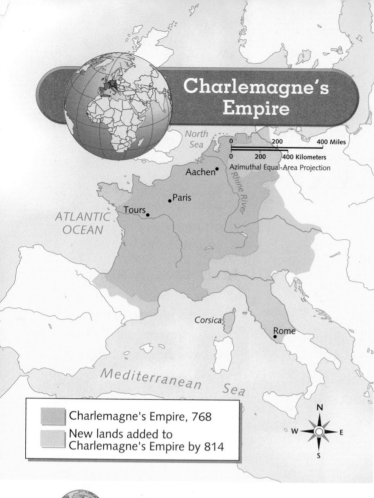

Charlemagne's Empire

North Sea

Aachen

Paris

Tours

ATLANTIC OCEAN

Rhine River

Corsica

Rome

Mediterranean Sea

0   200   400 Miles
0   200   400 Kilometers
Azimuthal Equal-Area Projection

N
W   E
S

Charlemagne's Empire, 768
New lands added to Charlemagne's Empire by 814

MAP THEME **Place** Charlemagne brought many people of western Europe together under one empire.

■ *About how many miles across was Charlemagne's empire at its widest point?*

Charlemagne had close ties with the **pope**, the leader of the Christian Church based in Rome. Both Charlemagne and his grandfather, Charles Martel, whose name means "Charles the Hammer," had helped popes by defending the city of Rome against other Germanic tribes. In the year 800 Pope Leo III rewarded Charlemagne by crowning him "Emperor of the Romans" on Christmas Day. Many people saw him as being like the Roman emperors of old.

The pope gave Charlemagne the title "Augustus," after the first Roman emperor. And Charlemagne tried to live up to the title. Like Augustus, Charlemagne wanted his government to be strong and his leaders to be wise. He saw it as his responsibility to teach

his leaders how to govern fairly. In the spring of each year, Charlemagne met with all of his nobles. These meetings, called the Fields of May, became famous. In meadows filled with flowers, Charlemagne set up tents and taught his nobles about law, religion, trade, and education.

Charlemagne truly respected learning. "Knowledge," he said, "must come before action." Charlemagne invited scholars from all over Europe to teach at the school he set up for his nobles' children. He also urged priests in all parts of the empire to teach "all those who with God's help are able to learn." While Charlemagne himself could not write, he read well. In fact, reading was one of his favorite activities.

Charlemagne's rule was a high point of the early Middle Ages. Even before Charlemagne's death in 814, however, Muslims from northern Africa attacked the empire's Mediterranean coast. Then Slavs and Magyars from eastern Europe invaded from the east. Vikings came from the north, from what is now Norway, Sweden, and Denmark. The empire Charlemagne had built fell apart. Once again Europe became a land of small kingdoms.

REVIEW *How did Charlemagne strengthen his empire through cooperation?*

Here Pope Leo III crowns Charlemagne as Emperor of the Romans.

Peasants usually worked in the fields of wealthy landowners who lived in large manors (right). Few people, rich or poor, could read the illustrated manuscripts (above) that were made during this time.

Life in the Middle Ages

For much of the Middle Ages, most Europeans lived in small villages which were parts of a manor. The **manor** was a large block of land made up of forests, meadows, farmland, the village, a church, and the house or castle of the noble who owned it all.

The peasants, or **serfs**, who worked on the manor lived in the village. Each day they walked from the village to the fields to work. They grew the food and made the goods needed to support the noble's family. The serfs worked on the land, but they were not allowed to own it. They were the noble's tenants. A **tenant** is someone who pays rent to a landowner.

In return for being allowed to use the noble's land, the serfs paid the noble in services and goods. Each week they worked on his land. At harvesttime, they gave him a part of their crops. In return, the noble protected the serfs from attacks by enemies from other villages.

The noble himself was a tenant of the king. Under the law of the time, the king owned all the land in his kingdom. He kept large parts of it for himself and divided the rest among the nobles who agreed to help him in times of war. These nobles were called **vassals**. A king's vassal agreed to perform services for the king in return for being given use of the land. The vassal also had to send soldiers to fight in the king's army, fight in battles himself, and collect the king's taxes.

A vassal's services were usually listed in a written agreement, or **contract**, with the king. (Unfortunately, most vassals could not read.) A typical contract started out like this:

> 66 As long as I shall live, I am bound to give you service and obedience. 99

The contract also listed the amount of land the vassal received, the buildings that went with it, and the number of peasants living on it. This system of trading protection for loyalty became known as the **feudal system**.

REVIEW *How did the feudal system work?*

The Church and the Crusades

From about 800 to about 1300, almost everyone in Europe lived on a manor and was ruled by a king. Although Europe was divided into many separate kingdoms, Europeans united under the Christian Church of Rome. The idea of **Christendom**, or feeling that all Christians from all kingdoms formed a community, was very important to people.

GEOGRAPHY

Jerusalem

The Dome of the Rock

Jews, Christians, and Muslims of today think of Jerusalem as a holy place, just as they did long ago. Jews gather daily to pray at Jerusalem's Western Wall—the last remaining wall of an ancient Jewish temple. Muslims visit the Dome of the Rock, honored as the site of Muhammad's journey to heaven. Christians visit sites such as the Church of the Holy Sepulchre, built on the site where Jesus was crucified and buried. Today Jerusalem is the capital of the country of Israel.

The Christian Church of the Middle Ages had more than just religious authority. It crowned emperors, as Pope Leo III crowned Charlemagne, and it sent soldiers to war.

Artwork of long ago shows the crusades from both a Muslim (left) and a Christian (below) point of view.

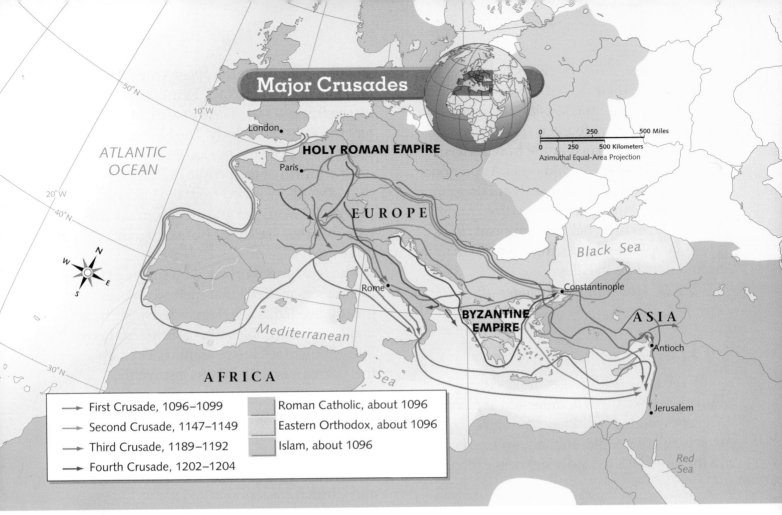

Major Crusades

London

ATLANTIC OCEAN

HOLY ROMAN EMPIRE

Paris

EUROPE

Rome

Black Sea

Constantinople

BYZANTINE EMPIRE

ASIA

Antioch

Mediterranean Sea

AFRICA

Jerusalem

Red Sea

0 — 250 — 500 Miles
0 — 250 — 500 Kilometers
Azimuthal Equal-Area Projection

- → First Crusade, 1096–1099
- → Second Crusade, 1147–1149
- → Third Crusade, 1189–1192
- → Fourth Crusade, 1202–1204

Roman Catholic, about 1096
Eastern Orthodox, about 1096
Islam, about 1096

Movement The crusades brought many Europeans into close contact with Muslims of southwestern Asia.

■ *About how many miles did the crusaders travel to get from Paris to Constantinople during the Second Crusade?*

In 1095 Pope Urban II called on all of Christendom to help seize control of the holy city of Jerusalem from the Seljuk Turks, who were Muslims. By this time the Seljuk Turks had gained control of the lands that were once part of the Muslim Empire, including the city of Jerusalem. Pope Urban said that the Turks would not let Christians visit Jerusalem and other holy places controlled by the Turks. The pope asked the people of Christendom to go to war for a holy cause. With cries of "God wills it! God wills it!," thousands of European Christians headed toward Jerusalem.

Excited volunteers tore cloth into strips, which they pinned to their clothes in the shape of a cross. Because these people took the cross as their sign, they were called **crusaders**. The wars these Christians fought were called crusades.

There were eight major crusades between 1095 and 1291. Some were called People's Crusades. Whole families left their homes and set out for Jerusalem. In every crusade people from across Europe marched together to battle. Even two armies of children marched off on what became known as the Children's Crusade. Most of them died of hunger on the long trip and never saw Jerusalem. In the wars for the Holy Land, thousands of Muslims and Christians died.

The crusaders never retook Jerusalem permanently. Yet the crusades did help the Europeans in another way. The crusades brought Europeans into close contact with Muslims and their way of life. The new ideas they learned from the Muslims changed European thinking forever.

Europeans returned home from the crusades, bringing spices and other Asian goods with them. A demand for such goods soon developed, leading to the growth of trade. This trade, in turn, helped European cities grow. People began moving from the manors to find new jobs in cities.

REVIEW *How did the crusades affect life in Europe?*

Disaster and Change

By the late Middle Ages, most cities in Europe were crowded, unhealthful places. Rickety wooden buildings rose above narrow streets full of people, animals, and garbage. In the late 1340s a deadly sickness called the

LEARNING FROM GRAPHS In the 1340s many Europeans died from the bubonic plague.
■ *About how many fewer people lived in England in 1377 than in 1347?*

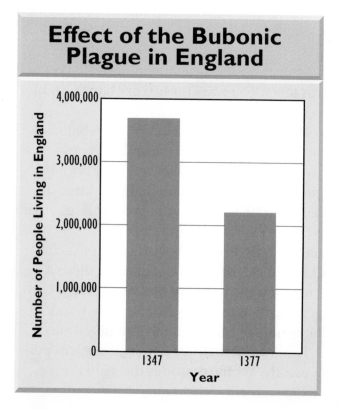

Effect of the Bubonic Plague in England

(Y-axis: Number of People Living in England — 0; 1,000,000; 2,000,000; 3,000,000; 4,000,000)
(X-axis: Year — 1347, 1377)

bubonic plague hit European cities. The bubonic plague, or Black Death, was spread by the fleas on rats. The disease caused blisters to form on the body. The blisters turned black just before the person died.

One-fourth of the people in Europe—more than 20 million—died from the bubonic plague. So many people died from the disease that they had to be buried together in huge graves.

The few farm workers who survived on the manors realized that their work was greatly needed. They demanded fairer treatment from the nobles who controlled their lives. Sometimes the peasants backed up their demands with revolts against the nobles.

During the late Middle Ages, many Europeans became unhappy with both the Church and the feudal system. The disagreements over authority between kings and Church leaders shocked some. Others blamed the kings and the popes for not being able to stop the plague.

REVIEW *How did the bubonic plague change Europe in the late 1340s?*

The Rise of Nation-States

Beginning in the late Middle Ages, strong kings began to take authority away from the nobles and Church leaders. Nation-states formed in many parts of Europe, especially in England, France, and Spain. Each **nation-state** had a strong central government and a single ruler—the monarch, or king. Each also had its own laws, government leaders, and full-time army. Language, culture, and customs also brought people together in these nation-states.

Hoping to hold on to some of their authority, powerful nobles tried to find ways to stop the king from taking it all. In 1215 a group of English nobles presented King John,

Magna Carta

Copy of the original Magna Carta

The following are 3 of the 63 demands the English nobles made in the Magna Carta.

[30] No sheriff, or bailiff of ours, or anyone else shall take the horses or carts of any free man for transport work save [except] with the agreement of that free man.

[31] Neither we nor our bailiffs will take, for castles or other works of ours, timber which is not ours, except with the agreement of him whose timber it is.

[40] To no one will we sell, to no one will we refuse or delay right or justice.

then the King of England, with a list of 63 demands in the form of a contract. This document came to be called the **Magna Carta**, or "Great Charter." King John was made to accept it. The Magna Carta forced the king to take responsibility for his actions. In other words, the king now had to follow laws like everyone else. For example, he could no longer take property without paying for it.

The Magna Carta was written by the nobles to protect themselves. However, parts of the charter later became the basis for laws in Europe that protected the freedoms of everyone. For example, the Magna Carta gave people the right to trial by jury.

The Magna Carta required the English monarch to have "the general consent of the realm [kingdom]" before ordering new taxes. The assembly of nobles who met to vote on taxes later became known as Parliament. Today the main lawmakers of Parliament are elected by the people.

The signing of the Magna Carta had long-lasting effects. For example, the Constitution of the United States has its roots in the ideas first expressed in the Magna Carta.

REVIEW *How did the nobles try to limit the authority of King John?*

LESSON 3 REVIEW

Check Understanding

1 **Remember the Facts** What key factors shaped life in Europe during the Middle Ages?

2 **Recall the Main Idea** How did individuals and groups affect governments during the Middle Ages in Europe?

Think Critically

3 **Personally Speaking** If the plague had not happened, do you think people would still have tried to change the feudal system? Explain your answer.

4 **Past to Present** How did the nobles' charter with King John help build the democracies of later times?

Show What You Know

Simulation Activity Museums of living history have actors act, dress, and talk the way people did long ago. With several classmates, create a scene that shows what life was like under the feudal system. Invite other classmates to ask questions about your "living history" scene.

Understand National Symbols

1. Why Learn This Skill?

Since the forming of the first nation-states, flags have been used as symbols of national identity. A flag stands for a nation's land, its people, and its government. It also expresses ideas or qualities valued by the people of a nation. Knowing the kinds of things flags represent can help you better understand today's nations and their histories.

2. Think About Flags

Flags were probably first used thousands of years ago. Egyptian soldiers went to battle carrying poles topped with streamers, hoping that they would persuade their gods to help them win. Later, Assyrians, Greeks, and Romans used flags in the same way. Their flags stood for their gods or their leaders.

During battles, generals often watched flags to follow the movement of the soldiers. Each side in a battle was represented by a flag. If their flag was captured, many soldiers would surrender. If the soldier carrying the flag was killed or wounded, others would pick it up and "rally around the flag" to prevent the enemy from capturing it.

In the Middle Ages, knights often decorated their shields with colors and other symbols to help their followers recognize them in their armor on the battlefield. Later, those symbols were used on flags, clothing, and other items. In the late Middle Ages, leaders of nation-states used those symbols on their national flags.

3. Understand the Process

The designs on many flags were used in heraldry, the system of colors, patterns, and picture symbols that knights used during the Middle Ages in Europe. Today the flags of nations also use color, patterns, and picture symbols in their flags.

- **Colors**

    Most national flags today use one or more of seven colors: black, blue, green, orange, red, white, and yellow. These colors were used in heraldry to stand for different qualities: blue for loyalty, red for courage, and white for freedom.

    Several nations use the same colors in their flags. Black, green, red, and white stand for Arab unity. They are used in the flags of present-day Iraq, Jordan, Kuwait, Sudan, Syria, the United Arab Emirates, and Yemen.

- **Patterns**

    Patterns on many present-day national flags are similar to those used in heraldry. Some knights in the Middle Ages used a stripe of white or yellow to separate two colors. That pattern is used in many flags of today. The flag of Egypt has a white stripe between stripes of black and red. The Mexican flag has a stripe of white between stripes of green and red.

- **Picture Symbols**

    The picture symbols used on some flags stand for a religion practiced by its nation's people. The cross, a symbol for Christianity, has been used on some flags. The crescent and star, a symbol of Islam, is on the flags of many Muslim nations. The Star of David appears on the flag of Israel. Stars often stand for unity. The number of stars in a flag is sometimes equal to the number of states or provinces united to form a country. The United States' flag has 50 stars.

Picture symbols can also show an important element of a nation's past. On the Mexican flag, an eagle on a cactus holds a snake in its mouth. This was the sign the Aztecs believed showed them where to build their capital city of Tenochtitlán. Argentina's flag shows a sun, which stands for the country's freedom from Spain.

The flags of some countries are shown below. You can find all the flags of the world in the Almanac section of this book, pages R10–R29.

4. Think and Apply

Draw a flag for your school or class, and write a paragraph to explain the symbols and colors you use. Display your flag on a classroom bulletin board along with those of your classmates.

BUILDING CITIZENSHIP

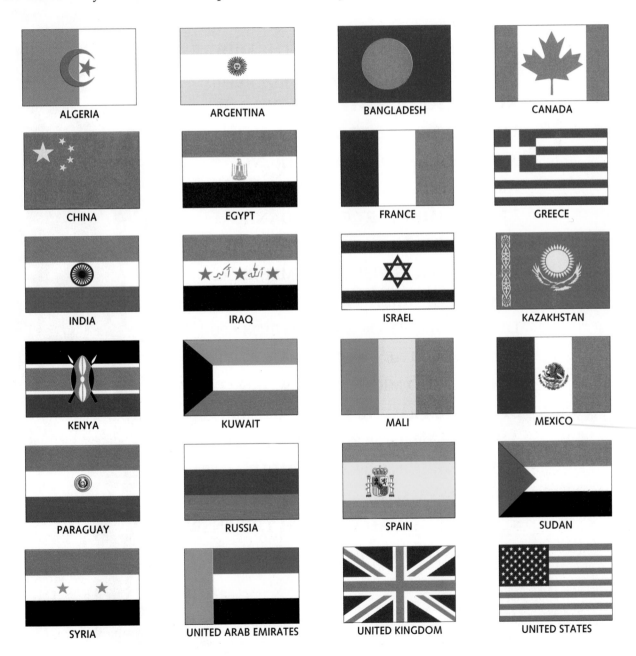

ALGERIA

ARGENTINA

BANGLADESH

CANADA

CHINA

EGYPT

FRANCE

GREECE

INDIA

IRAQ

ISRAEL

KAZAKHSTAN

KENYA

KUWAIT

MALI

MEXICO

PARAGUAY

RUSSIA

SPAIN

SUDAN

SYRIA

UNITED ARAB EMIRATES

UNITED KINGDOM

UNITED STATES

KNIGHTS
of the
MIDDLE AGES

THE FEUDAL SYSTEM OF THE MIDDLE AGES LED TO THE CREATION OF A NEW KIND OF SOLDIER—THE KNIGHT. THE LITERATURE SELECTION, *SIR DANA: A KNIGHT, AS TOLD BY HIS TRUSTY ARMOR,* TELLS ABOUT ONE SUCH KNIGHT. THE STORY OF SIR DANA BEGINS WHEN A CLASS OF PRESENT-DAY STUDENTS VISITS THE MEDIEVAL ROOM OF A GREAT MUSEUM. AS THEY LOOK AT A SUIT OF ARMOR FROM 600 YEARS AGO, THEY WONDER ABOUT THE KNIGHT WHO MIGHT HAVE WORN IT. THE STUDENTS IMAGINE THAT THE ARMOR ANSWERS THEIR QUESTIONS ABOUT THE LIFE OF SIR DANA IN THE MIDDLE AGES.

READ NOW SOME OF THE QUESTIONS THE STUDENTS ASK, ALONG WITH THE ANSWERS FROM SIR DANA'S TRUSTY ARMOR.

Knights went into battle with suits of armor. The metal plates protected them from sword attacks.

Sir Dana: A Knight

As Told by His Trusty Armor

Words and Pictures by Dana Fradon

 Hy did Sir Dana become a knight?

"Truth to tell, as the son of a knight, no thought was ever given to his being anything else. From the day of his birth, he was prepared for this lifelong task. As a child, Sir Dana played games that developed his physical skills.

"Using toy wooden swords, he and his friends pretended they were knights.

"They walked on stilts.

"They played catch with a ball made of leather or cloth stuffed with almost anything. Wool was best. It was light and held its shape.

"Sometimes they would hit the ball over a net or a raised mound of earth with a gloved hand. . . ."

 Hat's a squire?

"A squire was a knight's assistant, his apprentys,[1] you might say. A squire followed his knight on the way to battle, leading the knight's courser[2] and caring for his equipment. The knight rode his palfrey.[3]

"For the first few years, squires did not take part in battle. But as they grew older and stronger, many squires fought alongside their knights as equals, with much valor, and did great mischief[4] to the enemy. The great English knight Sir John Chandos met his death at the hands of a strong, experienced squire.

"Some men chose to remain squires their entire lives. Expensive it was to become a knight.[5] Living as an assistant to a rich lord or successful knight was often as good as being one."

[1] **apprentys:** medieval for *apprentice*
[2] **courser:** battle horse
[3] **palfrey:** regular riding horse
[4] **mischief:** damage
[5] A great lord needed to supply a new knight only with a horse, armor, and weapons. The new knight often had to pay for lavish feasting and ceremonies himself.

HOW OLD WAS SIR DANA WHEN HE BECAME A KNIGHT?

"Sir Dana was twenty-one, the age most squires became knights. But many a squire was made a knight while still a teenager.

"On the other hand, the great French knight Sir Bertrand du Guesclin—the Tenth Worthy[6]—did not become a knight until he was thirty-five.

"Mind you this: A king could confer knighthood on almost anyone he wished—at any age. Many a rich merchant bought the honor of knighthood with money. Some poor but able foot soldiers earned it on the field of battle through their bravery. The nobles, of course, were exceedingly wroth[7] at this backward entry into their class, but they could not entirely halt it.

"Squire Dana became a knight, and received the title Sir, in a ceremony many centuries old. Having taken a purifying bath the night before to cleanse him of his sins, he dressed all in white to signify his purity. He vowed to serve and defend God, the king of Domania, his fellow knights, womanhood, and the weak. And at all times to act in a just, gentlemanly, and chivalrous manner.

"Then the king girded him—fastened a sword and belt around Squire Dana's waist. Riding spurs were attached to his boots.

"After that an odd, *very* odd, thing happened. The king delivered the buffet, an open-handed blow to the cheek. Sometimes it was merely symbolic, and sometimes it was powerful enough to send a knight reeling.

"The buffet ended the ceremony. Some say its purpose was to make sure the young knight never forgot his vows."

---

[6] **Tenth Worthy:** tenth greatest knight of all time, so deemed by his countrymen
[7] **wroth:** medieval for *upset*

COULD A GIRL BE A KNIGHT? WAS JOAN OF ARC A KNIGHT?

"No! Why, a knight was not even supposed to ride a mare! It was believed that females had no place on the battlefield. However, here and there, women did go to war—and as leaders, too. Queen Philippa of England was said to have urged her troops to fight manfully at the Battle of Neville's Cross. She prevented a Scottish invasion, while her husband, King Edward III, and most of his knights were across the English Channel fighting the French. And the countess of Montfort led the defense of her castle and lands when her husband was a prisoner of the French. She was said to possess the courage of a man and the heart of a lion!

"I know not directly of Joan of Arc. She died, burned at the stake, in 1431. Sir Dana would have been one hundred years old by then. A great leader, she wore full armor as she led her troops against the English. A saint she became, but not a knight. . . ."

WHAT IS CHIVALRY?

"It was a code, the rules and values of knighthood, written and unwritten, going back at least to the ninth-century Anglo-Saxon king Alfred. It included a devotion to duty, fair play on the battlefield, honesty, good manners, and bravery. Also kindness toward the weak, respect for women, courtesy, generosity, and gentleness toward everyone. Above all, it pledged the knight to serve God. By Saint Denis! Not bad values, even for today, eh?

"Sad to say, these rules were much broken. Knights often killed needlessly. Ho! Is killing ever but needless? Chivalrous behavior was often forgotten in dealings with peasants, religious minorities, or anybody a knight disliked.

"If a captured knight promised to pay a ransom in exchange for being allowed to return home unharmed, he would almost always keep his word.

"If a king granted safe passage through his country to certain of the enemy—as during peace talks—his subjects were expected to honor his word.

"In a battle of the Hundred Years War, the blind king of Bohemia, showing much bravery and noble spirit, spoke to his several attendants. 'Gentlemen, friends, and

THERE MUST BE AN EASIER WAY TO GET TO BE A KNIGHT.

WHOOF!
WOUFF!
WUF!

brethren-at-arms—as I am blind, I request of you to lead me into battle that I may strike one stroke with my sword.' With their reins all tied together so they would not be separated, the king and his comrades rode into the fierce fray. The next morning they were found dead, still honorably tied together.

"If a knight broke a rule in a tournament, he dishonored himself and his comrades. For instance, on each charge of a joust, one or both knights could be violently unhelmed—at the least. It was an explosive shock to have a fully laced helmet ripped from your head. Sir Reginald de Roye, tilting[8] with Sir John Holland, attempted to soften this blow by fastening his helmet with but one slim thong. Thus his helmet flew off easily when struck.

Sir John's English comrades shouted, 'Ha! The French do not fight fair; why is not his helmet as well buckled on as Sir John Holland's? We say he is playing tricks.' They were sore put because they thought it was not chivalrous to seek clever, sneaky advantages.

"A friend of Sir Dana's, Sir Geoffrey de Charny, wrote three books on the meaning of chivalry, extending the code to include all men-at-arms, not just knights. His writings taught honor, compassion, moderation, cheerfulness, and above all the spirit of love. Sir Geoffrey was called the Perfect Knight, perhaps because he was not only a brave warrior but also a writer and philosopher. . . ."

---

[8] **tilting:** charging on horseback with a lance to knock an opponent to the ground

1. What was it like to be a knight?

2. The time of knights is often thought of as a time of excitement and adventure. Do you think you would have enjoyed being a knight if you had lived in Europe during the Middle Ages? Why or why not? What might have prevented you from becoming a knight?

3. Write a poem or song that you think tells the most important information about knights.

Knights on horseback (right) were common sights during the Middle Ages in Europe. Most knights served as vassals to lords, who lived in castles such as this one (below)—Bodiam Castle in what is now the United Kingdom. Few knights were wealthy enough to own their own castles.

500 •   •   700   •

527
• Justinian I
  becomes
  Byzantine
  emperor

570
• Muhammad
  is born

800
• Charlemagne
  is crowned
  "Emperor of
  the Romans"

CONNECT MAIN IDEAS

Use this organizer to show that you understand the development of the Byzantine Empire, the Muslim Empire, and Europe in the Middle Ages. Write a sentence or two that describes each topic listed below. A copy of the organizer appears on page 68 of the Activity Book.

Heirs of Rome and Persia

The Byzantine Empire

Byzantine emperors built on their Roman past while making needed changes.

1. _____

   _____

2. _____

   _____

The Muslim Empire

The religion of Islam affected people living in the lands into which it spread.

1. _____

   _____

2. _____

   _____

Europe in the Middle Ages

Individuals and groups affected governments and ways of life during the Middle Ages in Europe.

1. _____

   _____

2. _____

   _____

WRITE MORE ABOUT IT

Write a Letter Write a letter about a school rule you think should be changed to keep up with the times. If you think your school should keep part of the old rule, tell which part and explain why that part should be kept.

Write a Diary Entry Imagine that you are a European peasant-farmer during the Middle Ages. Write a diary entry that describes one day of your life. Include descriptions of where you live, your work, and the things you do for recreation.

900	1100	1300	1500

1095
• Pope Urban II calls for a crusade

1215
• The Magna Carta is signed

late 1340s
• Bubonic plague hits Europe

USE VOCABULARY

Write a term from this list to complete each of the sentences that follow.

Catholic   **orthodox**

Middle Ages   **tenant**

Muslim

1 Justinian wanted all the Byzantine people to follow _____, or officially accepted, Christianity.

2 The word _____ means "all-embracing."

3 A _____, or follower of Islam, believes that the Qur'an is God's word.

4 Historians call the years from 500 to 1500 in Europe the medieval period, or the _____.

5 A _____ is someone who pays rent to a landowner.

CHECK UNDERSTANDING

6 What was the Justinian Code? How did it relate to the old Roman codes?

7 How did Byzantine Empress Theodora influence Justinian?

8 What religious group considers Mecca to be a holy city?

9 What were some of the advances made by the people of the Muslim Empire?

10 What did Charlemagne do to strengthen his empire?

11 For what reason did people in Europe become crusaders?

12 The United States Constitution has its roots in the ideas first expressed in what English document?

THINK CRITICALLY

13 **Explore Viewpoints** How did different religious points of view cause conflicts in the Byzantine and Muslim empires?

14 **Think More About It** Why do you think Europeans' views of Muslims changed when Europeans traveled to Muslim lands?

15 **Cause and Effect** What effects did the bubonic plague have on Europe?

APPLY SKILLS

Understand Point of View Reread the quote by Theodoric on page 296. What does the quote say about Theodoric's point of view about the Byzantine Empire?

Understand National Symbols Reread the information on pages 316–317 about national symbols. Then create a flag to represent your family.

READ MORE ABOUT IT

Clothes and Crafts in the Middle Ages by Imogen Dawson. Dillon Press. This book provides detailed descriptions of the clothing worn during the Middle Ages, as well as unique craft ideas.

HARCOURT BRACE

Visit the Internet at
http://www.hbschool.com
for additional resources.

EMPIRES IN
ASIA AND THE
AMERICAS

"My descendants will wear gold, they will eat the choicest meats, they will ride the finest horses."

Genghis Khan, founder of the Mongol Empire

Image of Mongol conqueror Genghis Khan, who lived from 1162 to 1227

Growth for China

FOCUS

In what ways can leaders of today help their countries develop rich cultures?

Main Idea   As you read, look for the ways that Chinese rulers helped China develop a rich culture.

Vocabulary

draft
currency
porcelain

In the 1200s, while western Europe was still in the Middle Ages, China had a well-organized empire. Chinese cities, such as Beijing (BAY•JING), bustled with trade. Boats and barges carrying people and goods crowded the Grand Canal, which linked Beijing with Hangzhou (HAHNG•JOH).

Building the Grand Canal and an Empire

The Chinese empire of the 1200s really began in A.D. 589. In that year the Sui (SWEE) dynasty brought China together after it had been divided for 400 years.

Sui emperors ruled for only 30 years. Yet in that short time they built one of the wonders of ancient times—the Grand Canal. By using existing waterways between the Huang He and the Chang Jiang and by digging new ones, they created a 1,000-mile (about 1,610-km) waterway. In this way they connected China's most important rivers. The Grand Canal linked northern and southern China for the first time.

Sui emperors made the peasants build the Grand Canal, just as earlier emperors had made peasants build the Great Wall. More than a million people worked on the job, and many died from the heavy work. The emperors also taxed the people heavily to pay for the project. In 610 the canal was opened. But in 618 the peasants rebelled against these cruel rulers, ending the Sui dynasty.

As the Sui dynasty ended, another ruling family, the Tang, claimed the Mandate of Heaven. Tang rulers added to China's lands by moving west into central Asia, south into what is now Vietnam, and east into Korea. To protect China's northern border, the Tang rebuilt parts of the Great Wall and made it longer.

Empress Wu, who lived in the late seventh century, was the first woman to rule China.

327

Expanding China's empire required more soldiers, so Tang emperors made all male citizens serve in the army. Government officials used a **draft**, or system for choosing, to make sure China had enough soldiers whether the empire was at war or at peace. The Tang dynasty's powerful army kept China strong for 150 years.

REVIEW *In what ways did the Sui and Tang dynasties help build China's empire?*

The Tang gained control of China through military force. This clay figure represents a soldier in the Tang Imperial Guard. The job of the Imperial Guard was to protect the crown prince.

A Golden Age

Under the Tang dynasty China entered a Golden Age that lasted from 618 to about 750. During this time the Chinese developed their civilization in many ways.

Much of the activity during the Golden Age took place in the Tang capital of Chang'an. A present-day historian has described ancient Chang'an as "the largest, wealthiest, and most cosmopolitan city in the world." Because the city stood at one end of the famous Silk Road, about 2 million people lived in and around Chang'an.

Many people in Chang'an worked for the government. During the Golden Age the Tang emperors improved the government

Movement The Sui, Tang, and Song dynasties brought great growth to China.

■ *In what directions did the Tang and Song dynasties expand China?*

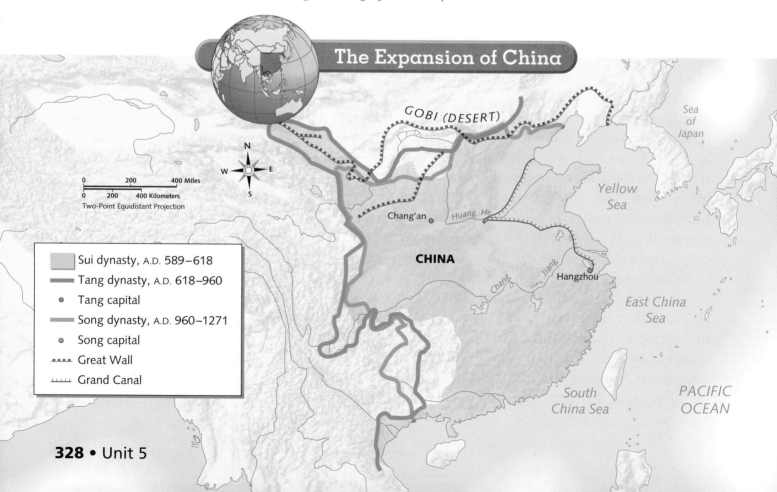

The Expansion of China

GOBI (DESERT)

Sea of Japan

Yellow Sea

Chang'an

Huang He

CHINA

Chang Jiang

Hangzhou

East China Sea

South China Sea

PACIFIC OCEAN

0   200   400 Miles
0   200   400 Kilometers
Two-Point Equidistant Projection

Sui dynasty, A.D. 589–618
Tang dynasty, A.D. 618–960
● Tang capital
Song dynasty, A.D. 960–1271
● Song capital
••••• Great Wall
ᴜᴜᴜ Grand Canal

This painting of court ladies and their servants (above) was found in a tomb near Chang'an. The Tang are remembered for many works of art including paintings, pottery, and statues (right).

civil service examination system. More than ever, government jobs were filled on the basis of ability rather than on social class.

Books to help people study for the civil service examinations became popular. To print books faster, Tang craftworkers improved the use of block printing. The Chinese had long printed with blocks of stone that had words carved in them. Now they began to make wood or metal blocks to use as ink stamps. In later years, printers invented movable type blocks for single characters. Better printing methods led to the invention of the first paper **currency**, or money. Paper currency was easier to carry around and exchange than heavy metal coins.

During the Tang dynasty the arts prospered. Potters made **porcelain**, a kind of clay pottery so thin that it looks almost clear. Chinese porcelain has been described as "so fine that the sparkle of water can be seen through it." The porcelain bowls and vases of the Tang were both beautiful and useful. Tang porcelain is still admired today.

Tang painters created beautiful landscapes and pictures of people and animals. The most famous Tang artist, Wu Dao-zu (WOO DOW•ZOO), worked with a "whirlwind brush," people said.

Poetry written during the Tang dynasty became as famous as Tang painting and porcelain. The work of one well-known poet, Li Bo (LEE BOH), reflects a pride in China's prosperity and cultural achievement. Li Bo, who lived from 701 to 762, wrote this of the Golden Age:

> 66 I desire to select and transmit the old, so that its splendor will last a thousand ages. 99

At this same time, the Chinese renewed their interest in religion. Tai Zung, the second Tang emperor, urged that people study Daoism and Buddhism. He also invited a priest to teach about Christianity. Under Tai Zung, Confucianism once again became China's official religion.

This painting from the Song dynasty shows the importance of both agriculture and the obedience of children to their parents in early China. How is each of these important ideas illustrated in the painting?

After about 750 the Tang dynasty grew weak because its emperors ruled poorly. By 900, leaders in some of China's distant lands began challenging Tang rule. In 960 one of them, Zhao Kuangyin (JOW KWAHNG•YIN), claimed the Mandate of Heaven and began the Song dynasty.

REVIEW *What new ideas developed during China's Golden Age?*

China Under the Song

By about 1050 China's population may have been more than 80 million. Most of these people were peasants, who lived in villages and worked on farms. Yet a large number of China's people also lived in cities and towns. Hangzhou, the capital of China after 1127, had a population of almost 1 million.

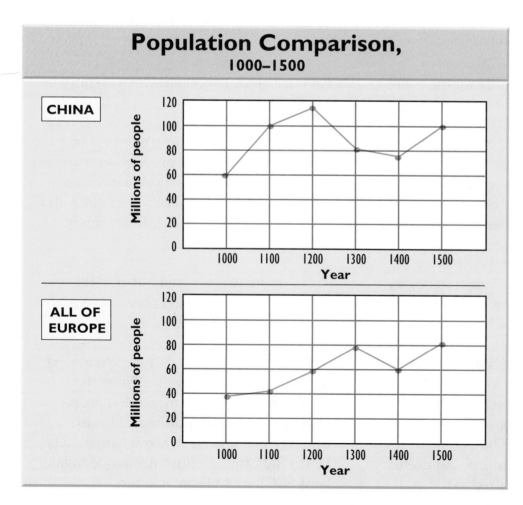

Population Comparison,
1000–1500

CHINA

ALL OF EUROPE

LEARNING FROM GRAPHS
The top graph shows the population of China during the years 1000 to 1500. The bottom graph shows the population of all the countries of Europe during the same years. By the year 1000 China had a population of about 60 million.

■ *In what year did China have almost 60 million more people than were in all of Europe?*

The cities of Song China bustled with activity. Busy street traffic reflected the many kinds of people who lived in China's cities. Merchants moved their goods in carts and on bamboo poles. Servants carried wealthy people in sedan chairs, comfortable seats with poles attached so that they could be moved from place to place. Homeless people lived in the streets. And when floods came or crops failed, people who had lost their homes and farms crowded into the cities.

Changes were also taking place on the farms. A new, quick-growing rice let farmers raise two crops of rice each year instead of one. Water-control projects in southern China allowed more fields to be used. As more food was grown, the farmers sold their surplus, or extra amount, in the many small market towns.

Like the peasants in Europe, peasants in Song China were tenant farmers. They paid rent to a landlord. Sometimes the rent was half of their crops. Chinese landlords, like the nobles of the European manors, had much power over the peasants. Day after day, the landlords forced the peasants to work in the fields from morning until late at night to pay their rent. Few children had time to learn to read or write because they also worked in the fields.

CULTURE

Rice

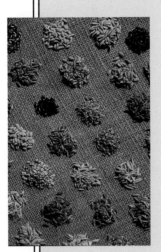

For the people of Song China, rice served as the main part of a meal, not a side dish. They ate huge amounts of the grain, perhaps as much as 2 pounds (about 1 kg) of cooked rice a day. They grew dozens of different kinds. Some had pretty colors. Others smelled like flowers when cooked. Rich families in Hangzhou even had their own kinds that they alone were allowed to eat.

The authority of the Song leaders did not last. By the early 1200s Mongol people from north of the Great Wall had conquered all of northern China. In 1271 Mongol leaders claimed the Mandate of Heaven and began the Yuan (yoo•AHN) dynasty.

REVIEW *What was life like for Chinese peasants during the Song dynasty?*

LESSON I REVIEW

Check Understanding

1 **Remember the Facts** How were Song China and western Europe alike? How were they different?

2 **Recall the Main Idea** How did the Sui, Tang, and Song leaders help China develop a rich culture?

Think Critically

3 **Think More About It** Why do you think the rule of the Tang dynasty is called the Golden Age of China?

4 **Cause and Effect** What are possible causes for a time of great achievements in any country? What effect might a time of great achievements have on a country?

Show What You Know

Generalizing Activity On the basis of what you have read up to this point, write a generalization about leaders during the Golden Ages of civilizations.

FOCUS

What events today bring world cultures together?

Main Idea As you read, look for ways the Mongols brought the Chinese into closer contact with other cultures.

Vocabulary

khan

plunder

The Mongol Empire

The Mongol people lived in a part of central Asia that today is called Mongolia. Like other people of the Asian steppe region, the Mongols were herders skilled as horse riders and warriors. Like nomads in most parts of the world, the Mongols lived in small clans. The Mongol clans often fought for grazing land and for water and firewood, which were scarce resources on the steppes.

From time to time a strong leader, or **khan**, brought some of these rival clans together. Because of their skills as riders and warriors, these united clans became an almost unstoppable fighting force. Under the leadership of the greatest of the khans, the Mongols conquered lands far and wide. The empire they created covered much of Asia.

Mongol Conquests

Known for his cruelty, the khan Temujin (TEM•yuh•juhn) struck fear in even the toughest Mongol warrior. At a meeting of clans in 1206, Temujin made himself leader over all the other khans. He took the title Genghis Khan, or "World Leader," and began to make conquests to live up to his new name.

Genghis Khan and an army of about 130,000 riders swept down from Mongolia into northern China. Leaving behind a trail of destruction, the Mongols captured Beijing and renamed it Khanbalik (kahn•buh•LEEK). For the first time, China had been conquered by outsiders.

Before his death in 1227, Genghis Khan told his sons, "A deed is not glorious until it is finished." They knew he wanted the conquering to continue. The sons of Genghis Khan took their father's words as an order, and so did their sons after them.

The Mongols claimed Korea and tried unsuccessfully to invade Japan. They also captured central Asia and much of western Asia. Many of the lands once under Muslim control faced great destruction as the Mongols fought to claim them.

The Mongol ruler Genghis Khan marched into China with his troops. What do you think was the outcome of the Mongol advances into China?

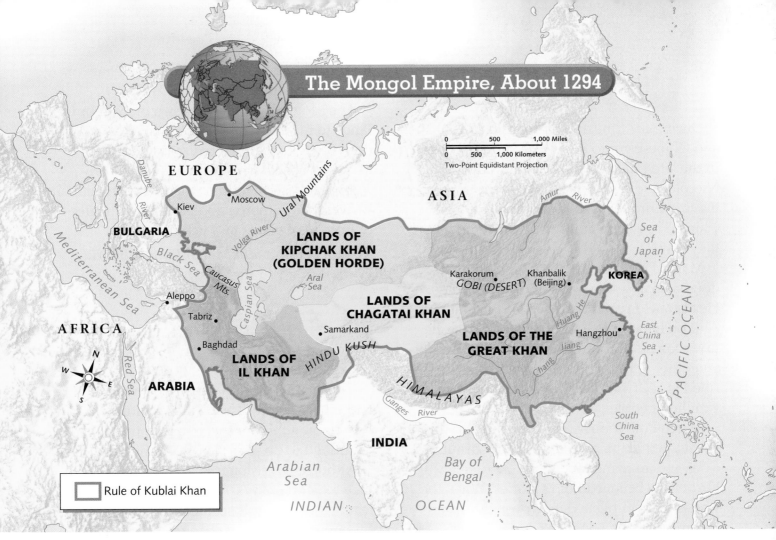

The Mongol Empire, About 1294

EUROPE

ASIA

Danube River

Kiev

Moscow

Ural Mountains

Amur River

BULGARIA

Volga River

LANDS OF
KIPCHAK KHAN
(GOLDEN HORDE)

Black Sea

Caucasus Mts.

Caspian Sea

Aral Sea

Karakorum

Khanbalik
(Beijing)

GOBI (DESERT)

KOREA

Sea of Japan

Mediterranean Sea

Aleppo

Tabriz

Samarkand

LANDS OF
CHAGATAI KHAN

Huang He

AFRICA

Baghdad

HINDU KUSH

LANDS OF THE
GREAT KHAN

Hangzhou

East China Sea

LANDS OF
IL KHAN

HIMALAYAS

Chang Jiang

ARABIA

Red Sea

Ganges River

South China Sea

INDIA

PACIFIC OCEAN

Arabian Sea

Bay of Bengal

INDIAN OCEAN

0   500   1,000 Miles
0   500   1,000 Kilometers
Two-Point Equidistant Projection

Rule of Kublai Khan

Regions The Mongol Empire was made up of several states called Khanates. The empire grew to fill much of what is today the country of China.

■ *Why do you think the Mongol Empire did not extend its borders farther?*

Batu, one of Genghis Khan's grandsons, led armies into Europe, tearing through what is now Russia, Poland, and Hungary. They **plundered**, or took goods by force, everywhere they went. They also killed many people or took them as slaves. The frightened Europeans began to call the Mongol invaders the Golden Horde. "Golden" was for the riches they stole and "horde" meant "army on horses."

By about 1260 the Mongols had created the largest empire the world had ever known. It reached from the shores of the Black Sea to the Pacific Ocean. It covered central Asia, much of Persia, parts of eastern Europe,

and all of China. In 1260 another grandson of Genghis Khan took the title Kublai Khan (KOO•bluh KAHN), or Great Khan, making himself head of the whole Mongol Empire.

Kublai Khan sent soldiers throughout the Mongol Empire to help bring about peace. With so much of Asia under Mongol control, merchants felt safe enough to travel the trade routes. They crossed Asia as they went to and from Europe and northern Africa, carrying ideas as well as goods between East and West.

REVIEW *How did the Mongols bring both fear and safety to the lands they conquered?*

An Exchange of Ideas and Goods

During the time of Mongol rule, Europeans and Chinese got to know one another better. In the late 1200s Marco Polo, his father, Niccolò, and his uncle Maffeo were among the first Europeans to spend much time in China. They were amazed by everything that they saw.

Marco Polo marveled at Chinese inventions such as gunpowder and the compass. He also held paper currency for the first time. And on his visit to Kublai Khan's palace, he saw room after room filled with gold, jewels, and other riches. The Polos were also astonished to see Chinese cities with more than 1 million people.

Marco Polo returned to Europe with silks, jewels, porcelain, and stories about beautiful cities and amazing inventions. At first, few Europeans believed Polo's stories. When the stories were published, however, Europeans became very interested in China and its riches. European merchants began searching for the best trade routes to find their share of China's treasures.

The Mongols wanted to learn more about lands to the west that Marco Polo had described. Rabban Bar Sauma, a Christian who had been born in China, traveled to Europe to visit kingdoms there. Everywhere he went, he gathered goods along with tales of European places and people.

REVIEW *How did Marco Polo help bring Chinese ideas to the West?*

The Mongol Way of Life

Chinese civilization dazzled Marco Polo and other visitors. The Chinese culture that had bloomed under the Tang and the Song continued to do so under the Mongols.

Although the Mongols conquered China, they took on many Chinese ways. The defeat by the Mongols seemed to change the Mongols more than it changed the Chinese. Chinese culture remained uniquely Chinese.

This early map (below) shows Marco Polo and his father and uncle with their caravan. The reports of their trip interested Europeans in Chinese products, such as this porcelain vase (right) from the Yuan dynasty.

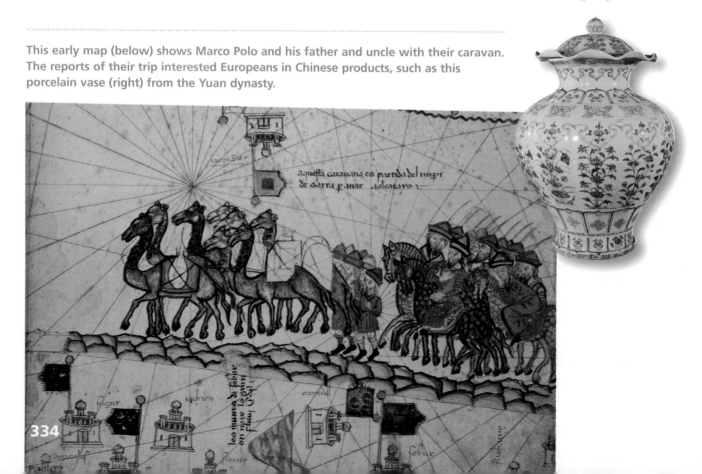

Kublai Khan, grandson of the fierce Genghis Khan, was skilled both as a statesperson and as a warrior.

The Mongol leader Kublai Khan ruled well and did much for China. He extended the Grand Canal and had the main roads fixed. His mail service, with more than 200,000 riders, reached the farthest parts of his empire. His strong armies kept the peace. Kublai Khan, however, is perhaps best known for bringing East and West together. Chinese cities became busy centers of trade as Westerners sought Chinese goods.

Although the Mongols had been cruel in their conquests, they tried to rule fairly. For example, the Mongols allowed people to practice their own religions. Even so, many Chinese did not like being ruled by the outsiders who had earlier destroyed so much.

The Mongols were better at fighting for more land than they were at governing it. Not long after Kublai Khan's death in 1294, the empire began to break up. It was too large for one person to rule. In addition, the peoples in the empire did not feel any connection with one another. Believing that the Mongols had lost the Mandate of Heaven, the people rebelled. In 1368 a rebel leader captured Khanbalik and formed a new dynasty, the Ming, which lasted almost 300 years.

REVIEW *For what is Kublai Khan most remembered?*

LESSON 2 REVIEW

Check Understanding

1 Remember the Facts What was Genghis Khan's role in shaping the history of China?

2 Recall the Main Idea How did the Mongols bring Chinese people into closer contact with other cultures?

Think Critically

3 Personally Speaking Marco Polo praised the Mongol army for the sense of safety it brought to China. If you had been a Chinese citizen during this time, how would you have felt about the Mongol army?

4 Past to Present How do people in the United States today learn about customs around the world?

Show What You Know

Research Activity Look through newspapers and magazines for something that has happened to bring together world cultures. Create a script for a television program that tells classmates how you think each culture was affected by this contact. Then act out the program as if you were on television.

Did the Mongols Help

Under the rule of Kublai Khan, China achieved many things. The Grand Canal was completed, an observatory was built, trade increased, and China became known everywhere for its wealth and greatness. One historian, speaking of the reign of Kublai Khan, said that it was "probably the most productive and beneficial of all the reigns of the Great Khans."

Not everyone living during the time of Kublai Khan, however, agreed that his rule was beneficial, or helpful, to the Chinese people. Some believed that the Chinese people suffered under the rule of the Mongol leader. Two people who held opposite views were Marco Polo, the European traveler who served in Kublai Khan's court for a number of years, and Cheng Sixiao (CHUHNG SOO•SHOO), a Chinese painter and poet. Read the following quotation from Marco Polo and the poem by Cheng Sixiao to learn how each thought the rule of Kublai Khan affected the Chinese people.

Marco Polo

66 The great khan sends every year his commissioners to ascertain [find out] whether any of his subjects have suffered in their crops of grain from unfavorable weather, from storms of wind or violent rains, or by locusts, worms, or any other plague; and in such cases he . . . furnishes them from his granaries with so much grain as is necessary for their subsistence, as well as for sowing their land. . . . He provides in like manner for their clothing, which he has the means of doing from his tenths of wool, silk, and hemp. . . . By reason of this admirable and astonishing liberality which the grand khan exercises toward the poor, the people all adore him as a divinity [god]. 99

The scene below shows Mongol farmers at work, irrigating rice fields.

or Hurt China?

Cheng Sixiao

66 In the past, in the age of the former emperor,
Who faced the sun for forty years,
The bright light of learning and refinement
    flooded the world,
And superior and heroic men stood before their
    ruler.
But once the barbarian soldiers invaded,
With sudden shock, Han rule was toppled.
To this day the proper ways of men are in chaos.
To lonely mountain valleys have fled all the
    worthies of the former age.
In that age of peace, the ways of the superior man
    flourished,
Men of talent appeared who were models of
    human achievement.
With their open hearts they looked on the sun
    and moon,
From their mouths flowed words of lofty and
    noble import. . . .
Today the likes of it are not to be seen.
As I look about there is darkness on all sides. 99

In the scene below, a Mongol army attacks Persian forces.

Compare Viewpoints

1. How did Marco Polo think the rule of Kublai Khan affected the Chinese people? How do you know?

2. How did Cheng Sixiao think the rule of Kublai Khan affected the Chinese people? How do you know?

3. Why might the viewpoint of a visitor to China during the time of Kublai Khan differ from that of a Chinese citizen?

Think and Apply

The people who live under the rule of a leader sometimes have a different view about their leader than people who view the leader from afar. What other leaders in history have given rise to these different views?

FOCUS

How can learning about other cultures affect societies?

Main Idea As you read, look for the ways in which the Japanese borrowed from and adapted Chinese culture.

Vocabulary

typhoon
Shinto
kami
regent
daimyo
samurai
shogun

Development of Japanese Culture

The many islands that make up Japan lie close to the eastern edge of the Asian mainland. The Japanese call their island country Nippon, or "land of the rising sun." Many experts believe that the first Japanese migrated from the Asian mainland. When they reached the islands, they met the Ainu people who already lived there. Ancient Japanese legends say the first emperor of Japan was the descendant of the sun goddess. The Japanese thought their emperor was not just a human being with the right to rule but a Tenno, or "heavenly prince." Because of this, one family has inherited the emperor's authority in an unbroken chain.

Japan's Early Development

Until the 400s the Japanese lived almost free from outside influence. Rough seas and fierce storms called **typhoons** kept other people away and stopped the Japanese from crossing the seas around them. Left alone, the Japanese developed strong feelings for their country. These feelings have shaped their culture for centuries.

The early Japanese were hunters and farmers, who had a great respect for nature. A central part of their culture was their religion, **Shinto**, or "the way of the gods." People who follow the Shinto religion believe that spirits called **kami** (KAH•mee) live in all natural things, such as stones, trees, and animals.

The Japanese believed that a different spirit protected each clan. Because of this belief, people felt great loyalty to their clans and clan leaders. The Japanese way of life, based on loyalty to clan leaders and respect for a godlike emperor, went on without change for hundreds of years.

REVIEW *What kept the early Japanese from contact with outsiders?*

The early Japanese believed that their emperor was a descendant of Amaterasu, the sun goddess. This picture, created in 1407, shows Amaterasu holding a globe with a rabbit inside.

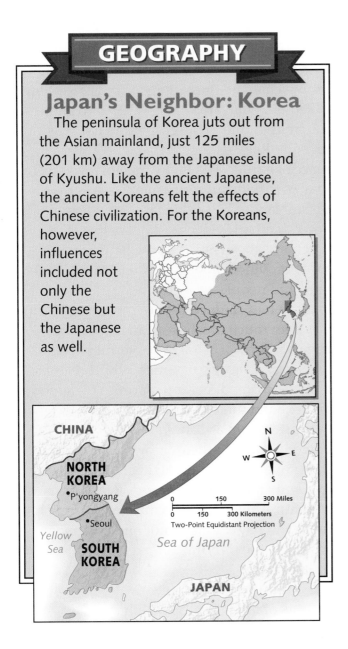

Japan's Neighbor: Korea

The peninsula of Korea juts out from the Asian mainland, just 125 miles (201 km) away from the Japanese island of Kyushu. Like the ancient Japanese, the ancient Koreans felt the effects of Chinese civilization. For the Koreans, however, influences included not only the Chinese but the Japanese as well.

CHINA

NORTH KOREA
• P'yongyang

• Seoul

Yellow Sea

SOUTH KOREA

Sea of Japan

JAPAN

0   150   300 Miles
0   150   300 Kilometers
Two-Point Equidistant Projection

China's Influence on Japan

Sometime during the first century A.D., the Japanese began to trade with people on the Asian mainland. Most likely, Korean merchants were the first to tell the Japanese about the Chinese civilization. The more the Japanese learned about China, the more interested they were.

In the mid-500s Chinese missionaries arrived in Japan. The missionaries brought not only Buddhism but also many Chinese customs. They introduced the Japanese to Chinese law, dress, architecture, art, and manners. The Japanese willingly accepted all these Chinese ways. In fact, for years the Japanese imitated the Chinese almost completely.

In 645, laws called the Taika (TY•kuh) reforms established a system of government for Japan based on Chinese government. But the Japanese changed some of the Chinese ways to meet their own needs. While the Chinese Mandate of Heaven passed from one dynasty to another, the Japanese rulers—the imperial family—claimed the right to rule for all time. And unlike the Chinese, the Japanese did not start a civil service. Instead, most of the government jobs were held by members of important clans.

As Japan began to use Chinese ideas about governing, the role of the emperor of Japan changed. Once simply a religious leader, the emperor now also became a political

LEARNING FROM TABLES The early Japanese based their way of writing on Chinese characters.
■ *On the basis of these samples, do you think an ancient Chinese reader could have read Japanese writing?*

Origin of Japanese Writing

ENGLISH WORD	CHINESE WRITING	JAPANESE WRITING (KANSI)
Sun	日	日
Moon	月	月
Tree	木	木
Rain	雨	雨
Mountain	山	山
Water	水	水

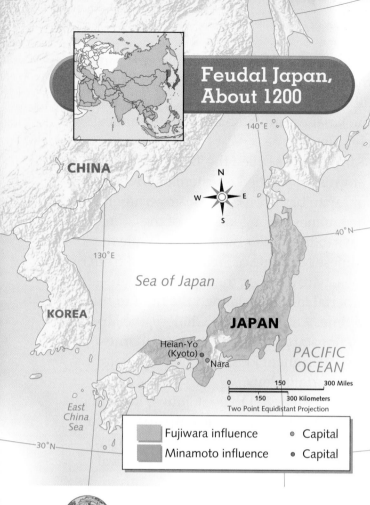

**Feudal Japan,
About 1200**

CHINA

Sea of Japan

KOREA

JAPAN

Heian-Yo
(Kyoto)

Nara

PACIFIC
OCEAN

East
China
Sea

0   150   300 Miles
0   150   300 Kilometers
Two Point Equidistant Projection

Fujiwara influence • Capital
Minamoto influence • Capital

Regions This map shows the main areas of influence of the Fujiwaras and the Minamotos.

■ *Which parts of Japan do you think each was less able to control?*

leader, as Chinese emperors were. For the first time, the people of Japan united under the emperor. This unity lasted for about 300 years.

Like the Tang rulers of China, the Japanese imperial family supported the arts. They encouraged the people to create great works of art. For example, Lady Murasaki Shikibu (MUR•ah•SAHK•ee SHEE•KEE•boo) wrote the world's first novel, called *The Tale of Genji* (GEN•jee). It is filled with descriptions of court life and sensitive poems about nature. *The Tale of Genji* is considered one of Japan's finest pieces of literature.

REVIEW *How did the role of the Japanese emperor change in the 600s?*

Feudal Japan

In the mid-800s the Japanese way of governing changed once more. About 858 a clan called the Fujiwara (FUJ•EE•WAH•rah) gained the right to rule in the emperor's name as regents. **Regents** are people who govern in place of a ruler. The Fujiwara, however, were unable to gain authority over Japan's most distant lands. The noble families who governed these provinces did not respect the regents as they respected the emperor. In these provinces nobles took control over the land and people.

As nobles claimed different parts of Japan, a system much like European feudalism began to form. The most powerful nobles, known as **daimyos** (DY•mee•ohz), or "great names," formed their own armies to defend and expand their lands. The soldiers, who became known as **samurai** (SAH•muh•ry), vowed loyalty to their daimyo. The daimyo then gave them land won in battle. Peasants lived on and farmed the land owned by the samurai. They gave the samurai food and money to pay for his armor and weapons. In return, the samurai agreed to protect them.

Samurai were much like the knights of feudal Europe. Only the sons of nobles could become samurai, and their training was long and hard. As part of their training, they hiked barefoot in freezing weather. Sometimes they went for days without eating. This helped them accept pain

Samurai armor was made up of a helmet, a mask, body armor, and leg armor. Leather strips were laced together to make this easy-to-wear armor.

This woodblock print by Japanese artist Yoshitora shows Japanese samurai in battle. At the far left the shogun Minamoto Yoritomo rides a black horse. What mood does this artwork create?

and hunger. "When [a samurai's stomach] is empty," their teachers told them, "it is a disgrace to feel hungry." Their training also taught them to be ready at all times for battle and not to fear death.

As time went on, the daimyos took part in governing Japan. Late in the 1100s a daimyo named Minamoto Yoritomo (MEE•nah•MOH•toh YOH•rih•TOH•moh) set up a military government. In 1192 Minamoto Yoritomo convinced the emperor to give him the title of **shogun** (SHOH•guhn), or "leading general." The shogun was supposed to be the emperor's chief army officer. However, the shogun really held all the authority.

Minamoto Yoritomo and the shoguns who came after him built on the feudal system. They gave land to loyal daimyos. In return, the daimyos promised to send soldiers to the shoguns in times of war. This system lasted until the 1330s, when daimyos began to question the authority of the shoguns. Daimyos fought one another for control of land. By the late 1400s Japan was divided by civil war.

REVIEW *What was Japanese feudalism like?*

LESSON 3 REVIEW

Check Understanding

1. **Remember the Facts**   How did the Japanese learn about Chinese culture?
2. **Recall the Main Idea**   How did the Japanese adapt Chinese culture to create their own civilization?

Think Critically

3. **Personally Speaking**   Why do you think the Japanese took up many Chinese ways and ideas? Why did they change some of them?
4. **Think More About It**   Why do you think feudal systems developed in both Japan and Europe?

Show What You Know

Drama Activity   In the early 1300s the Japanese developed a type of drama called the No play. The No play retells a historical event through the actors' hand and body movements. At the same time, key lines of the play are called out by a group of narrators. As a group, write your own No play about one event in the history of Japanese civilization. Assign parts, and practice your play. Then perform the play for the rest of the class. You may want to add costumes and music to capture the attention of your audience.

FOCUS

How do people today change their environment, and how do these changes affect them?

Main Idea Think about the ways in which people living in the Americas between 1100 and 1500 adapted to and changed their environment.

Vocabulary

chinampa
mesa
pueblo
Mound Builders

Civilizations in the Americas

In the 1400s the Japanese had plunged into "the time of the country at war." The Mongols had just lost the Mandate of Heaven. Europeans were recovering from the tragic Black Death. An ocean away, in the Americas, civilizations were reaching new heights.

In the late 1400s more than 45 million people lived in the Americas. From Alaska in the north to Tierra del Fuego in the south, the peoples of the Americas followed many different ways of life. Some groups of people lived as hunters and gatherers. Others settled in farming villages. Some of these villages grew into large cities with 150,000 to 250,000 people.

The Aztecs Build an Empire

Around 1200, groups of warlike nomads from the north invaded what is now central Mexico. The groups fought those who already lived there and one another for control of the region until one group, the Aztecs, won. With the land firmly under their control, the Aztecs settled it and became farmers.

According to legend, the Aztecs had moved south in search of a new homeland. Their war god, Huitzilopochtli (weet•see•loh•PAWCH•tlee), had promised they would find it where they saw an eagle sitting on a cactus with a snake in its mouth. Aztec warriors saw this sign on an island in Lake Texcoco (tes•KOH•koh) in central Mexico. There, about 1325, the Aztecs built their capital city, which they called Tenochtitlán (tay•nohch•teet•LAHN).

The island had few natural resources, such as stone and wood, for building. Also, the land was marshy, and it flooded often. The Aztecs, however, found ways to solve

The ancient Aztecs used this stone calendar, decorated with turquoise and shells, to keep track of the seasons.

The Aztecs believed in many gods and goddesses. They worshipped Quetzalcoatl (right) as the god who created humankind. The Aztecs also believed that Aztec warriors (above) would enter heaven if they died in battle. What other culture of the past thought it was a great honor to die in battle?

these problems. They drove large posts deep into the ground and built reed houses on top of them. They also made causeways, or bridges, to connect the island capital to the mainland. They constructed a dike 9 miles (14.5 km) long to protect the city from floods. In addition, they built two brick aqueducts to bring drinking water from the mainland. Using wood and stone they had gotten through trade and as tribute, they built large palaces and flat-topped pyramid temples. By the 1400s Tenochtitlán had become a huge city of more than 300,000 people.

The Aztecs had another problem. The island on which Tenochtitlán was built did not have much good farmland. To solve this problem, the Aztecs built **chinampas** (chee•NAHM•pahz), human-made islands formed by weaving branches together to make huge underwater baskets. The baskets were filled with mud taken from the lake bottom. On these "floating gardens" Aztec farmers grew corn, beans, peppers, and avocados.

Although the Aztecs settled as farmers, they continued their conquests. Armies of Aztec soldiers marched across central Mexico. The soldiers conquered one kingdom after another. By the 1500s the Aztecs controlled an empire that covered much of the land that is now present-day Mexico. The Aztec Empire grew to include as many as 5 million people. From every conquered people, the Aztecs demanded tribute in gold, silver, and cacao beans.

Like most early civilizations, Aztec society was divided into classes. The noble class made up the smallest part, while the farmers and slaves made up the largest. The slave class included people who had been taken as prisoners of war by the Aztecs. They had no rights. However, their children were born free rather than enslaved.

REVIEW *What did the Aztecs gain by adapting to and changing the environment?*

The Aztec Way of Life

In many ways Aztec civilization was like the civilization of the Mayas. The Aztecs had an accurate calendar and made much use of mathematics to help them grow larger crops. They also developed a system of hieroglyphic writing, just as the Mayas had done. Their craftworkers, like the Mayan craftworkers, made beautiful jewelry and decorations. They also constructed many well-organized cities with large buildings.

The Aztecs, like the Mayas, practiced a religion that included human sacrifice. The Aztecs believed that their gods needed the beating hearts of humans to survive. One reason the Aztecs fought wars was to capture prisoners they could use as sacrifices. At the height of Aztec power, around the year 1500, as many as 20,000 people died each year in Tenochtitlán's ceremonies.

The Aztec Empire lasted for fewer than 100 years. Peoples began to rebel against the Aztecs' harsh rule. Soon after, the Aztecs met their most fearsome enemy—the Spaniards who had come across the ocean from Europe.

REVIEW *How was Aztec civilization like Mayan civilization?*

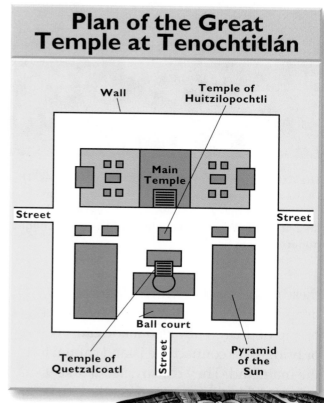

Plan of the Great Temple at Tenochtitlán

Wall

Temple of Huitzilopochtli

Street

Main Temple

Street

Ball court

Temple of Quetzalcoatl

Street

Pyramid of the Sun

LEARNING FROM DIAGRAMS This diagram (right) shows a typical walled religious center for the Aztec people. This temple was an important part of the Aztec city of Tenochtitlán (below).

■ *Why do you think a ball court was in the temple?*

344

Potatoes

The Incas grew more than 200 kinds of potatoes. They even knew how to freeze-dry their potato crop. First, they laid out potatoes in the chilly night air. The following morning they stamped out the water from the potatoes. Then they dried and stored them to be eaten during the winter when they were short of food.

The Inca Empire

The Incas in South America built their empire in much the same way the Aztecs built theirs. In time the Inca Empire covered almost half a million square miles (about 1.3 million sq km) along the Andes Mountains.

The Incas believed that they were descended from their sun god. Inca legends say that the Incas built their capital city of Cuzco (KOOS•koh) around 1200. In 1438, under a strong ruler named Pachacuti (pah•chah•KOO•tee), the Incas began to conquer many other kingdoms. By the 1500s Inca emperors ruled a wide area, which they called the Four Quarters of the World. In the empire lived 9 million people who spoke dozens of languages.

To hold the empire together, the Incas made the peoples they conquered follow the Inca way of life. The Incas believed that the many peoples of the empire would be less likely to rebel if everyone believed the same things and spoke the same language.

The Incas also brought unity to their empire by adapting to and changing their environment. They connected all regions of the empire with the capital city of Cuzco through a system of wide stone roads. They built bridges made of rope across deep mountain gorges, or narrow passes, where roads could not go. Runners passed messages to other runners along these roads and bridges.

Inca roads led to magnificent cities. The buildings in these cities were made of stones cut so carefully that they fit together perfectly. This way of building can still be seen in the ruins of the Inca city of Machu Picchu (MAH•choo PEE•choo) in present-day Peru.

The Incas also changed their environment to make life easier. They used their engineering skills to make the land more suited to farming. They began by building terraces—flat ledges cut into hillsides and edged by stone walls. Then, using both irrigation and fertilizer, the Incas raised beans, corn, squash, tomatoes,

Ruins of the Inca city of Machu Picchu (below) and a gold knife (left) used in Inca religious ceremonies

and many kinds of potatoes on these terraces.

Most of the food grown on these terraces went to government storehouses. It was used to feed the Inca armies and was given to anyone who needed it. In return for this food, the Inca rulers expected the people to work for them on their many building projects.

REVIEW *In what ways did the Incas benefit from adapting to and changing their environment?*

North American Cultures

The peoples of what are now the United States and Canada were too few and lived too far apart to build empires like those of the Aztecs or the Incas. Even so, Native Americans in this region adapted to and changed their environment to form complex cultures.

Native peoples in the southwestern part of what is now the United States used

Location Throughout the Americas native peoples formed unique cultures. Each culture was influenced in some ways by its land and resources.

■ *How do you think location affected the foods the first Americans ate? Which peoples do you think depended on fish and shellfish? Why?*

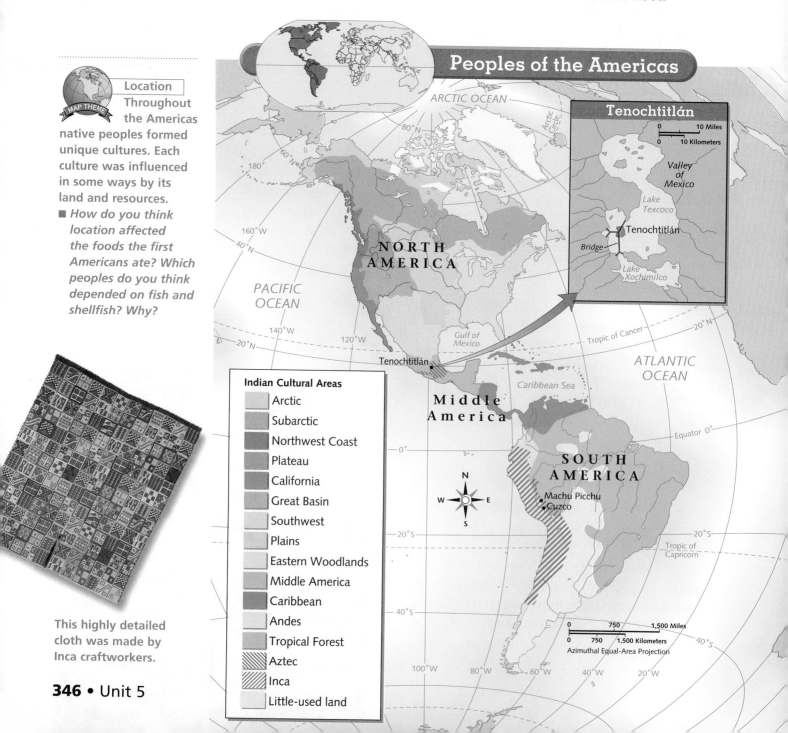

This highly detailed cloth was made by Inca craftworkers.

Peoples of the Americas

Indian Cultural Areas
- Arctic
- Subarctic
- Northwest Coast
- Plateau
- California
- Great Basin
- Southwest
- Plains
- Eastern Woodlands
- Middle America
- Caribbean
- Andes
- Tropical Forest
- Aztec
- Inca
- Little-used land

Tenochtitlán

irrigation to make the dry land better for growing crops. They built systems of ditches—some of them 10 miles (16 km) long—to carry life-giving water to the fields.

Even though their environment was harsh, it did provide some natural resources. The people formed pots from clay and made baskets out of grasses, woven tightly enough to hold water. They also built shelters several stories high on cliff ledges and on the tops of mesas. A **mesa** (MAY•sah) is a flat-topped hill with steep slopes. Some of these buildings, or **pueblos** (PWEH•blohs), had hundreds of rooms.

Across the continent of North America, life was quite different. In the Eastern Woodlands region lived people called the **Mound Builders**. Their civilization reached its peak between 1250 and 1400 with the Mississippian culture. This culture influenced the area from the Gulf of Mexico to the Great Lakes.

The Mound Builders got their name from the animal-shaped mounds of earth that they used to bury their dead or to build temples on. The largest settlement, Cahokia

These pueblos were built into a wall of the Mesa Verde canyon in what is now southern Colorado.

(kuh•HOH•kee•uh), near what is today St. Louis, Missouri, had 85 of these mounds. The largest of them covered 16 acres and was 100 feet (30.5 m) high. Cahokia may have had a population of 75,000. At the time, few European cities were even close to this size.

REVIEW *How did the native peoples of North America change their environment?*

LESSON 4 REVIEW

Check Understanding

1 Remember the Facts Where in the Americas did the Aztecs and Incas live?

2 Recall the Main Idea How did the native peoples of the Americas adapt to and change their environment?

Think Critically

3 Personally Speaking Do you think the changes the Aztecs and Incas made hurt the environment in any way? Explain.

4 Past to Present What changes are being made to the environment in your community today? What effects have they had?

Show What You Know

Multimedia Activity Work in a group to prepare and present a multimedia report to your class. Use library resources to find out which Native American groups lived in your state before 1500. Research their ways of life and how they adapted to and changed the environment to meet their needs. Also find out about family life, religion, government, education, and economy. Use any of the following as part of your report: posters, charts and graphs, slides, overhead transparencies, computers, music, dance, speeches, artwork, and models.

Compare Maps with Different Scales

1. Why Learn This Skill?

Places are drawn larger or smaller on maps, depending on how much area is to be shown. Maps that show a large area must use a small scale—places must be drawn small to fit everything in. Maps that show only a small area can use a larger scale. Drawing places large allows details to be shown. Knowing about different map scales can help you choose the best map for gathering the information you need.

2. Map Scales

The maps on these two pages show how scale can change depending on whether the map shows a close-up or faraway view of an area. Map A is a small-scale map. It shows a large area of land with little detail. Map C is a large-scale map. It shows a small amount of land in great detail. Map B has a larger scale than Map A and a smaller scale than Map C.

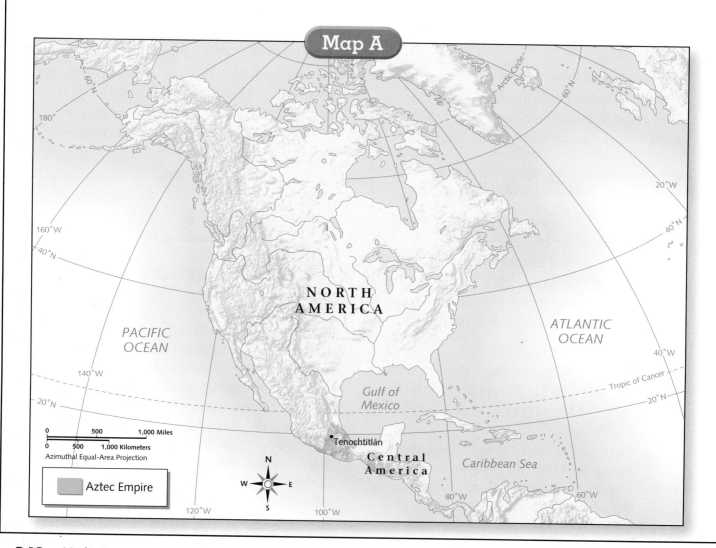

Map A

NORTH AMERICA

PACIFIC OCEAN

ATLANTIC OCEAN

Gulf of Mexico

Tropic of Cancer

•Tenochtitlán

Central America

Caribbean Sea

0   500   1,000 Miles
0   500   1,000 Kilometers
Azimuthal Equal-Area Projection

Aztec Empire

Map B

Tropic of Cancer

Gulf of Mexico

N
W E
S

Castillo de Teayo

Valley of Mexico
Lake Texcoco

Teotihuacán
Tlatelolco
Texcoco
Tlacopán
Tenochtitlán
Chapultepec

20°N

Zempoala

Cholula

Monte Albán

0   75   150 Miles
0   75   150 Kilometers
Azimuthal Equal-Area Projection

PACIFIC OCEAN

100°W

Aztec city

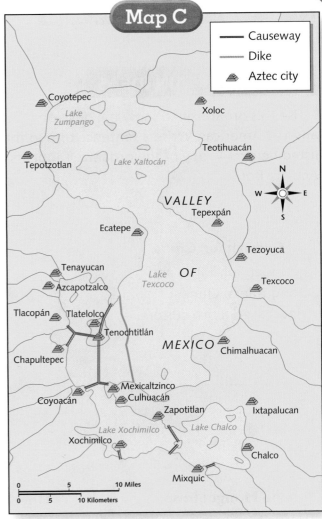

Map C

— Causeway
— Dike
🔺 Aztec city

Coyotepec

Lake Zumpango

Xoloc

Teotihuacán

Tepotzotlan

Lake Xaltocán

VALLEY

N
W E
S

Tepexpán

Ecatepe

Tezoyuca

Tenayucan

Lake Texcoco

OF

Azcapotzalco

Texcoco

Tlacopán   Tlatelolco

Tenochtitlán

MEXICO

Chapultepec

Chimalhuacan

Mexicaltzinco
Culhuacán

Coyoacán

Zapotitlan

Ixtapalucan

Lake Xochimilco   *Lake Chalco*

Xochimilco

Chalco

Mixquic

0   5   10 Miles
0   5   10 Kilometers

3. Understand the Process

Use the following questions as a guide to help you understand the best uses for small-scale and large-scale maps.

1 Find Tenochtitlán on all three maps. Notice the other cities near it. Which map shows the most cities of the Aztec Empire?

2 Suppose that you wanted to travel from Tenochtitlán to the Gulf of Mexico. On which map can you best measure the distance between them? Tell why.

3 Suppose that you wanted to measure Lake Texcoco's length from its most northern point to its most southern point. Which map would you use?

4 You have read about the causeways that connected Tenochtitlán to the mainland and about the city's dike. On which map can you find the causeways and the dike? Why do you think they appear on that map but not on the others?

4. Think and Apply

Think about how you use maps when you travel. Find two road maps with different scales—perhaps a road map of your state and a road map of a large city within your state. When would it be more helpful to use the state map, with the smaller scale? When would it be more helpful to use the city map, with the larger scale?

500   700

618
• Tang dynasty
  begins in China

645
• Taika reforms
  begin in Japan

CONNECT MAIN IDEAS

Use this organizer to show the development of empires in Asia and the Americas. Write a sentence or two that describes each topic listed below. A copy of the organizer appears on page 75 of the Activity Book.

Growth for China
Under Sui, Tang, and Song rulers, China developed a rich culture.

1. _____
2. _____

Empires in Asia and the Americas

The Mongol Empire
The Mongols brought the Chinese into closer contact with other cultures.

1. _____
2. _____

Development of Japanese Culture
The Japanese borrowed from and adapted Chinese culture.

1. _____
2. _____

Civilizations in the Americas
People living in the Americas between 1100 and 1500 adapted to and changed their environment.

1. _____
2. _____

WRITE MORE ABOUT IT

Write a Poem The Tang are remembered for their poetry and for other cultural achievements. Write a poem that describes a cultural achievement of the Tang.

Write a Description In your own words, describe how the Aztecs both adapted to and changed their environment to meet their needs.

900
• Feudalism in Japan

960
• Song dynasty begins in China

1271
• Mongols claim Chinese Mandate of Heaven

1500
• Height of Aztec power in the Americas

USE VOCABULARY

Use each term in a complete sentence that helps explain its meaning.

1. currency
2. daimyo
3. khan
4. mesa
5. plunder
6. porcelain
7. pueblo
8. samurai

CHECK UNDERSTANDING

9. Why was the Grand Canal important?

10. In what ways did Mongols hurt as well as help people in the lands they conquered?

11. Why did Europeans become interested in China?

12. How did the Mongols change Chinese policies toward outsiders?

13. From what culture did the early Japanese borrow ideas?

14. In what part of the Americas did the Aztecs live? In what part of the Americas did the Incas live?

15. Why did the Incas make the peoples they conquered follow the Inca way of life?

THINK CRITICALLY

16. **Think More About It** Describe what you think your daily life would be like if you were a Chinese peasant living under the rule of the Sui dynasty.

17. **Personally Speaking** Write your opinion of leaders, such as Genghis Khan and Kublai Khan, who brought destruction and positive change to the lands they conquered.

18. **Past to Present** Describe ways in which present-day peoples adapt to and change their environments to meet their needs. Tell which of these ways are useful and which you think are destructive.

19. **Cause and Effect** How does contact with people of different cultures affect people in the United States today?

APPLY SKILLS

Compare Maps with Different Scales Use the maps on pages 348 and 349 to answer these questions.

20. Suppose you want to describe the location of Tenochtitlán to a friend. Which map would best show the city in relation to places your friend probably knows?

21. Suppose you want to find the distance between Texcoco and Chapultepec. Which map would you use? Why?

22. What might a map of Tenochtitlán look like at an even larger scale?

READ MORE ABOUT IT

Aztec Times by Antony Mason. Simon and Schuster. Read this book to learn more about the Aztec way of life, including Aztec art, clothing, ornaments, science, and schools.

Visit the Internet at **http://www.hbschool.com** for additional resources.

Make Peace,

During much of the world's history, war or the threat of war has been a way of life for many of the world's people. Leaders such as Charlemagne and Genghis Khan used war to build great empires in Europe and Asia. Few of these empires lasted long after the deaths of their builders, however.

Times of peace often followed the horrors of war. During peaceful times, cultural exchanges that promoted science, technology, literature, and art took place within and between empires. Also, different ways of governing were tried. All these developments changed people's lives. Soon rulers began to see that peace could be as useful as war for empire building. Genghis Khan, though known far and wide as a mighty warrior, once said that much trouble could be avoided if peaceful agreements could be reached.

Many world leaders today have come to agree with what Genghis Khan said long ago. More can be gained if we make peace, not war!

In recent years, conflict raged among people in Israel, the Balkans, and Northern Ireland. However, leaders in these areas continue to support the peace process. As Prime Minister Tony Blair of the United Kingdom said, " . . . we only make progress if people give up violence for good."

Drawings by 11- and 12-year olds and a mural in Belfast, Ireland, show a desire for a more peaceful world.

Not War

Think and Apply

Listen to the news on television and radio or look through newspapers and magazines to find out where war has been ended or avoided. What actions were taken by world leaders and world organizations to end these conflicts? Report your findings to the class in the form of a television news broadcast.

HARCOURT BRACE

Visit the Internet at
http://www.hbschool.com
for additional resources.

CNN Turner Le@rning

Check your media center or classroom video library for the Making Social Studies Relevant videotape of this feature.

Palestinians and Jews parade for peace in Israel.

UNIT 5 REVIEW

Summarize the Main Ideas
Study the pictures and captions to help you review the events you read about in Unit 5.

Make a Generalization
Look closely at each scene. Based on what you see, make a generalization about life in different parts of the world between 500 and 1500.

1 The Byzantine Empire built on its Roman past while changing with the times.

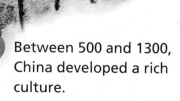

4 Between 500 and 1300, China developed a rich culture.

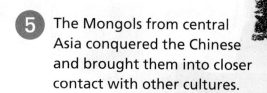

5 The Mongols from central Asia conquered the Chinese and brought them into closer contact with other cultures.

2 The people of the Muslim Empire are remembered for their achievements in science, geography, and mathematics.

3 In western Europe, many small independent kingdoms replaced the strong central government of the Roman Empire. During this time, Europeans answered the call to join the crusades.

6 The Japanese borrowed ideas from Chinese culture as they developed their own civilization.

7 People in the Americas adapted to and changed their environment as they built civilizations.

USE VOCABULARY

Work with a partner. Use one of the groups of terms below to write a short story.

Group A: crusader, feudal system, manor, bubonic plague

Group B: mesa, Mound Builders, pueblo

Group C: Catholic, icon, mosaic, orthodox, patriarch

CHECK UNDERSTANDING

1 What were some of the achievements of the Byzantine emperor Justinian?

2 What is the Qur'an, and why is it important to the religion of Islam?

3 How did the defeat of the Chinese by the Mongols affect both peoples?

4 In what ways did the Chinese influence Japanese civilization?

5 How did the Aztecs change their environment as they built Tenochtitlán?

6 How did Native Americans of the Southwest adapt to a dry environment?

THINK CRITICALLY

7 **Past to Present** What present-day groups are fighting over differences in religion?

8 **Explore Viewpoints** Why do you think some groups of people, such as the samurai of Japan, have been willing to go through great difficulty to reach their goals?

9 **Personally Speaking** Which of the cultures you read about in this unit interests you the most? Why?

APPLY SKILLS

Compare Maps with Different Scales Use Map A and Map B to answer the questions.

10 Which map would you use to identify ancient cities fewer than 100 miles (161 km) from Constantinople? Explain.

11 Which map would you use to find the size of Constantinople from east to west? Explain.

Map A: Byzantine Empire, 1204

Map B: Constantinople, 1204

REMEMBER

- Share your ideas.
- Cooperate with others to plan your work.
- Take responsibility for your work.
- Help one another.
- Show your group's work to the class.
- Discuss what you learned by working together.

ACTIVITY Present a
Dramatization

Work with a partner to dramatize a reporter's interview with Marco Polo. One partner should be Marco Polo, and the other should be the reporter. Work together to write questions for the reporter to ask Marco Polo. Then write the answers Marco Polo will give. Practice the dramatization. Then act it out for your class.

ACTIVITY Make a
Model

Work in a group to find out more about feudal life in Europe. Then work together to make a model of a manor. Label the parts of the model with small signs. Display your finished model in your classroom.

ACTIVITY Write a
Song

In a group, think about what your life would be like if you were members of one of the following groups: crusaders on the way to Jerusalem, Muslims defending their claim to the Holy Land, Japanese men and women living during the time of the shoguns, or Aztecs building Tenochtitlán. With group members, write the words of a song that describes your way of life.

Unit Project Wrap-Up

Make a Map Now that you have completed Unit 5, you and your classmates can complete your world map of early empires. First, label the regions where the empires were located. Then, use the notes that you have gathered to illustrate one or two scenes showing the culture of each empire. Include one or two sentences to describe each scene. You may wish to draw your scenes and write your sentences on separate sheets of paper. You can then display these papers alongside your map. Place your completed map on a classroom wall.

GROWTH OF TRADE

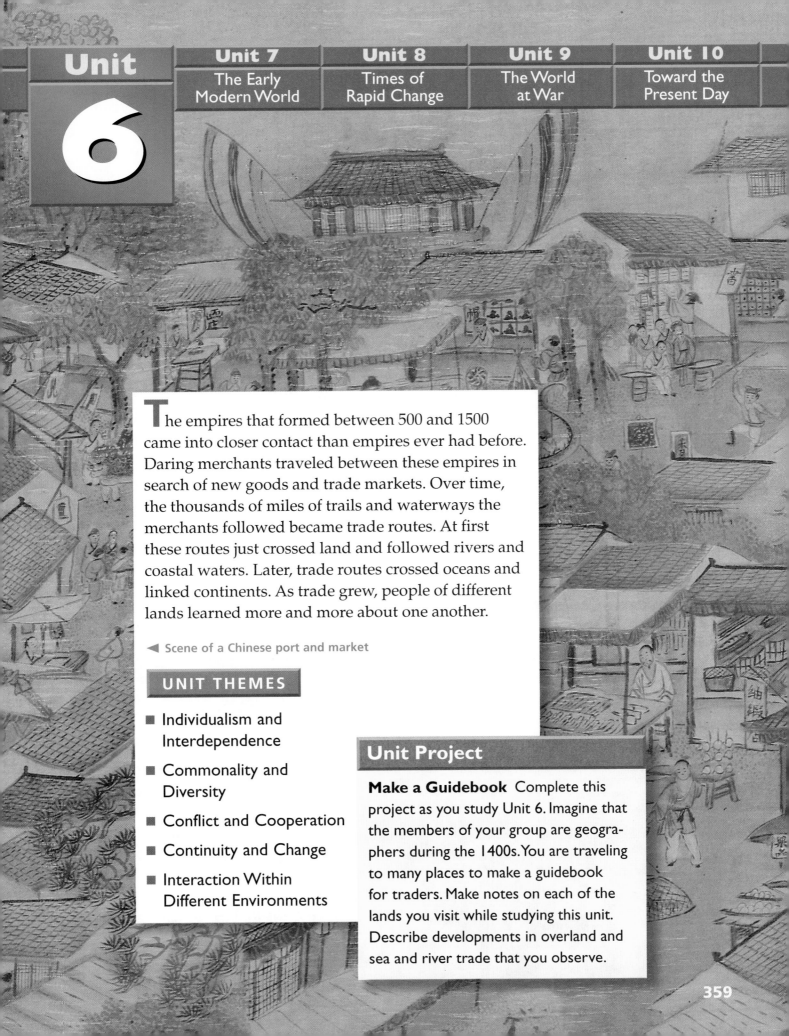

The empires that formed between 500 and 1500 came into closer contact than empires ever had before. Daring merchants traveled between these empires in search of new goods and trade markets. Over time, the thousands of miles of trails and waterways the merchants followed became trade routes. At first these routes just crossed land and followed rivers and coastal waters. Later, trade routes crossed oceans and linked continents. As trade grew, people of different lands learned more and more about one another.

◀ Scene of a Chinese port and market

UNIT THEMES

- Individualism and Interdependence
- Commonality and Diversity
- Conflict and Cooperation
- Continuity and Change
- Interaction Within Different Environments

Unit Project

Make a Guidebook Complete this project as you study Unit 6. Imagine that the members of your group are geographers during the 1400s. You are traveling to many places to make a guidebook for traders. Make notes on each of the lands you visit while studying this unit. Describe developments in overland and sea and river trade that you observe.

359

UNIT 6
PREVIEW

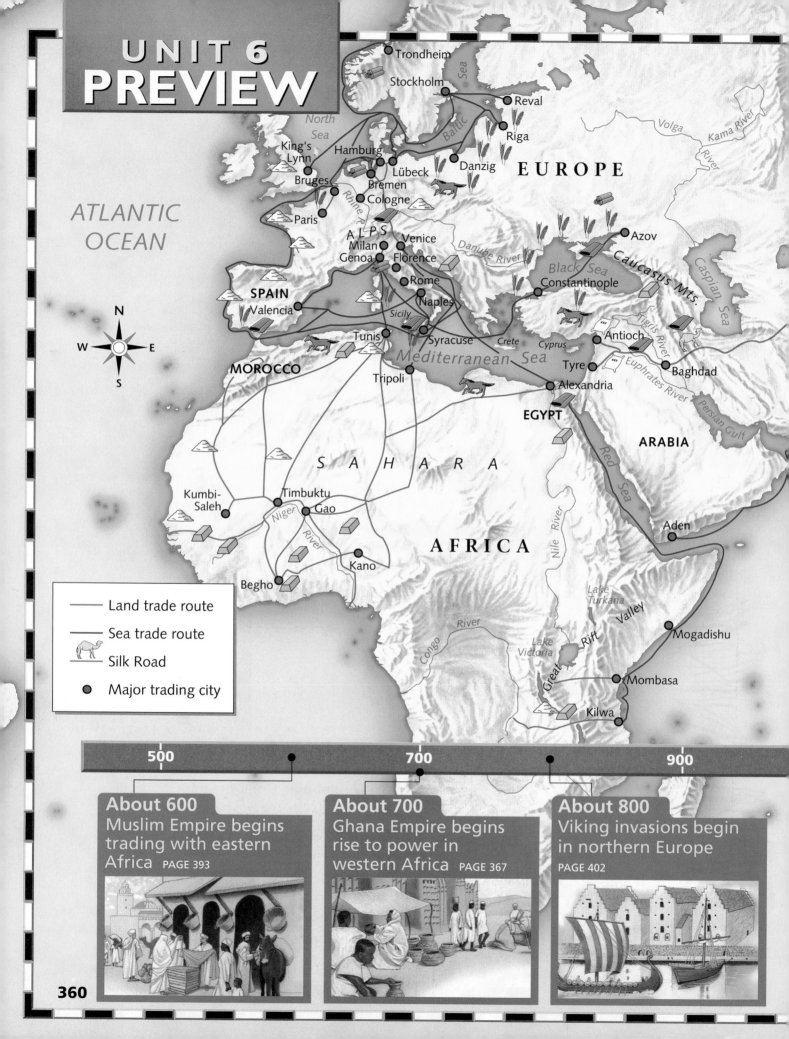

ATLANTIC OCEAN

North Sea

Trondheim
Stockholm
Reval
Riga
Danzig

EUROPE

Volga River
Kama River

King's Lynn
Hamburg
Lübeck
Bruges
Bremen
Cologne
Paris

Rhine River

ALPS
Milan
Genoa
Venice
Florence
Rome
Naples

Danube River

Azov

Black Sea
Caucasus Mts.
Constantinople

Caspian Sea

SPAIN
Valencia

Sicily

Syracuse
Tunis

Crete
Cyprus

Antioch
Tyre
Baghdad

Tigris River
Euphrates River

Persian Gulf

MOROCCO

Mediterranean Sea

Tripoli

Alexandria

EGYPT

ARABIA

SAHARA

Red Sea

Nile River

AFRICA

Kumbi-Saleh
Timbuktu
Gao
Kano
Begho

Niger River

Congo River

Aden

Lake Turkana

Great Rift Valley

Lake Victoria

Mogadishu

Mombasa

Kilwa

Land trade route

Sea trade route

Silk Road

● **Major trading city**

500   700   900

About 600
Muslim Empire begins trading with eastern Africa **PAGE 393**

About 700
Ghana Empire begins rise to power in western Africa **PAGE 367**

About 800
Viking invasions begin in northern Europe **PAGE 402**

360

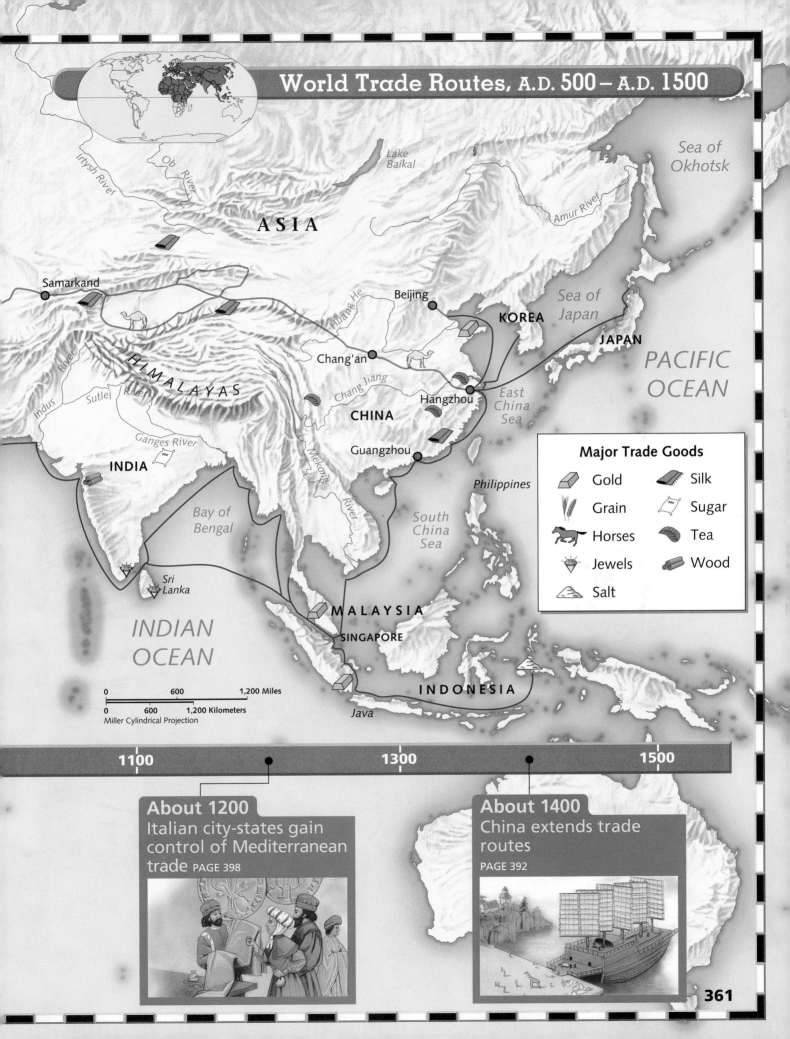

World Trade Routes, A.D. 500–A.D. 1500

ASIA

Irtysh River

Ob River

Lake Baikal

Amur River

Sea of Okhotsk

Samarkand

Beijing

KOREA

Sea of Japan

Huang He

JAPAN

PACIFIC OCEAN

Chang'an

Chang Jiang

Hangzhou

East China Sea

CHINA

HIMALAYAS

Indus River

Sutlej River

Ganges River

INDIA

Guangzhou

Mekong River

Philippines

South China Sea

Bay of Bengal

Sri Lanka

INDIAN OCEAN

MALAYSIA

SINGAPORE

INDONESIA

Java

Major Trade Goods

Gold		Silk	
Grain		Sugar	
Horses		Tea	
Jewels		Wood	
Salt			

0   600   1,200 Miles
0   600   1,200 Kilometers
Miller Cylindrical Projection

1100   1300   1500

About 1200
Italian city-states gain control of Mediterranean trade PAGE 398

About 1400
China extends trade routes PAGE 392

THE ROYAL KINGDOMS OF
Ghana, Mali, and Songhay
LIFE IN MEDIEVAL AFRICA

written by Patricia and Fredrick McKissack
illustrated by Higgins Bond

Muslim merchants traveling the north-south trade routes across the Sahara brought Arab culture and the religion of Islam to western Africa. In turn, the people of Africa shared their customs. Ideas moved back and forth as people traveled between Muslim and western Africa.

In 1324 Mansa Musa (MAN•sah MOO•sah), the ruler of the western Africa empire of Mali, made his hajj (HAJ), or pilgrimage, to the Muslim holy city of Mecca. Never before had the Muslims in such places as Egypt seen a visitor like Mansa Musa. Their ideas about the people of western Africa changed forever.

From 1307 to 1332 Mansa Musa ruled over the empire of Mali in western Africa.

THE GREAT HAJJ

Months before Mansa[1] Musa's departure from Mali, officials and servants began preparing for the long trip. Five hundred slaves, each carrying a six-pound staff[2] of gold, arrived in Cairo, Egypt, in July of 1324. Next came Musa and his entourage,[3] followed by a caravan of one hundred camels, each carrying three hundred pounds of gold. A hundred more camels carried food, clothing, and other supplies. All together sixty thousand people accompanied the mansa to Mecca.

Mansa Musa reached Cairo after eight months of travel. His Arab guide suggested that he visit the local ruler or sultan. Musa rejected the idea, saying he wasn't interested in making a social call. The guide convinced him that his actions might be taken as an insult by an important Muslim brother. So Musa agreed to make the visit.

It was customary that a visitor kneel and kiss the ground before the sultan. Mansa Musa flatly refused. He was richer and controlled more territory than the sultan of Egypt, so why, he asked, should he kowtow[4] before a lesser king? Once again the guide explained the custom to Musa. "Very well," Musa agreed, choosing diplomacy. "I will prostrate[5] myself before Allah, who created me and brought me into the world." Having done this, the sultan compromised, too. He welcomed Musa to come sit beside him, a sign that they were equals.

Musa continued to Arabia, where he completed his hajj. Merchants and travelers had teased Middle Easterners with stories about

---

[1] **mansa**: ruler
[2] **staff**: stick or pole
[3] **entourage**: group of people who take care of the needs of an important person
[4] **kowtow**: kneel and touch forehead to the ground as a sign of respect
[5] **prostrate**: lie flat, face down

Mansa Musa's Hajj, 1324

- - - -> Possible route of Mansa Musa's hajj

Movement Muslims are expected to make a pilgrimage, if possible, to Mecca on the Arabian Penninsula.

■ *How would you describe the route Mansa Musa took?*

the gold-rich empires south of the Sahara. When news spread that the king of Mali was in the city, people lined the streets to see him.

Everywhere Mansa Musa went he graciously paid for every service in gold and gave lavish gifts to his hosts. Merchants scrambled to get his attention, for it was not uncommon for Musa to buy up everything that was presented to him. Beggars lined the streets as he passed, hoping to receive a gold nugget.

By the time Mansa Musa left the Middle East, he had put so much gold into circulation, its value fell sharply. A reporter in the service of the Egyptian sultan reported that the Cairo gold market had been so saturated that it still had not fully recovered twelve years after Mansa Musa's fabulous hajj.

This unit tells more about Mansa Musa and his amazing trip. It also tells how people of different cultures learn more about one another through their trading contact.

OVERLAND TRADE

"They . . . travel in the desert as if it were upon the sea, having guides to pilot them by the stars or rocks in the deserts."

Description of how traders crossed the Sahara, by a twelfth-century Muslim writer

The desert is home to this present-day camel trader from Cairo, Egypt.

The Trading Empires of West Africa

FOCUS
Why do present-day countries seek trading partners?

Main Idea As you read, look for reasons the peoples of the West African empires traded with other peoples.

Vocabulary
savanna
tropical rain forest
tariff
mansa

Trade has always been important to the peoples of Africa. Early peoples traded surplus resources for resources that were scarce where they lived. Over the years trade networks developed. Then, between the years 700 and 1500, powerful West African empires that were based on trade developed. The wealth of these empires attracted traders and travelers from many other lands.

West African Beginnings

Africa is a giant among continents—the second largest in the world. Geographers usually describe the continent in terms of five regions—North Africa, West Africa, Central Africa, East Africa, and Southern Africa.

Much of Africa is a plateau broken in places by deep basins and valleys. The Great Rift Valley stretches about 3,500 miles (5,633 km) north and south through East Africa. It is one of the world's longest and deepest valley systems. Deserts also cover large parts of Africa. The Sahara, the world's largest desert, covers more than 3.5 million square miles (9 million sq km) of North Africa.

South of the Sahara lies West Africa. Much of West Africa is a grassy plain, or **savanna** (suh•VA•nuh). A tropical region covers West Africa's southern coast and much of Central Africa. This hot, wet land with trees so tall that they block the sunlight is a **tropical rain forest**.

Survival was easy for the early peoples of West Africa. The savanna was full of wild animals that could be hunted for food, and the fertile soil was perfect for growing crops. Because of this, West Africa's population grew quickly.

About 300 B.C. people in the savanna learned how to shape iron by heating it. The earliest known iron users in West Africa were the Nok people. They lived from about

This Nok sculpture was found in 1943 and is more than 2,000 years old. It is made of terra-cotta, or baked clay.

900 B.C. to A.D. 200 in the region that today is northern Nigeria (ny•JIR•ee•uh).

Iron changed the lives of the Nok people. It gave them stronger weapons for hunting and fighting. Iron tools also made it easier for them to clear land and grow crops. Because of these advantages, the Noks and other iron users grew powerful.

By the 700s iron users called the Soninkes had taken over much of the West African grassland. The land they lived on, alongside the Niger River, was fertile. The Soninkes made the most of their location by using water from the Niger to irrigate their land.

The Soninkes were not only skilled farmers but also good traders. Their location was ideal for a center of trade. The region lay between the forestlands south of the Niger and the desert lands of the Sahara in North Africa. North African merchants crossed the Sahara to trade with the Soninkes. As their main trade good, the Soninkes offered gold.

Gold, however, was a scarce resource in the grasslands where the Soninkes lived. To get gold to trade, they traded with the kingdom of Wangara, to the south. The Soninkes traded salt, which they had gotten from the Muslim merchants of North Africa, to the Wangaras for gold. Because the Wangaras had very little salt, they were willing to trade gold for it.

Africa offers much geographical diversity. The desert lands of the Sahara (left) provide a sharp contrast to the jungle of the tropical rain forest (top right). South of the desert lie the grasslands of the savanna (bottom right).

LEARNING FROM CHARTS The Soninkes were at the center of the gold-and-salt trade.
■ *Who ended up with the gold? Who ended up with the salt?*

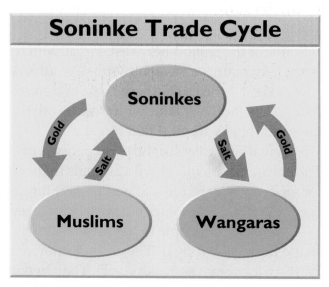

Soninke Trade Cycle

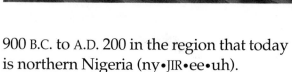

Once the Soninkes got the gold from the Wangaras, they traded it to North African merchants for more salt. This cycle of trade in gold and salt went on through the years. The Soninkes also served as the go-betweens for the trade of other goods. In doing so, they took Mediterranean goods such as paper, woven cloth, and perfumes to the peoples farther south in Africa.

Because the Soninkes made a profit at both ends of their trade cycle, they grew powerful and rich. Their wealth led to the development of the first great empire in West Africa.

REVIEW *How did the Soninkes trade salt and gold? What was the result?*

Ghana

The new West African empire soon became known by a title used by its rulers—*Ghana* (GAH•nuh), meaning "war chief." Ghana, which was located between the Senegal and upper Niger rivers, began its rise to power about 700. By the year 1000 the empire covered more than 100,000 square miles (258,980 sq km).

Much of what we know about early Ghana comes from the works of Muslim scholars. One of these scholars, al-Zuhri (al•ZUKH•ree), wrote about Ghana's rise to power. He said that the Ghanaians attacked peoples who

Regions Geographers divide Africa into five regions. Climate and resources vary from region to region.
■ *What kinds of climate does West Africa have?*

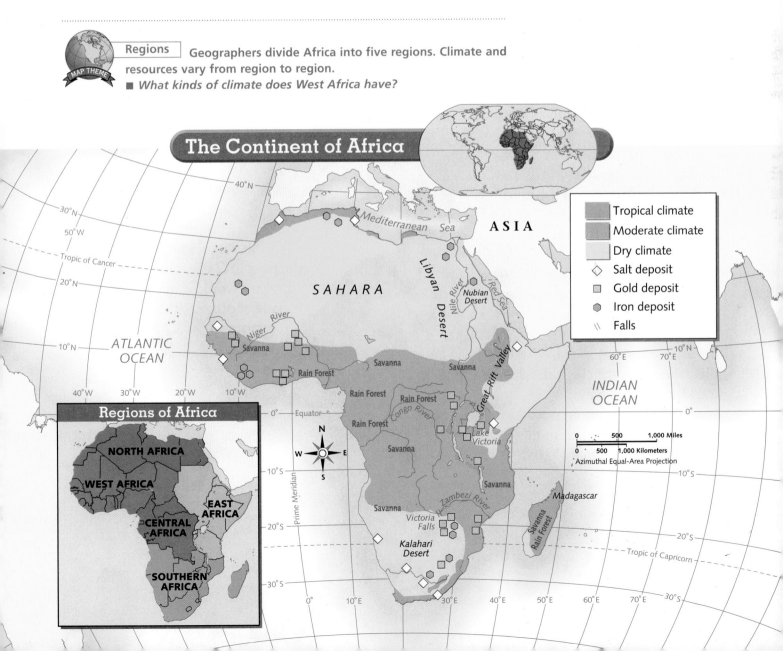

The Continent of Africa

Tropical climate
Moderate climate
Dry climate
◇ Salt deposit
▢ Gold deposit
⬡ Iron deposit
\\ Falls

Regions of Africa

NORTH AFRICA
WEST AFRICA
EAST AFRICA
CENTRAL AFRICA
SOUTHERN AFRICA

ATLANTIC OCEAN
INDIAN OCEAN
ASIA
SAHARA
Libyan Desert
Nubian Desert
Mediterranean Sea
Nile River
Red Sea
Niger River
Savanna
Rain Forest
Congo River
Great Rift Valley
Lake Victoria
Zambezi River
Madagascar
Victoria Falls
Kalahari Desert
Rain Forest
Savanna

0   500   1,000 Miles
0   500   1,000 Kilometers
Azimuthal Equal-Area Projection

were "ignorant of iron and who [fought] with ebony clubs." The Ghanaians, with their iron spears, easily defeated these peoples.

As time passed, each Ghanaian king won authority over more kingdoms in West Africa. The kings ordered the Ghanaian army to keep trade routes across the savanna safe from enemy attacks. The kings then charged **tariffs**, or taxes, on all goods passing through the savanna. The eleventh-century Muslim geographer al-Bakri (al•BAHK•ree) explained how these tariffs worked:

66 The king exacts [demands] the right of one dinar [an Arab coin] of gold on each donkey-load of salt that enters his country, and two dinars of gold on each load of salt that goes out. 99

The tariffs provided the funds needed to feed the soldiers in Ghana's army and support its government.

As the empire of Ghana grew, lands rich with gold came under its control. The "master of the gold," as the Ghanaian king was called, held a monopoly over the gold trade. As al-Bakri wrote, "All pieces of gold that are found in the empire belong to the king of Ghana, but he leaves to his people the gold dust." By claiming so much gold, the king of Ghana made sure that this metal did not become too easy to get. In this way, he kept the price of gold high.

Much of the gold trade took place near Ghana's capital city, Kumbi-Saleh (KOOM•bee SAH•lay). This city lay on one of the most important trade routes across the western Sahara. North African merchants brought to Kumbi-Saleh their most important trade good—pure salt from mines in the Sahara. At that time salt was used not only to add more flavor to food but also to keep meat from rotting. Salt was worth a lot in West Africa because it was a scarce resource there. At times a trader might have to pay 1 pound (454 g) of gold to get an equal amount of salt!

Besides gold, the North Africans traded for ivory, cotton goods, and animal skins. They also bought slaves, whom they later sold to owners of salt mines or large farms. In return, the North Africans traded horses, swords, glass, and wool clothing.

For more than 300 years, Ghana controlled trade in West Africa. Then, in the 1000s, quarrels between Ghana and a Berber trading center led to war. The Berbers, from northwestern Africa, won, and Ghana never became powerful again. By 1203 the empire had broken up into small kingdoms. In time the people of the fallen Ghana Empire would come under the rule of other African empires.

REVIEW *How did Ghana's kings get their wealth?*

Artifacts such as this bracelet and this sculpture of a bird called an ibis are evidence of metalworking skills in the empire of Ghana.

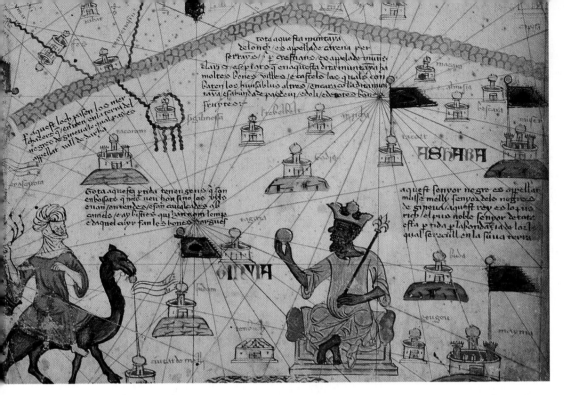

This section of a fourteenth-century map shows the great Mali Empire. The seated figure with a crown is the ruler Mansa Musa. Why has the mapmaker pictured Mansa Musa holding out a gold nugget to a trader?

Growth of Islam in West Africa

The Ghanaians were not the only ones to trade with Muslim merchants. In the ninth century the kingdom of Kanem (KAH•nem), which had risen on the shores of Lake Chad, began to grow through trade. Around the same time trading centers formed along the Niger River at Jenné (jeh•NAY) and at Gao (GOW).

Contact with the Muslim North Africans through trade began to change the lives of the people in West Africa. The Muslim traders showed West African traders how to use money instead of bartering. They also brought with them the Arabic language.

Most important, West Africans began to accept the religion of Islam. The kings of Ghana, Kanem, and Gao became Muslims in the 1000s. Later the rulers of other kingdoms and many African traders also accepted Islam. The great empires that rose in Ghana's place were based not only on trade but also on Islam.

REVIEW *How did North African traders change life in the West African trading kingdoms?*

Mali and Mansa Musa

About 25 years after the fall of Ghana, a new empire called Mali formed in West Africa. The people who founded Mali were called Malinkes (muh•LING•kayz). Under their Muslim leader Sundiata (sun•JAHT•ah), the Malinkes conquered many of the small kingdoms Ghana had once held, including those rich in gold. Mali's riches, like Ghana's, came from the gold-and-salt trade.

The **mansas**, or rulers, who followed Sundiata won more land for the Mali Empire. Mali grew to be nearly twice as large as the empire of Ghana had been. Mali's greatest growth came during the rule of Mansa Musa, from 1307 to 1332. During his rule Mansa Musa extended the empire to include the rich trading markets of Gao and Timbuktu (tim•buhk•TOO). The addition of lands brought even more wealth to the empire.

Mali became known for more than its wealth, however. Mansa Musa encouraged knowledge and study throughout his empire. A Muslim himself, Mansa Musa invited Arab scholars to come to Mali. Many did, and Mali became a center of learning. Students from as far away as Egypt and Arabia studied at the university at Timbuktu.

In 1324 Mansa Musa made his famous pilgrimage to Mecca, the Muslim holy city. All who saw him on his travels through North Africa and Southwest Asia were amazed. Mansa Musa's servants glittered in their fine clothing. His warriors carried golden spears. All along the way, Mansa Musa handed gifts to almost everyone he met.

The pilgrimage helped make Mansa Musa and the empire of Mali known far and wide. Mali's trading influence grew. Later rulers of Mali, however, were not as strong and wise as Mansa Musa had been. They could not hold on to the land that he had gained during his rule. Because of this, Mali's power began to slip away.

REVIEW *Why did people come to Mali during the rule of Mansa Musa?*

Place Over time three empires—Ghana, Mali, and Songhay—rose and fell in West Africa.

■ *Which of the empires extended the farthest north?*

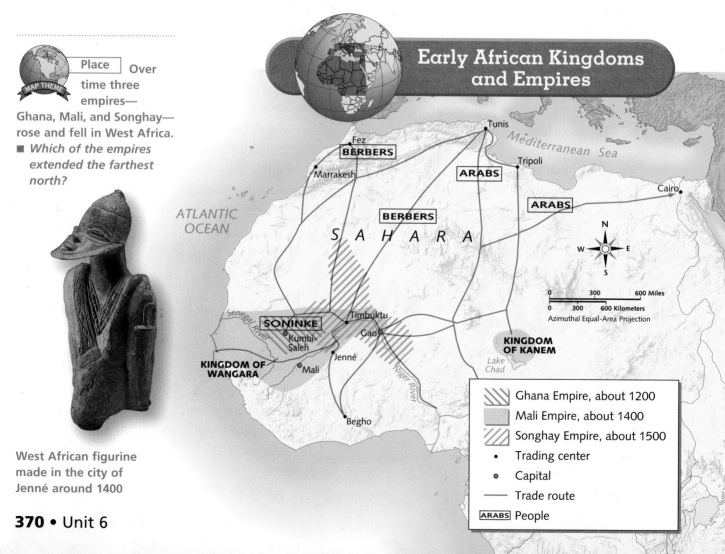

West African figurine made in the city of Jenné around 1400

Early African Kingdoms and Empires

BERBERS
Fez
Marrakesh
Tunis
Tripoli
Mediterranean Sea
ARABS
Cairo
ARABS
BERBERS
S A H A R A
ATLANTIC OCEAN

N
W E
S

0   300   600 Miles
0   300   600 Kilometers
Azimuthal Equal-Area Projection

Senegal River
SONINKE
Kumbi-Saleh
Timbuktu
Gao
Jenné
KINGDOM OF WANGARA
Mali
Niger River
KINGDOM OF KANEM
Lake Chad
Begho

Ghana Empire, about 1200
Mali Empire, about 1400
Songhay Empire, about 1500
• Trading center
• Capital
— Trade route
ARABS People

Songhay

As Mali weakened, another West African empire began to grow. By the late 1400s much of what had been Mali had become part of the Songhay (SAWNG•hy) Empire. Like Ghana and Mali before it, the Songhay Empire grew rich from its control of trade routes across the Sahara. The Songhays also took control of the main trading centers along the Niger River—Jenné, Timbuktu, and Gao. War canoes along the Niger protected these trading cities from attacks by raiders.

The Muslim traveler and geographer Leo Africanus (LEE•oh af•rih•KAY•nuhs) visited Songhay in the early 1500s. In Gao he found "rich merchants who travel constantly about the region with their wares." The people of Gao, he saw, had more than enough gold to spend on goods imported from Europe and North Africa.

Rulers who wanted the wealth and power of Songhay waited for a chance to capture it. In 1591 the ruler of Morocco in North Africa sent an army of about 4,000 soldiers to attack Songhay. The Songhay soldiers fought with

A sculpture made in the 1400s (left) and a tomb built in the 1500s are reminders of the Songhay Empire of long ago.

swords. Their attackers fought with weapons new to the Songhays—guns, which the Moroccans had gotten from southwestern Asia. The Songhays could not hold off the Moroccan attacks. The Songhays' defeat led to the end of the Songhay Empire. The trade routes across the Sahara were still used, but they became less important. European ships sailing Africa's Atlantic coast created a new route for West African trade.

REVIEW *Why did other peoples want the lands of the Songhay Empire?*

LESSON 1 REVIEW

Check Understanding

1 Remember the Facts What were three important West African empires?

2 Recall the Main Idea Why did the peoples of the West African empires trade with other peoples?

Think Critically

3 Think More About It Why did North African traders want gold? Why were the Wangaras willing to trade it?

4 Cause and Effect How did the conquering of kingdoms rich in gold help Ghana's economy?

5 Past to Present What natural resources are scarce in your state? How does your state get products made from these natural resources?

Show What You Know

Journal Activity Imagine that you are a North African merchant traveling with a caravan to one of the West African trading towns. Write journal entries about the trip across the Sahara, your arrival in West Africa, and the trading that takes place.

Compare Maps with Different Projections

1. Why Learn This Skill?

Over the centuries Arab, Chinese, and European mapmakers have developed different ways to show the round Earth in the form of a flat map. These different representations of the Earth are called **projections**. Every map projection has **distortions**, or parts that are not accurate. This is because the shape of the round Earth needs to be split or stretched to make it flat. Identifying these distortions will help you understand how map projections can best be used.

2. Map Projections and Their Uses

Different kinds of map projections have different kinds of distortions. Some map projections distort the shape or the size of the area shown. Some show distances to be greater or less than they actually are. One way that mapmakers classify map projections is by the properties that are distorted the least.

Map A is an equal-area projection. Notice that there is equal area on either side of the prime meridian and on either side of the equator. An **equal-area projection** shows the sizes of regions in correct relation to one another, but it distorts shapes. Because an equal-area projection shows correct size relations of regions, it is useful for comparing information about different parts of the world.

Map B is a conformal projection. Notice that the lines of longitude are all an equal distance

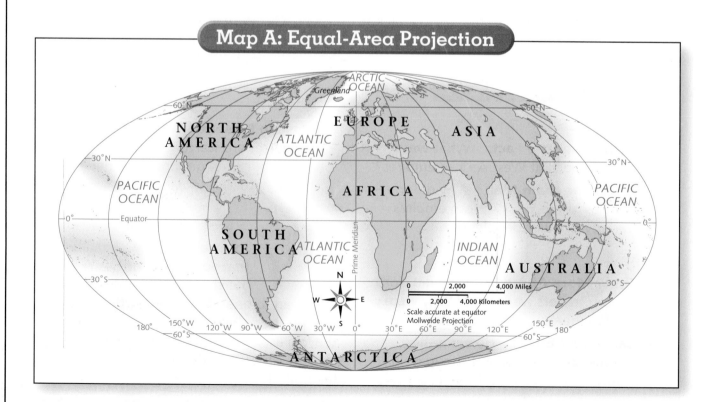

Map A: Equal-Area Projection

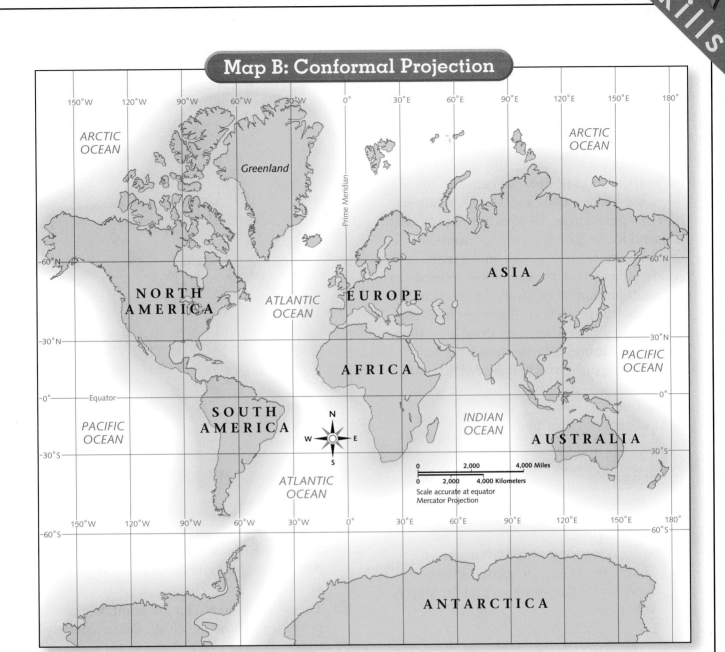

Map B: Conformal Projection

ARCTIC OCEAN

Greenland

Prime Meridian

ARCTIC OCEAN

NORTH AMERICA

ATLANTIC OCEAN

EUROPE

ASIA

30°N

PACIFIC OCEAN

AFRICA

Equator

SOUTH AMERICA

PACIFIC OCEAN

INDIAN OCEAN

AUSTRALIA

ATLANTIC OCEAN

| 0 | 2,000 | 4,000 Miles |
| 0 | 2,000 | 4,000 Kilometers |

Scale accurate at equator
Mercator Projection

ANTARCTICA

apart. On a globe the lines of longitude get closer together as they near the poles, where they meet. Also notice on Map B that the lines of latitude closer to the poles are farther apart. On a globe the lines of latitude are an equal distance apart. A **conformal projection** shows directions correctly, but it distorts sizes, especially of places near the poles. The Mercator (mer•KAY•ter) projection, shown above on Map B, is just one example of a conformal projection. Another type of map, the Robinson projection, is a combination of equal-area and

conformal projections. Map C is an example of a Robinson projection.

Map D is an **equidistant projection**. It shows accurate distances from a central point. Any place on the Earth can be chosen as the central point. Often the central point chosen is one of the poles. That kind of map is called a **polar projection**. Either the North Pole or the South Pole can be the center of a polar projection. Notice on Map D that the North Pole is at the center of the map. The lines of latitude are circles, and the circles farther from the center are larger. Lines of longitude on Map D are straight lines that extend from the center in all directions, like the spokes of a wheel.

A **great circle** is any imaginary circle that divides the Earth into equal parts. The equator is a great circle. Lines of longitude are great circles, too. Because the Earth's surface is curved, the shortest distance between any two places is not really a straight line but part of a great circle. An equidistant projection is useful for finding the distance from the central point to other places on the map. Another projection, the gnomonic projection, is also important when studying great circle routes. In this projection all straight lines are great circle routes. Therefore, these lines show the shortest routes between two places. Distances on this projection are not accurate, however.

3. Understand the Process

Compare and contrast Maps A, B, C, and D by answering the questions below. As you answer the questions, think about the advantages and disadvantages of each map projection.

1 South America is much larger than Greenland. Which projection shows Greenland's size more accurately, Map A or Map B?

Map D: Equidistant Projection

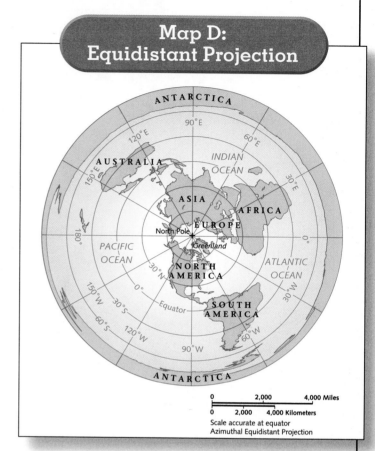

Scale accurate at equator
Azimuthal Equidistant Projection

2 The greatest east-west distance in Africa is about the same as the greatest north-south distance. Which projection shows Africa's shape more accurately, Map A or Map B?

3 The North Pole is a single point. Which projections show the North Pole accurately?

4 Which map can be called a polar projection?

5 On which maps do the lines of longitude get closer together toward the poles?

6 On which map or maps are the lines of longitude parallel, or equally far apart?

4. Think and Apply

Reread the information on map projections and study the maps. Write a paragraph about the advantages and disadvantages of using each kind of map.

Map C: Robinson Projection

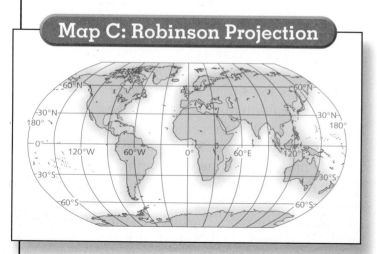

Trade Routes Linking Asia and Europe

FOCUS
How does trade change when countries grow?

Main Idea Look for ways in which the growth of unified empires led to trade among the peoples of Africa, Asia, and Europe.

Vocabulary
oasis
caravansary
cartographer

The caravan routes between North Africa and West Africa were just one part of a trade network that linked Africa with Asia and Europe. This network of trade routes stretched over thousands of miles. It crossed deserts, went around forests, and climbed mountain ranges. Travel along the trade routes brought many cultures together. This led to the exchange of language and cultural ideas as well as goods.

Trade in the Lands of Islam

By the end of the 700s, Muslims controlled lands that reached east to the Indus River, west to what is now Spain and Portugal, and south to the Sahara. The empire included many peoples—Indians, Syrians, Persians, Egyptians, and Spaniards, among others.

Little by little the different peoples under Muslim rule came together as one culture. Many of these people became Muslims, and peoples all over the Muslim lands began to speak Arabic. Muhammad is reported to have said, "Whoever speaks Arabic is an Arab."

The growing network of trade routes throughout Muslim lands also brought people together. This network included roads built by the Romans and the Persians as well as new roads. On the desert trade routes, the Arabian, or single-humped, camel was the main transportation. Well suited for desert trips, this "ship of the desert" could go for four days without water.

Painting of an Islamic pilgrimage, 1237

Desert travel was slow, however. On a good day camels could walk about 25 miles (40 km) in ten hours. Every two to three days, camel caravans needed to stop at an **oasis** (oh•AY•suhs), or water hole, to take on fresh water. Along the most-traveled routes, some of the watering places had **caravansaries** (kar•uh•VAN•suh•reez), inns where travelers could find food and shelter.

REVIEW *What helped connect the many peoples living in the lands controlled by the Muslims?*

A Time of Cultural Exchange

Trade brought wealth to the lands controlled by the Muslims. Merchants traveled far and wide, carrying new products to and from markets in southwestern Asia.

The goods brought back to Muslim lands had an important effect on life there. For example, gold changed the way Muslims traded. Even in the early days of trade, the Muslims used gold from West Africa to make coins called dinars. Over time the dinar became the standard coin for trade. Trade goods also changed the look of the land controlled by the Muslims. Muslim merchants brought fruit trees from Asia. Soon lemon and orange groves grew all along the Mediterranean.

Ideas traveled as freely as goods on the trade routes, and learning flourished in the Muslim Empire. Muslim scholars developed new ways to study medicine, mathematics, astronomy, and geography. For example, trade with India brought the Muslim world the number system that we know today as Arabic numerals.

LEARNING FROM DIAGRAMS The Muslims exchanged goods with peoples in Africa and Asia.

■ *From where did Muslim traders get gold? spices? silk?*

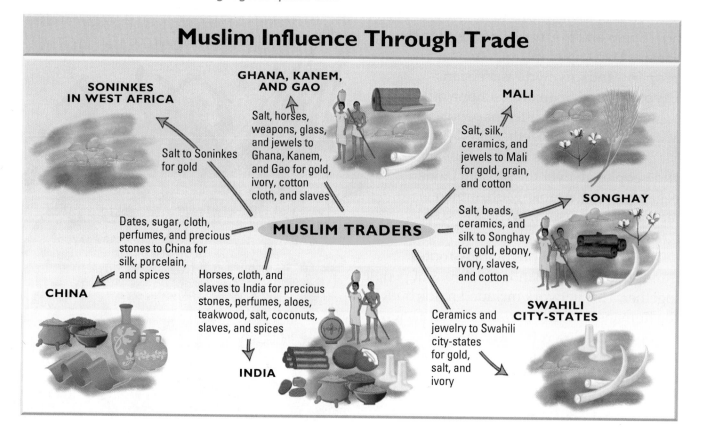

Muslim Influence Through Trade

SONINKES IN WEST AFRICA

GHANA, KANEM, AND GAO

MALI

Salt to Soninkes for gold

Salt, horses, weapons, glass, and jewels to Ghana, Kanem, and Gao for gold, ivory, cotton cloth, and slaves

Salt, silk, ceramics, and jewels to Mali for gold, grain, and cotton

MUSLIM TRADERS

Dates, sugar, cloth, perfumes, and precious stones to China for silk, porcelain, and spices

Salt, beads, ceramics, and silk to Songhay for gold, ebony, ivory, slaves, and cotton

SONGHAY

CHINA

Horses, cloth, and slaves to India for precious stones, perfumes, aloes, teakwood, salt, coconuts, slaves, and spices

INDIA

Ceramics and jewelry to Swahili city-states for gold, salt, and ivory

SWAHILI CITY-STATES

This painting (left) from a fifteenth-century manuscript illustrates the Muslims' skill in the practice of medicine. In Muslim pharmacies (below) many medicines were made.

With this number system Muslim mathematicians advanced the study of algebra (*al-jabr* in Arabic). Algebra deals with relationships among numbers. Algebra problems use variables, such as x and y. In ancient times the Egyptians had written about the idea of algebra. However, this branch of mathematics was fully developed only through the work of al-Khwarizmi (al•KWAR•uhz•mee) in Baghdad during the early 800s.

After hundreds of years of travel and trade, the Muslims had become expert geographers. Using the study of stars and the journals of travelers, Muslim **cartographers** (kar•TAH•gruh•ferz), or mapmakers, began to draw highly accurate maps. Their maps were used by European explorers of the 1400s and 1500s.

Literature, too, owed much to the flow of ideas along the trade routes. For example, many of the stories in *The Arabian Nights* may have first been told in India and Persia. At the height of the Muslim Empire, however, the stories had become a part of Arabic literature.

Everywhere in the Muslim lands, people read Arabic poetry, essays, biographies, and tales. Through literature they also learned about Islamic history, law, and science.

Muslims kept control of the trade network even during invasions by Seljuk Turks from central Asia and by European crusaders. Then, in the mid-1200s, the Mongols destroyed the Muslim trade center of Baghdad. After that, control of the land trade routes fell from Muslim hands.

REVIEW *What achievements of the Muslim Empire resulted from the exchange of ideas?*

This twelfth-century map of the world was made by the Muslim geographer al-Idrisi. What continents are shown on this map?

Trade on the Silk Road Continues

The Mongol invasions brought changes to Asia and Europe. The Mongols destroyed hundreds of cities and took thousands of lives. A Muslim poet who lived during the 1200s called the Mongols "an army as dense as the sands of the desert."

Yet when the Mongols set up governments in the lands they had taken, they also opened new trade opportunities. Like the Muslims, the Mongols brought many peoples together into one empire. From the Chinese in the southeast to the Russians in the northwest, the Mongols ruled over peoples of many cultures. Under Mongol rule warring peoples of the central Asian steppes came together in peace. A new wave of law and order made travel and trade much safer along the Silk Road.

The Silk Road, also called the Silk Route, was a way into Asia for European merchants and travelers. This was the route that Marco Polo had followed to China in 1274. As Europeans began to believe Marco Polo's reports of China's riches, more and more merchants set out for the East on the Silk Road. The trade centers of Italy made the most money from merchant travel on the Silk Road. In fact, the cities of Genoa, Venice, Florence, and Siena signed trade treaties with the Mongols. Merchants from these cities traveled deep into the Mongol Empire to buy spices, pearls, carpets, and silk.

Movement Marco Polo followed the general direction of the Silk Road in his travels to China.

■ *How would you describe the route he followed back to Venice?*

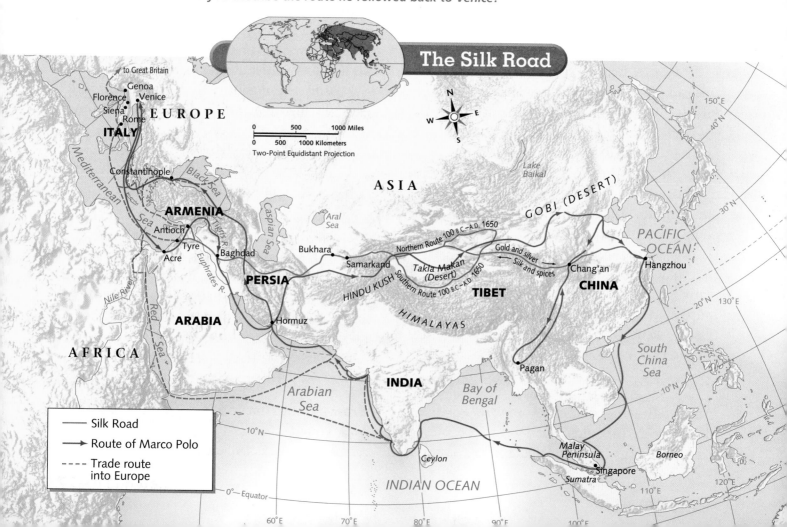

The Silk Road

Silk Road
Route of Marco Polo
Trade route into Europe

Then, in the 1300s, the Mongol Empire began to weaken. Civil war broke out in central Asia. Travel along the Silk Road became dangerous. Without safe land routes, Europeans depended more on sea routes to reach the treasures of China.

REVIEW *How did the Mongol Empire's control of the trade routes help Europeans?*

Trade in South Asia

Stories of the riches of India had been heard in Southwest Asia for centuries. One Muslim trader reported that "the Indian rivers are pearls, the mountains rubies, and trees perfumes." Such tales brought Muslim descendants of the Mongols from central Asia to India. Beginning in the early 1000s, they pushed south through the high mountain passes of the Hindu Kush range and conquered much of northern India.

The desire for gold, silver, precious jewels, and perfumes had brought the first Muslims to India. Now many other goods traveled back and forth. Coconuts, salt, and a scented

Two types of money used throughout the Mongol Empire were silver ax-shaped coins (left) and paper bank notes (above).

wood called aloe were among the goods that left India. Horses and fine woven cloth traveled south into India. In addition to goods, slaves—often prisoners of war—were carried in caravans going in both directions.

REVIEW *What were some of the goods that flowed into India? What were some of the goods that flowed out?*

LESSON 2 REVIEW

Check Understanding

1 Remember the Facts What bonds linked the many different peoples who lived in the Muslim Empire?

2 Recall the Main Idea How did the growth of the Muslim and Mongol empires lead to the trade of goods and ideas?

Think Critically

3 Think More About It How can the trade of goods lead to the trade of ideas?

4 Past to Present What are some present-day examples of trade leading to cultural exchange?

5 Personally Speaking What do you think was the most important idea traded during the period covered in this lesson? Explain.

Show What You Know

Map Activity Using an atlas or another reference work, make your own physical map of Africa and the southern part of Asia. Be sure to show the physical features of the region. Then imagine that you have the job of choosing a trade route from India to West Africa. Thinking carefully about landforms, draw a route that you might take. Explain your choice.

What Brought Success

For hundreds of years Arab people controlled the world's major trade routes. Historian Veronica Wedgwood says, "The Arabs had long been known as adventurous traders by sea and land." Control over trade allowed the Arabs to spread the message of Islam far and wide. Trade also helped the spread of knowledge and ideas.

While most historians agree that the people of the Muslim Empire were successful traders, they have different opinions about the reasons for their success. Read the following quotations from Fernand Braudel, James Simmons, and Francis Robinson. Each has his own belief as to why the Muslim people were able to become successful traders.

Fernand Braudel

" Muslim merchants enjoyed from earliest times the consideration, at least from their political rulers, which was rarely forthcoming in Europe. The Prophet [Muhammad] himself is said to have said: 'The merchant enjoys the felicity [happiness] both of this world and the next'; 'he who makes money pleases God.' This is almost sufficient in itself to indicate the climate of respectability attaching to commercial life; and there are plenty of concrete examples. "

Muslim traders with their camel caravans (above) were common sights about 1,000 years ago. Muslim scribes, architects, scientists, and philosophers (left) received the support of their leaders.

to Muslim Traders?

James Simmons

66 The domestication of the camel, not the invention of the wheel, liberated [freed] the early Arabs and allowed them to master the vast desert spaces and develop lucrative [profitable] trade routes. Great camel caravans, often numbering thousands of animals and their attendants, transported ivory, slaves, and exotic skins from . . . Africa, silks from India, and spices from southeastern Asia. Other caravans moved along the Incense Road from southern Arabia transporting myrrh, frankincense, and cinnamon northward through the deserts to the peoples beyond. Today we can hardly appreciate the enormous importance of incense in an ancient world where a general lack of sanitation required clouds of sweet-smelling smoke to cover noxious [disgusting] odors. 99

Francis Robinson

66 Muslim traders, making good use of the fortunate geographical position of the Islamic heartlands, came in the years before 1500 to control much of the international traffic along the trade routes of the world. . . . These arteries of world economy formed natural channels along which Islamic influences flowed; as Muslims came to dominate key areas of the system, their non-Muslim trading partners often came to embrace Islam as well, in part because business was so much smoother if men shared a common culture and a common law. 99

Compare Viewpoints

1. What does James Simmons believe is the reason the Muslim people were able to become successful traders? How do you know?

2. What does Francis Robinson believe is the reason the Muslim people were able to become successful traders? How does Robinson's viewpoint differ from Fernand Braudel's?

3. In addition to the reasons given by these three historians, what else do you think may have been a reason for the trading success of the Muslim Empire?

Think and Apply

People often disagree about the reasons an event happened or a situation came about in history. What are some examples of this kind of disagreement today?

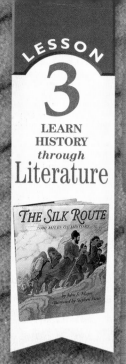

THE SILK ROUTE
7,000 MILES OF HISTORY

*by John S. Major
Illustrated by Stephen Fieser*

The Silk Route

7,000 Miles of History

Written by JOHN S. MAJOR

Illustrated by STEPHEN FIESER

The Silk Road, which connected empires in trade, was also referred to as the Silk Route. It was not actually a single road. Instead it was a general route traders followed to exchange goods over a wide area. On this route goods from China made their way to Central and Southern Asia and Europe, and goods from these places found their way to China.

Come along now with the merchants of long ago as they travel the Silk Route from Chang'an in China to the Byzantine Empire. On your journey, think about the ways in which trade linked the empires of the past.

THE JOURNEY BEGINS

The caravan includes many private merchants as well as Chinese government officials. Like the covered-wagon trains of the American West, members of the caravan travel together to help one another on the long, dangerous journey. Along the way they will face heat, hunger, thirst, and the ever-present possibility of bandit raids.

Few members of the original caravan will travel all the way to the Mediterranean. The silk and other goods that they are bringing from China will change hands several times along the way.

The caravan begins its journey, which will take many months. It is early spring. The caravan must get beyond the fierce western deserts before the heat of summer arrives. Leaving the city walls of Chang'an behind, it

The caravan faces rough travel across the dry desert sands of the Taklamakan.

passes through rich farmland. A Buddhist temple is on a nearby hillside.

DUNHUANG

The Buddhist religion came to China from India along the Silk Route around A.D. 100. The oasis town of Dunhuang, for centuries an important trading and supply center for caravans, soon grew into a great religious center as well. Hundreds of Buddhist cave-temples were cut into the soft rock of a nearby cliff. The cave-temples contain Buddhist statues; the walls are decorated with bright religious paintings.

Some of the merchants go to the cave-temples of Dunhuang to pray for a safe journey, while others buy supplies in the town market. Some Chinese officials take charge of a small herd of horses brought from the west by another caravan. They will escort the horses back to the capital; other officials will continue west to purchase still more of them.

TAKLAMAKAN

The Taklamakan is one of the world's driest deserts. Its name means "if you go in, you won't come out" in Uighur Turkish, one of the main languages of Central Asia. The caravan skirts the northern edge of the desert, just south of the snow-capped peaks of the Tian Shan Mountains. The route is very rough, passing around sand dunes, across rocky flats, and through tangled willow thickets[1] along dry riverbeds. But the caravan's two-humped Bactrian camels are strong and hardy.[2] They are used to this difficult country.

Many of the camels and camel drivers that set out from Chang'an turned back at Dunhuang. The merchants hired new ones

---

[1] **thickets:** thick growth of trees or bushes
[2] **hardy:** able to withstand bad conditions

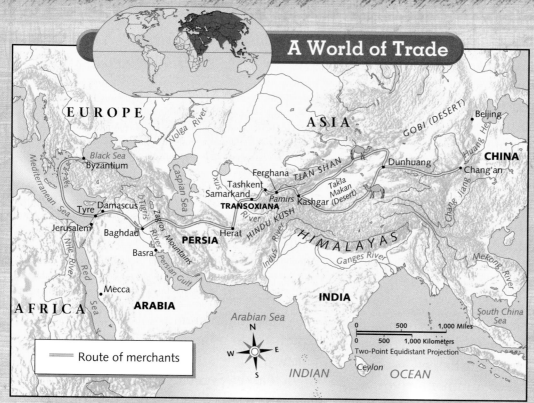

A World of Trade

Place

This map shows the route followed by the merchants in this story.

■ *What places are stops on the "Silk Route"?*

Route of merchants

for this stage of the journey, along with extra animals to carry food and water for crossing the desert. Such changes of men and animals will occur several times along the way from China to Damascus.

KASHGAR

Hot and tired after their trip across the Taklamakan Desert, the men and animals hurry to reach the oasis city of Kashgar. The pastures near the city are dotted with grazing animals and the camps of herding peoples: Uighurs in round felt yurts,[3] Turkomans and Tibetans in black tents.

Kashgar is famous for its fruit. Dates, melons, and grapes are grown in irrigated fields and vineyards. Everyone in the caravan looks forward to fresh food and water.

Some of the Chinese members of the caravan will end their journey here. They trade silk for dried dates, raisins, jade, and other local products to bring back to China. Others will continue on toward the west,

joined by new merchants, guards, and camel drivers with fresh animals from Kashgar.

THE PAMIRS

The Pamirs are a range of high mountains in eastern Afghanistan. Here the route winds through narrow, high-walled valleys beside rushing rivers. The camel drivers call this section of the Silk Route the "Trail of Bones" because of the many men and animals that have died along the way from falls and from sudden storms in the high, cold passes. The westbound caravan meets a caravan heading for China with luxury goods from Western lands and a herd of fine horses from Ferghana.

TASHKENT, KINGDOM OF FERGHANA

In the central market of Tashkent, the last remaining Chinese officials in the caravan trade bolts[4] of silk for horses that they will take back to China. The horses of

---

[3]**yurts:** circle-shaped tents

[4]**bolts:** rolls

Ferghana are considered by Chinese military leaders to be the strongest and toughest in the world.

Tashkent marks the eastern edge of the Persian cultural world. Some private merchants trade Chinese silk, porcelain, and other goods for Persian metalwork, glass, and musical instruments. They too will head back to China from here.

TRANSOXIANA

After making another stop, in the city of Samarkand, the caravan enters the wild country east of the Oxus (Amu Darya) River. No government rules this land; the nomads who live here will rob caravans if they get a chance to.

Traders from many lands meet at the market of Herat, in Persia.

Suddenly the caravan is attacked by a group of Turkoman bandits on horseback. After a fierce fight with swords and bows and arrows, the bandits are driven off. But some members of the caravan have been killed or wounded, and the bandits escape with a few heavily laden[5] camels.

HERAT

In this thriving Persian city, artisans produce fine metalwork, glassware, carpets, and other goods that can be sold for a high price in China. Herat is also, for the moment, on the eastern edge of the rapidly expanding Islamic world. A newly built mosque looms[6] over the city market.

[5] **laden:** loaded
[6] **looms:** appears in great form

Merchants from the caravan mingle in the market with local merchants and Turkoman nomads, as well as with Arabs from Baghdad and Damascus. Traders from India are here too, selling spices and brightly dyed Indian cloth. Muslim imams,[7] Zoroastrian priests, Nestorian Christian priests, and Buddhist monks tend to the religious needs of the cosmopolitan city.

The caravan will leave its last Bactrian camels in Herat. For the rest of the journey they will use dromedaries, the one-humped camels of Western Asia.

BAGHDAD

Baghdad is the greatest city of the Islamic world and a hub of world trade. Caravans crowd the roads leading to the city. An Arab merchant leads a group of African slaves bringing ivory, gold, and spices from Zanzibar. Ships coming upriver from the port at Basra bring spices and printed cotton cloth from India, pearls from the Persian Gulf, and precious stones from Ceylon (now Sri Lanka). Some of the goods will soon be heading east to China.

Only a handful of Chinese merchants remained with the caravan, and they will end their journey here. Most of the silk, porcelain, and other products from China have already changed hands several times along the way, increasing in value each time. The last remaining Chinese merchants will sell their goods for a fortune in Baghdad, but then they face a long, difficult, and dangerous trip home again.

---

[7] **imams:** prayer leaders at a mosque

A variety of goods from many parts of the world are exchanged in Baghdad.

DAMASCUS

Arab merchants have brought bolts of silk from Baghdad to Damascus. Only the finest silk cloth has traveled this far; it includes intricately[8] patterned brocades, brilliantly colored satins, and thin gauze to make nightgowns for aristocratic ladies. Wealthy Muslim women, heavily veiled, admire bolts of finished silk cloth in a shop.

TYRE

In the port city of Tyre, on the Mediterranean coast of Lebanon, goods are loaded on ships bound for cities farther to the west. Some of the silk that was traded in the market at Damascus will be sent to Byzantium,[9] the capital of the Eastern Roman Empire.

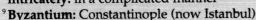

[8] **intricately:** in a complicated manner
[9] **Byzantium:** Constantinople (now Istanbul)

BYZANTIUM

In the main hall of a splendid palace, a Byzantine nobleman receives a visit from a bishop of the Orthodox Christian church. Both are dressed in rich garments of silk brocade. The palace women remain in an inner courtyard, out of sight of the men. A visiting prince from Russia, far to the north, awaits his turn to speak to the nobleman. Perhaps he will receive a small present of silk to take back home with him.

The garments worn by the wealthy people of Byzantium are made of silk cloth brought from China, more than 6,000 miles away. Few people in Byzantium have more than a vague idea of where China is or what its people are like, just as few Chinese know anything about the Eastern Roman Empire. Yet Chinese silk is sold in Byzantium, and Byzantine gold coins circulate in the markets of China. The two empires are linked together by trade, thanks to the brave and enterprising merchants of the Silk Route.

LITERATURE REVIEW

1. How did the Silk Route link different groups of people?
2. In what ways could a trade good have given one group of people an idea of the way of life of another group of people?
3. Make your own map of Europe and Asia. Be sure to include present-day borders. Then look at the map on page 360. Copy the trade route onto your map. Make a list of the present-day countries that now occupy the land through which the trade route went.

CHAPTER 11

REVIEW

500 — 700

About 700
- Soninke traders gain control of parts of West Africa

Connect Main Ideas

Use this organizer to describe the development of overland trade. Write two details to support each main idea. A copy of the organizer appears on page 82 of the Activity Book.

Overland Trade

The Trading Empires of West Africa

The peoples of West Africa grew strong through trade with others.

1. ____________________

2. ____________________

Trade Routes Linking Asia and Europe

The growth of unified empires led to trade among the peoples of Africa, Asia, and Europe.

1. ____________________

2. ____________________

Write More About It

Write a Diary Entry Imagine that you are an innkeeper at Kumbi-Saleh in Africa. Write a diary entry in which you describe the traders who stay at your inn. Include your thoughts about how trade affects relationships among different peoples.

Write a Personal History Describe a time when you traded with a friend. Perhaps you exchanged books, games, or sports cards. Explain why you decided to make the trade, and describe how the trade affected your relationship.

About 1000
• African trading empire of Ghana flourishes

About 1250
• Mongols destroy Muslim trading center of Baghdad

1274
• Marco Polo travels to China

1324
• Mansa Musa makes his pilgrimage to Mecca

USE VOCABULARY

Write a definition for each of the terms.

1. cartographer
2. mansa
3. oasis
4. savanna
5. tariff
6. tropical rain forest

CHECK UNDERSTANDING

7. How does Africa compare in size with the other continents?

8. How did learning to shape iron affect the lives of the Nok people of Africa?

9. What were the two main kinds of goods that the Soninkes traded?

10. What was the first great empire to rise in western Africa, and how did this empire grow in wealth?

11. How have we learned what we know about the ancient empire of Ghana?

12. How did trade with Muslims change the lives of people in western Africa?

13. Why was Mansa Musa's pilgrimage important?

14. What was the most common form of transportation on the desert routes used by Muslim traders?

15. How did trade influence life in the Muslim Empire?

16. How did the Mongol invasions affect Asia and Europe?

THINK CRITICALLY

17. **Cause and Effect** What caused the collapse of the Mali Empire?

18. **Past to Present** In what ways are present-day countries affected by their trading relationships?

19. **Think More About It** Why do you think people began to search farther and farther away for trading partners in the years 500 to 1500?

20. **Explore Viewpoints** Mansa Musa of Mali visited Egypt during his pilgrimage to Mecca. What different viewpoints might Egyptians have formed about the African ruler from his visit?

APPLY SKILLS

Compare Maps with Different Projections In your library, locate an atlas or another book containing many maps. Look through the maps to identify different projections. Make a list of the different types of projections that you find. Beside each projection name, describe the unique features of that projection.

READ MORE ABOUT IT

Ancient Ghana: The Land of Gold by Philip Koslow. Chelsea. This book details the fascinating history of ancient Ghana. The culture of ancient Ghana is also discussed.

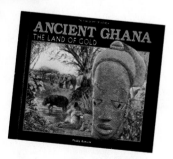

Visit the Internet at **http://www.hbschool.com** for additional resources.

SEA AND RIVER TRADE

"The number of ships increases. The endless flood of Vikings never stops growing bigger."

A French monk writing of the Vikings in the ninth century

Viking wood carving from about 1,100 years ago

Indian Ocean Trade

LESSON

1

FOCUS

How does trade link
different cultures
today?

Main Idea Read about
how trade around the
Indian Ocean linked
many peoples.

Vocabulary

monsoon
lateen sail
dhow
junk
diplomat
Swahili

Besides traveling over land routes, traders also went to sea. Far from home they found new sources of gold, fine cloth, ivory, glass, and porcelain. The trade of such goods at ports on the Indian Ocean brought many peoples together.

From Baghdad to Guangzhou

"This is the Tigris," the Muslim caliph al-Mansur (al•mon•SOOR) said in 762 when he chose Baghdad, in what is now Iraq, as his capital. "There is no obstacle between us and China. Everything on the sea can come to us on it." Baghdad did, indeed, become "the harbor of the world." Boats from Baghdad sailed down the Tigris to the deep harbor at Basra on the Persian Gulf. At Basra, merchants loaded their goods onto oceangoing ships. They then sailed out into the Indian Ocean and followed the sea routes to East Africa, India, and China.

Arab merchants set out for the East late in the year. When they planned their journeys, they took into account the climate of the region they were sailing to. Strong winds known as **monsoons** blow across the Indian Ocean. The winter monsoon blows from the northeast between November and March. The summer monsoon blows from the southwest between April and October.

Because of these steady winds, seagoing peoples in the Indian Ocean had developed the **lateen sail**. This triangle-shaped sail lets a ship travel into the wind. Arab ships, known as **dhows** (DOWZ), used lateen sails to travel east toward China when the northeast monsoon blew.

New knowledge about nature, improved ship design, and new navigation tools made traveling by sea easier than before. These Arab sailors are setting out on a trading expedition.

The Dhow

The dhow was a wooden boat with one or two sails. The boards it was made of were not held together with nails or wooden pegs, as on European ships. Instead, they were "stitched together with cords made of coco[nut] husk." Arab shipbuilders then spread a coating of oil, such as shark oil, over the boards to keep water out.

The first stop for the merchants was Muscat, at the tip of the Arabian Peninsula. There the ships took on fresh water. Then a month's sailing took them to the Malabar Coast of southwestern India. By late winter their ships had reached the Nicobar Islands in the eastern Indian Ocean. From there they sailed into the China Sea. By this time the summer monsoon had begun. The southwest wind carried the ships to Guangzhou (GWAHNG•JOH), China's major port.

The ships arrived in China loaded with the products of Arabia—dates, sugar, linen cloth, perfumes, and jewels. After trading these goods for others in Guangzhou, the Arab merchants made use of the winter monsoon to sail home. They returned with Chinese silks and porcelain bowls, cotton and pepper from India, and spices from the East Indies.

The round trip took about 18 months. The Arab merchants spent 6 months at home gathering new goods that they could trade and were ready to set out again with the next winter monsoon.

REVIEW *How did the people of Baghdad reach the people of Guangzhou for trading?*

Traders on the Indian Ocean

Arab dhows sailed across the Indian Ocean to China every year. However, Arab merchants did not have a monopoly on the east–west ocean trade routes. Jewish merchants from southwestern Asia traveled the sea routes from the Persian Gulf to China. Indian traders also sailed the seas, mostly in the eastern Indian Ocean.

Starting in the 800s, Chinese **junks**—wooden boats with four-sided sails—sailed to such places as the Malay Peninsula. In the early 1400s Chinese traders began to travel even farther. Under the command of Admiral Zheng He (JUHNG HUH), Chinese ships visited Siam, Indonesia, Ceylon, the Arabian Peninsula, and the eastern coast of Africa. Zheng He was not only a sailor but also a

In China, and in other parts of the world, women (left) often carried trade goods to markets and ports. Junks (below) are still used today to carry goods long distances.

Zheng He (seated) made many ocean voyages for the Chinese emperor. On his first trip, Zheng He commanded a fleet of more than 300 ships.

diplomat—a person skilled in developing treaties. Zheng got many of the peoples he visited interested in trading with China.

Even so, until the late 1400s Arab merchants were the leaders of trade on the Indian Ocean. Because their journeys were very long, Arab merchants set up communities in some of the larger trading ports they visited. Muslim settlements grew up in Sri Lanka, parts of Indonesia, and China.

The ways of the Muslim trading communities soon began to spread to the people living around them. Many of these people became Muslims. By the 1500s Arab merchants had taken their religion to southern India, Sri Lanka, and parts of Indonesia. Islam also

![MAP THEME icon] **Human-Environment Interactions** The Swahili city-states traded with the Bantu states in Africa and southwestern Asia.

■ *Why did the Swahili city-states form along the coast?*

spread to the lands along the western edges of the Indian Ocean.

REVIEW *How did Muslim ways and religion spread to countries bordering the Indian Ocean?*

The Swahili City-States

Arab dhows had been sailing to the east coast of Africa since the 600s. Arab traders wanted gold, ivory, animal skins, and—sometimes—slaves. They offered cloth, spices, pottery, and porcelain to the Africans.

Some of the Arab traders started communities in the trading ports of East Africa. They settled there, married African women, and raised families. By 900 a culture and a language that were part Arabian and part African had grown up along the coast. The people and the language they spoke were called **Swahili** (swah•HEE•lee). Most Swahilis became Muslims, but they also followed many African traditions and customs.

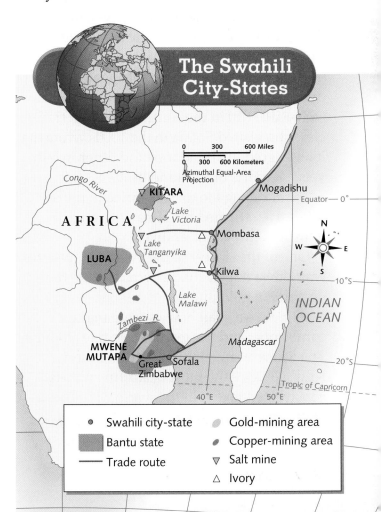

The Swahili City-States

0   300   600 Miles
0   300   600 Kilometers
Azimuthal Equal-Area Projection

Congo River

KITARA

AFRICA

Lake Victoria

Mogadishu

Equator — 0°

Mombasa

Lake Tanganyika

LUBA

N
W   E
S

Kilwa

—10°S

Lake Malawi

INDIAN OCEAN

Zambezi R.

Madagascar

MWENE MUTAPA

Great Zimbabwe   Sofala

—20°S

Tropic of Capricorn

40°E   50°E

● Swahili city-state	Gold-mining area
Bantu state	Copper-mining area
— Trade route	▽ Salt mine
	△ Ivory

This detail of a painting on silk by the artist Shen Tu is called *The Tribute Giraffe with Attendant*. It shows a giraffe brought to China from Africa in 1419 by Admiral Zheng He as a gift for the Chinese emperor.

Over the years the East African trading ports grew into independent city-states. By the 1300s there were as many as 40 trading cities along the eastern coast of Africa. The trade centers stretched from Mogadishu (moh•guh•DIH•shoo) in the north to Sofala (soh•FAHL•uh) in the south. A Muslim traveler who visited Sofala in the 1000s wrote that it had "gold in abundance and other marvels." Reports of this kind brought Chinese admiral Zheng He to East Africa in the early 1400s. He returned to China with amazing treasures and exotic animals.

One of the richest of the Swahili city-states was Kilwa (KIL•wah). Its wealth came from its trade in gold and could be seen everywhere. Kilwa's tall houses were made of coral stone, and its people wore fine clothing. The Muslim traveler Ibn Battuta called Kilwa "one of the most beautiful and best-constructed towns in the world."

REVIEW *How did the Swahili city-states develop?*

Great Zimbabwe

The people of the Swahili city-states did not produce the goods that they traded to the Arabs and others. Instead, they traded for these goods. The people of Sofala and Kilwa traded salt, tools, and cloth to people from Central Africa for gold. The ancestors of these Central Africans had migrated from West Africa hundreds of years before. These people, whom historians call Bantu speakers, settled in all parts of East Africa and Southern Africa.

Around 1200 a Bantu-speaking group called the Shonas (SHOH•nuhz) took control of the Central African mines from which

Movement Bantu-speaking people began their migration from West Africa.
■ *In what direction did these people move?*

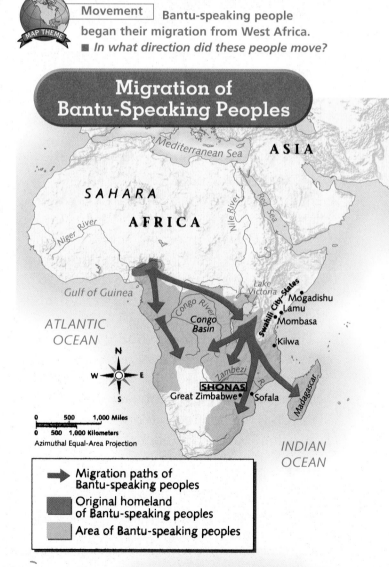

Migration of Bantu-Speaking Peoples

➡ Migration paths of Bantu-speaking peoples

■ Original homeland of Bantu-speaking peoples

Area of Bantu-speaking peoples

In what is today the African country of Zimbabwe stand the remains of the royal court walls of Great Zimbabwe (inset).

Sofala's and Kilwa's gold came. This made the Shonas very wealthy. They also gained wealth from the large herds of cattle they kept. The Shonas came to rule a large empire in Central Africa. They built their capital at Great Zimbabwe. As a sign of their wealth, the Shona kings had a huge stone wall built around the royal court. More than 30 feet (about 9 m) tall, the wall closed in an area as long as a football field and about four times as wide.

The Shona Empire lasted for more than 200 years, trading gold to the Swahili city-states. Then, around 1450, the Shonas left Great Zimbabwe. Why they left is not known.

REVIEW *What part did the people of the Shona Empire play in trade across the Indian Ocean?*

LESSON I REVIEW

Check Understanding

① **Remember the Facts** Which people made the most use of the Indian Ocean for trade?

② **Recall the Main Idea** How did trade around the Indian Ocean link the peoples of Asia and Africa?

Think Critically

③ **Personally Speaking** Why do you think African traders did not take to the seas in search of trade as Arab traders did?

④ **Cause and Effect** What effect did gaining control of gold mines in Central Africa have on the Shonas?

Show What You Know

Letter-Writing Activity Imagine that you are a crew member on one of Admiral Zheng He's ships. Write a letter to a friend in China telling what you saw on your visit to one of the Swahili city-states. You should also mention goods and items from the city-state that you are returning to China with.

FOCUS

How do countries today become leaders in trade?

Main Idea Read about how some city-states became leaders of trade in the Mediterranean Sea and in the Black Sea.

Vocabulary

Greek fire

doge

The Mediterranean and the Black Sea

For many centuries the Mediterranean and Black seas both were "Roman lakes," controlled by the Roman Empire. Over these bodies of water, goods moved back and forth among the empire's many regions. When the Roman Empire broke up, problems developed over control of trade on these seas.

Byzantine Trade

During the sixth century Emperor Justinian I brought the Mediterranean and the Black seas under Byzantine rule. Constantinople, his capital, was between the two seas and served as a center of trade for both. "Into her harbors sailed expectantly the vessels of the world's trade," a poet of the time wrote.

Byzantine trade was carried on in many places besides the shores of these two seas. Byzantine merchant ships sailed through the Red Sea and across the Indian Ocean to India. Smaller boats crossed the Black Sea and journeyed up the Dnieper (NEE•per) River to trade with the Rus (ROOS) of Kiev (KEE•ef) in what is now Ukraine. Camel caravans followed land routes to China.

Traders on all these routes took many goods back to Constantinople. Furs, salt, wax, and honey came from Kiev. Ivory, porcelain, jewels, silk, and spices came from India and China. A tax on all trade goods that went through Constantinople made the empire very rich.

For hundreds of years the Byzantine navy kept the sea routes safe. The navy was able to control the seas by using a secret weapon called Greek fire. **Greek fire** was a chemical

The Byzantine Empire grew rich by controlling trade routes. These silver spoons and this ceiling painting from the Palace of Constantine and Helena show Byzantine wealth.

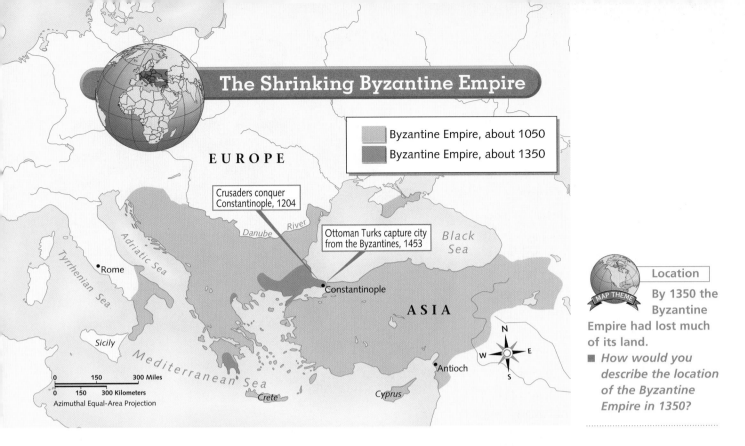

The Shrinking Byzantine Empire

Byzantine Empire, about 1050
Byzantine Empire, about 1350

EUROPE

Crusaders conquer Constantinople, 1204

Ottoman Turks capture city from the Byzantines, 1453

Danube River

Adriatic Sea

Tyrrhenian Sea

•Rome

Sicily

Black Sea

Constantinople

ASIA

Mediterranean Sea

•Antioch

Crete

Cyprus

0   150   300 Miles
0   150   300 Kilometers
Azimuthal Equal-Area Projection

N W E S

Location

MAP THEME

By 1350 the Byzantine Empire had lost much of its land.

■ How would you describe the location of the Byzantine Empire in 1350?

mixture that caught fire when water hit it. One shot of Greek fire could set a ship on fire. The ships of Muslims and others who wished to take control of the Mediterranean risked becoming targets of the Byzantine navy.

REVIEW *How did trade make the Byzantine Empire wealthy?*

Muslims in the Mediterranean

From the earliest days of Mediterranean trade, the Muslims had tried to take control of it. In 649 Muslims took over the island of Cyprus in the eastern Mediterranean. About 150 years later, Muslims from Tunis, Morocco, and Spain took control of important Mediterranean islands, including Crete and Sicily. From these islands they were able to protect Muslim trade ships that sailed along the coast of North Africa. In this way the Muslims kept safe the western link of a Muslim trade network reaching all the way to China.

In the late 900s the Byzantines took back Cyprus and Crete. Then their government

ordered all merchants in the empire to stop sending wood and iron to Muslim lands. Byzantine leaders hoped that this action would keep the Muslims from building new boats to sail on the Mediterranean. But not all Byzantines obeyed the order. The Italian cities of Amalfi and Venice, which were far from the rest of the empire, paid no attention to it. For the most part, Amalfi and Venice acted as independent city-states, without ties to a larger government.

Amalfi's wealth came from trade with the Muslim Empire. Amalfi, located along the Tyrrhenian Sea, did not want to lose its trading partner just because of an order from the Byzantine government. Venice had also grown rich by trading with the Muslims. So the people of Venice, on the northern shores of the Adriatic Sea, felt the same way. As it turned out, it was the Venetians—not the Muslims of North Africa—who took control of Mediterranean trade from the Byzantines.

REVIEW *Why was gaining control of Mediterranean islands important to the Muslims of North Africa?*

The Rise of the Italian City-States

Venice, as an eleventh-century document said, was a city-state "that does not plow, sow, or gather vintage." Instead, the Venetians "buy grain and wine in every port." Trade was certainly the most important activity in Venice. Its merchants bought wood, wool, and iron from western Europe. Then they sold these goods in the eastern Mediterranean ports of the Muslim Empire. The traders returned to Venice with silks, spices, and ivory, which they then sold in Europe.

Other Italian ports did much the same. In the western lands along the Mediterranean, the city-states of Pisa and Genoa formed strong ties with the Muslim ports of North Africa. Ships from Pisa and Genoa carried linen, cotton, jewels, perfumes, and spices south across the Mediterranean Sea. The ships returned with leather goods, animal skins, grain, and other items for further trade.

Venetian wool traders (above)
Amethyst vessel from Venice (left)

In the late 1000s, Normans, who controlled a small area of land in what is now France, sailed through the Strait of Gibraltar looking for new lands to conquer. Because Venice fought against the Normans, the Byzantines rewarded the city-state by letting Venetian traders pass through Constantinople without paying taxes.

The Italian City-States

Trade route
City-state

Movement

Merchants from the Italian city-states traveled by land and sea to trade.

■ *Why do you think Venetian merchants traveled in so many different directions?*

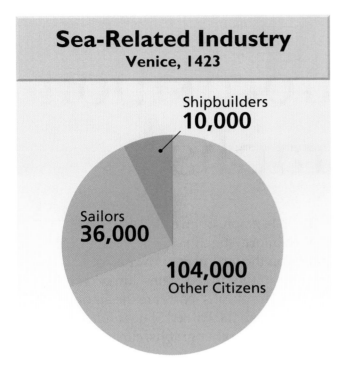

Sea-Related Industry
Venice, 1423

Shipbuilders
10,000

Sailors
36,000

104,000
Other Citizens

LEARNING FROM GRAPHS Venice's location on the Adriatic Sea made it an important sea-trade center.
■ *About what percent of citizens were sailors or shipbuilders?*

The Byzantines were sorry, however, when the Venetians helped the Normans drive the Byzantines from Italy. Then, in 1204, the **doge** (DOHJ), or leader, of Venice told crusaders on their way to the Holy Land to attack Constantinople. After three days of fighting, the city fell. Venice quickly took over most of the Byzantine lands along the eastern shores of the Mediterranean.

Venice now controlled the important trading routes in the eastern Mediterranean and in the Black Sea. Genoa controlled the western Mediterranean. As time passed, Venice won control of all Mediterranean trade.

At about this same time, inland city-states, such as Milan and Florence, also started to trade. In 1252 Florence and other city-states began making their own gold coins. Florentine florins and Venetian ducats soon replaced Arab dinars as coins used for trade in the Mediterranean lands.

The Italian city-states, with Venice in the lead, held a monopoly on trade in the Mediterranean for more than 200 years. Then, in 1453, Constantinople was taken by the Ottoman Turks. The Mediterranean and Black seas became Turkish waters. At about the same time, many European countries became jealous of the Italian city-states' control of trade. These countries began sailing out into the Atlantic Ocean in search of another route to Asia. These voyages set the stage for a time of exploration by Europeans.

REVIEW *What ended the Italian city-states' monopoly on Mediterranean trade?*

LESSON 2 REVIEW

Check Understanding
1 **Remember the Facts** What groups wanted to gain control of the Mediterranean Sea trade?

2 **Recall the Main Idea** How did the Italian city-states gain control of the trade routes in the Mediterranean and Black seas?

Think Critically
3 **Past to Present** How might countries today benefit from trading with the United States?

4 **Think More About It** Study a map of the Mediterranean region. How did the geography of the region help Genoa and Venice become important in trade?

Show What You Know
Poetry Activity The people of Venice took great pride in their achievements. Imagine that you are a Venetian living in the early 1400s. Write a poem that describes your pride in being a Venetian. Share your poem with a classmate.

Compare Information with Graphs

1. Why Learn This Skill?

Suppose you want to prepare a report on trade in the world today. You want to show a lot of information in a brief, clear way. One way you might do this is by making graphs. A **graph** is a diagram for showing relations between numbers. Knowing how to read and make graphs will help you see and compare large amounts of information.

2. Bar, Circle, and Line Graphs

Different kinds of graphs show information in different ways. A **bar graph** uses bars and is especially useful for quick comparisons. Notice that the bars on the graphs of imports and exports are horizontal. On a horizontal bar graph, the bars go from left to right. Bar graphs can be vertical, too. On a vertical bar graph, the bars go from bottom to top.

A **circle graph**, often called a pie chart, divides information into parts. The circle graphs on the next page show the total amounts of the United States' imports and exports. The graphs' parts are the amounts of trade between the United States and certain countries. Like other graphs, circle graphs can help you make comparisons. You can compare the parts to each other or to the whole. To be useful, a circle graph should have only a few parts. If it has many parts, it becomes crowded and unclear.

A **line graph** shows change over time. The line graph on the next page shows how the amount of goods exported from the United States changed between the years 1970 and 1995. Each dot shows how much trade took place in one year, and a line connects all the dots. Depending on the information, the line may go up or down or stay at the same level.

Top Five Trading Partners of the U.S.: Imports

5% China
5% Germany
7% Mexico
46% 24 other countries
18% Japan
19% Canada

Top Five Trading Partners of the U.S.: Exports

5% Germany
5% The United Kingdom
9% Mexico
50% 22 other countries
11% Japan
20% Canada

Line graphs are most useful in showing a **trend**, or the way something changes over time.

3. Understand the Process

Compare the information in the bar, circle, and line graphs by answering the following questions. Think about the advantages and disadvantages of each kind of graph.

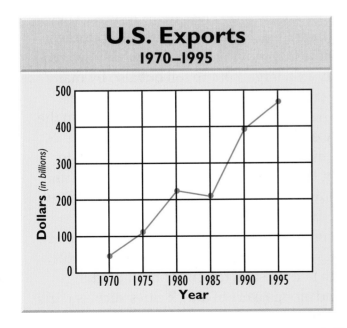

U.S. Exports
1970–1995

Dollars (in billions) / Year

1 Which graph or graphs would you use to find how much machinery the United States imports? Explain your choice.

2 Which graph or graphs would you use to find how much of the United States' international trade of products is with Japan? Explain your choice.

3 Which graph or graphs would you use to find how much change there was in the United States' exports between the years 1970 and 1980? Explain your choice.

4 Do you think the information on the bar graphs can be shown on circle graphs? Explain your answer.

5 Do you think the information on the line graph can be shown on a circle graph? Explain your answer.

4. Think and Apply

Using the graphs on these pages, write a paragraph summarizing information about the United States' international trade in recent years. Share your paragraph with a partner, and compare your summaries.

FOCUS

How does the addition of new territory affect trade?

Main Idea As you read, think about how the addition of new territories affected trade in northern Europe.

Vocabulary

saga
territorial expansion
Hansa
embargo

The Northern Seas

The silks and spices of Asia reached even the most northern parts of Europe. Seafaring people of the north formed their own trading networks to carry these goods. Their ships sailed the Atlantic Ocean and the North and Baltic seas and traveled up many rivers. Over time two great trading cultures developed—those of the Vikings and the members of the Hanseatic (han•see•A•tik) League.

Viking Adventurers

In one Icelandic **saga**, or adventure story about the brave deeds of people, a young hero says to his father, "Give me a longship and crew therewith, and I go a-viking." The word *a-viking*, which meant "raiding overseas," soon came to describe the warriors who carried out the attacks—the Vikings. But why did the Vikings leave their northern lands to attack other people?

During the 700s the population of Scandinavia—the present-day countries of Denmark, Norway, and Sweden—grew quickly. After a while the land could not feed all the people who lived there. Many Scandinavians took to the seas each summer to search for food and items to steal. They traveled in their longships, or narrow, flat-bottomed boats. These fast-moving longboats were powered not only by a large, square sail but also by many strong rowers who served as fighters as well.

The Vikings often attacked at night or in the very early morning in order to take people by surprise. They killed everyone who tried to fight them. Often they carried off women and children to sell as slaves. What they could not steal, they set on fire.

The people along the coasts of northwestern Europe were the first to be attacked by Vikings. An English priest wrote, "Never has Britain known such terror." Later the Vikings began to sail inland along rivers to attack cities such as Paris, Bordeaux, and Seville.

Designed to cover the head and face, this helmet protected early Viking raiders as they attacked.

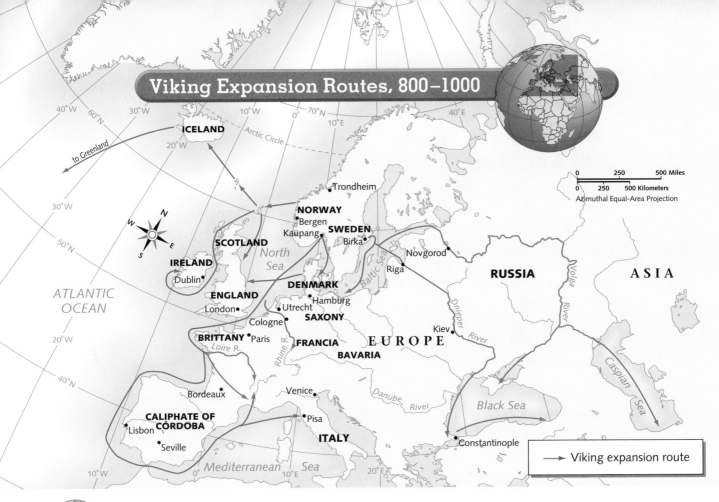

Viking Expansion Routes, 800–1000

ICELAND
to Greenland
Arctic Circle
Trondheim
NORWAY
Bergen
Kaupang
SWEDEN
Birka
Novgorod
Riga
RUSSIA
ASIA
Volga River
SCOTLAND
North Sea
IRELAND
Dublin
ATLANTIC OCEAN
ENGLAND
London
DENMARK
Hamburg
Utrecht
Cologne
SAXONY
Kiev
Dnieper River
BRITTANY
Paris
Loire R.
Rhine R.
FRANCIA
EUROPE
BAVARIA
Caspian Sea
Bordeaux
Venice
Danube River
Black Sea
CALIPHATE OF CÓRDOBA
Lisbon
Pisa
ITALY
Constantinople
Seville
Mediterranean Sea

0   250   500 Miles
0   250   500 Kilometers
Azimuthal Equal-Area Projection

→ Viking expansion route

Movement From Scandinavia—the present-day countries of Denmark, Norway, and Sweden—the Vikings traveled in many directions.
■ *How would you describe the route the Vikings took to get to Pisa in what is today Italy?*

In time the Vikings began to settle on the lands they had attacked. This **territorial expansion**, or adding of new lands, gave the Vikings the room they believed they needed. To the east, Swedish Vikings pushed deep into what today is Russia. The Danes, from the land that is now called Denmark, took control of parts of England and France. In the west, Norwegians settled Iceland, Greenland, and parts of Scotland and Ireland. They even began a settlement in North America.

With settlement, a-viking became a thing of the past, remembered only in the sagas. Over time, trading became the Vikings' main economic activity.

REVIEW *Why did Scandinavians take up a-viking, and why did they stop their raids?*

Longships (far left) enabled the Vikings to travel easily and to capture riches. The Vikings traded the captured riches or used them to make items such as this gold brooch (near left).

Chapter 12 • **403**

The Vikings in North America

Historians had long wondered if the Vikings had really gotten as far west as North America. Strong evidence was found in North America in the 1960s when a group of Viking-style houses was found in Newfoundland. One artifact dug up there was a stone weight similar to those used on Viking spindles for making yarn. Scholars knew that in Viking society, women did the spinning and weaving. They also knew that women did not go on voyages unless the Vikings planned to begin a settlement. From all these facts, historians concluded that the Vikings must have settled in North America.

The Rus

After a while many trade routes connected the lands of the Vikings. The most widely used routes were those in the east. Early in the Viking age, raiders from Sweden settled on the Baltic shores of present-day Latvia. They then traveled inland until they reached the Dnieper and Volga rivers. Some Vikings sailed downstream on the Dnieper and set up a trading center at Kiev. Others followed the Volga downstream from the trading center of Novgorod (NAHV•guh•rahd).

The people of this part of eastern Europe— the Slavs—called the Vikings the *Rus*. The word *Russia* may have come from this name. Stories of the Rus and their trading reached far and wide. Muslim geographer Ibn Rustah noted during the 900s that the only business of the Rus was "trade in sable and squirrel skins and other kinds of skins, selling them to those who will buy from them."

Goods were not the only things that traveled on the eastern trade routes, however. In the late 900s Byzantine missionaries traveled north, taking Christianity to the Rus of Kiev.

The Rus and other descendants of the Vikings kept the lead in trade on the northern waterways until the 1200s. The people of western Europe grew to depend on these northern traders for furs and other luxuries. Later, however, other European traders began to follow the sea routes of the north in search of these goods.

REVIEW *What trade routes did the Rus control?*

Merchants in Europe Unite

European merchants faced many problems, such as bandits on land and pirates at sea. They also had to pay a tax at almost every port in which they stopped. In the early

This "Great Crane of Danzig" helped people load and unload heavy cargo at the town of Bruges in northern Europe. What activities are taking place in this scene?

1200s some merchants in northern European towns decided they could better protect themselves by working together. They formed groups called **Hansas** (HAN•suhz). Hansa members shared the costs of trading, such as renting ships and paying guards for trade caravans.

Around 1240 the Hansas of the German ports of Lübeck and Hamburg signed a treaty. They agreed to protect each other's merchants. Over the next hundred years, the merchants of about 200 northern European towns joined this Hanseatic League.

The league had its own navy. At times it used this navy to fight wars to protect its members and to gain new trade agreements. More often the league used economic power. **Embargoes**, or bans on trade, worked as well as war for getting the kind of trade agreements the league wanted.

The Hanseatic League controlled the northern sea trade for more than 100 years. Then during the 1400s the center of European trade shifted to ports on the Atlantic Ocean.

REVIEW *Why was the Hanseatic League formed?*

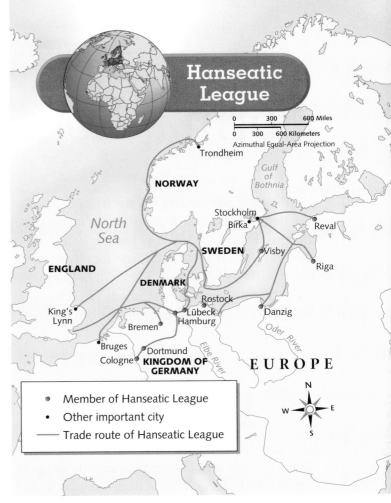

Hanseatic League

0   300   600 Miles
0   300   600 Kilometers
Azimuthal Equal-Area Projection

- ● Member of Hanseatic League
- • Other important city
- — Trade route of Hanseatic League

Movement   Trade routes throughout the North Sea and the Baltic Sea connected the towns of the Hanseatic League.

■ *What do you think would have happened to the merchants of a town such as Riga if they had not joined the Hanseatic League?*

LESSON 3 REVIEW

Check Understanding

1 Remember the Facts Where did the Vikings, and later the Hanseatic League, trade?

2 Recall the Main Idea How did Viking territorial expansion help the Vikings and the Hanseatic League become leaders of trade?

Think Critically

3 Past to Present Where is territorial expansion taking place today? How does it compare to expansion that took place in earlier times?

4 Think More About It When merchants work together, as the Hanseatic League merchants did, what happens to competition? How does this affect consumers?

Show What You Know

Simulation Activity Imagine that you are a leader of the Hanseatic League. You want to get more towns to join the league. Create a presentation that tells the advantages trade towns would gain by becoming league members.

Form a Logical Conclusion

1. Why Learn This Skill?

A **logical conclusion** is a decision or an idea reached by thoughtful study of all the known facts. To form a logical conclusion, you must be able to put new facts and ideas together with those you already know. This will help you see why things happened as they did in the past, as well as why things happen in your own life today.

2. Remember What You Have Read

By the 1960s historians had raised the question *Did the Vikings build settlements in North America?* There was evidence that the Vikings had traveled to North America, but no evidence proved that they had stayed there for any length of time. Then a discovery provided

The spindle part (bottom) uncovered by scientists Helge Ingstad and Anne Stine (top) proved to the world that the Vikings built settlements in North America.

Norwegian scientists Helge Ingstad and Anne Stine the evidence that was needed.

At the village of L'Anse aux Meadows, in Newfoundland, in present-day Canada, Ingstad, Stine, and their helpers uncovered eight homesites that looked like Viking homesites. They also found many artifacts that could have been made by the Vikings. Soon after, Anne Stine found a ring made of stone. This was clearly a piece of a Viking spindle, a very important tool for spinning wool. This spindle was just like the ones found in other places where the Vikings had lived. With this evidence, Ingstad and Stine were able to conclude that the Vikings had built homes and lived for a time in North America.

3. Understand the Process

There are many ways to form a conclusion. One way is to follow these steps:

• Form a question about the subject or the situation, such as *Did the Vikings build settlements in North America?*
• Think about evidence you already have that might help you answer the question.
• Gather new evidence that might give you the answer to your question.
• Think carefully about what the new evidence tells you.

4. Think and Apply

Write as many as ten clues that lead to the identification of a place in your community, such as the library. Read the clues one by one to a partner. How many clues does it take before your partner can form a logical conclusion as to what the place is? Discuss with your partner how each clue led to the conclusion.

Conquering the Pacific

FOCUS
What problems do explorers face today?

Main Idea Read to find out how people solved problems to explore and settle the islands in the Pacific Ocean.

Vocabulary
atoll
lagoon
outrigger
star path
archipelago

For hundreds of years merchants sailed up and down the coasts of the Pacific Ocean in search of trade. At first, few chose to risk their lives by sailing into the open ocean. Yet over time people did set out into the Pacific to explore and settle the islands there.

The Pacific Islands

With Asia on its west side and the Americas on its east side, the Pacific Ocean is the world's largest body of water. At its widest point, the Pacific stretches 12,300 miles (19,794 km), or about halfway around the world. It is larger than all the world's land surfaces put together.

Although they take up little of its space, more than 20,000 islands dot the Pacific Ocean. Some of the Pacific islands were formed by volcanoes. Some of these volcanoes are still active. The volcanic islands are often made up mostly of mountains and hills. These types of islands are called the high islands. Other islands are **atolls**, islands formed from coral reefs. In the centers of these atolls are **lagoons**, or small bodies of water. Many of these islands are very beautiful. The islands formed from coral are called the low islands.

The Pacific islands are divided into three groups. To the northeast of Australia lies Melanesia (meh•luh•NEE•zhuh), or "dark islands." North of Melanesia lies Micronesia (my•kruh•NEE•zhuh), or "small islands." To the east of these two groups is Polynesia (pah•luh•NEE•zhuh), or "many islands." The Polynesian islands are small and very far apart. For example, Easter Island, which is only 50 square miles (129 sq km) in area, lies about 1,500 miles (2,414 km) from its nearest neighbor.

Fear of the unknown was the greatest barrier to travel in the Pacific. People on the rim of the ocean did not want to sail away into the unknown. A few did, but they rarely returned to tell what they had seen.

REVIEW *What was the greatest barrier to early travel in the Pacific Ocean?*

A view from the volcanic island of Bora Bora in the Pacific Ocean

Trade Along the Pacific Coasts

Chinese traders sailed the waters of the Pacific from earliest times. Chinese seafaring, however, almost came to an end when the Han emperors took up Confucianism. Confucianism said it was not right for people to take long voyages while their parents were alive. It also taught that trade was not a worthwhile activity.

By the 800s ideas about sea travel began to change. The wealth of the Arab, Persian, and Indian merchants who visited the port of Guangzhou got many Chinese interested in trade. Soon Chinese merchant ships began sailing south to the Malay Peninsula and Sumatra, an island that is today part of Indonesia. Others sailed north to Korea and Japan.

By the 1100s the Chinese government knew that sea trade could help improve the

The 1100s were a time of increased sea trade for China. Chinese ships traveled the Pacific and Indian oceans.

country's economy. As Emperor Gao Zong (GOW ZAWNG) said:

> 66 Profits from maritime commerce [sea trade] are very great. If properly managed, they can amount to millions. Is this not better than taxing the people? 99

The government provided money to improve harbors and shipping. By mid-century, government profits from overseas trade had doubled. The government also offered rewards for new ship plans and ideas that would improve sea travel. By the start of the 1200s, the Chinese had the fastest ships in the South Seas. They controlled the waters from Guangzhou to Korea and Japan. Also, they had started to control the trade in the South China Sea westward toward the Indian Ocean. From this time on, the Indian Ocean—not the Pacific—became the center of Chinese sea travel.

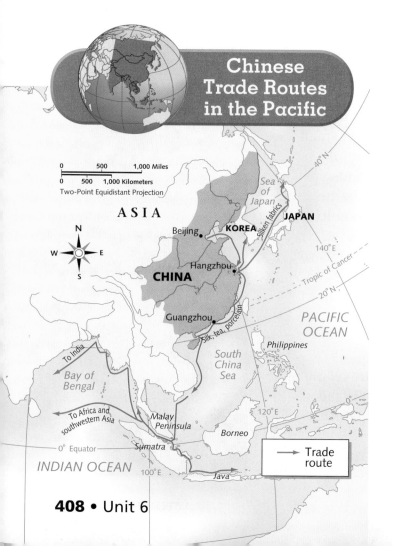

Chinese Trade Routes in the Pacific

0   500   1,000 Miles
0   500   1,000 Kilometers
Two-Point Equidistant Projection

ASIA

Sea of Japan

JAPAN

Beijing   KOREA

Silken fabrics

140°E

Hangzhou

Tropic of Cancer

CHINA

20°N

Guangzhou

PACIFIC OCEAN

Silk, tea, porcelain

Philippines

South China Sea

To India

Bay of Bengal

120°E

To Africa and southwestern Asia

Malay Peninsula

Borneo

0° Equator

Sumatra

INDIAN OCEAN   100°E

Java

→ Trade route

Human-Environment Interactions

Chinese traders sailed the Pacific.

■ *Why do you think Chinese sea traders stayed fairly close to the mainland?*

These statues were created by the early people of Easter Island in the southeastern Pacific Ocean. The statues, which weigh as much as 50 tons each, were carved from volcanic rock and placed on stone platforms. Exactly how the rock was moved and why the statues were created are still unknown.

Across the Pacific many peoples traveled along the coasts of North and South America. A rich trade route linked the regions that today are Mexico and Peru as early as the 700s. By the 1500s the Salangone—who lived near what is today Ecuador—controlled much of the trade along the coast. A Spanish document of the time described the water transportation of the Salangone as sailing rafts built of balsa wood. These sailing rafts were large enough to carry several people and many goods.

REVIEW *Who controlled coastal trade at either end of the Pacific?*

Out into the Pacific

The sturdy design of the balsa-wood rafts led some historians to wonder if Native Americans had ever traveled across the open ocean. Some even wondered if Native Americans could have sailed west with the winds to the Pacific islands. In the 1940s Thor Heyerdahl (THAWR HAY•er•dahl), a Norwegian explorer, proved that such a trip was possible. He built a balsa-wood raft and sailed it from Peru in South America to Polynesia. Even so, most archaeological evidence suggests that people settled the Pacific islands from Asia.

The people of almost every Pacific island have a legend about their earliest people. Scholars do not think all these old stories are true. However, they do feel that the legends give a picture of the interests of the people. One Polynesian tale praises a navigator as

66 The king of the black purple deep,
    The king of the depths unknown. 99

HERITAGE

Passing on Knowledge

The Pacific islanders had different ways of passing on what they learned about navigation. The people of some islands passed on their learning in chants and songs that everyone learned. People of other islands chose certain families to keep the knowledge of the sea. These "navigator" families held an important place in their society. Still other islanders began schools where young people were trained in navigational skills.

The legends support the idea that settlement of the Pacific islands was not an accident. It happened because planned exploration and migration took place over a long period of time. It began as far back as 1500 B.C. when daring sailors set out from the larger islands off the Asian mainland. They arrived first in Melanesia. Later generations pushed north and east into Micronesia and Polynesia. By about A.D. 800, seafarers had settled every island in the Pacific that people could live on. In doing so, said one scholar, they "achieved the greatest feats of maritime navigation in all human history."

Obviously, the Pacific islanders put great thought into their travels. Their boats were small but well suited to ocean travel.

Outriggers, or wooden frames placed on each side, kept the boats from tipping over in rough seas. Large triangular sails called crab claws powered the boats. These sails, like lateen sails, allowed the boats to travel into the wind. To navigate, the Pacific islanders used the sun and the stars. They also studied **star paths**, the way the stars in the night sky seem to move because of the Earth's rotation.

When they migrated, the Pacific islanders took everything they would need in a new home. They loaded their boats with animals and plants and took along people who knew how to farm and make tools.

After the age of exploration and migration, the Pacific islanders continued to make sea journeys. Some people sailed back and forth

Movement In time, people settled on every livable island in the Pacific.

■ *What group of islands did the Asian explorers probably visit first?*

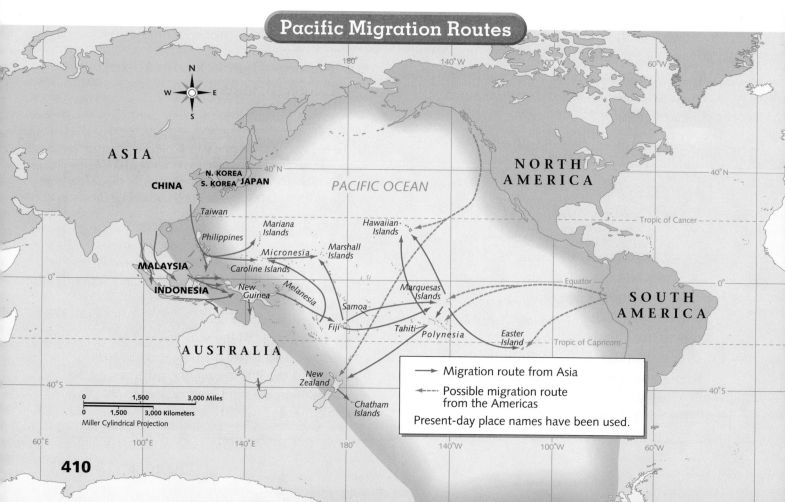

Pacific Migration Routes

ASIA

N. KOREA
S. KOREA JAPAN
CHINA

PACIFIC OCEAN

NORTH AMERICA

Taiwan

Mariana Islands

Hawaiian Islands

Philippines

Marshall Islands

Micronesia

MALAYSIA   Caroline Islands

INDONESIA   New Guinea   Melanesia   Marquesas Islands

Samoa

SOUTH AMERICA

Fiji   Tahiti   Polynesia   Easter Island

AUSTRALIA

New Zealand

Chatham Islands

Tropic of Cancer

Equator

Tropic of Capricorn

→ Migration route from Asia

◄--- Possible migration route from the Americas

Present-day place names have been used.

0   1,500   3,000 Miles
0   1,500   3,000 Kilometers
Miller Cylindrical Projection

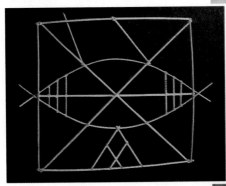

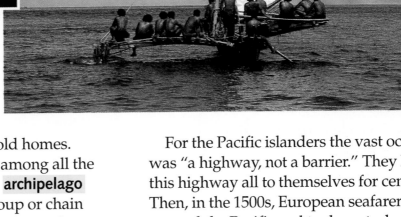

Long ago, Micronesians made maps out of sticks (above). In Micronesia and elsewhere in the Pacific, outrigger canoes are still used (right).

between their new and their old homes. Also, traders regularly sailed among all the islands in an archipelago. An **archipelago** (ar•kuh•PEH•luh•goh) is a group or chain of islands. Trade linked archipelagos that were far apart, such as Tahiti and Hawaii, which are separated by nearly 2,400 miles (3,862 km) of ocean.

For the Pacific islanders the vast ocean was "a highway, not a barrier." They had this highway all to themselves for centuries. Then, in the 1500s, European seafarers entered the Pacific and took control of its waters.

REVIEW *How did the Pacific islanders make the ocean a "highway"?*

LESSON 4 REVIEW

Check Understanding

1 **Remember the Facts**   Where did the earliest trade on the Pacific Ocean take place?

2 **Recall the Main Idea**   How were the Pacific islanders able to explore and settle the thousands of islands in the Pacific Ocean?

Think Critically

3 **Past to Present**   How was early exploration of the Pacific Ocean like present-day space or undersea exploration?

4 **Think More About It**   A historian called the Pacific islanders "sea-attuned" people. *Attune* means "in touch with." What do you think the historian meant by "sea-attuned"?

5 **Explore Viewpoints**   Some Chinese people believed that long trading voyages were wrong because older parents were left alone. Others believed that trading voyages were a good idea because wealth gained through trade reduced taxes. Which idea do you support? Give reasons for your decision.

Show What You Know

Questioning Activity   Work in a group of five. List five questions you have about the early peoples of the Pacific Ocean. Each group member should use reference materials to find the answer to one question. Finally, the group members should share their findings.

500   700

About 600
• Arab ships begin traveling to the eastern coast of Africa

762
• Baghdad rises as Muslim trading center

CONNECT MAIN IDEAS

Use this organizer to describe the development of sea and river trade. Write three details to support each main idea. A copy of the organizer appears on page 90 of the Activity Book.

Indian Ocean Trade
Trade around the Indian Ocean linked many peoples.

1. _____
2. _____
3. _____

The Mediterranean and the Black Sea
Some city-states became leaders of trade in the Mediterranean Sea and in the Black Sea.

1. _____
2. _____
3. _____

Sea and River Trade

The Northern Seas
The addition of new territories affected trade in northern Europe.

1. _____
2. _____
3. _____

Conquering the Pacific
People solved problems to explore and settle the islands in the Pacific Ocean.

1. _____
2. _____
3. _____

WRITE MORE ABOUT IT

Write a Report Write a one-page report that describes the different resources each member of a family can provide. Give examples of how family members can depend on one another, and explain how this can help the whole family.

Write a Journal Entry Imagine that you are a Muslim sea trader who has just returned home from a voyage. Write a journal entry that describes how people at home react to the goods you brought from China, India, and the East Indies.

About 900
• Swahili culture thrives in eastern Africa

1204
• Venice conquers Constantinople

About 1400
• Admiral Zheng He extends Chinese trade routes

1453
• Constantinople captured by Ottoman Turks

Use Vocabulary

Write a sentence or two to explain the meaning of each of these terms.

1. atoll
2. dhow
3. Greek fire
4. lagoon
5. lateen sail
6. monsoon
7. outrigger

Check Understanding

8. Why was ancient Baghdad called the harbor of the world?

9. How did lateen sails improve sea trade?

10. How did Arab trade affect the communities in the trading ports of East Africa?

11. What types of goods did Byzantine traders bring back to Constantinople?

12. What led to the rise of Venice as a trading center?

13. Who were the Rus? What goods did the Rus supply people in western Europe with?

14. What kept the Chinese from exploring the Pacific Ocean for many years?

Think Critically

15. **Past to Present** What are some personal characteristics that you think present-day traders might have in common with early sea traders?

16. **Explore Viewpoints** What different views do you think people living in the 1200s may have had about sailing out onto the world's oceans?

17. **Cause and Effect** The United States depends on resources from many different countries. What are the positive and negative effects of this dependence?

Apply Skills

Compare Information with Graphs Use the graphs on pages 400 and 401 to answer these questions.

18. Which graph would you use to find the year in which United States exports totaled about $394 billion?

19. Imagine that you have been asked to prepare a graph showing how many automobiles the United States imported between 1970 and 1995. Which of the graphs shown might you use as a model? What type of graph is it?

Form a Logical Conclusion Use the steps on page 406 to support this conclusion: People from Asia settled the Pacific islands. Use this book and other books to gather evidence to support the conclusion.

Read More About It

Technology in the Time of the Vikings by Peter Hicks. Raintree Steck-Vaughn. This book provides descriptions of Viking technology.

 Visit the Internet at **http://www.hbschool.com** for additional resources.

The International

A thousand years ago the Chinese city of Chang'an (now Xian) lay at the eastern end of the Silk Road, the main world trade route of its day. In the city market, merchants sold goods from distant lands—sandalwood from Indonesia, cloves from India, and incense from eastern Africa. Some merchants offered Persian dates and pistachios. The smells of Burmese pepper rose from the marketplace.

In the United States today, any shopping mall has more kinds of goods from more places in the world than the Chang'an marketplace offered. Present-day mall merchants might sell coffee and fruit grown in South America, cotton shirts from India, athletic shoes made in South Korea, compact disc players from Japan, and American products from nearly every state in the Union.

The international exchange of goods that is now a part of everyday life began hundreds of years ago with the traders who traveled the world. It was their idea to find new products and bring them to market. Thanks to those daring adventurers, you can choose among basketball shoes made in many places—some as far away as South Korea!

Marketplace

Think and Apply

Like an early trader, search for products made in other parts of the world. Look around your home for such products, and mark on a world map the places where they were made. Then, look closely at your map. Where were most of the products you found made? Were certain kinds of goods more likely to come from certain areas? Work with a partner to write a short report that explains your findings.

HARCOURT BRACE

Visit the Internet at
http://www.hbschool.com
for additional resources.

CNN
Turner
Le@rning

Check your media center or classroom video library for the Making Social Studies Relevant videotape of this feature.

Sonora market in Mexico City

UNIT 6 REVIEW

VISUAL SUMMARY

Summarize the Main Ideas
Study the pictures shown in this visual summary to help you review the events you read about in Unit 6.

Make a Map
Sketch your own map of the world. Do not show borders of present-day countries. Label the continents, oceans, and major seas. Think about what you see on the visual summary and what you have read about trade in this unit. Add to your map written descriptions of trade activities in different parts of the world between 500 and 1500.

1 Between 500 and 1500, West Africans traded with many other peoples. Because of this trade, they were able to build wealthy empires.

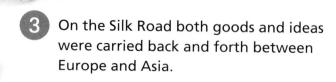

3 On the Silk Road both goods and ideas were carried back and forth between Europe and Asia.

5 Venice and other Italian city-states came to control trade around the Mediterranean Sea and the Black Sea.

2 As the Muslim Empire grew, it formed trade networks with the peoples of Asia, Africa, and Europe.

4 Travel on the Indian Ocean brought together people in Asia and Africa, leading to the exchange of goods and ideas.

7 People had to solve many problems as they explored the islands in the Pacific Ocean.

6 In northern Europe the Vikings took new territories, which brought them more trade. Northern European merchants joined together to expand their own trade.

UNIT 6 REVIEW

USE VOCABULARY

Write the word that correctly matches each definition. Then use each word in a sentence.

archipelago   **oasis**

dhow   **savanna**

embargo   **tariff**

Hansa

1 a grassy plain

2 a tax on goods

3 a water hole

4 an Arab ship that used lateen sails

5 a ban on trade

6 a group whose members shared the costs of trading

7 a group or chain of islands

CHECK UNDERSTANDING

8 Why did the population of early peoples in West Africa grow quickly?

9 How did the location of the Soninke people contribute to their success as traders?

10 How did the king of Ghana keep the price of gold high?

11 Why was salt worth a great deal in West Africa?

12 What factors helped bring people together in the ancient Muslim Empire?

13 Who controlled the gold mines of Central Africa?

14 Why was territorial expansion important to the Vikings?

15 How did membership in the Hanseatic League help merchants?

16 What was the greatest barrier to travel in the Pacific?

THINK CRITICALLY

17 **Past to Present** How has technology changed the way peoples trade throughout the world today?

18 **Think More About It** Imagine that every country in the world could produce everything it needed. How do you think the lack of interdependence among countries would affect the world?

19 **Cause and Effect** Explain why trade between the years 500 and 1500 increased both understanding and conflict between cultures.

APPLY SKILLS

Compare Maps with Different Projections Identify the projections of these maps as polar, conformal, or equal-area.

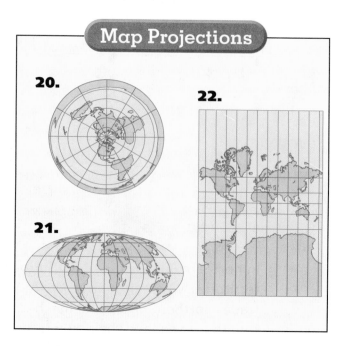

Map Projections

20.

21.

22.

418 • Unit 6

REMEMBER

- Share your ideas.
- Cooperate with others to plan your work.
- Take responsibility for your work.
- Help one another.
- Show your group's work to the class.
- Discuss what you learned by working together.

 ACTIVITY

Make Flow Charts

Work with a partner to make a flow chart that shows how people depend on one another when they produce goods and services for export. Make another flow chart that shows how people depend on one another when they obtain imported goods and services. Include goods and services from businesses, factories, farms, and schools. Present the flow charts to your class when they are finished.

 **ACTIVITY**

Draw a Map

Work with three or four classmates to make a map that shows world trade between the years 500 and 1500. On your map, identify each continent. Also, show different trading cultures and the trading networks they formed. Compare your map with those of other groups.

 **ACTIVITY**

Make a Diorama

Review what you have learned about the African kingdoms of Ghana, Mali, and Songhay. Then work in a group to create a diorama that highlights one of these kingdoms.

Unit Project Wrap-Up

Make a Guidebook Review the notes you have taken to help you write your guidebook. Each member could write about one of the places discussed in Unit 6. Maps should be included to show the location of trade centers and the trade routes used to reach them. You may also wish to add illustrations to your guidebook.

THE EARLY MODERN WORLD

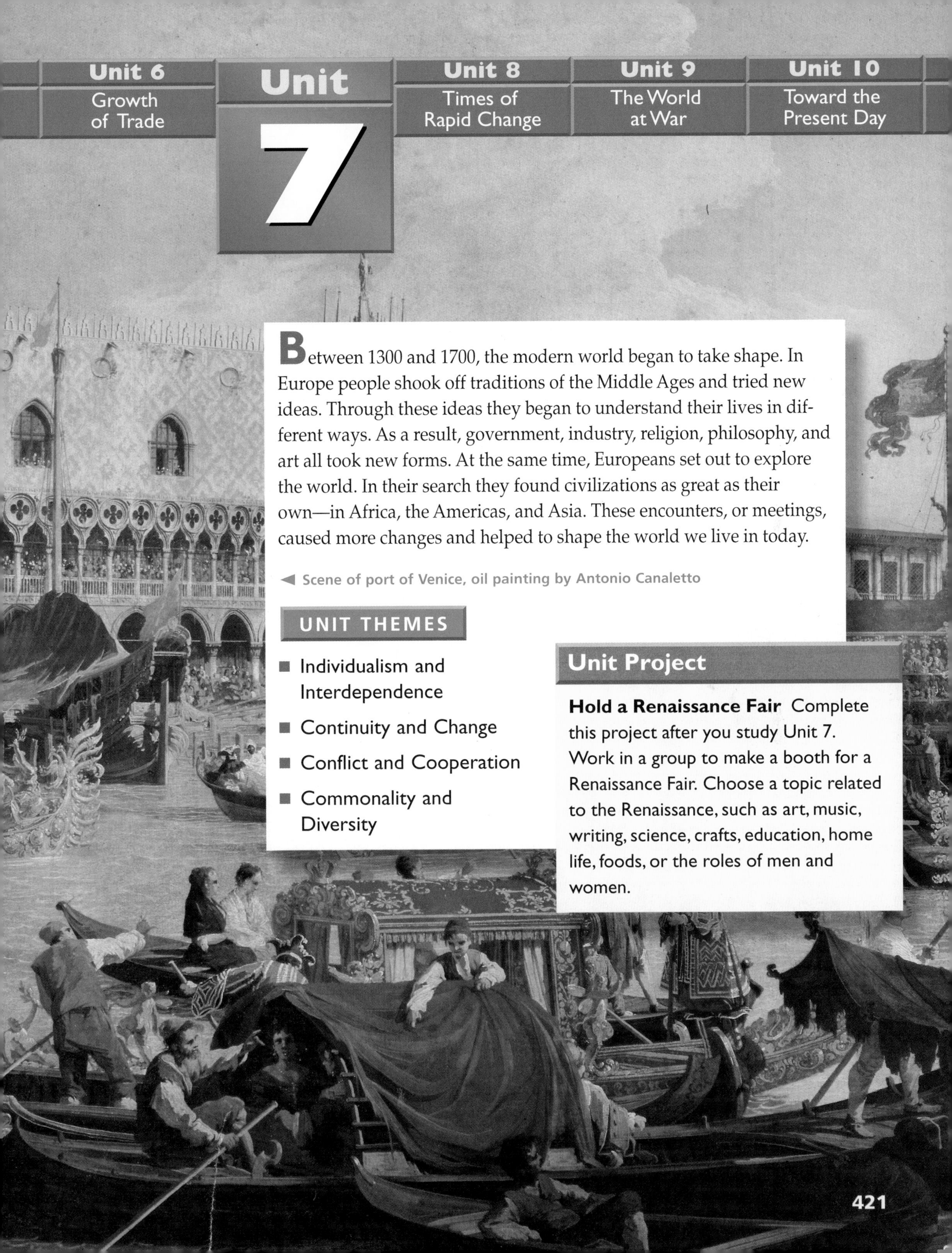

Between 1300 and 1700, the modern world began to take shape. In Europe people shook off traditions of the Middle Ages and tried new ideas. Through these ideas they began to understand their lives in different ways. As a result, government, industry, religion, philosophy, and art all took new forms. At the same time, Europeans set out to explore the world. In their search they found civilizations as great as their own—in Africa, the Americas, and Asia. These encounters, or meetings, caused more changes and helped to shape the world we live in today.

◄ Scene of port of Venice, oil painting by Antonio Canaletto

UNIT THEMES

- Individualism and Interdependence
- Continuity and Change
- Conflict and Cooperation
- Commonality and Diversity

Unit Project

Hold a Renaissance Fair Complete this project after you study Unit 7. Work in a group to make a booth for a Renaissance Fair. Choose a topic related to the Renaissance, such as art, music, writing, science, crafts, education, home life, foods, or the roles of men and women.

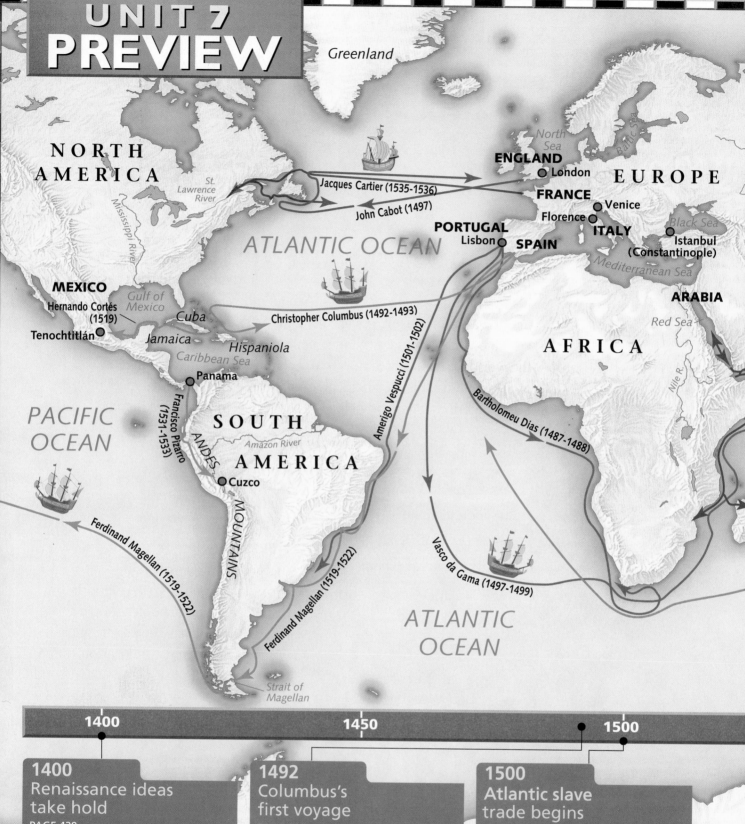

UNIT 7 PREVIEW

Greenland

NORTH AMERICA

St. Lawrence River

Mississippi River

Jacques Cartier (1535-1536)

John Cabot (1497)

ENGLAND
○ London

EUROPE

North Sea

Baltic Sea

FRANCE

○ Venice

Florence ○

ITALY

Black Sea

PORTUGAL

Lisbon ○ **SPAIN**

○ Istanbul (Constantinople)

Mediterranean Sea

ATLANTIC OCEAN

Christopher Columbus (1492-1493)

Amerigo Vespucci (1501-1502)

MEXICO

Hernando Cortés (1519)

Gulf of Mexico

Cuba

Jamaica

Hispaniola

Caribbean Sea

Tenochtitlán ○

○ Panama

ARABIA

Red Sea

AFRICA

Nile R.

Bartholomeu Dias (1487-1488)

PACIFIC OCEAN

Francisco Pizarro (1531-1533)

ANDES

SOUTH AMERICA

Amazon River

○ Cuzco

MOUNTAINS

Ferdinand Magellan (1519-1522)

Vasco da Gama (1497-1499)

ATLANTIC OCEAN

Ferdinand Magellan (1519-1522)

Strait of Magellan

1400	1450	1500

1400
Renaissance ideas take hold
PAGE 429

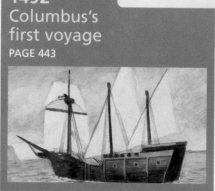

1492
Columbus's first voyage
PAGE 443

1500
Atlantic slave trade begins
PAGE 449

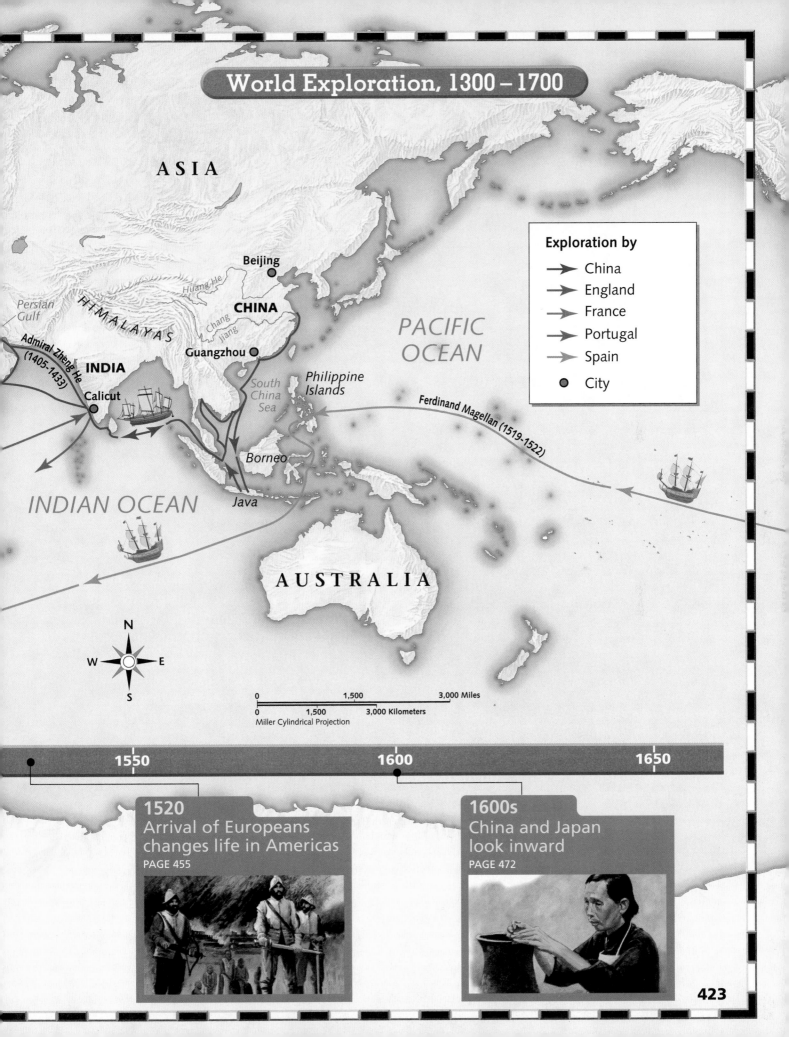

World Exploration, 1300–1700

ASIA

Persian
Gulf

HIMALAYAS

Admiral Zheng He
(1405-1433)

INDIA

Calicut

Huang He

Beijing

CHINA

Chang
Jiang

Guangzhou

South
China
Sea

Philippine
Islands

Borneo

Java

PACIFIC
OCEAN

Ferdinand Magellan (1519-1522)

INDIAN OCEAN

AUSTRALIA

Exploration by
→ China
→ England
→ France
→ Portugal
→ Spain
● City

N
W   E
S

0		1,500		3,000 Miles
0	1,500		3,000 Kilometers	

Miller Cylindrical Projection

1550   1600   1650

1520
Arrival of Europeans
changes life in Americas
PAGE 455

1600s
China and Japan
look inward
PAGE 472

I, Juan de Pareja

by Elizabeth Borton de Treviño

The Middle Ages gave way to a period in which individuals examined their world more closely. Writers, scholars, scientists, and artists all took new directions in their work. Artists started to use new materials and new techniques to capture real life on the canvas on which they painted.

Read now about a Spanish artist who was swept up in the spirit of this age. His story is told by his enslaved servant, Juan (also called Juanico). Juan tells us about an artist living in a time of individualism and creativity.

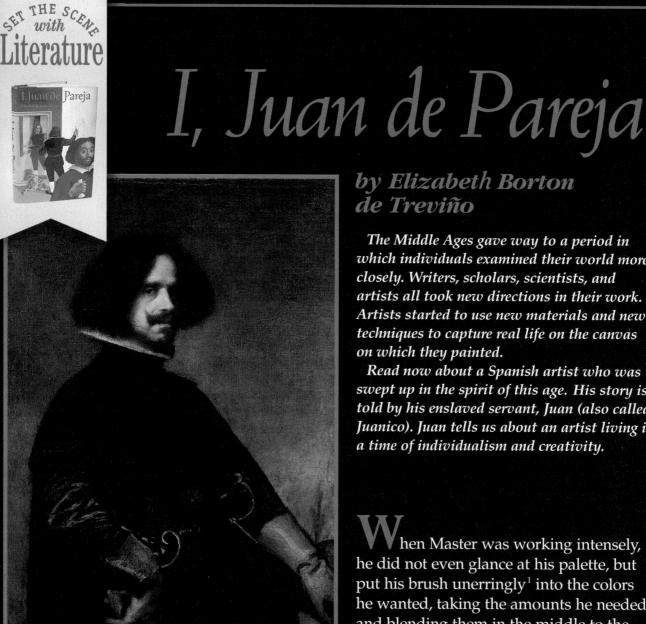

The story *I, Juan de Pareja* (WAHN day pah·REH·hah) is based on the real life of the enslaved servant of Spanish artist Diego Velázquez (vah·LAHS·kays). Shown above is a self-portrait painted by Velázquez.

When Master was working intensely, he did not even glance at his palette, but put his brush unerringly[1] into the colors he wanted, taking the amounts he needed and blending them in the middle to the shades he required. I have seen him thus mix up the same shade time and time again, without glancing, and taking them straight to the canvas; they were always perfect.

His strokes on the canvas, too, sometimes seemed slapdash, rough and unintelligible, if one stood as close to the canvas as he. But a little distance away, and those spots and dashes of light cream or ivory would resolve themselves into a delicate frill of lace, or the daintiest of highlights on satin. Time after time I verified this, and it always seemed magical to me. Master never commented on my astonishment, but often I saw a slight smile curl the quiet mouth beneath the dark silky mustache.

---

[1] **unerringly:** without mistake

Oil painting of Juan de Pareja by Velázquez

This painting, *The Tapestry Weavers* by Velázquez, shows an artist's use of sitters.

And he never chatted while he worked. It was the sitter who spoke, and Master merely put in a word now and again, should there come an expectant silence. Then he would murmur, "Ah?" or "Possibly," or "Just so."

But he studied people. Once he said to me, when the sitter had gone home, and Master was working on a background, "I like to watch people when they talk about themselves, Juanico. Then they reveal to you what they really are. Women, for instance, love themselves; they speak of themselves as if they were talking about a beloved relative who is to be pardoned any foolishness. Men, on the other hand, seem to admire themselves. They speak of themselves like judges who have already brought in a verdict of 'Not guilty.'"

I ventured, "Isn't it difficult to show people their true selves when you paint them, Master?"

"No. Nobody ever knows what he really looks like. Bring me some more of the ochre."

And he was silent again.

Once in a while he would paint me, to keep his hand in, or would ask me to model some difficult fabric.

After he had taught the apprentices[2] to draw vases and fruits and cheeses and hams and all manner of objects, he began to let them sketch people. Then I was often told to pose for them. Then I had my revenge on Cristobal and I helped Alvaro, turning myself subtly so as to ruin Cristobal's drawing and holding myself very still when I noticed Alvaro's eyes on me. Master scolded me for this and watched me, but all the same I was sometimes mischievous.[3] I was always sorry

---

[2] **apprentices:** people who are in training
[3] **mischievous:** full of mischief

when Master criticized Alvaro's work and praised Cristobal's, and one day he answered the distress he saw that this caused me, by telling me his reason.

"Art must be true," he said. "It is the one thing in life that must rest on solid truth. Otherwise, it is worthless."

Then one day there was a knock at the door, and soon after, Mistress came running into the studio, pale with excitement. Behind her, pacing slowly, followed a messenger from the King. He handed a rolled parchment[4] to Master, bowed, and turned. Mistress ran ahead of him to open the door for his departure. The apprentices and I stood silent and respectful as Master unrolled the parchment and read it. He rolled it up again, and took up his palette and brush once more. I remember that he was painting a bronze vase, and I had been at great pains to keep moving it so the sunlight should continue to strike it at the same point every moment.

Diego!" burst forth Mistress. "Tell me, please! Don't make me wait to know! What was in the King's message?"

"I am to paint his portrait," he answered at length, frowning.

"Oh, God be praised! How wonderful!"

"And I am to be given a studio in the palace."

Mistress collapsed onto a chair, which creaked ominously,[5] and she had to fan herself. Little black curls escaped from her pompadour[6] and fell down over her forehead. This meant she was to move in court circles. It meant a fortune, dignity, honors, position beyond anything she had dreamed of.

But Master was silent and pale as he continued to paint the vase. At last he murmured, under his breath, and only I heard, "I hope they haven't sent some courtier[7] to select and prepare a studio for me. It must have light. Light. Nothing else matters. . . ."

---

[4] **parchment:** animal skin used to write on

[5] **ominously:** in a way that threatens
[6] **pompadour:** a hair style
[7] **courtier:** royal attendant

In this oil painting by Velázquez, the family of Spanish King Philip IV visits the artist in his studio at the king's palace.

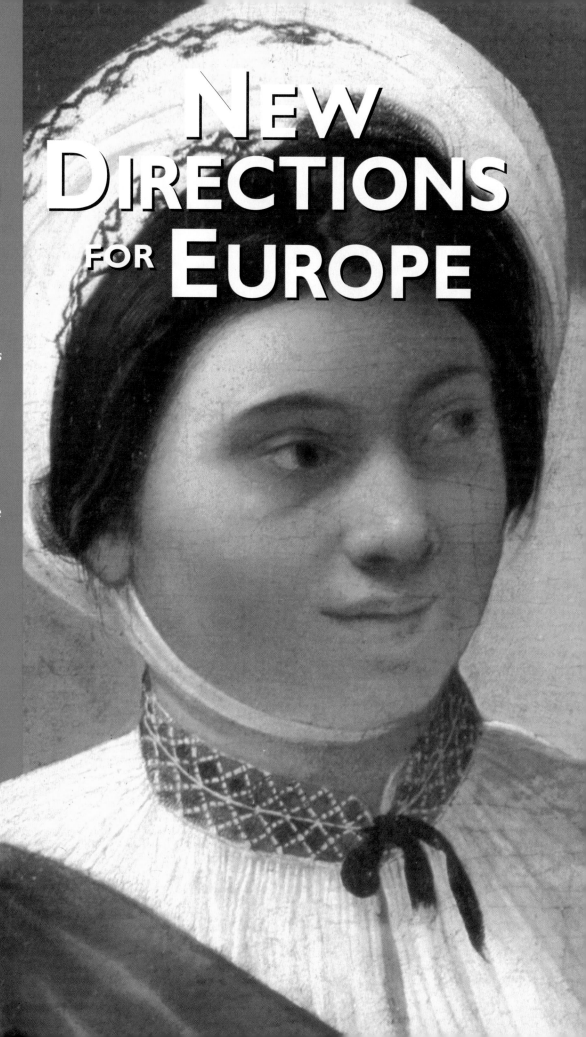

NEW DIRECTIONS FOR EUROPE

*"O, wonder!
How many goodly
creatures are there
here! How beauteous
mankind is! O brave
new world That has
such people in't!"*

Spoken by Miranda
The Tempest
William Shakespeare

Both the nonreligious
subjects, such as this
woman, and the
religious subjects
painted by sixteenth-
century artist
Michelangelo Merisi da
Caravaggio look like
real people.

Rebirth of Ideas in Europe

FOCUS

How might greater freedom for the individual help bring about an age of creative ideas?

Main Idea As you read, think about how changes in European thought encouraged individualism and creativity.

Vocabulary

Renaissance
patron
perspective
movable type
telescope
gravity
scientific method

As Europe emerged from the Middle Ages, people began to look at the world differently. They rejected old ways and started to explore new ideas. Yet some of their ideas were not really new. Many came from the learning of early Greece and Rome. Others came from cultures in Asia and Africa. Encounters with Muslims during the Crusades had given Europeans a better understanding of the importance of learning. Using all their new ideas, Europeans entered an age of thought, learning, art, and science. We call this time, which lasted from about 1400 to 1600, the **Renaissance** (REH•nuh•sahns), a French word meaning "rebirth."

The Renaissance Begins in Italy

Renaissance ideas first took hold in Italy. During the Middle Ages, Italian city-states such as Venice, Naples, Milan, Florence, and Genoa served as important centers of trade between East and West. Merchants from the city-states brought back not only goods from the East but also ideas about philosophy, science, geography, and technology. These ideas inspired a new interest in learning in Italy.

The Italian merchants who sailed to the East and the bankers who paid for their trips became rich and powerful. The wealthy merchant and banking families soon took over as the government leaders of the city-states.

The new leaders placed high value on learning. They believed that it was important to study Greek and Roman classics. The Greeks' love of beauty and the Romans' practical ideas about government strongly appealed to them.

For years the city-states had competed with one another for control of trade in the Mediterranean. Now they competed to become known as Europe's greatest center of learning.

This portrait is typical of Renaissance painting, which captured everyday life.

Chapter 13 • **429**

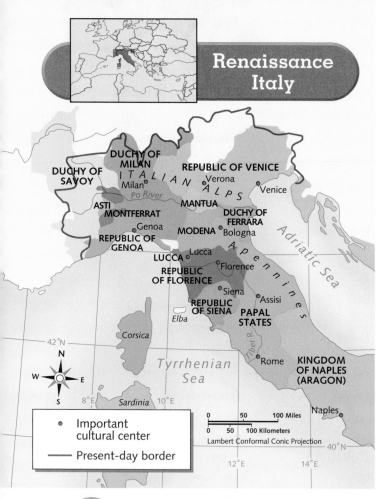

Renaissance Italy

The wealthy merchants and bankers in the various city-states became **patrons**, or supporters, of the arts. They paid artists to create paintings and sculptures and promised to give scholars money if they would come to live in their city-state. The Medici (MED•uh•chee) family of Florence gave much of their wealth to help the careers of artists and thinkers. Such encouragement helped make the Renaissance possible.

REVIEW *What contributed to the rebirth of ideas in Italy?*

Learning About the World

The Italian patrons supported scholars who believed in an idea unheard of during the Middle Ages—the importance of the individual. In the Middle Ages, scholarly thinking had focused on God and religion. The ideas and actions of individuals were not considered worthy of study.

The scholars of the Renaissance studied all the old Greek and Roman works they could find. Many of the works came to them by way of Muslim scholars, who had saved the works when few Europeans were interested in them. Others had been stored in European monasteries.

The study of the Greek and Roman works led Renaissance scholars to a new way of thinking about the world. They believed that people needed to understand how things worked. Anything and everything had to be looked at closely, not just religion. They felt that a person's life should be judged by the things he or she did, not just by faith.

Gaining knowledge was a focus of the Renaissance. This painting of a school in 1516 shows how important learning to read had become.

This painting (above) by the artist Raphael is a good example of the use of artistic perspective. Notice how all parts of the painting lead the eye to a center point (above right).

This new way of thinking first appeared in literature. Writers of the Renaissance borrowed many of their ideas from the Greek and Roman classics that had been written much earlier. However, the writers of this time chose to write in their own languages rather than in Latin or Greek.

REVIEW *What was the relationship between Greek and Roman culture and Renaissance thinking?*

Changes in Art

Renaissance ideas about the importance of the individual also changed art and artists. In the Middle Ages, artists used only religious subjects, and their works looked formal and stiff. Renaissance artists, however, studied Greek and Roman works and produced art that was far more lifelike and that showed both religious and nonreligious subjects. People in Renaissance paintings and sculptures looked like real human beings, and their faces showed feelings. Even the backgrounds in these paintings looked real, because Renaissance painters used **perspective**. This technique allows an artist to show a difference between things that are close and things that are far away.

As art changed, the way people viewed artists also changed. In the Middle Ages, people thought of artists as craftworkers, much like carpenters or bricklayers. Groups of artists, called guilds, controlled where and for whom artists could work, and artists could not choose their subjects. During the Renaissance, however, patrons competed to attract the best artists of the time. As a result, artists could choose for whom they would work, and many were well paid.

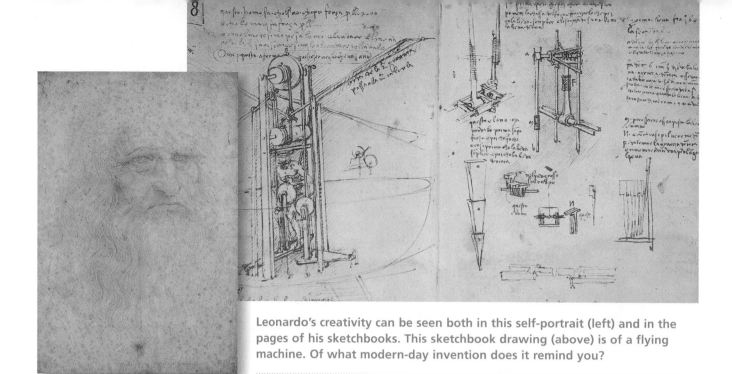

Leonardo's creativity can be seen both in this self-portrait (left) and in the pages of his sketchbooks. This sketchbook drawing (above) is of a flying machine. Of what modern-day invention does it remind you?

Without a doubt, the greatest genius of the Renaissance was Leonardo da Vinci (lee•uh•NAR•doh duh VIN•chee). Leonardo lived from 1452 to 1519, but his accomplishments could have filled a dozen lifetimes. He was a scientist, an engineer, an inventor, a philosopher, and a writer as well as an artist. Leonardo filled notebook after notebook with his ideas and drawings. He sketched plants, animals, and the bones and muscles of the human body. He also filled his pages with "the imagining of things that are to be," such as a flying machine.

Leonardo's paintings stand as his greatest work. For centuries people have been trying to guess the secret behind the smile of his *Mona Lisa.* His attention to detail in *The Last Supper* still leaves people amazed.

Renaissance artist Michelangelo Buonarroti (my•kuh•LAN•juh•loh bwaw•naw•RAW•tee) also showed skill in many fields. His sculptures of David and Moses have the power of the greatest Greek sculptures. The magnificent dome of St. Peter's Church in Rome shows his ability as an architect. The glory of his painting can be seen in the scenes from the Bible that cover the ceiling of the Sistine (SIS•teen) Chapel. Pope Julius II, the patron

who supported these paintings, once complained that Michelangelo worked too slowly. The artist's answer showed the spirit of Renaissance artists: "It will be finished when I have done all that I believe is required to satisfy Art."

REVIEW *How did art change during the Renaissance?*

CULTURE

The *Mona Lisa*

Leonardo da Vinci spent three years painting the world-famous portrait known as the *Mona Lisa.* The work shows the artist's skill in blending colors and using light and shadow. Everyone agrees that the *Mona Lisa* is a masterpiece. But no one knows the identity of the woman who inspired it. Some people say she was the wife of a Florentine merchant, Francesco del Giocondo (joh•KOHN•doh). Others believe that she lived only in Leonardo da Vinci's mind.

The Spread of Ideas

Renaissance ideas spread through Europe with the help of an invention from Germany. During the fourteenth century, Europeans had printed books by carving words and pictures into a block of wood. The block was then inked and stamped onto paper. The whole block had to be recarved if anything on it needed to be changed.

About 1450 a German printer named Johannes Gutenberg (yoh•HAHN•uhs GOO•tuhn•berg) became the first European to print with **movable type**. Gutenberg's printing press used many small pieces of metal, each with a single number or letter of the alphabet. These metal pieces could be arranged in trays to form rows of words and could be easily changed. The printing process became much faster and easier.

In 1455 Gutenberg printed a 1,200-page Bible, using a printing press with movable type. Soon after that, printing presses appeared in all the major cities of Europe. Because books could be printed in large numbers, they became cheaper. This meant that more people could buy them. Through the printed page the ideas of the Renaissance quickly spread to all parts of Europe.

Renaissance ideas reached into Spain, France, and England, bringing about some of the greatest writing of the time. English literature flourished during the time Elizabeth I ruled England. She loved poetry and drama and supported many English writers. The greatest writer of England's Golden Age—perhaps of all time—was William Shakespeare, who wrote poems and plays. Ordinary people, nobles, and royalty alike crowded London's Globe Theatre to see Shakespeare's plays. People still enjoy his works today. In fact, several of his plays have been made into movies. As English poet Ben Jonson noted, "He was not of an age but for all time."

REVIEW *How did the printing press affect the Renaissance?*

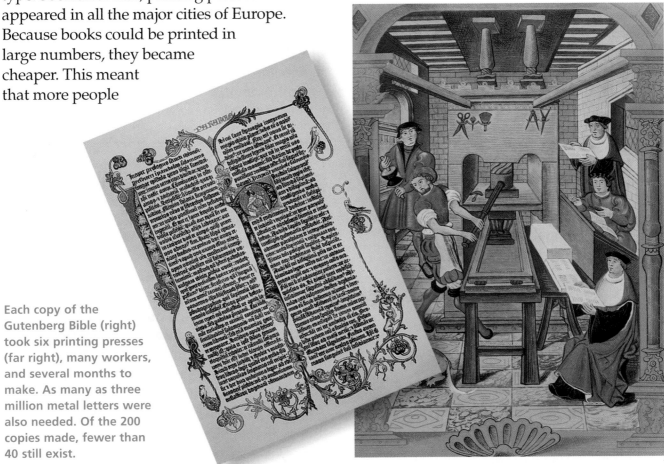

Each copy of the Gutenberg Bible (right) took six printing presses (far right), many workers, and several months to make. As many as three million metal letters were also needed. Of the 200 copies made, fewer than 40 still exist.

Revolution in Science

The questioning spirit of the Renaissance affected science as well as literature and the arts. More and more, scientists began to explore how the physical world works. One important Renaissance scientist was a Polish astronomer named Nicolaus Copernicus (nik•uh•LAY•uhs koh•PER•nih•kuhs). In the 1500s he presented calculations that showed the Earth revolves around the sun. This idea disputed beliefs that the Earth was the center of the solar system.

In the early 1600s Galileo Galilei (ga•luh•LAY•oh ga•luh•LAY•ee), an Italian scientist, proved Copernicus's theory. Galileo had heard about an instrument that could make faraway objects seem close. He set out to make such an instrument. With the help of his **telescope**, he showed that the Earth did indeed move around the sun.

Galileo's work upset religious leaders. They felt that Galileo's ideas went against Church teachings, and they tried to make him say that he was wrong. Old and ill, Galileo gave in. However, legend says that as he lay dying, Galileo said, "And yet it [the Earth] *does* move!"

This notebook of Copernicus and this model of Galileo's telescope are both examples of the new ideas of Renaissance scientists.

The work of Copernicus and Galileo interested an English mathematician named Isaac Newton. In 1687 Newton wrote a book explaining that objects are held to the Earth by a force called **gravity**. The same force, Newton said, keeps the planets circling the sun. In developing his theory, Isaac Newton followed a **scientific method**. Scientific methods require that ideas be tested through observing and experimenting. Scientists still work this way today.

REVIEW *What are some of the scientific contributions that Copernicus, Galileo, and Newton made?*

LESSON 1 REVIEW

Check Understanding

1 **Remember the Facts** Why is the Renaissance a good name for the age of learning?

2 **Recall the Main Idea** In what ways did changes in European thought encourage individualism and creativity?

Think Critically

3 **Think More About It** Today we often call someone who is skilled in many fields a Renaissance man or a Renaissance woman. Do you think this is a good name? Explain your answer.

4 **Cause and Effect** What helped the new learning spread so quickly throughout Europe? What changes did this spread of ideas bring?

Show What You Know

Art Appreciation Activity
Work in a group to find Renaissance art in books or magazines. Identify the works and the artists. Your group should then take on the role of a panel of art experts. Discuss how each painting or piece of sculpture reflects the ideas of the Renaissance.

Changes in Europe

By the mid-1500s the Renaissance in Italy had lost much of its force. Although its gift of learning and art remained, trade, wealth, and power began to shift to other parts of Europe—especially Spain, France, and England.

FOCUS

What might cause a society today to change over time?

Main Idea As you read, look for reasons that European society gradually changed.

Vocabulary

Reconquista
clergy
indulgence
heresy
Protestant
Reformation

New Monarchies

Since about 1100, Christian kings had been trying to drive the Moors out of Spain. The Moors were Muslims who had come from North Africa. In the 1400s King Ferdinand, who ruled the Spanish kingdom of Aragon (AR•ah•gohn), and Queen Isabella, who ruled the Spanish kingdom of Castile (ka•STEEL), led the effort to expel the Moors.

In 1469 Ferdinand and Isabella married. Several years later, they united their kingdoms and other parts of Spain under one rule. They believed, though, that true unity would come for Spain only if it were a completely Catholic country.

Their plan to make Spain all Catholic was called the **Reconquista** (ray•kohn•KEES•tah), or Reconquest. They immediately began driving the Muslims from Spain. By 1492 they had claimed all the land that the Moors once ruled. In the same year they drove more than 200,000 Jews from Spain. By the end of 1492, Ferdinand and Isabella had united Spain under one religion and one government.

The task of uniting France fell to Louis XI. In 1461 he became ruler of a divided kingdom. France had just won the Hundred Years' War with England. But the French people were tired of fighting and of special rights for the nobles. Powerful French nobles took

King Ferdinand of Aragon and Queen Isabella of Castile ruled Spain from 1479 to 1516.

435

care of their own needs first, treated others poorly, and refused to listen to their king. Louis XI saw the need to bring peace, order, and unity to France.

Louis immediately went to work. First he crushed the power of the nobles. Then he began to give special favors to the merchants in the growing towns and cities. He knew that they controlled business and finance and had the money to pay taxes. For the middle-class merchants, taxation was better than the disorder caused by warring nobles. Therefore, they supported Louis. By the time Louis died in 1483, he ruled all of France.

The uniting of England took much longer. After the Hundred Years' War, leading noble families quarreled about which one had the strongest claim to the English crown. In 1485 Henry Tudor, the Earl of Richmond, defeated Richard III at the Battle of Bosworth and became King Henry VII. Henry at once began to unite the country. He married a niece of Richard III to unite the warring families and make his claim to the throne stronger. Then he moved against the most powerful noble families who still opposed him. He seized

Merchants lined this sixteenth-century Paris street. Why did Louis XI favor the merchants in the growing cities?

The Reconquista

Reconquered by 1085
Reconquered by 1150
Reconquered by 1270
Reconquered by 1492

0   100   200 Miles
0   100   200 Kilometers
Azimuthal Equal-Area Projection

Place   By 1492 Spain had come under the control of Ferdinand and Isabella.
■ *By what date had they conquered Granada?*

their private armies and made them give up some of their lands. He chose lesser nobles and people from the middle class to help him govern. When Henry VII died in 1509, England was peaceful and united under a strong central government.

REVIEW *How did each of the new monarchies establish its authority?*

Life in Europe

Renaissance ideas and strong monarchs transformed Europe in many ways, but for most people life did not change much. At the beginning of the 1500s, most of the people of Europe lived in small villages. Poor families lived in huts of wood and straw, as people had during the Middle Ages. Tenant farmers, who worked long and hard, still had to hand over a part of their harvest to landowners.

By the mid-1500s life for peasant farmers had become worse than ever. The demand for wool was rising steadily. Landowners saw that they could make huge profits from raising sheep. To gain more pastures for sheep, they threw thousands of families off the land. The lucky ones found work on other farms. Some unlucky ones became beggars. Others became robbers. Still others headed for the towns and cities in search of jobs.

The arrival of large numbers of jobless people from the country made life harder for those already in the towns and cities. Employers hired the newcomers because they were willing to work for any amount of pay. Townspeople who had been working for years were suddenly out of jobs.

Europe's wealthy lived a life of leisure while its peasants lived a life of hardship.

In contrast to the poor, the wealthy nobles and merchants lived lives of luxury, dividing their time between palaces in the cities and manor houses in the country. They became patrons of the arts and spent a lot of money entertaining.

REVIEW *What caused life to change for European peasant farmers in the mid-1500s?*

LEARNING FROM GRAPHS In the 1500s many Europeans moved from the countryside to the cities.
- *How many times larger was the population of London in 1600 than in 1500?*

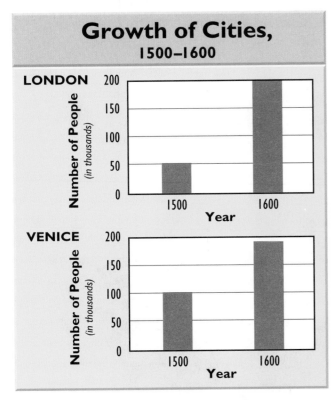

Growth of Cities,
1500–1600

A Weakened Church

In 1513 a member of the Medici family of Florence became the leader of the Catholic Church as Pope Leo X. It is said that he wrote to his brother, "God gave us the papacy [office of the pope]—let us enjoy it." Leo X did indeed enjoy himself. He spent church money freely on himself and as a patron of the arts. To replace the money, Leo sold positions in the church to whoever could pay the most.

Most Christians in Europe never met the pope, but they did see their local priest. While many priests served the church well, some behaved in less desirable ways. Some Europeans warned that poor judgment among members of the clergy, or church officers, would cause trouble.

The Inquisition

"Come with me. The Inquisitor wishes to speak with you." This command struck fear into the hearts of fifteenth-century Europeans. It meant that they had been ordered to appear before the Inquisition. This was a religious court whose task was to find and punish nonbelievers. Victims of the Inquisition were tortured, sent to prison, or killed by being burned alive. Pope Gregory IX set up the first Inquisition in the 1230s. Ferdinand and Isabella started a new Inquisition in 1478 as a way to make the Catholic religion stronger in Spain. The Spanish people lived under this Inquisition for more than 300 years.

Trouble came much sooner than most people expected. Leo X wanted to rebuild St. Peter's Church in Rome. To get the money for this work, he began to sell **indulgences**, or pardons for sins. Selling indulgences had been common in the church. One church official stated, "The Lord desireth not the death of a sinner but that he live and pay." Leo X's new indulgences were different, however. They promised forgiveness for sins that people might commit in the future!

A priest named Martin Luther saw the sale of indulgences taking place in the public square of the German town of Wittenberg (WIH•tuhn•berg). The idea that forgiveness could be bought with money shocked Luther. That forgiveness for future sins could be bought shocked him even more. Luther wondered whether he should take independent action, since few other people seemed to care. After much thought, he decided to challenge the practice of selling indulgences.

REVIEW *What were indulgences? Why did Martin Luther feel that they were wrong?*

The Reformation

At noon on October 31, 1517, Luther nailed his 95 Theses (THEE•seez), or statements of opinion, to the door of the Castle Church in Wittenberg. The papers listed Luther's complaints against his own church.

A church court quickly put Luther on trial. It convicted him of **heresy**, or denying the beliefs of the church. Charles V, the leader of the Holy Roman Empire—of which the German states were a part—also put Luther on trial. In both trials Luther explained that he did not intend to hurt the church. He only wanted to identify and solve its problems. At the same time, however, he refused to deny or change any of his ideas. Luther was told, therefore, that he was no longer a member of the church.

Charles V declared Martin Luther an outlaw. No one in the empire was to help

This papal bull, or letter from the pope (below), demanded that Martin Luther (left) change his ideas.

Movement The earliest Protestants lived in the area known today as Germany.
■ *What was the major direction in which the Protestant religion spread?*

Luther. However, Frederick the Wise, a German prince, ignored the emperor's order and gave Luther a place to live.

By now Luther had begun to question the roles of priests and the pope. He came to believe that the Bible held all the religious teachings people needed to know. From his safe place Luther translated the Bible from Greek to German, the people's language. The improved printing press made it possible for many people to have Luther's translation of the Bible.

Over time, many Germans became followers of Luther, forming the Lutheran Church. Catholic leaders tried to stamp out this new church. Some Germans strongly protested these actions and, as a result, became known as **Protestants**. The movement that gave rise to Protestant churches was called the **Reformation** because its goal was to reform the Catholic Church.

The Protestant Reformation spread from Germany to other parts of Europe, including

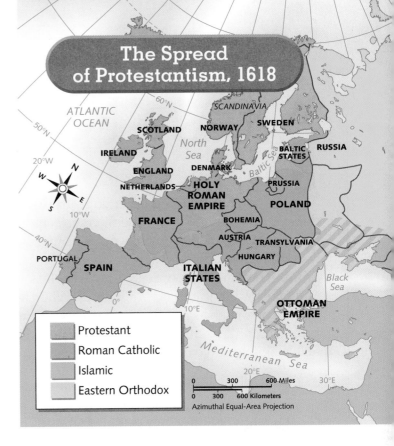

The Spread of Protestantism, 1618

Legend:
- Protestant
- Roman Catholic
- Islamic
- Eastern Orthodox

0 300 600 Miles
0 300 600 Kilometers
Azimuthal Equal-Area Projection

Scandinavia, England, Scotland, and the Netherlands. Hundreds of new Christian churches were founded there. The Catholic Church remained strong in Spain, Portugal, Italy, France, Ireland, and parts of eastern Europe. However, the rise of Protestantism caused the Catholic Church to reform.

REVIEW *How did the Reformation change Europe?*

LESSON 2 REVIEW

Check Understanding

1 Remember the Facts What was the Reformation? What effect did it have on Europe?

2 Recall the Main Idea What factors caused great change during this time period?

Think Critically

3 Explore Viewpoints Catholics viewed Protestants as heretics (people guilty of heresy). Protestants saw themselves as reformers. Give reasons why each side thought the way it did.

4 Cause and Effect How did Renaissance ideas and inventions contribute to the Reformation?

Show What You Know

Journal-Writing Activity Imagine that you are a student in Germany during the mid-1500s. Write journal entries describing the changes to life in your town caused by Martin Luther's actions.

Act as a Responsible Citizen

1. Why Learn This Skill?

Nations, churches, and other large groups depend on their citizens or members to act responsibly. To be responsible, people must keep informed about what is happening in the group. They must choose thoughtful leaders and take part in the group's activities. When a large group such as a nation or church faces problems, its citizens or members may need to take action to solve those problems.

2. Remember What You Have Read

You have read about the problems faced by the Catholic Church in the early 1500s. Many of its members took part in a movement called the Reformation. The movement's goal was to reform, or change, the actions of some church officials, such as those who were selling indulgences. Martin Luther, a leader of this movement, nailed his protest of 95 Theses to the door of the Wittenberg Castle Church. This got the attention of church leaders and of Charles V, leader of the Holy Roman Empire. Luther was not the only person to make a difference in the Reformation. Hundreds of clergy and other leaders, especially those in Germany, worked to solve the Catholic Church's problems.

Martin Luther posts his 95 Theses.

3. Understand the Process

Acting as a responsible citizen or group member is not always as difficult as it was for Martin Luther and his followers, who often risked their lives. It can be as simple as keeping informed or voting. However, it almost always needs some special thought and action.

Here are some steps that people today can follow to act as responsible citizens of the United States:

1. They can inform themselves about the problems in their country.
2. They can think about ways to solve these problems.
3. They can decide how to bring about change in ways that would be good for the whole country.
4. Each person can decide how he or she can help, acting either alone or with others.

4. Think and Apply

Some acts of responsible citizenship, such as voting, can be done only by adults. Others can be done by citizens of any age. The four steps above can help anyone act as a responsible citizen. Use the four steps as you think of ways in which you and your classmates can act as responsible citizens of your community.

Europeans Explore the Globe

FOCUS
What leads people to explore the unknown?

Main Idea As you read, look for reasons European nations began to explore and claim lands overseas.

Vocabulary
caravel
circumnavigation
Armada

As early as the fifteenth century, several European countries wanted to break the Italian and Muslim monopolies on trade with the East. To do this, they looked for new sea routes to Asia. The race to find these new routes began Europe's Age of Exploration.

The Fall of Constantinople

In the early 1400s Venice was the leader in European trade with the East. A chain of Venetian trading posts reached from the eastern Mediterranean to the Black Sea. The routes beyond the Black Sea were controlled by Muslim traders, who took a share of the profits.

A threat to this trade arrangement arose when the Ottoman Turks began pushing west. In 1453 these Muslims captured the city of Constantinople. Constantinople had long served as the crossroads of the sea trade between Europe and Asia. The people of Venice saw the danger and fought to keep their trading empire. Yet by 1500 the Ottoman Empire controlled the trade routes to the East.

The capture of Constantinople by the Muslim Ottomans shocked Europeans, but they did not really feel sorry for Venice. Many European nations had already begun to look for new water routes to the East so that they would no longer have to pay Venetian traders. Such routes would allow them to trade directly with Asia and keep all the profits. The Europeans' search for a new route focused on the Atlantic Ocean.

REVIEW *How did the fall of Constantinople affect European trade with Asia?*

In mid-1453 the Ottoman Turks captured Constantinople from the Venetians.

Sailors of the fifteenth century relied on tools of navigation such as this compass and this map showing sea monsters.

Europeans Look Toward the Atlantic

Perhaps some word of the Viking explorations across the Atlantic had reached Spain and Portugal. That might explain why many people began to think that a huge piece of land was in the ocean to the west. Many Europeans also now believed that a sea route to Asia could be found by crossing the Atlantic.

Ships of the early 1400s were not strong enough to make a long ocean voyage. In the mid-1400s, though, shipbuilders in Portugal began to build a type of ship called a **caravel**. This ship used square or lateen sails to travel long distances swiftly and withstand heavy seas.

At the same time, European sailors became better navigators. They learned to use the compass and the astrolabe, and they had much better maps than before. Many of their maps came from Muslim geographers. With these tools European sailors were finally prepared to search for a sea route.

REVIEW *What developments allowed sailors to sail out into the Atlantic Ocean?*

Portugal and Spain Lead the Way

Sailors from Portugal were the first to sail out into the Atlantic. Small and fairly poor, Portugal wanted a share of the trade with Asia. Its leaders felt sure that trade would bring wealth to Portugal.

The Portuguese expeditions into the Atlantic began mainly because of one man, Prince Henry the Navigator. He never went on a voyage of exploration himself, yet he turned Portugal into a world sea power. About 1419 Henry began a school for navigators. There he brought together the best mapmakers, scientists, and ship designers from many lands. He put their ideas into use by paying for voyages of exploration along Africa's Atlantic coast.

Henry died in 1460, but the Portuguese continued their expeditions along Africa's western coast. In 1488 Bartholomeu Dias (DEE•ahsh) sailed around the southern tip of Africa and entered the Indian Ocean. Though Dias's crew made him turn back, he had opened a new way to the East. Ten years later, Vasco da Gama sailed as far as India.

He returned to Portugal in 1499 with a cargo of Indian spices and jewels. The sale of the cargo brought 60 times what the trip had cost! The Portuguese quickly set up trading posts along the coasts of Africa and India. From there Portuguese ships pushed deeper into Asian waters. By the late 1500s a network of Portuguese trading posts reached from Africa's Atlantic coast to China.

About the time of Dias's voyage, another sailor, named Christopher Columbus, met with the king of Portugal. Columbus, an Italian, felt sure that a ship could reach Asia by sailing west across the Atlantic. After being rejected by the king of Portugal, Columbus took his idea to Ferdinand and Isabella of Spain. He promised them great wealth and new lands. He also said he would take the Catholic religion to the people of Asia. Ferdinand and Isabella agreed to help.

On August 3, 1492, Columbus set sail with three ships. A little more than two months later, on October 12, he landed on a small island in the Caribbean Sea, which he named San Salvador ("Holy Savior"). Columbus was sure that he had reached the Indies, so he called the island's people Indians. When he returned to Spain in 1493, he received a hero's welcome.

Columbus made three more voyages, but he never knew that he had found a new

Movement At the end of the fifteenth century, sailors from Spain and Portugal set off to explore the world.
■ *Which explorer traveled mainly along the Tropic of Cancer?*

Vasco da Gama

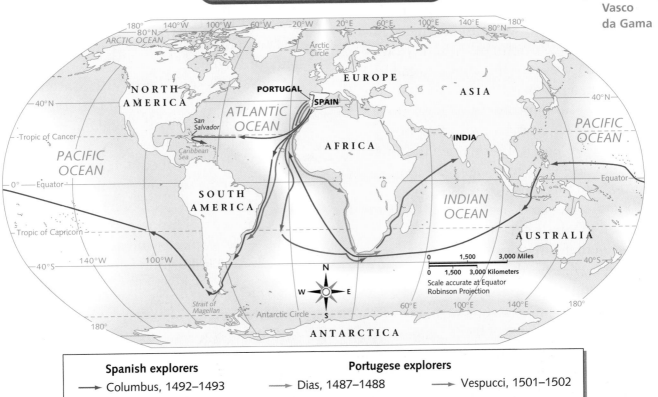

Voyages of Exploration

Spanish explorers
→ Columbus, 1492–1493
→ Magellan, 1519–1522

Portugese explorers
→ Dias, 1487–1488
→ Da Gama, 1497–1499
→ Vespucci, 1501–1502

Christopher Columbus is remembered for his voyages across the Atlantic, which forever changed ways of life in Europe and the Americas.

land. Others soon realized this, however. In 1501 Amerigo Vespucci (uh•MAIR•ih•goh veh•SPOO•chee), an Italian sailing for Portugal, explored the coast of what is now Brazil. He drew careful maps and wrote about what he saw. "It is lawful to call [the continent] a new world," he said, "because none of these countries were known to our ancestors." A mapmaker read Vespucci's observations and in 1507 named the "new" continent America in his honor.

At about this time Spain and Portugal signed a treaty that divided the undiscovered world between them. They drew an imaginary line north and south through the world as they knew it. Spain had the right to explore all lands west of the line. Portugal could explore all lands east of the line.

Under this treaty Spain was able to continue searching for a westward route to Asia. In 1519 five ships led by Ferdinand Magellan (mah•JEH•lahn) left Spain. Magellan sailed across the Atlantic, around the tip of South America, and into the Pacific Ocean. He then sailed on to Asia. Magellan was killed in a battle in the Philippines, but his sailors completed the trip around the world.

This **circumnavigation** of, or journey around, the world showed three important points. It proved that a ship could reach Asia by sailing west. It proved that there was a water route around the world. And it gave geographers a new way to calculate the size of the world.

REVIEW *Why were the voyages led by Portugal and Spain important?*

English Exploration

The English began to search for new trade routes shortly after Columbus sailed across the Atlantic. King Henry VII paid for the voyages of the Italian explorer John Cabot, who also searched for a western route to Asia. In 1497 and 1498 Cabot sailed along the northeast coast of North America and claimed the land for England.

Henry VII's son, Henry VIII, concentrated more on religious change and less on exploration. Under his rule, England became a Protestant country. It was Henry VIII's daughter, Elizabeth I, who made England a sea power. After she came to the throne in 1558, she provided money to support a group of young sea captains, including Francis Drake, John Hawkins, and Walter Raleigh. Some of the sea captains were pirates as

This portrait of Elizabeth I shows her on the day she was crowned as the queen of England.

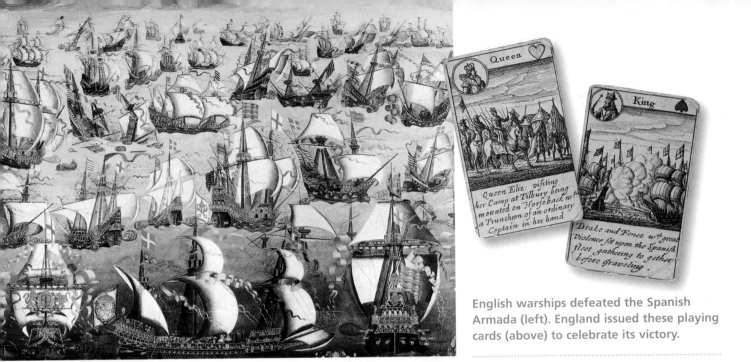

English warships defeated the Spanish Armada (left). England issued these playing cards (above) to celebrate its victory.

well as explorers. Elizabeth ignored their piracy because their attacks on Spanish and Portuguese ships filled her treasury with gold and silver.

The Spanish king, Philip II, became very angry about Queen Elizabeth's pirate-explorers. He also wanted to force Protestant England to return to the Catholic Church. In 1588 Philip put together a fleet of 130 warships, called the **Armada** (ar•MAH•dah), to attack England. The Spanish warships were not as fast as England's, and the English drove the Spanish ships away. A fierce storm destroyed the Armada as it tried to return to Spain by sailing around the northern tip of Scotland. This sea battle showed that Spain was weakening as a world power and that England was gaining strength.

REVIEW *What event showed that England was becoming a world power?*

LESSON 3 REVIEW

Check Understanding

1 Remember the Facts Where did Europeans look for a sea route to Asia?

2 Recall the Main Idea What led European nations to explore and claim lands on other continents?

Think Critically

3 Personally Speaking Imagine that you are about to start a voyage of exploration in the 1400s. How would you prepare yourself physically, mentally, and emotionally?

4 Cause and Effect How did the Renaissance help bring about the age of European exploration?

5 Past to Present Where do people go on today's great journeys of exploration? Why are people exploring these areas?

Show What You Know

Letter-Writing Activity
Explorers of long ago often had to persuade somebody, usually a monarch, to pay for their expeditions. Imagine that you want to set out on a voyage of exploration for Portugal, Spain, or England. Write a letter to the monarch of that country. Explain why conditions are right for your voyage and how helping you would help the monarch.

About 1400
• Renaissance ideas take hold in Italy

About 1450
• Gutenberg develops movable type

1492
• Columbus's first voyage to the Americas

CONNECT MAIN IDEAS

Use this organizer to show that you understand the ideas and effects of the Renaissance in Europe. Write two details to support each main idea. A copy of the organizer appears on page 96 of the Activity Book.

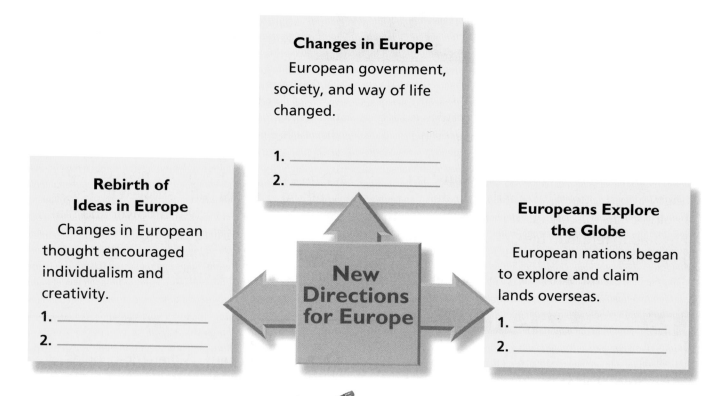

Changes in Europe
European government, society, and way of life changed.

1. _____
2. _____

Rebirth of Ideas in Europe
Changes in European thought encouraged individualism and creativity.

1. _____
2. _____

New Directions for Europe

Europeans Explore the Globe
European nations began to explore and claim lands overseas.

1. _____
2. _____

WRITE MORE ABOUT IT

Write Dialogue William Shakespeare, perhaps the greatest playwright of all time, lived during the period described in this unit. Try your hand at playwriting. Select one of the following scenes: a European artist speaks to a patron; Galileo Galilei defends his ideas; King Ferdinand and Queen Isabella discuss plans for the Reconquista; an explorer tries to find a sponsor. Then write one page of dialogue for the characters in the scene you have chosen.

Write a Ship's Log Imagine that you are a crew member sailing with one of the European explorers, such as Vasco da Gama, Christopher Columbus, or Ferdinand Magellan. How did this explorer affect your life? What did you learn about the explorer? Write two log entries: one for the day you were most inspired by this explorer and one for the day you were most upset. Give details about each of the days you have chosen, and tell why you felt as you did.

1550   1600   1650   1700

1588
• England defeats
  the Spanish Armada

1687
• Newton publishes
  work on gravity

USE VOCABULARY

Write the term that matches each definition.
Then use each term in a complete sentence.

Armada   caravel

indulgence   Reformation

Renaissance   scientific method

1. a French word meaning "rebirth"

2. a type of ship

3. a pardon for sins

4. the testing of ideas through observing and experimenting

5. a Spanish naval fleet

6. a sixteenth-century movement to change the Catholic Church

CHECK UNDERSTANDING

7. How did Renaissance art differ from art of the Middle Ages?

8. What famous individual of the Renaissance was a scientist, a writer, a philosopher, an engineer, an inventor, and an artist?

9. Who was Johannes Gutenberg, and how did he help spread new learning in Europe?

10. What is the relationship between Martin Luther and Protestants?

11. Who was Prince Henry, and what effect did he have on exploration?

12. What two European nations were the first to begin overseas exploration?

13. Where did Columbus land in 1492?

14. Why was the ocean voyage of Magellan and his crew important?

THINK CRITICALLY

15. **Think More About It** What were some benefits of the Reconquista to Spain? What were some ways the Reconquista may have hurt Spain?

16. **Personally Speaking** What changes in Europe between 1400 and 1700 do you think were most important? Why?

17. **Cause and Effect** What might have been the effect on world exploration if Italian and Muslim traders had not controlled the trade routes to the East?

APPLY SKILLS

Act as a Responsible Citizen
Look through recent newspapers and magazines to find an article that shows someone acting as a responsible citizen. Write a brief description of the action that person took and the results of that action.

READ MORE ABOUT IT

The Apprentice by Pilar Molina Llorente, translated by Robin Longshaw. Farrar, Straus & Giroux. A young boy discovers the hard work that goes with being an apprentice in Renaissance Italy.

Visit the Internet at
http://www.hbschool.com
for additional resources.

EUROPE, AFRICA, AND THE AMERICAS INTERACT

"When the people of Malindi saw [the Portuguese], they knew they were bringers of war and corruption, and were troubled with very great fear."

The Chronicle of Kilwa, describing the arrival of Vasco da Gama's fleet in East Africa

Brass sculpture of an oba (king) of Benin

Africa and Europe

As the Middle Ages drew to a close in Europe, new kingdoms arose in Africa south of the Sahara. Like the ancient West African empires, these kingdoms grew mainly because of trade. For many of the African kingdoms, the arrival of Europeans in Africa seemed to mean more trade, wealth, and power. They would soon learn that they were mistaken.

African Societies

A military defeat in 1591 led to the fall of the Songhay Empire. Soon another great empire, Kanem-Bornu (KAHN•em BAWR•noo), gained control of trade across the Sahara. The kingdom of Kanem had risen around Lake Chad in the 800s. Through trade with North Africa, Kanem grew wealthy and strong. Eventually, Kanem joined with the nearby kingdom of Bornu. By 1600 the soldiers of Kanem-Bornu had created a huge empire.

Kanem-Bornu's time of greatest growth came in the late 1500s under the rule of Idris Aloma (EE•drees al•OH•muh). Idris improved his army by importing the most up-to-date weapons and hiring military advisers to teach his soldiers the newest ways to fight. Idris was a devout Muslim who tried to spread his faith to the lands he governed. He also replaced Kanem-Bornu's old laws with ones based on Islamic law. But the rulers who followed Idris did not have his leadership abilities, and Kanem-Bornu slowly weakened.

To the southwest of Kanem-Bornu, in the West African forests, other trading kingdoms formed. By 1500 Benin (buh•NIN) was perhaps the most important. Benin grew rich by trading in spices, ivory, cloth, tools, and slaves. From a great palace in the walled city of Benin, the oba (OH•buh), or king, ruled a huge empire. Its lands filled much of what is now south-central Nigeria.

FOCUS
What happens when people are forced to migrate against their will?

Main Idea As you read, consider how Europeans forced many Africans to leave their homeland.

Vocabulary
plantation
triangular trade
Middle Passage
racism

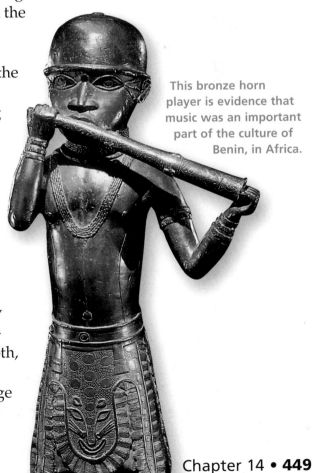

This bronze horn player is evidence that music was an important part of the culture of Benin, in Africa.

Great African Kingdoms

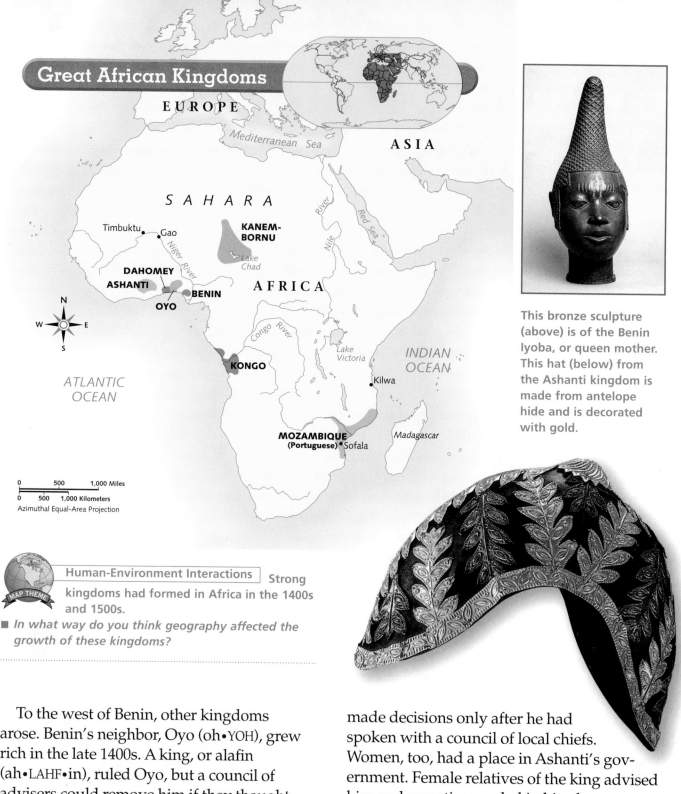

EUROPE

Mediterranean Sea

ASIA

SAHARA

Timbuktu • Gao

KANEM-BORNU

Niger River

Lake Chad

DAHOMEY

ASHANTI

BENIN

OYO

AFRICA

River

Red Sea

Nile

ATLANTIC OCEAN

Congo River

KONGO

Lake Victoria

INDIAN OCEAN

• Kilwa

MOZAMBIQUE (Portuguese) • Sofala

Madagascar

0   500   1,000 Miles
0   500   1,000 Kilometers
Azimuthal Equal-Area Projection

This bronze sculpture (above) is of the Benin Iyoba, or queen mother. This hat (below) from the Ashanti kingdom is made from antelope hide and is decorated with gold.

MAP THEME Human-Environment Interactions Strong kingdoms had formed in Africa in the 1400s and 1500s.

■ *In what way do you think geography affected the growth of these kingdoms?*

To the west of Benin, other kingdoms arose. Benin's neighbor, Oyo (oh•YOH), grew rich in the late 1400s. A king, or alafin (ah•LAHF•in), ruled Oyo, but a council of advisers could remove him if they thought he was not a good leader. In Dahomey (duh•HOH•mee), which rose in the mid-1600s, government was very different. There the king controlled everything without any fear of being removed.

The kingdom of Ashanti (uh•SHAHN•tee), founded at about the same time as Dahomey, was ruled in yet a different way. The king

made decisions only after he had spoken with a council of local chiefs. Women, too, had a place in Ashanti's government. Female relatives of the king advised him and sometimes ruled in his place.

Far to the south, at the mouth of the Congo River, the kingdom of the Kongo grew strong in the 1400s. The people thought of their king, the manikongo, as a god. As in the kingdoms to the north, the Kongo's economy was based on trade.

REVIEW *What did the African kingdoms have in common? How were they different?*

Europeans in Africa

The arrival of Europeans in Africa brought many changes to these kingdoms. The Portuguese were the first Europeans to establish settlements. The Africans were willing to trade, and they allowed the Portuguese to set up stations all along the African coast. Local African rulers rented the stations to the Portuguese in return for a part of the profits and a promise of protection from their enemies in Africa. These stations were heavily armed, almost like forts. Most stations also had Catholic priests, who had come to teach the Africans about Christianity.

At first the Portuguese traded for spices, gold, and ivory. As time went on, however, slaves came to be the main export of African trade. Events across the Atlantic in the Americas brought about this change. Settlers had started colonies in all parts of North, Central, and South America. These settlers mined the mineral wealth of the Americas. They also started huge farms, called **plantations**, on which they grew sugarcane, pineapples, cotton, tobacco, and coffee. Work in the mines and fields was very hard. Few Europeans were willing to do it, so owners of mines and plantations used slave labor. The Portuguese looked to Africa for these slaves.

REVIEW *How did the Portuguese carry on trade in Africa?*

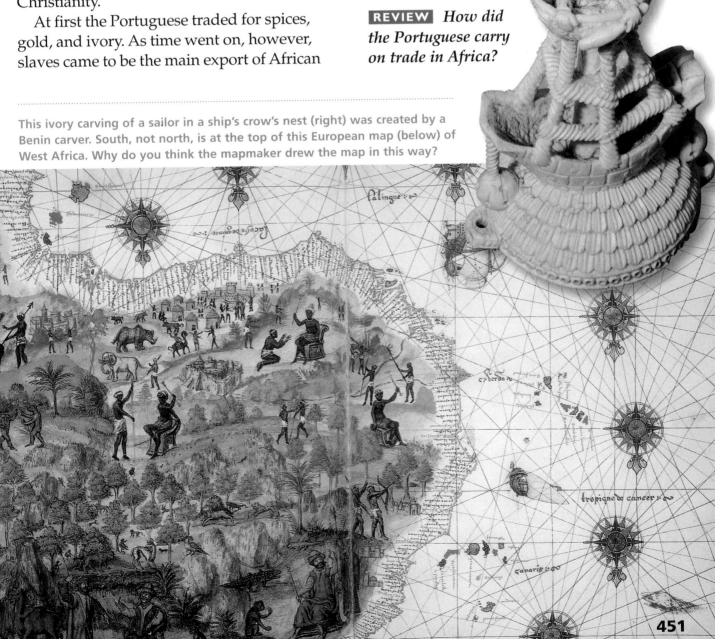

This ivory carving of a sailor in a ship's crow's nest (right) was created by a Benin carver. South, not north, is at the top of this European map (below) of West Africa. Why do you think the mapmaker drew the map in this way?

Olaudah Equiano
About 1750–1797

Olaudah Equiano was born about 1750 in what today is Nigeria. At the age of 11 or 12, Equiano was captured and sold into slavery. He was shipped to Virginia, where he worked on a plantation. He was then sold to an officer in the British navy. After serving with his owner in the French and Indian War, Equiano was sold to a West Indian merchant. In time Equiano made enough money to buy his freedom. In 1777 he settled in England, where he wrote a book about his life as a slave. He also became a leader in the movement to bring an end to slavery.

The Slave Trade

Slavery was not new. It had existed since earliest times. Conquered people had been enslaved by the Sumerians, the Egyptians, the Greeks, and others. Slaves worked on building projects in the Roman Empire. Slavery had also been practiced in Africa for centuries. Up to that time, however, most African slaves were prisoners of war or criminals working off their punishment. Slaves were treated fairly well and might one day become free.

European slavery was different. African slaves were thought of as property, to be bought and sold as their owners saw fit. This type of slavery was for life. An enslaved person had little hope of ever becoming free. Children of a slave were born slaves and would remain enslaved all their lives.

First the Portuguese and then other Europeans took part in the transatlantic slave trade. Slave traders went into the African countryside, capturing anyone they could. They then sold their captives to European traders at stations along the coast. These traders loaded the captured people

on ships for the journey to the Americas. The traders showed no mercy. They separated "fathers from sons, husbands from wives, brothers from brothers," one Portuguese observer said.

Life on the slave ships was horrible. The more slaves aboard, the greater the traders' profits. So traders jammed people into every bit of space. For much of the long voyage across the Atlantic, the captured Africans were chained together in the cargo holds. A former slave named Olaudah Equiano (oh•LOW•duh ek•wee•AHN•oh) said that the air "became unfit for respiration [breathing] from a variety of loathsome smells, and brought on a sickness among the slaves, of which many died. . . ."

Perhaps as many as one African in five died on this terrible trip. Those who lived to reach the Americas were sold at auction. The sale of human life was part of a system called the **triangular trade**. First, traders sailed from Europe to Africa with iron, cloth, guns, and liquor. In Africa the traders exchanged these goods for enslaved people. Next, during what is sometimes called the **Middle Passage**, the enslaved people were shipped across the Atlantic to the Americas. There the traders sold the enslaved people for products from the plantations. These products were taken back to Europe, completing the triangle.

For more than 300 years, Africa was the focus of the slave trade. Eventually, many Europeans, especially religious leaders, began to feel that slavery was cruel and wrong. In 1807 the British government put a stop to Britain's part in the slave trade. Soon other countries did the same. Newly enslaved people were no longer taken to the United States. However, a cruel war would follow before slavery ended there in 1865.

REVIEW *How did the system of triangular trade operate?*

Effects of the Slave Trade

As many as 10 million enslaved Africans were taken to the Americas during the time of the slave trade. Many others died.

The slave trade had a terrible effect on the economy of Africa. In some places so many people were taken that the land was left almost empty. There were few people to work the fields or care for the herds. Also, the African kingdoms that took part in the slave trade made such large profits that they ignored all other economic activities. When the slave trade and its profits ended, the once-great African trading kingdoms were left with nothing.

Movement Triangular trade involved selling of both goods and people.
■ *How do you think this trade pattern would have been different if everyone at the time felt that people could not be sold?*

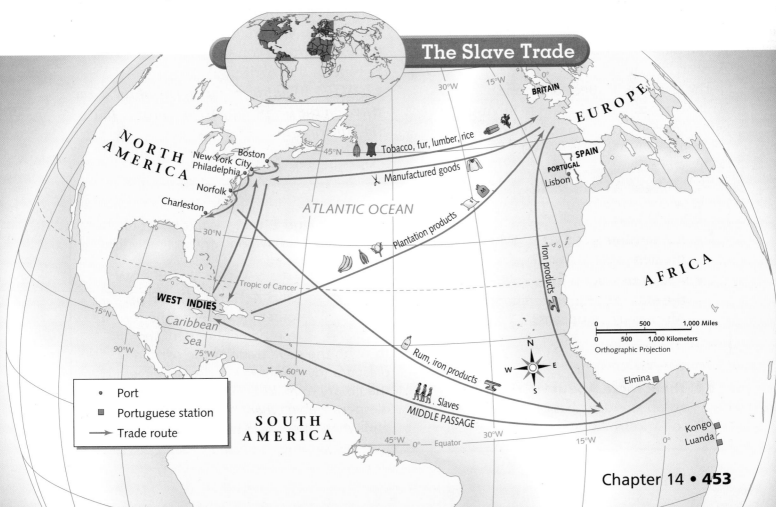

The Slave Trade

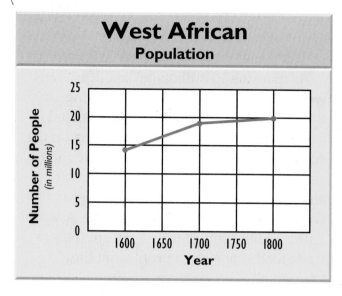

West African
Population

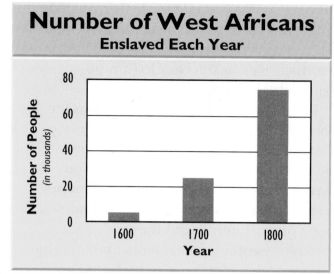

Number of West Africans
Enslaved Each Year

LEARNING FROM GRAPHS Between 1700 and 1800 the population of West Africa did not grow greatly.

■ *Do you think the slave trade affected this slowing of population growth? Why or why not?*

The slave trade also had a deep and lasting effect on African society. At first Africans sold mostly prisoners of war to Europeans. But as the demand for slaves grew, Africans started raiding nearby communities. As a result, many wars broke out among the African kingdoms.

The slave trade affected Europeans and Americans, too. To take part in buying and selling people, traders and owners had to act without feeling. They had to think of the Africans they enslaved as inferior to them. In lands affected by slavery, **racism**—a feeling of being better than other people because of their color—spread. Racism has been a continuing source of concern in the Americas, in Europe, and in Africa.

REVIEW *What were the effects of the slave trade on the people of Africa, Europe, and the Americas?*

LESSON 1 REVIEW

Check Understanding

1 Remember the Facts What created the demand for slaves?

2 Recall the Main Idea What were the effects of the forced migration of Africans by Europeans?

Think Critically

3 Think More About It How did Europeans deny basic human rights to Africans?

4 Cause and Effect What effect did the slave trade have on African family life?

Show What You Know

Map Activity Historians sometimes refer to the forced resettlement of Africans through the slave trade as the African *diaspora* (dy•AS•puh•ruh). Use resources in the library to make a map of the African diaspora. Show where Africans came from and where they were taken as slaves.

A Time of Encounter

FOCUS
What happens when different cultures come into contact?

Main Idea As you read, think about how the arrival of Europeans in the Americas affected life in both the Western and Eastern hemispheres.

Vocabulary
conquistador
immunity
Columbian exchange
encomienda
coureurs de bois

Across the Atlantic from Africa, the Americas also began to feel the effect of European political and economic activity. The cultures of the Americas and Europe would never be the same.

Spain Builds an Empire

Columbus had promised Ferdinand and Isabella new lands and wealth. On his later voyages to the Americas, he tried to keep this promise. He started colonies on some Caribbean islands and looked for gold. Other people, also seeking treasure, soon followed Columbus.

The Spanish called these treasure seekers **conquistadors** (kahn•KEES•tah•doors), or "conquerors." One of the first of the conquistadors was Hernando Cortés (er•NAHN•doh kawr•TEZ). In 1519, attracted by stories of great wealth to be found, Cortés set out to explore Mexico.

When Motecuhzoma (maw•tay•kwah•SOH•mah), the Aztec emperor, heard of Cortés's arrival, he thought that Cortés might be the Aztec god Quetzalcoatl (khet•zahl•koo•WAH•tahl). According to Aztec legend, Quetzalcoatl would one day appear as a bearded, light-skinned man, which was almost exactly the way Cortés looked. In addition, Cortés and his army rode horses and had weapons unknown to the Aztecs. When Cortés arrived in the Aztec capital, Tenochtitlán, Motecuhzoma offered him gifts of gold. The golden jewelry that the Aztecs offered amazed Cortés. The conquistador wanted more.

Cortés's greed led the Aztecs to turn against him. In a surprise attack on June 30, 1520, they drove the Spaniards from Tenochtitlán. The following year, however, Cortés returned with a larger army. The Spaniards burned the Aztec city.

—Cortés's gold gave other conquistadors the desire to search for riches. In 1526 Francisco Pizarro (fran•SIS•koh pee•ZAR•oh) led an expedition to the Inca Empire in South America. The

This ivory horn, used for holding gunpowder, shows both a Spanish ship and Aztec gods.

455

Inca emperor, Atahuallpa (ah•tah•WAHL•pah), agreed to meet with Pizarro and was taken prisoner. In return for his freedom, Atahuallpa promised Pizarro a large room filled with gold. Atahuallpa kept his word, but Pizarro had him killed anyway. The Spaniards then conquered the Inca Empire easily.

Chasing dreams of gold, other conquistadors explored much of the Americas. Within 100 years of Columbus's first voyage, the Spanish ruled a large empire in the Americas. They did not control all of South America, however. In 1500 Pedro Cabral (kah•BRAHL) had claimed what is now the country of Brazil for Portugal.

REVIEW *How did Spain create an empire in the Americas?*

The Aztecs honored their gods with temples, sculptures, and ceremonies. This bell is decorated with the image of an Aztec god.

Spanish Encounters

Almost at once, ships began to carry gold, silver, and precious stones from the Americas back to Spain. This wealth of goods helped Spain become the richest, most powerful nation in the world during the 1500s.

As the Spanish moved through the Americas, they learned about many new foods. Corn, beans, squash, peppers, peanuts, tomatoes, and chocolate soon were added to the European diet. Some foods, such as the peanut, traveled beyond Europe to become important foods in Africa and Asia. Perhaps the food that caused the greatest change was the potato. Cheap and plentiful, the potato kept many poor people from starving. This caused a great population increase in Europe. One non-food crop—tobacco— also found its way to Europe.

The Spaniards who settled in the Americas brought European animals and plants with them. Cattle, chickens, pigs, sheep, chickpeas, sugarcane, and wheat changed the way the peoples of the Americas ate. The horse, which had been unknown in the Western Hemisphere, changed transportation, hunting, and warfare.

Routes of Cortés and Pizarro

NORTH AMERICA

40°N

60°W

ATLANTIC OCEAN

MEXICO Gulf of Mexico

Tropic of Cancer

Tenochtitlán

Veracruz Cuba Jamaica Hispaniola

Caribbean Sea

Panama

0° — Equator

Tumbes

SOUTH AMERICA

PACIFIC OCEAN

Cajamarca

ANDES MTS.

Cuzco

N W E S

100°W

→ Route of Hernando Cortés
→ Route of Francisco Pizarro
• Conquered city

0   500   1,000 Miles
0 500 1,000 Kilometers
Robinson Projection

Movement Conquistadors headed for the Americas.
■ *How would you describe the location of Cortés's final destination in the Americas?*

At the same time, the Spanish brought deadly diseases such as influenza, smallpox, and measles to the Americas. The people of the Americas had never been exposed to many of these diseases. Therefore, they had not developed an **immunity**, or resistance, to them and usually died if they became ill with them. As many as 90 percent of the native peoples may have died from European diseases.

Historians refer to the movement of people, animals, plants, diseases, and ideas between Europe and the Americas as the **Columbian exchange**. People and their cultures were certainly one of the most important parts of this exchange.

In Spanish America some European colonists established what came to be known as the **encomienda** (en•koh•mee•EN•dah) system. Under this system Native Americans had to work for the colonists and accept their religion. In return, the colonists were supposed to make certain that these people were well fed and were taught the Catholic faith. Many colonists, however, treated the people as slaves. When the Native Americans died from overwork and disease, the colonists replaced them with African slaves. They treated the Africans as poorly as they had the Native Americans.

Slowly the cultures of the Spanish, the Africans, and the Native Americans began to mix in Spanish America. For example, many Native Americans and slaves accepted the Catholic religion. The Spanish adopted the lifeways of the African slaves and the Native Americans that were suited to the American environment. This mixing of cultures created a new Latin American way of life.

REVIEW *What exchanges took place between Europe and the Americas?*

Tenochtitlan.

Malintzin, at right

Malintzin
About 1501–1550

When Hernando Cortés landed on the Yucatán Peninsula, he came into contact with the Mayas. As a peace offering, the Mayas gave him 20 slaves. Among them was a young Aztec princess named Malintzin (mah•LINT•chin). Cortés called the young woman Doña Marina and made her his interpreter. In time Malintzin became one of Cortés's most trusted advisers. He felt that the conquest of the Aztecs would have been almost impossible without her. For the same reason, many people in Mexico today think Malintzin was a traitor. In fact, some Mexicans call a person who betrays his or her own people a *Malinchista*.

French Encounters

Meanwhile, far to the north, encounters between Native Americans and Europeans produced a very different American culture. The explorations of Jacques Cartier (ZHAHK kar•TYAY) in the 1530s gave France a claim to lands in what is now Canada. Cartier reported that the lands lying along the St. Lawrence River had many fur-bearing animals and that the Native Americans in the region were willing to trade. French traders soon began bartering with the Indians for furs and skins, which brought high prices in Europe.

Trade grew as the French became friendly with both the Algonkin (al•GON•kin) and the Huron Indians. French trappers known as **coureurs de bois** (koo•RER duh BWAH), or "runners of the woods," trapped animals and traded with the Native Americans. They lived in Algonkin and Huron villages and adopted the peoples' languages and customs. As they traveled, they learned much about the geography of the area. Their reports gave the Europeans their first information about North America's interior lands.

French priests also journeyed into the interior to teach native peoples the Catholic faith. Many behaved like the *coureurs de bois.* People said that Father Jacques Marquette "could be a Huron with the Hurons, an Algonkin with the Algonkins, one with any among whom he lived and worked." Marquette traveled nearly the whole length of the Mississippi River. Those who followed Marquette claimed for France the lands around the Great Lakes and the Ohio River. There they found people making claims for another European country—England.

REVIEW *How did the coureurs de bois become accepted by the Native Americans?*

English Encounters

The earliest English settlers arrived on the east coast of North America. For the most part, Native Americans were friendly to them. They taught the settlers how to grow corn, pumpkins, squash, and beans. They

Movement Beginning in the 1500s, many of the resources of the Americas were shipped to Europe, Asia, and Africa.
■ *What products raised by the Incas moved across the Atlantic?*

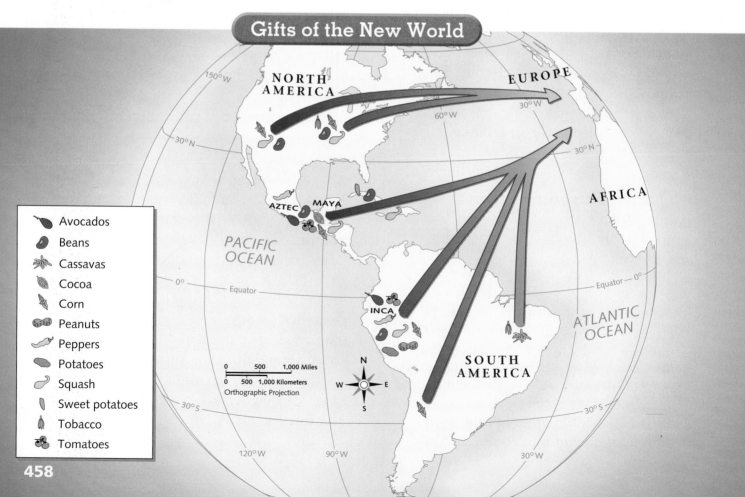

Gifts of the New World

Avocados
Beans
Cassavas
Cocoa
Corn
Peanuts
Peppers
Potatoes
Squash
Sweet potatoes
Tobacco
Tomatoes

NORTH AMERICA

EUROPE

AFRICA

AZTEC
MAYA

PACIFIC OCEAN

INCA

ATLANTIC OCEAN

SOUTH AMERICA

0   500   1,000 Miles
0   500   1,000 Kilometers
Orthographic Projection

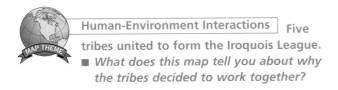

Human-Environment Interactions Five tribes united to form the Iroquois League.
■ *What does this map tell you about why the tribes decided to work together?*

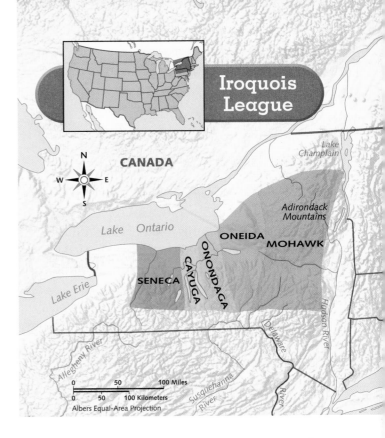

Iroquois League

CANADA

Lake Champlain

Lake Ontario

Adirondack Mountains

ONEIDA MOHAWK

ONONDAGA

CAYUGA

SENECA

Lake Erie

Allegheny River

Hudson River

Delaware River

Susquehanna River

0   50   100 Miles
0 50 100 Kilometers
Albers Equal-Area Projection

showed the settlers the best places to fish and to gather shellfish.

With the help of the Native Americans, the English settlers survived their early years in North America. Soon they began to do well as farmers. Their success brought more settlers from England. To grow more food for the increasing population, the colonists started to feel the need for more land. Because of this, they began to drive the Native Americans off the lands on which they lived and hunted. As the number of new colonists grew, more and more Native Americans were pushed westward.

Tribes who spoke the Iroquois language lived farther inland. These tribes united to form the Iroquois League. An unwritten constitution, or set of rules, kept peace among the members. Leaders from each tribe met in a Grand Council. The council declared war, made peace treaties, and protected League members. The colonists made treaties with the League because of the League's strength. Peace lasted for a time, but later the League broke apart. However, a plan similar to the Iroquois idea of bringing together different groups in a league would be used by the writers of the U.S. Constitution more than 100 years later.

REVIEW *How did Native Americans help the English settlers?*

LESSON 2 REVIEW

Check Understanding

1 **Remember the Facts** Where in the Americas did the earliest English settlers arrive?

2 **Recall the Main Idea** How did the arrival of Europeans in the Americas affect life in both the Western and Eastern hemispheres?

Think Critically

3 **Think More About It** Do you think conflict between the people of the Americas and the Europeans had to happen? Why or why not?

4 **Cause and Effect** What were the positive and negative effects of the Columbian exchange?

Show What You Know

Chart Activity Create an illustrated chart that identifies the people, animals, plants, diseases, and ideas that moved between Europe and the Americas in the Columbian exchange. Share and discuss your work with classmates.

Compare Maps

1. Why Learn This Skill?

Symbols, such as color, can have different meanings on different maps. For example, on one map the color red may stand for a certain elevation. On another map red may stand for a certain number of people per square mile or square kilometer. In some cases, however, symbols on two maps may have similar meanings. When symbols such as color have a similar meaning on two different maps, they can help you compare information.

2. Understand the Process

To compare information on different maps, you can follow these steps:

1 Identify the subject and time period shown on each map.

2 Find out from each map key what the symbols stand for.

3 Think about what you can learn by comparing the maps that you could not learn from looking at one map alone.

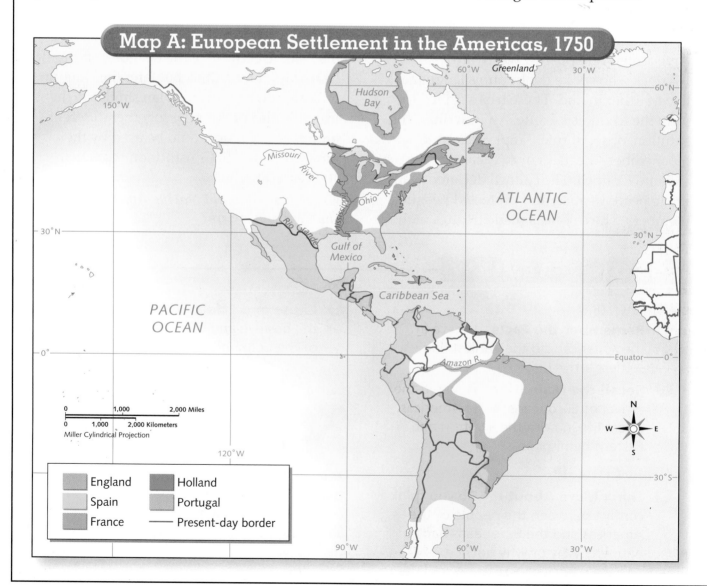

Map A: European Settlement in the Americas, 1750

- England
- Spain
- France
- Holland
- Portugal
- Present-day border

Use the steps to compare Map A and Map B. Then answer the questions.

a. What does the title of Map A tell you?

b. What area is shown on Map A? What does the map show you about that area?

c. What time period is shown on Map A? What does the map show you about that time?

d. What does the title of Map B tell you?

e. What area is shown on Map B? What does the map show you about that area?

f. What time period is shown on Map B? What does the map show you about that time?

g. Compare Map A and Map B. Is there a connection between the European countries that settled certain areas and the languages spoken in those areas today? Explain.

h. What do the two maps show together that you could not learn from one map alone?

3. Think and Apply

Use an atlas or an encyclopedia to find at least two kinds of maps of your state. Use the steps listed in Understand the Process to compare the maps. Then use what you learn from the two maps to write a paragraph describing your state.

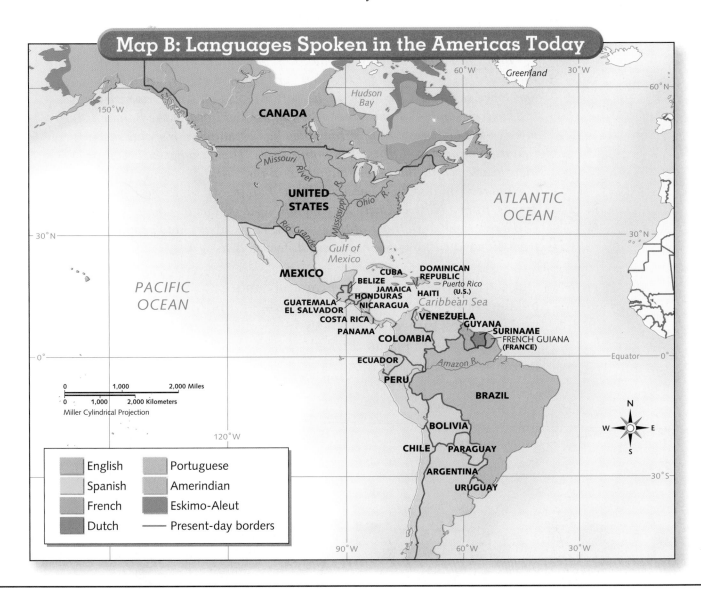

Map B: Languages Spoken in the Americas Today

English
Spanish
French
Dutch
Portuguese
Amerindian
Eskimo-Aleut
Present-day borders

MORNING GIRL

WRITTEN BY MICHAEL DORRIS

ILLUSTRATED BY DOROTHY SULLIVAN

When Christopher Columbus landed on San Salvador Island in the Bahamas in 1492, he brought together very different cultures that had developed separately. In doing so, he set the world on a historic new course.

The first people Columbus met, the Tainos, had lived in the Bahamas for more than 1,500 years. In that time they had established a social system that did not accept violence. Columbus said, "There cannot be better or more gentle people than these anywhere in the world."

Now read an imaginary account of the Europeans' first meeting with the Tainos, from a Native American viewpoint. As you read, compare Morning Girl's reactions with those of the visitors. Think about how people from different cultures can hold very different ideas.

I stepped over my mat very carefully and left the house. I set my feet into the hard-packed places, turned sideways to avoid the leaves of plants, ducked beneath low branches. From my quick dream I chose the idea of water, maybe because I was thirsty, maybe because the day was already hot and the thought of waves on my skin made me feel better, maybe because the sea promised me a story.

Smoke was not yet rising from cook fires, so I knew it was early. No wonder the sea called. It must be lonely, a feeling I could understand: today, I was in no one's good thoughts. Star Boy was unhappy with me, and now Mother and Father were, too, for their own reasons. They would be distant toward me until I helped them to forget my unsisterly words.

I wished there were someone I could complain to, someone who would easily forgive me either for being too nice, as I was to Star Boy at the feast, or too harsh, as I was last night. I missed the new sister who had never come home. I was sure I would never have argued with her. It seemed to me wrong that she had received no name. Grandmother said that we hadn't known her well enough . . .

and yet I *did* know her. She was in my thoughts often, as she was this morning. Then I had an idea so surprising that I stopped walking: *I* could give the new sister a name, just between her and me. I closed my eyes, held my breath, and found exactly the right one: She Listens. Now she was real.

I looked at the place where I was, to remember it. The island was all green and brown, the flowers red and yellow, the sky a deep and brilliant blue. At my feet, the tip of something white stuck from the sand. I stooped, dug with my fingers, and pried out a small, empty conch, washed so gently by the sea that not a single chip was missing— just the way Star Boy insisted for the shells he liked to keep. My gift would be the start of his new collection, replacing what the storm had borrowed. Things would be the way

they had been, only better. I put the conch into a bowl of dried seaweed, where I could find it later, and ran into the water.

Dawn made a glare on the ocean, so I splashed through the shallow surf and dived without looking. I felt the hair lift from around my head, felt a school of tiny fish glide against my leg as I swam underwater. Then, far in the distance, I heard an unfamiliar and frightening sound. It was like the panting of some giant animal, a steady, slow rhythm, dangerous and hungry. And it was coming closer.

I forgot I was still beneath the surface until I needed air. But when I broke into sunlight, the water sparkling all around me, the noise turned out to be nothing! Only a canoe! The breathing was the dip of many paddles! It was only *people* coming to visit, and since I could see they hadn't painted themselves to appear fierce, they must be friendly or lost.

I swam closer to get a better look and had to stop myself from laughing. The strangers had wrapped every part of their bodies with colorful leaves and cotton. Some had decorated their faces with fur and wore shiny rocks on their heads. Compared to us, they were very round. Their canoe was short and square, and, in spite of all their dipping and pulling, it moved so slowly. What a backward, distant island they must have come from. But really, to laugh at guests, no matter how odd, would be impolite, especially since I was the first to meet them. If I was foolish, they would think they had arrived at a foolish place.

"I won't make a mistake," I told She Listens. "I won't be too good, and I won't say too much because I might choose the wrong words."

I kicked toward the canoe and called out the simplest thing.

"Hello!"

One of the people heard me, and he was so startled that he stood up, made his eyes small, as fearful as I had been a moment earlier. Then he spotted me, and I waved like I've seen adults do when visitors arrive, my fingers spread to show that my hand was empty.

The man stared at me as though he'd never seen a girl before, then shouted something to his relatives. They all stopped paddling and looked in my direction.

"Hello," I tried again. "Welcome to home. My name is Morning Girl. My mother is She Wins the Race. My father is Speaks to Birds. My brother is Star Boy. We will feed you and introduce you to everyone."

All the fat people in the canoe began pointing at me and talking at once. In their excitement they almost turned themselves over, and I allowed my body to sink beneath the waves for a moment in order to hide my smile. One must always treat guests with respect, I reminded She Listens, even when they are as brainless as gulls.

When I came up they were still watching, the way babies do: wide eyed and with their mouths uncovered. They had much to learn about how to behave.

"Bring your canoe to the beach," I shouted, saying each word slowly so that they might understand and calm themselves. "I will go to the village and bring back Mother and Father for you to talk to."

Finally one of them spoke to me, but I couldn't understand anything he said. Maybe he was talking Carib or some other impossible language. But I was sure that we would find ways to get along together. It never took that much time, and acting out your thoughts with your hands could be funny. You had to guess at everything and you made mistakes, but by midday I was certain we would all be seated in a circle, eating steamed fish and giving each other presents. It would be a special day, a memorable day, a day full and new.

I was close enough to shore now for my feet to touch bottom, and quickly I made my

way to dry land. The air was warm against my shoulders, and there was a slight breeze that disturbed the palm fronds strewn on the ground. I squeezed my hair, ran my hands over my arms and legs to push off the water, and then stamped on the sand.

"Leave your canoe right here," I suggested in my most pleasant voice. "It will not wash away, because the tide is going out. I'll be back soon with the right people."

The strangers were drifting in the surf, arguing among themselves, not even paying attention to me any longer. They seemed very worried, very confused, very unsure what to do next. It was clear that they hadn't traveled much before.

I hurried up the path to our house, but not before She Listens reminded me to take the white conch shell from the seaweed where I had left it. As I dodged through the trees, I hoped I hadn't done anything to make the visitors leave before I got back, before we learned their names. If they were gone, Star Boy would claim that they were just a story, just my last dream before daylight. But I didn't think that was true. I knew they were real.

LITERATURE REVIEW

❶ How did Morning Girl show she meant the strangers no harm? Do you think the strangers understood this? Explain why or why not.

❷ What did Morning Girl think of the visitors? Based on what you have read, what do you think the visitors thought of Morning Girl?

❸ With classmates, act out what you think happened the next time Morning Girl encountered the visitors.

Compare Information on a Double-Line Graph

1. Why Learn This Skill?

As you have learned, a line graph shows changes over time. These changes are called trends. Some line graphs have one line. Others have two or more. Graphs with two or more lines allow you to compare trends. The double-line graph on page 467 compares trends in the populations of Native Americans and Europeans for a period of more than 250 years—from Columbus's first voyage until the year 1750.

2. Remember What You Have Read

Beginning in the 1490s, Europeans caused many changes in the lives of the people they encountered in the Americas. The Europeans brought new weapons, animals, and crops that changed the way many Native Americans hunted as well as the foods they ate. The Europeans also brought new diseases that killed as many as 90 percent of the native peoples in North America and South America.

In the period from the 1490s to 1650, the Native American population became much smaller. Besides the deaths caused by disease, there were many deaths in battle as Native Americans defended their lands from soldiers and settlers.

3. Understand the Process

The graph on page 467 is a double-line graph. The number scale on the left-hand side of the graph shows the population in millions. The number 100, at the top of the graph, stands for 100 million. The numbers along the bottom are years. The dots above these years show the

For centuries Native Americans lived alone in the Americas. Different groups of Native Americans developed different ways of life. In the painting titled *Ju-ah-kis-gaw* (left), artist George Catlin shows a mother and child of one of the many groups. The arrival of the Europeans brought many changes to the ways of life in the Americas. The embroidered cloth (above) shows the Spanish conquistador Cortés and his Native American interpreter, Malintzin.

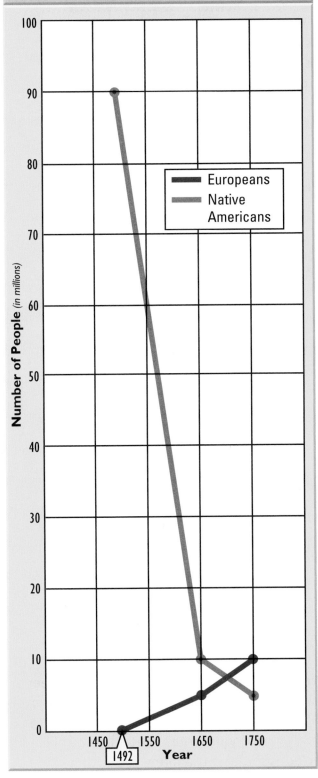

Population of Native Americans and Europeans, 1492–1750

Number of People (in millions)

Europeans
Native Americans

100
90
80
70
60
50
40
30
20
10
0

1450 | 1492 | 1550 | 1650 | 1750

Year

estimated population of each group in the Americas for three different times.

You read a double-line graph the same way you read a single-line graph. Find the black lines for the years 1450 and 1550. Notice that a blue dot is positioned about halfway between the two lines, at the year 1492. This dot is part of the blue line that shows the European population in the Americas. It is on the population scale at 0. This means that there were almost no Europeans living in the Americas in 1492.

Now move your finger up to the second dot, which is part of the red line that shows the Native American population. This dot is on the population scale at 90, meaning that about 90 million people lived in the Americas around the time Europeans arrived.

Next, find the dots for the European and Native American populations for 1650 and 1750. Then answer the questions.

1. What were the Native American and European populations in 1650? in 1750?

2. During which time period did the population of Native Americans drop more sharply? How large was the drop?

3. In 1750 about how much larger was the population of Europeans than that of Native Americans?

4. What prediction can you make about the direction the line for European population would go if it continued to 1850?

5. What prediction can you make about the direction the line for Native American population would go if it continued to 1850?

4. Think and Apply

Think about what you have learned about line graphs with two or more lines. With a partner, brainstorm kinds of information that can be shown on this type of graph. Then write a paragraph summarizing the best uses for double-line graphs.

1400

1450

About 1400
• Rise of Kingdom
of Kongo in Africa

CONNECT MAIN IDEAS

Use this organizer to describe the first interactions between Africa, Europe, and the Americas. Write three details to support each main idea. A copy of the organizer appears on page 106 of the Activity Book.

Europe, Africa, and the Americas Interact

Africa and Europe
Europeans forced many Africans to leave their homelands.

1. _____
2. _____
3. _____

A Time of Encounter
The arrival of Europeans in the Americas affected life in both the Western and Eastern hemispheres.

1. _____
2. _____
3. _____

WRITE MORE ABOUT IT

Write a Story Write a story about a young African who has heard that people in nearby communities have been captured and sold as slaves. Describe the young person's feelings on hearing this news. Will this news affect your character's life? If so, how?

Write a Menu Imagine that you have been asked to prepare a dinner for a celebration called the Americas' Gifts to the World. What foods would you serve? Write a menu that includes some of the many foods that came from the Americas.

1492
• Columbus's first voyage to the Americas

1519
• Cortés begins exploration of Mexico

About 1530
• Cartier explores what is now Canada for France

USE VOCABULARY

Use each term in a complete sentence that helps explain its meaning.

1 conquistador
2 encomienda
3 immunity
4 Middle Passage
5 plantation
6 triangular trade

CHECK UNDERSTANDING

7 What did the newer African kingdoms of the 1500s have in common with the older West African empires?

8 What did Idris Aloma do to bring about growth for Kanem-Bornu?

9 What role did women play in the government of Ashanti?

10 What was the Middle Passage?

11 What led the conquistadors to explore the Americas?

12 What happened as the English in the Americas needed more land for settlers and crops?

13 What was the Iroquois League?

THINK CRITICALLY

14 **Think More About It** How did the Portuguese who rented stations along the African coast change the history of Africa?

15 **Past to Present** In what ways are people in the United States still battling racism? What is being done to overcome this problem?

16 **Cause and Effect** What effect do you think Cortés had on Aztec culture?

APPLY SKILLS

Compare Maps Use the maps on pages 460 and 461 to answer these questions.

17 What countries had settlements in South America by 1750?

18 What languages are spoken in South America today?

19 What relation does there seem to be between European claims in South America and the languages spoken there today?

Compare Information on a Double-Line Graph Look in a reference book for the average monthly high and low temperatures for two cities. Use this information to create a double-line graph, with a set of lines for each city. Write five questions that can be answered by studying your graph. Exchange questions and graphs with a classmate. Answer the questions you have received.

READ MORE ABOUT IT

Tomatoes, Potatoes, Corn, and Beans: How the Foods of the Americas Changed Eating Around the World by Sylvia A. Johnson. Atheneum. This book provides detailed descriptions of foods native to the Americas.

Visit the Internet at **http://www.hbschool.com** for additional resources.

CHANGES IN ASIA

"Even though some of the western methods are different from our own . . . there is little about them that is new."

Qing Emperor Kangxi (1662–1722) explaining why China had turned away from European ideas

This painting on silk shows a Ming dynasty empress.

China and Japan
in Early Modern Times

FOCUS

How do peoples' views of their role in the world change over time?

Main Idea As you read, look for changes in the ways the people of China and Japan saw themselves in relation to the rest of the world.

Vocabulary

isolation
calligraphy
Bushido
haiku

While Europe was going through the Renaissance and the Age of Exploration, the societies of China and Japan were also changing. For a time, China renewed contact with the outside world, but this did not go on for long. Soon it closed its borders to outsiders. Japan, too, tried to keep outsiders away. At this time, both countries counted on history and tradition to bring order and keep peace.

Renewed Growth for China

During the mid-1300s the Mongols' dynasty weakened. Convinced that the Mongols had lost the Mandate of Heaven, the Chinese people rebelled. One of the rebel leaders, a former Buddhist monk, took power in 1368. Taking the name Hong Wu, he began the Ming dynasty.

On taking power, Hong Wu said, "I intend to reign like the Tang and Song." True to his word, Hong Wu set up a government based on Confucian ideas. He then started to rebuild the war-torn land. He restored fields, irrigation systems, canals, and roads. Under his program China's economy improved and the population grew. During his later years, however, Hong Wu became very cruel. He had thousands of people thrown into prison or killed. When he died in 1398, few people were sad.

Yong Le (YUHNG LEH), Hong Wu's son, wanted to make China a major force in Asia. He entered into an alliance with Korea and conquered parts of what is now Vietnam. Yong Le also paid for the great ocean voyages of Admiral Zheng He. Through these voyages the Chinese learned much about the rest of the world. At the same time, the fleets gave the world a glimpse of China's strength and wealth. Everywhere the fleets

A traditionally dressed Ming official of the 1600s

During the Ming dynasty, artworks such as this painting (above) and this porcelain vase (right) were created in a distinctly Chinese style. What Ming policies helped to create such a unique style?

visited, people learned of the splendor of the Ming dynasty.

REVIEW *How did China grow under Hong Wu and Yong Le?*

China Looks Inward

Yong Le died in 1424, and China's interest in seafaring ended soon after. In 1433 government officials stopped all oceangoing voyages and destroyed Zheng He's records.

Why did this happen? Perhaps the voyages became too costly. Or perhaps Ming officials agreed with what an earlier emperor had said: "China's territory produces all goods in abundance, so why should we buy useless trifles from abroad?"

Whatever the reason, the Ming rulers would not let merchants trade outside of China. China turned to a policy of **isolation**, or separation from others. For centuries China had been physically separated from most of the world's people. Now the Chinese purposely tried to keep themselves apart from others.

Ming emperors set about building China's strength from within. They made the Great Wall stronger and repaired the Grand Canal. The Ming rulers also offered help to farmers.

While Chinese merchants could not trade with the outside world, they did very well within lands controlled by China. Merchants transported farm products, cloth, iron, and precious metals along China's waterways. Some villages on the waterways became market towns, and many cities grew.

The Ming period was a time of growth for Chinese culture. Ming emperors encouraged learning. Some scholars wrote histories of earlier dynasties. Ming artists took styles of earlier times and improved on them. Two examples are the Chinese art of **calligraphy** (kuh•LIH•gruh•fee), or beautiful handwriting, and the making of porcelain.

Other Ming artists painted beautiful landscapes. Their paintings, however, did not look real. When told that European artists could show perspective, Ming painters were not interested. The Ming wanted to preserve traditional ideas, not adopt new ones.

REVIEW *What important developments took place under Yong Le's successors?*

Pressure from the Outside

The Ming dynasty had turned its back on the outside world, but the outside world still had an interest in China. Foreign traders wanted China's fine porcelain and silks. In 1513 the Portuguese arrived in Guangzhou, hoping to trade with China.

The Portuguese would not give up easily. In 1557 the Chinese allowed them to set up a trading post on an island near Macao (muh•KOW). Later, Spanish, Dutch, and English traders joined the Portuguese. The Ming government, however, kept tight control on contact between the Europeans and the Chinese people.

Surprisingly, the Ming allowed Catholic missionaries into China. These missionaries went there mainly to win converts. Yet they had respect for knowledge and showed interest in Chinese learning. For the most part, though, the Chinese seemed to care little about European knowledge.

In the end, conflicts from within brought down the Ming dynasty. While the people of the Ming period fought one another, invaders from Manchuria in the north swept into China. In the mid-1600s the Manchus set up the Qing (CHING) dynasty. After 300 years the Mandate of Heaven had once again fallen into foreign hands.

REVIEW *What caused the Ming dynasty to fall?*

Regions The empire of the Qing dynasty included all the land that once belonged to the Ming dynasty as well as much additional territory.
■ *What natural feature was the southern border of the land of the Qing?*

The Ming and Qing Dynasties

MANCHURIA

MONGOLIA

TIEN SHAN

Takla Makan (Desert)

KUNLUN SHAN

Plateau of Tibet

HIMALAYAS

GOBI (DESERT)

Mukden

Beijing

Sea of Japan

KOREA

JAPAN

Yellow Sea

Huang He

East China Sea

PACIFIC OCEAN

Chang Jiang

Tropic of Cancer

INDIA

Land controlled by the Ming dynasty, about 1600

Land added by the Qing (Manchu) dynasty, about 1800

Guangzhou

Macao (Portuguese)

VIETNAM

South China Sea

Taiwan

0   250   500 Miles
0   250   500 Kilometers
Two-Point Equidistant Projection

473

Tokugawa Japan

The Japanese also came face to face with Europeans. During the mid-1500s Portuguese merchants arrived at Japanese ports. Some daimyos eagerly traded with the Portuguese. They also welcomed the Christian missionaries who followed the traders.

In the year 1603, when Tokugawa Ieyasu (toh•ku•GAH•wah ee•uh•YAH•soo) became shogun, Japan's attitude toward Europeans changed. The new shogun feared that Christianity would threaten Japan's unity. He drove Christian missionaries out of Japan and allowed European traders to land only at the port of Nagasaki (nah•guh•SAH•kee). A later shogun stopped even this contact. He prevented the Japanese from leaving their islands or having any dealings with foreigners. By 1639 Japan was closed to the rest of the world.

This "closed country" policy was one step the Tokugawa shoguns took to unify Japan.

Unlike the samurai, Japanese ninjas, such as the one shown in this woodblock print, were trained as spies.

They also reformed the feudal system by limiting the authority of the daimyos.

In addition, the Tokugawa shoguns began a rigid class system. They adapted the Confucian idea of classes to Japanese society. Below the shogun were the daimyo and the samurai, or soldiers. Samurai were highly respected. However, they did not lead easy lives. They had to live by a harsh code called **Bushido** (BU•shih•doh), or "the way of the warrior." Above all, Bushido demanded samurai loyalty to the daimyo.

Farmers, who were next in the social rank, had difficult lives as well. Government leaders took part of their crops in taxes. Landlords took their share, too. This left

Japan Under Tokugawa Shogunate

CHINA

Hokkaido

Sea of Japan

JAPAN · Sakata

KOREA

Honshu · Edo (Tokyo)

Kyoto ·

· Osaka

PACIFIC OCEAN

Nagasaki

Shikoku

East China Sea

Kyushu

140°E

130°E

40°N

140°E

30°N

0   150   300 Miles

0   150   300 Kilometers

Two-Point Equidistant Projection

✹ Capital city

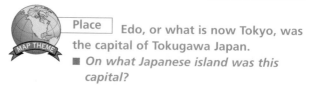

Place — Edo, or what is now Tokyo, was the capital of Tokugawa Japan.

■ *On what Japanese island was this capital?*

many Japanese farmers with barely enough to live on.

In contrast, those at the bottom of the social ladder—craftworkers and merchants—often did well economically. Cities were noisy with the sounds of people working at dozens of trades. Merchants grew rich by buying and selling goods and by lending money to samurai and tenant farmers.

As the merchants grew richer, they became patrons of the arts and literature. Perhaps the most popular writing form of Tokugawa times was the **haiku** (HY•koo), a 17-syllable poem. Without a doubt, the best haiku poet was Matsuo Basho (maht•SOO•oh BAH•shoh). Most of Basho's poems were about nature and had hidden meanings. Some, like this one translated by poet Harry Behn, were humorous:

Craftworkers in Tokugawa Japan had a low social standing but many economic opportunities. These workers were probably paid well for the armor they made.

66 There goes my best hat
as down comes rain on my bald
pate, plop! plop! Oh, well . . . 99

The Tokugawa shoguns' focus on traditional ways brought peaceful times. The Japanese made little progress in science and technology, however, and this hurt their economy.

Dutch traders, who were allowed to visit Japan once a year, brought news of exciting changes in the West. Soon some Japanese began to call for an end to the "closed country" policy.

`REVIEW` *What was Bushido?*

LESSON I REVIEW

Check Understanding

1 **Remember the Facts** What was the "closed country" policy?

2 **Recall the Main Idea** What changes took place in the way China and Japan saw themselves in relation to the rest of the world?

Think Critically

3 **Think More About It** How did the Ming emperors and the Tokugawa shoguns unite their nations and keep order and peace?

4 **Personally Speaking** Do you think that a policy of isolation was wise or unwise for China and Japan? Explain your answer.

Show What You Know

Poetry Activity Find out more about the haiku form of poetry. Practice writing one or two haiku about nature. Then write a haiku that describes the effect of isolation on Tokugawa Japan. Read your haiku to the class.

FOCUS

How can moving to a new place affect both the culture of the newcomers and the culture of the people they meet there?

Main Idea Look for ways the policies of the Ottoman and Mogul empires affected the people they conquered.

Vocabulary

Janissary
grand vizier
sultan

The Ottoman and Mogul Empires

During early modern times, two major Muslim empires grew to rival the greatness of the empires of Europe and the Americas. By the mid-1500s these two Muslim powers controlled lands that reached from southeastern Europe to Tibet. United by a common religion—Islam—the two empires developed cultures that were similar in many ways, including their treatment of the people they conquered.

The Ottoman Empire

The empire of the Ottomans formed gradually. Migrating to southwestern Asia from central Asia, the Ottomans began claiming new lands around 1300. In 1453 the Ottomans, who were Muslim, moved into Asia Minor and captured the city of Constantinople.

When Sultan Mehmed (meh•MET) II captured the city of Constantinople, he believed he had made a prediction come true. The Muslim prophet Muhammad had foretold the rebirth of Constantinople as a great Islamic city. Mehmed made the city, now called Istanbul (is•tuhn•BOOL), the capital of the Ottoman Empire. Under Mehmed, Istanbul again became the greatest city in the Mediterranean region.

A learned man himself, Mehmed valued education. He started colleges and built a magnificent library, hoping to return Istanbul to its former glory as a center of learning. He even invited Christian and Jewish scholars to come to Istanbul. Non-Muslims were allowed to follow the laws of their own religions and their own religious leaders. They paid a special tax called *jizya* to the Ottoman government.

At the same time, Mehmed was a warlike ruler who dreamed of re-creating the Eastern Roman Empire under

The capture of Constantinople strengthened the Ottoman Empire. Sultan Mehmed II began calling the city Istanbul.

Janissaries were soldiers who had been captured by the Ottomans or recruited as young boys and trained for years as fierce warriors.

Islamic rule. To make this dream true, Mehmed built a large and powerful army and an efficient government.

The Ottoman army got its soldiers from every corner of the empire. The best-trained, however, were the soldiers known as **Janissaries** (JA•nuh•sair•eez). Most were former Christians who had been captured or recruited as young boys and then became Muslims. Years of hard training prepared them for one thing—war—and taught them unquestioning loyalty to the sultan. With the Janissaries at its head, Mehmed's army pushed the boundaries of the empire deep into southeastern Europe.

Mehmed often chose non-Turks to govern parts of the empire. The Ottomans picked the most promising from among their enslaved youths to train for government service. After converting to Islam, these boys were sent to special schools. After they finished their training, they were given jobs as officials and advisers. This bureaucracy of slaves made Mehmed's empire run smoothly.

Later sultans built on the foundations laid by Mehmed II. The greatest of these sultans was Süleyman (SOO•lay•mahn) I, who came to power in 1520.

REVIEW *What steps did Mehmed II take to achieve his dream of building a great empire?*

Süleyman the Magnificent

The people of the Ottoman Empire called Süleyman the Lawgiver, but Europeans knew him as Süleyman the Magnificent. Süleyman led his armies into central Europe, capturing the city of Belgrade in 1521. The following year his navy conquered the island of Rhodes. This victory gave the Ottomans control of much of the eastern Mediterranean. Over the next few years, Süleyman seized much of Hungary.

This miniature painting by an Ottoman artist shows a master philosopher and his students.

Besides being a military leader, Süleyman was a patron of the arts. He encouraged poetry and painting and had the architect Sinan (suh•NAHN) plan new buildings for Istanbul.

Süleyman was called the Lawgiver because he made sure that all the people he ruled were treated fairly. He showed by his own example that officials could behave honestly. For advice Süleyman depended on Ibrahim Pasha (ih•brah•HEEM PAH•shah), his **grand vizier** (vuh•ZIR), or chief minister. Europeans who met Ibrahim were surprised to discover that he had once been a slave. Süleyman also asked for the advice of his favorite wife, Roxelana (rahk•suh•LAHN•uh). Like Ibrahim, she had also been a slave.

Süleyman often started wars to gain territory. Yet he brought peace to the lands he conquered. A Venetian ambassador reported:

66 I know of no State which is happier than this one. It . . . is rich in gold, in people, in ships, and in obedience; no state can be compared with it. 99

In 1566 Süleyman died during his last invasion of Europe. With Süleyman's death, the Ottoman Empire slowly began to fade. It lasted until the twentieth century, but it never regained the strength it had under Süleyman.

REVIEW *Why was Süleyman called the Lawgiver?*

Regions After the Ottomans captured Constantinople, they continued to conquer land in Europe.
■ *How would conquering southwestern Europe have benefited the Ottomans?*

The Ottoman Empire

ATLANTIC OCEAN

PORTUGAL
FRANCE
SPAIN
EUROPE
RUSSIA
Danube
Vienna 1683
River
HUNGARY
Mohács 1526
Belgrade
ITALY
Aral Sea
Algiers
Black Sea
Caucasus Mts.
Caspian Sea
ASIA
Lepanto 1571
Constantinople (Istanbul)
ARMENIA
Athens
Asia Minor
Tigris R.
Mediterranean Sea
Rhodes
Crete
Cyprus
Euphrates River
Baghdad
PERSIA
Tripoli
Jerusalem
Persian Gulf
Cairo
AFRICA
ARABIA
EGYPT
Nile River
INDIAN OCEAN

0   300   600 Miles
0   300   600 Kilometers
Two-Point Equidistant Projection

N W E S

Extent of empire by 1680
Battle site

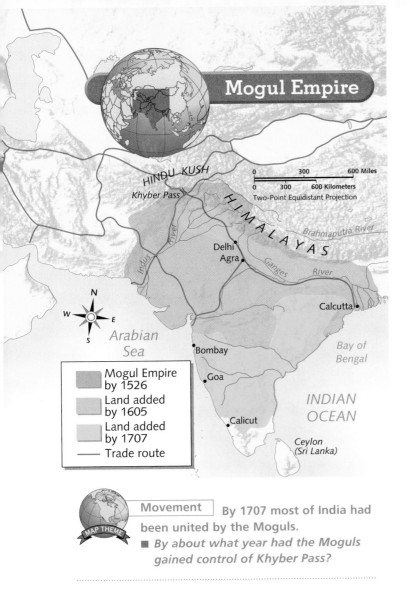

Mogul Empire

HINDU KUSH

Khyber Pass

H I M A L A Y A S

Indus River

Brahmaputra River

Delhi
Agra

Ganges River

Calcutta

Arabian Sea

Bombay

Goa

Bay of Bengal

INDIAN OCEAN

Calicut

Ceylon (Sri Lanka)

0   300   600 Miles
0   300   600 Kilometers
Two-Point Equidistant Projection

N W E S

Legend:
- Mogul Empire by 1526
- Land added by 1605
- Land added by 1707
- — Trade route

Movement By 1707 most of India had been united by the Moguls.

■ *By about what year had the Moguls gained control of Khyber Pass?*

India's Mogul Empire

Farther southeast, in India, another Muslim empire took shape in the 1500s. Much earlier Muslim Turks had gained control of almost all of India. This began a period of unified rule in India that historians call the Delhi sultanate. Under the Muslim **sultans**, or rulers, many Hindus became Muslims. By 1500 the Delhi sultans had begun to lose their hold in India. Central Asian Muslims swept through the Khyber Pass in 1526 and claimed northern India. Their leader, Babur (BAH•ber), founded the Mogul (MOH•guhl) Empire.

The greatest of the Mogul emperors was Babur's grandson, Akbar (AK•ber), who ruled from 1556 to 1605. Akbar, unlike the Delhi sultans, allowed Hindus to freely practice their own religion. He also got rid of the tax

that had been placed on Hindus. Under Akbar, Hindus and other non-Muslims were allowed to become government officials.

Akbar also worked to improve India's economy. He lowered the farmers' taxes and made land reforms. These changes brought about a huge increase in agricultural production. Akbar encouraged merchants to trade with both China and Europe.

Akbar was a man of learning who supported the arts. Among his interests were architecture, painting, and literature. Mogul artists of his time painted in an original style, capturing the smallest of details.

In addition to the arts, religion interested Akbar. He studied not only Islam but also Hinduism, Buddhism, and Christianity. He welcomed priests of all religions in India and eagerly debated them about their beliefs.

A daring military leader, Akbar kept pushing the boundaries of the Mogul Empire south. By 1605, he had united nearly all of India under Mogul rule.

REVIEW *What impact did Akbar have on the Hindus in his empire?*

Babur (the top left figure in this miniature) founded the Mogul Empire. This detailed work of gold (right) belonged to the ruler Akbar.

479

The Taj Mahal was built as a monument to Mumtaz Mahal, Shah Jahan's wife. She died in 1631, only three years after Shah Jahan became emperor. He is buried by her side beneath the floor of the Taj Mahal.

India After Akbar

Those who ruled after Akbar did not have his ability. His son Jahangir (juh•HAHN•gir) liked hunting more than governing. He left the running of the empire to his wife, Nur Jahan (NOOR juh•HAHN), who ruled well and fairly.

The next Mogul ruler, Shah Jahan (SHAH juh•HAHN), came to power in 1628. He was a cruel man with a surprising love of beauty. He personally directed the construction of some of the world's most beautiful buildings. The Taj Mahal (TAHZH muh•HAHL) stands today as Shah Jahan's greatest cultural contribution.

Made of white marble inlaid with gold and precious stones, the Taj Mahal took 22 years to build.

In 1658 Shah Jahan's son Aurangzeb (ow•ruhng•ZEB) seized power. He ended the policy of treating Hindus as equals. Also, to pay for his military campaigns, he taxed the people heavily. Because of his actions Hindus and Muslims alike rebelled. The Mogul Empire became much smaller. The loss of central control in India made it easier for Europeans to gain land there.

REVIEW *How did later Mogul emperors help make it easy for Europeans to take over much of the Indian subcontinent?*

LESSON 2 REVIEW

Check Understanding

1 Remember the Facts What did the Ottomans and the Moguls have in common?

2 Recall the Main Idea How did Ottoman and Mogul policies affect the peoples they governed?

Think Critically

3 Think More About It Would Süleyman be a successful world leader today? Explain your answer.

4 Cause and Effect How did Akbar's treatment of Hindus help unify the Mogul Empire?

Show What You Know

Speech Activity Imagine that you are a historian living in the Ottoman Empire or the Mogul Empire in the 1600s. Give an oral report on how life has changed in the empire from the early 1500s up to your time.

Read a Population Pyramid

1. Why Learn This Skill?

A **population pyramid** is a graph that shows how a country's population is divided by age. It also shows what part of each age group is made up of males and of females. A pyramid's shape depends on the country's birth rate (the number of births each year for every 1,000 people) and death rate (the number of deaths each year for every 1,000 people). The shape also depends on the amount of immigration to and from the country. Knowing how to read a country's population pyramid can tell you a lot of information about that country.

2. Understand the Process

The population pyramids below show the present-day populations of the United States and India by age groups.

The pyramids are made up of several bars. Each bar extends left and right from the center line. The bars show the percentage of males and of females in each age group.

Look at the shapes of the two pyramids. The shape of the United States' pyramid shows that its population is growing very slowly. The United States has a higher percentage of people over the age of 50 than India has. Less than 8 percent of the United States' population is under age 5. The shape of India's pyramid is quite different. Its rows get much shorter as the pyramid gets higher. This shows that the population of India is very young.

3. Think and Apply

Use the graphs to answer the questions.

1 What percentage of the population of the United States is in your age group?

2 Are there more males or more females in this group?

3 Which of the two countries has a larger percentage of people under 15 years old?

4 What generalizations can you make about the populations of the two countries?

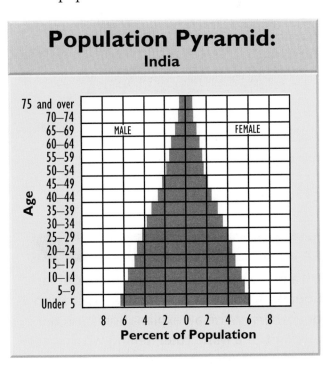

Population Pyramid: United States

Population Pyramid: India

1350   1400   1450

1368
• Ming dynasty gains
Mandate of Heaven
in China

1433
• Ming government
stops oceangoing
voyages

CONNECT MAIN IDEAS

Use this organizer to show that you understand changes in Asia between 1300 and 1700. Write two details to support each main idea. A copy of the organizer appears on page 111 of the Activity Book.

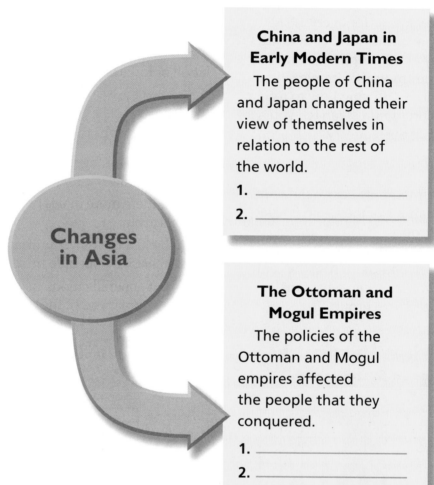

China and Japan in Early Modern Times

The people of China and Japan changed their view of themselves in relation to the rest of the world.

1. _____
2. _____

Changes in Asia

The Ottoman and Mogul Empires

The policies of the Ottoman and Mogul empires affected the people that they conquered.

1. _____
2. _____

WRITE MORE ABOUT IT

Write an Explanation In the 1400s China turned to a policy of isolation, or separation from others. Write an explanation from the viewpoint of a Ming ruler, telling why this policy was necessary.

Write a Persuasive Letter Imagine that you are a merchant in Japan. Write a letter to the government explaining why Portuguese merchants should or should not be allowed to enter Japanese ports.

1520
• Süleyman I rules Ottoman Empire

1603
• First Tokugawa shogun in Japan

1605
• Akbar unites most of India under Mogul rule

USE VOCABULARY

Write a term from this list to complete each of the sentences that follow.

Bushido   **haiku**   **sultan**

calligraphy   **Janissary**

1 ____ was "the way of the warrior."

2 ____ is beautiful handwriting.

3 A ____ was a well-trained Ottoman soldier.

4 A ____ is a 17-syllable poem.

5 A ____ is a Muslim ruler.

CHECK UNDERSTANDING

6 In what ways did Chinese culture grow during the Ming period?

7 What was the first European nation to set up a trading post in China?

8 What brought an end to China's Ming dynasty? What dynasty followed the Ming? How did this dynasty gain control?

9 Why did Tokugawa Ieyasu drive Christian missionaries from Japan?

10 What is the present-day name of the city of Constantinople?

11 What made Akbar such a good ruler for the Moguls?

THINK CRITICALLY

12 **Cause and Effect** Suppose China had continued to explore the world in the late 1400s. What effect might this have had on today's world?

13 **Think More About It** Some boys volunteered to be Janissaries in the Ottoman army. Why do you think they did this?

14 **Explore Viewpoints** At certain times in history, United States citizens have wanted a policy of isolation. What are some of the good points of isolation? What is good about not being isolated?

APPLY SKILLS

Read a Population Pyramid Use the population pyramids on page 481 to answer these questions.

15 In India, what age group has the most people? What age group has the fewest people?

16 In the United States, what age group has the most people? What age group has the fewest people?

17 Why do you think the shapes of the population pyramids for India and the United States are so different?

READ MORE ABOUT IT

The Boy and the Samurai by Erik Christian Haugaard. Houghton Mifflin. Saru, an orphan, helps a samurai flee to a more peaceful life.

HARCOURT BRACE

Visit the Internet at **http://www.hbschool.com** for additional resources.

Chapter 15 • **483**

F·O·O·D
America Gave the World

Who could imagine Italian food without tomatoes? Irish stew without potatoes? Indian curry without chili peppers to make it hot? Or Ghanaian stew without peanuts?

Yet none of these traditional foods of Europe, Asia, and Africa could have developed without ingredients that came from the Americas. When the earliest Americans began to farm, they domesticated many wild plants unknown in other parts of the world. Throughout both continents, they developed corn, several kinds of beans, including kidney beans, snap beans, and lima beans, and squashes like zucchini and pumpkins. North American Indians called corn, beans, and squash the "three sisters." Together these foods gave Native Americans a balanced diet.

Different areas of the Americas made their own contributions to the world's dinner tables. On islands throughout the Caribbean, native peoples raised peanuts and sweet potatoes. In the eastern woodlands of North America, peoples collected sap from maple trees and boiled it down into maple syrup and sugar. In the jungles of Central America, other peoples found cacao beans and vanilla pods. In the high Andes, still others grew potatoes and preserved them by freeze-drying. Chili peppers, avocados, cranberries, tomatoes, and eggplants are all foods that originated in the Americas.

So, the next time you enjoy popcorn, spaghetti, pumpkin pie, a baked potato, or hot chocolate, think about the Native American farmers. It was they who gave key ingredients to these popular foods.

Think and Apply

Think about the different foods you eat during one week. Then use library resources to find out where key ingredients of these foods first came from. Using this information, create a quiz on these foods and places for friends and family members.

BUILDING CITIZENSHIP

HARCOURT BRACE

Visit the Internet at
http://www.hbschool.com
for additional resources.

CNN Turner Le@rning

Check your media center or classroom video library for the Making Social Studies Relevant videotape of this feature.

VISUAL SUMMARY

Summarize the Main Ideas
Study the pictures and captions to help you review the events you read about in Unit 7.

Dramatize the Story
This visual summary shows the meeting of different cultures. Select one such meeting and act out this encounter.

1 Changes in European ways of thinking encouraged individualism and creativity, bringing about a period now known as the Renaissance.

4 The lifeways of people in the Americas changed with the arrival of Europeans.

2 European nations began to explore and claim land overseas.

3 Europeans changed life in Africa by enslaving many people there and forcing them to leave their homelands.

5 China and Japan tried to keep from being changed by other cultures.

6 The growth of the Ottoman and Mogul empires affected the ways of life of the peoples they conquered.

487

USE VOCABULARY

Use each term in a sentence that will help explain its meaning.

1. patron
2. perspective
3. movable type
4. telescope
5. clergy
6. heresy
7. Columbian exchange
8. circumnavigation
9. racism
10. Bushido

CHECK UNDERSTANDING

11. What change took place in European art during the Renaissance?

12. What effect did Martin Luther's actions have on religion in Europe?

13. What led Europeans to explore overseas?

14. How did Spain and Portugal divide the undiscovered world between them?

15. How was the life of an African slave in 1700 different from the life of a slave who lived centuries earlier?

16. How did Hong Wu rebuild China during the Ming dynasty?

17. What steps did the Tokugawa shoguns take to unify Japan?

THINK CRITICALLY

18. **Think More About It** Why did the Renaissance scholars think it was important to understand how things worked?

19. **Explore Viewpoints** What viewpoint did Ferdinand and Isabella hold about religion in Spain? What viewpoint do you think the Moors held? What viewpoint do you think Jews living in Spain held?

20. **Past to Present** How is the world today affected by the encounters of Europeans and Native Americans?

21. **Cause and Effect** How did China's isolation preserve traditional ideas about art?

22. **Personally Speaking** Suppose you were asked to rename this unit. What name would you choose? Why?

APPLY SKILLS

Compare Maps Use the map below and the one on page 439 to answer the questions.

23. Which European countries were mostly Protestant in 1618? Which are mostly Protestant today?

24. What generalization can you make about religions in Europe today compared to religions in Europe in 1618?

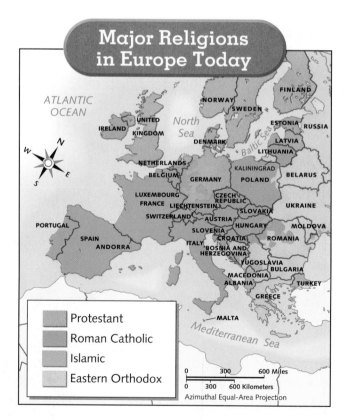

Major Religions in Europe Today

ATLANTIC OCEAN

NORWAY · FINLAND · SWEDEN · IRELAND · UNITED KINGDOM · North Sea · DENMARK · ESTONIA · RUSSIA · LATVIA · LITHUANIA · Baltic Sea · NETHERLANDS · BELGIUM · GERMANY · KALININGRAD · POLAND · BELARUS · LUXEMBOURG · FRANCE · LIECHTENSTEIN · CZECH REPUBLIC · SLOVAKIA · UKRAINE · SWITZERLAND · AUSTRIA · HUNGARY · MOLDOVA · PORTUGAL · SLOVENIA · CROATIA · ROMANIA · SPAIN · ANDORRA · ITALY · BOSNIA AND HERZEGOVINA · YUGOSLAVIA · BULGARIA · MACEDONIA · ALBANIA · TURKEY · GREECE · MALTA · Mediterranean Sea

- Protestant
- Roman Catholic
- Islamic
- Eastern Orthodox

0 300 600 Miles
0 300 600 Kilometers
Azimuthal Equal-Area Projection

REMEMBER

- Share your ideas.
- Cooperate with others to plan your work.
- Take responsibility for your work.
- Help one another.
- Show your group's work to the class.
- Discuss what you learned by working together.

Tell a
Story

Imagine you are an Aztec storyteller. It is your responsibility to remember and retell the history of the Aztecs. Retell the story of the encounter between Motecuhzoma and Cortés.

Write a
Letter

Imagine you are part of the group that traveled with Jacques Cartier on his explorations of Canada. Write a letter to a friend in your homeland of France, describing how you bartered with the Indians for furs and skins.

Design a
Scene

Draw a scene that could be painted on a porcelain vase. The scene should show one of the following:

- Chinese reaction to outsiders during the Ming dynasty
- the growth of Chinese culture during the time of the Ming dynasty
- the rigid class system of the Tokugawas of Japan

Unit Project Wrap-Up

Hold a Renaissance Fair Review the notes you have taken so that your group can give a presentation on your topic during the fair. Use cardboard, paint, ribbons, flowers, and other items to decorate your booth. Your group may want to dress in Renaissance costumes.

TIMES OF RAPID CHANGE

OSWEGO STARCH FACTORY

FIRE PROOF STOREHOUSE

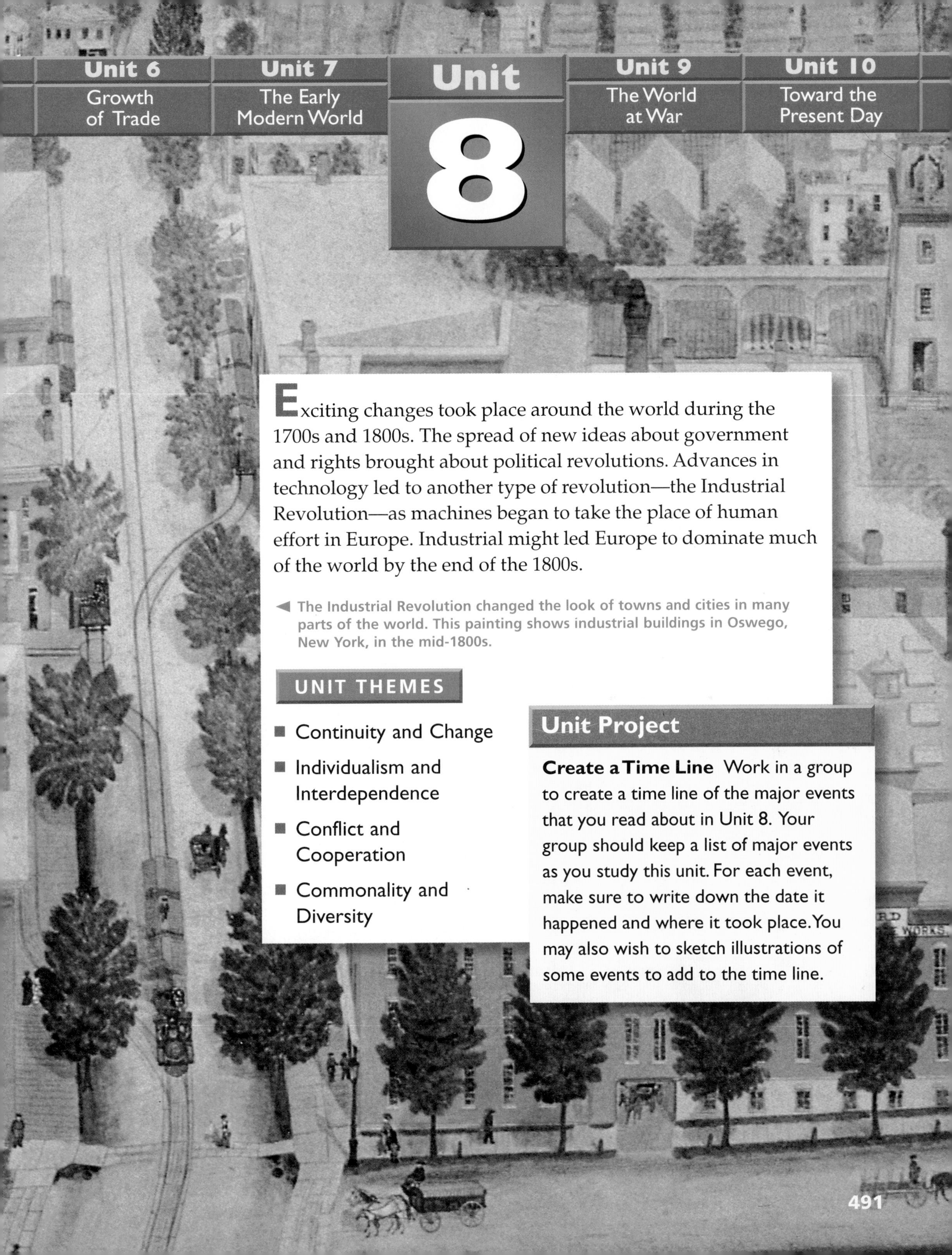

Exciting changes took place around the world during the 1700s and 1800s. The spread of new ideas about government and rights brought about political revolutions. Advances in technology led to another type of revolution—the Industrial Revolution—as machines began to take the place of human effort in Europe. Industrial might led Europe to dominate much of the world by the end of the 1800s.

◄ The Industrial Revolution changed the look of towns and cities in many parts of the world. This painting shows industrial buildings in Oswego, New York, in the mid-1800s.

UNIT THEMES

- Continuity and Change
- Individualism and Interdependence
- Conflict and Cooperation
- Commonality and Diversity

Unit Project

Create a Time Line Work in a group to create a time line of the major events that you read about in Unit 8. Your group should keep a list of major events as you study this unit. For each event, make sure to write down the date it happened and where it took place. You may also wish to sketch illustrations of some events to add to the time line.

491

UNIT 8 PREVIEW

Greenland

Iceland

ALASKA
(UNITED STATES)

CANADA

NORTH AMERICA

Great Lakes

Montreal

PACIFIC
OCEAN

San Francisco

UNITED STATES

Mississippi River

New York City

Los Angeles

ATLANTIC
OCEAN

N
W E
S

HAWAII
(UNITED STATES)

Gulf of Mexico

Cuba

MEXICO

BRITISH HONDURAS

0   1,000   2,000 Miles
0   1,000   2,000 Kilometers
Miller Cylindrical Projection

Mexico City

HONDURAS

GUATEMALA
EL SALVADOR
COSTA RICA

NICARAGUA

Caribbean Sea

VENEZUELA

Caracas

BRITISH GUIANA

DUTCH GUIANA

COLOMBIA

FRENCH GUIANA

ECUADOR

Amazon River

BRAZIL

SOUTH AMERICA

Lima

Salvador

PERU

BOLIVIA

Raw Materials		Industry	
	Cocoa		Coal mining
	Coffee/Tea		Copper mining
	Cotton		Textile manufacturing
	Diamonds		Iron and steel manufacturing
	Gold		Machinery and hardware
	Rubber		
	Sugar		
	Tobacco		
	Wood		

PARA.

Rio de Janeiro

CHILE

Buenos Aires

URUGUAY

ARGENTINA

1775   1800   1825

1776
American colonies declare independence
PAGE 499

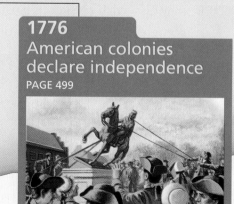

1825
Most of Latin America is independent
PAGE 510

European Interests Around the World, 1870

NORWAY
SWEDEN
BRITAIN
North Sea
DEN.
NETH.
Berlin
London
Paris
GER.
FRANCE
AUSTRIA-HUNGARY
SPAIN
Rome
ITALY
GREECE
Constantinople
OTTOMAN EMPIRE
ALGERIA
MOROCCO
TRIPOLI
Cairo
Suez Canal
EGYPT
ARABIA
OMAN
Mediterranean Sea

EUROPE
Moscow
RUSSIA
Volga R.
Black Sea
Caspian Sea
Aral Sea
AFGHANISTAN
PERSIA
Persian Gulf
BELUCHISTAN
Indus R.
Ganges R.
INDIA
Goa
(PORTUGAL)

ASIA
Lake Baikal
Huang He
HIMALAYAS
Chang
Jiang
CHINA
Peking
Sea of Japan
Hong Kong
(BRITAIN)
Manila
South China Sea
Philippine Islands

FRENCH INDO-CHINA

Nile R.
Red Sea
AFRICA
Lagos
GOLD COAST
GABON
RÍO MUNI
ZANZIBAR
ANGOLA
INDIAN OCEAN
PORT. EAST AFRICA
Cape Town
CAPE COLONY
Port Natal

DUTCH EAST INDIES

AUSTRALIA
Melbourne

Legend

- ● City
- - - - - Undefined border

Controlled by

- Britain
- Denmark
- France
- Netherlands
- Portugal
- Spain
- Independent nation
- Unclaimed by European powers

Timeline

1850 — 1875 — 1900

About 1850
Industrial Revolution underway in Britain
PAGE 515

1860
Garibaldi frees much of southern Italy
PAGE 536

493

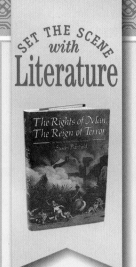

THE RIGHTS
OF MAN,
THE REIGN
OF TERROR

THE STORY OF THE FRENCH REVOLUTION

Written by Susan Banfield

In the 1700s powerful monarchs ruled the nations of Europe. Most lived in luxury in their palaces, completely isolated from the people they ruled. These monarchs did not know what the lives of their people were like—nor did they seem to care.

Read now how the rich—in this case, King Louis (LOO•ee) XVI—and the poor in France began the day. Think about the contrast between the ways of life of the two families described in the story.

This portrait of French king Louis XVI by Francois Callet shows
the wealth of the royal family before the French Revolution.

The King yawned as one of his valets[1] threw back the heavy brocade[2] curtains that surrounded the royal bed on four sides. The light that streamed through the tall casement windows now flooded the entire room. The King rose at once. After he had said his morning prayers, the elaborate process of dressing him began. First, one of his valets shaved him. Then, one at a time, each nobleman who had earned the privilege of waiting on the King handed him the article that was officially his to present. One might hand him his stockings, another his satin breeches,[3] yet another his garters.[4] Once he had been dressed, the King's hair was carefully curled and powdered.

Meanwhile, a similar little drama was being enacted[5] in the bedroom of the Queen. There, at the center of a circle of softly swishing silks, stood Queen Marie Antoinette. She shivered in the chill morning air as she waited for the appointed lady-in-waiting to hand her her undergarments. Several others then helped her into her dress—one of the three new ones she had bought for that week.

The royal husband and wife would not see each other until noon Mass.[6] They would then take the midday meal together, seated side by side at a small table. Dinner was far from an intimate meal for two, however. The women of the royal family and other noblewomen of the court sat on stools encircling the royal table. Beyond them was a crowd of spectators eager for the chance at a glimpse of their rulers. Servants brought out one heavy silver serving dish after another. The King, conscious of the dozens of pairs of eyes that followed his every move, might help his wife to the dishes she fancied[7] that day, but it was unlikely that there would be any further conversation between them. That would have been too informal.

Meanwhile, the sun was also rising on a crude mud cottage in Picardy.[8] Jean Flavier and his family could not see it, as windows were a luxury way beyond their means. But the light creeping in under the door let them know it was time to be up and about. Jean's wife Marie shivered as she quickly pulled on her tattered old linen dress and wooden shoes.

She ripped off a piece of bread for herself and her youngest son. The bread was made of grain so coarsely ground that pieces of straw still stuck in the loaf. Marie wrapped another hunk of the bread for her husband to take out to the fields, sticking in a few small apples along with it.

In sullen silence Jean Flavier took the small parcel that his wife pressed into his hand. Feelings of rage and hopelessness swirled inside him. The bailiff[9] was due to come any day to inquire about the grain they had borrowed from the lord last winter. After the Church took its due from their small garden, what was left would scarcely last them till Christmas. Surely their house would be stripped.

The sun was rising up above the trees now. Jean knew he was late again in setting out for the fields. But he could not seem to care.

As you read more about Europe in the 1700s, you will discover that this contrast between the lives of the rich and the poor helped bring about a revolution in France.

---

[1] **valets:** (va•LAYS) male servants
[2] **brocade:** heavy cloth with raised designs
[3] **breeches:** short pants reaching to just below the knees
[4] **garters:** straps for holding up long stockings
[5] **enacted:** acted out
[6] **Mass:** a Roman Catholic religious service

[7] **fancied:** liked; had a fondness for
[8] **Picardy:** (PIH•ker•dee) region in northern France
[9] **bailiff:** official who makes arrests

This painting, *The Delivery Woman* by Jean Baptiste Chardin, shows what life was like for the poor of France.

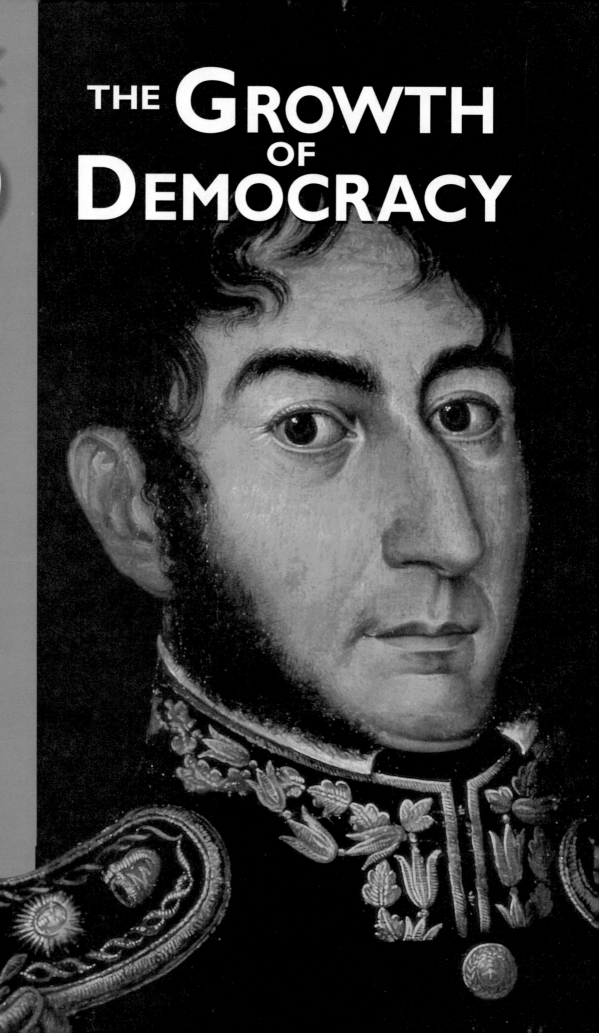

THE GROWTH OF DEMOCRACY

"Hear, O mortals, the sacred cry of Liberty."

Beginning of Argentina's national anthem, *Himno Nacional*

Portrait of José de San Martín

Democratic Revolutions

FOCUS
Why do leaders of today take different types of actions?

Main Idea Look for ways different leaders affected history during the 1700s.

Vocabulary
Declaration of
  Independence
English Bill of Rights
Enlightenment
confederation
Constitution of the
  United States
  of America
Bill of Rights
Declaration of the
  Rights of Man
  and of the Citizen
Reign of Terror
Napoleonic Code

By the 1700s strong monarchs ruled most European countries. Many of them held absolute authority and gave few rights to those they ruled. In some countries people began to call for greater freedom and a greater voice in the running of the government. In time determined individuals stepped forward to lead the fight for independence and freedom.

The American Revolution

During the summer of 1776, American colonists took to the streets to celebrate. "Church bells rang," an observer said. "Cannons were discharged, and every face appeared joyful." The colonists had just heard readings of the **Declaration of Independence**. This document proclaimed the colonies' freedom from Great Britain. Great Britain was the name given to the Kingdom of England and Wales and the Kingdom of Scotland when they united.

For Thomas Jefferson, the main author of the Declaration, the reason for declaring independence was simple. The British, he said, did not care about the rights of the American colonists. Yet the rights of individuals had roots deep in the history of Britain. The Magna Carta, signed in 1215, became the base of laws that protected the rights of everyone in Britain. More than 470 years later, in 1689, the **English Bill of Rights** granted even more individual rights.

In the Declaration, Jefferson told what these British laws were supposed to protect. He explained that people have certain rights and that "among these are Life, Liberty, and the pursuit of

Minutemen, volunteers who could be ready with a minute's notice, fought for American independence.

The painting (right) by Louis Couder shows General Washington at the Siege of Yorktown during the American Revolution. The sign (above) seeks soldiers for Washington's Army.

Happiness." He said that when a government violates, or fails to protect, these rights, the people have a responsibility to change the government or end it. In the case of the American colonists, the change was a very great one—a revolution.

English Bill of Rights

Below are some of the important points of the English Bill of Rights of 1689:

Suspending of laws . . . by [royal] authority without consent of parliament is illegal.

The freedom of speech and debates . . . in Parliament [should not be] questioned in any court. . . .

United States Bill of Rights

Amendment 1
Congress shall make no law respecting an establishment of religion, or prohibiting the free exercise thereof; or abridging the freedom of speech, or of the press; or the right of the people peaceably to assemble, and to petition the government for a redress of grievances.

The ideas that inspired the American Revolution came from thinkers of the **Enlightenment**. This movement, which began in France in the early 1700s, focused on ways to create a government that would protect the rights of individuals. Leaders of the Enlightenment believed that reason—the act of thinking things through—would lead the way to a more nearly perfect society. Some important thinkers of the Enlightenment were the philosophers Voltaire (vohl•TAIR), Jean-Jacques Rousseau (ZHAHN•ZHAK roo•SOH), and John Locke.

Jefferson's writings, which reflected Enlightenment ideas, made him the voice of the American Revolution. It was George Washington, however, who led the colonists to victory in their Revolutionary War with Britain. Washington took command of the American forces in 1775. With tattered clothing and few supplies, the American farmer-soldiers were an unusual army. Washington knew that he had to keep their hopes high even if he believed they had little chance of winning. With this in mind, Washington treated his soldiers with respect. They repaid him with loyalty.

In 1781, after six years of fighting, the colonists won their independence. Now they needed to continue the work of forming a government. Because the former colonists disliked the idea of strong government, the United States became a **confederation**, or loose group of governments. The central government had little authority.

Under this government, the states did not always cooperate. Many state leaders agreed that a change was needed. In 1787 Washington led a meeting that drew up a new plan for government—the **Constitution of the United States of America**.

The Constitution established a democratic republic, in which citizens select people to represent them in government. In some ways the republic of the United States was like the Roman government of long ago. However, the writers of the Constitution made sure that they balanced the freedoms of the citizens with the need for a strong government. Under the Constitution the states and the central government shared authority.

The central, or national, government was divided into three branches—one to make the laws, one to interpret them, and one to enforce them. Each of these branches was designed to check and balance the authority of the others. A **Bill of Rights** was added to the Constitution in 1789. It protected individual rights—including freedom of speech and freedom of religion.

One important difference between this new democratic government and those of the past was that its highest leaders were

Abigail Adams, wife of the second U.S. President, John Adams, believed that women should take part in making laws.

Eastern North America, 1783

0   200   400 Miles
0   200   400 Kilometers
Albers Equal-Area Projection

BRITISH NORTH AMERICA

Lake Superior
Lake Michigan
Lake Huron
Lake Ontario
Lake Erie
Mississippi River
Ohio River

Maine (Part of Mass.)
NEW HAMPSHIRE
MASSACHUSETTS
NEW YORK
RHODE ISLAND
CONNECTICUT
PENNSYLVANIA
NEW JERSEY
DELAWARE
MARYLAND
VIRGINIA
NORTH CAROLINA
SOUTH CAROLINA
GEORGIA

SPANISH LOUISIANA

SPANISH FLORIDA

ATLANTIC OCEAN

Gulf of Mexico

BAHAMA ISLANDS

CUBA

Caribbean Sea

HAITI

- United States
- British possession
- Spanish possession
- French possession
- Disputed territory

Regions In 1763 the British controlled all the land east of the Mississippi. By 1783, they had lost most of this land.

■ *What did the British control in 1783?*

responsible to the people who elected them. In the United States of the late 1700s, though, only white male property owners could vote. The Constitution gave women few rights. It also did little for Africans in the United States, whether free or enslaved. Even so, the Constitution stated a very important idea— that the government belonged to the people. This idea would soon echo around the world.

REVIEW *What roles did Thomas Jefferson and George Washington play in the American Revolution?*

The French Revolution

France, long an enemy of Britain, sided with the Americans in their fight for independence. Helping the Americans, however, drained the French treasury. The fact that French royalty lived in luxury did not help. Louis (LOO•ee) XVI, the king of France, decided he could solve his country's money problem by raising taxes. So in 1788 he called for a meeting of the Estates-General.

The Estates-General was made up of representatives from France's three estates, or social classes. The First Estate—the clergy—and the Second Estate—the nobles—owned most of the land, held most of the high government positions, and paid little in taxes.

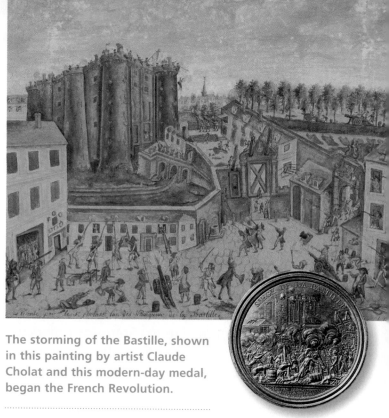

The storming of the Bastille, shown in this painting by artist Claude Cholat and this modern-day medal, began the French Revolution.

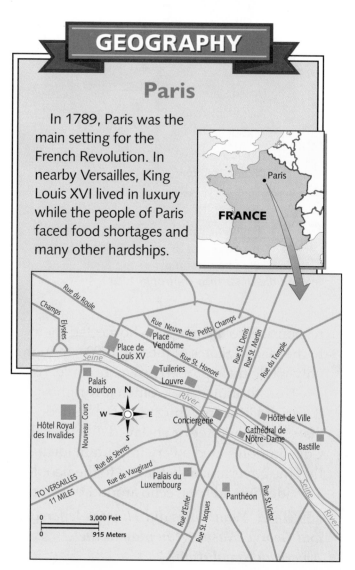

GEOGRAPHY

Paris

In 1789, Paris was the main setting for the French Revolution. In nearby Versailles, King Louis XVI lived in luxury while the people of Paris faced food shortages and many other hardships.

FRANCE

Paris

Rue du Roule
Champs Élysées
Rue Neuve des Petits Champs
Place Vendôme
Place de Louis XV
Rue St. Denis
Rue St. Martin
Rue du Temple
Seine
Rue St. Honoré
Tuileries
Louvre
Palais Bourbon
N
W E
S
River
Nouveau Cours
Hôtel Royal des Invalides
Conciergerie
Hôtel de Ville
Cathédral de Nôtre-Dame
Bastille
Rue de Sèvres
Rue de Vaugirard
Palais du Luxembourg
TO VERSAILLES 11 MILES
Panthéon
Rue St. Victor
Rue d'Enfer
Rue St. Jacques
Seine River

0 3,000 Feet
0 915 Meters

The Third Estate included everyone else, from doctors to merchants to peasants. Its members had little say in the government but paid nearly all the taxes.

The members of the Third Estate resented paying the most taxes when the rich lived in luxury and paid little. To make matters worse a poor wheat harvest made bread hard to get and very expensive. Many people were forced to spend money on taxes instead of on the food they needed to survive.

Every time the Third Estate tried to set up a fairer way of taxing, the votes of the other Estates stopped it. In June 1789 the Third Estate broke away from the Estates-General. It called itself the National Assembly and claimed the right to make laws.

Shocked by this action, Louis XVI brought soldiers into Paris. The people of France decided they would need weapons if the soldiers attacked. On July 14, 1789, an angry crowd marched through the streets of Paris, shouting, "To the Bastille! To the Bastille!" The Bastille (bas•TEEL) was a prison where Louis XVI's army also kept weapons. The crowd stormed the Bastille, killed many guards, and took the weapons. They then destroyed the Bastille, freeing the prisoners. The French Revolution had begun!

REVIEW *How did Louis XVI's actions help start the French Revolution?*

A Time of Terror

To keep violence from spreading, the National Assembly quickly passed new laws. It ended the special rights held by the First and Second Estates. It also approved the **Declaration of the Rights of Man and of the Citizen**. The document promised freedom of speech and religion and equal treatment of all citizens under the law.

These rights were not given to women, even though some women had been leaders of the attack on the Bastille. Later, in 1789, women led a march all the way from Paris to Louis XVI's palace at Versailles (ver•SY). The purpose of the march was to protest the lack of bread to feed their families.

Many women were angry that they received so little respect for what they had done. One woman, Olympe de Gouges (oh•LAMP duh GOOZH), wrote a paper titled *The Rights of Woman*, calling for fair treatment for all people. Still the National Assembly did nothing about women's rights.

In 1791 the National Assembly adopted a new constitution for France. The king would remain on the throne, but an elected assembly would make the laws.

Louis XVI publicly agreed to the new constitution. Secretly, however, he asked the monarchs of other countries to invade France with their armies and overthrow the revolutionaries. Learning of this, an angry crowd put the king and his wife, Marie Antoinette (an•twuh•NET), in prison. Soon after that, a new assembly met to write another constitution. The new constitution stripped Louis of all his authority and made France a republic.

At the same time, a group of young revolutionaries took over the government. They wanted to break with the past and build a new society for France. They began in January 1793 by ordering Louis XVI executed. The executioners used a machine called a guillotine (gih•luh•TEEN), which beheaded its victims with a swift drop of a heavy blade. The executions of Marie Antoinette and hundreds of nobles followed.

Shocked by this violence, a number of European countries formed an alliance to fight the French Republic. In addition, rebellions against the revolution sprang up across France. The revolutionaries reacted with a **Reign of Terror**, or a period of violence and rule by fear, against their political enemies. Anyone who questioned the revolution was killed. In 1794 the National Assembly ordered the arrest and execution of the

This eighteenth-century drum (left) was used during the time of the French Revolution. The engraving (far left) shows women marching to Versailles to protest a bread shortage. A poor harvest had made bread expensive and hard to get. Because members of the Third Estate had to pay high taxes, they could not afford to buy the bread.

revolutionaries. The next year the Directory, a group of five people, took over the French government.

REVIEW *Why did the focus of the French Revolution change from human rights to terror?*

Napoleon Bonaparte

Throughout the Reign of Terror, France fought the armies of the European alliance. A French officer named Napoleon Bonaparte (nuh•POH•lee•uhn BOH•nuh•part) won great fame fighting the enemies of France.

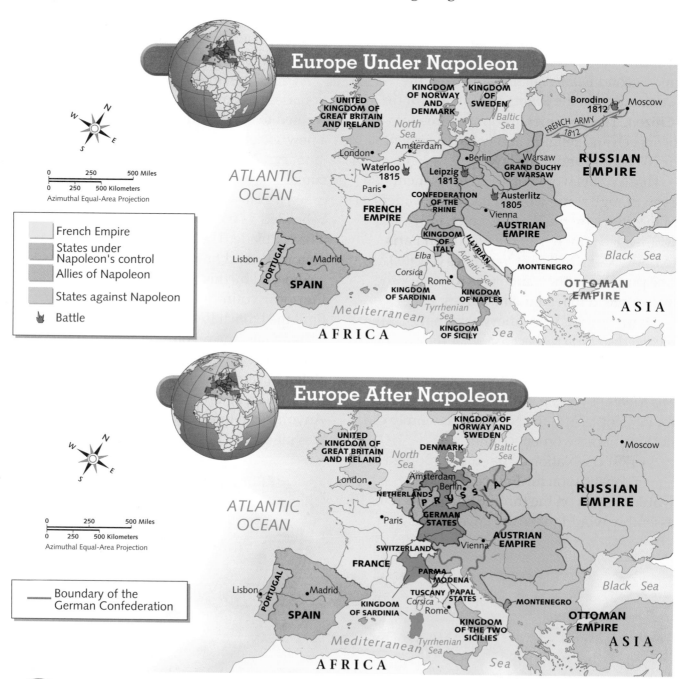

Europe Under Napoleon

French Empire
States under Napoleon's control
Allies of Napoleon
States against Napoleon
⚜ Battle

Europe After Napoleon

—— Boundary of the German Confederation

Regions After Napoleon's defeat, France lost control of much of the territory it had gained.

■ *In what ways was the shape of the French Empire under Napoleon different from the shape of France after 1815 following the leader's defeat?*

Napoleon (center and on coin) brought his code of law to every country he conquered. His last stand was the Battle of Waterloo (left).

Napoleon supported the ideas of the revolution but also had a hunger for power. In November 1799 he overthrew the Directory and took control of the French government.

Napoleon soon changed the French way of governing. Perhaps his most important action was to oversee the writing of a set of laws known as the **Napoleonic Code**. This code guaranteed some of the freedoms people had fought for in the revolution. French law is still based on it today.

Despite his interest in law and rights, Napoleon ruled with an iron hand. In 1804 Napoleon went so far as to crown himself Emperor of France. He then led his army on a campaign to spread the ideas of the revolution. By 1812 the empire reached from Spain to the Russian border.

Napoleon's ambition eventually led to his downfall. In the summer of 1812, he marched into Russia with an army of 600,000 soldiers. Unexpectedly, his supplies ran out as the harsh winter weather set in. French soldiers died by the thousands. At the end, only 100,000 ragged soldiers were left.

Other defeats followed the disaster in Russia. Napoleon's empire began to crumble. Armies from Britain and its European allies finally defeated Napoleon at the Battle of Waterloo in 1815.

REVIEW *How did Napoleon affect Europe?*

LESSON 1 REVIEW

Check Understanding

1. **Remember the Facts** How were Louis XVI and Napoleon alike? How were they different?

2. **Recall the Main Idea** How did different types of leaders affect the revolutions in America and France during the late 1700s?

Think Critically

3. **Past to Present** Can you think of a recent political event in which one person changed the outcome? Explain your answer.

4. **Cause and Effect** How did the American Revolution help bring about the French Revolution?

5. **Think More About It** If bread had been plentiful in France, do you think the Third Estate still would have sought greater individual rights?

Show What You Know

News-Writing Activity Imagine that you are a reporter working for a weekly newspaper in the late 1700s. Write a brief article describing one of the leaders mentioned in the lesson. Focus on how that individual's qualities helped him or her influence the way events developed.

Read a Political Cartoon

1. Why Learn This Skill?

Some cartoons have a serious message purposely planned to make you think. A cartoon on the editorial page of a newspaper presents the artist's point of view about people and current events in politics and government. This kind of cartoon is called a **political cartoon**. Knowing how to read a political cartoon can help you understand its meaning and the artist's point of view.

2. Early Political Cartoons

In 1754 Benjamin Franklin drew one of the first political cartoons. In his cartoon Franklin urged the 13 British colonies in North America to unite for protection against the French and the American Indians. Franklin's cartoon showed the colonies as parts of a cut-up snake, with the caption *Join, or Die*.

By the middle 1800s drawing cartoons had become a popular way for artists to express their ideas and opinions. Honoré Daumier (ah•nuh•RAY dohm•YAY) became the leading cartoonist in France in the years after Napoleon's rule. In 1835 the French artist drew a cartoon in which he attacked the

You are free to speak by Honoré Daumier

French government for not allowing free speech. Daumier's cartoon carried the caption *You are free to speak*.

3. Understand the Process

To understand the meaning of a political cartoon, you first need to identify its details. Look for a caption or any writing on the drawing that can help you identify the people or the setting. Many cartoonists use symbols, like Franklin's snake. You will need to identify the ideas the symbols stand for. In Daumier's cartoon, unbalanced scales carved on the judge's desk stand for injustice.

Cartoonists often use exaggeration when drawing people. The way the people look can help you know the artist's opinion of these people. What tells you that Daumier did not like the government officials he drew?

4. Think and Apply

Choose a current event, and begin collecting political cartoons about it. Make a booklet of the cartoons, and write a short description explaining each one. Draw your own political cartoon to add to the booklet.

Join, or Die by Benjamin Franklin (Note: The colonies of Delaware and Georgia are not represented.)

Democratic Ideas in Latin America

LESSON 2

FOCUS
Why do people seek to change their government?

Main Idea As you read, look for reasons the peoples of Latin America wanted to change their governments.

Vocabulary
peninsular
Creole
hacienda
mestizo
mulatto
junta

Across the Atlantic Ocean, in what is often called Latin America, Spain and Portugal had created huge empires. Latin America consists of Mexico, Central America, South America, and nearby islands. The region got its name because most of its people speak languages that come from Latin, such as Spanish and Portuguese. In the 1700s the colonies in Latin America were under the complete control of Spain or Portugal. People who lived in those colonies had little say in the government. However, the spirit of revolution soon spread to Latin America from North America and France. Before long the Latin American colonies wanted independence.

Colonial Society and Religion

Society in colonial Latin America was divided into several social classes. Family and place of birth decided a person's social rank. Members of the highest class were called **peninsulars**. These were people born in Spain and Portugal, on Europe's Iberian Peninsula. Peninsulars held the important jobs in the government, the army, and the Catholic Church. They usually did not live permanently in Latin America.

Creoles (KREE•ohlz), people who had Spanish or Portuguese parents but had been born in Latin America, made up the next class. Many Creoles owned mines, ranches, or **haciendas** (ah•see•EN•dahs)—huge farms or plantations—and were very wealthy. Some Creoles held positions in local government, yet they were not respected by the peninsulars. As a German traveler said, "The lowest, least educated, and uncultured European believes himself superior to the white born in the New World."

The owner (right) and the manager (left) of a Mexican hacienda

This painting, by an unknown eighteenth-century artist, shows a Mexican mestizo shoemaker and his family.

Far below the peninsulars and the Creoles came people of mixed blood. **Mestizos** (mes•TEE•zohs), people of both European and native descent, lived mainly in the Spanish colonies. **Mulattoes** (moo•LAH•tohs), people of both African and European descent, were the most common mix in Portuguese America. Over the years millions of enslaved Africans had been brought to Latin America.

Some mestizos and mulattoes owned small farms. Most, however, were poor. Even so, people of mixed blood had a better life than Africans and Indians.

Africans and Indians were at the bottom of the social ladder in Latin America. Some free Africans lived in the towns and cities. Most Africans, however, were slaves on sugarcane, coffee, or tobacco plantations. Indians were free, but they were looked upon as little more than slaves. Most worked on haciendas and ranches for very low pay.

The Catholic Church was important to people of all classes in Latin America. Catholic priests, who came to the Americas with the early explorers and conquistadors, converted millions of Indians to the Catholic faith. The missionaries did not treat the Indians as equals, but most felt a duty to help them. Often the missionaries alone protected the Indians against bad treatment by colonial landowners.

Religion was the center of life for both rich and poor. The largest building in a Latin American town was always its church. Every important religious holiday brought crowds to the towns for parades and carnivals. Also, for many people in Latin America, the church was the only place where they could get an education.

REVIEW *How was society in colonial Latin America organized?*

The church was an important part of every Latin American town. Below is an early Latin American church, Santa Prisca Cathedral in Taxco, Mexico, built around 1750. The inset shows an inside view of another Latin American church from about this same time.

Moves Toward Latin American Independence

Many people were unhappy with colonial Latin American society and government, especially the Creoles. The Creoles had blood ties to Europe, but they did not think of themselves as Spanish or Portuguese. They resented being told what to do by a government across the sea. The representatives of that government, the peninsulars, behaved as if they thought they were better than the Creoles. This angered the Creoles. They wanted to be free of the peninsulars' rule and to control their own lives.

Many Creoles had traveled and studied in Europe and knew about the ideas of the Enlightenment. They knew that their neighbor to the north, the United States, had thrown off its colonial ruler. They also were

Latin America, 1830

(1821) Year of independence

UNITED STATES
Gulf of Mexico
MEXICO (1821)
CUBA
PUERTO RICO
BRITISH HONDURAS
UNITED PROVINCES OF CENTRAL AMERICA (1823)
HAITI (1804)
VENEZUELA (1830)
BRITISH GUIANA
DUTCH GUIANA
FRENCH GUIANA
Isthmus of Panama
NEW GRANADA (1830)
ECUADOR (1830)
PERU (1821)
BRAZIL (1822)
BOLIVIA (1825)
PARAGUAY (1811)
CHILE (1818)
URUGUAY (1828)
ARGENTINA (1816)
ATLANTIC OCEAN
PACIFIC OCEAN
Tropic of Cancer
Equator
Tropic of Capricorn

0   750   1,500 Miles
0   750   1,500 Kilometers
Robinson Projection

Regions By 1830 most Latin American countries had gained independence.
■ *Which colonies in South America had not gained their independence by 1830?*

BIOGRAPHY

Tupac Amarú
1742–1781

A revolt against Spanish rule in Latin America took place in Peru in 1780 before the successful revolt in Haiti. It was led by Tupac Amarú (too•PAHK ahm•ar•OO), a descendant of the last Inca ruler. For years Tupac Amarú had tried to get rights for the Inca people through the courts. Nobody listened, however. In 1780 Tupac Amarú led an uprising. "From this day forth," he told his people, "no longer shall the Spaniard feast on your poverty." Tupac Amarú was taken prisoner and executed in 1781. Although the uprising lasted for two more years, the Inca people were unable to free themselves from Spanish rule.

aware of the democratic revolution going on in France. These two revolutions showed them that people could fight for freedom and win.

The Creoles, however, did not lead the first successful revolt in Latin America. People in the French colony of St. Domingue (SAN duh•MANG) in the Caribbean fought the first war for independence.

In 1793 the French government abolished slavery in all its colonies. The freed slaves in St. Domingue, however, wanted more than an end to slavery. They wanted independence. Led by Toussaint-Louverture (TOO•san LOO•vair•tyoor), who had been a slave, they fought the French army for control of the colony and won. In 1804 they founded the

Chapter 16 • **509**

independent country of Haiti. Others, including the dissatisfied Creoles, would soon follow Haiti's lead.

REVIEW *Why did the Creoles dislike being ruled by distant governments?*

Independence for Latin America

Events in France had provided the spark for the revolution in Haiti. These same events lit the fires of revolution throughout Latin America. In 1808 Napoleon conquered Spain and put his brother Joseph on the throne. The Creoles did not accept Joseph as the rightful king. With him on the throne, the Creoles saw no reason to stay loyal to Spain.

In 1810 Creoles in the city of Buenos Aires (BWAY•nohs EYE•rays) in Argentina formed an independent governing council, or **junta** (HUN•tah). This council replaced Spanish rule in the southern part of South America. Then in 1816 Argentina's Creoles declared total independence from Spain.

Creoles in the northern city of Caracas (kah•RAH•kahs), Venezuela, also set up a junta in 1810. Their leader, Simón Bolívar (see•MOHN boh•LEE•var), wanted to break with Spain and to create a United States of South America. It was not easy to meet those goals, however. Creoles and peninsulars loyal to Spain fought against Bolívar. Then in 1814 the rightful Spanish king won back his throne and sent soldiers to South America to take back the land controlled by Bolívar.

Bolívar proved to be a skilled military leader. His soldiers were loyal to him and showed confidence in him. By 1822 Bolívar and his soldiers had freed New Granada (now Colombia), Venezuela, and Ecuador from Spanish rule. Because of this success, Bolívar became known as the Liberator.

Another leader, José de San Martín (sahn mar•TEEN), led the fight for independence in southern South America. In 1817 San Martín started a daring and dangerous campaign. He led an army of 5,000 soldiers from Argentina across the snowcapped Andes Mountains to attack Spanish soldiers

Simón Bolívar, shown on a military campaign (left), freed many South American countries. General José de San Martín announced the independence of Peru at Plaza de Armas (below) in 1821.

in Chile. Soldiers of African heritage made up more than one-fourth of his army. They had been promised their freedom in return for military service. As one of San Martín's generals said, "They were distinguished throughout the war for their valor, constancy, and patriotism."

San Martín's army drove the Spanish out of Chile. San Martín moved into Peru, where he encountered Bolívar and his freedom fighters. San Martín soon withdrew. He did not want any disagreements over who would lead the fight. Bolívar went on to free Peru from Spanish rule. By 1825 almost all of Spanish South America had gained independence.

In Mexico the revolution took a different route. In 1810 a Creole priest named Miguel Hidalgo (ee•DAHL•goh) led a rebellion of Indians and mestizos. He called for independence, the return of

Indian lands to the Indians, and an end to slavery. In less than two months, 80,000 people joined him. However, Hidalgo could not control this huge, angry army. Soldiers stopped the rebels at the gates of Mexico City. Hidalgo was executed, but the revolution did not end. Independence for Mexico finally came in 1821, when Creoles, army officers, and the clergy united to demand a break with Spain.

Brazil, a Portuguese colony, gained independence peacefully. Prince Pedro, the son of the king of Portugal, ruled the huge colony. He listened to the Brazilians' demands for freedom. In 1822 Pedro said, "I proclaim Brazil forevermore separated from Portugal." Then he tore the symbol of Portugal from his hat and tossed it to the ground. Three years later, Portugal agreed to grant Brazil its independence.

Prince Pedro freed Brazil from the rule of Portugal and of his father, King John VI.

REVIEW *How were the pathways to independence different in Brazil, Mexico, and Spanish South America?*

LESSON 2 REVIEW

Check Understanding

1. **Remember the Facts**   What three European countries controlled the Latin American colonies?

2. **Recall the Main Idea**   Why did people in the Latin American colonies seek to change their governments?

Think Critically

3. **Past to Present**   In which countries today are people trying to bring about changes in their governments? Why do they want to make these changes?

4. **Think More About It**   Would the Latin American countries have rebelled against Spain and Portugal if the American and French revolutions had not taken place? Explain your answer.

5. **Cause and Effect**   How did events in Europe help start revolutions in Latin America?

Show What You Know

Speech-Writing Activity
Imagine that you are a Creole leader in the early 1800s. You want your friends to join the independence movement. Write a brief speech that explains why you think your colony should break away from Spanish rule.

CHAPTER 16

REVIEW

1750 — 1775

1776
- American colonies declare independence

CONNECT MAIN IDEAS

Use this organizer to show that you understand how democracy spread to several countries. Write three details to support each main idea. A copy of the organizer appears on page 115 of the Activity Book.

The Growth of Democracy

Democratic Revolutions

Different kinds of leaders affected history in France and in what is now the United States during the late 1700s.

1. ______________________
2. ______________________
3. ______________________

Democratic Ideas in Latin America

The peoples of Latin America wanted changes in their governments.

1. ______________________
2. ______________________
3. ______________________

WRITE MORE ABOUT IT

Write a News Story Write a news story about an event of the 1700s that changed history. You might write about the storming of the Bastille in France, George Washington leading his army into battle, or one of the Latin American revolutions. Present your story to the class as though you were a news reporter at the scene.

Write a Biographical Sketch Research and then write a biographical sketch about one of these people: Thomas Jefferson, George Washington, Napoleon, Abigail Adams, or Simón Bolívar. Include information on how this individual tried to bring change to the world. If you wish, add illustrations. Then share your completed biography with others.

1800	1825	1850

1789
• French Revolution begins

1815
• French Emperor Napoleon is defeated

1825
• Almost all of Spanish South America is independent

USE VOCABULARY

Write the term that correctly matches each meaning.

Enlightenment	**peninsular**
mestizo	**Reign of Terror**
Napoleonic Code	

1 a person who was born in Spain or Portugal but lived in Latin America

2 a movement to create a perfect society that would protect individual rights

3 a period of rule by fear

4 laws that guaranteed freedoms that people fought for in the French Revolution

5 a person of European and native South American heritage

CHECK UNDERSTANDING

6 According to Thomas Jefferson, why were the American colonists fighting for independence?

7 How did King Louis XVI decide to solve his country's money problems?

8 What role did the Bastille play in the fight for rights in France during the late 1700s?

9 What was the result of the Reign of Terror?

10 What lands did Napoleon bring under his control?

11 Where was Napoleon finally defeated?

12 Who were the Creoles?

13 Which was the first Latin American country to gain independence?

THINK CRITICALLY

14 **Past to Present** How would life in the United States be different if the Declaration of Independence had never been written?

15 **Think More About It** Do you think followers of the Enlightenment would be satisfied with the democratic societies of today? Explain your answer.

16 **Cause and Effect** What effect do you think the American Revolution had on people in Latin America?

APPLY SKILLS

Read a Political Cartoon Create a political cartoon that shows an opinion for or against an event in this chapter. Do you think your cartoon would have been popular or unpopular at the time of the event? Explain. Exchange your cartoon with that of a classmate. See if you understand the message of the cartoon you receive.

READ MORE ABOUT IT

The American Revolution by Alden R. Carter. Franklin Watts. This book discusses the causes, campaigns, events, as well as the aftermath of the American Revolution.

HARCOURT BRACE

Visit the Internet at **http://www.hbschool.com** for additional resources.

THE BEGINNING OF THE
INDUSTRIAL AGE

"It is the Age of Machinery, in every outward and inward sense of the word."

Thomas Carlyle, nineteenth-century British historian

The Industrial Revolution

LESSON
1

FOCUS
How can technology change people's ways of life?

Main Idea As you read, look for ways the new technology of the Industrial Revolution changed life in Britain.

Vocabulary
Industrial Revolution
crop rotation
textile
cottage industry
factory
patent
raw material
entrepreneur

New ideas about government brought about political revolutions in the late 1700s. New technology brought about another great change, the **Industrial Revolution**. This revolution, which began in Britain, forever changed the way people lived and worked.

Changes in Agriculture

Around the mid-1700s some British farmers began to use new technology in agriculture. Instead of wooden plows, they used iron ones. Instead of scattering seeds on top of the soil, they used the seed drill invented by a farmer named Jethro Tull. This invention planted seeds in neat rows. A farming method called crop rotation was also developed during 1732. **Crop rotation** means alternating the kind of crops planted in a field from year to year. Because different crops use different nutrients, the soil remains fertile. Crop rotation made it possible to plant farmland for a longer period of time.

More than technology brought changes to agriculture during this time. A growing demand for wool created the need for more land on which to graze sheep. Wealthy farmers bought up many small plots of land and then fenced in large areas to use as private pastures. Up to this point farmers had been able to use some of this land for raising crops and as pastureland to feed their animals. They could no longer do this now that the land was enclosed, or fenced. They either had to rent land from the owners of large farms or stop farming altogether.

Many of these farmers soon left the countryside to look for work in towns and cities. They

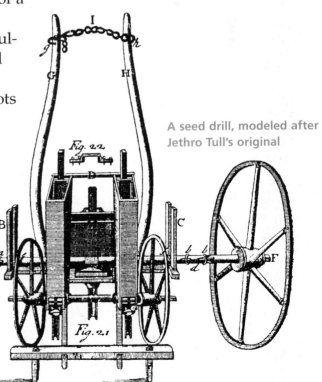

A seed drill, modeled after Jethro Tull's original

This 1834 engraving (left) shows calico cloth being made in a British factory. Before the mid-1700s textile-making was a cottage industry (above).

arrived just as the Industrial Revolution was beginning.

REVIEW *What new ways of farming did British farmers introduce?*

The Age of Machines

The Industrial Revolution started quietly with people tinkering in back rooms and workplaces all over Britain. The result was an explosion of technology that improved the way products were made.

During the early days of the Industrial Revolution, most of the new technology was developed for the **textile**, or cloth, industry. Until the mid-1700s textile making was a **cottage industry**. Families worked in their small homes, or cottages, to make cloth from cotton and wool supplied to them by a merchant. First, they spun the cotton and wool into thread by hand. Then they wove the thread into cloth on wooden looms. They returned the finished cloth to the merchant, who paid them for their work.

Soon people looked for ways to speed up production. The invention of the flying shuttle in 1733 made it possible to weave cloth twice as fast as on the old looms. Flying shuttles worked so well that it was hard to

get enough thread for them. As many as five people had to spin thread to make enough to use with just one flying shuttle.

In 1764 James Hargreaves, a weaver, solved this problem with the invention of the spinning jenny. With the jenny, one worker could spin eight threads at the same time.

Two other inventions, the spinning frame and the power loom, not only increased cloth production but also changed where the work was done. Families could not afford to buy these machines. Besides, the machines were too big to fit into a house. So rich textile merchants would buy a number of the machines and put them in **factories**—large buildings where goods are made. Workers were forced to move near these locations.

Because the large spinning and weaving machines depended on the power of running water, early factories were built near fast-flowing rivers. This changed in 1769, when James Watt built an efficient steam engine.

By 1800 about 1,200 steam engines were in use across Britain. They powered machines that spun thread or wove cloth, and later even powered locomotives. Steam became the power of the Industrial Revolution.

REVIEW *How did new technology change the textile industry?*

Britain Leads the Way

The Industrial Revolution began in Britain partly because of the inventions of people like James Watt and James Hargreaves. Experimenting was encouraged throughout Britain. Business owners ran contests and offered prizes for the best new ideas. Almost every large city had a science club, where inventors could meet and talk about their projects. All of this led to a rush of inventions. More than 1,000 new machines received patents in Britain between 1760 and 1789. A **patent** is a legal document guaranteeing that only the inventor has the right to make and sell the new idea or product.

Several other factors helped the British lead the Industrial Revolution. First, Britain had many natural resources, such as iron and coal. Iron was used to make machine parts. Coal was burned to run steam engines. Second, Britain's colonies supplied industries with low-cost cotton, lumber, wool, and other **raw materials** used to manufacture goods. Also, growing numbers of people in Britain and its colonies meant that more manufactured goods were needed. British factory owners looked for ways to meet this growing demand.

Through trade Britain had become a very wealthy country. British banks had large amounts of money to lend to entrepreneurs (ahn•truh•pruh•NERZ). An **entrepreneur** is a person who takes a financial risk by putting up money to start a business. Of course, there is always some risk that the business will fail and that the owner will lose the money. Some British entrepreneurs failed, but many did very well.

REVIEW *Why did Britain lead the way in the Industrial Revolution?*

James Watt showed that steam engines could produce large amounts of power. This steam engine was based on Watt's design.

LEARNING FROM TIME LINES The period from the late 1700s through the 1800s is remembered as a time of invention.

■ *Why did the invention of different types of machines increase after 1769?*

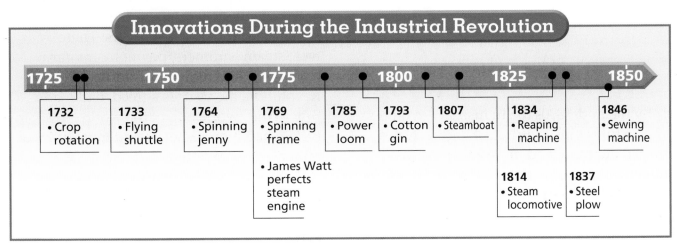

Innovations During the Industrial Revolution

1725 — 1750 — 1775 — 1800 — 1825 — 1850

- 1732 • Crop rotation
- 1733 • Flying shuttle
- 1764 • Spinning jenny
- 1769 • Spinning frame
- 1769 • James Watt perfects steam engine
- 1785 • Power loom
- 1793 • Cotton gin
- 1807 • Steamboat
- 1814 • Steam locomotive
- 1834 • Reaping machine
- 1837 • Steel plow
- 1846 • Sewing machine

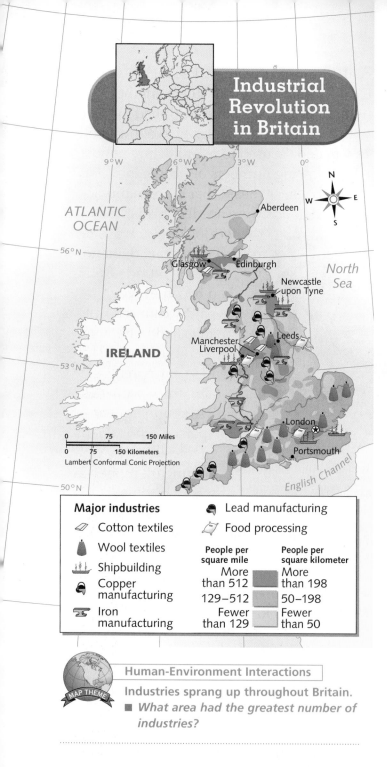

Industrial Revolution in Britain

Major industries

- 🡢 Cotton textiles
- 🡢 Wool textiles
- ⚓ Shipbuilding
- 🡢 Copper manufacturing
- 🡢 Iron manufacturing
- 🡢 Lead manufacturing
- 🡢 Food processing

People per square mile		People per square kilometer
More than 512		More than 198
129–512		50–198
Fewer than 129		Fewer than 50

Human-Environment Interactions

Industries sprang up throughout Britain.
■ *What area had the greatest number of industries?*

New Ways of Working and Living

By the mid-1800s the Industrial Revolution was in full swing in Britain. Huge factories turned out more and more goods each day, greatly affecting workers' lives. Cities became crowded because many families came from the country in search of work. They jammed into poorly built houses. Streets were filthy, and the air was full of smoke from the factory chimneys. Unhealthful living conditions led to the spread of disease. Illnesses claimed the lives of many, especially young children.

People faced difficult working conditions as well. Most men worked at least 12 hours a day 6 days a week for very low pay. Women and children worked just as long and just as hard but for even less pay. As one textile worker said in 1832,

> 66 Whilst the engine runs the people must work—men, women, and children are yoked together with iron and steam. 99

Children often had the most dangerous jobs. Some were made to climb on the spinning machines to repair broken threads—while the machines were running!

Over time the Industrial Revolution did improve the lives of workers. Although wages were low, they were steady. Workers could buy meat and vegetables once in a while to go with their daily bread and cheese.

REVIEW *What was life like for working people during the Industrial Revolution?*

Worldwide Impact

In 1851 Britain hosted a show called the Great Exhibition in the Crystal Palace in London. People came from all over Europe and the United States to get a good look at Britain's technological wonders. There were steam hammers, power looms, farm machinery, and more. The Industrial Revolution, the visitors agreed, had made Britain the "workshop of the world." By 1851 Britain had more factories and more miles of railroad than any other country.

By 1851 the United States, Germany, Belgium, and France had also started to industrialize. These countries used Britain as a model for their own industrial revolutions.

The smoke from factories made cities grim places to live in (left). Nineteenth-century factories often relied on child labor (above).

Economic success gave Britain and the other industrial nations new strength in dealing with other nations and peoples. In search of new markets—places to sell their goods—they expanded their colonies in Asia. They also forced China and Japan into signing new trade agreements. Next, the European industrial countries turned to Africa. This huge continent had plenty of inexpensive raw materials for Europe's factories and possible markets for its goods.

The strength of the industrial nations sent a clear message to the world: industrial countries would be the winners. In Asia, the country of Japan listened to this message. The Japanese government quickly passed laws that helped make it easier to build new industries. By 1900 Japan, too, was having an industrial revolution.

REVIEW *What steps did the industrial countries take to find new markets and new sources of raw materials?*

LESSON 1 REVIEW

Check Understanding

1 **Remember the Facts**   What were some of the machines that changed the textile industry?

2 **Recall the Main Idea**   How did the new technology of the Industrial Revolution change life in Britain?

Think Critically

3 **Past to Present**   Name one recent development in technology. How has it changed everyday life?

4 **Think More About It**   In your opinion, which invention developed during the Industrial Revolution has changed everyday life the most? Why?

Show What You Know

Simulation Activity   With a small group, hold a meeting of a science club similar to the ones in Britain in the late 1700s. At the meeting, discuss the latest technology of the period and how it affects people's lives.

Read and Compare Population Maps

1. Why Learn This Skill?

The two maps on these pages show the population of cities in Europe and the Mediterranean region in 1715 and 1815. Map A shows the area before the Industrial Revolution. Map B shows the area after it changes because of the industrialization that began in Britain. Knowing how to read and compare population maps of cities can help you see patterns in the way cities grow during times of great economic progress.

2. Understand the Process

Look at the keys of both population maps. The map keys tell you that the different sizes of the dots stand for different ranges of population. The smallest dot on the maps stands for a city with a population of 30,000 to 50,000 people. The next largest dot stands for a city of 50,000 to 80,000 people. The largest dot, which appears on Map B only, stands for a city of more than 500,000 people. These symbols

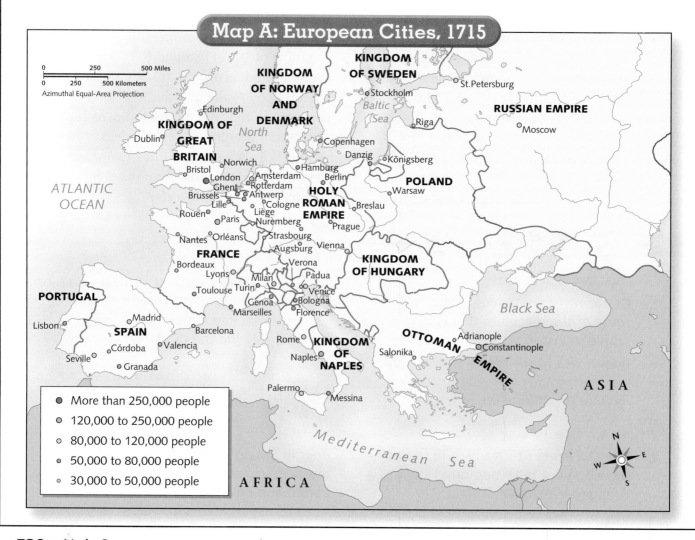

Map A: European Cities, 1715

0   250   500 Miles
0   250   500 Kilometers
Azimuthal Equal-Area Projection

KINGDOM OF SWEDEN
KINGDOM OF NORWAY AND DENMARK
KINGDOM OF GREAT BRITAIN
RUSSIAN EMPIRE
HOLY ROMAN EMPIRE
POLAND
FRANCE
KINGDOM OF HUNGARY
PORTUGAL
SPAIN
KINGDOM OF NAPLES
OTTOMAN EMPIRE

ATLANTIC OCEAN
North Sea
Baltic Sea
Black Sea
Mediterranean Sea

St.Petersburg · Stockholm · Moscow · Edinburgh · Dublin · Riga · Copenhagen · Danzig · Königsberg · Norwich · Bristol · London · Amsterdam · Hamburg · Berlin · Ghent · Rotterdam · Warsaw · Brussels · Antwerp · Breslau · Lille · Cologne · Rouen · Liège · Prague · Paris · Nuremberg · Nantes · Orléans · Strasbourg · Augsburg · Vienna · Bordeaux · Verona · Lyons · Padua · Toulouse · Turin · Milan · Venice · Génoa · Bologna · Marseilles · Florence · Madrid · Barcelona · Rome · Lisbon · Córdoba · Valencia · Naples · Salonika · Adrianople · Constantinople · Seville · Granada · Palermo · Messina

AFRICA · ASIA

- More than 250,000 people
- 120,000 to 250,000 people
- 80,000 to 120,000 people
- 50,000 to 80,000 people
- 30,000 to 50,000 people

do not give exact populations, but they do help you compare city sizes. Now use the information on both maps to answer the questions that follow.

1 Which city, London or Paris, had more people in 1715?

2 Did London or Paris have more people in 1815? Explain your choice.

3 What other cities in Europe were about the size of Paris in 1815?

4 What city or cities had more than 120,000 people in 1715?

5 What cities had more than 120,000 people in 1815?

6 What are five cities that appear on both maps and that had fewer than 50,000 people living in them in 1715?

7 What generalization can you make about the population growth of cities in countries where the Industrial Revolution took place?

8 What generalization can you make about the population growth of cities between 1715 and 1815?

3. Think and Apply

Study the population information given on the maps. Then use charts, graphs, or tables to show the same information for some of the cities. You might make a table comparing the ten largest cities in 1715 with the ten largest in 1815. You might make a bar graph comparing the numbers of cities in Britain, France, Italy, Germany, and Russia. Display your charts, graphs, and tables on a classroom bulletin board.

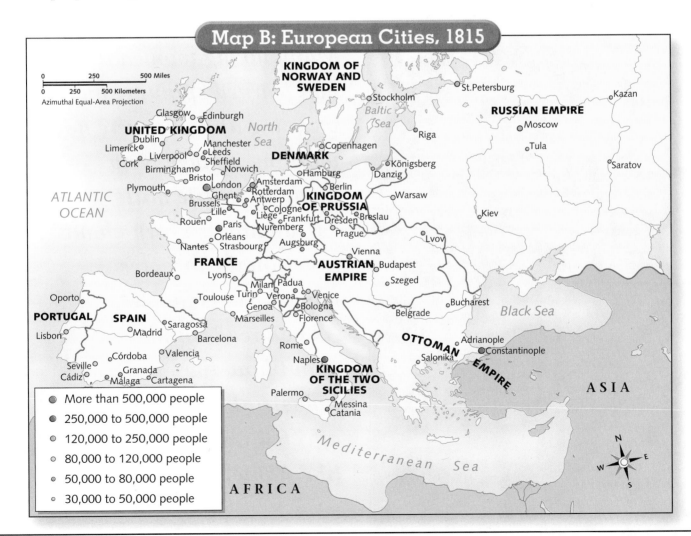

Map B: European Cities, 1815

Legend:
- More than 500,000 people
- 250,000 to 500,000 people
- 120,000 to 250,000 people
- 80,000 to 120,000 people
- 50,000 to 80,000 people
- 30,000 to 50,000 people

THE Clock

by James Lincoln Collier and
Christopher Collier

By the early 1800s the Industrial Revolution had begun to take hold in the northeastern United States. Many young women who had learned spinning and weaving at home were now working in huge New England textile mills.

Read now a story about a fictional character named Annie Steele. As you read, think about how the Industrial Revolution affected textile workers like Annie.

Scene at an American textile mill in the 1800s

ON Monday I started to work at the mill. There were eight of us girls, and we were put up on the second story in a room of our own to keep us from distracting the boys. I was glad about that in one way, for it made me blush when the boys winked at me like that; but in another way I was disappointed, for I was mighty curious about those New York boys, and wanted to hear their stories and find out what New York was like.

But still, it was nice to be with some girls. I knew most of them from church, anyway, although not as well as I knew Hetty Brown. Hetty's ma was an old friend of my ma, going way back to when Ma first came to Humphreysville with Pa. Naturally, we visited back and forth with them, especially during the winter, at times when things on the farm were slow. Hetty was short and plump, and always looked on the bright side of things. If you told Hetty you weren't feeling good, she'd say it was probably something you ate and you'd feel better soon; and if you said it looked like rain, she'd say it wouldn't last long. Hetty was cheerful to be around.

All the girls worked on slubbing billies. A slubbing billy was really a machine for spinning. But instead of having one little spindle for twisting the wool into yarn, it had eight big ones. It looked like a table without a top—just a frame on legs. The spindles were at one end, about three feet from the other end. The yarn stretched from one end to the other. At the opposite end from the spindles there were two girls, each with a big basket of rolags.[1] We worked just like I did at home in the parlor at the spinning wheel, picking up the rolls of wool, twisting them between our thumb and fingers onto the end of the spinning yarn. You had to watch out for the same things as home—bunching, or stretching too much so the connection broke. Only we didn't march back and forth by the

---

[1] **rolags:** rolls of wool to be spun

Young women operate looms at a Massachusetts factory.

walking wheel[2]; we just stood in one place all day; and that was much more tiresome than all that walking.

There were some other differences too. First off, the noise. You could hear the great wheel creaking as it turned in the water outside, below the slubbing-room window. And you heard the main axle that came from the waterwheel into the mill, turning its gears and making all the belts turn that then turned the axles that went to each machine. And then every machine made its own whirring, or clanking, or banging, or humming. You had to speak up real loud to be heard.

The other big difference was the speed the spindles turned at without stopping. There would be no time out for tea, I could see that. Hetty told me that each of our machines could turn out three or four times as much yarn in a day as the fastest spinner could on a wheel. And the machine yarn was stronger and smoother than the homespun, she said. Pa was right about one thing; the wages I earned would buy a lot more yarn than I could spin in the same time at home. Except, of course, that's not what Pa was going to spend my wages on.

They rang the mill bell at four-thirty in the morning to wake everybody up. But if the wind was wrong we couldn't hear it out on the farm, so George[3] would wake me up. George slept in the back of the house and when the animals started moving around in the morning they'd wake him up. He'd climb up the loft ladder, put his head over the top, and call my name. I'd jump up and dress in two minutes, come down the loft ladder, and grab a piece of johnnycake[4] to eat on the way to the mill. It didn't take me more than twenty minutes to get to the mill, if I hurried.

---

[2] **walking wheel:** a high wheel used in spinning; the spinner has to walk back and forth
[3] **George:** Annie's brother
[4] **johnnycake:** a kind of bread made with cornmeal

They rang the mill bell again at five o'clock. We were supposed to be ready to start work then. At seven o'clock the bell rang again for breakfast, and again at noon for dinner, and again at five o'clock to let us quit and go home. From where I stood at the slubbing billy in the wool mill, I could see the bell tower, which was on the cotton mill. There was a clock in the bell tower, and I could see that, too, and now I knew what it meant to work by clock time, instead of sun time.

With sun time, the way we always worked before, and our grandpas and grandmas before us, and their grandpas and grandmas before them, you could rest a little when you were tired, and take a drink of something when you were thirsty, or a bite of bread and cheese when you were hungry. But with clock time you weren't allowed to get tired or hungry or thirsty on your own; you had to wait until the clock told you it was time to be thirsty or tired. I wasn't used to it.

Back on the farm Ma and me would spin all the livelong day half the winter, it seemed like. And if it wasn't spinning it was cutting and sewing to make frocks for ourselves and trousers and shirts for Pa and George. But now and again, when we felt like it, we'd stop working and rest. Ma'd make tea and we'd eat a baked apple left over from supper with cream on it, and talk. Ma would tell about Mrs. Reed's school, or how handsome Pa was when he was courting her, and I'd tell about being a teacher when I was grown up,

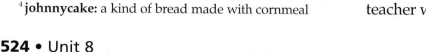

and the eagle I'd seen the day before in the top of the pine trees.

But you couldn't do that on clock time. You had to wait until the bell said you could rest and eat and talk about things. Oh, it didn't take me but two days to come to hate that bell and that clock in the tower. But there wasn't anything to change that. I just had to get used to being hungry when I was told to be hungry.

LITERATURE REVIEW

1 How did the Industrial Revolution affect Annie Steele's life?

2 Would you rather have worked as a spinner at home or in a factory? Explain your answer.

3 On graph paper, design a model factory. Develop a floor plan that will increase production. Take into account the workers' health and their interest in their jobs.

Factory workers head for home after a hard day's work at a New England factory in this engraving based on the work of American artist Winslow Homer.

FOCUS

How can economic differences cause conflicts between people?

Main Idea As you read, look for ways that economic differences led to conflicts between social classes in Europe and the United States.

Vocabulary

economic system
traditional economy
command economy
market economy
demand
supply
capitalism
laissez-faire
free enterprise
strike
labor union
socialism
utopian

Capitalism and Classes

T he European industrial countries grew rich in the 1800s, but the wealth was not shared equally. Some people became very wealthy, while others stayed very poor. In many countries the gap between rich and poor grew wider, leading to social conflict.

Adam Smith and Capitalism

One of the reasons Britain led the way in the Industrial Revolution was its economic system. An **economic system** is the way a country produces and uses goods and services.

Today there are three main kinds of economic systems. A **traditional economy** is one that does not see much change over time. For example, children do the same jobs that their parents and their parents before them did. If the parents are farmers, the children too will be farmers. For the most part, people with a traditional economy spend most of their time raising food for themselves. They are able to produce little surplus. Without a surplus to sell, the people are not able to buy better tools or improve their ways of farming. They continue to work as they always have.

In a **command economy** the government owns almost all land and natural resources. It has complete control over farms and factories. That is, the government of a country commands the direction the economy takes. Government leaders decide what is to be produced and in what quantity. And the government tells how much workers earn and how much goods will cost.

This nineteenth-century painting, *Industry of the Tyne*, shows workers in Britain.

In the 1800s countries that practiced free enterprise grew rich and powerful. Shown in this nineteenth-century painting are merchants at the Cloth Hall in Leeds, England.

In a **market economy** the people decide which goods and services they will buy. Every day individual people make choices about how they will spend their money. In addition, they decide how they will earn their living.

A market economy works on the principle of supply and demand. When an individual buys a product or service, he or she is showing a **demand** for that product or service. If there is a great demand, the provider will increase the **supply**, or amount offered for sale. The provider will do this in order to make a greater profit.

During the Middle Ages, Britain had a traditional economy. Under the feudal system, most people worked as their parents did, and they earned just enough to survive. They had little say in their own economic affairs. Peasants were expected to work for nobles, who seldom shared the profits of the peasants' labor.

In the 1700s Britain adopted an economic system that today we would consider to be a market economic system. This system is known as **capitalism**. Entrepreneurs in Britain invested money, or capital, in businesses. They hoped that the businesses would do well and make more money for them. The key to capitalism was that the individuals had control of how they would earn money.

About the time the Industrial Revolution began, a Scottish economics professor named Adam Smith wrote a book titled *The Wealth of Nations* (1776). In this book Smith explained how capitalism works.

This system, he said, works because of "the natural effort of every individual to better his own condition." He explained, "It is not from the benevolence [kindness] of the butcher, the brewer, or the baker that we expect our dinner, but from their regard to their own interest."

In other words, business owners do not make and sell goods because they are kind people. They do it because they want to make a profit. Still by acting to help themselves, the business owners help everyone. They give jobs and wages to workers. By having to compete with other businesses, they offer consumers better goods.

Smith felt that in a capitalist system the government did not have to become involved in a country's economy. He encouraged the idea of **laissez-faire** (le•say-FAYR), letting the economy continue without interference from the government. Smith believed that the principles of supply and demand would naturally take place and keep the economy going.

Businesses would boom, there would be more jobs, and the country would gain much wealth. Over time everyone would share a portion of these riches.

Smith's ideas, which became known as **free enterprise**, pleased the working class. In fact, these ideas became the "battle plan" for the Industrial Revolution. Just as Smith had predicted, the countries that followed the free enterprise approach grew rich and powerful.

REVIEW *According to Adam Smith, how would capitalism benefit both owners and workers?*

Economic Classes in Europe

As capitalism took hold in Europe, economic classes saw change. As always, the wealthy landowners, the aristocracy, were considered the upper class. With the beginning of the agricultural revolution, the landowners had turned to large-scale farming. Rather than farming the land themselves, they rented it to tenant farmers.

Joining the aristocracy at the top of the economic ladder were those business owners who had grown extremely rich in the Industrial Revolution. Unlike the aristocracy, the business owners were a part of the upper class because of the money they earned, not because of the family into which they were born.

Perhaps the greatest change during this period was the growth of the middle class. The middle class consisted of the bankers, merchants, shopkeepers, and professional people such as doctors and lawyers. Also in the middle class were the business owners who had made money in the Industrial Revolution.

At the bottom of the social ladder were the factory and farm workers. Both of these groups worked from dawn to dusk for very low wages. They were called members of the working class.

For centuries the members of the aristocracy had separated themselves from other people. Now the Industrial Revolution was bringing others into their social circles. At the same time, differences grew between the middle class and the working class. Members of the middle class lived in different types of neighborhoods than the working class. Parents in the middle class could afford to send their children to school to train for well-paying jobs and better futures. The working class had little hope of ever leaving the crowded slums where they lived.

REVIEW *How were Europeans divided into social classes as the Industrial Revolution took hold?*

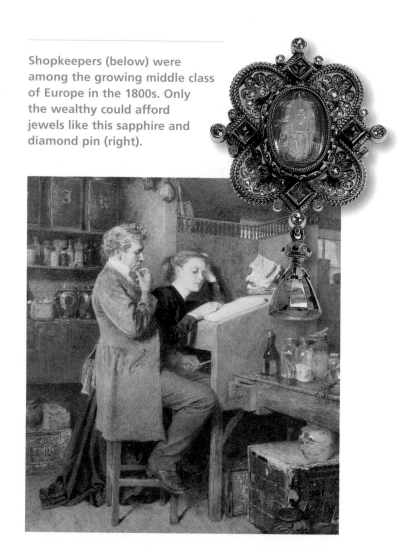

Shopkeepers (below) were among the growing middle class of Europe in the 1800s. Only the wealthy could afford jewels like this sapphire and diamond pin (right).

Conflict Among the Classes

Disagreements soon arose among the economic classes. Upper-class people had a low opinion of business. Socially, they looked down on the wealthy members of the middle class. In turn, the middle class claimed that the upper class did nothing to earn its wealth. The landlords simply waited for the rents to come in. The economist John Stuart Mill agreed. "They grow richer . . . in their sleep," he wrote, "without working, risking, or economizing."

Working people were angry at the middle class. They were unhappy that they were forced to work long hours at low pay in poor working conditions. They believed that business owners treated them like a raw material, such as iron or coal, to be bought at the lowest price possible.

Over time the working people's anger grew. Without their labor, they believed, there would be no wealth. They wanted a share of the riches that they produced. To back up their demands for better wages, some workers went on **strike**—they stopped working. Unfortunately for the workers, many of these strikes were poorly planned. Besides, there were many new workers ready to take their jobs. Some workers thought they could get better results if they formed groups called **labor unions**. At first most people were against these workers' groups. Many European governments passed laws against unions. By the end of the 1800s, however, these laws had been changed. Unions spoke for the workers, organizing major strikes that won them better working conditions and higher wages.

REVIEW *Why did conflicts arise among the social classes in Europe?*

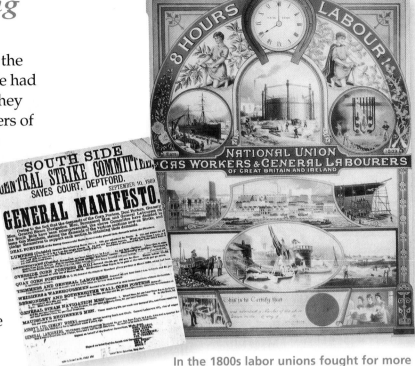

In the 1800s labor unions fought for more pay and better working conditions. This manifesto (left), or written statement of a viewpoint, was printed during the Great London Dock Strike, and this paper (right) was a certificate of membership in a gasworkers' union. Both were typical signs of the times.

Calls for Change

For some people, strikes and labor unions did not change the economic system enough. They said capitalism should be replaced with a system called socialism. Under **socialism** the government owns all industries and runs them for the benefit of all the people. Socialists said that capitalism made life hard for working people. To have a better life, they said, all people should work together and share equally the results of their labor.

The early socialists believed that socialism would work best in small communities. They set up a number of model towns where all the people jointly owned all houses and factories. The people also shared the money they made from their work. Many of these model communities were in the United States because land there was cheap and easy to get. One such community was New Harmony,

Robert Owen started several cooperative communities. His New Harmony in Indiana (left) was short-lived. In 1832 Owen explained many of his ideas in *The Crisis* (below), which he wrote with his son.

Indiana. It was founded in the 1820s by Robert Owen, a wealthy British business owner. Owen hoped that New Harmony would be a place where "all will be equal in their condition." Owen and people who shared his views were called **utopians**, or believers in a perfect society. For the most part, the utopias failed.

Some socialists thought that a community based on cooperation was not the answer. The leader of this group was a German writer named Karl Marx. He argued that history had moved through many stages. Each stage had been marked by struggles among social classes. In the age of capitalism, the conflict was between the wealthy middle class and the poor working class. Marx believed that this conflict would lead to a revolution,

Karl Marx urged workers to fight against capitalism.

which the working class would win. After this revolution a new social system without classes would develop.

Marx published his ideas in 1848. He called for the workers to revolt against the ruling classes, but workers did not rise to Marx's call. Even so, his words sent chills through the governments and business leaders of Europe during the second half of the 1800s.

REVIEW *What did utopians call for?*

Life in the United States

The United States also faced social and economic division during the 1800s. Two different economic systems separated the new nation. The southern United States continued an economic and social system based on agriculture. Plantation owners and their families, like the lords and ladies of Europe during the Middle Ages, made up the upper class. The middle class included owners of smaller farms, merchants, and business people. Next came the workers and poor farmers. Below this class were the people who made it possible for the very small upper class to have its wealth and privileges—enslaved Africans.

Horatio Alger's *Risen from the Ranks* (left) and this New York City residence of the Vanderbilts (below) both showed the United States as the land of opportunity.

The North developed a three-class economic and social system as it accepted capitalism and the Industrial Revolution. In the upper class were wealthy land and industry owners who were born in the United States. The upper class also included immigrants or former members of the middle class who had made their fortunes in industry.

The middle class included business owners and merchants. Below them were the working people. The workers of the North faced many of the same problems the workers of Europe faced—low wages, long hours, and poor working conditions.

Even so, American industrialists did not have the same fears of socialist revolution as European industrialists did. In the democratic United States, working people were able to take action to help themselves by voting. Also, Americans, for the most part, were better off economically than Europeans.

Most Americans looked on the United States as a land of opportunity. Anyone, they felt, could start with nothing and rise to wealth through hard work. This feeling was described in the "rags-to-riches" stories written by Horatio Alger. As one of Alger's characters said, "I don't mean always to be a newsboy or errand boy. I shall work my way upward as fast as I can, and in time I may come to fill a good place in society."

Eventually, American workers did form unions, though. They also used strikes to get better pay, shorter working days, and improved working conditions.

REVIEW *Why was there less class conflict in the United States than in Europe?*

LESSON 3 REVIEW

Check Understanding

1 Remember the Facts What is the difference between capitalism and socialism?

2 Recall the Main Idea How did economic differences affect social classes in Europe and in the United States?

Think Critically

3 Past to Present Do economic differences cause conflict in the United States today? Explain your answer.

4 Explore Viewpoints Why did many workers believe they needed to form labor unions? Why were many business owners against such unions?

Show What You Know

Letter-Writing Activity Work with a partner. One of you is a European business owner in the second half of the 1800s. The other is an unhappy industrial worker. The business owner should write a letter to the editor of the local newspaper, expressing an opinion about the activities of workers. Then the worker should write a reply to the opinion presented in the first letter.

CHAPTER 17
REVIEW

1700

1750

1732
• Crop rotation
  introduced

1733
• Flying shuttle
  invented

CONNECT MAIN IDEAS

Use this organizer to describe the beginning of the Industrial Age. Write three details to support each main idea. A copy of the organizer appears on page 121 of the Activity Book.

The Beginning of the Industrial Age

The Industrial Revolution

The new technology of the Industrial Revolution changed life in Britain and elsewhere.

1. _____
2. _____
3. _____

Capitalism and Classes

Economic differences led to conflicts between social classes in Europe and the United States.

1. _____
2. _____
3. _____

WRITE MORE ABOUT IT

Write a Report Research an occupation of the 1700s, and write a report on how the Industrial Revolution changed the way that job was done. Conclude your report by comparing the way technology might change a similar job today. Include at least one table that compares and contrasts.

Write a Diary Entry Write a diary entry about your first day at a job in a factory in England around 1750. What was your life like before you started your job? What did you do at the factory? How did you feel when you got home? Explain why you liked or disliked this change in your life.

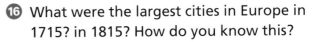

1800   1850

1769
• James Watt builds
  working steam
  engine

1776
• *The Wealth of Nations*
  is written

1837
• Steel plow
  invented

1851
• Britain hosts the
  Great Exhibition

USE VOCABULARY

For each group of terms, write a sentence or two that explains how the terms are related.

1. capitalism, free enterprise
2. Industrial Revolution, cottage industry, textile
3. patent, entrepreneur
4. socialism, utopian
5. strike, labor union

CHECK UNDERSTANDING

6. What is crop rotation?
7. Why did textile making stop as a cottage industry?
8. How did the Industrial Revolution affect children?
9. Why was Britain called "the workshop of the world"?
10. How are a command economy and a market economy different?
11. Who was Adam Smith, and what ideas did he write about that became known as "free enterprise"?
12. What did early socialists believe?
13. Why did most people think of the United States as a land of opportunity?

THINK CRITICALLY

14. **Past to Present** In the 1700s the Industrial Revolution affected the lives of many people. Today the technological revolution is doing the same. How has this revolution affected your life?

15. **Explore Viewpoints** Why do you think the ideas of socialism were popular with the middle and lower classes in Europe?

APPLY SKILLS

Read and Compare Population Maps Use the maps on pages 520 and 521 to answer these questions.

16. What were the largest cities in Europe in 1715? in 1815? How do you know this?
17. Which city had more people in 1815, Constantinople or St. Petersburg? How do you know this?
18. Based on the information shown on the population maps, what generalization can you make about European cities from 1715 to 1815?

READ MORE ABOUT IT

Lyddie by Katherine Paterson. Lodestar. Lyddie Worthen of Vermont plans to earn some money and gain her independence by becoming a factory worker in Lowell, Massachusetts, in the 1840s.

HARCOURT BRACE   Visit the Internet at
http://www.hbschool.com
for additional resources.

Chapter 17 • **533**

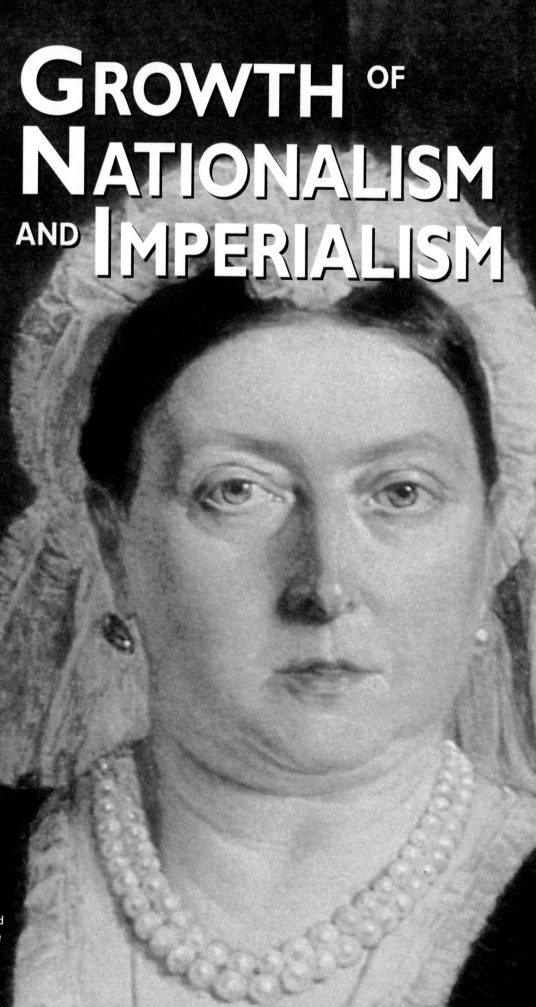

GROWTH OF NATIONALISM AND IMPERIALISM

"We, the undersigned chiefs, with a view of bettering the condition of our country and people, do this day [give] to the . . . Company, for ever, the whole of our territory."

from a treaty prepared by a British company seeking to gain land in Africa

Queen Victoria, ruler of the United Kingdom of Great Britain and Ireland throughout much of the nineteenth century

534

Rise of Nationalism

FOCUS

What are some reasons why people today feel proud of their country?

Main Idea As you read, think about how people in the 1800s began to develop a sense of belonging to a country.

Vocabulary

nationalism

kaiser

Today most people feel that they are a part of the country in which they live. Through much of recorded history, however, many people felt a part of only a town, city, or region. For most people a sense of belonging to a country did not exist.

Nationalism Grows

All through history, people have felt a sense of belonging to their family and to the place where they were born. Some people also felt loyalty to a monarch. Yet for a long time, a person usually did not feel a link with other people who lived under the same government.

This attitude began to change at the end of the eighteenth century. The Americans felt pride in their new country. The French, too, were proud that they had fought together to gain a greater voice in government during the French Revolution. Because of this united action, they began to think of one another as members of the same large group who shared the same beliefs, hopes, and fears. They felt a sense of **nationalism**, or loyalty to a nation.

Working together as the French people did can promote nationalism. The geography of a region can also add to the growth of national feeling. A map of France shows that the country has natural boundaries— oceans, mountains, and rivers—on almost all sides. These boundaries helped give the French people a sense of identity. In addition, a language, religion, or race can unite a people as a nation.

Early nineteenth-century map of western Europe

In some countries people have come together as a nation, even though they seem to share very little. The people of the United States have a variety of heritages, follow different religions, and are of different races. Still, they have a strong sense of belonging to a nation. Their shared love of freedom defines the United States and gives its people their national identity.

In the 1800s strong nationalist feelings spread across the European nations and the rest of the world. Throughout the world, nationalism affected people and their dealings with others.

REVIEW *What conditions encourage the rise of nationalism?*

Italian Nationalism

Italy experienced the rise of nationalism early. In the 1830s Italy was a collection of separate states and kingdoms. The Catholic Church ruled Rome and the states around it. Members of the Austrian and French royal families ruled a number of small Italian states. Some of the other states were ruled by Italian nobles.

Unification of Italy, 1870

LOMBARDY 1859
Milan
VENETIA 1866
PARMA 1860
MODENA 1860
SAN MARINO
Florence
TUSCANY 1860
PAPAL STATES 1860
KINGDOM OF SARDINIA 1859
Corsica (FRANCE)
Rome
Naples
Sardinia
Tyrrhenian Sea
Adriatic Sea
EUROPE
KINGDOM OF THE TWO SICILIES 1860
Sicily
Mediterranean Sea
AFRICA

0   75   150 Miles
0   75   150 Kilometers
Lambert Conformal Conic Projection

1860 Date joined with Kingdom of Italy

Giuseppe Garibaldi devoted his life to fighting for Italian unity. In his autobiography he tells of his life as an adventurer, a sailor, and a nation builder.

PRICE TWO SHILLINGS.
GARIBALDI AN AUTOBIOGRAPHY.
EDITED BY ALEXANDRE DUMAS.
LONDON: ROUTLEDGE WARNE & ROUTLEDGE.

Many people believed that these separate states and kingdoms should unite to form a single nation. A leader of these people was the lawyer and writer Giuseppe Mazzini (joo•SEP•ay maht•SEE•nee). He pointed out that the mountains and coast formed Italy's natural boundaries. The land within those boundaries should be one country, he said. In 1831 Mazzini founded Young Italy, a nationalist group. Its goal was to unite Italy into one democratic republic governed by and for the Italian people.

Mazzini spread his ideas with great passion. He urged Italians to think of themselves as one people. "Do not say *I*," he wrote, "say *we*." He also called on the Italians to free the country from foreign rulers.

Mazzini may have been the voice of Italian freedom, but Giuseppe Garibaldi was its heart. An adventurer and a sailor, Garibaldi joined Young Italy in 1834. His work for Italy's freedom earned him a death sentence, which he escaped by fleeing to South America. Returning to Italy in 1848, he took part in a short revolution that failed. This time he escaped to the United States. Before he left, he called on his soldiers with these words:

Regions By 1870 the many kingdoms on the Italian peninsula had become one nation with Sardinia's King Victor Emmanuel as its leader.

■ *Which area was the last to join Italy?*

This painting shows Garibaldi's volunteer army—known as the Red Shirts—in action during the battle of Calatafimi, near Naples, in southern Italy.

66 This is what I have to offer: hunger, cold, the heat of the sun; no wages, no barracks, no ammunition. . . . Those of you who love your country and love glory, *follow me*. 99

In 1860 Garibaldi returned. He and a thousand followers, all wearing red-shirted uniforms, captured the island of Sicily. Garibaldi and his Red Shirts then sailed to the mainland, taking Naples. Soon they had freed much of southern Italy.

Meanwhile, Count Camillo di Cavour (kah•VUR), chief minister of the Kingdom of Piedmont-Sardinia, had united much of the north. Cavour convinced Garibaldi to set up a kingdom of Italy. King Victor Emmanuel of Sardinia became the first ruler of this new nation. Italy became fully united in 1870, when Victor Emmanuel's soldiers finally captured Rome.

REVIEW *How did Mazzini, Garibaldi, and Cavour help unite Italy?*

German Unification

In the early 1800s Germany, like Italy, was a collection of separate states. Since 1815 these states had been united in a confederation, or loose alliance, which had little authority. One of the main goals of the alliance was to stop any nationalist feelings and keep the German states independent.

Not everyone agreed that the states should stay separate. King Wilhelm, who in 1861 had become the ruler of Prussia, one of the most powerful states, believed that Germany was meant to be united under Prussian rule. "All that remains to be determined," he said, "is when and how." The when and the how were largely decided by Otto von Bismarck, who became the chancellor, or prime minister, of Prussia in 1862.

Bismarck immediately made it clear that he thought the world was run "not by speeches and decisions" but by "iron and blood." In 1864 Bismarck declared war on Denmark. He then attacked and defeated Austria.

Unification of Germany, 1862–1871

North Sea

SWEDEN

DENMARK

Baltic Sea

0   100   200 Miles
0   100   200 Kilometers
Azimuthal Equal-Area Projection

SCHLESWIG 1866

HOLSTEIN 1866

OLDENBURG 1867

MECKLENBURG-SCHWERIN 1867

HANOVER 1866

NETHERLANDS

PRUSSIA

BRUNSWICK

ANHALT

★ Berlin

PRUSSIA 1866

BELGIUM

HESSE-CASSEL 1866

THURINGIA 1867

SAXONY 1867

RUSSIAN EMPIRE

NASSAU 1866

DARMSTADT 1871

BAVARIA 1871

ALSACE-LORRAINE From France 1871

WÜRTTEMBERG 1871

BADEN 1871

FRANCE

SWITZERLAND

AUSTRO-HUNGARIAN EMPIRE

Danube River

BOSNIA   SERBIA

1867 Year state became part of Germany

★ Capital

Place Otto von Bismarck led Prussia's campaign to unite Germany.

■ *Which became part of the united nation first, southern Germany or northern Germany?*

In 1871 all the German states, except for Austria, had joined with Prussia and its "Iron Chancellor" to form a new German Empire. They named King Wilhelm I of Prussia **kaiser** (KY•zer), or emperor, and they named Bismarck chancellor of the empire.

Bismarck worked hard to make Germany strong. He sponsored laws that gave help to industry and took steps to build up the army and navy. In time Germany became the leading power in Europe.

REVIEW *How did Bismarck unite Germany?*

National Feeling Grows in Japan

Japanese national pride did not grow out of a wish to unite many different states but out of concern over threats from other countries. In 1853 two American warships sailed into the harbor of Edo (present-day Tokyo). The Japanese feared the ships' huge guns would be used against their nation. The commander of the ships, Matthew Perry, told the Japanese that he wanted peace. At the same time he insisted that they open their ports to American traders.

Since the arrival of the first Europeans in Japan, the Japanese had argued among themselves about how they should deal with foreigners. Some wanted to allow Western traders into the country. Others believed that opening the country to outside influences would destroy the Japanese way of life. Perry's visit worried the Japanese government. The shogun knew that Japan's army would have difficulty keeping the United States out of Japan.

Perry returned the following year with seven heavily armed ships. Knowing they had no choice, the Japanese signed a treaty, or agreement, with the United States.

King Wilhelm I (right) and Otto von Bismarck (left) discuss battle plans during an 1870 war with France.

This Japanese woodblock print (left) shows United States Commodore Matthew Perry's arrival in Japan in 1853. Above is a Japanese figurine from the same period.

This opened two ports to American merchants. Soon after that, Japan signed treaties with the European powers.

Many Japanese people hated the treaties. One samurai wrote of his shame: "Now the Japanese sword is tarnished, and the warrior's spirit is broken." With the cry "Honor the emperor; expel the barbarians," samurai attacked and killed many foreigners. Then, in 1868, these samurai overthrew the shogun and restored the emperor to power. The emperor called his reign *Meiji* (MAY•jee), or "enlightened rule." This time in Japanese history is called the Meiji Restoration.

The emperor and his advisers took advantage of the new nationalist feeling and challenged the West. To compete with the new industrial nations, Japan had to become more modern. Meiji officials looked to the West for the technology that would make this change possible. However, they did not want to change the "spirit of old Japan." By the early 1900s the Meiji government's program of "Eastern ways, Western science" had made Japan a world power.

REVIEW *What caused the rise of nationalism in Japan?*

LESSON 1 REVIEW

Check Understanding

1 Remember the Facts What is nationalism? In what ways do people develop a feeling of nationalism?

2 Recall the Main Idea What helped unite people in Europe and in Japan?

Think Critically

3 Past to Present What are the main causes of nationalist feelings today?

4 Think More About It What do you think is the strongest cause of nationalism? Support your choice with information from the lesson.

Show What You Know

Simulation Activity Imagine that you and your classmates are students in Italy, Germany, or Japan during the time when nationalism grew in one of these countries. Act out a scene in which you and your classmates discuss the growing sense of nationalism in your country.

Evaluate Information and Sources

1. Why Learn This Skill?

You can get information from many sources, such as television, radio, newspapers, the Internet, and reference books. Before you use this information, however, you need to evaluate it. To **evaluate** information is to decide whether or not you can trust it.

2. Information and Sources

One kind of information is facts. A **fact** is a statement that can be proved to be true. Suppose you are reading a story about Japan. In the story you read the statement "Japan is about the same size as the state of California." You can check whether the statement is true by finding the areas of both Japan and California in an almanac or another source and comparing the two.

Some kinds of information cannot be proved so easily. Archaeologists study ancient cultures about which little may be known. Instead of using written sources of information, archaeologists find and study ancient buildings, tools, and other artifacts. Based on their studies, they form opinions. An **opinion** is a statement of someone's belief or judgment. Although some opinions can be supported by fact, opinions are not trusted as much as facts.

For historians, written or picture records are important sources of information. They describe or show facts and help to explain their meaning. These records may be firsthand accounts, or **primary sources**, that tell the authors' own ideas. Others are secondhand accounts, or **secondary sources**, that tell about other people's ideas.

B

3. Understand the Process

To evaluate information and its sources, you can follow these steps:

- Study the material carefully. What kind of material is it? Is it based on firsthand information or on the accounts of others?
- Think about the audience. For whom was this message meant? Whether it was meant for a certain audience may have affected what was written and the way it was written.
- Check for **bias**, or a leaning toward or against someone or something. Watch for words or phrases that show a one-sided view.
- When possible, compare sources. Study more than one source on a topic if you can. Comparing sources gives you balanced information.

Now that you know more about evaluating information and sources, study the pictures on these pages and answer the questions. Picture A is a drawing made by a Japanese artist after seeing an American steamship arrive in his country in 1853. Picture B is a drawing another

artist made of the American fleet after it returned from Japan in 1854.

① Is Picture A based on firsthand information or on the accounts of others? Explain.

② For whom do you think Picture A was meant? Explain.

③ Does Picture A show bias? What details in the picture show the Japanese artist's feelings about Americans? Explain.

④ In what ways is Picture A like Picture B? How is it different?

⑤ Which of the pictures is a better source for what the American steamships really looked like? Why is it better?

4. Think and Apply

With a partner, preview the illustrations in the next lesson. Identify them as primary or secondary sources. Then follow the steps in Understand the Process to study the pictures more closely. Discuss the advantages and disadvantages of using these illustrations as sources of information.

FOCUS

Why do some nations try to control the governments and economies of other nations?

Main Idea As you read, think about why the Western industrial nations wanted colonies in Africa and Asia.

Vocabulary

imperialism
indirect rule
direct rule
cash crop
sepoy
Great Mutiny
Open Door policy

Life changed greatly for the people living in the interior of Africa during the 1800s. In this scene an enslaved African works under the watchful eye of a European colonist.

Age of Imperialism

To keep their factories humming, the industrialized countries needed many kinds of raw materials. They also needed markets for their manufactured goods. In the 1800s they found both in Africa and Asia.

The Scramble for Africa

Europeans had been increasing their contact with the Africans since the 1400s. That contact, for the most part, was limited to the African coasts. Europeans knew little about Africa's interior. It was not until the 1800s that Europeans began to explore these central parts.

Perhaps the most famous of the explorers was the Scottish doctor and missionary David Livingstone. Livingstone arrived in Africa in 1841 and spent more than 30 years exploring its interior. Livingstone kept a journal in which he described the land and people he met. When the journal was published in Europe, it quickly became a best-seller. Reading the journal, European business leaders realized that they could get rich in Africa.

Traders soon followed the explorers. To feed the machines of the Industrial Revolution, Europeans wanted timber, rubber, and other raw materials from Africa. They also wanted Africans to buy their goods. European trade in Africa quickly became big business, and large companies were formed by European traders. The companies tried to get their governments to conquer the lands where they did business.

During the 1870s many European governments did just that. They established colonies and took control of African lands to protect their trade. The Europeans believed that they acted not only from a legal right but also from a duty. They saw it as their responsibility to bring their way of life to the "less-fortunate" Africans. In time the European countries began to compete with one another to add more lands to their colonial empires. Such empire building is called **imperialism**.

The European scramble to control parts of Africa went on until 1884. In that year representatives from 14 European nations met in Berlin, Germany, to divide Africa among themselves. Each country got the regions where it had the most settlements and trading posts. No African representatives were invited to the meeting. The Europeans did not think it necessary to let the Africans say how they felt about the European takeovers. Because of this, the division did not take into account the physical geography of the continent or the similarities and differences in religions, languages, and ways of life in Africa.

By 1900 the Europeans had colonies almost everywhere in Africa. Different countries ruled their colonies in different ways. Many of the British colonies were governed by **indirect rule**. African officials were allowed to run their own communities, but British officials handled important matters that affected the colony as a whole. In contrast, most French and German colonies were governed by **direct rule**. This means that European officials handled all colonial affairs.

Whatever the form of government that was set up, European officials ran the economy of each colony. To get the resources they wanted, the Europeans built mines, factories, and plantations. Often the Europeans treated the African workers like slaves.

The Europeans made African farmers grow **cash crops**—crops raised to sell rather than to use at home. These crops were then exported to markets in Europe, where they were sold for European profit. Up to now, African farmers had always grown what they needed to feed their families. Now they had less land and less time to grow their own food. They became dependent on European traders for the things they needed.

REVIEW *Why did the European countries build colonial empires in Africa?*

African Reaction

The European colonial powers changed life in Africa enormously. Some Africans accepted these changes, but others fought to keep their lands and their ways of life. The people of East Africa fiercely resisted German

The African colonies provided raw materials to the industrialized Western nations. Below is a nineteenth-century East African coffee estate.

rule. "If it should be friendship that you desire, then I am ready for it, today and always," one leader told the Germans. "If it should be war you desire, then I am ready, but never to be your subject." The Germans answered with a war that took the lives of more than 100,000 East Africans.

In West Africa, Samori Touré, ruler of a Muslim empire, declared that he would never surrender to the French. His 30,000 well-trained soldiers held off the French armies for more than 15 years. In 1898, however, the French took Samori prisoner in a surprise attack. Soon after that, his empire fell.

Samori Touré, ruler of a Muslim West African empire, tried to resist European imperialism.

The British also faced stiff opposition. For years Muslims kept them out of what is today Sudan, in northeastern Africa. The peoples of southern Africa, too, made the British fight for every inch of land they took. In West Africa the Ashanti (uh•SHAHN•tee) waged a number of wars before they finally gave in to the British.

REVIEW *How did African leaders respond when European countries came to take control?*

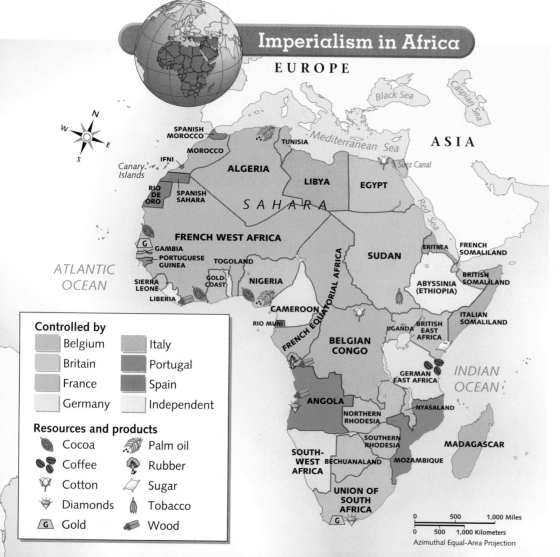

Imperialism in Africa

EUROPE

ASIA

Black Sea

Caspian Sea

Mediterranean Sea

Suez Canal

Red Sea

SPANISH MOROCCO

TUNISIA

MOROCCO

IFNI

Canary Islands

ALGERIA

LIBYA

EGYPT

RIO DE ORO

SPANISH SAHARA

SAHARA

FRENCH WEST AFRICA

GAMBIA

PORTUGUESE GUINEA

TOGOLAND

GOLD COAST

SIERRA LEONE

LIBERIA

NIGERIA

CAMEROON

RIO MUNI

FRENCH EQUATORIAL AFRICA

SUDAN

ERITREA

FRENCH SOMALILAND

BRITISH SOMALILAND

ABYSSINIA (ETHIOPIA)

ITALIAN SOMALILAND

UGANDA

BRITISH EAST AFRICA

BELGIAN CONGO

GERMAN EAST AFRICA

ANGOLA

NORTHERN RHODESIA

NYASALAND

SOUTHERN RHODESIA

MADAGASCAR

SOUTH-WEST AFRICA

BECHUANALAND

MOZAMBIQUE

UNION OF SOUTH AFRICA

ATLANTIC OCEAN

INDIAN OCEAN

N
W E
S

Controlled by
- Belgium
- Britain
- France
- Germany
- Italy
- Portugal
- Spain
- Independent

Resources and products
- Cocoa
- Coffee
- Cotton
- Diamonds
- Gold
- Palm oil
- Rubber
- Sugar
- Tobacco
- Wood

0   500   1,000 Miles
0   500   1,000 Kilometers
Azimuthal Equal-Area Projection

Regions
MAP THEME

By 1884 most of Africa had been claimed by Europe.
■ *Why do you think European countries wanted colonies in different parts of Africa?*

Queen Victoria ruled over the United Kingdom of Great Britain and Ireland during its time of greatest expansion. The time of her reign, from 1837 to 1901, is often called the Victorian Age.

Egypt and the Suez Canal

By 1900 Britain controlled African lands from the Mediterranean coast to the southern tip of the continent. One of the most important of these lands was Egypt. Egypt was formally a part of the Ottoman Empire, but it had acted independently for many years. Several Egyptian rulers had requested that Europeans help them make their country more modern. As a result, European countries such as Britain and France had much influence in Egypt. Still, until the mid-1800s, they did not try to take full control of the country.

Between 1859 and 1869, French engineers dug a canal through the Isthmus of Suez which connects northeastern Africa and western Asia. The Suez Canal allowed direct water travel between the Mediterranean and Red seas, shortening the sea route from Europe to Asia. Instead of going all the way around Africa, ships could now go through the Suez Canal, saving several months of travel. Suddenly the European trading nations showed much more interest in Egypt.

In 1875, money problems forced Egypt to sell its shares in the Suez Canal. Britain quickly bought the shares and took control of this important waterway. In the early 1880s Egyptian nationalists rebelled, hoping to drive out the Europeans. The British government sent soldiers to Egypt to stop the rebellion. The British explained this action by stating that they had to protect the canal. For many years the British remained in control of the canal and of Egypt.

REVIEW *Why did European nations show interest in Egypt after the building of the Suez Canal?*

British India

Control of the Suez Canal gave the British a fast route to India, their most prized colony.

The official opening of the Suez Canal, in 1869, is shown on this lithograph.

Lord Curzon, a high official, said, "As long as we rule India we are the greatest power in the world. If we lose it we shall drop straight away to a third-rate power."

In 1600 Queen Elizabeth I had given the East India Company the right to control trade between India and England. This group of merchants built trading posts at large Indian ports, such as Bombay, Calcutta, and Madras. The company grew rich in trade goods.

In the 1700s, however, things began to go badly for the East India Company's business. The Mogul Empire, which had ruled India for more than 200 years, started to collapse, and princes of the individual Indian states fought for control of Mogul lands. Also, merchants from other European countries tried to take away some of the Indian trade. To protect their business, company leaders made agreements with the Indian princes. They also formed their own army of **sepoys** (SEE•poyz), Indian soldiers led by British officers. Through treaties and war the company improved its position in India. By the mid-1800s the company controlled much of the Indian subcontinent.

The East India Company brought British government and British ways to the lands it controlled. Spreading British culture was not

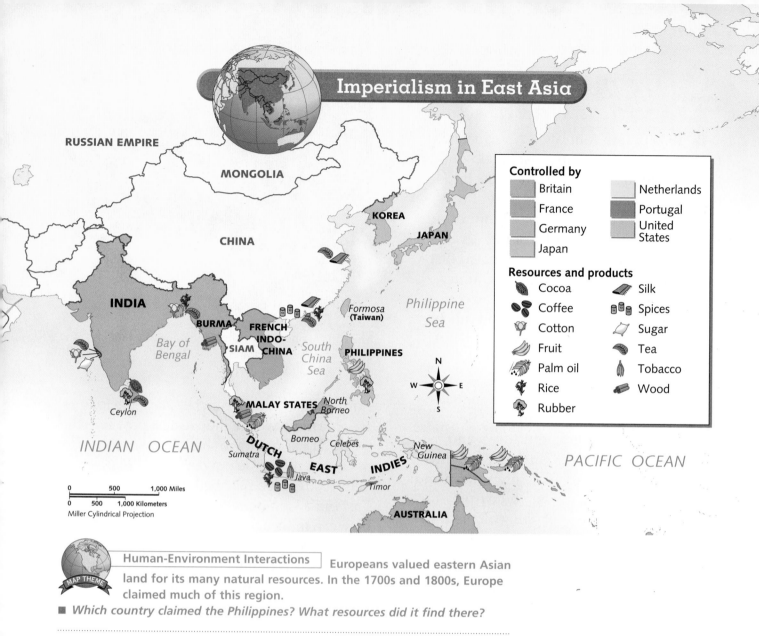

Imperialism in East Asia

Controlled by

- Britain
- France
- Germany
- Japan
- Netherlands
- Portugal
- United States

Resources and products

- Cocoa
- Coffee
- Cotton
- Fruit
- Palm oil
- Rice
- Rubber
- Silk
- Spices
- Sugar
- Tea
- Tobacco
- Wood

Human-Environment Interactions Europeans valued eastern Asian land for its many natural resources. In the 1700s and 1800s, Europe claimed much of this region.

■ *Which country claimed the Philippines? What resources did it find there?*

the company's main purpose, though. The company was in business to take India's raw materials for British industry and sell British industrial goods in India. It also tried to prevent Indians from starting their own businesses and put many Indian industries out of business.

Many Indians became angry about the East India Company's rule. More than anything else, they disliked having to adopt British ways. In 1857 anger flared into rebellion. Thousands of sepoys, backed by the Indian people, mutinied, or turned against, the company. Fighting went on for more than a year. When British soldiers were sent to India, the **Great Mutiny** finally ended.

After the mutiny the East India Company gave control of its Indian lands to the British government. Britain's Queen Victoria became empress of India. A viceroy was appointed to govern "British India" through regional governors and councils. Some Indian leaders were on these councils, but they had little say in making decisions.

Some order now returned to India, but Britain was mainly concerned about its interests, not those of the Indian people. Many Indian people wanted independence from the British.

REVIEW *How did the East India Company gain authority in India? How did it lose that authority?*

Carving Up China

Trade brought the Western countries to China, just as it had brought Europeans to India and Africa. In the early 1800s it seemed as if all the industrialized nations wanted China's goods. The Chinese, on the other hand, seemed quite happy to live without anything made in the West. The small amount of trade the Chinese carried on with the outsiders came through one port, Guangzhou. Chinese leaders wanted to keep the foreigners on the coast, away from most of their large cities. This would keep the Chinese people from learning Western ways.

Western traders wanted China to open up more ports for trade. To do this, they knew they had to offer something the Chinese wanted. The East India Company found just such a product—opium. Opium is a dangerous, habit-forming drug made from the poppy plant. Poppies grew well on company lands in India. Company traders began smuggling opium from India into China. More and more Chinese became addicted to opium.

In 1839 the Chinese tried to stop the drug trade by destroying British supplies of opium stored at Guangzhou. This led to the Opium War between Britain and China. Using gunboats, the British were able to defeat the Chinese. In a treaty, signed in 1842, China gave Britain special trading rights. Soon all the imperialistic nations of Europe wanted the same rights as the British. In 1894 the Japanese, who felt that some Chinese lands belonged to them, declared war on China. They seized the Chinese island of Formosa (present-day Taiwan). By this time Britain, France, Germany, Russia, and the United States also controlled parts of China.

The Chinese reacted angrily to this control by outsiders. In 1900 the Boxers, a secret Chinese society, began attacking missionaries

This Chinese porcelain bowl shows the factories of foreign traders.

and foreign officials. The leaders of a number of nations sent soldiers, who quickly put down the Boxer Rebellion. The leaders then agreed to follow an Open Door policy. An **Open Door policy** means that all countries have an equal opportunity to trade freely in a certain place. This policy allowed Westerners to keep control of China.

REVIEW *How did foreign powers come to control much of China?*

LESSON 2 REVIEW

Check Understanding

1 **Remember the Facts**   What is imperialism?

2 **Recall the Main Idea**   Why did the Western industrial nations want colonies in Africa and Asia?

Think Critically

3 **Think More About It**   How do you think Africa, India, and China might have developed without Western control?

4 **Cause and Effect**   How did Western influence change farming in Africa? What were the effects of these changes?

Show What You Know

Map Activity   Use an outline map of the world to show the empires of the European nations at the beginning of the 1900s. Color-code the different colonial empires. Give your map a title and a key. Write a caption for your map to explain why the European countries built large empires. You may need to use library resources to do this activity.

Were European Imperialists

During the 1800s the industrial nations in Europe competed with one another in a race to build global empires. Britain was so successful in gaining colonies throughout the world that the British people boasted, "The sun never sets on the British Empire."

The main reason for European imperialism was to gain control of trade. But most Europeans also believed that the people they conquered were in need of their help and guidance. Read the following points of view from people in China, Central Africa, and India to learn how each person viewed the European imperialists. Did these conquered people consider the Europeans helpful or harmful?

A Mangbetu leader in Africa

"Foreigners have always deceived us. . . . We have been the prey in succession [one after another] to the Zandes [a Central African people], the Turks, and the Arabs. Are the whites worth more? No, beyond doubt. But whatever they may be, our territory is today freed from the presence of any foreigners, and to introduce another would be an act of cowardice. I do not wish to be a slave to anyone, and I will fight the whites."

Girischandra Ghose, a writer from India

"The final cause of the advent [arrival] of the English in India is to forward the progress of mankind toward perfection. They are the destined instrument in the hand of Providence [God] for this great work. . . . The march of civilization throughout the world is forward. . . . Progress is a necessary condition of creation. . . . The course of nature is perpetual [unending] development."

The Great Indian Peninsula Revolving Terminus in Bombay was one of the many structures built during the time of British imperialism in India.

Helpful or Harmful?

Counterpoints

Under British control, India saw a contrast in the treatment of Indians and British subjects.

Lin Zexu, a government official in China

❝Of all that China exports to foreign countries there is not a single thing which is not beneficial . . . the things that must be had by foreign countries are innumerable . . . foreign countries cannot get along for a single day without them. If China cuts off these benefits . . . then what can the barbarians rely upon to keep themselves alive? . . . On the other hand, articles coming from the outside to China can only be used as toys. We can take them or get along without them. They are not needed by China.❞

Compare Viewpoints

1. How does Lin Zexu view the European imperialists? How do you know?

2. How does the Mangbetu leader view the coming of Europeans to Central Africa? How do you know?

3. How is the viewpoint of Girischandra Ghose different from the viewpoints of Lin Zexu and the Mangbetu leader? Do you think that most people in India held the same view as Ghose? Explain.

Think and Apply

BUILDING CITIZENSHIP

People who live in different places often have different views. You have read that people from three different places in the world had different views on European imperialism. At what other times in history have people of different places disagreed about the actions of a nation or group of nations?

1831
• Giuseppe Mazzini founds nationalist group Young Italy

CONNECT MAIN IDEAS

Use this organizer to describe the growth of nationalism and imperialism. Write three details for each main idea. A copy of the organizer appears on page 127 of the Activity Book.

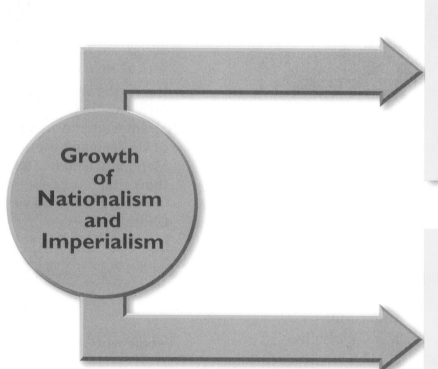

Rise of Nationalism

People in the 1800s developed more of a sense of belonging to a country.

1. _____
2. _____
3. _____

Growth of Nationalism and Imperialism

Age of Imperialism

The Western industrial nations claimed colonies in Africa and Asia.

1. _____
2. _____
3. _____

WRITE MORE ABOUT IT

Write an Explanation Write down what comes to mind when you think of the term *nationalism*. Then write an explanation of the term as it might appear as an article in an encyclopedia.

Write a Speech Imagine that you are living in Africa at the time of European imperialism. Write a speech that tells people of the effects that imperialism has had on you and your community.

1850		1875	1900

1839
• Opium War between China and Britain

1857
• Great Mutiny in India

1868
• Meiji Restoration in Japan

1870
• European "scramble for Africa" begins

1898
• West African leader Samori is captured by the French

USE VOCABULARY

Write a term from this list to complete each of the sentences that follow.

direct rule

imperialism

nationalism

Open Door policy

sepoy

1 _____ means that a country continues to add lands to its colonial empires.

2 An _____ means that all countries have an equal opportunity to trade freely in a certain place.

3 _____ is a feeling of loyalty to a country.

4 Under _____ European officials handled all the affairs of African colonies.

5 In colonial India, a _____ was an Indian soldier led by a British officer.

CHECK UNDERSTANDING

6 What are three things that can give people a shared sense of identity?

7 How did Giuseppe Garibaldi affect the history of Italy?

8 What method did Otto von Bismarck use to unite Germany?

9 What made Japanese nationalism during the 1800s different from nationalism in many European nations at the same time?

10 Why did European countries try to control lands in Africa?

11 What was the importance of the Suez Canal to Britain?

12 What was the result of the Great Mutiny in India?

13 What was the Boxer Rebellion?

THINK CRITICALLY

14 **Think More About It** How can nationalism make a country stronger? How can nationalism make a country weaker?

15 **Past to Present** What factors make people today unite for a common purpose?

APPLY SKILLS

Evaluate Information and Sources
Imagine that you have been asked to write a report on how European imperialism affected ways of life in Africa.

16 Would you use primary sources, secondary sources, or both? Why?

17 Do you think you might find bias in sources on this topic? Why or why not?

READ MORE ABOUT IT

Commodore Perry in the Land of the Shogun by Rhoda Blumberg. Lothrop, Lee & Shepard. This book explains Commodore Matthew Perry's role in opening Japan to the rest of the world in the 1850s.

HARCOURT BRACE

Visit the Internet at **http://www.hbschool.com** for additional resources.

Chapter 18 • **551**

Technology

During the Industrial Revolution the pace of technology seemed to explode. Inventions such as the steam engine and the power loom sped up the production of all kinds of goods. These large, roaring machines changed the way people lived and worked.

Present-day inventors still search for ways to make technology faster, better, and less expensive. Often they are able to make new inventions smaller and more efficient as well.

Computers, once the size of a large room, have become small enough to fit in a briefcase. Modern computer chips work 10,000 times faster than the first computer chip, which was invented in 1971. In recent years, more and more people have been able to own computers as costs have come down.

New technology is also making space exploration less expensive. This is because space engineers are now able to build smaller spacecraft to do bigger jobs. Planning the mission takes less time, too. The first mission to Mars in the 1970s took eight years to plan and carry out at a cost of $3 billion. The 1997 Pathfinder mission to Mars took just four years of planning and cost only $250 million. Administrator Daniel S. Goldin said that the Pathfinder mission "embodies the spirit of NASA and serves as a model for future missions that are faster, better, and cheaper."

Now scientists and engineers are working to develop machines so small that they can be seen only with a microscope. Examples include robots, engines, pumps, and motors that can fit on the tip of a needle. These miniature machines will lower costs, improve safety, and help bring about a cleaner environment. They will be very different from the big, noisy machines of the Industrial Revolution!

The Pathfinder mission to Mars used the space rover *Sojourner* to study the planet's surface.

Space technology was not always as compact as the Pathfinder mission. In 1975 NASA launched the Viking spacecraft, large compared to today's standards.

Today

Think and Apply

BUILDING CITIZENSHIP

With a partner, research and write a report about recent technology. Include information about some of the latest inventions, short biographies on the inventors, ways these inventions have changed since their introduction, and the role these inventions have in daily life. Share your report with classmates.

HARCOURT BRACE

Visit the Internet at **http://www.hbschool.com** for additional resources.

CNN Turner Le@rning

Check your media center or classroom video library for the Making Social Studies Relevant videotape of this feature.

The black and white photograph on this page shows a far different scene of technology than the other photographs on the page. In this 1946 picture a scientist uses a mainframe computer to solve mathematical problems. The top picture shows a present-day engineer using a robotic arm to build a circuit board. At bottom is the world's smallest abacus, which can be seen only with a microscope.

VISUAL SUMMARY

Summarize the Main Ideas
Study the pictures and captions to help you review the events you read about in Unit 8.

Write Creatively
Imagine that you are one of the people shown in this visual summary. Quickly write down your thoughts and feelings. Are you happy? sad? afraid? proud? Explain why.

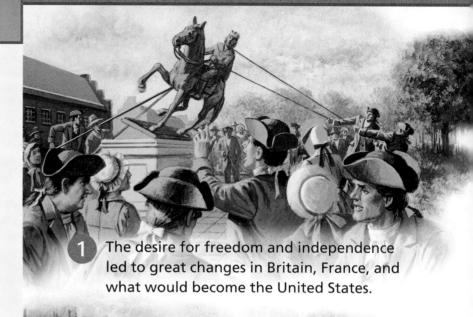

1 The desire for freedom and independence led to great changes in Britain, France, and what would become the United States.

3 The new technology of the Industrial Revolution changed life in Britain and in other parts of the world.

5 In the latter part of the 1800s, more and more people began to develop a sense of nationalism, or loyalty to a nation.

2 The spirit of revolution spread to Latin America. The peoples of Latin America wanted to change their ways of life and their governments.

4 Economic differences among social classes in Europe led to conflicts.

6 During the Age of Imperialism, industrialized nations in the West took control of the governments and economies of nations in Africa and Asia.

USE VOCABULARY

Write each term in a sentence that will help explain its meaning.

1. Constitution of the United States of America
2. Bill of Rights
3. Declaration of the Rights of Man and of the Citizen
4. hacienda
5. junta
6. traditional economy
7. imperialism
8. Open Door policy

CHECK UNDERSTANDING

9. Who were Jean-Jacques Rousseau and Voltaire? To what eighteenth-century movement did they contribute ideas?

10. What was the relationship between King Louis XVI and the French Revolution?

11. What caused the Creoles of Latin America to try to change their government?

12. What effect did the spinning jenny and other new machinery have on the textile industry?

13. How were the ideas of Adam Smith and Karl Marx different?

14. What was Germany's political structure like before unification in 1871?

15. How did completion of the Suez Canal affect ships traveling between Europe and Asia?

THINK CRITICALLY

16. **Think More About It** In what ways did the Enlightenment affect politics in the eighteenth century?

17. **Past to Present** Is the struggle for individual freedom still important? Explain.

APPLY SKILLS

Read and Compare Population Maps Look closely at the two maps shown below. Then answer the questions.

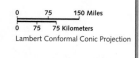

18. About how much larger is the population of London today than it was in 1815?

19. What patterns do you notice in the populations of the large cities in Britain?

Population Maps: Great Britain

- ● More than 5 million people
- ● 1 million to 5 million people
- ● 500 thousand to 1 million
- • Fewer than 500 thousand

0   75   150 Miles
0   75   75 Kilometers
Lambert Conformal Conic Projection

COOPERATIVE LEARNING WORKSHOP

REMEMBER
- Share your ideas.
- Cooperate with others to plan your work.
- Take responsibility for your work.
- Help one another.
- Show your group's work to the class.
- Discuss what you learned by working together.

ACTIVITY

Present an Oral Report

In Chapter 18 you learned about the colonies in Africa and Asia that were controlled by the Western industrialized nations. In a group, select one such colony. Then find out more about that colony. Next, prepare and present an oral report that communicates the information you have found. Be sure to tell how colonization affected the people of Africa or Asia.

ACTIVITY

Make a Poster

Work in a group to create a poster about some of the democratic revolutions discussed in this unit. Label each scene with the name of the country you are showing.

ACTIVITY

Hold a Class Fair

The Industrial Revolution caused great change in the way people lived and worked in the nineteenth century. In your classroom, hold a fair about "revolutionary" ideas for the twenty-first century. With a group of six or seven classmates, make an exhibit of photographs, drawings, or models that show how people will live and work in the new century. Group members should explain each exhibit while other students view it.

Unit Project Wrap-Up

Create a Time Line As a group, review the list of events you have made and decide which ones to show on your time line. To make the time line, use one long sheet of paper or several individual sheets taped together. For each event, show its date and the place where it happened and describe the event. Place each event in order on the time line. Make sure to title the time line and add illustrations to some of the events shown. Display the time line on a bulletin board or wall.

THE WORLD AT WAR

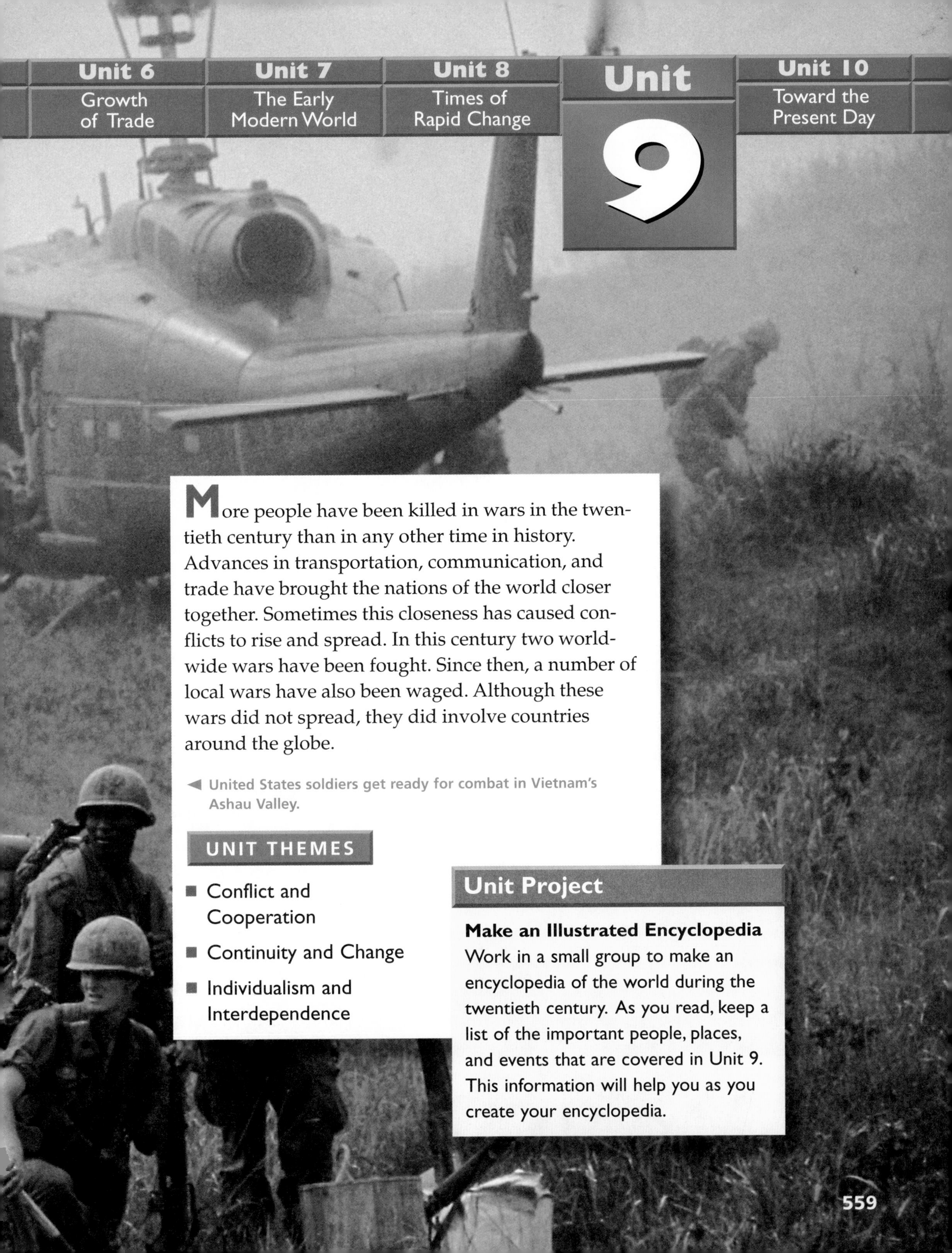

More people have been killed in wars in the twentieth century than in any other time in history. Advances in transportation, communication, and trade have brought the nations of the world closer together. Sometimes this closeness has caused conflicts to rise and spread. In this century two worldwide wars have been fought. Since then, a number of local wars have also been waged. Although these wars did not spread, they did involve countries around the globe.

◄ United States soldiers get ready for combat in Vietnam's Ashau Valley.

UNIT THEMES

- Conflict and Cooperation
- Continuity and Change
- Individualism and Interdependence

Unit Project

Make an Illustrated Encyclopedia
Work in a small group to make an encyclopedia of the world during the twentieth century. As you read, keep a list of the important people, places, and events that are covered in Unit 9. This information will help you as you create your encyclopedia.

559

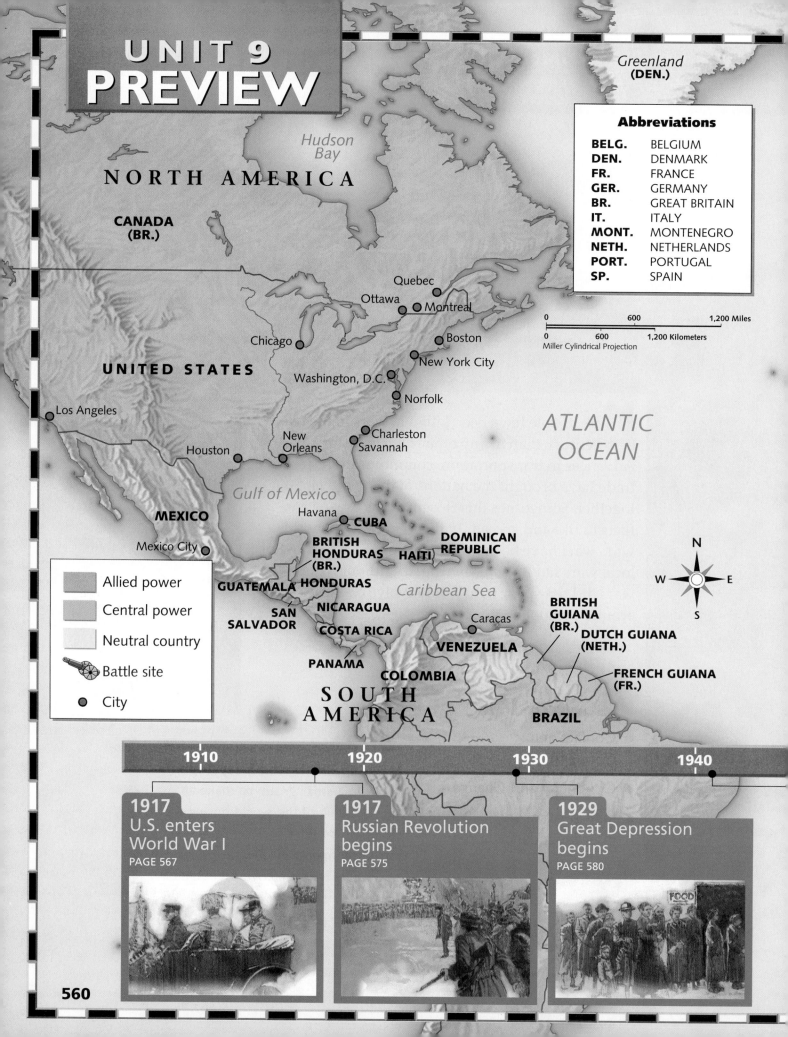

1917
U.S. enters World War I
PAGE 567

1917
Russian Revolution begins
PAGE 575

1929
Great Depression begins
PAGE 580

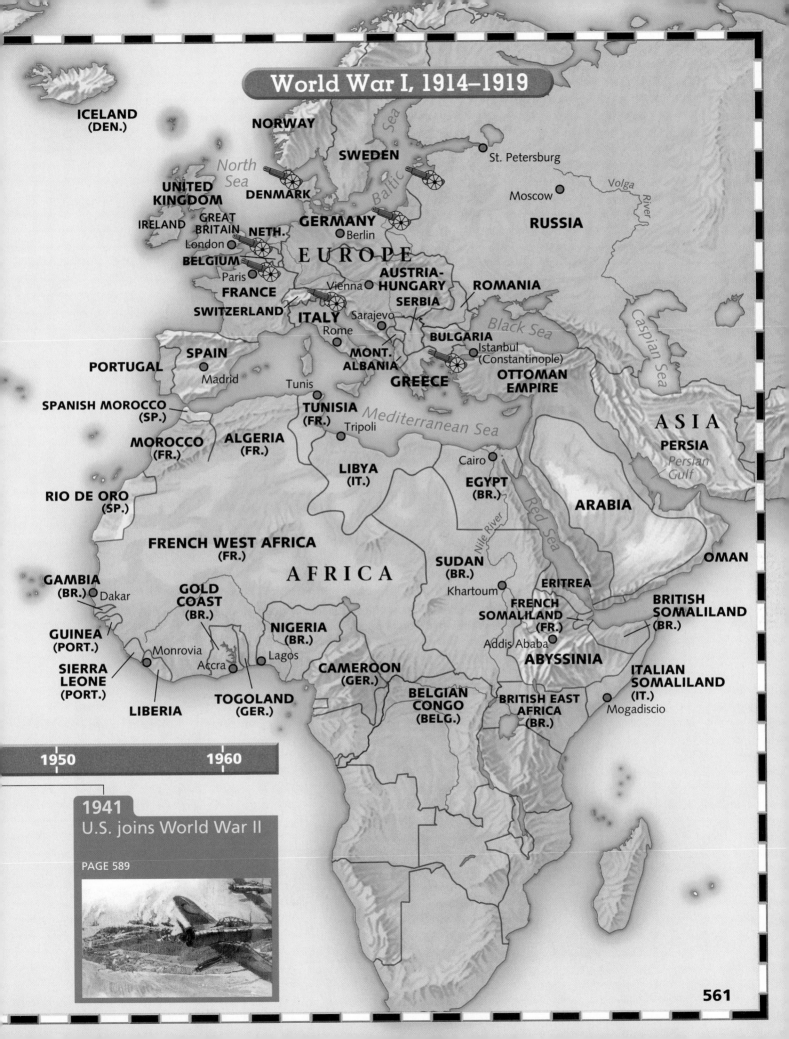

World War I, 1914–1919

ICELAND
(DEN.)

NORWAY

SWEDEN

North Sea

Baltic Sea

St. Petersburg

Moscow

Volga River

UNITED KINGDOM

DENMARK

IRELAND

GREAT BRITAIN

NETH.

London

BELGIUM

Paris

FRANCE

SWITZERLAND

GERMANY
• Berlin

EUROPE

AUSTRIA-HUNGARY

Vienna

ITALY
Rome •

MONT.
ALBANIA

SERBIA

Sarajevo

ROMANIA

Black Sea

BULGARIA

Istanbul
(Constantinople)

GREECE

OTTOMAN EMPIRE

RUSSIA

Caspian Sea

ASIA

PERSIA

Persian Gulf

SPAIN

Madrid •

PORTUGAL

SPANISH MOROCCO
(SP.)

MOROCCO
(FR.)

ALGERIA
(FR.)

Tunis •

TUNISIA
(FR.)

Tripoli •

Mediterranean Sea

LIBYA
(IT.)

Cairo •

EGYPT
(BR.)

Nile River

Red Sea

ARABIA

OMAN

RIO DE ORO
(SP.)

FRENCH WEST AFRICA
(FR.)

AFRICA

SUDAN
(BR.)

Khartoum •

ERITREA

FRENCH SOMALILAND
(FR.)

BRITISH SOMALILAND
(BR.)

GAMBIA
(BR.)

Dakar •

GOLD COAST
(BR.)

NIGERIA
(BR.)

Addis Ababa •

ABYSSINIA

GUINEA
(PORT.)

Monrovia •

Accra •

Lagos •

CAMEROON
(GER.)

ITALIAN SOMALILAND
(IT.)

SIERRA LEONE
(PORT.)

LIBERIA

TOGOLAND
(GER.)

BELGIAN CONGO
(BELG.)

BRITISH EAST AFRICA
(BR.)

Mogadiscio •

1950   1960

1941
U.S. joins World War II

PAGE 589

SCENE OF WAR

written by Mildred Aldrich

War affects everyone, not just the soldiers who fight in it. It becomes part of the way of life of all men, women, and children in a battle-torn country. Read now as Mildred Aldrich, an American living in France, describes the coming of war to the French countryside in 1914.

This painting by Claude Monet (moh•NAY) shows stacks of grain in the French countryside. The painting represents the artist's first impressions of an outdoor scene.

Artist Jules Brenton captures on canvas a scene of French women gathering leftover grain from a field.

A dozen times during the afternoon I went into the study and tried to read. Little groups of old men, women, and children were in the road, mounted on the barricade that the English had left. I could hear the murmur of their voices. In vain I tried to stay indoors. The thing was stronger than I, and in spite of myself, I would go out on the lawn and, field glass in hand, watch the smoke. To my imagination every shot meant awful slaughter, and between me and the terrible thing stretched a beautiful country, as calm in the sunshine as if horrors were not. In the field below me the wheat was being cut. I remembered vividly afterward that a white horse was drawing the reaper, and women and children were stacking and gleaning.[1] Now and then the horse would stop, and a woman, with her red handkerchief on her head, would stand, shading her eyes a moment, and look off. Then the white horse would turn and go plodding on. The grain had to be got in if the Germans were coming, and these fields were to be trampled as they were in 1870.

It was just about six o'clock when the first bomb that we could really see came over the hill. The sun was setting. For two hours we saw them rise, descend,[2] explode. Then a little smoke would rise from one hamlet, then from another; then a tiny flame—hardly more than a spark—would be visible; and by dark the whole plain was on fire, lighting up Mareuil[3] in the foreground, silent and untouched. There were long lines of grain stacks and mills stretching along the plain. One by one they took fire, until, by ten o'clock, they stood like a procession of huge torches across my beloved panorama.[4]

As you read this unit, you will find out how wars touched the lives of millions of people.

[1] **gleaning:** gathering grain left scattered in a field

[2] **descend:** fall
[3] **Mareuil:** (muh•ROY) a town in France
[4] **panorama:** complete view in all directions

CHAPTER

19

The Early Twentieth Century

"There's just one thing that I know, mister. Our hungry babies must be fed. . . ."

Jim Garland, American songwriter

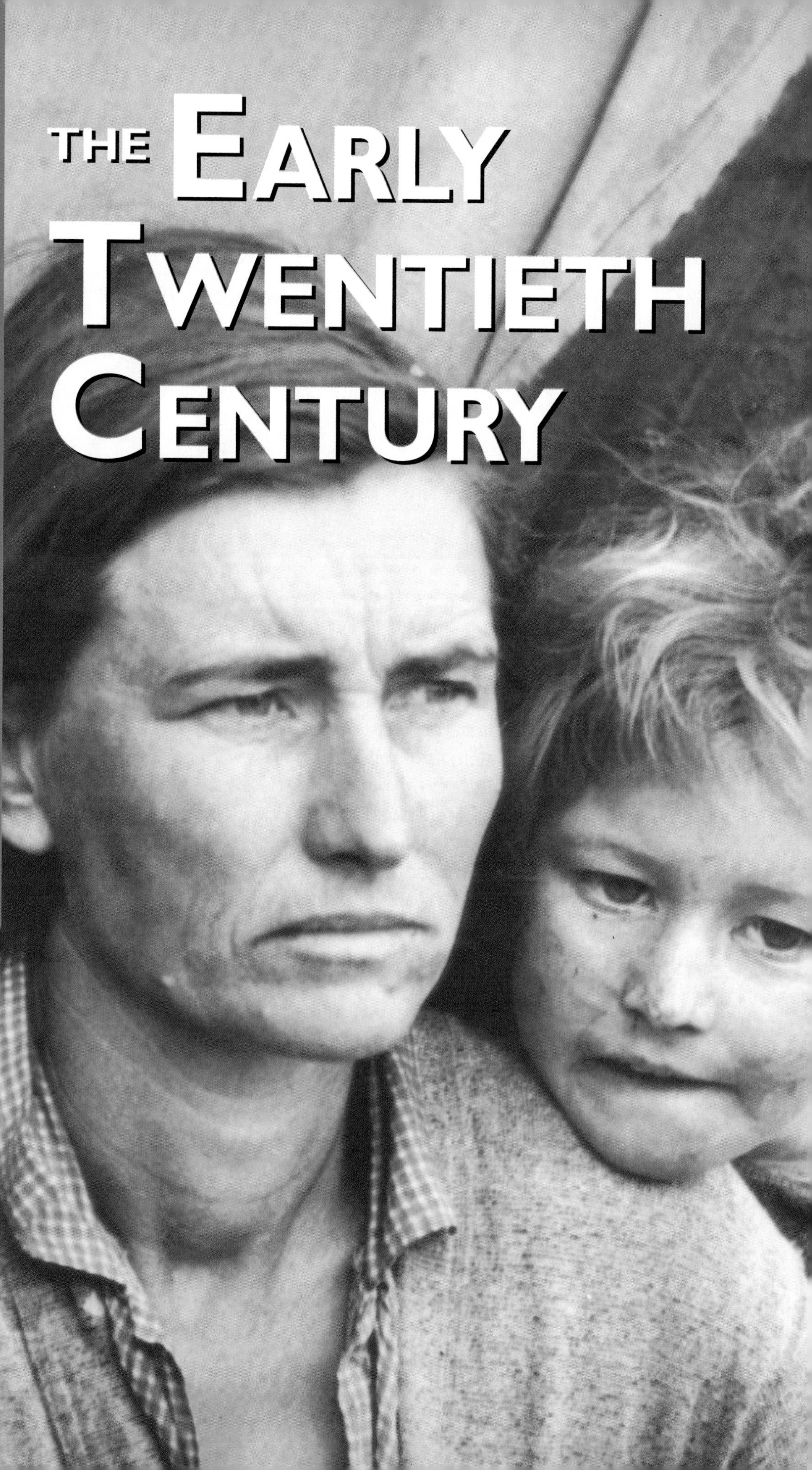

This photograph is one of many taken by the American photographer Dorothea Lange during the Great Depression.

World War I

LESSON

1

FOCUS

What brings about war between different peoples?

Main Idea As you read, think about how alliances of nations led to World War I.

Vocabulary

militarism
conscription
arms race
armistice

N apoleon's plan to conquer all of Europe in the early 1800s placed much of the continent into war. After Napoleon's defeat in 1815, European leaders avoided war by not letting any one country get too strong. This balance of power kept the peace among nations for much of the nineteenth century. Then, in the late 1800s, this balance broke down as rivalries, or competition, among the European nations grew stronger. These rivalries would send Europe and the rest of the world into war.

Unsettled Conflicts

The spirit of nationalism, or strong feelings of pride in a nation, which arose in Europe in the late 1800s, created many conflicts. Often strong national pride drove countries to take actions that helped their own people but not others. Many times this competition led to disputes. Although war was usually avoided by making agreements, nobody was really happy with the results. Angry feelings continued.

Conflicts also arose in regions where people who wanted to rule themselves were not allowed to do so. Throughout the Balkan Peninsula such nationalist feelings were especially strong. Many different peoples lived in this region, including Hungarians, Greeks, Albanians, Turks, and German-speaking Austrians. Slavic peoples such as Serbs, Croats, Bulgarians, and Slovenes also made the Balkans their home. Some of these ethnic groups—ruled by Austria-Hungary—wanted to build independent nations. Other groups, such as the Bulgarians and the Serbs, already had independence. They wanted others who shared their culture to gain their freedom from Austria-Hungary or from the Ottoman Empire and join them.

REVIEW *How did nationalism create conflicts in Europe at the end of the nineteenth century?*

In the early 1900s many world leaders built up their armies and navies. Here German emperor Wilhelm II speaks to a ship's crew.

Preparing for War

The growing tensions among European nations led to a spirit of **militarism**, or strong interest in armed power. Many European leaders believed that if they used force, they would soon get whatever they wanted. Therefore, they began to build up their nations' military power.

A number of European countries formed huge armies. They kept their armies large through **conscription**, the drafting of young men to serve in the armed forces for a set number of years. These nations also spent a lot of money on weapons and built their own large naval forces. All of Europe became involved in an **arms race**, or competition to have the most weapons.

As the number of weapons grew, so did people's fear of war. European leaders began to form alliances, or agreements, with other nations. These alliances included the promise to help one another against enemies in case of war.

In 1882 Austria-Hungary, Germany, and Italy formed the Triple Alliance. Fearing the strength of this alliance, France allied itself with Russia in 1893. As the arms race sped up, the British joined the French and the Russians. This alliance became known as the Triple Entente (ahn•TAHNT).

The system of alliances created a balance of power among the major nations. Yet it also divided Europe into two sides. Even a minor event might start a war. Such an event soon came to be in the Balkans.

REVIEW *Why did the European nations build up their military power?*

The World at War

In 1908 Austria-Hungary seized the Balkan provinces of Bosnia (BAHZ•nee•uh) and Herzegovina (hairt•suh•goh•VEE•nuh). This angered the Serbs who lived there. They thought that these provinces should be part of Serbia. By 1914 tempers could no longer be controlled.

On June 28, 1914, Archduke Francis Ferdinand, who was to be the future ruler of Austria-Hungary, arrived in the Bosnian capital, Sarajevo (sair•uh•YAY•voh). As he and the archduchess rode through the streets in an open car, a young Serbian nationalist shot and killed them. The leaders of Austria-Hungary thought that the Serbian government had something to do with the assassination. A month later Austria-Hungary declared war on Serbia.

The system of alliances quickly went into operation. The Russians supported their fellow Slavs, the Serbs. Austria-Hungary's main ally, Germany, declared war first on Russia and then, France. Britain responded by declaring war on Germany. By early August 1914 most of Europe was at war. Britain, France, Russia, and their allies soon became known as the Allied Powers, or Allies. Germany, Austria-Hungary, and their allies were called the Central Powers.

In time, the conflict reached beyond Europe. Japan had made agreements with

This 1914 photograph shows Archduke Ferdinand and the archduchess just one hour before their assassination.

the Allies, so it declared war on Germany and attacked German territory in the Pacific Ocean and in China. The war spread to southwestern Asia when the Ottoman Empire entered on the side of the Central Powers. Fighting also broke out in eastern Africa, where British and Belgian troops attacked German colonies. Around the globe British colonists in Australia, Canada, India, and New Zealand also joined the fight. As Australia's prime minister said, "Remember that when the [British] Empire is at war so is Australia at war."

The United States tried to stay out of the war. Many Americans felt the war was a European problem and none of their

German (above) and American (right) war posters

business. Those against having the United States in the war were called isolationists. For the most part, President Woodrow Wilson agreed with the idea of isolation. He said he hoped that Americans would remain "impartial in thought as well as in action." Then in 1917 German submarines attacked United States ships that were trading with Germany's enemies. Also, the British found out about a German plan to draw Mexico into the war by helping the Mexicans regain land that had been lost to the United States.

The United States citizens were outraged. President Wilson realized there was only one thing to do. On April 2, 1917, he asked Congress to declare war to "bring peace and safety to all nations and make the world itself at last free." Four days later the United States entered the war on the side of the Allies. American soldiers would travel overseas to fight in World War I—the Great War, as it was called at the time.

REVIEW *How did the assassinations of Archduke Francis Ferdinand and his wife lead to war?*

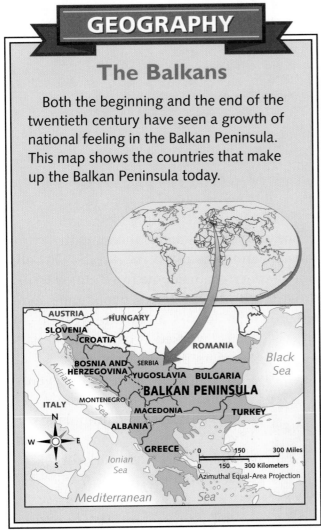

GEOGRAPHY

The Balkans

Both the beginning and the end of the twentieth century have seen a growth of national feeling in the Balkan Peninsula. This map shows the countries that make up the Balkan Peninsula today.

AUSTRIA
HUNGARY
SLOVENIA
CROATIA
ROMANIA
BOSNIA AND HERZEGOVINA
SERBIA
Black Sea
Adriatic Sea
YUGOSLAVIA BULGARIA
BALKAN PENINSULA
MONTENEGRO
ITALY
MACEDONIA
TURKEY
ALBANIA
N
W E
S
GREECE
0   150   300 Miles
0 150 300 Kilometers
Azimuthal Equal-Area Projection
Ionian Sea
Mediterranean Sea

Europe in 1918

0 | 250 | 500 Miles
0 | 250 | 500 Kilometers
Azimuthal Equal-Area Projection

Legend:
- Allied Power
- Central Power
- Neutral nation
- Triple Alliance
- Triple Entente
- Western Front trench
- ⊛ Capital
- ⚶ Battle site

Regions In the early 1900s, most countries in Europe supported either the Triple Entente or the Triple Alliance.

■ *What three world powers made up the Triple Entente? What three world powers made up the Triple Alliance?*

Role of Women in the War

The entry of millions of men into the war caused women to take on new roles. On both sides women on the home front mined coal, drove trucks, swept streets, maintained and repaired railroad cars, and made weapons. They also worked as bank tellers, mail carriers, and police officers.

Women also took part in events closer to the war itself. Some served as nurses and ambulance drivers. Others joined the army and navy and worked as clerks or telegraph operators.

REVIEW *What new roles did women take on during World War I?*

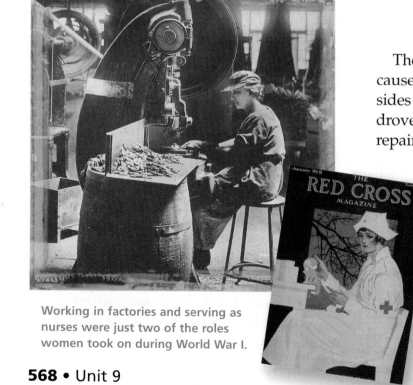

Working in factories and serving as nurses were just two of the roles women took on during World War I.

Soldiers Killed
in World War I

Germany	🪖🪖🪖🪖🪖🪖🪖🪖🪖🪖🪖🪖🪖🪖🪖🪖🪖	
Austria-Hungary	🪖🪖🪖🪖🪖🪖🪖🪖🪖🪖🪖🪖	**CENTRAL POWERS**
Ottoman Empire	🪖🪖🪖🪖	
Russia	🪖🪖🪖🪖🪖🪖🪖🪖🪖🪖🪖🪖🪖🪖🪖🪖🪖	
France	🪖🪖🪖🪖🪖🪖🪖🪖🪖🪖🪖🪖🪖🪖	**ALLIES**
British Empire	🪖🪖🪖🪖🪖🪖🪖🪖🪖	
Italy	🪖🪖🪖🪖🪖🪖🪖	
United States	🪖🪖	🪖 = 100,000 people

LEARNING FROM GRAPHS United States soldiers (left) and German soldiers (right) were among the many troops who fought in World War I. Millions of soldiers lost their lives.

■ *Which side lost more soldiers, the Allied Powers or the Central Powers?*

War in an Industrial Age

When the war began, people thought it would not last long. However, the war kept on without a winner. For more than three years, neither side gained much territory.

Enemy soldiers faced each other across a long line of deep trenches, or ditches. The trenches protected them from machine-gun fire. The trenches, though, were horrible places. Soldiers were forced to eat, sleep, and fight in the same spot for weeks at a time. Sickness was everywhere. Rain and mud added to the soldiers' misery.

Troops could only defend their territory from the trenches. To gain territory, soldiers had to leave their trenches and attack the enemy head-on. Soldiers dreaded the command "over the top," which forced them out of the trenches. Outside the trenches lay a "no-man's land" of barbed wire and exploding mines. At best, trips over the top meant tiny gains of territory. They always brought death for some soldiers.

By the end of the war, more than 8 million soldiers would be killed. An additional 20 million would be wounded. Many others would suffer from a nervous condition called shell shock.

The high numbers of injuries and deaths during the war resulted partly from new technology. Inventors had produced many deadly new weapons, such as machine guns, tanks, and a poisonous spray called mustard gas. The new guns could fire shells at targets that were miles away. A direct hit by one of these shells killed many soldiers and scattered bodies everywhere. "Death roars around one," a German soldier said, "a hail of machine-gun and rifle bullets; every moment one expects to be hit."

REVIEW *How did new technology add to the destruction during World War I?*

A Fragile Peace

By the summer of 1918, the war seemed to be coming to an end. A revolution had overthrown the Russian government in 1917. Soon the new government signed a peace treaty with the Central Powers. With the war against Russia over, the Central Powers sent all their forces to western Europe.

New Nations After World War I

The peace treaty that ended World War I brought many changes. Germany lost some of its land. The old empire that was known as Austria-Hungary was broken up and reduced to two small countries. In addition, the independent countries of Poland, Czechoslovakia (che•kuh•sloh•VAH•kee•uh), Yugoslavia (yoo•goh•SLAH•vee•uh), Finland, Estonia, Latvia, and Lithuania were created. Later a new international organization called the League of Nations reduced the Ottoman Empire to the independent state of Turkey. New borders were drawn in the lands once part of the Ottoman Empire, creating Iraq, Syria, Lebanon, Palestine, and Trans-Jordan, all under French or British control.

They thought this would bring them victory. The Allies, however, had fresh American troops. They soon won several battles. It now looked as if the Allies would win.

President Wilson turned his attention to the peace that would follow. He wanted a treaty that would create a lasting peace. His proposal for peace became known as the Fourteen Points. The points included arms reductions by all nations and open rather than secret peace agreements. For Wilson one point was more important than all the others. He wanted the nations of the world to form an international association to keep the peace.

By late October the Germans were ready to end the war's killing and destruction. On November 11, 1918, Germany signed an **armistice** (AR•muh•stuhs), or agreement to stop fighting. Two months later a meeting took place in Paris to decide peace terms.

The delegates signed a document called the Treaty of Versailles on June 28, 1919.

Regions The Treaty of Versailles caused borders in Europe to change. Compare this map with the map on page 568.

■ *What new countries were formed in Europe because of the treaty?*

Europe After the Treaty of Versailles

As World War I drew to a close, United States President Woodrow Wilson (far right) wrote a peace proposal that became known as the Fourteen Points (near right).

• FOURTEEN POINTS •

Listed below is one of the Fourteen Points proposed by United States President Woodrow Wilson at the end of World War I.

14. A GENERAL ASSOCIATION OF NATIONS MUST BE FORMED UNDER SPECIFIC COVENANTS FOR THE PURPOSE OF AFFORDING MUTUAL GUARANTEES OF POLITICAL INDEPENDENCE AND TERRITORIAL INTEGRITY [RIGHTS] TO GREAT AND SMALL STATES ALIKE.

The delegates agreed to some of Wilson's points, including the creation of a new international organization called the League of Nations. For the most part, however, the treaty was very different from the document of peace Wilson wanted.

For one thing, the treaty dealt very harshly with Germany. The Germans had to take full responsibility for the war. They also had to pay huge sums of money to the Allied nations to repair damages caused by the war. The German army and its supply of weapons were to be cut back. Germany also had to give up territory in Europe, Africa, and the Pacific.

The treaty left many people bitter. The Germans were angry about the harsh treatment they received. The Italians had wanted to gain more land as a reward for their role on the side of the Allies. Also, the United States did not join the League of Nations because many Americans wanted to return to a policy of isolation. The uneasy peace that followed the war would last no more than 20 years.

REVIEW *How did the Treaty of Versailles punish Germany?*

LESSON I REVIEW

Check Understanding

1 Remember the Facts What were the two major alliances in Europe in the years leading up to World War I? What nations were in each?

2 Recall the Main Idea How did the system of alliances among European nations lead to World War I?

Think Critically

3 Cause and Effect How did nationalism create tensions in Europe in the early 1900s?

4 Past to Present How have nationalist feelings affected recent international conflicts?

Show What You Know

List Activity President Wilson's Fourteen Points were designed to help the nations of the world work out their differences peacefully. Think about ways in which your classmates could work out their differences without fighting. Then make a poster titled *Points for Keeping Peace at School* that lists your ideas. Discuss them with classmates.

Understand Time Zones

1. Why Learn This Skill?

The measurement of time is important to many people's daily activities. Trains, buses, and airplanes must keep to time schedules. Television and radio programs must start at certain times. Imagine the problems people would face if every community had its own way of measuring time! In the 1880s most of the countries of the world agreed to follow a system of standard time zones to end confusion about times. Modern travel and communication make understanding time zones even more important than it was in the 1800s.

2. Time Zones

Time on Earth is measured by meridians. You have learned the word *meridian* as another name for a line of longitude. The prime meridian, or line of 0° (degrees) longitude, passes through Greenwich (GREH•nich), which is a suburb of London, England. Many years ago an observatory was built there. It had very accurate tools that scientists used to tell the exact time of day. Because of this the meridian that passes through Greenwich was chosen as the prime meridian, or the starting point for the world's time zones.

All the time zones lie east or west of the prime meridian. There are 24 standard time zones, 12 of them to the east of Greenwich and 12 to the west. Each time zone covers 15 degrees of longitude. Every 15 degrees east or west, the standard time changes by one hour.

All the time zones to the east of the prime meridian are ahead of Greenwich time. All zones to the west are behind Greenwich time. The meridian where the east and west time zones meet is known as the International Date Line. It is 12 time zones from the prime meridian, so when it is noon in Greenwich, it is midnight at the International Date Line, the time when the date changes.

Clocks Around the World

NEW YORK
7:00 A.M.

BUENOS AIRES
9:00 A.M.

LONDON
NOON

CAIRO
2:00 P.M.

DELHI
5:30 P.M.

TOKYO
9:00 P.M.

3. Understand the Process

The map shows all 24 standard time zones. It tells what time it is in each zone when it is noon at the prime meridian. By international agreement, all places within the same time zone have the same time. When it is 7:00 A.M. in Montreal, Canada, it is also 7:00 A.M. in Lima, Peru, and in New York City.

Look at the times at the top of the map. The time in each time zone is one hour ahead or one hour behind the times in the neighboring zones. If you go east from Greenwich, the time in each zone you come to is one hour later than the last. When it is noon in Greenwich, it is 1:00 P.M. in Vienna, Austria. Vienna is in the first time zone to the east of Greenwich. Meanwhile, it is 9:00 P.M. in Tokyo, Japan, which is in the ninth time zone to the east. As you go west from Greenwich, the time in each zone is one hour earlier. When it is noon in Greenwich, it is 6:00 A.M. in Mexico City.

You can also see on the time zone map that the boundary between two time zones does not always follow the meridian exactly. The boundary may zigzag in places so that neighboring cities and towns can keep the same time. In some places the people in a time zone have chosen not to use the time of their zone. Notice on the time zone map that all of India uses a time that is 30 minutes ahead of the time in Pakistan. Also notice that Australia's central time zone is 90 minutes ahead of its western time zone. Such places are shown on the map as having nonstandard time zones.

4. Think and Apply

Write five word problems about time zones, and give them to a partner to solve. Here is an example: "At 9:00 P.M. Maria telephones from Mexico City, Mexico, to her sister in Buenos Aires, Argentina. What time is it in Buenos Aires?"

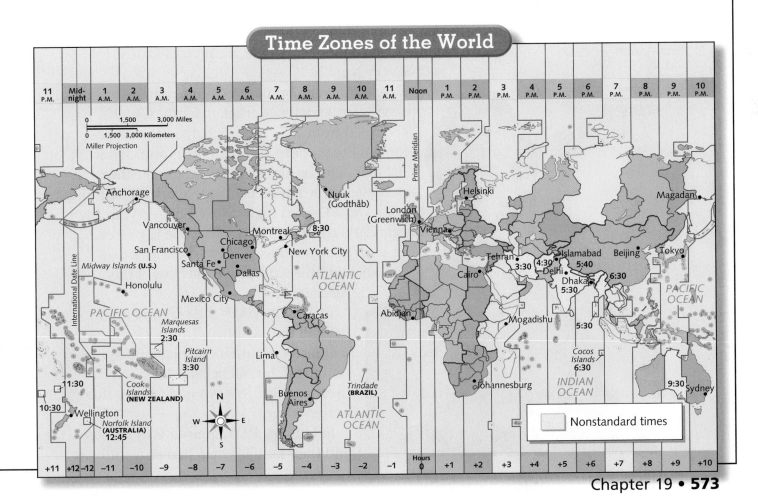

Time Zones of the World

FOCUS

How can a country change political systems and yet remain much the same?

Main Idea As you read, think about how the government of Russia changed and yet stayed much the same after the revolution of 1917.

Vocabulary

autocrat
czar
communism
soviet
collective
purge
totalitarian

The Russian Revolution

Since the late 1400s, **autocrats**, or leaders with unlimited authority, had ruled Russia. These autocrats often treated their people badly. By the early 1900s the Russian people wanted change. They overthrew their rulers and set up a new form of government.

Czarist Russia

In the 1400s, after 200 years of Mongol rule, the Russian provinces were able to gain their freedom. Moscow, a province that had gained great strength, managed to drive out the Mongols. Most of the Russian lands became united under a leader known as Ivan III. Later, the leader of Russia would be known as the **czar** (ZAR), meaning "caesar," or ruler.

Russia's czars extended the country's borders and built Russia into a rich nation. However, most czars treated the people very harshly.

Even czars who brought positive changes to Russia were sometimes cruel. Peter the Great, who ruled from 1682 to 1725, helped Russia become more modern and built the grand city of St. Petersburg as his capital. To complete the project, however, he forced people to work on building the city and collected high taxes from everyone in Russia. Catherine the Great, who came to power in 1762, supported learning and the arts. But she did little to improve the lives of the Russian people.

By the late 1800s the czar and nobles held all the wealth and authority. Peasants and factory workers owned almost nothing. Czar Nicholas II, who came to the throne in 1894, wanted to keep things as they were.

In January 1905 thousands of workers and their families marched peacefully to

Catherine the Great of Russia

the czar's palace in St. Petersburg to ask for reforms, or improvements. Their requests were met by bullets from the czar's troops. The people answered by going on strike, which brought the country to a stop. Reluctantly Nicholas II agreed to make reforms, but little changed.

When Russia became involved in World War I, Nicholas II insisted on taking charge of the war effort himself. Russia suffered defeat after defeat. The people blamed their czar for their losses.

While Nicholas led the war effort, Czarina (zah•REE•nuh) Alexandra took over the everyday running of the government. A peasant from Siberia named Rasputin (ra•SPYOOT•uhn), who claimed to be a holy man with special powers, influenced her greatly. Seeing their country being run by a priest—who might be a fake—made the Russian people even angrier than they had been before. In 1916 a group of nobles killed Rasputin. By this time the czar had completely lost the loyalty of the people.

REVIEW *Why were the Russian people unhappy with their leaders?*

Revolution!

The angry Russian people formed many groups that worked for political change. Some groups wanted democracy. Others were made up of revolutionaries who followed the ideas of Karl Marx. Of special interest to them was Marx's idea that socialism would lead to communism. **Communism** is a system in which all property and all means of production, such as factories and farms, belong to the people as a group. The revolutionaries who supported that system came to be known as communists.

By early 1917 food had become hard to find in the Russian capital of St. Petersburg. Late in the winter, Russian workers marched through the streets, demanding bread. "End the war!" and "Down with the czar!" they shouted. Soon, riots broke out and rebellion quickly spread across the country. Finally, even soldiers refused to obey government orders to put down the revolt.

Czarina Alexandra and Czar Nicholas II (top) seemed to care little that their subjects faced hard lives. In the photograph at right, Russian men and women wait in line for food during the early 1900s. What kinds of emotions do you think these people felt?

575

On March 15 Czar Nicholas II gave up his throne. At the same time, leaders in the Duma (DOO•muh), or parliament, set up a temporary government. The czar had been overthrown by a revolution of the workers. Marx believed that a worker revolution was one step toward a new way of life based on communism. However, the leaders of the temporary government wanted democracy, not communism. The communists would not have control of the revolution until later—under a leader who went by the name of Lenin (LEH•nuhn).

REVIEW *How did Czar Nicholas II fall from power?*

The poster (above left) asks, "Have you volunteered for the Red Army?" In the painting (above) the Red Army marches through Moscow.

This painting shows the second All-Russian Congress of Soviets. The members of the congress appointed Lenin (center) to head the newly formed Soviet Union.

The Communists Come to Power

As a young man, Lenin became a follower of Karl Marx. He helped found a Marxist group that later became known as the Russian Social Democratic Labor Party. Lenin strongly believed that only active revolutionaries should be allowed to become party members. This idea split the party in two. Those who followed Lenin became known as Bolsheviks (BOHL•shuh•viks).

After the fall of the czar, Lenin called for an end to the new democratic government. He believed that a communist government should lead Russia. Lenin and the Bolsheviks won many followers by promising, "Peace, Land, and Bread." These were the things the peasants and workers wanted most.

In early November 1917 Lenin and the Bolsheviks took control of the government. First, they signed peace treaties with the Central Powers and withdrew from World War I. Then, they made the Communist party the only legal political party in Russia. They also formed a secret police force, called the Cheka (CHAY•kuh). Saying "He who is not

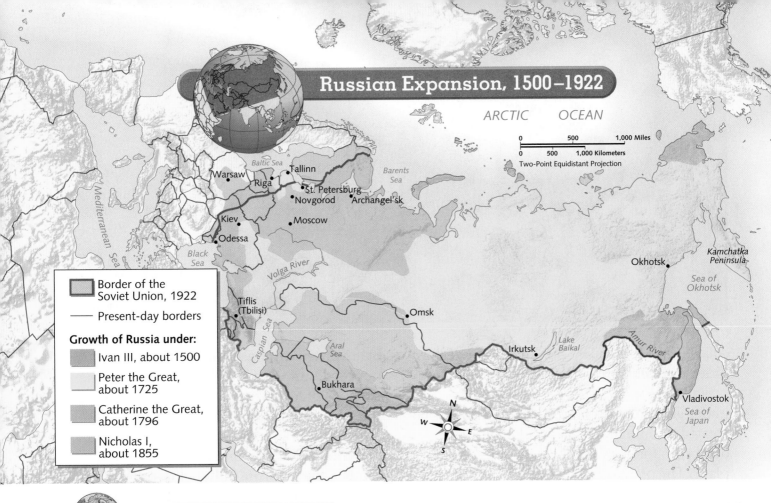

Russian Expansion, 1500–1922

ARCTIC OCEAN

0 500 1,000 Miles
0 500 1,000 Kilometers
Two-Point Equidistant Projection

Legend:
- Border of the Soviet Union, 1922
- Present-day borders

Growth of Russia under:
- Ivan III, about 1500
- Peter the Great, about 1725
- Catherine the Great, about 1796
- Nicholas I, about 1855

Map labels: Warsaw, Riga, Tallinn, Baltic Sea, St. Petersburg, Novgorod, Archangel'sk, Barents Sea, Kiev, Moscow, Odessa, Black Sea, Volga River, Tiflis (Tbilisi), Caspian Sea, Aral Sea, Bukhara, Omsk, Irkutsk, Lake Baikal, Amur River, Okhotsk, Kamchatka Peninsula, Sea of Okhotsk, Vladivostok, Sea of Japan, Mediterranean Sea

Human-Environment Interactions Over the centuries Russia grew to include much of northern Asia.

■ *Under whose rule did Russia grow most in size?*

---

with us is against us," Lenin ordered the Cheka to track down anyone against his government. The Cheka killed or put into prison tens of thousands of men and women. The government of the czars had been replaced by one that was just as cruel.

Not all Russians were happy to see the Bolsheviks in control. Some who opposed them put together a fighting force called the White Army. The Bolsheviks then formed the Red Army. A civil war between Red and White followed. By 1921 the Red Army had defeated the White. The Bolsheviks were in control, but Russia was in ruins and many Russians were dead. Among the civil war's victims were Czar Nicholas II and his family, who had been executed by the Bolsheviks.

REVIEW *What did the Bolsheviks promise the Russian people?*

Stalin and Totalitarianism

In 1922 Russia was renamed the Union of Soviet Socialist Republics (USSR). The word **soviet** refers to the workers' groups that carried out the revolution. Lenin started rebuilding the country. After Lenin died in 1924, Joseph Stalin (STAH•luhn) took over the job of running the Union of Soviet Socialist Republics, or Soviet Union.

Stalin believed that his most important task was to make the Soviet Union one of the world's strongest nations. To produce more food, he ordered that farms be grouped together into **collectives**. These were large farms on which people worked together as a group. Stalin's secret police killed or put into prison peasants who were against the

Millions of people were sent to slave labor camps during purges ordered by Stalin (above). At left are the barracks, or sleeping quarters, of one such labor camp.

collectives. He then had hundreds of huge factories built and forced people to work in them.

Stalin placed all parts of the economy under government control. In doing so he created a command economy. He then laid out a path for economic growth in five-year plans. The plans set up production schedules for farms and factories. By the late 1930s Stalin had met his goal of making the Soviet Union a leading industrial nation. But his success came at a high cost.

Most Soviet people now had jobs and enough food, but not much more. They had no voice in the government. In fact, when citizens protested and called for change,

Stalin ordered **purges**. All those who opposed him were killed or put into prison. Millions of his purge victims were sent to forced labor camps in Siberia.

The Soviet Union became a world power under Stalin's government. It also became a **totalitarian** (toh•ta•luh•TAIR•ee•uhn) state—a state in which the government has complete control over people's lives. Even with all the changes, however, Soviet citizens had no more freedom or political power than earlier Russian citizens had under the czars.

REVIEW *How did Stalin build a totalitarian state?*

LESSON 2 REVIEW

Check Understanding

1 **Remember the Facts** Who led the Bolsheviks to power?

2 **Recall the Main Idea** In what ways were the government and the economy of Lenin and Stalin different from those of the czars? How were they similar?

Think Critically

3 **Explore Viewpoints** Lenin and Stalin seemed to believe that any action to help the revolution was all right. Do you think the leader of a democratic nation would have shared such a view? Explain your answer.

4 **Personally Speaking** If you had been a Russian peasant or worker in 1917, would you have supported Lenin? Why or why not?

Show What You Know

Writing Activity Russian revolutionaries often discussed the ideal society. Describe in writing your ideal society. Tell how it would be created.

The Great Depression

LESSON 3

FOCUS

How can events in one country affect life in other countries?

Main Idea As you read, find out how an economic crisis in the United States added to problems in other countries.

Vocabulary

Great Depression
inflation
propaganda

In 1929 United States President Herbert Hoover said, "We have reached a higher degree of comfort and security than has ever existed before in the history of the world." For a while it looked as if he was right. After World War I, the United States and many other nations made economic progress. Unfortunately, the good times that followed the war did not last. The United States looked prosperous, but it had hidden economic problems.

A Depression in the Making

The United States has always had a market economy. That is, the people decide which goods and services to buy and sell. They make choices about how to earn their living and spend their money.

Just after World War I, Americans made decisions to buy huge amounts of goods. Factories increased production to meet the demand of buyers. Over time, however, demand fell. People could not afford to keep buying more goods. Warehouses and stores soon overflowed with unsold goods. Even so, industries made more and more products, thinking that someone would buy them.

Government policies made the problem worse. To protect American farms and industries, the government put high taxes on goods imported into the United States. This made it harder for other countries to sell their goods in the United States. If they could not sell their own goods, they could not afford to buy American goods. The American economy suffered because of this.

As doubts about the strength of the economy grew, many people in the United States began to invest in the stock market. They bought and sold shares of stock in the hope of making a

Hard times during the Great Depression forced many people to wait in long lines at food kitchens.

quick profit. Many people did make huge profits. But stockbrokers, or people who bought and sold stock for others, allowed buying on credit. The buyer paid the stockbroker only a small part of the actual price of the stock at the time of the sale. The broker expected the buyer to pay the rest of the price at a later date.

In October 1929 some major stock market investors, worried about the economy, began selling their stock. Panic set in. Soon nearly everyone wanted to sell stock, but few people wanted to buy. Stock prices went way down, or crashed. Brokers demanded the money that was owed them. Most investors, however, did not have the money to pay back what they owed. Many investors and brokers lost all their money.

Economic problems grew rapidly. Few people had money for goods and services. Factories already had full warehouses, so they cut back production and laid off workers. More and more people lost their jobs and worried about paying rent or making house payments. Many tried to

withdraw their savings from banks. Most banks could not pay back so many people so quickly, though. Hundreds of banks closed.

As sources of money became scarce, more businesses closed. The failure of businesses left even more people without jobs. As the 1930s began, the United States began the worst economic decline in the world's history—the **Great Depression**.

REVIEW *What economic problems were hidden by the prosperity of the 1920s?*

Depression Spreads

The stock market "crash" ruined the economies of nations around the world. Many Americans had invested large amounts of money in Europe after World War I. After the crash they could not afford to keep their money invested abroad. The European economy, already weak, suffered even more from the loss of American dollars. Banks closed, and people who had deposited money could not get it back. Factories shut down, putting millions out of work. In Asia,

The Great Depression was the time of the worst economic trouble in the history of the world. This Oklahoma family travels in search of a better life. Oklahoma was part of the United States region that became known as the Dust Bowl. A series of dust storms and droughts ruined many farms in this region.

Africa, and South America, demand for raw materials dropped. Many people there suffered poverty and hunger. By the early 1930s the world economy was in a mess. World trade and production were down, and unemployment was the highest it had ever been.

As the depression dragged on, people who were out of work felt that their governments did not care about them. With unrest growing daily, people everywhere looked for political leaders who might offer them hope.

REVIEW *How did the Great Depression affect the world economy?*

Roosevelt and the New Deal

In 1933 most Americans felt they had found a leader who could help them. The

President Roosevelt's "fireside chats" over the radio offered hopeful news about the economy of the United States.

new President, Franklin D. Roosevelt, had bold ideas to save the economy and was not afraid to try them out. "The only thing we have to fear is fear itself," he said.

Roosevelt proposed new laws and programs to help people quickly. He also urged Congress to pass laws to reform the economic system. Roosevelt called the new laws and programs the New Deal. The New Deal provided money to allow farmers to keep their land and to help people who were out of work. It created millions of new jobs by paying for many public works. An important New Deal law was the Social Security Act of 1935. This gave money to people who were retired, disabled, or unable to work for other reasons.

The New Deal changed the way the United States government operated. Never before had the government taken such a direct role in people's lives. Even so, the American democratic system remained basically unchanged. In some other countries, however, the search for solutions to the Great Depression meant an end to democracy.

REVIEW *What steps did President Roosevelt take to bring the United States out of the Great Depression?*

LEARNING FROM GRAPHS The stock market crash brought about a time of high unemployment.
■ *In what year did the United States face the highest unemployment?*

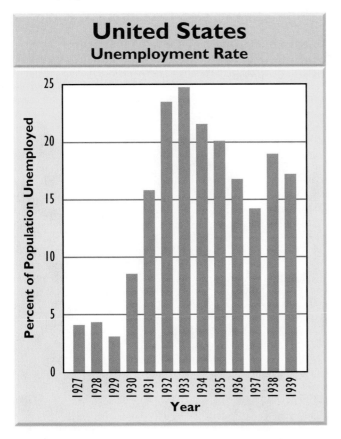

United States
Unemployment Rate

(bar graph: Percent of Population Unemployed vs. Year, 1927–1939)

Ein Volk, ein Reich, ein Führer!

"One People, one Empire, one Leader!" reads this 1938 poster of Adolf Hitler.

Hitler and the Rise of the Nazis

After World War I, Germany became a federal republic. During the 1920s and 1930s, the German republic had terrible problems. Jobs were hard to find. Also, high **inflation**—a continuing increase in prices—made German money almost worthless.

Most German people had lost faith in their government. Many complained bitterly against the government for signing the Treaty of Versailles. They felt the treaty had turned Germany into a poor, weak country. They wanted a strong leader who would make Germany powerful again. Some thought that leader was Adolf Hitler.

Hitler had fought in World War I and felt the shame of Germany's loss. Shortly after the war, he began to look for a way to make up for the defeat. In 1920 he helped form a highly nationalistic, anticommunist group called the National Socialist, or Nazi (NAHT•see), party.

At first the party had little influence, and few people joined. However, when the Great Depression started, more and more people began listening to Hitler's emotional speeches. Many Germans liked his idea that the Germans were a "superrace," a group of people better than all others. Business people liked his promises to rebuild Germany's ruined economy.

By 1933 the Nazis had more elected representatives in the Reichstag (RYKS•tahk)—the German legislature—than any other party. Hitler forced Germany's president to make him chancellor, and he forced the Reichstag to give him control of the government. He then took the title of führer, leader of the German people.

As führer, Hitler banned all political parties except the Nazi party and put an end to elections. He also formed a strong secret police

German money had so little value that people often chose to burn it as fuel rather than use it to buy firewood.

The Nazis and German Youth

The Nazis were successful partly because of support from young people. By 1930 a Nazi youth organization controlled student government at many German universities. By 1933 more than 40 percent of Nazi party members were under 30 years old. Once in power, Hitler set up the Hitler Youth for younger students. Many thousands joined. Some were so loyal that they turned in their own parents as traitors to the government.

force called the Gestapo. The Gestapo arrested anyone who disagreed with Hitler's government. At the same time, Hitler began to rebuild Germany's army.

To get the people to accept all these actions, Hitler used propaganda. **Propaganda** is the spreading of information or rumors to help or hurt a cause. To spread his propaganda, Hitler took control of newspapers, radio stations, and schools. He also screamed speeches filled with hate to huge crowds.

A key part of Hitler's message was that Germany's political and economic troubles were the fault of the Jewish people. Hitler argued that the Jews had to lose their economic power and their place in society for Germany to become strong again. The Nazi party propaganda convinced many Germans that Hitler was right. Most did not complain when he passed laws that took away Jewish citizens' rights and property.

REVIEW *How did Hitler and the Nazis take control in Germany?*

LESSON 3 REVIEW

Check Understanding

1. **Remember the Facts** What event marked the beginning of the Great Depression in the United States?

2. **Recall the Main Idea** How did economic problems in the United States lead to problems in other countries?

Think Critically

3. **Think More About It** How were the political reactions to the Great Depression in Germany different from those in the United States?

4. **Past to Present** Do you think a ruler like Hitler could gain power today? Explain why or why not.

Show What You Know

Chart Activity Prepare a chart that shows how the economic problems of the Great Depression created a "vicious circle" in the United States.

CHAPTER 19
REVIEW

1900   1910

1914
• World War I
  begins

1917
• U.S. enters
  World War I

• Russian
  Revolution

CONNECT MAIN IDEAS

Use this organizer to describe the early twentieth century. Write three details to support each main idea. A copy of the organizer appears on page 133 of the Activity Book.

The Early Twentieth Century

World War I

Alliances of nations led to World War I.

1. _____
2. _____
3. _____

The Russian Revolution

The Russian government changed yet stayed much the same after the Russian Revolution of 1917.

1. _____
2. _____
3. _____

The Great Depression

An economic crisis led to the Great Depression and affected countries around the world.

1. _____
2. _____
3. _____

WRITE MORE ABOUT IT

Write a News Story Imagine that you are a news reporter in the early 1900s. Write a news story to tell the people of the United States about life in Europe in the months before the Great War. Describe how events in Europe affect the United States.

Write a Song Imagine that you are a songwriter during the Great Depression. Write one or more verses of a song that describes the hardships people are facing. Once you have written your song, you may want to perform it for your family or your class.

1920	1930	1940	1950

1918
• World War I ends

1929
• Great Depression begins

1933
• Franklin Roosevelt declares New Deal

• Adolf Hitler becomes leader of Germany

USE VOCABULARY

For each pair of terms, write a sentence or two that explains how the terms are related.

1. armistice, arms race

2. autocrat, czar

3. communism, collectives

4. conscription, militarism

5. purge, totalitarian

CHECK UNDERSTANDING

6. Which countries formed the Triple Alliance? Which countries formed the Triple Entente?

7. Why did Austria-Hungary declare war on Serbia in 1914?

8. How did the role of women change during World War I?

9. Why was the peace that followed the Treaty of Versailles an "uneasy peace"?

10. How did the Bolsheviks encourage the peasants and workers of Russia to support them?

11. Who was affected by the United States' stock market crash of 1929?

12. What problems in Germany helped Hitler rise to power?

THINK CRITICALLY

13. **Cause and Effect** What effect do you think the new roles of women during World War I had on everyday life after the war?

14. **Think More About It** Why did the democratic system in the United States stay unchanged after World War I? Why did democracy end in some other parts of the world?

15. **Explore Viewpoints** Why do you think the German people listened to Hitler?

APPLY SKILLS

Understand Time Zones Use the time zone map on page 573 to answer these questions.

16. Sarah is traveling by automobile west from New York City. Her trip will cross two time zones. Should she set her watch back or forward for each time zone she crosses?

17. Justin lives in Chicago. He wants to communicate by computer to a pen pal in Cairo, Egypt. Justin sends his message at 9 A.M. What time is it in Cairo when Justin sends his message?

READ MORE ABOUT IT

Out of the Dust by Karen Hesse. Scholastic. Through a series of poems, 14-year-old Billie Jo relates the hardships of life in Oklahoma during the Great Depression.

HARCOURT BRACE

Visit the Internet at
http://www.hbschool.com
for additional resources.

THE LATER
TWENTIETH CENTURY

"From Stettin in the Baltic to Trieste in the Adriatic, an iron curtain has descended across the Continent."

Sir Winston Churchill, former British prime minister, 1946

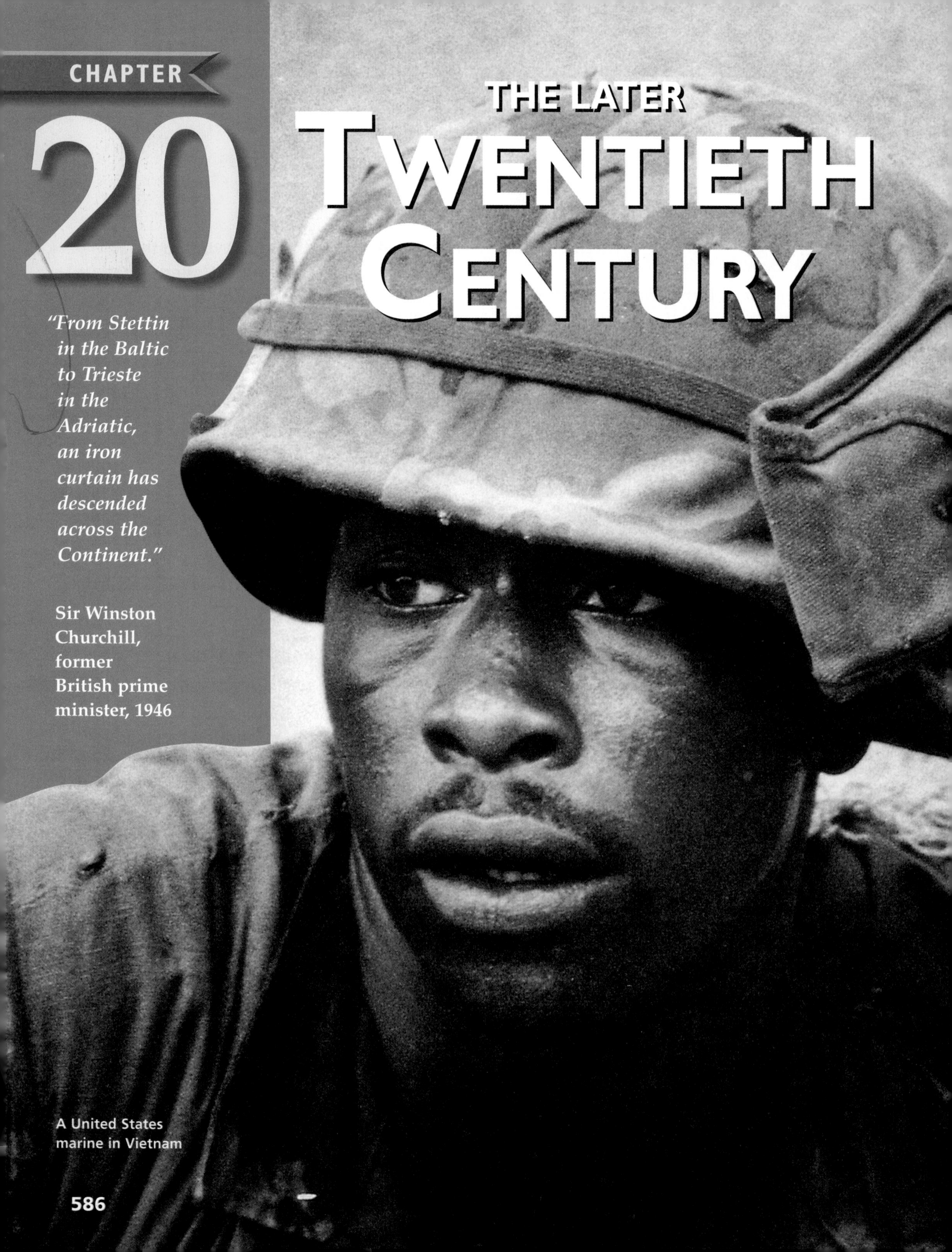

A United States marine in Vietnam

World War II

FOCUS
How can the desire of
some people to control
others lead to war?

Main Idea As you
read, find out how
some people's attempts
to control others led
to a second war that
involved the whole
world.

Vocabulary
fascism
appeasement
concentration camp
genocide
Holocaust
refugee

By 1939 Hitler had turned his slogan "One People, One Empire, One Leader" into reality. His Nazi party ruled Germany's government, army, and press. Through his propaganda and fiery speeches, Hitler had gained control over the minds and emotions of the German people. In time Germany would join forces with Italy and Japan to try to control much of the world.

Seeds of War

Hitler's Nazi party followed a set of political ideas known as **fascism** (FA•shih•zuhm). Fascists valued strong government control, military strength, and intense nationalism. They admired strong leaders and cared little for the freedoms and rights that are important to democracy.

Many Italians were unhappy with the small gains of land they received under the Treaty of Versailles. They also disliked the way their government had handled the country's economic problems. Many wanted change.

Led by Benito Mussolini (moo•suh•LEE•nee), the Fascist party quickly gained support among the Italian people. The Fascists soon took steps to take power. "Either they will give us the government or we shall seize it," Mussolini said boldly. The Italian king gave in to pressure and named Mussolini prime minister in 1922. Mussolini banned all political parties except the Fascist party. He then set up a secret police force and limited the freedom of the press.

Around this time Japan also had a change in government. There, however, the army, rather than a political party, took charge. A group of army officers gained control of the country and promised to build a great empire.

By the mid-1930s Japan, Italy, and Germany were making their dreams of empire a reality. In 1935 Italy conquered the African country of Ethiopia. In 1937 the Japanese military swept into the middle of China. In 1938 the Germans took control of Austria and parts of Czechoslovakia.

Benito Mussolini with his highest-ranking officers

World War II
Military Forces

Number of Troops (in millions)

AXIS			ALLIES					
Germany	Japan	Italy	United States	USSR	China	Britain	India	Poland

Country

LEARNING FROM GRAPHS Troops from around the world took part in World War II.
■ *Which nation supplied more troops, Italy or China?*

European leaders did very little to stop the German and Italian takeovers. They did not want to risk another world war. Also, many of them thought that the fascists' desire for glory and power would soon be met. This policy of not opposing the fascists became known as **appeasement**.

In 1939 the Germans showed that they would not be satisfied. They seized the rest of Czechoslovakia and attacked Poland. Britain and France felt that Hitler had gone too far. They declared war on Germany.

REVIEW *What were some of the reasons for the start of war in 1939?*

Bombs (near right) dropped during air raids caused much destruction. In this 1940 photograph (far right) Winston Churchill inspects bomb damage.

Worldwide Conflict

Hitler's soldiers had been training for war for years. Once their tanks and dive-bombers went into action, German forces seemed unstoppable. By 1940 Germany had taken over Poland, Denmark, Norway, Belgium, the Netherlands, and France.

Britain remained undefeated. The British leader, Winston Churchill, inspired his people to resist. Even in the worst times, Churchill encouraged his people with words like these:

> 66 We shall fight on the beaches, we shall fight on the landing grounds, we shall fight in the fields and in the streets, we shall fight in the hills; we shall never surrender. 99

Failing to take Britain in 1940, Hitler turned his attention elsewhere. With Mussolini he planned to conquer the Mediterranean region. And even though Hitler had made a peace agreement with Stalin, he attacked the Soviet Union in mid-1941. After the attack, the Soviet Union joined the Allies.

Meanwhile, the Japanese rapidly added to their Asian empire. They captured other areas of China and much of Indochina, the eastern part of a peninsula just south of China. They also began to move across the Pacific, capturing island after island.

Some of the many faces of war: (left to right) African American artillery troops, American troops in Tunisia, a wartime poster for recruiting women.

Then, in 1941, Germany, Italy, and Japan—the Axis Powers—faced a number of setbacks. In December 1941 the Japanese bombed the United States naval base at Pearl Harbor in Hawaii. Immediately the United States joined Britain and the Soviet Union in the war against the Axis Powers. Also, the Germans were caught up in a long and bitter struggle against Soviet military forces and Soviet winters. The advantage the Axis Powers had once held over the Allies began to slip away.

Allied forces began to win several important battles. In late 1942 and in 1943, the Allies won victories against the Germans and Italians in North Africa and Sicily. Early in 1943 the German army was forced to pull back from the Soviet Union. Soviet troops then began to move into eastern Europe on their way to Germany. The Italians surrendered in September 1943. Meanwhile, the Allies were also winning naval battles in the Pacific.

REVIEW *Which events in 1941 proved to be turning points in the war? Why?*

The War Ends

In mid-1944 the Allies felt ready to take on Hitler's forces in northern Europe. Their plan involved landing large numbers of Allied soldiers on the beaches of Normandy in northern France. From France, the Allies planned to push toward Germany. The June 6 invasion—code-named D day—did not go smoothly. Some troops landed on the beach only to find steep cliffs ahead. German soldiers immediately began shooting.

But the Allies held the beaches. Within a month they had moved far inland. By late August they had taken Paris from the Germans and had destroyed German cities in bombing raids. On May 7, 1945, the Germans surrendered, ending the war in Europe.

In the Pacific the Allies were slowly driving the Japanese back. First they began taking Japanese-held islands. Then in the spring of 1945, the Allies bombed Japanese cities. They destroyed Japan's war industries and left most of its cities in ruins. The Japanese, however, showed no signs of surrender.

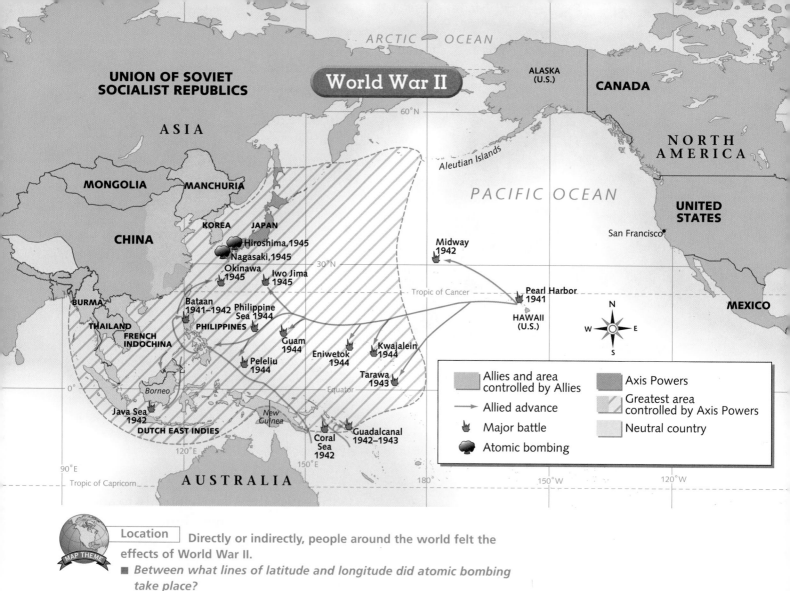

UNION OF SOVIET
SOCIALIST REPUBLICS

ARCTIC OCEAN

ALASKA
(U.S.)

CANADA

ASIA

NORTH
AMERICA

MONGOLIA   MANCHURIA

Aleutian Islands

PACIFIC OCEAN

UNITED
STATES

CHINA

KOREA   JAPAN

San Francisco

Hiroshima,1945
Nagasaki,1945

Midway
1942

Okinawa
1945
Iwo Jima
1945

Tropic of Cancer

Pearl Harbor
1941

MEXICO

BURMA

Bataan
1941–1942   Philippine
Sea 1944

HAWAII
(U.S.)

N

THAILAND
FRENCH
INDOCHINA

PHILIPPINES

Guam
1944

Eniwetok
1944

Kwajalein
1944

W   E

S

Peleliu
1944

Tarawa
1943

Borneo

Equator

Java Sea
1942

New
Guinea

DUTCH EAST INDIES

Coral
Sea
1942

Guadalcanal
1942–1943

AUSTRALIA

	Allies and area controlled by Allies		Axis Powers
→	Allied advance		Greatest area controlled by Axis Powers
	Major battle		Neutral country
	Atomic bombing		

Location Directly or indirectly, people around the world felt the effects of World War II.

■ Between what lines of latitude and longitude did atomic bombing take place?

On August 6, 1945, the United States dropped a terrible new weapon, the atomic bomb, on the Japanese city of Hiroshima (hir•uh•SHEE•muh). The explosion of the atomic bomb sent shock waves that knocked down buildings miles away. Its heat melted stone and steel and turned human bodies into gases. This "rain of ruin from the air" killed more than 70,000 people and destroyed much of Hiroshima. Three days later a second atomic bomb exploded over the city of Nagasaki (nah•guh•SAH•kee). Once again, the explosion caused terrible damage. Finally the Japanese offered to surrender.

REVIEW *How did the Allies gain victory in Europe and in the Pacific during World War II?*

The Holocaust

As the Allies marched through Europe, they began to realize the full horror of what the Nazis had done. Hitler believed that to rebuild after World War I, Germany had to rid itself of "undesirable" people. In this way the pure German Aryan race, as he called it, could become a master race and conquer the world. Hitler put into action his plan to get rid of all those he thought were inferior—especially the Jews. Gypsies, persons with disabilities, and opponents of Nazism were also targets of Hitler's hate.

The first arrests of Jews began in the early 1940s. Those who were arrested were sent to a type of prison called a **concentration camp**.

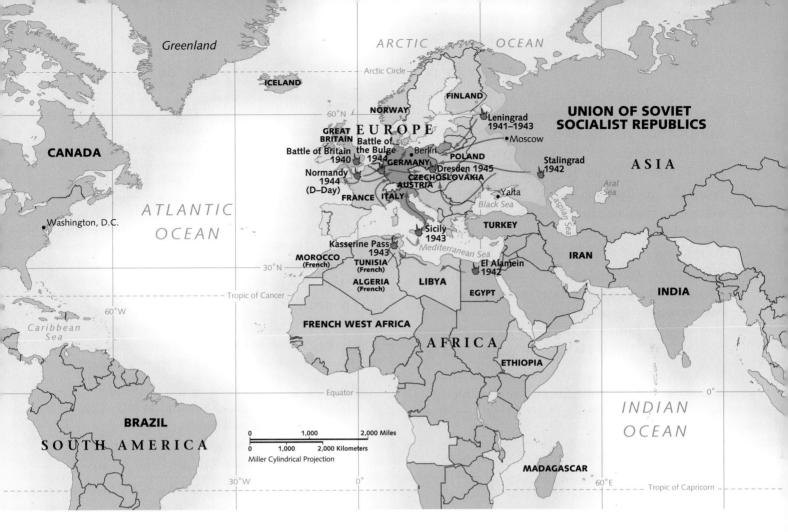

Many of the prisoners in the camps served as slave labor for the German war effort. Others were killed.

To avoid capture many Jews were forced to go into hiding. The Frank family of Amsterdam, a city in the Netherlands, will long be remembered for how they lived in secret. The Franks had earlier fled Germany because Jews there were being terrorized. When Jews in Amsterdam started being sent to concentration camps, the Franks hid above their family business. Anne, the younger daughter, kept a diary about her family's life in hiding. Her diary gives us a touching description of the pain that many suffered during this time. Tragically, Anne was discovered by the Nazis and sent to a concentration camp, where she died.

The Nazis purposely made camp conditions terrible. In most camps guards beat inmates for no reason. In some, such as Auschwitz (OWSH•vits), Nazi doctors used prisoners for strange and cruel medical experiments.

During the winter of 1941–1942, Germany's leaders developed what they called the Final Solution to the Jewish Problem. Their Final Solution was **genocide**, the killing of an entire group of people.

Young prisoners at Auschwitz (below); Anne Frank (right)

The Germans' plan was to kill all the Jews in Europe. Jews were herded like cattle into boxcars and taken to special concentration camps, such as Auschwitz, Majdanek (my•DAH•nek), Dachau (DAH•kow), Sobibór, and Treblinka. When they got there, they were sent to "bathhouses," where they were told they would take showers. But the bathhouses were really gas chambers. A poisonous gas came out of the showers, and within minutes the Jews were dead. Their bodies were then burned in huge ovens nearby.

The mass killing of the Jewish people is now known as the **Holocaust**. By the end of the war, 6 million Jews had died in the death camps, as the concentration camps came to be called. The Nazis also had killed 6 million non-Jews.

REVIEW *What reason did the Germans have for killing Jews and other people?*

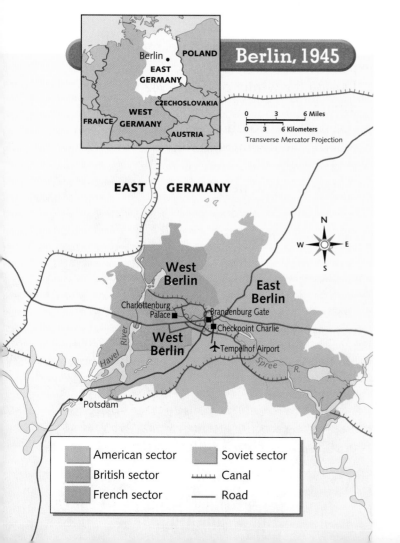

Berlin, 1945

EAST GERMANY

West Berlin

East Berlin

Charlottenburg Palace

Brandenburg Gate

Checkpoint Charlie

West Berlin

Tempelhof Airport

Havel River

Spree R.

Potsdam

American sector	Soviet sector
British sector	Canal
French sector	Road

After the War

The costs of World War II were enormous. Perhaps as many as 50 million soldiers and civilians died in the war. Across Europe, Japan, and other places where fighting had occurred, cities were in ruins. In some cities more than 90 percent of the buildings were too badly damaged to be used. Large numbers of survivors became **refugees**—people who leave their homes to seek shelter and safety elsewhere.

The world needed to be rebuilt. Even before the fighting had ended, Allied leaders Roosevelt, Churchill, and Stalin had begun to make plans for the postwar world. There were conferences at Yalta, on the Black Sea, and at Potsdam, in Germany. At these conferences it was agreed that Germany's weapons would be taken away and Germany would be divided into four zones. Britain, the United States, the Soviet Union, and France would govern these zones. Berlin, the German capital, located in the eastern Soviet zone, would be divided in a similar way. A new international organization, the United Nations, would replace the old League of Nations and help prevent new wars.

The future of eastern Europe was not decided. The Soviet Union had set up communist governments in several eastern European nations. Stalin wanted these governments to remain. The United States and Britain did not. It soon became clear that the alliance that had won the war was already starting to come apart.

REVIEW *What were the results of the Yalta and Potsdam conferences?*

Regions After the war the city of Berlin was divided into four sectors, or parts.

■ *In which part was Charlottenburg Palace?*

The United Nations

INTERNATIONAL COURT OF JUSTICE
Hears and decides legal disputes between nations

Interprets the UN Charter and international law

Made up of 15 elected judges

SECURITY COUNCIL
Deals with disputes between nations

Recommends settlements for disputes

May send troops to settle disputes

Made up of 5 permanent members (France, Britain, China, Russia, and the United States) and 10 elected members

TRUSTEESHIP COUNCIL
Deals with territories that are not self-governing

Because there are presently no United Nations trust territories, the Trusteeship Council no longer meets regularly.

GENERAL ASSEMBLY
Discusses and makes recommendations about world problems

Controls UN finances

Made up of one representative from each member nation

SECRETARIAT
Manages day-to-day business of the UN

Made up of an elected Secretary-General and a staff of interpreters, guides, writers, and clerks

ECONOMIC AND SOCIAL COUNCIL
Studies and makes recommendations about economic and social problems

Promotes human rights

Works with specialized agencies and commissions

Made up of 54 representatives

LEARNING FROM CHARTS The chart above shows the six main agencies of the United Nations. Each agency has its own duties and responsibilities.
■ *Which agency decides whether the UN will send peacekeeping troops to a war-torn nation?*

LESSON 1 REVIEW

Check Understanding

1 Remember the Facts   What were the three major Axis Powers?

2 Recall the Main Idea   How did the desires of some people to control others lead to a world war?

Think Critically

3 Cause and Effect   What factors led to the rise of fascism in Europe?

4 Explore Viewpoints   What arguments might people in the United States have made against getting into the war?

5 Past to Present   Do people today still try to gain control over other people? Explain your answer, using present-day examples.

Show What You Know
News-Reporting Activity
Imagine that you are a radio news reporter at the start of World War II. Write a brief report explaining the rise of fascism. Be sure to answer the questions Who? What? Where? When? Why? and How? about your subject. If you have a tape recorder, you might tape your report and "broadcast" it to the class.

Use a Double-Bar Graph

1. Why Learn This Skill?

A good way to compare statistics is by making a graph. **Statistics** are facts shown with numbers. **Double-bar graphs**, such as those in this lesson, make it easy to compare two sets of statistics.

2. Statistics of World War II

World War II was the most destructive war in world history. More people were killed or wounded in World War II than in any other war. No one knows how many civilians died. Millions of people in war-torn areas died from hunger or disease when food production and health services stopped. Bombing raids often destroyed the records that showed how many

people were killed. In all, as many as 20 million Soviet civilians and 10 million Chinese civilians may have died.

Much more is known, however, about the casualties—people killed or wounded—in the military. Of the more than 70 million people who served in the armed forces of the Allies and the Axis Powers, about 17 million were killed and another 17 million were wounded.

A United States Army nurse feeds a wounded soldier in this 1943 photograph taken during World War II.

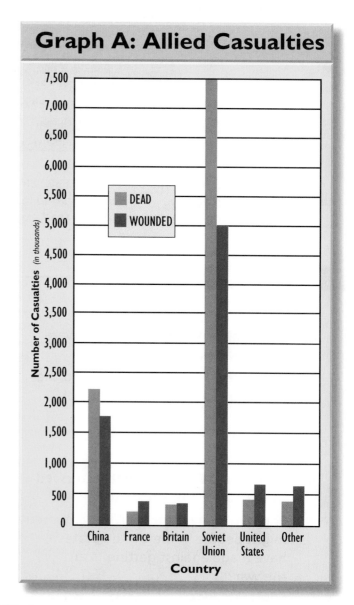

Graph A: Allied Casualties

Number of Casualties *(in thousands)*

Legend: DEAD, WOUNDED

Y-axis: 0, 500, 1,000, 1,500, 2,000, 2,500, 3,000, 3,500, 4,000, 4,500, 5,000, 5,500, 6,000, 6,500, 7,000, 7,500

X-axis (Country): China, France, Britain, Soviet Union, United States, Other

3. Understand the Process

The double-bar graphs on these two pages show by country the numbers of those who were killed and those who were wounded. Graph A shows the Allies' casualties, and Graph B shows the Axis Powers' casualties. Use these steps as a guide to study the graphs.

1 Look at the words and numbers along the bottom and left-hand side of each graph. Countries are listed along the bottom, and the numbers of people are listed along the left-hand side.

2 Notice that there are two different kinds of bars for each country. The red bar shows the number who died. The blue bar shows the number who were wounded.

3 Read each graph by running your finger up to the top of each bar and then left to the number. If the top of the bar is between two numbers, the correct number is between those two.

4 Compare the heights of the red bars. Which country had more people killed?

5 Compare the heights of the blue bars. Which country had more people wounded?

6 Compare the heights of the red bar and the blue bar for any one country. Which bar is higher? How much higher is one bar than the other?

7 Now compare the heights of all the bars to compare casualties among all the countries. How do the double-bar graphs help you understand the human cost of World War II?

4. Think and Apply

Make a double-bar graph of your test scores in social studies and in your other subjects. List the subjects along the bottom of your graph. Along the left-hand side, list possible test scores by tens from 0 percent on the bottom to 100 percent at the top. For each subject, make two bars to show your next two test scores. Remember to use different colors or solids and stripes for the first and second tests. Study your completed graph. What does it tell you?

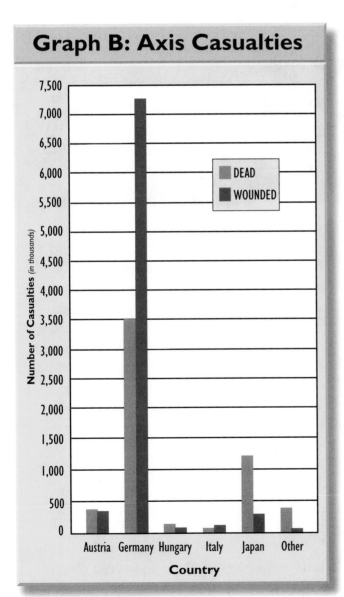

Graph B: Axis Casualties

DEAD
WOUNDED

Number of Casualties (in thousands)

7,500
7,000
6,500
6,000
5,500
5,000
4,500
4,000
3,500
3,000
2,500
2,000
1,500
1,000
500
0

Austria   Germany   Hungary   Italy   Japan   Other

Country

Number the STARS

written by Lois Lowry   illustrated by Tony Meers

As the Nazis marched across Europe, they subjected Jewish people to special abuse. They forced Jews to live in segregated areas called ghettos. They also made Jews wear yellow Stars of David, six-pointed stars that are a symbol of Judaism. Later, as the Nazis began their Final Solution, they sent millions of Jewish people to concentration camps.

Now read about how a Danish couple protected a Jewish child, Ellen, by pretending she was their oldest daughter, who had actually died. As you read, consider how responsible people should be for protecting the rights of others.

*A*nnemarie eased the bedroom door open quietly, only a crack, and peeked out. Behind her, Ellen was sitting up, her eyes wide.

She could see Mama and Papa in their nightclothes, moving about. Mama held a lighted candle, but as Annemarie watched, she went to a lamp and switched it on. It was so long a time since they had dared to use the strictly rationed electricity after dark that the light in the room seemed startling to Annemarie, watching through the slightly opened bedroom door. She saw her mother look automatically to the blackout curtains, making certain that they were tightly drawn.

Papa opened the front door to the soldiers.

"This is the Johansen apartment?" A deep voice asked the question loudly, in terribly accented Danish.

"Our name is on the door, and I see you have a flashlight," Papa answered. "What do you want? Is something wrong?"

"I understand you are a friend of your neighbors the Rosens, Mrs. Johansen," the soldier said angrily.

"Sophy Rosen is my friend, that is true," Mama said quietly. "Please, could you speak more softly? My children are asleep."

"Then you will be so kind as to tell me where the Rosens are." He made no effort to lower his voice.

"I assume they are at home, sleeping. It is four in the morning, after all," Mama said.

Annemarie heard the soldier stalk across the living room toward the kitchen. From her hiding place in the narrow sliver of open doorway, she could see the heavy uniformed man, a holstered pistol at his waist, in the entrance to the kitchen, peering in toward the sink.

Another German voice said, "The Rosens' apartment is empty. We are wondering if they might be visiting their good friends the Johansens."

"Well," said Papa, moving slightly so that he was standing in front of Annemarie's bedroom door, and she could see nothing except the dark blur of his back, "as you see, you are mistaken. There is no one here but my family."

"You will not object if we look around." The voice was harsh, and it was not a question.

"It seems we have no choice," Papa replied.

"Please don't wake my children," Mama requested again. "There is no need to frighten little ones."

The heavy, booted feet moved across the floor again and into the other bedroom. A closet door opened and closed with a bang.

Annemarie eased her bedroom door closed silently. She stumbled through the darkness to the bed.

"Ellen," she whispered urgently, "take your necklace[1] off!"

Ellen's hands flew to her neck. Desperately she began trying to unhook the tiny clasp. Outside the bedroom door, the harsh voices and heavy footsteps continued.

"I can't get it open!" Ellen said frantically. "I never take it off—I can't even remember how to open it!"

Annemarie heard a voice just outside the door. "What is here?"

"Shhh," her mother replied. "My daughters' bedroom. They are sound asleep."

"Hold still," Annemarie commanded. "This will hurt." She grabbed the little gold chain, yanked with all her strength, and broke it. As the door opened and light flooded into the bedroom, she crumpled it into her hand and closed her fingers tightly.

Terrified, both girls looked up at the three Nazi officers who entered the room.

One of the men aimed a flashlight around the bedroom. He went to the closet and looked inside. Then with a sweep of his gloved hand he pushed to the floor several coats and a bathrobe that hung from pegs on the wall.

There was nothing else in the room except a chest of drawers, the blue decorated trunk in the corner, and a heap of Kirsti's dolls piled in a small rocking chair. The flashlight beam touched each thing in turn. Angrily the officer turned toward the bed.

"Get up!" he ordered. "Come out here!"

Trembling, the two girls rose from the bed and followed him, brushing past the two remaining officers in the doorway, to the living room.

---

[1] **necklace:** The necklace was a gold chain with a Star of David attached to it.

Annemarie looked around. These three uniformed men were different from the ones on the street corners. The street soldiers were often young, sometimes ill at ease, and Annemarie remembered how [one] had, for a moment, let his harsh pose slip and had smiled at Kirsti.

But these men were older and their faces were set with anger.

Her parents were standing beside each other, their faces tense, but Kirsti was nowhere in sight. Thank goodness that Kirsti slept through almost everything. If they had wakened her, she would be wailing—or worse, she would be angry, and her fists would fly.

"Your names?" the officer barked.

"Annemarie Johansen. And this is my sister—"

"Quiet! Let her speak for herself. Your name?" He was glaring at Ellen.

Ellen swallowed. "Lise," she said, and cleared her throat. "Lise Johansen."

The officer stared at them grimly.

"Now," Mama said in a strong voice, "you have seen that we are not hiding anything. May my children go back to bed?"

The officer ignored her. Suddenly he grabbed a handful of Ellen's hair. Ellen winced.

He laughed scornfully. "You have a blond child sleeping in the other room. And you have this blond daughter—" He gestured toward Annemarie with his head. "Where did you get the dark-haired one?" He twisted the lock of Ellen's hair. "From a different father? From the milkman?"

Papa stepped forward. "Don't speak to my wife in such a way. Let go of my daughter or I will report you for such treatment."

"Or maybe you got her someplace else?" the officer continued with a sneer. "From the Rosens?"

For a moment no one spoke. Then Annemarie, watching in panic, saw her father move swiftly to the small bookcase and take out a book. She saw that he was holding the family photograph album. Very quickly he searched through its pages, found what he was looking for, and tore out three pictures from three separate pages.

He handed them to the German officer, who released Ellen's hair.

"You will see each of my daughters, each with her name written on the photograph," Papa said.

Annemarie knew instantly which photographs he had chosen. The album had many snapshots—all the poorly focused pictures of school events and birthday parties. But it also contained a portrait, taken by a photographer, of each girl as a tiny infant. Mama had written, in her delicate handwriting, the name of each baby daughter across the bottom of those photographs.

She realized too, with an icy feeling, why Papa had torn them from the book. At the bottom of each page, below the photograph itself, was written the date. And the real Lise Johansen had been born twenty-one years earlier.

"Kirsten Elisabeth," the officer read, looking at Kirsti's baby picture. He let the photograph fall to the floor.

"Annemarie," he read next, glanced at her, and dropped the second photograph.

"Lise Margrete," he read finally, and stared at Ellen for a long unwavering moment. In her mind, Annemarie pictured the photograph that he held: the baby, wide-eyed, propped against a pillow, her tiny hand holding a silver teething ring, her bare feet visible below the hem of an embroidered dress. The wispy curls. Dark.

The officer tore the photograph in half and dropped the pieces on the floor. Then

he turned, the heels of his shiny boots grinding into the pictures, and left the apartment. Without a word, the other two officers followed. Papa stepped forward and closed the door behind him.

Annemarie relaxed the clenched fingers of her right hand, which still clutched Ellen's necklace. She looked down, and saw that she had imprinted the Star of David into her palm.

LITERATURE REVIEW

1. What made Annemarie think the men were not ordinary soldiers?

2. How did Annemarie and her parents show courage and cleverness in protecting Ellen from the Nazis?

3. Write a diary entry that Ellen Rosen might have written the day following the events described in the story. Be sure to include how Ellen felt about the actions of the Johansens.

FOCUS

How can differing ideas about economics and government lead to conflict today?

Main Idea As you read, think about how differing ideas about economics and government led to tensions and fighting in the years after World War II.

Vocabulary

superpower
Cold War
containment
limited war
détente

Cold War Tensions

After World War II the United States and the Soviet Union became the world's most powerful nations. Tensions between these two **superpowers** soon arose. Americans and Europeans feared that the Soviets wanted to make other nations communist and would use force to meet this goal. Such fears led to a new kind of conflict, the **Cold War**. During this time the two superpowers did not fight face to face. They did, however, prepare for war with all kinds of weapons. Both sides wanted to have not only the most weapons but also the most powerful weapons.

The Superpowers Compete in Europe

In 1946 Winston Churchill said that an "iron curtain" had "descended across the Continent" of Europe. He noted that all the nations to the east of this curtain were under Soviet control. Churchill had good reason to say this. The Soviet Union had promised free elections in the eastern European nations it had freed from Nazi control. But the Soviets had not kept their promise. Instead, they banned all opposition to the communist governments they had set up in those nations.

Many Americans urged their government to adopt a policy of **containment**. That is, they wanted to develop ways to keep the Soviets from gaining control of other countries. In 1947 President Harry S. Truman said that the United States would give money and supplies to help any nation that wanted to keep out the Soviets. Truman also suggested that the United States was prepared to give

The European Recovery Program (ERP), or Marshall Plan, helped European countries rebuild their economies.

E·R·P

You hold the Key

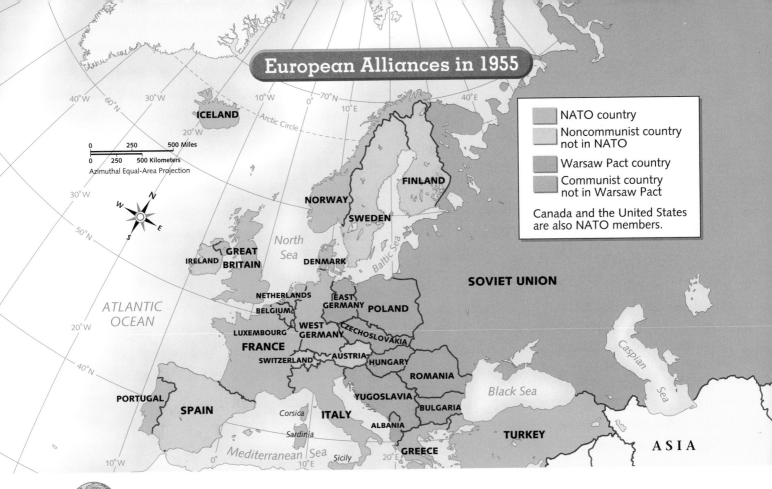

European Alliances in 1955

	NATO country
	Noncommunist country not in NATO
	Warsaw Pact country
	Communist country not in Warsaw Pact

Canada and the United States are also NATO members.

ICELAND
Arctic Circle
NORWAY
FINLAND
SWEDEN
North Sea
GREAT BRITAIN
IRELAND
DENMARK
Baltic Sea
SOVIET UNION
NETHERLANDS
EAST GERMANY
POLAND
BELGIUM
ATLANTIC OCEAN
LUXEMBOURG
WEST GERMANY
CZECHOSLOVAKIA
FRANCE
SWITZERLAND
AUSTRIA
HUNGARY
ROMANIA
Caspian Sea
PORTUGAL
YUGOSLAVIA
Black Sea
SPAIN
Corsica
ITALY
BULGARIA
Sardinia
ALBANIA
TURKEY
ASIA
Mediterranean Sea
Sicily
GREECE

Regions By 1955 most European nations had joined an alliance.
■ *In what part of Europe were most of the Warsaw Pact members located? In what part of Europe were most of the NATO members located?*

military help to any such nation. This new policy became known as the Truman Doctrine.

Truman also saw to it that the European Recovery Act, or the Marshall Plan, passed Congress in 1948. This plan provided $13 billion to help the European countries rebuild their economies. Truman believed that an economically healthy Europe would have little interest in communism.

To speed up the work of the Marshall Plan, Britain, France, and the United States decided to unite their zones in Germany and create a new German government. The Soviet Union saw this action as a threat to its control of eastern Germany. Immediately the Soviets blocked all land and water routes between the western part of Germany and the western zone of Berlin. Britain and the United States

then began sending supplies by air to Berlin. In May 1949, after 11 months, the Soviets ended the blockade.

The Western countries continued with their plans to form the democratic Federal Republic of Germany. The Soviets created the communist German Democratic Republic, or East Germany, in their zone. The city of Berlin was also divided into two parts.

In 1949 the Western powers formed a military alliance called the North Atlantic Treaty Organization (NATO) to help defend themselves against Soviet attack. In 1955 Soviet leaders organized the eastern European nations into an opposing alliance called the Warsaw Pact.

REVIEW *What was the Western response to the threat of Soviet expansion?*

The Spread of Communism in Asia

The Cold War soon spread beyond Europe to Asia. In 1945, communists fought to take over the Chinese government. In October 1949 they set up a communist state called the People's Republic of China. Beijing, then known as Peking, became its capital.

The conflict between communism and democracy next spread to Korea. After World War II Korea had been divided into two parts, with Soviet forces in the north and American troops in the south. With the Soviets' help, a communist government took control of North Korea. In June 1950, North Korean soldiers crossed the border into South Korea in an attempt to reunite the country under communism. The United States and the United Nations quickly sent troops to help the South Koreans. The Soviet Union and newly communist China gave aid to the North Koreans. Tensions between the communist and non-communist nations reached an all-time high level. Many people felt that these tensions might explode into another world war.

President Truman wanted to keep the conflict from spreading. Still, he decided that the conflict would be a **limited war**. This meant that the United States would not insist on total victory. This decision made it less likely

Location | North Korea hoped to unite all of Korea under one communist government.

■ *Why would you expect heavy fighting on the land around 38°N?*

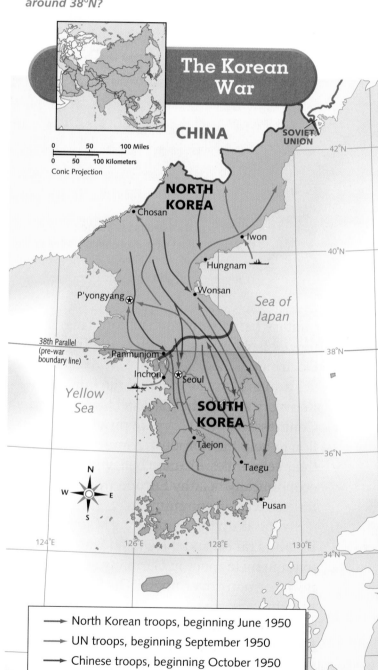

The Korean War

CHINA

SOVIET UNION

NORTH KOREA
Chosan
Iwon
Hungnam
Wonsan
P'yongyang
Sea of Japan

38th Parallel (pre-war boundary line)
Panmunjom
Inchon
Seoul
Yellow Sea
SOUTH KOREA
Taejon
Taegu
Pusan

0   50   100 Miles
0   50   100 Kilometers
Conic Projection

42°N
40°N
38°N
36°N
34°N

124°E   126°E   128°E   130°E

N W E S

→ North Korean troops, beginning June 1950
→ UN troops, beginning September 1950
→ Chinese troops, beginning October 1950
→ UN troops, beginning January 1951
— Boundary line, formed July 1953
⊛ Capital

Refugee women and children pass American soldiers marching into the Naktong River area of Korea.

that atomic, or nuclear, weapons would be used. This was a fear because the Soviet Union had tested its first nuclear bomb in 1949.

In 1953 both sides agreed to end the war. Their truce set a new border between North Korea and South Korea, near the 38th parallel. Although the fighting in Korea stopped, the Cold War continued.

REVIEW *Why were Cold War tensions at their worst in the early 1950s?*

Khrushchev and Kennedy

In 1958 Nikita Khrushchev (nuh•KEE•tuh KRUSH•chawf) became leader of the Soviet Union. As the Soviet leader, Khrushchev used harsh methods to control the eastern European communist countries. At the same time, he led Western nations to believe there could be peace. "Peaceful coexistence among different systems of government is possible," Khrushchev said. As a step in improving Soviet–American relations, he visited the United States.

This thaw in the Cold War did not last long. In the 1960s the United States and the Soviet Union came very near to war. In May 1961 Khrushchev demanded that United States President John F. Kennedy remove all American troops from West Berlin. The Soviets said the troops were a threat to East Germany. President Kennedy refused. Khrushchev threatened to use nuclear weapons if the Americans did not leave. Kennedy still stood firm.

In August, East German troops set up a fence of bricks and barbed wire between East and West Berlin. They wanted to stop East Germans from running to freedom in West Berlin. Kennedy answered by sending more troops to the city. Khrushchev also sent more troops. The danger of war seemed very real. Then the Soviet troops left.

U.S. President Kennedy and Soviet leader Khrushchev shake hands in Vienna in 1961 (above). Berliners look over the wall that divided their city (right). How do you think the division of Berlin affected those who lived there?

Tensions eased after this, but the fence stayed. In time the East Germans replaced the barbed wire with the concrete Berlin Wall. The wall soon became a symbol of the Cold War and the division between the free world and the communists.

Shortly after the Berlin crisis, another conflict came about. This time the location was Cuba, a small island nation south of Florida. In 1959, revolutionaries led by Fidel Castro had taken control of the island. The Castro government quickly formed close ties with the Soviet Union.

The strength of those ties became clear in 1962. Americans learned that the Soviet

Union had built launching sites for nuclear missiles in Cuba, less than 100 miles (161 km) from the coast of Florida. President Kennedy ordered a blockade of ships around Cuba to stop the Soviets from shipping military supplies to the island. When Soviet cargo ships began sailing toward the blockade, war seemed certain.

Suddenly the Soviet ships turned around. "We're eyeball to eyeball," United States Secretary of State Dean Rusk said, "and I think the other fellow just blinked." Within a week the Soviets agreed to take away the missiles. In return, Kennedy agreed not to invade Cuba. In 1963 the two superpowers signed a treaty ending the testing of nuclear bombs above ground or underwater.

REVIEW *What became an important symbol of the Cold War?*

Vietnam

Vietnam, a country in Indochina, became the focus of the next Cold War conflict. At the end of World War II, Vietnamese leaders had declared independence from their colonial ruler, France. The French, however, wanted to take back control of the country. The United States supported France because Ho Chi Minh (HOH CHEE MIN), the

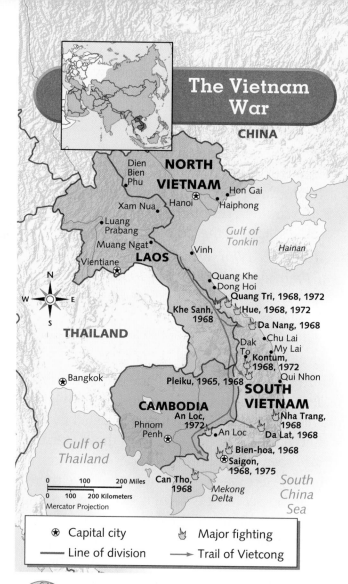

The Vietnam War

CHINA

Dien Bien Phu

NORTH VIETNAM

Hon Gai

Xam Nua · Hanoi ⊛ · Haiphong

Luang Prabang

Muang Ngat·

Vientiane ⊛

LAOS

· Vinh

Gulf of Tonkin

Hainan

Quang Khe
· Dong Hoi
Quang Tri, 1968, 1972
Khe Sanh, 1968
Hue, 1968, 1972
Da Nang, 1968

THAILAND

Dak To · Chu Lai
· My Lai
Kontum, 1968, 1972
Qui Nhon

· Bangkok

Pleiku, 1965, 1968

SOUTH VIETNAM

CAMBODIA

An Loc, 1972

Phnom Penh ⊛

· An Loc

Nha Trang, 1968
Da Lat, 1968

Gulf of Thailand

Bien-hoa, 1968
⊛ Saigon, 1968, 1975

0   100   200 Miles
0 100 200 Kilometers
Mercator Projection

Can Tho, 1968

Mekong Delta

South China Sea

⊛ Capital city   Major fighting
— Line of division   → Trail of Vietcong

Location The present-day country of Vietnam was once divided into warring parts.

■ *In which part of Vietnam did most of the fighting take place?*

American soldiers carry the wounded out of a South Vietnamese jungle in 1967.

Vietnamese leader, had communist ties. By 1954, after years of fighting, the French were defeated. An agreement was reached to divide Vietnam into northern and southern parts.

With the help of China and the Soviet Union, Ho Chi Minh built a communist state in the north. He also gained a strong following among people in the south. These Vietcong, or "Vietnamese Communists," began a campaign to overthrow the government of South Vietnam. War then broke out between North and South Vietnam. In the

A helicopter brings fresh troops into battle (above). A young Vietnamese girl cuddles a baby in the middle of a war zone (right).

early 1960s the United States began helping South Vietnam. The Soviet Union sided with North Vietnam.

By 1969 there were 550,000 American troops in Vietnam. Yet victory seemed no nearer, and Americans were dying every day. Millions of Vietnamese in the north and south also were killed. Fighting spread to other countries in the region as well.

America's role in the war caused conflict in the United States. Some Americans believed that the United States had a duty to fight communism. Others believed that the United States should not be involved in another country's battle. Those who opposed the war held protests and marches.

More and more Americans began to question their government's reasons for fighting in Vietnam. Therefore, United States leaders tried to end their country's role in the war. In 1973 North Vietnamese and American leaders reached a cease-fire agreement. Soon after that, United States troops withdrew.

About 58,000 Americans had died in the war, and 360,000 had been wounded. In 1974 North Vietnam again attacked South Vietnam. By April 1975 the Communists had gained control of all of Vietnam. Not until 1994 did the United States again begin trade and communication with the Vietnamese.

After its withdrawal from Vietnam, the United States government began a new policy toward communist nations. Called **détente** (day•TAHNT), the policy was meant to relax tensions between the communists and the free world. In the spirit of détente, American leaders

SICK OF THE WAR IN VIETNAM

This button reflects the mood of Americans opposed to the war.

began talks with China. They also signed an agreement with the Soviet Union to limit the making of nuclear weapons.

In 1979 tensions flared once again. In that year leaders of the Soviet Union sent troops to its neighbor Afghanistan to keep that country's failing communist government in power. President Jimmy Carter responded by stopping grain sales to the Soviet Union. President Carter also refused to allow U.S. teams to play in the 1980 Summer Olympics, which were held in the Soviet Union. In addition, he threatened to send American troops to Afghanistan. The spirit of détente had temporarily disappeared.

REVIEW *Why did United States leaders decide to end their country's role in Vietnam?*

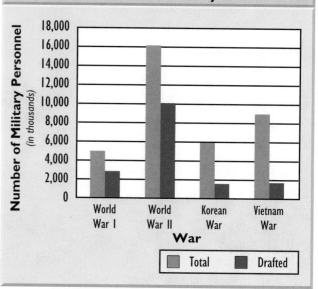

United States Forces
in Twentieth-Century Wars

LEARNING FROM GRAPHS This graph shows the number of soldiers who fought for the United States in each of four wars.
■ *About how many more U.S. soldiers fought in World War II than in the Vietnam War?*

War medals (left) and the Vietnam Veterans Memorial in Washington, D.C. (below)

LESSON 3 REVIEW

Check Understanding

1 Remember the Facts What was détente?

2 Recall the Main Idea How did differing ideas about government lead to tensions after World War II?

Think Critically

3 Think More About It How might division of a country into two parts affect that country's people?

4 Cause and Effect What events caused tensions to ease between the superpowers?

Show What You Know

Political Cartoon Activity Create a political cartoon that illustrates the idea of a cold war. Write a caption to explain your cartoon, if needed.

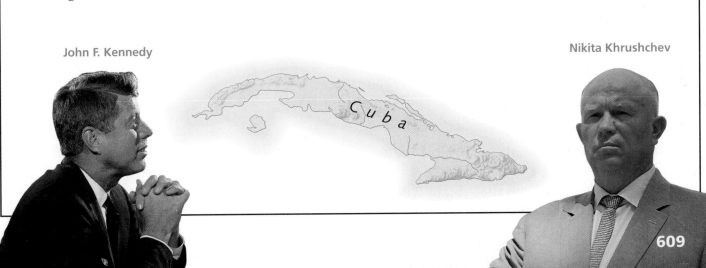
Make Decisions

1. Why Learn This Skill?

Every action you take has a consequence, or result. Some consequences are short-term—they happen right away and last a short time. Other consequences are long-term—they happen in the future and last a long time. An action can also have either positive or negative consequences—or both. To make thoughtful decisions, you need to think about all the possible consequences before you take action.

2. Remember What You Have Read

You have read that the leaders of the superpowers during the Cold War had to make many difficult decisions. In the Cuban Missile Crisis of 1962, United States President John F. Kennedy and Soviet leader Nikita Khrushchev both had to make important decisions.

President Kennedy had to decide what to do to stop the Soviets from shipping military supplies to Cuba, the island nation 90 miles (145 km) south of Florida. No matter what action he decided to take, he risked the consequence of going to war with the Soviet Union. He could have ordered a military attack on Cuba. Instead, he ordered a shipping blockade to stop Soviet cargo ships from landing in Cuba.

In turn, Khrushchev had to decide what to do in response to the United States' blockade. He could have ordered his ships to try to sail through the blockade. Instead, Khrushchev ordered the ships to return to the Soviet Union.

3. Understand the Process

To make a difficult decision, you can use a set of steps that many people use. Following these steps can help you make your decision more thoughtfully.

1. Identify your goal.
2. Think about the problem that is keeping you from reaching your goal.
3. List the actions you could take. Begin with those you think would have the most positive consequences, and end with those you think would have negative consequences.
4. Make the choice that seems best.
5. Put your choice into action.
6. Think about whether your choice helped you reach your goal.

4. Think and Apply

Think about a decision you made at school. What steps did you follow? What choice did you make? What were the consequences? Do you think you made a thoughtful decision? Explain.

John F. Kennedy

Nikita Khrushchev

Cuba

1930 •
1939
• World War II begins

1945 •
1945
• World War II ends

1950
• United Nations is established

1950
• Korean War begins

CONNECT MAIN IDEAS

Use this organizer to tell about the later twentieth century. Write several sentences to describe each of the following topics. A copy of the organizer appears on page 140 of the Activity Book.

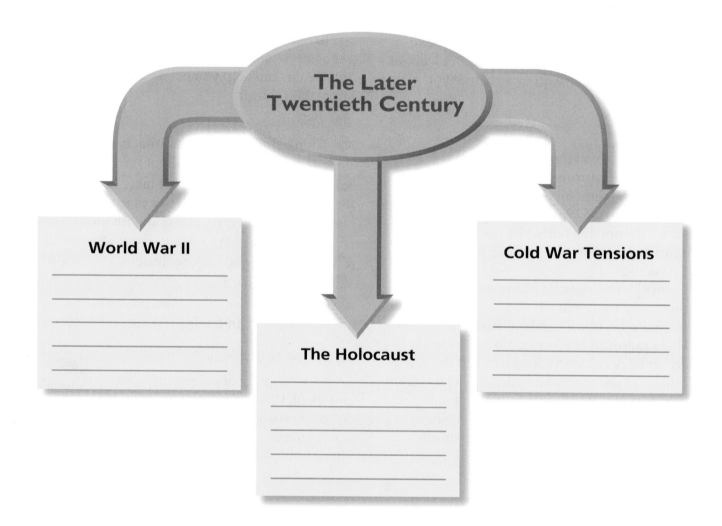

The Later Twentieth Century

World War II
_____
_____
_____
_____

The Holocaust
_____
_____
_____

Cold War Tensions
_____
_____
_____
_____

WRITE MORE ABOUT IT

Write an Interview Many people lost their lives in concentration camps, but some survived. Write five questions that you might ask a survivor of a concentration camp.

Write a Tribute Write a paragraph honoring the men and women who lost their lives as civilians or soldiers in a twentieth-century conflict.

Timeline:

1970 — **1990** — **Present**

- **1959** • Fidel Castro takes control in Cuba
- **1961** • Berlin Wall is built
- **1969** • Height of United States involvement in Vietnam War
- **1973** • United States troops leave Vietnam
- **1994** • United States and Vietnam begin trade and communication

USE VOCABULARY

Use each term in a complete sentence that helps explain its meaning.

1. appeasement
2. containment
3. détente
4. genocide
5. limited war
6. superpower

CHECK UNDERSTANDING

7. What event caused Britain and France to declare war on Germany in 1939?
8. What events led to the surrender of Germany and Japan in World War II?
9. What organization replaced the League of Nations, and what is its main purpose?
10. What happened to Germany after World War II?
11. Why did President Truman want the Korean conflict to be a limited war?
12. Why did the United States take part in the Vietnam War?

THINK CRITICALLY

13. **Past to Present** Could an event like the Holocaust happen today? Explain.
14. **Personally Speaking** Do you think the United States should give military support to countries involved in war? Explain.
15. **Explore Viewpoints** Some people believe it was necessary for the United States to use atomic bombs on Japanese cities during World War II. Others disagree. What reasons might each group give to support its view?

APPLY SKILLS

Use a Double-Bar Graph Use the double-bar graphs on pages 594 and 595 to answer these questions:

16. According to the bar graphs, were there more deaths among the Axis Powers or among the Allies?
17. Which country had more casualties, China or Japan?

Make Decisions Answer these questions about making a decision:

18. What is the first thing you should do when making a decision?
19. Why would you want to think about possible negative consequences?
20. Why is it important to think about whether you made the right decision?

READ MORE ABOUT IT

The Land I Lost: Adventures of a Boy in Vietnam by Huynh Quang Nhuong. HarperCollins. This book is a collection of the author's childhood memories of his village in Vietnam.

Visit the Internet at **http://www.hbschool.com** for additional resources.

Chapter 20 • **611**

On the top of a hill in France stands a statue of a woman. Her head is bowed and one arm hangs at her side. A robe covers her hair, her shoulders, and part of her face. She appears to be deep in thought and very sad. This statue is a memorial built to honor the more than 3,500 Canadians who died in battle on this hill during World War I.

Many people who lived during an event keep the memory of it in their hearts and minds. Memorials such as this statue keep the important events alive for future generations. Former United States senator Bob Dole said, "Countries have their solemn memorials so that . . . coming generations will not forget the . . . experience of war and risk its repetition."

All over the world, war memorials are built to record history, to preserve the past, and to remind people of the costs of freedom. On the wall of the Korean War Veterans Memorial at the National Mall in Washington, D.C., is written "Freedom is not free." This message reminds visitors of the men and women who died fighting for democracy in the Korean War.

Near the Korean War Memorial are many other memorials, such as the Women in Military Service for America Memorial, the United States Holocaust Memorial Museum, and the Vietnam Veterans Memorial. Visitors have left more than 25,000 mementos, including teddy bears and sealed letters, beside the wall at the Vietnam Memorial. These mementos show that memorials help keep alive for people the important events of the past.

"Mother Canada" watches over the Canadian National Vimy Memorial in France (left). A pair of boots are left at the Vietnam Veterans Memorial, Washington, D.C. (right).

Think and Apply

Find out about recent world events by listening to the news, looking through books or magazines, or by using the Internet. Identify one event that you think is deserving of a monument to honor it. Write a short report explaining why you think the monument should be built. Then, make a drawing that shows what you think the monument should look like.

HARCOURT BRACE

Visit the Internet at **http://www.hbschool.com** for additional resources.

CNN Turner Le@rning

Check your media center or classroom video library for the Making Social Studies Relevant videotape of this feature.

The Korean War Memorial (above) and the Women's Vietnam War Memorial (below right) at the National Mall, Washington, D.C. (below)

UNIT 9 REVIEW

Summarize the Main Ideas
Study the pictures and captions to help you review the events you read about in Unit 9.

Examine the Scenes
Look closely at each scene. What details are shown for each period? After you have looked at all the scenes, write your own description for each.

1 The assassination of the Serbian archduke Francis Ferdinand launched rival European nations into World War I.

5 Jews and other people suffered greatly during the Holocaust. Millions were put into concentration camps and killed.

2 The Russian people rebelled against their czar, forcing him to give up the throne. In time, the Communist party came to power, yet the citizens of what became the Soviet Union still had little freedom or political authority.

FOOD

3 An economic crisis in the United States developed into the Great Depression and affected people around the world.

4 The actions of countries that became known as the Axis Powers led to a second war that involved the whole world—World War II.

6 Differing ideas about government and economics led to tensions and fighting in the years after World War II. The Korean War and the Vietnam War were major conflicts during this time.

USE VOCABULARY

Write the term that correctly matches each definition.

Cold War	inflation	refugee
Holocaust	propaganda	totalitarian

1. a continuing increase in prices
2. the spreading of information or rumors to help or hurt a cause
3. the mass killing of the Jewish people
4. having complete control over people's lives
5. a person who is forced to leave his or her home to seek safety and shelter elsewhere
6. a conflict that led to an arms buildup by the world's superpowers

CHECK UNDERSTANDING

7. What caused European nations to develop a spirit of militarism in the years before World War I?
8. What was the spark that started World War I?
9. Why were the Germans angry about the terms of the Treaty of Versailles?
10. Why did the Germans arrest Jews and other groups of people in the 1940s?
11. Where was World War II fought?
12. What world superpower supported South Vietnam? Why? What superpower supported North Vietnam? Why?

THINK CRITICALLY

13. **Think More About It** How was World War I different from wars that had been fought in the past?

14. **Cause and Effect** How did Hitler's belief in a "master race" lead to the Holocaust?
15. **Explore Viewpoints** Woodrow Wilson wanted a lasting peace to follow World War I. What seemed most important to those who signed the Treaty of Versailles?

APPLY SKILLS

Understand Time Zones World War II was fought around the world and crossed many time zones. On December 7, 1941, at 7:55 A.M., the Japanese bombed Pearl Harbor in Hawaii. Use the time zone map below to answer these questions about the bombing of Pearl Harbor.

16. When the Japanese bombed Pearl Harbor, what time was it in Washington D.C.?
17. What time was it and what date was it in Tokyo, Japan?

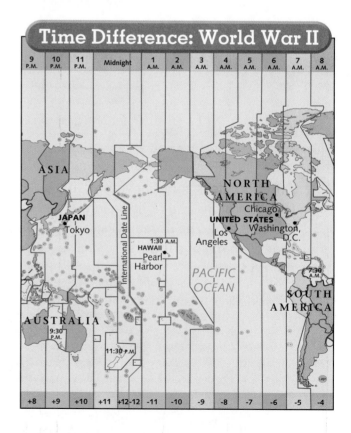

Time Difference: World War II

REMEMBER

- Share your ideas.
- Cooperate with others to plan your work.
- Take responsibility for your work.
- Help one another.
- Show your group's work to the class.
- Discuss what you learned by working together.

Create a
Remembrance

Brainstorm with a group of three or four students to think of ways to encourage young people to remember the Holocaust. You might suggest creating artwork, a song, or a poem, or you might have other ideas. Once you have considered different ideas, select one, make a plan, and act on your plan.

Develop a
Peace Plan

With three or four classmates, develop your own Fourteen Points for Peace. Include all the ways you think countries can avoid future wars. Show your Fourteen Points on a poster for display in your classroom.

Hold a
Class Debate

Imagine that the year is 1967. The people of the United States are divided because of the Vietnam War. Hold a class debate about United States involvement in the Vietnam War. Form two debate teams. One team should argue for involvement. The other should argue for withdrawal.

Unit Project Wrap-Up

Make an Illustrated Encyclopedia As a group, complete your encyclopedia by reviewing the list you have made while studying Unit 9. Write brief reports on all the events you listed and place them in your encyclopedia in the order that they happened. Be sure to feature maps to help explain each event. Also include separate articles about important people and places related to the events. Place these in the encyclopedia as you think appropriate. Keep your encyclopedia in the classroom so that others may use it.

TOWARD THE PRESENT DAY

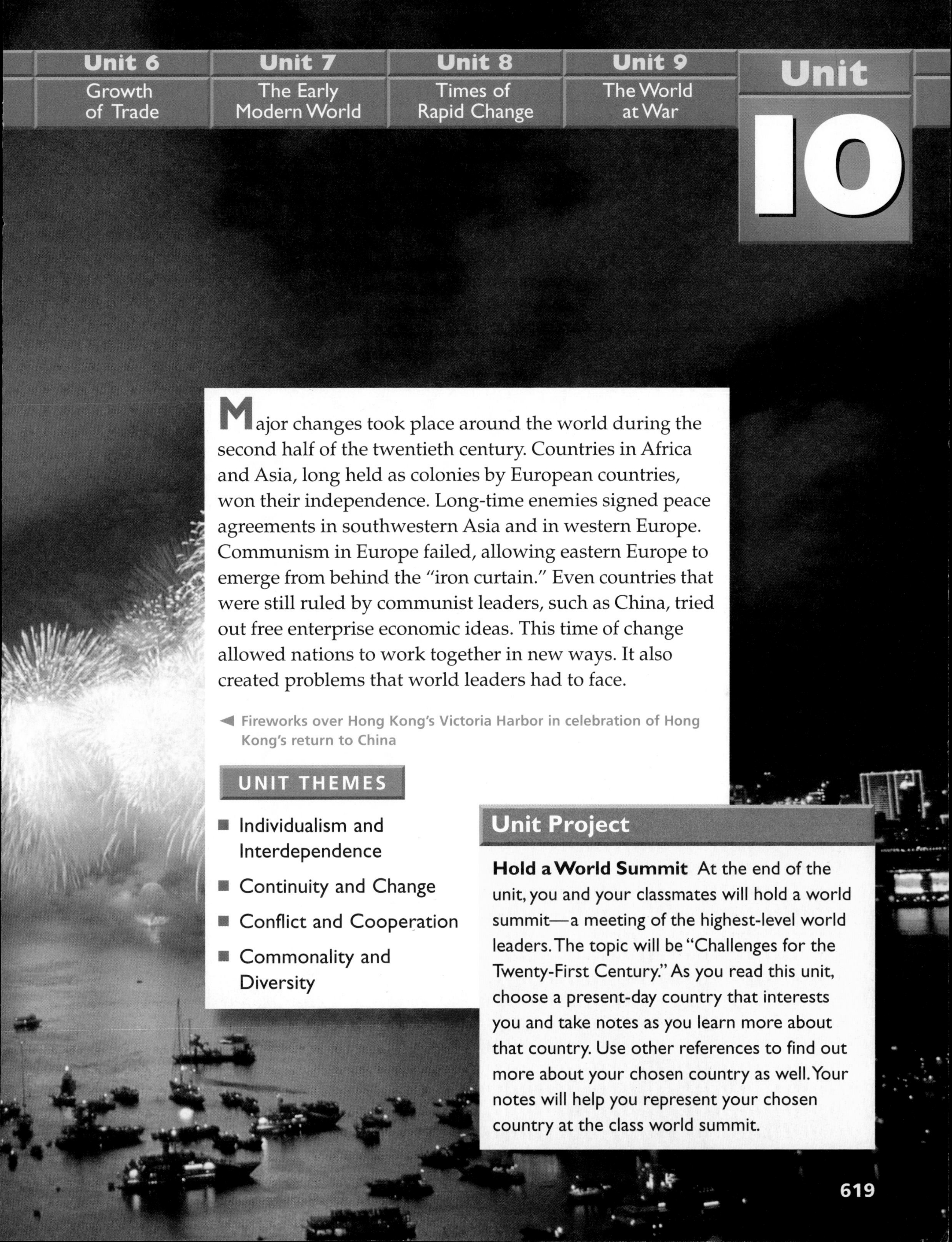

Major changes took place around the world during the second half of the twentieth century. Countries in Africa and Asia, long held as colonies by European countries, won their independence. Long-time enemies signed peace agreements in southwestern Asia and in western Europe. Communism in Europe failed, allowing eastern Europe to emerge from behind the "iron curtain." Even countries that were still ruled by communist leaders, such as China, tried out free enterprise economic ideas. This time of change allowed nations to work together in new ways. It also created problems that world leaders had to face.

◀ Fireworks over Hong Kong's Victoria Harbor in celebration of Hong Kong's return to China

UNIT THEMES

- Individualism and Interdependence
- Continuity and Change
- Conflict and Cooperation
- Commonality and Diversity

Unit Project

Hold a World Summit At the end of the unit, you and your classmates will hold a world summit—a meeting of the highest-level world leaders. The topic will be "Challenges for the Twenty-First Century." As you read this unit, choose a present-day country that interests you and take notes as you learn more about that country. Use other references to find out more about your chosen country as well. Your notes will help you represent your chosen country at the class world summit.

UNIT 10
PREVIEW

Greenland
(DENMARK)

RUSSIA

ALASKA
(U.S.)

CANADA

★ National capital

• Major city

Vancouver

Ottawa

UNITED STATES

New York City
Washington, D.C.

ATLANTIC
OCEAN

1994
Canada, Mexico, and the United States sign the North American Free Trade Agreement.

Los Angeles

MEXICO

Havana

BAHAMAS

CUBA

HAITI

DOMINICAN REPUBLIC

HAWAII
(U.S.)

PACIFIC   OCEAN

Mexico City

BELIZE

JAMAICA

HONDURAS

GUATEMALA
EL SALVADOR
NICARAGUA
COSTA RICA

PANAMA

VENEZUELA

GUYANA
SURINAME
FR. GUIANA
(FRANCE)

Bogotá

COLOMBIA

ECUADOR

Equator

Amazon River

ALB.	ALBANIA	LITH.	LITHUANIA
ARM.	ARMENIA	LUX.	LUXEMBOURG
AUS.	AUSTRIA	MAC.	MACEDONIA
AZER.	AZERBAIJAN	NETH.	NETHERLANDS
BELG.	BELGIUM	REP. CONGO	REPUBLIC OF THE CONGO
BOS.-HER.	BOSNIA AND HERZEGOVINA	ROM.	ROMANIA
C.A.R.	CENTRAL AFRICAN REPUBLIC	SEN.	SENEGAL
C.d'I.	CÔTE D'IVOIRE	S.L.	SIERRA LEONE
CRO.	CROATIA	SLK.	SLOVAKIA
CZH. REP.	CZECH REPUBLIC	SLN.	SLOVENIA
DEM. REP. OF CONGO	DEMOCRATIC REPUBLIC OF THE CONGO	SWITZ.	SWITZERLAND
EQ. GUI.	EQUATORIAL GUINEA	U.A.E.	UNITED ARAB EMIRATES
G.B.	GUINEA-BISSAU	U.S.	UNITED STATES
HUNG.	HUNGARY	YUGO.	YUGOSLAVIA
LEB.	LEBANON		

PERU
Lima

BRAZIL

Brasília

BOLIVIA

São Paulo

Rio de Janeiro

1980–1990
Democracies replace dictatorships in most Latin American countries.

PARAGUAY

Tropic of Capricorn

URUGUAY

30°S

NEW ZEALAND

0   1,500   3,000 Miles
0   1,500   3,000 Kilometers
Miller Cylindrical Projection

CHILE

Buenos Aires

ARGENTINA

1980   **1985**   **1990**

1977
China begins new economic program
PAGE 628

1991
End of communism in Europe
PAGE 684

The World Today

1989
The Berlin Wall falls as communist rule in eastern Europe ends.

1995
The four-year civil war in Bosnia and Herzegovina officially ends with the signing of a peace agreement.

1989
College students demonstrating in Beijing, China, demand political freedom at Tiananmen Square.

1991
The Soviet Union breaks apart.

1995
Israeli Prime Minister Yitzhak Rabin is assassinated.

1993
Apartheid ends in South Africa.

1997
After an eight-month-long civil war, Zaire is renamed the Democratic Republic of the Congo.

1997
Hong Kong becomes part of China after being under British control since 1839.

1998
Asian countries face economic decline.

ICELAND
NORWAY
UNITED KINGDOM
IRELAND
London
Paris
Madrid
PORTUGAL
SPAIN
Casablanca
MOROCCO
WESTERN SAHARA (MOROCCO)
MAURITANIA
SEN.
GAMBIA
G.B.
GUINEA
S.L.
LIBERIA
C. d'I.
TOGO
EQ. GUI.
SÃO TOMÉ AND PRÍNCIPE
CABINDA (ANGOLA)

FINLAND
SWEDEN
ESTONIA
LATVIA
LITH.
NETH. DENMARK
BELG.
GERMANY
LUX.
POLAND
BELARUS
CZH. REP.
SLK.
UKRAINE
AUS. HUNG.
MOLDOVA
SWITZ.
FRANCE
SLN.
CRO. BOS.
YUGO.
HER.
ROM.
ITALY
MAC.
BULGARIA
ALB.
GREECE
Rome
Algiers
TUNISIA
ALGERIA
LIBYA
MALI
NIGER
CHAD
SUDAN
NIGERIA
BURKINA FASO
BENIN
GHANA
Lagos
CAMEROON
C.A.R.
GABON
REP. CONGO
DEM. REP. OF CONGO
Kinshasa
ANGOLA
UGANDA
RWANDA
BURUNDI
TANZANIA
KENYA
Nairobi
Addis Ababa
ETHIOPIA
SOMALIA
DJIBOUTI
ERITREA
YEMEN
ZAMBIA
MALAWI
ZIMBABWE
NAMIBIA
BOTSWANA
MOZAMBIQUE
MADAGASCAR
COMOROS
SEYCHELLES
SWAZILAND
LESOTHO
SOUTH AFRICA
Pretoria

Moscow
RUSSIA
KAZAKHSTAN
MONGOLIA
Beijing
CHINA
Huang He
Chang Jiang
Shanghai
NORTH KOREA
Seoul
SOUTH KOREA
JAPAN
Tokyo
TAIWAN
Hong Kong
UZBEKISTAN
KYRGYZSTAN
TAJIKISTAN
TURKMENISTAN
GEORGIA
ARM.
AZER.
TURKEY
CYPRUS
SYRIA
LEB.
ISRAEL
IRAQ
IRAN
AFGHANISTAN
PAKISTAN
New Delhi
INDIA
Calcutta
Mumbai (Bombay)
NEPAL
BHUTAN
BANGLADESH
MYANMAR (BURMA)
LAOS
THAILAND
Bangkok
CAMBODIA
VIETNAM
PHILIPPINES
Manila
SRI LANKA
MALDIVES
BRUNEI
MALAYSIA
SINGAPORE
INDONESIA
Jakarta
PAPUA NEW GUINEA
JORDAN
KUWAIT
BAHRAIN
QATAR
U.A.E.
OMAN
SAUDI ARABIA
Cairo
EGYPT
Nile R.
Volga R.

INDIAN OCEAN
MAURITIUS
REUNION (FRANCE)
Equator

AUSTRALIA
Melbourne

Arctic Circle
Tropic of Cancer
Tropic of Capricorn
30°E   60°E   90°E   120°E   60°N   30°N   0°

1995 ———— Present

1994
South African elections open to all
PAGE 676

1998
Renewed peace talks in Middle East
PAGE 667

1998
Asian economic crisis
PAGE 633

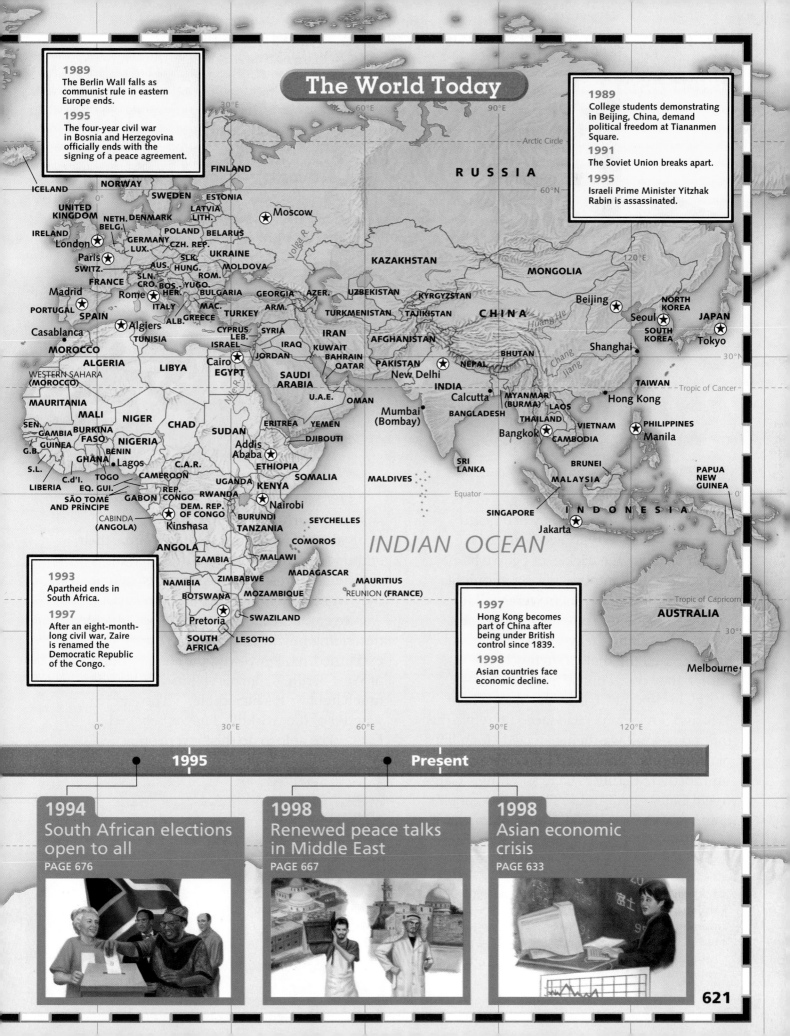

THE BERLIN WALL

by Doris M. Epler

Late in 1989 communism began to fall apart in eastern Europe. On November 9 the East German government stunned the world by announcing that it planned to begin opening its borders—including the Berlin Wall—at midnight. Read now about the excitement of East Berliners as they heard this news. As you read, think about why the opening of the Berlin Wall interested not only those in Berlin but also people around the world.

In East Berlin, people began to go to the Wall to see if what they had heard was true. It was. Within two hours of the announcement, the trickle[1] of people had turned into jubilant[2] crowds. By midnight, thousands of East Berliners were walking, biking, or driving to crossing points in the Wall and entering the western half of the city—something that, just a few hours earlier, they could only dream of.

At Checkpoint Charlie, the place where U.S. and Soviet tanks had faced off while the infamous[3] Wall was being erected,[4] long lines of cars and people moved into West Berlin unimpeded.[5] Berliners were shouting, "Gates open! Gates open!" and "The Wall is gone!" Some exuberant[6] Germans even scampered to the top of the Wall, now that all fear of being shot was gone.

As East Berliners drove their cars down the splendid Kurfürstendamm, West Berlin's equivalent of New York's Fifth Avenue, their enthusiasm grew. They had dreamed of entering the western zone for years, and now they were seeing their dreams come true. It was an emotional time—many had difficulty describing how they felt. One woman exclaimed, as she viewed the shop windows of West Berlin, "There is so much color, so much light." "It's incredible," "The eighth wonder of the world!" "I never believed I would be able to do this!" were other

---

[1] **trickle:** movement of just a few at a time
[2] **jubilant:** joyful
[3] **infamous:** evil
[4] **erected:** built
[5] **unimpeded:** not blocked
[6] **exuberant:** high-spirited

remarks. Of the West Berliners, one East German student said, "It's amazing how warmly we were greeted. We were applauded. They cried. They were just as happy as we were."[7] A blind man, guided by a seeing-eye dog, remarked, "I just wanted to smell the air of a free Berlin."[8]

East German guards, who hours before would have shot anyone trying to escape, now posed happily as people snapped pictures of the scene. "The East German soldiers don't know what to do now," said one West Berliner. "They behave a bit crazy tonight, so calm and so quiet."[9] One man rushed across the border carrying a copy of a newspaper that proclaimed, in an enormous headline, "Berlin is Berlin Again!" The guards, who previously would have confiscated[10] such material, merely reached out eagerly to see the newspaper.

The celebrations continued all through the night and into the morning. People began to dance on top of the Wall. Others blew trumpets, embraced, and laughed while tears streamed down their faces. The ringing of chisels and hammers could be heard as people began to chip away at the once-impregnable[11] barrier.

The next day more crossings were opened, including the Glienicke Bridge, the site of many East-West spy exchanges. A hundred thousand East Berliners inundated[12] the western zone. Among them was an East Berlin man who had borrowed three books from the American Memorial Library in West Berlin the day before the Wall went up. Now, twenty-eight years later, he returned the books—in excellent condition. (Presumably, no late-book fines were imposed.)

In this unit you will read more about the opening of the Berlin Wall and other events of the late twentieth century that have had far-reaching effects on world affairs.

---

[7] Quotation from *Newsweek*, "The Fall of the Wall," November 20, 1989
[8] Quotation from *Maclean's*, "Free at Last!" November 20, 1989
[9] Quotation from *Newsweek*, "The Fall of the Wall," November 20, 1989
[10] **confiscated:** taken by authority

---

[11] **impregnable:** not possible to overcome
[12] **inundated:** flooded

On November 9, 1989, the gates of the Berlin Wall opened (photo on page 622). Excited Berliners (below) climbed the Berlin Wall to celebrate the fact that the "Wall of Shame" would no longer separate Berlin and its people. Germans of all ages (inset) soon began to chip pieces from the wall.

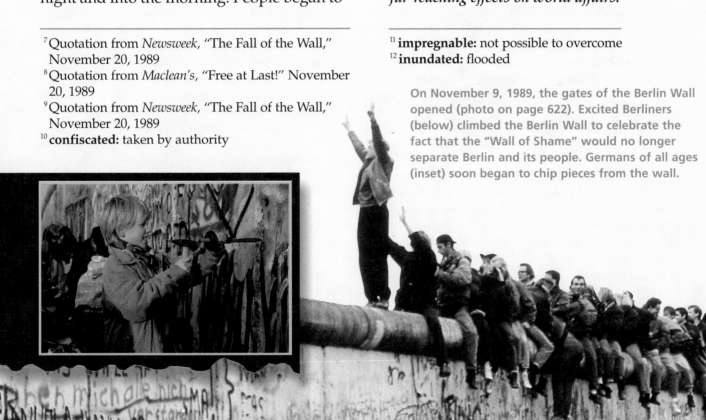

CHAPTER

21 Economic Challenges

"All the big questions confronting the world in the century ahead are basically economic."

Bruce W. Nelan, American journalist, 1992

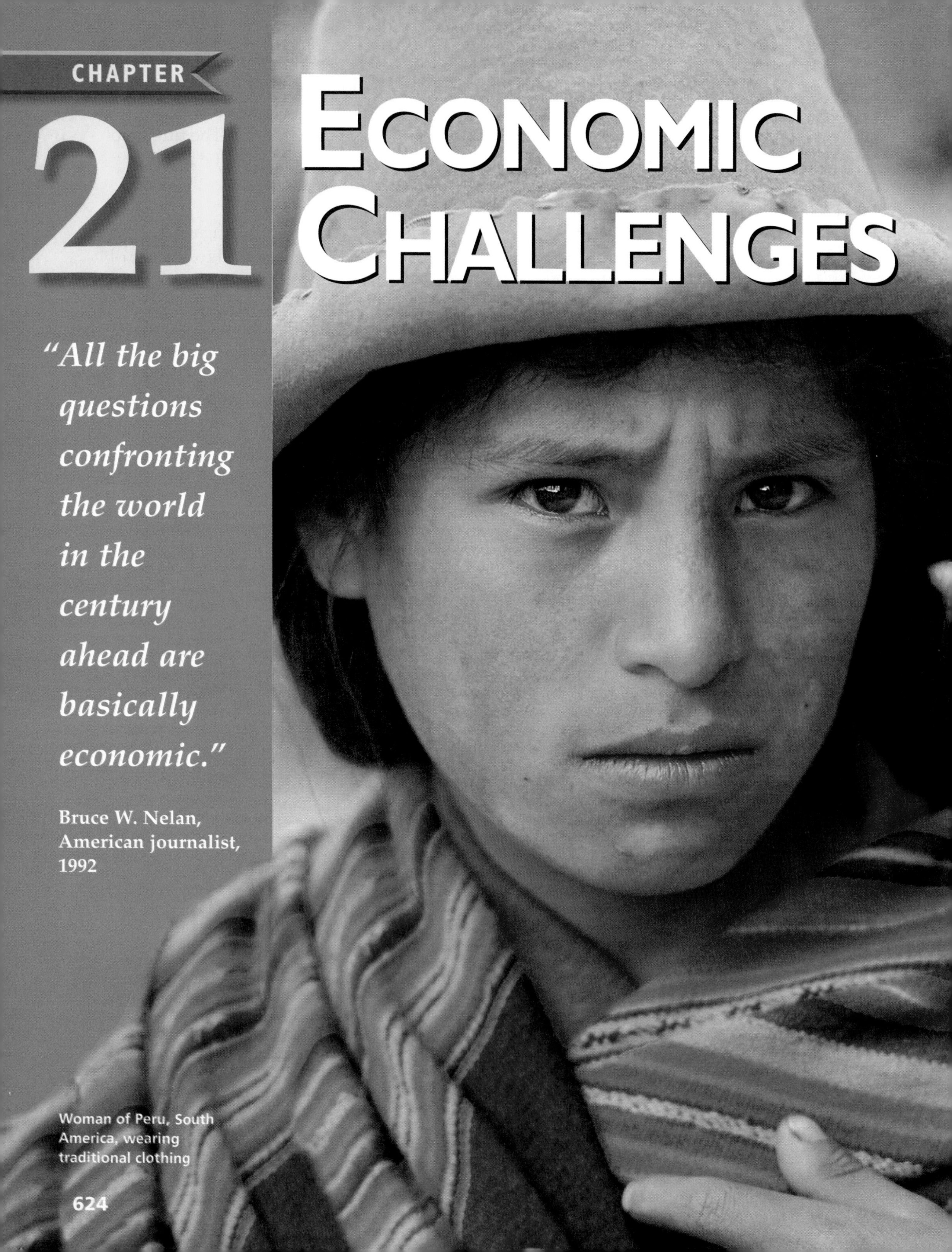

Woman of Peru, South America, wearing traditional clothing

China in the Modern World

FOCUS
How is a country's economy affected by the ideas and actions of its leaders?

Main Idea As you read, find out how China's industry, agriculture, and trade changed as the country's leaders changed.

Vocabulary
warlord
Long March
commune
Cultural Revolution
Red Guard
quota

At the beginning of the twentieth century, China was mainly a rural, agricultural country with a traditional economy. Economic growth was slow because foreign powers controlled many of China's resources. Later, the introduction of communism did not help economic conditions.

Chinese Nationalism

By the early 1900s parts of China were controlled by other countries. The Qing emperors seemed unable to stop this, but many young Chinese demanded change. "The foreigners must leave," they said. At the same time, they wanted China to learn foreign ways and become a modern country.

A new political party, the Guomindang (GWOH•min•dahng), or People's Nationalist party, grew out of the calls for change. Its leader, Sun Yat-sen (SUN YAHT•SEN), wanted to create a republic based on the "Three Principles of the People"—nationalism, democracy, and a strong economy. Sun Yat-sen thought that China needed to get rid of foreign control, form a democratic government, and find a way to become an industrial power.

By 1911 the Nationalists had forced the last Qing emperor to step down. Sun Yat-sen became the president of a new Chinese republic. The new government, though, was not able to unite China. Warlords, individuals with their own small armies, had taken over many parts of the country. The warlords refused to follow the orders of the Nationalist government. The Nationalists seemed to have little chance of success in bringing the Chinese people together.

The situation changed in 1925, when Sun Yat-sen died. Chiang Kai-shek (jee•AHNG KY•SHEK) became leader of the Nationalists. Chiang soon built up the Nationalist army and began defeating the warlords.

Sun Yat-sen (center) visits the site of an ancient Chinese tomb in 1912.

At the same time, the Nationalist party split. The newly formed Communist party wanted the peasants to have more say in government. Chiang, supported by wealthy landowners, disagreed with this and took action against the Communists.

By 1934 the Nationalist armies had forced the Communists into a small area in southeastern China. About 100,000 Communists began a walk of 6,000 miles (9,656 km) across China to safety in the northwest. This hard journey, now known as the **Long March**, took more than a year. Nationalists attacked all along the way. Fewer than 20,000 people survived the march. Yet on the way they found a leader—Mao Zedong (MOW ZUH•DUNG).

REVIEW *Why were the Nationalists unable to unite China?*

Communism in China

In the northwest, which was now under Communist rule, Mao Zedong lowered taxes and gave the peasants control of the land. In the rest of China, Chiang Kai-shek was unable to bring about much economic change. More and more peasants joined the Communists, hoping for a better life.

Years before the Long March, Mao had made this prediction:

66 Several hundred million peasants . . . will rise like a tornado or tempest— a force so extraordinarily swift and violent that no power, however great, will be able to suppress it. 99

As Mao had hoped, an army of peasants rose up. After a long and violent war, this peasant army drove out the Nationalists. In 1949 Mao set up a communist state, the People's Republic of China. Chiang and his followers escaped to the island of Taiwan (TY•WAHN). There they set up their own government, which they called the Republic of China.

Mao began to change every area of Chinese life to fit his ideas. He appointed Communists to all leadership positions. He then divided the country into many small districts. In each district the people ran the factories and farms where they worked. Still, the real authority belonged with the central government, which was controlled by Mao and other Communist leaders. Together they created five-year plans to set economic goals for the country.

Mao Zedong (left) led Chinese Communist forces. Followers of Mao are shown (picture at far right) after the completion of the Long March in 1934. During that 6,000-mile journey, marchers crossed 24 rivers and 18 mountain ranges.

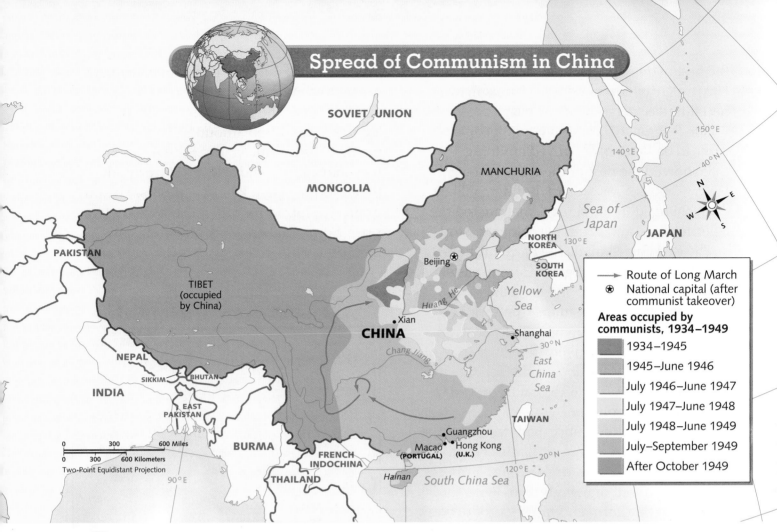

Spread of Communism in China

SOVIET UNION

MONGOLIA

MANCHURIA

PAKISTAN

TIBET
(occupied
by China)

Beijing ✪

NORTH
KOREA

SOUTH
KOREA

Yellow
Sea

Sea of
Japan

JAPAN

NEPAL

• Xian

CHINA

Huang He

Shanghai

East
China
Sea

SIKKIM

BHUTAN

Chang Jiang

INDIA

EAST
PAKISTAN

TAIWAN

0   300   600 Miles
0   300   600 Kilometers
Two-Point Equidistant Projection

BURMA

FRENCH
INDOCHINA

Guangzhou

Macao   • Hong Kong
(PORTUGAL)   (U.K.)

THAILAND

Hainan   South China Sea

Legend:
→ Route of Long March
✪ National capital (after communist takeover)

Areas occupied by communists, 1934–1949
- 1934–1945
- 1945–June 1946
- July 1946–June 1947
- July 1947–June 1948
- July 1948–June 1949
- July–September 1949
- After October 1949

Movement In 1934 the Long March took the Chinese Communists to safety in the northwest. Just 15 years later the Communists controlled all of China.
■ *Why do you think the Long March did not follow a more direct route?*

Mao's first five-year plan in 1953 called for rapid growth of industry. It also forced most peasants to live in **communes**, farming communities where people shared housing, food, and work. For the most part, Mao's plan worked. Leaders were pleased to see an increase in farm production and industry.

Mao's second five-year plan, the Great Leap Forward, tried to do much more. It created hundreds of large communes, where as many as 25,000 people lived and worked. The goal was to bring China's production levels up to those of Western nations. As a result of poor planning, industry nearly came to a stop. Also, bad harvests from 1959 to 1961 left millions of people starving. China had failed to take the Great Leap Forward.

Some members of the Communist party criticized Mao's plans. They believed production would increase only through rewards to workers. Mao accused them of "walking the capitalist road." Their goal, Mao said, was to return to the days of the emperors.

REVIEW *What steps did Mao Zedong take to change the Chinese economy?*

The Cultural Revolution

In 1966 Mao decided that too many people were refusing to accept his ways. What China needed, he said, was a **Cultural Revolution** to cut people's ties to the past. Mao felt that high school and college students would be the best people to lead this revolution. Having grown up under communism, they had little respect for China's past.

The **Red Guard**, as these young people came to be known, destroyed anything that showed the past or the ways of the West—books, works of art, buildings. They even changed traffic signals, making red the color for "go" and green the color for "stop."

The Red Guard made life hard for those who they felt were not good Communists. The people they questioned lost their jobs and their membership in the Communist party. Many were thrown into jails or sent to work camps. Some were killed.

In time even Mao thought the Red Guard had gone too far. In 1968 he called an end to the Cultural Revolution.

The Cultural Revolution had destroyed the Chinese economy. Large numbers of managers, factory workers, and peasant farmers had been put out of work by the Red Guard. Because of this, farm and factory production dropped. It would take many years for China to recover from this economic disaster.

REVIEW *How did the Cultural Revolution affect life in China?*

New Freedoms, New Challenges

After Mao died in 1976, two groups of Communist party leaders fought for control. The moderates—the group that won— believed that the country's economy would improve by forming closer ties with Western nations. The leaders of the losing group, which was headed by Mao's widow, Jiang Qing, were put in jail.

In 1977 Deng Xiaoping (DUHNG SHOW•PING) became the leader of the moderates. Deng soon announced a new economic program based on the Four Modernizations. The leader's plan aimed at improvements in four areas: farming, manufacturing, armed forces,

and technology. Under this plan the government gave managers more control over farms and factories. The government still set **quotas**, or required amounts of particular goods to be produced. But farmers and factory managers could sell any extra goods they produced and keep the profits. The program also introduced the idea of free enterprise. Some Chinese were allowed to start their own businesses.

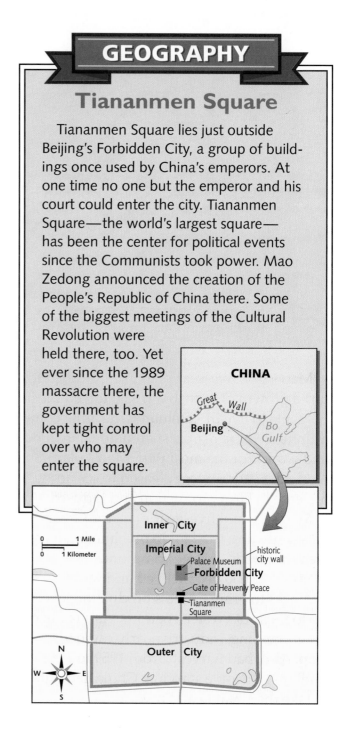

GEOGRAPHY

Tiananmen Square

Tiananmen Square lies just outside Beijing's Forbidden City, a group of buildings once used by China's emperors. At one time no one but the emperor and his court could enter the city. Tiananmen Square—the world's largest square— has been the center for political events since the Communists took power. Mao Zedong announced the creation of the People's Republic of China there. Some of the biggest meetings of the Cultural Revolution were held there, too. Yet ever since the 1989 massacre there, the government has kept tight control over who may enter the square.

CHINA

Great Wall

Beijing

Bo Gulf

0   1 Mile
0   1 Kilometer

Inner City

Imperial City

Palace Museum

Forbidden City

historic city wall

Gate of Heavenly Peace

Tiananmen Square

Outer City

N W E S

The taste of economic success made the Chinese people want even more changes. During the late 1980s thousands called for political changes as well as economic ones. In early 1989, students protested peacefully day after day in Tiananmen (TYAHN•AHN•MEN) Square in Beijing. The students demanded political freedom. As the weeks went by, their cry for democracy grew stronger.

The Chinese government decided to take action. On June 4, 1989, troops fired on the students in Tiananmen Square. "Tell the world our government has gone mad!" an angry young woman said to Western journalists. By the next day the army had moved into the Square and thousands of students lay dead or wounded. Many others were put in prison.

The Tiananmen Square killings shocked people around the world. Some governments cut trade ties with China. Chinese leaders responded by saying that other governments had no right to criticize their actions. The Chinese government then made all traces of the massacre disappear—as though the killings had never taken place!

In the early 1990s Chinese leaders gave back some freedoms to the people and began to rebuild economic ties with Western

Employees at an electronics store in China hand out advertisements for products. This scene is just one sign of free enterprise in China.

countries. Today China has one of the world's fastest-growing economies. After Deng Xiaoping's death in 1997, China's new leader, Jiang Zemin (JEE•AHNG zuh•MIN), promised to continue free enterprise in China. Politically, however, the country remains a long way from being a democracy.

Today, more than 1 billion people live in China. With China's large population comes the problem of how to feed so many people. Since the late 1970s China has tried to keep its population from growing by requiring families to have no more than one child.

REVIEW *How did Deng Xiaoping change China's economy?*

LESSON I REVIEW

Check Understanding

1 **Remember the Facts**   What was the Great Leap Forward? What was the Four Modernizations program?

2 **Recall the Main Idea**   How did China's economy change after Mao?

Think Critically

3 **Explore Viewpoints**   Which leader, Mao Zedong or Deng Xiaoping, helped China's economy more? Explain.

4 **Personally Speaking**   How would you feel if you were free to make decisions about earning your living but not about choosing your leaders? Do you think the two freedoms belong together? Do you think one can exist without the other? Explain.

Show What You Know

Time-Line Activity   Use library resources to create a time line showing events relating to the Chinese economy from 1911 to the present.

Read a Cartogram

1. Why Learn This Skill?

As you know, population is not evenly spread around the world. Some areas are nearly empty, while other areas are very crowded. Some small countries and continents have larger populations than large countries and continents. Many different factors—such as available resources, elevation, climate, historical events, and people's ways of life—affect an area's population.

One interesting way to show population is to use a kind of map called a cartogram. A **cartogram** is a map that gives information about places by the size shown for each place. Knowing how to read a population cartogram can help you find out in which countries of the world many or few people live.

2. Population Cartograms

A cartogram is not like most maps. On most maps, the size of each country or continent is based on its land area. On a cartogram, the size of the country or continent is based on a geographical statistic. On the cartogram on page 631, size is based on population.

A population cartogram shows the countries of the world as the sizes they would be if everyone had the same amount of land. A country with many people would be much bigger than a country with few people. When countries are shown this way, you can quickly compare populations around the world. A population cartogram does not, however, show the number of people in an area.

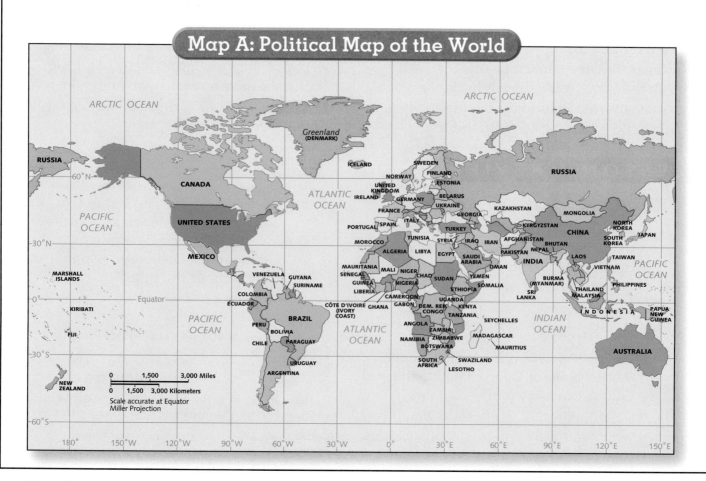

Map A: Political Map of the World

3. Understand the Process

Map A is a political map of the world. The size of each country is based on its land area. Compare the size of Russia with the size of China. Which is larger? Map B is a population cartogram. The size of each country is based on its population. Compare the sizes of Russia and China again. Although China has a smaller land area than Russia, it is shown larger than Russia on the cartogram because it has more people.

Locate Australia and Japan on Map A. You can see that Australia has a much larger land area than Japan. Now find Australia and Japan on the cartogram. Which of these countries has the larger population?

Continue to compare land area and population by answering these questions.

1 Which country in Africa has the largest population?

2 Which country in Africa has the greatest land area?

3 Which country in North America has the second-largest population?

4 Which country in North America has the second-largest land area?

5 Which continent has the largest population? Tell how you know.

6 Which continent has the fewest people? Tell how you know.

4. Think and Apply

With a partner, brainstorm other uses for cartograms. What other statistics could be shown this way to help people compare and contrast countries of the world? If these types of statistics are available in your local library, locate them and make your own cartogram. Then prepare a list of questions that could be answered by looking at your cartogram. Ask several classmates to take your cartogram quiz. Accept a classmate's challenge to take his or her cartogram quiz as well.

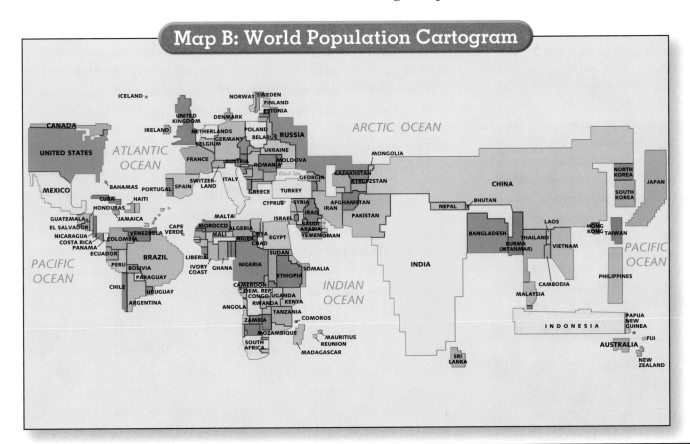

Map B: World Population Cartogram

FOCUS

How does a country grow rich and powerful?

Main Idea As you read, look for things Japan did to gain importance in the industrial world.

Vocabulary

gross domestic product
balance of trade
standard of living
megalopolis
trade surplus
protectionism
free port

Japan Becomes a World Power

Japan became an industrial nation in the late 1800s, many years after countries in Europe had industrialized, but long before China had. By the 1930s Japan had become the major industrial power in Asia. In the 1940s, however, World War II destroyed Japan's economy.

Japan Rebuilds

After World War II, it seemed that Japan's economy might never recover. United States Army troops led by General Douglas MacArthur occupied the country. Japanese emperor Hirohito (hir•oh•HEE•toh) had lost his authority. Military leaders who had led Japan into war had been put on trial, found guilty, and punished. Industries could produce little because most factories lay in ruins.

After the war the Japanese immediately began to rebuild. At first they had a great deal of help from the United States. United States leaders thought it was in the world's best interest to assist their former enemy. Government loans and money from United States companies helped the Japanese build new factories.

The rebuilding program began with the textile, or cloth, industry. Before World War II, Japan had made beautiful silks. The new textile factories made not only silk but cotton and other fabrics as well. The Japanese then built up their iron and steel industry. Japan soon became a world leader in steel production. Its factories also made large numbers of electric appliances and other goods. Transistor radios, toys, and a variety of gadgets were exported all over the world.

By the 1970s Japan was the third-highest producer of goods in the world. It led all other nations in building ships, and it was second only to the United States in making cars. What Japan did was remarkable because it has so few natural resources. It has to import almost everything that it needs for its industries.

After World War II, Japan rebuilt quickly. Now Japan is a leader in the production of high-technology items like the bullet train pictured here.

Surprisingly, the war that destroyed most of Japan's industry also helped the country succeed in starting over. When the Japanese rebuilt their factories, they used the latest technology. This put Japan ahead of most other industrial nations, whose factories had older equipment.

Even so, the people of Japan were the main reason the country did so well. The goal of rebuilding their country united the Japanese. They realized that they would have to cooperate to reach this goal. The Japanese people were willing to put the good of their country first. They worked long hours and saved much of their money.

Using the money that was deposited in savings accounts, banks made loans to help rebuild Japanese industries. The Japanese government helped by lowering taxes for businesses. It also set up high tariffs to keep out goods from other countries, forcing the Japanese people to buy Japanese goods.

REVIEW *What made Japan's growth possible?*

Problems Below the Surface

Today Japan is one of the world's industrial leaders. Its **gross domestic product** (GDP), the total value of a country's goods and services produced within the country's borders each year, is more than three

Computers and other electronic goods are produced in factories throughout Japan.

trillion dollars. Japan also has a favorable **balance of trade**. This means that it exports, or sells to other countries, more than it imports, or buys from other countries.

At the same time, the last years of the twentieth century brought economic trouble for Japan. The country suffered its worst economic setback since World War II. By the century's close, Japan's GDP had dropped to almost half of what it was just five years before. Its **standard of living**—a measure of how well people live in a certain place—also dropped.

Japan's falling economy created new problems. The country's once booming stock prices slid steadily downward. Japan's workers, once sure of lifetime jobs, began to face layoffs.

Japan faces other problems as well. One such problem relates to the combination of growth and limited space. After World War II,

LEARNING FROM GRAPHS Japan's gross domestic product remains one of the highest in the world.
■ *How much higher is Japan's GDP than Germany's?*

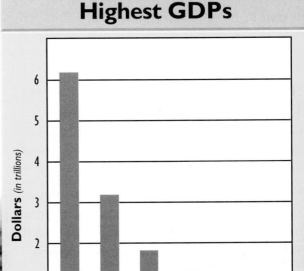

Countries with the Highest GDPs

Highly industrialized nations often must deal with environmental problems such as smog. This air pollution threatens people's health and well-being. Smog often covers the city of Tokyo, Japan.

Japan's industries grew quickly. As more land was used for industry, less could be used for houses. The cost of homes became very high. Nearby cities seemed to grow to meet one another, forming a **megalopolis**. In the large cities many middle-class Japanese could afford only tiny, two-room apartments in high-rise buildings. Today most large cities are overcrowded and have a shortage of houses and apartments. In these cities pollution also threatens people's health.

REVIEW *What problems faced Japan near the end of the twentieth century?*

Japan and Trade

Despite its economic setbacks, Japan has a favorable balance of trade with nearly every one of its trading partners. It has a **trade surplus** with the United States. This means that it exports to the United States more goods than it imports from our country.

Some Americans have claimed that Japan built this trade surplus in unfair ways. In the 1970s and 1980s, more and more Japanese

cars were shipped to the United States. Because of the cars' high quality and low prices, many people bought them instead of American cars. United States automobile makers closed factories and laid off workers partly as a result of Japan's stiff competition.

American feelings about this issue grew stronger in the 1990s. Some politicians urged the government to use a policy of

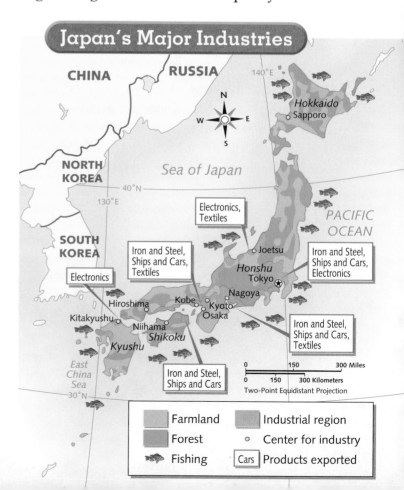

Place Japan produces a wide variety of goods and services.

■ *Where in Japan are textiles produced?*

634 • Unit 10

protectionism in dealing with Japan. Such a policy calls for actions, such as raising tariffs, to protect a market from imports.

In 1994 the United States government said it would take such actions if Japan did not end "procedures that lock American or other foreign products out of the Japanese market."

In July 1995 the United States and Japan agreed on a plan to open up the Japanese automobile market to American producers. Many people believed that this was a good first step toward a more balanced trade.

REVIEW *How did Japan respond to United States concerns about Japanese trade practices?*

Japan's Competitors

Japan is no longer the only industrial power in Asia. South Korea, Taiwan, Hong Kong, and Singapore have industrialized as well. These places now compete with Japan to export products to places throughout the world.

South Korea borrowed money from Japan and used Japanese ideas to build its manufacturing industry. Today South Korea is a leader in building ships and making textiles. Its low-priced goods compete with those of Japan in the electronics and automobile markets. Taiwan, too, exports electronic goods, textiles, and machinery.

Hong Kong's most important industries include textiles, electronics, plastics, and toys. Many foreign companies have built factories in Hong Kong because people there work for low pay. Foreign companies also like Hong Kong's status as a **free port**. This means that the government does not charge tariffs on imports or exports.

Hong Kong is located on the coast of China. For more than 150 years, however, Hong Kong was under British control. In 1997 Hong Kong once again became part of China. Even experts admit that they cannot predict how this political change will affect Hong Kong's economy in the future.

Hong Kong at night

GEOGRAPHY

Hong Kong

Located off the southern coast of China, Hong Kong includes Kowloon, which is on the mainland, and about 200 islands. Kowloon and one of the largest of these islands—the island of Hong Kong—form a fine natural harbor. British ships began using the harbor to trade with China around 1700. Britain took control of the area in 1842, after the Opium War. The colony, however, did not begin its rise to economic power until after World War II. Many people wonder if Hong Kong's economy will keep growing under Chinese control.

CHINA

CHINA

HONG KONG

0   5 Miles
0   5 Kilometers

Tsing Yi
Kowloon Peninsula — Kowloon
Victoria Harbor
Lantau Island
★ Victoria
Hong Kong Island
Lamma Island
Soko Islands
South China Sea
Po Toi Islands

N W E S

Recently, much of Asia suffered economic decline as these scenes show: Japanese stock listings in Tokyo (right); trade worries (below).

The nation of Singapore lies at the tip of the Malay Peninsula, on the Strait of Malacca (muh•LA•kuh). Its location makes Singapore an ideal stop for ships from all over the world and has helped it become a trade leader.

In recent years South Korea, Taiwan, Hong Kong, and Singapore have experienced economic setbacks similar to Japan's. Only time will tell if these countries will regain their economic strength.

Some non-Asian countries along the Pacific Rim are also challenging Japan for trade dollars. Among these are Australia and New Zealand. Mines in Australia supply precious metals, iron ore, coal, and petroleum. Australia also exports wool and cereals. New Zealand produces a variety of foods for export. It is also a source of cork, wood, wool, and machinery.

REVIEW *Which industrial powers share economic leadership of Asia with Japan?*

LESSON 2 REVIEW

Check Understanding

1 **Remember the Facts** What problems did Japan face at the end of World War II?

2 **Recall the Main Idea** How did Japan gain importance in the industrial world?

Think Critically

3 **Think More About It** What do you think is Japan's greatest problem today? Explain.

4 **Explore Viewpoints** What have American leaders said about the ways in which Japanese companies conduct business? What might the Japanese say in response?

Show What You Know

Simulation Activity With a group of classmates, create your own country. Give it a name, a location, and a population. Create a flag and perhaps a national anthem. Next list the country's resources. Then draw up a plan for how your country can become a leading industrial power in the world.

Read a Climograph

1. Why Learn This Skill?

Climate affects the foods people can grow in a place and the kinds of shelter and clothing they need to live there. One way to learn more about the climate of a place is to study a climograph. A **climograph** shows the average monthly temperature and the average monthly precipitation for a place. Knowing about the climate can help you understand more about a place and its people.

2. Understand the Process

A climograph shows both temperature and precipitation information. It is a line graph and a bar graph in one. Temperatures are shown as a line graph. Amounts of precipitation are shown as a bar graph. Along the bottom of a climograph are the months of the year.

Along the left-hand side of a climograph is a Fahrenheit scale to measure temperature. A dot is placed to show the average temperature for each month. These dots are connected with a line. By studying the line, you can see which months are hotter and which are colder.

Along the right-hand side of a climograph is a scale to measure precipitation in inches. A bar is drawn up to the average amount for each month. By studying the heights of the bars, you can see which months are drier and which are wetter.

The climograph shown here gives weather averages for the Japanese city of Tokyo. Japan's climate is much like that of the eastern United States. It is colder in the north and warmer in the south. Tokyo is located in Japan's warmer southern region. Study the climograph, and answer the questions about the temperature and precipitation of the city.

1 Which are the warmest and coldest months in Tokyo?

2 Which are the wettest and driest months in Tokyo?

3 What is the average temperature for Tokyo in January? in May? in October?

4 What relationship is there between the temperature and amount of precipitation in Tokyo?

5 What generalizations can you make about the climate of Tokyo?

3. Think and Apply

Use an almanac or other reference source to create a climograph for your town or city. Compare your climograph with that for Tokyo. Share your findings with a friend or a family member. What does the information tell you about the place where you live?

Climograph Tokyo, Japan

FOCUS

What happens when nations grow and change?

Main Idea Look for problems the South American nations have faced while growing and changing in the twentieth century.

Vocabulary

hydroelectric power
developing country
subsistence farming
nationalize
favela
deforestation

South America

Although Japan is a small island nation with few natural resources, it has become a leading industrial power. Compared to Japan, the countries of South America have many more natural resources. Even so, most of those countries have had a hard time building strong economies.

The Geography of South America

South America has a variety of physical features. Among these are the Andes, the world's longest mountain range. These mountains curve about 4,500 miles (7,242 km) down the Pacific coast of South America from Venezuela to Tierra del Fuego (TEE•air•ah del FWAY•goh) at the tip of Argentina. The mighty Amazon River in northern South America is second only to the Nile River in length, but it has a much greater volume of water. Angel Falls in Venezuela, at 3,212 feet (979 m), is the world's highest waterfall.

South America also has many climates and types of plants. The huge tropical rain forest of the Amazon River basin occupies much of the continent. Amazonia, as the rain-forest region is called, covers about 2.5 million square miles (6.58 million sq km). One-third of the world's plant and animal species live in this hot, wet region.

South America has desert lands, too. The Atacama (a•tuh•KAH•muh) Desert in northern Chile gets almost no rain. Few plants or animals can live in such a dry climate.

As much as 80 percent of the land in South America is good for farming. Beneath the soil lie many minerals—oil, iron ore, copper, tin, silver, lead, zinc, gold, and precious stones. Many rivers can be used for making hydroelectric power. **Hydroelectric power** is electricity produced by water power.

REVIEW *What are the main features of the geography of South America?*

Angel Falls, the world's highest waterfall, is on Auyán-Tepuí mountain in eastern Venezuela.

The South American Economy

Even with their rich resources, most South American countries are considered to be **developing countries**. Such countries usually have fast-growing populations, use few resources, and base their economies on agriculture. Since the end of World War II, the population of South America has more than doubled. Such fast growth can cause problems for a country's economy.

South America does not lack resources, but the resources often are not used as well as they could be. Much land that could be farmed is not being used. It is held by the rich, who think of the land only as wealth, not as a resource for producing food. Despite this, nearly half of South America's workers are farmers. Most carry on **subsistence farming**, raising only enough food for their families. They are not able to produce surplus crops to sell. Because of this, they do not earn money for their crops. Without any profits coming in, they cannot buy better farm tools to improve the way they grow crops. They must continue to live in poverty.

South American countries are trying to use their resources in better ways. In some plains areas farmers now raise cattle to take advantage of good land for grazing. Many countries have begun to look for better ways to use their mineral resources as well. Chile, for example, has about 25 percent of the world's copper, and this metal has become Chile's most important source of income.

These changes have brought problems as well as benefits. For example, some South American countries have gone into debt trying to improve their mining industries. South American countries still face economic challenges.

REVIEW *How have the countries of South America tried to change their economies?*

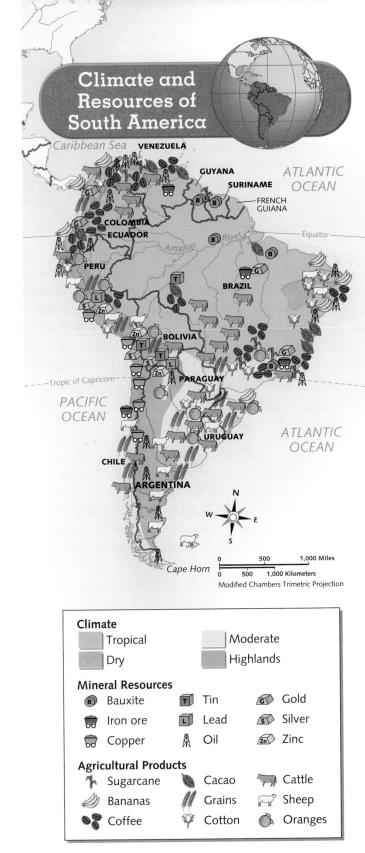

Climate and Resources of South America

Climate
- Tropical
- Dry
- Moderate
- Highlands

Mineral Resources
- B Bauxite
- Iron ore
- Copper
- T Tin
- L Lead
- Oil
- G Gold
- S Silver
- Zn Zinc

Agricultural Products
- Sugarcane
- Bananas
- Coffee
- Cacao
- Grains
- Cotton
- Cattle
- Sheep
- Oranges

Human-Environment Interactions South America has many different climate regions and a wide variety of natural resources.

■ *In what type of climate are bananas grown? What agricultural resources are found in the interior of South America?*

Venezuela and Colombia

Venezuela and Colombia are located in northwestern South America. In many ways their economies are similar.

A series of military dictators had control of Venezuela during much of the first half of the twentieth century. For the most part they let foreign companies control the country's greatest resource—oil. In 1958 a group of military leaders who wanted to set up a democracy seized control of the country. A freely elected government took office the following year and began working to improve education, health care, and other social services.

In the 1970s the government of Venezuela **nationalized** the oil industry. That is, it took control of the industry on behalf of the nation's people. Oil soon became the most important part of the country's economy. High prices for oil in the 1970s and 1980s helped make Venezuela a rich country. However, not all people shared in the wealth. Many people remained poor, especially those living in the countryside.

In the late 1980s oil prices fell, and so did the Venezuelan economy. As oil prices rose

Oil production has helped make Venezuela one of the richest countries in South America.

again in the early 1990s, the economy improved. Unfortunately, as long as Venezuela depends on a single product, its economy will slide up and down. Recent finds of iron ore may help the economy become more stable.

Colombia's economy also depends on a single product. Coffee makes up about half of Colombia's exports. In the 1970s coffee prices were fairly low. So peasant farmers turned to an illegal crop that was in high

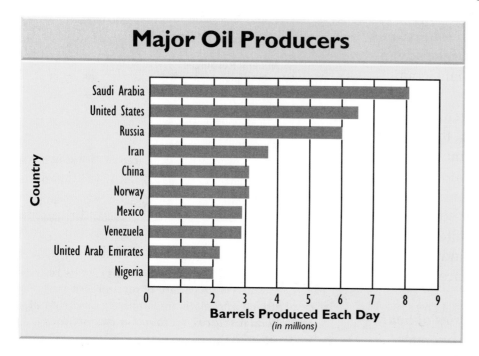

Major Oil Producers

Country:
- Saudi Arabia
- United States
- Russia
- Iran
- China
- Norway
- Mexico
- Venezuela
- United Arab Emirates
- Nigeria

Barrels Produced Each Day (in millions): 0 1 2 3 4 5 6 7 8 9

LEARNING FROM GRAPHS
Countries from around the globe make up the list of the world's top oil producers. Seven countries around the world produce more oil than Venezuela.

■ *About how many millions of barrels of oil does Venezuela produce in a day? About how many more barrels of oil does Saudi Arabia produce in a day?*

demand—coca leaves. The addictive drug cocaine is made from these leaves. This drug is smuggled from Colombia to the United States and other countries.

Soon gangs began to fight for control of the drug trade. Violence became part of everyday life. At the same time, guerrilla bands, or small groups of fighters, began trying to overthrow the government. By the 1990s the violence had decreased. Still, drug-related crimes and political unrest continue in Colombia today.

REVIEW *What do the economies of Venezuela and Colombia have in common?*

Chile

Political changes have greatly affected Chile's economy. In 1970 the people of Chile elected Salvador Allende (ah•YEN•day) as president. Allende immediately began to change the economy from free enterprise to socialist. He put most industries under the control of the national government. Then he gave the workers a say in how those industries would be run. He also ordered that the industries pay their workers more and set limits on how high the prices of goods could rise.

By demanding basic human rights, protesters helped bring an end to Augusto Pinochet's dictatorship in Chile.

At first these actions seemed to work, and business boomed. Then prices for copper, Chile's main export, fell. Inflation soared and the economy failed. Many Chileans in the middle and upper classes demanded change.

In September 1973 General Augusto Pinochet (pee•noh•CHET) seized power and became dictator. Allende and many of his supporters were killed. Pinochet declared that the constitution was no longer in effect. He got rid of all political parties. He sold industries owned by the government to private businesses and removed the tariffs on imports. He also stopped pay raises for workers and put strong control on the activities of labor unions.

After ten years of Pinochet's rule, inflation was lower and the economy had improved. However, most workers were suffering. By the early 1980s more people than ever were out of work. Without the tariffs many of Chile's industries found it hard to compete with cheap imports, and they went out of business. Chile depended on copper even more than before.

By the late 1980s the people of Chile had grown tired of Pinochet's dictatorship. In March 1989 they removed him from office through free elections. The new government allowed other countries to invest in Chile and brought about a more open economy. The country is now learning how to produce more of its own food by irrigating its desert lands. Chile's exports are also rising dramatically. Today Chile remains the world's largest exporter and producer of copper.

REVIEW *How did General Augusto Pinochet change the Chilean economy?*

Brazil

In the first half of the twentieth century, Brazil's economy was based almost entirely on coffee. Today, however, Brazil is the most heavily industrialized of all the South

American countries, and it exports a variety of products.

The drive to build new industries for Brazil began under President Getúlio Vargas (zheh•TOO•lyoo VAR•guhs), who held office from 1930 to 1945. Brazilian industry got another boost in the 1950s under President Juscelino Kubitschek (zhoo•seh•LEE•noh KOO•buh•chek). President Kubitschek promised "50 years of progress in 5." A new capital, Brasília (bruh•ZIL•yuh), and 11,000 miles (17,702 km) of new highways were built.

Today such goods as automobiles, ships, and steel make up more than half of Brazil's exports. Brazil also exports farm products, such as bananas, oranges, beef, coffee, and cacao—the beans used to make cocoa. These activities have made Brazil's economy the strongest in all of South America.

As Brazil enters the twenty-first century, it is experiencing some growing pains. Not all Brazilians share in the economic success. The rich are very rich and live in fine homes in the cities. Yet in the **favelas** (fuh•VEH•luhz), or slums outside the cities, poor families live in one-room shacks. Like many cities around the world, Brazilian cities face the problem of overcrowding. The current government is trying to solve this problem by providing well-built, affordable housing.

Careless development of Brazil's resources has caused a huge problem for Amazonia—and for the whole Earth. Farmers and timber companies have been clearing huge sections of rain forest. The Brazilian government has passed environmental laws to try to stop such **deforestation**, or clearing of forests. This deforestation can have many negative effects. It may cause landslides, flooding, and other disasters. At least 4,000 square miles (10,359 sq km) of Brazilian rain forest are still being destroyed each year.

Destroying the rain forest harms the whole world. Workers usually clear the land to make room for farms by burning many trees. These huge fires cause pollution and leave the soil bare. The rain forest's soil has few natural nutrients. When heavy rains fall on the bare soil, the nutrients are washed away. This means that farmers can grow crops for only two or three years after clearing. People must clear land if they want to continue farming.

The loss of rain forest trees also changes the world's air and climate. All trees produce oxygen, which we need in order to breathe.

Many places in Brazil, such as the Monumental Axis (below), offer positive signs of a growing economy. At the same time, this favela (right) in Rio de Janeiro is an example of the poverty that many of Brazil's people face.

More than 1,500 kinds of birds live among the thousands of different kinds of trees in the rain forests of South America (right). Parts of the rain forest have been cleared for farmland (below).

Trees also take in carbon dioxide. With fewer trees, there is more carbon dioxide in the atmosphere. The burning of the trees adds even more carbon dioxide. This increased carbon dioxide may be causing a warming of the Earth's atmosphere. Rising temperatures and drier conditions could hurt farming around the globe. Such a climate change might cause polar ice to melt, raising the levels of ocean water and flooding coastal lands. Some scientists refer to this possible warming as the "greenhouse effect," or "global warming."

Clearing the rain forest hurts people in other ways as well. Many native peoples have to find new places to live because they have lost their forest homes. As they come into contact with new people, they are exposed to new diseases. Also, away from their homes, they may lose touch with their own culture. The loss of the rain forest also means the loss of thousands of plants that cannot grow anywhere else. We will never know if these plants could have been important to science, perhaps even for curing diseases.

REVIEW *What economic and environmental problems does Brazil face?*

LESSON 3 REVIEW

Check Understanding

1 Remember the Facts   Why are most South American countries called developing countries?

2 Recall the Main Idea   What problems have South American countries faced while developing their economies?

Think Critically

3 Personally Speaking   Which of their economic problems do you think South American countries need to deal with first? Why do you think so?

4 Cause and Effect   Why are changes in world prices for copper, coffee, and oil a problem for some South American countries?

Show What You Know

Article-Writing Activity Choose one South American country, and imagine that you have just become its leader. Write an article titled "The Economy: Today's Problems, Tomorrow's Hopes." Post your article on a class bulletin board for others to read.

How Should World

To help their economies grow, all countries need to decide on the best uses for their resources. To use their resources one way, they give up the possibility of using them in other ways. This is called a **trade-off**. If countries clear parts of their rain forests in order to use the land, the trade-off is that they will no longer have the forests.

When a country makes an economic choice, what it gives up is the **opportunity cost** of what it gets. If countries keep their rain forests, it costs them the opportunity to use the land for farming, mining, or logging. If they clear their rain forests, it costs them the use of the forests and the benefits of the forests to the Earth itself.

People have many different viewpoints about the economic choices countries should make about their rain forests. Some people think that rain forests should be preserved at all costs, and that development should not be allowed in them. Others argue that not using the natural resources found in rain forests is unfair to the people who need them.

How and whether to use rain forests is often the subject of debate. El Yunque rain forest in Puerto Rico (above) remains undisturbed. Work on a mining project continues in Brazil on land that was once a rain forest (right).

Jonathan Burton

Writer Jonathan Burton believes in finding ways to use the rain forests to make money for the economy.

"One proposal is to harvest the forests for useful and renewable resources instead of cutting them down. A 1989 study showed that an acre in the Peruvian Amazon would be worth $148 if used for cattle pasture, $1,000 if cut for timber, and $6,820 if selectively combed for fruits, rubber, and other products. Using this method, known as 'sustainable development,' countries could gain economic benefits and at the same time preserve one of the planet's most biologically diverse areas."

Resources Be Used?

Zoran Bosnic

Zoran Bosnic, who works for the Brazilian government, believes that Brazil must be free to clear parts of its rain forests for industrial use.

66 Europe and America [the United States] destroyed their forests to become industrial powers, but when it comes to the Amazon they say, 'Stop!' Brazil has a debt, people to feed and employ. The economy is under terrific pressure. It must industrialize as soon as possible. 99

Santos Adam Afsua

Santos Adam Afsua, a Peruvian Indian, believes that the people who live in the rain forests should be the ones to make decisions about them.

66 We live to protect the forest with the best ecological and environmental knowledge that we possess, a knowledge we inherited from our ancestors. We do this with the understanding that we will continue living there, and we have to protect this forest because we have to think of future generations. . . . We have come to meet with the different environmental organizations to tell them, first of all, that the only people that can really conserve the environment are our people. 99

Compare Viewpoints

1. Why does Jonathan Burton believe that sustainable development is the best use of rain forest resources?

2. Why does Zoran Bosnic believe that it is necessary to clear parts of rain forests for industrial use?

3. How is the viewpoint of Santos Adam Afsua different from those of Jonathan Burton and Zoran Bosnic?

Think and Apply

People often have different viewpoints about the best way to solve a problem. Which of the three ideas given do you think is the best? Why? What other ideas do you have about using the resources of rain forests?

This rain forest is in Marenco, Costa Rica.

FOCUS

How might cooperation among neighboring countries affect the economies of those countries?

Main Idea As you read, think about how Canada, Mexico, and the United States are working together economically.

Vocabulary

bilingual
ratify
secede
Great Society
national debt
bloc

North America and Free Trade

C anada, Mexico, and the United States have all made great economic progress during the twentieth century. Still, as a new century begins, they all face economic challenges.

A Northern Giant

The beginning of the twentieth century seemed to promise a bright future for Canada. In the late 1890s gold had been discovered in the Yukon Territory, in Canada's far northwest. Canadians soon found that they had other natural resources that the world wanted. Their nickel, copper, zinc, and other metals turned out to be worth as much as the Yukon gold. Canada's forests became valuable as well, because people needed wood pulp to make paper. Also, the land of south-western Canada proved to be good for wheat farming and for ranching.

In 1931 Canada gained its independence from Britain. Not long after, Canada, like many other nations, suffered through the Great Depression. People all over Canada lost their jobs. After World War II, Canada began to recover. Canadians built up their iron, steel, and aluminum industries and discovered deposits of oil, natural gas, and minerals.

Today Canada has a strong economy and one of the world's highest standards of living. But Canada, like many other countries, has problems such as inflation and unemployment. In addition, Canada has some problems that are purely Canadian.

Canada, like the United States, has a federal form of government. But the provinces of Canada have more authority than the states that make up the United States. The federal

In the Canadian gold rush of 1898, people dug for gold in the streets of this Yukon town.

government and the provinces cannot agree on which should run Canada's oil industry and have more of the profits.

Canada faces still another problem. In 1763 Britain took over Quebec from the French. Since that time, Canada has been a country with two main cultures and languages. French Canadians are a minority in Canada, but in Quebec they make up more than 80 percent of the population. French is Quebec's official language. For many years the people of Quebec have wanted their language and culture recognized by all of Canada.

In 1969 the Official Languages Act made Canada a **bilingual** country, a nation with

two official languages. Then in the late 1980s the Canadian government planned to recognize the people of Quebec as a "distinct society" within Canada. The other Canadian provinces, however, refused to **ratify**, or approve, this. Many people in Quebec called for the province to **secede**, or separate, from Canada. In October 1995 the people of Quebec narrowly voted to remain part of Canada. Leaders of the movement that fought to separate vowed to continue trying for an independent Quebec.

REVIEW *Why does Quebec want to secede from the rest of Canada?*

Regions

Canada has a great wealth of resources.

■ *For what resources is Quebec known?*

The city of Quebec, capital of the Canadian province of Quebec, is a major tourist center.

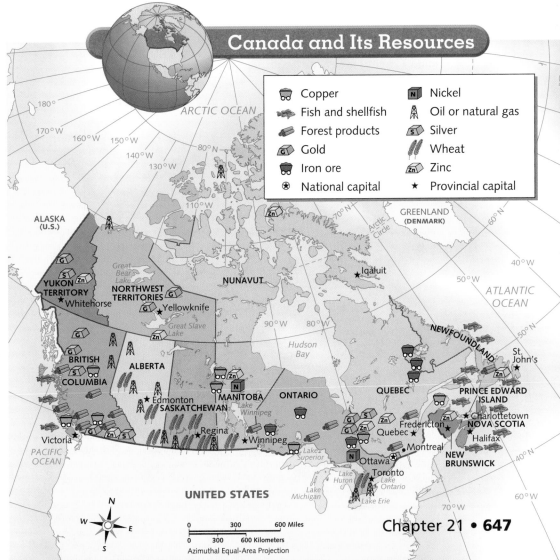

Canada and Its Resources

Symbol	Resource	Symbol	Resource
Copper		Nickel	
Fish and shellfish		Oil or natural gas	
Forest products		Silver	
Gold		Wheat	
Iron ore		Zinc	
National capital		Provincial capital	

ARCTIC OCEAN

180°
170°W
160°W
150°W
140°W
130°W
110°W
80°N
70°N
60°N
50°N
40°N

GREENLAND (DENMARK)
Arctic Circle

ALASKA (U.S.)

YUKON TERRITORY
★Whitehorse

NORTHWEST TERRITORIES
★Yellowknife

Great Bear Lake
Great Slave Lake

NUNAVUT
★Iqaluit

ATLANTIC OCEAN

BRITISH COLUMBIA
★Edmonton
ALBERTA
SASKATCHEWAN
★Regina

MANITOBA
Lake Winnipeg
★Winnipeg

ONTARIO

Hudson Bay

QUEBEC
★Quebec
Fredericton
NEW BRUNSWICK

NEWFOUNDLAND
★St. John's

PRINCE EDWARD ISLAND
★Charlottetown
NOVA SCOTIA
★Halifax

Victoria
PACIFIC OCEAN

★Ottawa
Toronto
Montreal

Lake Superior
Lake Huron
Lake Michigan
Lake Ontario
Lake Erie

UNITED STATES

90°W
80°W
70°W
60°W

N W E S

0   300   600 Miles
0   300   600 Kilometers
Azimuthal Equal-Area Projection

Chapter 21 • 647

Progress in Mexico

Since World War II, Mexico has faced the same economic problems as its neighbors in Central and South America. Slowly, the Mexican economy has come to depend less on agriculture and more on industry. The most important industry is now oil refining. Instead of exporting the oil in its crude form—as it comes from the ground—the Mexican government refines it first. Refined oil products are worth more than crude oil exports. Refining also provides more jobs for the Mexican people.

To build its industries, Mexico used aid from the United States. Both the United States government and private businesses loaned money to Mexican business people. Companies in the United States also set up *maquiladoras* (mah•kee•lah•DOH•rahs), or border industries, in Mexico. Mexican workers at the *maquiladora* plants make finished goods using parts shipped from the United States.

While the *maquiladora* system has created jobs for many Mexican men and women, it has had some unwelcome effects in Mexico as well. For example, pollution has increased greatly because of the factories.

Over the years Mexico has made much economic progress. Today it is one of the most highly industrialized countries in Latin America. However, because Mexico's economy depends so much on the price of oil, the country has problems when oil prices fall. Mexico also owes a lot of money to other countries.

Perhaps the biggest problem Mexico faces is its fast population growth. Mexico City alone has grown by 3 million people in the past ten years. It may have another 10 million by the year 2025. In Mexico City thousands of

Human-Environment Interactions Rapid population growth is one challenge Mexico faces as it enters the twenty-first century.
■ *In which of Mexico's states are the country's most populated cities?*

Mexico

1. AGUASCALIENTES
2. QUERÉTARO
3. TLAXCALA
4. MÉXICO
5. DISTRITO FEDERAL
6. MORELOS

- ● More than 10 million people
- ● 1–10 million people
- • Fewer than 1 million people
- ✪ National capital

This new university in Mexico City (above), high tech worker (bottom right), and modern assembly line (top right) reflect Mexico's rapid growth.

poor people have made their homes next to garbage dumps. They pick through the trash, trying to find something they can sell. Elsewhere in Mexico the poor face equally hard conditions.

People in Chiapas (chee•AH•pahs), Mexico's poorest state, were angry that their living conditions were so bad. Indian tribes in Chiapas rebelled in early 1994, asking for major economic and political changes. Government and rebel leaders worked out an end to the fighting. In 1998 Mexico's government stepped up efforts to work out an agreement to bring long-lasting peace to Chiapas.

REVIEW *How are Mexico's economic problems similar to those of other Latin American countries?*

A Leading Economic Power

In the United States, industries making goods for use in World War II created new jobs. This put money into the economy and helped pull the United States out of the Great Depression. By the mid-1950s the country was doing well. Labor union leader George Meany told union members, "You've never had it so good!" At the same time, however, many people lived in poverty.

In the mid-1960s President Lyndon Johnson felt that the federal government needed to do something for poor people. He proposed to Congress what he called the Great Society. In the Great Society, he said, every American would have the chance for a good life. His Great Society programs covered civil rights, health care, education, and housing.

At the same time, the United States became heavily involved in the Vietnam War. The government borrowed money to pay for the Great Society at home and for the war in Vietnam. Because government spending was so high, the economy weakened.

Both President Richard Nixon, who followed Johnson, and the next two Presidents, Gerald Ford and Jimmy Carter, faced high inflation because of increased government spending. Each tried something new to solve the problem, but all failed.

President Ronald Reagan, who was elected in 1980, also had a plan to help the economy.

He believed that the United States had spent too much money helping the poor. Reagan reduced government spending and cut taxes. Inflation decreased. Defense spending rose, however. The government then borrowed more money by selling bonds to individuals and banks. The **national debt**—the amount of money that is owed by the government—increased greatly.

The end of the twentieth century offered a brighter economic picture for the United States. Under President Bill Clinton the nation achieved a balanced budget.

Today many Americans stress that the United States must continue to be an economic superpower. Economically strong countries, they believe, will have the most influence on world events.

REVIEW *What is meant by the term National Debt?*

NAFTA

In 1994 a trade arrangement was made that affects the United States, Canada, and Mexico. It is called the North American Free Trade Agreement, or NAFTA. Under the agreement these three countries will, over a 15-year period, remove all tariffs and other forms of protectionism among them.

The goal of the agreement is to encourage the three countries to buy more of one another's goods.

Business leaders in all three countries hope NAFTA will lead to a powerful North American free-trade **bloc**, or group of

Free-Trade Groups in the Americas

Alaska (U.S.)
CANADA
N
W   E
S
UNITED STATES
ATLANTIC OCEAN
MEXICO
HONDURAS
GUATEMALA   NICARAGUA
EL SALVADOR
COSTA RICA   VENEZUELA
COLOMBIA
PACIFIC   ECUADOR
OCEAN
PERU   BRAZIL
0   1,000   2,000 Miles
BOLIVIA
0   1,000   2,000 Kilometers   PARAGUAY
Robinson Projection   CHILE
URUGUAY
ARGENTINA

- North American Free Trade Agreement
- Central American Common Market
- Latin American Integration Association
- Southern Cone Common Market

Regions Most countries in the Americas have entered into trade agreements with their Western Hemisphere neighbors.
■ *According to the map, of what trade groups is Mexico a member?*

650 • Unit 10

countries with the same interests. This free-trade bloc, they believe, will help North American companies compete against Asian and European companies.

In 1993 a number of Central American countries signed their own free-trade agreement. Some South American countries have done the same. Business leaders from places as far north as Canada and as far south as Argentina believe that one day all the countries of the Western Hemisphere will be part of a single free-trade agreement.

REVIEW *What do North American business leaders hope NAFTA will achieve?*

Representatives from Mexico, the United States, and Canada sign the North American Free Trade Agreement (top). U.S. Presidents (from left to right) Gerald Ford, Jimmy Carter, George Bush, and Bill Clinton attend the signing of NAFTA side agreement (bottom).

LESSON 4 REVIEW

Check Understanding

1 **Remember the Facts** What does NAFTA stand for?

2 **Recall the Main Idea** How are Canada, Mexico, and the United States working together economically?

Think Critically

3 **Think More About It** Why do you think some people supported NAFTA while others opposed it?

4 **Cause and Effect** How can the lowering of tariffs help both consumers and industries that produce consumer goods?

Show What You Know
Letter-Writing Activity
Write a letter to a local business leader. Ask whether NAFTA has changed his or her business, and if so, what changes has it brought? Report to your classmates on what you learn.

Chapter 21 • **651**

1900   1920

1911
• Chinese republic is formed

1931
• Canada gains independence from Britain

CONNECT MAIN IDEAS

Use this organizer to show that you understand recent world events. Write several sentences to describe the economic challenges that each of the countries or groups of countries listed below have faced in recent times. A copy of the organizer appears on page 148 of the Activity Book.

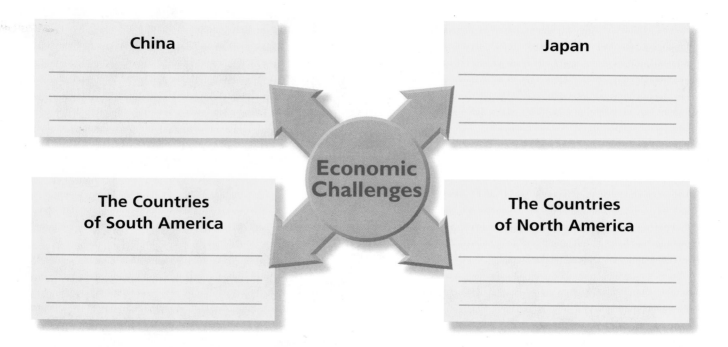

China

Japan

Economic Challenges

The Countries of South America

The Countries of North America

WRITE MORE ABOUT IT

Write a Biography Research and write a one-page biography on one of the following Chinese leaders or would-be leaders: Sun Yat-sen, Chiang Kai-shek, Mao Zedong, Jiang Qing, Deng Xiaoping, or Jiang Zemin. At the end of your report, describe the characteristics you think a good leader should have. Then tell whether the individual you selected had or has the characteristics needed to be a good leader.

Write a Description What do you think life is like economically for the people of Japan today? Write a one-page description of a day in the life of a Japanese worker. Be sure to describe living and working conditions.

Write Your Opinion Do you think Quebec will try again to secede from the rest of Canada? If so, will it be successful? Explain why you hold the opinion you do.

1940	1960	1980	present

1949
• The communist People's Republic of China is formed

1989
• Free elections remove Augusto Pinochet from office in Chile

1997
• Hong Kong becomes part of China

USE VOCABULARY

For each pair of terms, write a sentence or two that explains how the terms are related.

1 commune, Cultural Revolution

2 developing country, subsistence farming

3 Great Society, national debt

4 ratify, secede

5 trade surplus, protectionism

CHECK UNDERSTANDING

6 What political party grew out of China's demand for change in the early 1900s?

7 What type of change has China recently made—political or economic?

8 How did the United States help Japan rebuild its economy after World War II?

9 What is a developing country?

10 How has Brazil's economy changed since the first half of the twentieth century?

11 What makes Canada a bilingual country?

THINK CRITICALLY

12 **Cause and Effect** What were the effects of Mao's Cultural Revolution in China?

13 **Personally Speaking** Do you think the United States was right to help Japan rebuild after World War II? Explain.

14 **Explore Viewpoints** What are some reasons why some people want to save the rain forests? What are some reasons why others want to use the resources of the rain forests?

APPLY SKILLS

Read a Cartogram Draw a cartogram that compares the populations of Arizona, Nevada, New Mexico, California, and Texas. To find state populations, look in an almanac. Then, answer these questions.

15 Which state shown in your cartogram has the largest population?

16 Which state shown in your cartogram has the smallest population?

17 Is there a relation between population and size among these states? Explain.

Read a Climograph Select a large city in the United States. Look in an almanac to find that city's average temperature and precipitation for each month of the year. Make a climograph of that information. Then, exchange climographs with a classmate. Write a paragraph describing the information shown in your classmate's climograph.

READ MORE ABOUT IT

The Red Scarf Girl: A Memoir of the Cultural Revolution by Ji Li Jiang. HarperCollins. An autobiography of a young girl living in China during the Cultural Revolution.

Visit the Internet at
http://www.hbschool.com
for additional resources.

RELIGIOUS INFLUENCES

"Here religion is the strongest feature of civilizations, at the heart of both their present and their past."

Historian Fernand Braudel, describing the people of southwestern Asia

Young Muslim woman from North Africa

654

The Indian Subcontinent

FOCUS

How can religious beliefs shape people's lives?

Main Idea As you read, look for ways that religion has affected the history of the Indian subcontinent.

Vocabulary

satyagraha
passive resistance
discriminate
harijan
Mahatma
boycott
minority rights

At the beginning of the twentieth century, most people in India agreed about one thing—they wanted the British to leave. Yet as they worked toward this goal, religious differences divided them. Religious conflict has continued to affect the Indian subcontinent to the present day.

Gandhi Works for Independence

In 1893 Mohandas Gandhi (moh•HAHN•dahs GAHN•dee), a young Indian lawyer who had studied in London, took a job in South Africa. Shortly after he arrived, he went by train to visit some clients. As he had always done in Britain, he bought a first-class ticket. As soon as he got on the train, the conductors threw him out. Nonwhites could not travel first class, they told him. Gandhi realized that much work needed to be done to gain rights for the Indian people who lived in South Africa.

Gandhi remembered what his mother had taught him. A very religious woman, she had instructed him to respect all forms of life and to never hurt anyone or anything. With her teachings in mind, Gandhi came to believe that people must pay back bad actions with good ones, until those doing wrong grow tired of their actions. He called this idea **satyagraha** (suh•TYAH•gruh•huh), or "soul force." People practicing *satyagraha* must use peace instead of violence to bring about change. This approach to handling conflict is also known as **passive resistance**.

The Indians in South Africa used Gandhi's passive resistance with some success. By the time Gandhi left South Africa, the government had removed

Mohandas Gandhi

the harshest laws that **discriminated**—or treated unfairly because of race or other reason—against Indians.

In 1914 Gandhi returned to India to help it win its independence from Britain. To show his support for the movement to free India, he wore traditional Indian clothing instead of his English suits. He gave away nearly everything he owned and lived very simply. Then he began to teach the idea of passive resistance. He said people should work for independence without violence. All people, whatever their race or religion, should be respected, he said, even India's outcasts, the untouchables. Gandhi began calling the untouchables by another name— **harijans** (har•ih•JAHNZ), or "children of God."

When the people of India heard how he lived and what he taught, many thought Gandhi was a holy man. They began to call him **Mahatma** (muh•HAHT•muh), or "Great Soul."

REVIEW *What way of working to gain rights did Gandhi encourage?*

Prime Minister Nehru reviews a troop of soldiers at an Independence Day ceremony in Bombay, India.

Indian Independence

Indian calls for independence grew louder and louder. The British answered by trying to stop the protests in any way they could. In April 1919, British Brigadier-General Reginald H. Dyer ordered soldiers to fire on peaceful protesters in the city of Amritsar (uhm•RIT•ser). About 400 people were killed and another 1,200 were wounded. Gandhi, feeling that there was no way to cooperate with the British, called for passive resistance across all of India.

This campaign of noncooperation took many forms. Some government leaders quit their jobs. Many workers stayed at home. Sometimes Gandhi and his followers simply sat down in the middle of a street, which, of course, stopped traffic. Gandhi also called

on his followers to **boycott**, or refuse to buy, British goods. In all these ways the Indians brought business and government almost to a stop without using violence.

The British did not know how to deal with passive resistance. They tried to keep Gandhi away from his followers. In fact, they put him in jail several times. However, Gandhi was a strong leader even from behind prison walls. He wrote to his followers, urging them to continue their actions. He also prayed and went on long hunger strikes, refusing to eat until his demands were met.

By the end of World War II, the British saw that they were losing India. In 1947 they passed governing power to Jawaharlal Nehru (juh•WAH•her•lahl NAIR•oo). Nehru was a wealthy Brahman who had been working for India's independence since 1916. He seemed the ideal person to lead his country to freedom.

REVIEW *How did Gandhi help achieve India's freedom from Britain?*

Hindus and Muslims

Gandhi and Nehru wanted an independent India in which people of all religions could live in peace. Hindus and Muslims on the Indian subcontinent had been quarreling for hundreds of years. Their religions and their ways of life were very different.

Because there were fewer Muslims than Hindus in India, Muslims felt unsafe there. They believed they would never be guaranteed minority rights. **Minority rights** are freedoms given to groups of people who make up a small part of a population. Muslim leader Muhammad Ali Jinnah (JIH•nuh) demanded that his people have their own homeland. It should be in the north, he said, where there were more Muslims than Hindus. Reluctantly, Nehru and Gandhi agreed.

As August 15, 1947—the day set for Indian independence—came closer, millions of Muslims rushed north and millions of Hindus streamed south. People from both sides attacked each other. A million or more died, most of them Muslims.

Muslims crowd into railroad cars to travel to the land that is now Pakistan, where they would not be a minority.

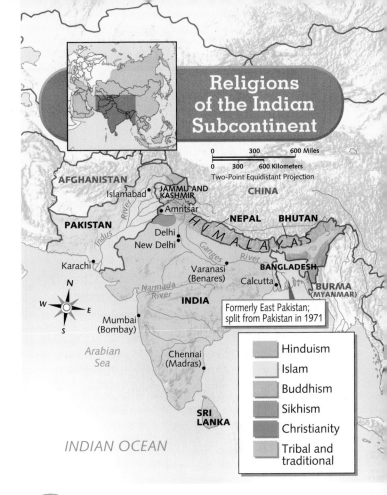

Religions of the Indian Subcontinent

0   300   600 Miles
0   300   600 Kilometers
Two-Point Equidistant Projection

AFGHANISTAN
Islamabad • JAMMU AND KASHMIR
Amritsar •
CHINA
PAKISTAN
Delhi •
New Delhi •
NEPAL   BHUTAN
HIMALAYAS
Karachi •
Ganges River
Varanasi (Benares) •
BANGLADESH
Calcutta •
BURMA (MYANMAR)
Narmada River
INDIA
Mumbai (Bombay) •
Formerly East Pakistan; split from Pakistan in 1971
Arabian Sea
Chennai (Madras) •
SRI LANKA
INDIAN OCEAN

- Hinduism
- Islam
- Buddhism
- Sikhism
- Christianity
- Tribal and traditional

Regions Most of the people who live in India today practice the religion of Hinduism.

■ *Where in India are other religions practiced?*

The Indian independence agreement created not one new country, but two. The northwestern and northeastern corners of British India became Pakistan. The rest became India, led by Nehru. Today most of the people of Pakistan are Muslims, while most of the people of India are Hindus.

During the fighting between the Hindus and the Muslims, Gandhi was killed. In January 1948 he was shot by a Hindu who believed that Gandhi was hurting his people by saying that Hindus and Muslims should work together. When telling the country of Gandhi's death, Nehru said, "The light has gone out of our lives." Around the world, many people agreed.

REVIEW *Why did Muslims move north while Hindus moved south?*

Chapter 22 • **657**

Nuclear Testing

In May 1998 India and Pakistan reopened the nuclear arms race for southwestern Asia. Nearly 24 years after its first nuclear explosion, India conducted five underground nuclear tests southwest of New Delhi. Indian prime minister Bihari Vajpayee strongly supported the testing. He believed India needed to prove to the world that it is a nuclear state.

Around the world, reactions to the testings varied. Many countries criticized India for its action. The most significant reaction to the testings came from Pakistan, India's northwestern neighbor. In response to India's testing, Pakistan conducted five nuclear tests of its own.

Both countries ignored their commitment to the Comprehensive Test Ban Treaty, which forbids all nuclear testing. As a result, the United States cut economic aid to India and Pakistan. Representatives from both countries met and after much discussion, have agreed to sign a treaty ending testing.

More Religious Differences

Religious differences caused many conflicts between the two new nations. The biggest problem was the northern state of Kashmir. Its ruler, a Hindu, chose to join India, not Pakistan. However, most of Kashmir's people were Muslims, so Pakistan felt that it should get the state. This disagreement brought India and Pakistan to war in 1947 and again in 1965. Even today the Kashmir problem is not settled.

In the 1980s another religious problem developed. This one involved a different religious group, the Sikhs (SEEKS). This group, which began in the 1500s, combines ideas from both Hinduism and Islam. From the beginning the Sikhs have struggled with both Hindus and Muslims. In time the Sikhs demanded a land of their own for their safety.

Some Sikhs turned to violence to gain their own homeland. Indian Prime Minister Indira (in•DIR•uh) Gandhi, the daughter of Nehru, was determined to end the trouble. In June 1984 Gandhi ordered the army to attack the Golden Temple in Amritsar, which the Sikhs

LEARNING FROM GRAPHS More than three-fourths of the world's Hindus live in India.

■ *Of the world's approximately 6 billion people, about how many practice Hinduism?*

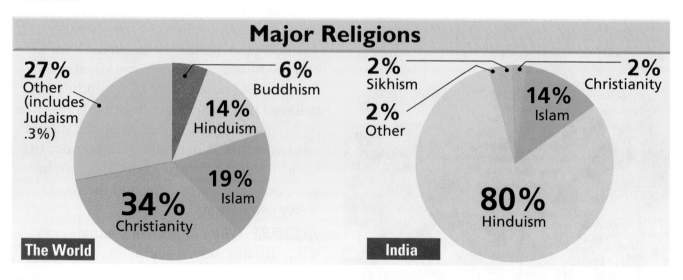

Major Religions

The World
- 27% Other (includes Judaism .3%)
- 6% Buddhism
- 14% Hinduism
- 19% Islam
- 34% Christianity

India
- 2% Sikhism
- 2% Other
- 2% Christianity
- 14% Islam
- 80% Hinduism

had turned into a fort. Almost 1,000 Sikhs died in the fighting. Many Sikhs wanted revenge for their losses. In October 1984 two of Gandhi's own bodyguards—both Sikhs—shot and killed her.

In the 1990s, Hindu leaders in India kept religious hatred alive. In Pakistan, Muslim leaders did the same. At the peak of this hatred, India and Pakistan conducted nuclear testing as a way of showing their military strength. It is clear that religious and political conflict remains a topic of concern for southern Asia.

REVIEW *Who are the Sikhs?*

Indira Gandhi reviews her troops.

Role of Women in Southern Asia

In the past, Hindu and Muslim traditions in India limited women's public roles. In the later part of the twentieth century, however, women began to take a more active part in governing. For example, Indira Gandhi was a leader in Indian politics for more than 19 years. Also, in 1988 Benazir Bhutto (BOO•toh) became prime minister of Pakistan. This made her the first woman in modern times to lead a Muslim country. Bangladesh (bahn•gluh•DESH), which gained independence from Pakistan in 1971, also elected a woman leader in the 1990s.

Although many Indian women stay at home, especially in rural areas, things are changing. In the cities more women are going to school, and many work outside the home. Some have become doctors, lawyers, and business leaders.

REVIEW *What two women have been important political leaders in India and Pakistan?*

LESSON 1 REVIEW

Check Understanding

1 Remember the Facts Why did the agreement for Indian independence call for the creation of two countries—India and Pakistan?

2 Recall the Main Idea How did religion shape the history of the Indian subcontinent?

Think Critically

3 Think More About It What do you think Gandhi meant by the term *satyagraha,* or "soul force"?

4 Cause and Effect How has India's history reflected conflict between Hindus and Muslims?

Show What You Know

Speaking Activity Search newspapers, magazines, and books to find an event in which nonviolent resistance proved to be the best way to handle a social or political problem. Describe what you learn to a family member or classmate.

Use Different Types of Population Maps

1. Why Learn This Skill?

In Chapter 21 of Unit 10, you learned that cartograms use size to show population. Cartograms are not the only means mapmakers have to show population, however. Other ways to show population on maps are with dots and with color. Knowing how to read different kinds of population maps can make it easier for you to find out where few or many people live in the world and how many people live in each place.

2. Understand the Process

The population of the world is not spread evenly across the seven continents. Map A uses dots to show the **population distribution** of India, or where people live on the subcontinent. Each dot on the map stands for 100,000 people. In some places on the map, the dots are so close that they run together. In these places, many people live close together. In other places on the map, there are no dots. Such places either have fewer than 100,000 people or have no people.

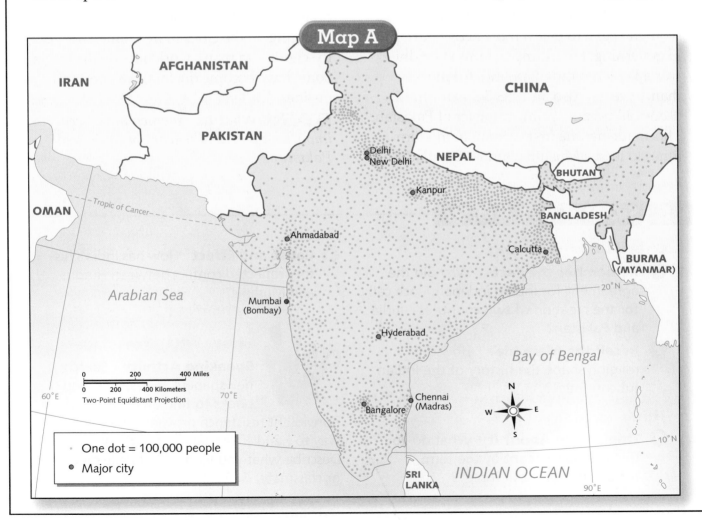

Map A

One dot = 100,000 people
Major city

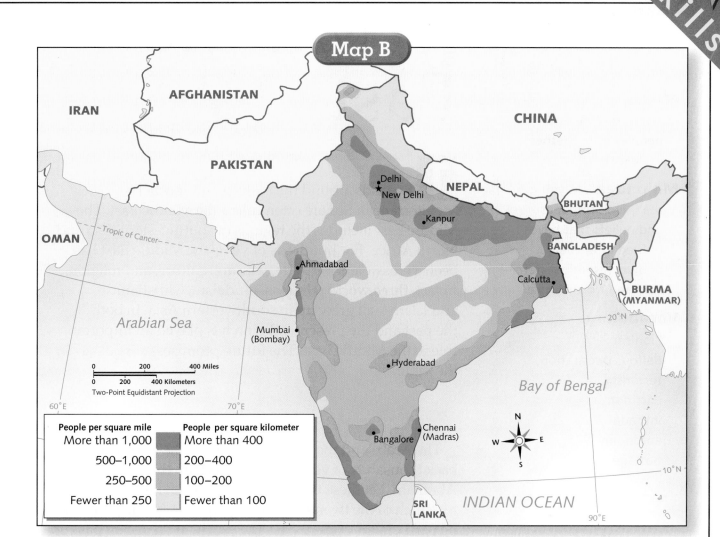

Map B

People per square mile | People per square kilometer
More than 1,000 | More than 400
500–1,000 | 200–400
250–500 | 100–200
Fewer than 250 | Fewer than 100

Where there are a great many people living close together, the population is *dense*. Where there are only a few people living far apart, the population is *sparse*. Both these terms describe population density. **Population density** is the average number of people living on a square unit of land. You can find this figure by dividing the number of people living on a given amount of land by the area of that land.

Dense populations are usually found in areas where the climate allows a long growing season. In India, good farming areas have very dense populations. Nearness of natural resources can also affect population density. But population density depends most of all on how easy communication and trade are. This explains why the coasts of India have dense populations.

Map B uses color to show the population density of India. Yellow stands for areas with populations of fewer than 250 people per square mile. Green stands for areas with populations of between 250 and 500 people per square mile. Orange stands for areas with populations of between 500 and 1,000 people per square mile. Red stands for areas with dense populations of more than 1,000 people per square mile.

3. Think and Apply

With a partner, study the population maps of India on these pages. Together, prepare a list of five questions you might have your classmates answer to better understand how to use these population maps.

FOCUS

How can different peoples live together in peace?

Main Idea As you read, look for ideas and beliefs that have unified or divided people in southwestern Asia and North Africa.

Vocabulary

Zionism
Balfour Declaration
terrorism
partition
intifada
autonomy
hostage

The Middle East

T he lands around the eastern and southern Mediterranean Sea are often called the Middle East. The Middle East includes the regions of southwestern Asia and North Africa. For hundreds of years the Middle East has been a crossroads for trade, warfare, culture, and religion. In fact, three world religions—Judaism, Christianity, and Islam—all grew up in southwestern Asia. In both the past and the present, religion has played an important role in the Middle East. The future promises more of the same.

Arabs and Jews

The Arabs and the Jews have roots in the Middle East going back thousands of years. They both claim the same ancestor—Abraham. Yet these two peoples have been fighting each other for much of the twentieth century. The reasons for this conflict lie partly in the ancient past and partly in the recent past.

The early Jews and Arabs settled in southwestern Asia thousands of years ago. In A.D. 70, however, the Romans destroyed the Jewish capital of Jerusalem. Not long after that they forced many Jews from the region, which the Jews had called Judah. The Romans then referred to the region as Palestine, removing the Jewish people's connection with the land they had once controlled.

Over the centuries Jews settled in nearly every part of the world. Those who left never forgot their homeland, however. Jews around the world end their Passover Seder (SAY•der)—the religious ceremony reminding them of their ancestors' departure from Egypt—with these words: "next year in Jerusalem."

Jewish (left) and Arab (right) merchants share market space to sell their fruit in Jerusalem.

As time passed, much changed in the land that had become known as Palestine. After the rise of Islam in the seventh century A.D., most Arabs became Muslims. Like the Jews and Christians, they considered Jerusalem a holy city. The Arab Muslims built an empire that governed most of the land in the Middle East. The Muslim Empire is remembered for its many achievements in science, medicine, and art.

In time, however, the Arabs lost control of much of their empire, including Palestine. For 400 years, beginning in the early 1500s, the land fell under the rule of another Muslim group, the Ottoman Turks. The Arabs longed to be free of Ottoman control.

During the late nineteenth and early twentieth centuries, many Jews began to come to the Middle East. Anti-Semitic, or anti-Jewish, activities in eastern Europe caused many Jews to leave and settle in Palestine. As more and more Jews settled there, some Jewish leaders decided to build a modern Jewish state. This idea grew into a movement called **Zionism**.

Arab nationalism also began to grow around this time. Arabs throughout the Middle East looked forward to a time when they would have their own independent states.

During World War I, the British wanted the Jewish people to support the Allied war effort. In 1917 the British government issued the **Balfour Declaration**. This document stated that the British favored "the establishment in Palestine of a national home for the Jewish people." At the same time, the declaration stated that "nothing shall be done which may prejudice the civil and religious rights of existing non-Jewish communities." The British hoped that the wording of the Balfour Declaration would please the Jews, yet not anger the Arabs.

After World War I, control of Palestine went from the Ottomans to the British.

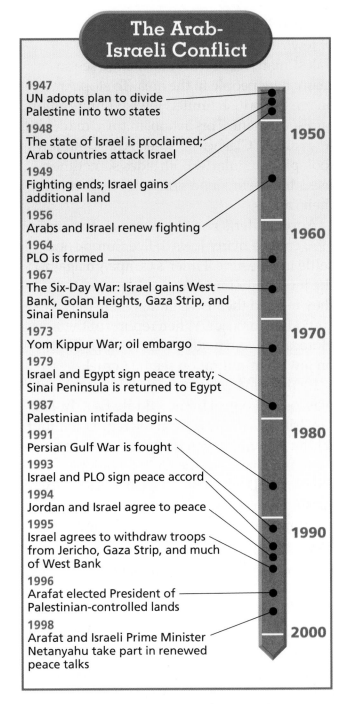

The Arab-Israeli Conflict

1947
UN adopts plan to divide Palestine into two states

1948
The state of Israel is proclaimed; Arab countries attack Israel

1949
Fighting ends; Israel gains additional land

1956
Arabs and Israel renew fighting

1964
PLO is formed

1967
The Six-Day War: Israel gains West Bank, Golan Heights, Gaza Strip, and Sinai Peninsula

1973
Yom Kippur War; oil embargo

1979
Israel and Egypt sign peace treaty; Sinai Peninsula is returned to Egypt

1987
Palestinian intifada begins

1991
Persian Gulf War is fought

1993
Israel and PLO sign peace accord

1994
Jordan and Israel agree to peace

1995
Israel agrees to withdraw troops from Jericho, Gaza Strip, and much of West Bank

1996
Arafat elected President of Palestinian-controlled lands

1998
Arafat and Israeli Prime Minister Netanyahu take part in renewed peace talks

1950
1960
1970
1980
1990
2000

LEARNING FROM TIME LINES The years since Israel's independence have brought both war and the promise of peace.

■ *Do you think other events belong on this time line? If so, which ones?*

According to the new League of Nations, Britain was to get Palestine ready for independence. Both the Jews and the Arabs believed that they would soon be given the right to their own homelands.

The British soon began allowing thousands of Jews to immigrate to Palestine. The Palestinian Arabs were alarmed to see so many new people in the area. To stop Arab anger, the British limited Jewish immigration and settlement. This action, in turn, made the Jews angry. Clashes between Arabs and Jews took place regularly. Both sides sometimes used **terrorism**, or acts of violence, to further their causes.

Adolf Hitler's rise to power in Germany in 1933 caused many Jews to flee Europe and settle in Palestine. Hitler's campaign against the Jews, the Zionists argued, proved that they needed their own land, where they could live in peace. When reports of the Holocaust were made public, British limits on Jewish immigration seemed cruel.

By this time war-weary Britain saw that it was losing control in the Middle East. In 1947 the British withdrew from the region without taking action. They placed the Palestine question in the hands of the United Nations. On November 29, 1947, the UN decided to **partition**, or divide, Palestine into two separate states—one Jewish and one Arab.

REVIEW *Why did Jews and Arabs both feel that Palestine was their homeland?*

Arab-Israeli Conflict

Jews around the world joyously welcomed the creation of their own state, Israel, in 1948. Arabs, however, did not accept the decision of the United Nations. Five Arab nations declared war on Israel and invaded the new country. The Arabs began making great advances. Within a few months, however, Israeli troops drove back the Arab armies. When both sides agreed to a cease-fire in January 1949, Israel had already taken much of the Arab part of Palestine. The rest of the Arab land became part of the country of Jordan.

During and after the war, more than 700,000 Arabs left Israel for neighboring Arab

Having escaped death in the Nazi camps, these Jewish refugees hope to find peace in Palestine.

states. Many of them lived and suffered in refugee camps there. Meanwhile, thousands of other Arabs remained in Israel and became citizens. Most Arabs, however, refused to accept Israel's existence as a nation.

Over the years Israel and the Arab nations clashed again and again. The superpowers of the time—the United States and the Soviet Union—soon became involved in the Middle Eastern conflict. The United States became Israel's most important ally. The Soviet Union backed some of the Arab countries.

In the 1950s most Arab countries united under the leadership of Egyptian president Gamal Abdel Nasser. The Israelis, surrounded by Arab neighbors who did not want them, began to build a strong army. The Israeli army, with the help of British and French forces, weakened Arab military strength in a 1956 war.

In 1967 Egypt, Syria, and Jordan prepared to attack Israel again. However, the Israelis acted first and drove back the Arab forces. During what is now called the Six-Day War, Israel captured large areas of land from Egypt, Syria, and Jordan. Israel gained control of the Sinai Peninsula, the Golan Heights, the Gaza Strip, and the West Bank. It also united the city of Jerusalem, which had been divided since 1948.

When Nasser died in 1970, Anwar as-Sadat (suh•DAT) became president of Egypt. In 1973, on Yom Kippur—the holiest day of the year for the Jewish people—Sadat launched a surprise attack on Israel. The Arabs made early gains, but later the Israelis took back most of those gains.

The Arabs then turned to economic weapons. The Arab countries supplied more than one-third of the oil used by noncommunist countries. For a few months Arab members of the Organization of Petroleum Exporting Countries (OPEC) refused to sell oil to countries they felt supported Israel. Many countries had to search for other sources of oil. The Arab OPEC members lifted the oil embargo in 1974. However, the idea that OPEC might do this again worried

Israel: 1947 to Present

0 ___ 25 ___ 50 Miles
0 ___ 25 ___ 50 Kilometers
Transverse Cylindrical Projection

Security zones

Land gained after Six-Day War, 1967, and still occupied

Land gained after Six-Day War, 1967; some Palestinian self-rule

Land gained after Six-Day War, 1967

Land gained after 1948 War

Israeli troops have withdrawn from area

Jewish state under 1947 partition plan

Land gained after Six-Day War, 1967, and returned to Egypt

LEBANON
SYRIA
GOLAN HEIGHTS
Acre
Haifa
Nazareth
Lake Tiberias (Sea of Galilee)
Mediterranean Sea
Tel Aviv
WEST BANK
Amman
Jericho
Jerusalem
Bethlehem
Hebron
Dead Sea
GAZA STRIP
Gaza
Beersheba
ISRAEL
JORDAN
EGYPT
Negev
Sinai Peninsula

Under Palestinian control

Place The shape of the land controlled by Israel has changed since 1947.

■ *Why do you think Israelis and Palestinians disagree about control of Jerusalem?*

Palestinian refugees in the Gaza Strip in 1954

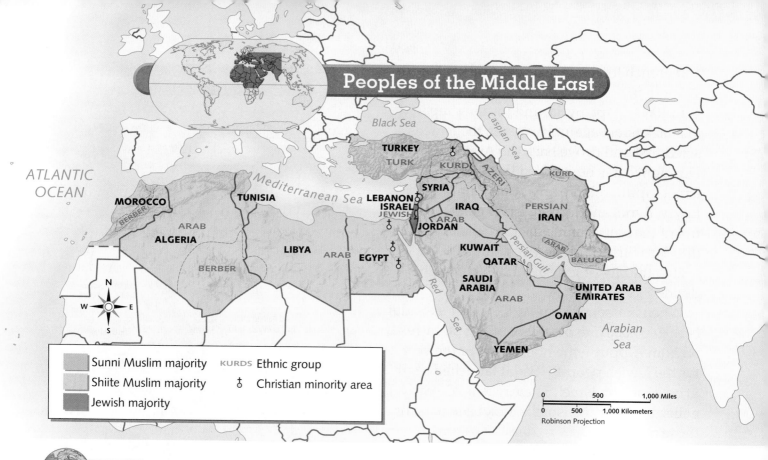

Peoples of the Middle East

Sunni Muslim majority
Shiite Muslim majority
Jewish majority
KURDS Ethnic group
☥ Christian minority area

0   500   1,000 Miles
0   500   1,000 Kilometers
Robinson Projection

Place The majority of the peoples of the Middle East are Arabs, but other peoples live in the region as well. The names printed in red on the map show some of the major ethnic groups in the Middle East.

■ *In what Middle Eastern country are most people Persian? How else are the people there different from others in the Middle East?*

Japan, the United States, and other countries that depended on imported oil.

Palestinian Arabs also took another type of action against Israel. In 1964, at a meeting of Arab leaders, a group called the Palestine Liberation Organization (PLO) was formed. The group's purpose was to organize the Palestinians in their struggle for a homeland. PLO members often used terrorist tactics in Israel and then in the lands taken over by the Israelis in the Six-Day War.

In 1969 Yasir Arafat (AH•ruh•faht) became chairperson of the PLO. Throughout the 1970s Arafat and the PLO became known and widely feared for their sudden attacks on civilian and military targets.

In the late 1980s a change in the Palestinian struggle took place. Many young Palestinians who had spent their lives under Israeli occupation in the territories of the West Bank and the Gaza Strip began to take part in the struggle. The Palestinians started an **intifada** (in•tee•FAH•duh), or people's uprising, in areas occupied by Israel. The Israelis tried to crush the intifada, but the outside world criticized their actions. The young Palestinians became more determined than ever. "Palestine is ours, and we shall shed our blood for it," they chanted.

REVIEW *What role did oil play in the conflict between Israel and the Arab nations?*

Working for Peace

The Israelis and the Arabs have fought one another for many years. Some leaders on both sides, though, have tried to bring peace to their region. An important step forward came in 1977, when Anwar as-Sadat agreed to visit Israel. He flew to Jerusalem, where he met with Israeli prime minister Menachem Begin (muh•NAH•kuhm BAY•gin).

Later in 1977 American President Jimmy Carter invited Sadat and Begin to the United States. Carter hoped that if the two talked openly, they might overcome their differences. This did happen, in 1978, and the three leaders signed an agreement called the Camp David Accords. The agreement laid out a plan for a peace treaty, which Israel and Egypt signed in 1979. In 1980 Egypt became the first Arab country to recognize Israel as a nation. Two years later Israel gave back much of the Egyptian land it had taken in the Six-Day War. The PLO was not included in the peace talks and therefore did not feel that the agreement applied to them.

In the 1990s Israel and the PLO held secret peace talks. After months of negotiations, often stopped because of continuing violence against both sides, an agreement was reached in late 1993. The agreement, signed by Israeli prime minister Yitzhak Rabin (rah•BEEN) and Yasir Arafat, called for Israel to give limited **autonomy**, or the right of a state to rule itself, to Palestinian areas.

In mid-1994 Rabin and Arafat established limited self-rule for Palestinians in the Gaza Strip and in the city of Jericho and its surrounding areas. Shortly afterward, Israel began to withdraw its troops from Jericho and the Gaza Strip.

For their work toward peace, Rabin, Arafat, and Israeli foreign minister Shimon Peres (shee•MOHN PAIR•es) were awarded the

Yasir Arafat, Shimon Peres, and Yitzhak Rabin receive the 1994 Nobel Peace Prize for their work toward peace.

Nobel Peace Prize in late 1994. In 1995 the Israelis began to pull troops out of the West Bank, allowing the Palestinians more control there as well. However, other Palestinian–Israeli issues, such as who should have control of Jerusalem, remained unsettled. Both the Palestinians and the Israelis claim the city as their capital.

The Israelis and the Palestinians were not the only ones to work toward peace in the Middle East in the 1990s. In 1994 Jordan signed a peace treaty with Israel. Also Syria and Israel have held peace talks.

However, the end of 1995 brought tragedy to the Middle East. At a rally for peace, Yitzhak Rabin was assassinated by an Israeli, who was angry that Israel had turned over control of some lands to the Palestinians. Israel's next prime minister, Benjamin Netanyahu (neh•tahn•YAH•hoo), slowed the peace process. During this time terrorist attacks against Israel increased. In 1998 Netanyahu and Arafat met face to face to discuss ways to end their conflict.

REVIEW *What major peace agreements did the Arabs and Israelis sign between 1979 and 1994?*

Islamic Renewal

While Jews and Arabs moved toward peace, another important development was taking place in the Middle East. Since the nineteenth century, Muslims in countries across the region were concerned that Western ideas had begun to replace the Islamic way of life. During the 1960s and 1970s, many Muslims returned to a more traditional practice of Islam. They attended prayer regularly and wore Muslim dress. They also wanted to make Islamic law, or *Shari'a*, the basis for governing Muslim nations.

Perhaps the most dramatic example of this Islamic renewal came in Iran in the late 1970s. Iran differs from most other Islamic nations in the region. Most of its people are Persians rather than Arabs. Also, most Iranians have long disagreed with other Muslim groups about religious issues.

Starting in the 1950s Mohammad Reza Pahlavi (rih•ZAH PA•luh•vee), Iran's shah, or ruler, tried to modernize the country and turn it into an industrial power. Many Iranians objected to the Western ways introduced by the shah. They felt that Iran should become a truly Islamic state. The strongest attacks on the shah's programs came from religious leader Ayatollah Khomeini (eye•uh•TOH•luh koh•MAY•nee). In January 1979 a revolt by Khomeini's supporters and others forced the shah to leave Iran.

Khomeini then took over the government. He quickly made it clear that Western powers were no longer welcome in Iran. The United States soon learned *how* unwelcome its citizens were. In November 1979, Iranian students took over the United States Embassy in the city of Tehran, taking more than 50 Americans hostage. A **hostage** is a prisoner who is held until certain demands are met. The students wanted the United States government to return the shah—who was being treated for cancer at an American hospital—to face trial. The shah died in July 1980, but the hostages were not freed until January 1981.

The Iranians planned to spread their Islamic revolution to other Muslim countries. Saddam Hussein (suh•DAHM hoo•SAYN), the leader of Iraq, wanted to keep this from happening. He also wanted to capture a part of Iran's land. In 1980 war broke out between the two countries. As fighting raged, Khomeini urged the Shiites in Iraq to overthrow their Sunni leader. The war dragged on for eight years. Neither side gained a clear victory.

Ayatollah Khomeini died in 1989. New Iranian leaders have spent less time spreading revolution and more time building the economy. Still, the renewal of traditional Islamic beliefs and practices has continued.

REVIEW *What is meant by Islamic renewal?*

The Persian Gulf War

Not all conflicts in the Middle East relate to religion. One such conflict gained worldwide attention in the early 1990s. That event was the Persian Gulf War.

Saddam Hussein, the president of Iraq, ordered his army to invade the oil-rich country of Kuwait so that he would not have to pay a debt owed. Almost immediately the United Nations stated that the attack was wrong and took steps to make Iraq suffer economically. It set January 15, 1991, as the deadline for Iraq to pull out of Kuwait. But Iraq stayed.

When Iraq would not cooperate with the United Nations, countries such as the United

The U.S. hostages appear happy after finally being released from captivity in Iran (below). The Ayatollah Khomeini (inset) granted their release in 1981.

WELCOME BACK TO FREEDOM

The Persian Gulf War was different from past wars. Women soldiers played greater roles than ever before (above). Advanced technology allowed live television reports (upper right) and the use of U.S. stealth bombers (lower right).

States, Saudi Arabia, Egypt, and France joined forces to free Kuwait. After all, they did not want Iraq to control Kuwait's oil. The United States and its allies began Operation Desert Storm—a series of air- and ground-bombing attacks. The Iraqis were quickly forced to leave Kuwait.

This war was different from any other war in the history of the world. People around the world watched and listened to their televisions to hear up-to-the-minute reports on the events of the war. Also, the war was fought almost completely with high-technology weapons that had never been used in battle. In addition, American women soldiers played an important role in the war.

REVIEW *Why did the Iraqis invade Kuwait?*

LESSON 2 REVIEW

Check Understanding

1. **Remember the Facts** What links do Jews and Arabs have to the Middle East?

2. **Recall the Main Idea** How have ideas and beliefs both united and divided people in the Middle East?

Think Critically

3. **Cause and Effect** How do you think the creation of the state of Israel affected events in the Middle East?

4. **Personally Speaking** What do you think gives people the right to live where they do?

Show What You Know

Current Events Activity Look in newspapers and magazines to find articles about conflicts and peace efforts in the Middle East. Using these articles, make a class bulletin board display. Update the display as new events occur.

CHAPTER 22 REVIEW

1980

1984
• Indira Gandhi is assassinated

Connect Main Ideas

Use this organizer to describe religious influences in the world today. Write three details to support each main idea. A copy of the organizer appears on page 153 of the Activity Book.

Religious Influences

The Indian Subcontinent
Religion has greatly affected the history of the Indian subcontinent.
1. ______________
2. ______________
3. ______________

The Middle East
Ideas and beliefs have both united and divided people in southwestern Asia and North Africa.
1. ______________
2. ______________
3. ______________

Write More About It

Write a Biographical Sketch Find out more about Mohandas Gandhi. Then prepare a one-page biographical sketch on the life of this Indian leader. Describe his background and his beliefs. Also, explain how his idea of passive resistance led not to conflict but to cooperation and finally to independence for India.

Write a History In your own words, tell the background of the Arab-Israeli conflict. Be sure that your report is fair to both sides. Use illustrations, time lines, and maps.

Write Questions Write five questions you might ask someone who fought in the Persian Gulf War.

1994
• Limited self-rule for Palestinians

1998
• Israelis and Palestinians renew peace talks
• India and Pakistan conduct nuclear tests

USE VOCABULARY

Write the term that correctly matches each meaning.

boycott   Mahatma

discriminate   terrorism

hostage   Zionism

1 a prisoner who is held until certain demands are met

2 "Great Soul"

3 to refuse to buy goods

4 acts of violence

5 the movement that called for a modern Jewish state in the homeland of the Jewish people

6 to treat unfairly because of race or other reasons

CHECK UNDERSTANDING

7 What event made Gandhi realize that much work was needed to gain rights for Indian people in South Africa?

8 What important lesson did Gandhi learn from his mother? How did this affect Gandhi?

9 What forms of noncooperation did Gandhi and his followers use in India?

10 To which three religions is the Middle East an important region?

11 What was the Balfour Declaration?

12 What was the result of the Six-Day War?

13 What is the Palestine Liberation Organization, or PLO? What is its goal?

14 Why was the Persian Gulf War fought?

THINK CRITICALLY

15 **Cause and Effect** What effects did passive resistance have on the British and their control of India?

16 **Explore Viewpoints** The Israelis want to keep control over all of Jerusalem. The Palestinians believe that part of Jerusalem should be under their control. Why do you think the two peoples cannot agree about the future of Jerusalem?

17 **Past to Present** In 1995, terrorists bombed a United States federal building in Oklahoma City. How do acts of terrorism, in this country and throughout the world, affect everyone?

APPLY SKILLS

Use Different Types of Population Maps Use the maps on pages 660 and 661 to answer these questions.

18 How would you describe India's population?

19 Which parts of India have the most people?

READ MORE ABOUT IT

Gandhi by Leonard Everett Fisher. Atheneum. This book explains how Gandhi led India toward independence.

HARCOURT BRACE

Visit the Internet at **http://www.hbschool.com** for additional resources.

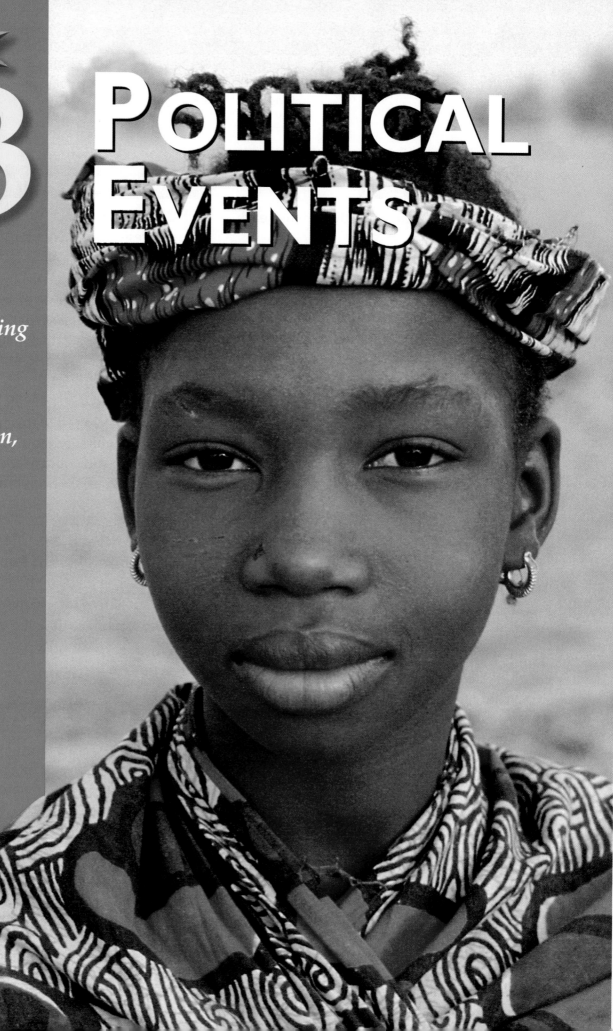

POLITICAL EVENTS

"We are starting a new era of hope, of reconciliation, of nation building."

Nelson Mandela, upon winning the presidency of South Africa in 1994

Young girl from the country of Senegal in Africa

672

Africa South of the Sahara

FOCUS
What challenges do newly independent nations face?

Main Idea As you read, think about some of the problems African nations have faced after winning independence.

Vocabulary
Afrikaans
apartheid
Bantustan

At the beginning of the twentieth century, only two African countries—Ethiopia and Liberia—had their independence. The others were under European control. By mid-century, however, nearly all the countries south of the Sahara had won freedom.

Winning Independence

Africans had resisted European rule from the beginning. Yet it was not until after World War II that a group of young leaders began to push for independence. They had one demand—freedom now! In the end the European powers had to free their African colonies.

Some former colonies gained their freedom peacefully. In the Gold Coast a young African named Kwame Nkrumah (KWAH•mee en•KROO•muh) formed the Convention People's Party (CPP) with this aim of "self-government now." The CPP organized strikes, boycotts, and demonstrations against British rule. In 1951 the British agreed to hold national elections. The CPP won easily, and the British asked Nkrumah to form a government under their direction. In 1957 the British gave full independence to the Gold Coast. The new African nation took the name Ghana, after the western African empire of earlier times.

The former British colony of Kenya, in eastern Africa, did not win freedom so peacefully. Most whites in Kenya had settled in the central highlands, a very good area for farming. They then passed laws to keep Africans from owning land there. These laws angered Kenya's largest ethnic group, the Kikuyus (kee•KOO•yooz). After all, their ancestors had held the central highlands for hundreds of years.

Prime Minister Kwame Nkrumah of Ghana in 1958

The Kikuyu leader Jomo Kenyatta (JOH•moh ken•YAHT•uh) wanted a fair share of these lands for his people.

In the early 1950s some Kikuyus formed the Mau Mau. The goal of this political group was to drive the whites from Kenya, by violence if necessary. The British met Mau Mau attacks with more violence. During the five-year Mau Mau rebellion, about 18,000 black Africans died.

In time the British realized that holding on to Kenya was impossible. They began to prepare the country for independence. Elections were held in 1963. The Kenya African National Union (KANU) won, and Jomo Kenyatta, KANU's leader, became the first prime minister of independent Kenya.

REVIEW *How was Kenya's path to independence different from Ghana's?*

The Colonial Legacy

Whether or not they won their independence peacefully, the new nations in Africa faced problems left over from colonial days. When the European powers carved the continent into colonies, they drew boundaries to suit themselves. In some cases the borders separated people of the same ethnic group. In other cases they grouped together people of very different backgrounds. The African nation of Nigeria, for example, became home to more than 250 ethnic groups.

Nigeria won independence from Britain peacefully in 1960. From the start, however, the government struggled with the country's ethnic differences. In 1967 one of the largest groups, the Igbos (EEG•bohz), seceded from Nigeria and started their own country, called Biafra (bee•AH•fruh). This set off a civil war that lasted more than two years. A million people died—many from hunger—before the Biafrans gave up.

In some cases European rulers encouraged fighting among groups within their colonies. They believed that if Africans fought one another, they would never be able to unite against colonial rule. For example, colonial rulers tried to divide the peoples of the Belgian Congo, now known as the Democratic Republic of the Congo. To the Belgians' surprise, the people set aside their differences to work for independence.

Most Kenyans live in rural areas. However, more and more people are moving to cities, such as Nairobi (left and below), Mombasa, and Kisumu.

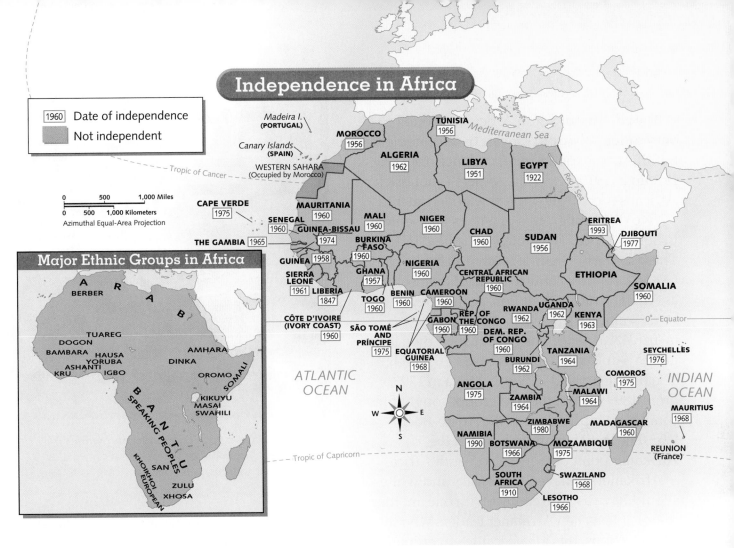

Independence in Africa

1960 Date of independence

Not independent

Major Ethnic Groups in Africa

ARAB
BERBER
TUAREG
DOGON
BAMBARA HAUSA
YORUBA
ASHANTI
KRU IGBO DINKA
AMHARA
OROMO
SOMALI
BANTU SPEAKING PEOPLES
KIKUYU
MASAI
SWAHILI
SAN
KHOIKHOI
EUROPEAN
ZULU
XHOSA

Madeira I. (PORTUGAL)
Canary Islands (SPAIN)
Tropic of Cancer
WESTERN SAHARA (Occupied by Morocco)
CAPE VERDE 1975
0 500 1,000 Miles
0 500 1,000 Kilometers
Azimuthal Equal-Area Projection

MOROCCO 1956
TUNISIA 1956
Mediterranean Sea
ALGERIA 1962
LIBYA 1951
EGYPT 1922
Red Sea

MAURITANIA 1960
SENEGAL 1960
THE GAMBIA 1965
GUINEA-BISSAU 1974
GUINEA 1958
SIERRA LEONE 1961
LIBERIA 1847
CÔTE D'IVOIRE (IVORY COAST) 1960
MALI 1960
BURKINA FASO 1960
GHANA 1957
TOGO 1960
BENIN 1960
SÃO TOMÉ AND PRÍNCIPE 1975
NIGER 1960
NIGERIA 1960
CAMEROON 1960
GABON 1960
REP. OF THE CONGO 1960
EQUATORIAL GUINEA 1968
CHAD 1960
CENTRAL AFRICAN REPUBLIC 1960
DEM. REP. OF CONGO 1960
SUDAN 1956
ERITREA 1993
DJIBOUTI 1977
ETHIOPIA
RWANDA 1962
UGANDA 1962
BURUNDI 1962
KENYA 1963
SOMALIA 1960
0° Equator
TANZANIA 1964
SEYCHELLES 1976

ATLANTIC OCEAN
N W E S
ANGOLA 1975
ZAMBIA 1964
MALAWI 1964
COMOROS 1975
INDIAN OCEAN
MAURITIUS 1968
ZIMBABWE 1980
MADAGASCAR 1960
NAMIBIA 1990
BOTSWANA 1966
MOZAMBIQUE 1975
REUNION (France)
Tropic of Capricorn
SOUTH AFRICA 1910
SWAZILAND 1968
LESOTHO 1966

Place Independence came to African nations at different times during the twentieth century.

■ *What places became independent countries in the 1990s?*

The colony gained its freedom from Belgium in 1960 and changed its name simply to Congo.

This cooperation did not last long. The regional conflicts that the Belgians had encouraged soon surfaced once again. After Congo's independence, the province of Katanga, which is rich in resources, seceded. In the political unrest that followed, Congo's first prime minister, Patrice Lumumba (luh•MUHM•buh), was assassinated.

The United Nations sent troops to stop the violence in Congo. Yet after they left, fighting began again. Then, in 1965, General Mobutu Sese Seko (muh•BOO•too SAY•say SAY•koh) took control. He united Congo by setting up

a government that allowed only one political party. He would hear no arguments against government policies.

The newly independent African nations also often faced serious economic problems. In most cases the colonial powers had not allowed the colonies to develop more than one resource or cash crop. After gaining independence, many countries stayed too dependent on this single source of income. Ghana, for example, exported little besides cacao, the beans used to make cocoa. When world prices for cacao fell in the mid-1960s, Ghana's economy also fell.

REVIEW *What types of problems did the new African nations face?*

South Africa

The country of South Africa developed very differently from the rest of the continent. South Africa won its independence from Britain in 1910, but white settlers—not black Africans—controlled the new government.

Two different groups of whites had settled in South Africa. The Dutch came first, in 1652. These settlers were first known as the Boers (BOHRZ). As they came to think of themselves as Africans rather than Europeans, they began calling themselves Afrikaners (a•frih•KAH•nerz). They spoke their own language, **Afrikaans**, which is based on Dutch. The British arrived in South Africa in 1795. From 1899 to 1902 the two groups fought for control of South Africa in the Anglo-Boer War. The British won the war, yet the Afrikaner point of view ruled South Africa.

Afrikaners believed that blacks and whites should have as little contact with one another as possible. When Afrikaner leaders won the 1948 elections, this idea became government policy. The Afrikaners called the policy **apartheid** (uh•PAR•tayt), which means "apartness."

Life under apartheid was hard for black South Africans. Although they made up more than two-thirds of South Africa's population, black South Africans had few rights. They could own land and govern themselves only within certain areas of the country. These were known as **Bantustans** (ban•too•STANZ), or "homelands." Black South Africans had to have permits to live outside the Bantustans. Even then they could not live in the same neighborhoods as white South Africans, and they did not have the right to vote.

Protests against South African racism had begun long before apartheid. The African National Congress (ANC) was founded in 1912 to fight for the rights of black South Africans. After 1948 the ANC began using passive resistance to demonstrate against

This photo shows a bus bearing a "non-whites only" sign, a typical example of the policy of apartheid, or separation of the races, in South Africa.

apartheid. In 1960 the South African government banned the ANC and jailed many of its leaders.

Shocked by the actions of the South African government, other countries limited or ended trade with South Africa. The South African government stuck to its policy of apartheid. At last things changed after Frederik Willem de Klerk became president of South Africa in 1989.

De Klerk, an Afrikaner, knew that sooner or later the black majority in South Africa would gain control of the country. De Klerk removed the ban on the ANC and ended many apartheid laws. He also freed ANC leader Nelson Mandela, who had been in prison for more than 25 years. De Klerk then met with black leaders to work out a way to share power.

By November 1993 the leaders agreed to open South African elections to all races. On April 27, 1994, black and white South Africans waited in line together to vote.

"My heart tells me it's the best day of my life," said one new voter. "I don't have to carry a pass. I can work anywhere in the country I want. I am free."

The election resulted in victory for Mandela and his party. In one of his first speeches as president, Mandela told of a new South Africa, "in which all South Africans, both black and white, will be able to walk tall, without any fear in their hearts."

Since the end of apartheid, South Africa has worked hard to become a more unified country. Its leaders continue to seek equality and economic success for all the people of South Africa.

REVIEW *What is apartheid? How did it end in South Africa?*

Present-Day Concerns

In the past few years, democracy has begun to spread across Africa. In 1989, 35 African nations were governed as single-party states. By 1994 most of these nations had given up this political system and held multiparty elections. In addition, more nations are trying forms of free enterprise.

Today African nations face problems other than politics and economics. Lack of rain has ruined many harvests and has led to famine. In Somalia, drought and famine led to civil war in the early 1990s. Clans of Somalis fought over the little water and food they had. Some clans even stole food and supplies sent from around the world. Meanwhile, millions of people died from starvation.

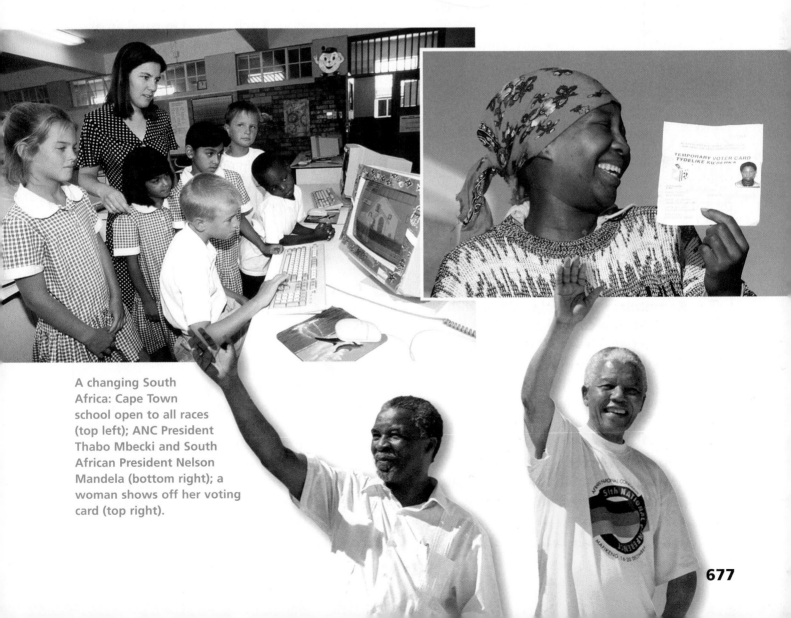

A changing South Africa: Cape Town school open to all races (top left); ANC President Thabo Mbecki and South African President Nelson Mandela (bottom right); a woman shows off her voting card (top right).

Rwandan refugees leave the Democratic Republic of the Congo (formerly Zaire) to return to their homeland.

Eventually, the United Nations sent more food and supplies as well as troops to make sure that help got to those who needed it.

The countries of Rwanda and Burundi were also divided by civil war in the early 1990s. Both countries consist of two different cultures: the Hutus and the Tutsis. Each group wanted to control the government at the expense of the other. In Rwanda, in 1994, the Hutus killed hundreds of thousands of Tutsis. Millions more were forced to flee for safety in Zaire. Two years later the leader of Zaire ordered all Tutsis out of that country. The Tutsis rebelled and, led by Laurent Kabila, took over Zaire. Kabila made himself president and renamed the country the

Democratic Republic of the Congo. In 1997 many Rwandan refugees, who had been living in the forests of the former Zaire, returned to their homeland.

Population growth is another concern for Africa. More people live on the continent than ever before. Lack of food in rural areas has brought many people to Africa's few large cities, causing overcrowding there.

The African people know that solving their problems will not be easy. Their determination is their strength, though. It should lead them to a stronger, more democratic, and more prosperous tomorrow.

REVIEW *What problems do African nations still face?*

LESSON 1 REVIEW

Check Understanding

1 **Remember the Facts** When did most African countries south of the Sahara gain their independence?

2 **Recall the Main Idea** What problems have African nations faced since winning independence?

Think Critically

3 **Cause and Effect** How did the policies of colonial powers later cause problems for newly independent African nations?

4 **Past to Present** What lessons might other nations learn from South Africa's recent history?

Show What You Know

Map Activity Using atlases, almanacs, and encyclopedias as resources, create two maps. One map should show the European colonies in Africa around the beginning of the twentieth century. The other should show the independent African nations and the year each nation won its freedom.

Journey to Jo'burg

written by Beverley Naidoo　　**illustrated by Beatrice Lebreton**

For more than 40 years, apartheid ruled the lives of black South Africans. Read now about Naledi, Tiro, and their baby sister, Dineo, who live with their grandmother in a black homeland. To support the family, their mother has taken a job with a white family in Parktown, a suburb of Johannesburg. When young Dineo becomes very ill, Naledi and Tiro travel to Johannesburg to find their mother and bring her home. On their journey they learn what it really means to live under apartheid. As you read, think about how you might have felt if you were forced to live under this system.

A New Friend

As they turned toward the road, there was a bus with the word "PARKTOWN" in big letters on the front. It was slowing down a little way up the road and the doors were opening. Through the front windscreen they could see the driver was black.

"Come on, Tiro!" called Naledi, pulling him by the arm. They were just about to jump aboard, when someone shouted at them in English, "What's wrong with you? Are you stupid?"

Startled, they looked up at the angry face of the bus driver and then at the bus again. White faces stared at them from inside as the bus moved off.

Naledi and Tiro stood on the side of the road, shaken, holding hands tightly, when a voice behind them said, "Don't let it bother you. That's what they're like. You'd better come out of the road."

A young woman put out her hand to bring them onto the pavement.

"You must be strangers here if you don't know about the buses. This stop has a white sign, but we have to wait by the black one over there."

She pointed to a small black metal signpost.

"You must also look at the front of the bus for the small notice saying 'Non-whites only.'"

"I'm sorry. We forgot to look," Naledi explained.

"It's not you who should be sorry!" said the young woman forcefully. "They should be sorry, those stupid people! Why shouldn't we use any bus? When our buses are full, their buses are half empty. Don't you be sorry!"

The children glanced at each other. This person was different from their mother. Mma never spoke out like that.

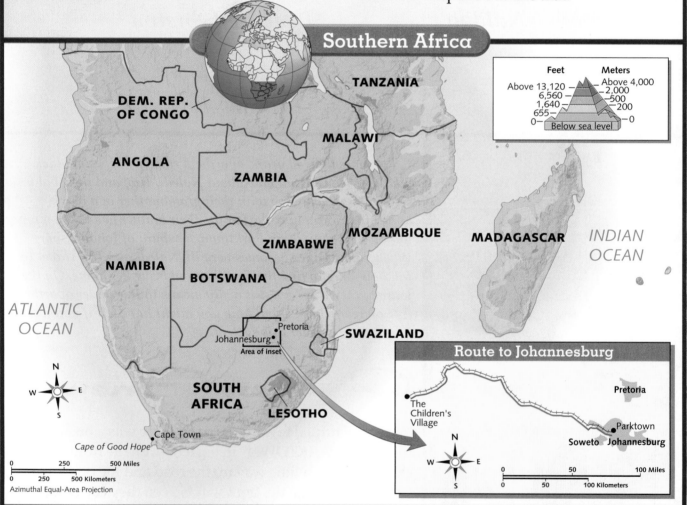

Southern Africa

TANZANIA

DEM. REP. OF CONGO

MALAWI

ANGOLA

ZAMBIA

MOZAMBIQUE

MADAGASCAR

INDIAN OCEAN

ZIMBABWE

NAMIBIA

BOTSWANA

ATLANTIC OCEAN

Pretoria

Johannesburg
Area of inset

SWAZILAND

SOUTH AFRICA

LESOTHO

Cape Town
Cape of Good Hope

N
W E
S

0   250   500 Miles
0   250   500 Kilometers
Azimuthal Equal-Area Projection

Feet   Meters
Above 13,120 — — Above 4,000
6,560 — — 2,000
1,640 — — 500
655 — — 200
0 — — 0
Below sea level

Route to Johannesburg

The Children's Village

Pretoria

Parktown
Soweto   Johannesburg

N
W E
S

0   50   100 Miles
0   50   100 Kilometers

Movement   The story takes place in the country of South Africa at the southern tip of the continent of Africa. The inset shows the route the children followed.

■ *About how many total miles did Naledi and Tiro travel?*

The young woman asked where they were going. Naledi took out the letter, and when the young woman looked at the address, she exclaimed, "But this is near where my mother works. I'm on my way to visit her today, so I can show you the place."

"Thank you, Mma." The children smiled. Lucky again.

"By the way, I'm Grace Mbatha. Now who are you both, and where are you from? You speak Tswana the way my mother does. Maybe you live near my mother's people."

So, once again, the children began their story.

Luckily the bus wasn't full when it arrived. Grace had warned them that in the rush hour you were almost squeezed to death. As the bus trundled along, stopping and starting with the traffic, there was a chance to stare out the windows. Tiro thought the cyclists were very brave, riding in between all the cars. Naledi kept trying to see the tops of the tall buildings, twisting her neck around until it began to hurt!

The bus now heaved its way up a steep hill and soon they were leaving the city buildings, seeing the sky again, as well as trees, grass lawns and flowers either side of the road. Behind the trees were big houses, such as they had never seen before. Grace smiled at the way the children were staring, amazed.

"Don't you know the people in this place have a lot of money? My mother looks after two children in a very big house, and there is another person just to cook, and another person to look after the garden."

Naledi and Tiro listened with interest. Mma never liked to talk much to them about her work when she was at home, although once they had overheard Mma talking to Nono about the child whom she looked after. Mma had said, "The little girl is very rude. She thinks I belong to her mother. You should hear how she can shout at me."

Naledi wanted to ask Grace to tell them some more, but she was still a little shy, and soon they had reached their stop.

They stepped off the bus onto a wide pavement along a street lined with great leafy trees.

"That's the road where your mother works at number twenty-five. My mma works at number seventeen in the next road down there. Can you manage now?"

The children nodded, and then Grace added, "If you need somewhere to stay tonight, you can come back with me to Soweto. I'm going home at six o'clock, O.K.?"

Tiro and Naledi thanked Grace, although they were a little puzzled about needing somewhere to stay. After all, they would be with their mother now and they would be going home with her as quickly as possible, back to Dineo.

As they turned to go down the road, they suddenly felt very excited—and anxious too. So much had been happening that they hadn't been thinking all along of their little sister.

Please let her be all right now pounded in Naledi's brain.

Half walking, half running, they made for number 25.

Mma

There it stood, a great pink house with its own grass lawn and trees in front, even its own road leading up to the front door! The two children stopped at the wide iron gates, looking up to it. The gates were closed, with a notice on them: "BEWARE OF THE DOG."

"Are we allowed in?" Tiro whispered.

"We must go in," Naledi replied, opening the gate a little.

Nervously they slipped in and slowly walked up the drive to the large front door.

Before they dared to knock, they heard a fierce barking from inside, which made them grip each other's hands, ready to run back to the street. Then they heard a sharp voice inside call out, in English, "Joyce, see who it is!"

The door opened.

As Mma gasped, the children flung themselves at her and she clasped them in her arms, hugging them. Tears welled up in her eyes as the children sobbed against her.

"What is wrong? What is wrong?" Mma cried softly.

"Who is it, Joyce?" came a brisk voice from behind. The dog was still barking.

"Be quiet, Tiger!" ordered the brisk voice,

and the barking stopped.

Mma stifled her sobs.

"Madam, these are my children."

"What are they doing here?" asked the white lady.

"Madam, I don't know. They haven't told me yet."

"Dineo is very ill, Mma." Naledi spoke between sobs. "Her fever won't go away. Nono and Mmangwane don't want to trouble you, but I told Tiro we must come and bring you home."

Mma gasped again and held her children more tightly.

"Madam, my little girl is very sick. Can I go home to see her?"

The Madam raised her eyebrows.

"Well, Joyce, I can't possibly let you go today. I need you tonight to stay in with Belinda. The Master and I are going to a very important dinner party."

She paused.

"But I suppose you can go tomorrow."

"Thank you, Madam."

"I hope you realize how inconvenient this will be for me. If you are not back in a week, I shall just have to look for another maid, you understand?"

"Yes, Madam."

The children couldn't follow everything the Madam was saying in English, but her voice sounded annoyed, while Mma spoke so softly. Why does the white lady seem cross with Mma? It's not Mma's fault that Dineo is sick, Naledi thought.

The children huddled close to Mma's starched white apron. They hadn't seen her in this strange servant's uniform before.

As Mma led the children through to the kitchen, they glanced across at open doors leading into other large rooms. A wide staircase also led upward. Never had they imagined a house could be this size!

In the kitchen Mma gave them a drink of water and some porridge she had cooked earlier. The kitchen seemed like a picture out of a magazine Mma had once brought home from the Madam. Their mother must have been busy cleaning that afternoon, because glistening plates of different sizes, cups and saucers, and delicate glasses were neatly stacked close to a large empty cupboard.

Naledi noticed that Mma took the tin plates and mugs for them from a separate little cupboard. While they ate, Mma quickly got on with her work.

When she had finished, she took the children to her room at the back of the yard. The children looked around the little room with interest. On the big iron bed was a white cover which Mma had neatly embroidered.

It must be strange sleeping all on your own, thought Tiro. At home they all shared a room.

When the children noticed the electric light, Mma said they could try it. But after Tiro had flicked it on and off about ten times, Mma told him to stop.

Bringing the children close to her now, Mma sat down at last and asked them to tell her fully what had happened.

The Madam had made it clear to Mma that the police wouldn't like it if the children spent the night in Parktown. So when Naledi spoke about Grace and her offer to take them to Soweto, Mma seemed of two minds. She knew Grace's mother well, but Soweto was also dangerous.

After getting the Madam's permission to go out for a little, Mma took her children by the hand and they walked to number 17 in the next road. They went around to the back of the house and found Grace still there.

"These two will be just fine with me," Grace assured Mma.

It was arranged that Grace and the children would meet Mma at Johannesburg station at seven the next morning. Mma gave Grace some money for the fares and, close to tears again, she hugged the children goodbye.

"Cheer up, you two," said Grace. "You can come and meet my brothers."

LITERATURE REVIEW

1. What features of the apartheid system did Naledi and Tiro learn about on their journey and in Parktown?

2. What does the Madam think of Mma? How does her treatment of Mma show her attitude?

3. Compare the ways that Grace and Mma act when they are treated badly. Write about how you would feel and act if you were treated that way.

FOCUS

How can greater freedom change the way of life in a country?

Main Idea As you read, discover how new freedoms in the former Soviet Union changed life all over Europe.

Vocabulary

perestroika
glasnost
dissident
common market

Changes for the People of Europe

Many changes came to both Europe and Asia during the last years of the twentieth century. After World War II eastern Europe and large parts of northern and central Asia were controlled by the Soviet Union and closed to the outside world. All that changed as the century ended.

Gorbachev's Reforms

In the early 1980s the Soviet Union was without question a world superpower. Yet beneath its military strength lay troubling economic and social problems. Years of poor planning by its leaders had destroyed the economy. There was never enough food or goods. Also, factories built in Stalin's time dumped chemicals into the water and the air. These chemicals polluted the environment, causing sickness and death. In addition, the people of the Soviet Union had few freedoms.

In early 1985 Mikhail Gorbachev (mee•kah•EEL gawr•buh•CHAWF) came to power in the Soviet Union. Gorbachev had new ideas about governing the country. In 1986 he announced a plan for a "moral revolution." Two keys to this plan were the policies of **perestroika** (pair•uh•STROY•kuh) and **glasnost** (GLAZ•nohst).

Perestroika, or "restructuring," meant a rebuilding of the Soviet political and economic systems. Under this policy Gorbachev reduced the authority of the Communist party and formed a new legislative body. He also called for open elections. When these elections took place, many longtime members of the Communist party were voted out of office.

Gorbachev's economic reforms took most of the authority for production decisions away from central planners and gave it to local farm and factory managers. Gorbachev also started a reward system to boost productivity.

Mikhail Gorbachev was the last leader of the Soviet Union.

Glasnost, or "openness," gave Soviet citizens new freedom to speak out without fear of being punished. The news media gained the freedom to report information that once had been hidden. Gorbachev also changed the Soviet policy toward religion so that people could now practice their beliefs openly. In addition, he set free from prison many **dissidents**—people who had spoken out against the government.

With the introduction of *glasnost*, some people began to speak out very strongly. In fact, people living in the Soviet Baltic republics—Lithuania, Latvia, and Estonia—called for total independence.

REVIEW *What new ideas did Gorbachev have about governing?*

The Collapse of Communism

Citizens of eastern European Communist countries that were not actually a part of the Soviet Union but under its control also wanted more freedom. In the past the Soviet Union had stepped in and even used its army when any communist government faced demands for more freedom from its citizens. But by 1989 Gorbachev realized that it was no longer possible to stem the tide of change. He decided to keep the Soviet Union out of political developments in eastern Europe.

Poland's system changed first. During the 1980s a workers' group called Solidarity led a campaign for a more democratic government. Led by Lech Walesa (vah•LEHN•sah), Solidarity called for strikes across Poland. After years of struggle, Communist leaders agreed to hold free elections. In August 1989 Communist rule in Poland ended, and Solidarity took control of the government. Poland soon became a democracy. Its command economy was transformed into a market economy.

Widespread peaceful demonstrations in 1989 brought new freedoms to people in Bulgaria, Hungary, and Czechoslovakia, too. Their communist governments promised reforms and free elections.

In Romania the move toward democracy proved more violent. For years President Nicolae Ceauşescu (chow•SHES•koo) had ruled the country with threats and force. When Romanians took to the streets to demand change, Ceauşescu ordered the army to stop the revolt. Instead, many soldiers sided with the people. By the end of 1989, Ceauşescu had been removed from office. The new leaders promised to put the country on the path toward democracy.

Perhaps the greatest changes came in East Germany. Huge protests in 1989 had little effect on the East German government. It rejected all calls for reform. More and more unhappy

Germans celebrate the anniversary of the reuniting of Germany; Berlin's Brandenburg Gate is in the background.

685

The Collapse of Communism

Former Communist Countries

EAST GERMANY, POLAND, CZECHOSLOVAKIA, HUNGARY, ROMANIA, YUGOSLAVIA, BULGARIA, UNION OF SOVIET SOCIALIST REPUBLICS

Commonwealth of Independent States

Place The collapse of communism brought many changes for the former Soviet Union. The union broke up into 15 independent countries.
■ *What new nations were formed from the former Soviet Union?*

East Germans found ways to leave the country. Many got permission to visit other communist countries and then fled to West Germany. On

This photograph shows Boris Yeltsin campaigning in 1991 for the presidency of the Russian Republic, which was then part of the Soviet Union. Later that year the breakup of the Soviet Union made Russia an independent country. Yeltsin continued as its president.

November 9, 1989, East German leaders said that they would open their borders. In Berlin joyous demonstrators gathered at the hated Berlin Wall, which had divided the city. They climbed on top of it, breaking off chunks of concrete with whatever they had at hand. The wall that had separated East and West Berlin for twenty-eight years finally crumbled. In October 1990 the two Germanys united to form the Federal Republic of Germany.

Elections in other eastern European countries also created new democratic governments. People who had been against the communists now found that they were the ones in control. They quickly cut themselves off from the Soviet Union, because they felt that their future lay with the West. They

Russians in Moscow express concern over the country's economic troubles.

also withdrew from the Warsaw Pact, the economic and political alliance led by the Soviet Union. By mid-1991 this organization no longer existed.

People in the Soviet Union watched carefully what was happening in eastern Europe. Some watched with hope. Others, including many communist leaders, watched with fear. In August 1991 some longtime Communist Party leaders tried to overthrow Gorbachev and take back the freedoms Gorbachev had given the people. Even though they failed, Gorbachev's authority was weakened.

More and more people in the Soviet Union wanted full democracy, not just a change in the Communist ways. "You can't ride two horses at once," said Boris Yeltsin (YELT•suhn), the president of the Russian Republic, the largest state in the Soviet Union.

In December 1991 Yeltsin and the presidents of the other Soviet republics declared that the Soviet Union no longer existed. In its place they set up a loose association, or group, called the Commonwealth of Independent States (CIS). Gorbachev stepped down and handed over authority to Yeltsin. The CIS was created to build a new market economy for its member countries. By 1995, 12 of the 15 former Soviet republics had joined the CIS. These republics are Armenia, Azerbaijan (a•zer•by•JAHN), Belarus, Georgia, Kazakhstan (ka•zak•STAN),

Kyrgyzstan (kir•gi•STAN), Moldova, Russia, Tajikistan (tah•jih•kih•STAN), Turkmenistan (terk•meh•nuh•STAN), Ukraine (yoo•KRAYN), and Uzbekistan (uz•beh•kih•STAN).

The fall of communism completely changed international relations. The breakup of the Soviet Union brought the Cold War to an end. The former communist countries now wanted to cooperate with the countries of the West. In 1991, for example, during the Persian Gulf War, some joined with the West to drive Iraq out of Kuwait. In 1998, however, Russia was faced with an economic crisis. Russia's money lost more than 50 percent of its value in less than a month. Also, Russia's government became unstable. The failing health of Russia's president Boris Yeltsin did not help. In addition, communism seemed to show renewed strength. It is clear that Russia faces an uncertain future.

REVIEW *What led to the fall of communism in eastern Europe and the Soviet Union?*

Conflict in Europe

Not every change that happened in Europe after the fall of communism was positive. People in the Balkans turned back to their old religious, ethnic, and national rivalries. After World War I the different peoples of that region had been forced to become citizens of a newly created nation called Yugoslavia. Their union had always been an uneasy one because of differences among the nation's three main ethnic groups: Muslims, Serbs, and Croats. Then with the fall of communism in 1989, a number of ethnic groups demanded their independence from Yugoslavia.

In 1991 people in the Yugoslavian republics of Slovenia (sloh•VEE•nee•uh) and Croatia voted to break away from Yugoslavia. The Serbs in Croatia feared living under the authority of the Croats. They called on the Yugoslavian republic of Serbia for help. In 1991, Serbia attacked Croatia. During the fighting, about 10,000 people were killed. Thousands more became refugees. By 1992 the Serbs had taken over about one-third of Croatia's territory.

In 1992 the republic of Bosnia also declared its independence. Right away, people from each ethnic group in Bosnia—Muslims, Serbs, and Croats—began using violence to drive out people from other groups. At the same time the Serbs tried to take a large part of Bosnia and make it part of Serbia. Croatia began taking over the areas of Bosnia where many Croats lived.

The United Nations sent in troops to restore peace. Finally, in 1995, leaders representing Serbs, Croats, and Muslims agreed to peace for Bosnia.

The troubles in the Balkans did not end with the peace agreements in Bosnia. In the late 1990s the Yugoslavian province of Kosovo, where about 80 percent of the population has an Albanian heritage, began to fight for independence from Serbia. The Serbian president sent in forces to try to stop the uprising. Thousands of Albanians died. Hundreds of thousands more were driven far from their homes.

Under world pressure, the Serbian government has begun to restore peace in Kosovo. Many Albanians continue to use nonviolent actions to win Kosovo's freedom.

On the other side of Europe, cultural and religious differences also caused conflict. For many years fighting has taken place over the question of freedom in Northern Ireland. Northern Ireland is part of the United Kingdom of Great Britain. The rest of Ireland is an independent country. The Irish Republican Army, or IRA, has used terrorism and other means in hopes of reuniting the two parts of Ireland. Many people in Northern Ireland, however, want to remain part of Britain.

In 1998 the different sides involved in the conflict agreed to talk about ways to achieve peace in the region. The agreements reached in these talks are believed by many to be meaningful steps toward peace.

REVIEW *What are some of the reasons for conflict in the former Yugoslavia? in Ireland?*

Bosnian refugees (below) are forced to leave their homes and flee to other countries. Peace-keeping troops (right) patrol an area of Sarajevo, Bosnia, a city hard hit by the war.

Signs of violence (right) and peace (left) in Northern Ireland

The United States of Europe?

When meeting with western European leaders, Mikhail Gorbachev often spoke of the "common house of Europe." He meant that all Europeans shared a heritage. After the fall of communism, many people felt that this heritage would help bring eastern and western Europe closer together. Perhaps a "United States of Europe" would develop.

Many years before, in 1957, several western European nations had formed an economic union, or **common market**. The purpose of this European Economic Community (EEC) was to make sure the economic policies of its member nations did not conflict. The EEC set as its goal the creation of the European Union (EU). The EU would be a single economic market with no tariffs on goods and no rules on crossing national borders.

The EU began in 1993—but it was not like its planners had imagined. Many member nations felt that the original plans gave too much control to the EU's governing body. Also, members could not agree on what to do about the former Yugoslavia.

While many dreamed of all Europeans coming closer together, some countries, such as Germany, found it difficult to keep their own people together. Most Germans were happy when the eastern and western parts of their country were united in 1990. But their joy did not last long. People in the former East Germany felt that the new government was not doing enough to help them make the change from communism to capitalism. People in the former West Germany felt that the government was doing too much.

Reunification has proved to be more difficult and more expensive than the people of Germany realized it would be. It will take much time and money to modernize the former East Germany.

Eastern European nations, too, had trouble bringing their people together. Then Czechoslovakia broke into two separate nations—the Czech Republic and Slovakia. This division caused some problems, but the people on both sides were happy that there was no bloodshed. "Look what happened to our neighbors in Yugoslavia," one said.

More Europeans than ever before now enjoy freedom. Even though many divisions still exist, the dream of creating a "United States of Europe" lives on. Eleven of the fifteen countries of the EU have agreed to use a common money. This money, called the euro, is one more step toward a united Europe.

REVIEW *What problems made it hard for European nations to unite in the late twentieth century?*

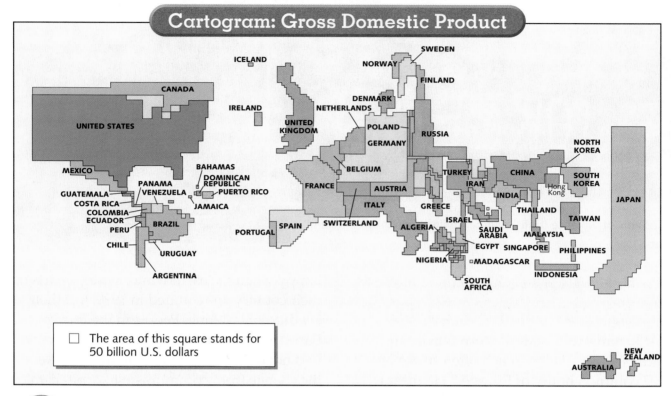

Cartogram: Gross Domestic Product

ICELAND

SWEDEN

NORWAY

FINLAND

CANADA

IRELAND

DENMARK
NETHERLANDS

UNITED
KINGDOM

POLAND

RUSSIA

UNITED STATES

GERMANY

NORTH
KOREA

BELGIUM

TURKEY

CHINA

SOUTH
KOREA

MEXICO

BAHAMAS

DOMINICAN
REPUBLIC

FRANCE

AUSTRIA

IRAN

INDIA

Hong
Kong

JAPAN

PANAMA

VENEZUELA

PUERTO RICO

GUATEMALA

COSTA RICA

JAMAICA

ITALY

GREECE

THAILAND

TAIWAN

COLOMBIA

ECUADOR

PERU

BRAZIL

PORTUGAL

SPAIN

SWITZERLAND

ALGERIA

ISRAEL

SAUDI
ARABIA

MALAYSIA

CHILE

EGYPT

SINGAPORE

PHILIPPINES

URUGUAY

NIGERIA

MADAGASCAR

INDONESIA

ARGENTINA

SOUTH
AFRICA

☐ The area of this square stands for
50 billion U.S. dollars

NEW
ZEALAND

AUSTRALIA

Place Economic success is the goal of countries around the world. This
cartogram shows how the world would look if nations' sizes were based on GDP.
■ *What country has the highest GDP in Europe?*

LESSON 3 REVIEW

Check Understanding

1 Remember the Facts What were the goals of *perestroika* and *glasnost*?

2 Recall the Main Idea How did new freedoms in the former Soviet Union change life all over Europe in the late 1980s?

Think Critically

3 Explore Viewpoints Some people blamed Mikhail Gorbachev for not going far enough or fast enough with his reform programs. Others praised him for beginning a new Europe. How could people have such widely differing viewpoints about the same person?

4 Past to Present What part, if any, should the United States take in creating a new Europe? What can the United States learn from past experiences, such as the civil war in the Balkans? Explain your answer.

5 Think More About It There are many ethnic groups in the United States. Regional differences also separate many Americans. Why do you think the individual states do not want to be totally free and independent from one another?

Show What You Know

Journalism Activity Imagine that you are a journalist who works for a European newspaper. Write a news story showing how the changes made by Mikhail Gorbachev in the Soviet Union led to the Europe of today.

Resolve Conflicts

1. Why Learn This Skill?

Disagreements are a part of everyday life. There are many ways to handle disagreements with other people. You can walk away and let strong feelings fade over time. You can try to show the other person your way of thinking. You can also **compromise**, or give up some of what you want in order to reach an agreement. Knowing how to compromise gives you another way to handle, or resolve, disagreements.

2. Remember What You Have Read

Many people believe that without compromise many of the world's problems will never be solved. Through compromise, leaders of nations or groups within a nation are sometimes able to resolve conflicts.

Much of the conflict in Northern Ireland began as a result of differences between religious and political groups. For 400 years the mostly Catholic Irish lived under the rule of the mostly Protestant English. This situation has led to hard feelings between Catholics and Protestants in Ireland. Since 1922 only Northern Ireland has remained under British rule. Resolving conflicts there has proved difficult. Yet in 1998 great strides were taken when leaders from Northern Ireland, Ireland, and Britain compromised to develop a peace plan for the region.

3. Understand the Process

To be able to compromise is as important for you as it is for world leaders. To compromise, you can use the following steps.

1. Before you begin to talk with the person you disagree with, be prepared to give up some things you would like in order to solve the disagreement.
2. Tell clearly what you want.
3. Decide which of the things that you want are most important to you.
4. Present a plan for compromise. Listen to the other side's plan.
5. Talk about any differences in the two plans.
6. Present another plan for a compromise, giving up something else. Continue talking until both sides agree on a compromise.
7. If either side becomes angry, take a break and calm down before you go on talking.
8. If there are many people on each side of the disagreement, each side should choose one or two people to do most of the talking.

4. Think and Apply

Think of a disagreement that you or your class might be facing in school. Form groups to discuss it, using the steps in Understand the Process. Vote on which plan for compromise should be chosen.

British Prime Minister Tony Blair (right) and Irish Prime Minister Bertie Ahern (left) were among the many leaders who worked together to help bring peace to Northern Ireland.

1990

1990
• Federal
  Republic
  of Germany
  is formed

1991
• Soviet Union
  collapses

CONNECT MAIN IDEAS

Use this organizer to describe recent political events. Write two details to support each main idea. A copy of the organizer appears on page 158 of the Activity Book.

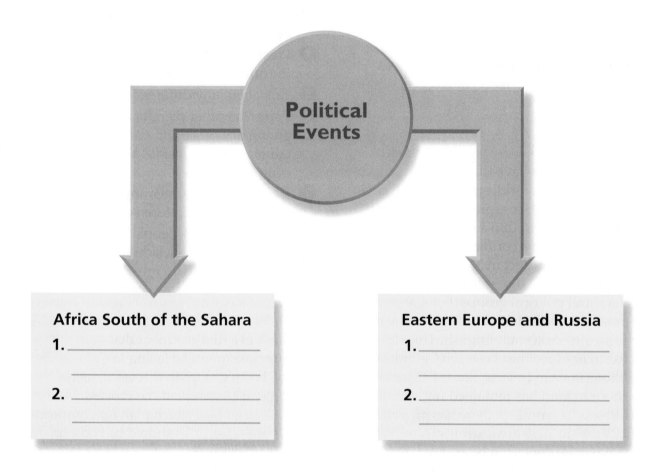

Political Events

Africa South of the Sahara

1. _____

   _____

2. _____

   _____

Eastern Europe and Russia

1. _____

   _____

2. _____

   _____

WRITE MORE ABOUT IT

Write a Letter Imagine that you are an eleven- or twelve-year-old living in South Africa. Write a letter to a pen pal in the United States explaining recent changes in South Africa. As background, tell what life was like before the changes.

Write an Article From newspapers, magazines, and television news programs, find out about the latest developments in the Balkans. Then write your own article that might appear in a current-events magazine for eleven and twelve-year-olds.

1995   2000

1994
• Mandela elected president of South Africa

1995
• Bosnia peace agreement

1998
• Northern Ireland peace agreement

USE VOCABULARY

Write a term from this list to complete each of the sentences that follow.

Afrikaans   **common market**

apartheid   **perestroika**

1. Dutch settlers in South Africa spoke their own language, known as _____.

2. The EEC is an economic union, or _____, of European nations.

3. Under the policy of _____, Gorbachev formed a new legislative body.

4. For many years South Africans lived under a political system known as _____, which separated people of different skin color.

CHECK UNDERSTANDING

5. Who was Kwame Nkrumah? What was his goal?

6. Who became the first prime minister of an independent Kenya?

7. What actions did President de Klerk take toward ending apartheid in South Africa?

8. Who became the first president of the new South Africa? What role had this leader played in the country in the past?

9. How did *perestroika* affect leadership in the Soviet Union?

10. The breakup of which country led to a war in the Balkans?

THINK CRITICALLY

11. **Cause and Effect** What were some of the effects of colonial rule on African nations?

12. **Past to Present** Make a prediction about the way of governing one year from today in each of these countries: Russia, Poland, Bosnia, South Africa, the United States.

13. **Explore Viewpoints** How do you think people your age who live in the former Soviet Union feel about the changes there? How do you think people there who are the age of your grandparents feel about the changes?

APPLY SKILLS

Resolve Conflicts Think about a conflict between you and a friend or family member. Then write several paragraphs about ways you can solve this conflict. Answer these questions in your writing: What compromises are you willing to make? What compromises are you unwilling to make?

READ MORE ABOUT IT

My Palace of Leaves in Sarajevo by Marybeth Lorbiecki. Dial. Through letters written to her American cousin, 12-year-old Nadja tells about life in war-torn Bosnia.

HARCOURT BRACE

Visit the Internet at **http://www.hbschool.com** for additional resources.

FORCES FOR
Unity AND Division

As the world enters the twenty-first century, it seems that people are as divided as ever. Serbs, Bosnians, and Croats have fought a terrible war. Palestinian Arabs and Israelis do not have lasting peace. Some Muslims and Hindus are fighting one another on the Indian subcontinent. There are many national, regional, and ethnic rivalries in Africa, Asia, Europe, and the Americas in which groups fight one another over civil rights and land.

In spite of these conflicts, some groups and leaders are helping to bring people together. Many international organizations have been formed to promote economic, social, and cultural cooperation. In addition to the United Nations, the main organizations are the Association of Southeast Asian Nations, the Caribbean Community and Common Market, the League of Arab States, the Commonwealth of Independent States from the former Soviet Union, the Organization of African Unity, and the Organization of American States. These groups work for unity in their regions of the world.

Think and Apply

Find out more about one of the international organizations. Write a letter asking for information, and do library research. Based on the information you gather, write an article summarizing the group's recent achievements.

HARCOURT BRACE

Visit the Internet at **http://www.hbschool.com** for additional resources.

CNN Turner Le@rning

Check your media center or classroom video library for the Making Social Studies Relevant videotape of this feature.

World leaders at a World Summit for Social Development, in Copenhagen, Denmark

31ST ASEAN MINISTERIAL MEETIN
24-25 JULY   PHILIPPI

Asian leaders gather to discuss issues important to their region of the world.

Israeli Prime Minister Benjamin Netanyahu (left) and Palestinian President Yasir Arafat (right) shake hands with United States Secretary of State Madeleine Albright (center) during 1998 peace negotiations.

VISUAL SUMMARY

Summarize the Main Ideas
Study the pictures and captions to help you review the events you read about in Unit 10.

Predicting Events
In the future, world events may be very different from the way they are shown here. What do you think the future will hold for cultures around the world? On a separate sheet of paper, draw scenes that you think might show the world in the year 2025. Then write a brief summary for each scene.

1 China's industry, agriculture, and trade changed as Mao Zedong introduced communism to the country. In recent years the Chinese people have gained some economic freedoms but no political freedoms.

5 Ideas and beliefs both unite and divide the peoples of the Middle East.

4 Religious beliefs have played a part in the shaping of the present-day countries in the Indian subcontinent.

2 Following its defeat in World War II, Japan rebuilt and became a leader in industry. In recent years, Japan's economy has experienced a decline.

3 The countries of South America have faced many economic and environmental challenges while growing and changing in the twentieth century.

6 After winning independence African nations faced a number of challenges. Only recently have all the people in South Africa begun to have equal rights.

7 The decline of communism in eastern Europe has brought many changes.

UNIT 10
REVIEW

USE VOCABULARY

Write each term in a sentence that will help explain its meaning.

1 quota

2 gross domestic product

3 standard of living

4 deforestation

5 terrorism

6 partition

7 autonomy

8 apartheid

CHECK UNDERSTANDING

9 What important event occurred on June 4, 1989, in China's Tiananmen Square?

10 Why does Japan have a favorable balance of trade?

11 Why are many of the South American nations known as developing countries?

12 Why was NAFTA created?

13 What is "passive resistance"?

14 Why is Nelson Mandela important to South Africa's history?

THINK CRITICALLY

15 **Cause and Effect** What effect have the conflicts in the Middle East and in Bosnia had on the United States?

16 **Think More About It** Why is autonomy so important to the Palestinian people? Why are the Israelis cautious about granting autonomy to the Palestinians?

17 **Past to Present** How is your life affected by each of the following: the end of apartheid, the collapse of communism in eastern Europe and the former Soviet Union, war and peace in the former Yugoslavia, the Arab-Israeli conflict, and NAFTA?

APPLY SKILLS

Compare Population Maps In Unit 10 you have read about problems in Japan caused by the growth of industry and population. Use the map below to answer the questions.

18 Which colors cover most of the country? What does this show about Japan and its population?

19 Where has most of Japan's population settled? Why do you think this is so?

20 Are there areas in Japan with fewer than 100 people per square mile? If so, where are these areas? Why do you think this is so?

21 What do you think will happen if Japan's population continues to grow? What are some possible solutions to Japan's problem of overpopulation? Which solutions are best? Why?

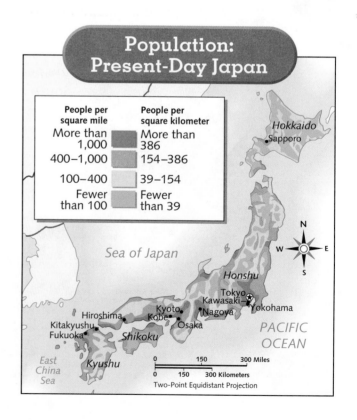

Population: Present-Day Japan

People per square mile	People per square kilometer
More than 1,000	More than 386
400–1,000	154–386
100–400	39–154
Fewer than 100	Fewer than 39

Hokkaido
Sapporo

Sea of Japan

Honshu

Tokyo
Kawasaki
Yokohama
Kyoto
Nagoya
Kobe
Hiroshima
Osaka
Kitakyushu
Fukuoka
Shikoku

PACIFIC OCEAN

East China Sea

Kyushu

0   150   300 Miles
0   150   300 Kilometers
Two-Point Equidistant Projection

COOPERATIVE LEARNING WORKSHOP

REMEMBER

- Share your ideas.
- Cooperate with others to plan your work.
- Take responsibility for your work.
- Help one another.
- Show your group's work to the class.
- Discuss what you learned by working together.

ACTIVITY

Make a Scrapbook

Important world events happen daily. Look through recent newspapers and magazines for articles and pictures about the latest political events in eastern Europe and in the member countries of the CIS. Then, with several classmates, make a scrapbook that contains the most important articles and pictures. For each article, write a brief description.

ACTIVITY

Conduct an Interview

Mohandas Gandhi was a leader in India's independence movement. What would it have been like to talk with him about his life and his ideas? Work with a classmate to make a list of ten questions you would have asked the Indian leader. The questions could focus on any of these topics: his early life, his views on conflict and cooperation, his religious beliefs. Once you have completed your questions, work with your partner to think of answers that Gandhi might have given. Then, with one of you playing the part of the interviewer and the other playing the part of Gandhi, present your interview to the class.

ACTIVITY

Present a Report

Work in a group to learn more about one of the African countries that became independent during the twentieth century. Find out about the nation's languages, peoples, colonial history, present-day ways of governing, and other topics of interest. Then, with your group, make an oral presentation about the country you have researched.

Unit Project Wrap-Up

Hold a World Summit Review the notes you have written about your selected country, and write a list of concerns you want to discuss. Make a sign that shows the country you represent. Then, either with your whole class or as part of a small group, take part in a world summit meeting.

For Your Reference

Contents

How to Gather and Report Information

To write a report, make a poster, or do many other social studies projects, you may need information that is not in your textbook. You would need to gather this information from reference books, electronic references, or community resources. The following guide can help you in gathering information from many sources and in reporting what you find.

HOW TO USE REFERENCE TOOLS

Reference works are collections of facts. They include books and electronic resources, such as almanacs, atlases, dictionaries, and encyclopedias. In a library a reference book has *R* or *REF*—for *reference*—on its spine along with the call number. Most reference books may not be taken home. They are for use only in the library. Many libraries also have electronic references on CD-ROM and the Internet.

▶ WHEN TO USE AN ENCYCLOPEDIA

An encyclopedia is a good place to begin to look for information. An encyclopedia has articles on nearly every subject. The articles are in alphabetical order. Each gives basic facts about people, places, and events. Some electronic encyclopedias allow you to hear music and speeches and see short movies.

▶ WHEN TO USE A DICTIONARY

A dictionary can give you information about words. Dictionaries explain word meanings and show the pronunciations of words. A dictionary is a good place to check the spelling of a word. Some dictionaries also include the origins of words and lists of foreign words, abbreviations, well-known people, and place names.

▶ WHEN TO USE AN ATLAS

You can find information about places in an atlas. An atlas is a book of maps. Some atlases have road maps. Others have maps of countries around the world. There are atlases with maps that show crops, population, products, and many other things. Ask a librarian to help you find the kind of atlas you need.

▶ WHEN TO USE AN ALMANAC

An almanac is a book or electronic resource of facts and figures. It shows information in tables and charts. However, the subjects are not in alphabetical order. You will need to use the index, which lists the subjects in alphabetical order. Most almanacs are brought up to date every year. So an almanac can give you the latest information.

These students are researching information that they need to prepare a report on ancient civilizations in the Americas.

Skills Handbook • **R3**

▶ HOW TO FIND NONFICTION BOOKS

Nonfiction books give facts about real people and things. In a library all nonfiction books are numbered and placed in order on the shelves. To find the nonfiction book you want, you need to know its call number. You can find the call number by using a card file or a computer catalog, but you will need to know the book's title, author, or subject. Here are some sample entries for a book on the early Mayas, a Native American people.

Subject Card

```
            INDIANS OF CENTRAL AMERICA.

REF      Meyer, Carolyn.
972.81        The mystery of the ancient Maya / Carolyn
MEYE     Meyer and Charles Gallenkamp. -- New York :
         Atheneum, 1985.

             ix, 159 p. : ill. ; 24 cm.

             ISBN 0-689-50319-9
```

Title Card

```
            The mystery of the ancient Maya

         REF      Meyer, Carolyn.
         972.81        The mystery of the ancient Maya / Carolyn
         MEYE     Meyer and Charles Gallenkamp. -- New York :
                  Atheneum, 1985.

                      ix, 159 p. : ill. ; 24 cm.

F1435.M56 1985       ISBN 0-689-50319-9
```

```
              REF      Meyer, Carolyn.
              972.81        The mystery of the ancient Maya / Carolyn
              MEYE     Meyer and Charles Gallenkamp. -- New York :
                       Atheneum, 1985.

                           ix, 159 p. : ill. ; 24 cm.

                           "A Margaret K. McElderry book."
                           Includes index.
                           SUMMARY: Explores the advanced civilization
                       and unsolved mysteries of the Mayas, who
                       reigned for six centuries and then
                       disappeared.
              F1435.M56 1985   ISBN 0-689-50319-9
```

Author Card

F1435.M56 1985   REF 972.81
                      84-24209 /AC/r90

Computer Catalog

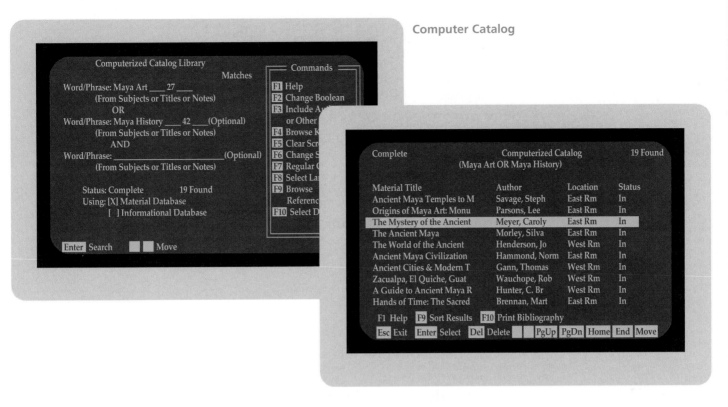

```
      Computerized Catalog Library                        ┌── Commands ──┐
                                    Matches
                                                          F1  Help
Word/Phrase: Maya Art ___ 27 ___                          F2  Change Boolean
        (From Subjects or Titles or Notes)                F3  Include A
              OR                                               or Other
Word/Phrase: Maya History ___ 42 ___ (Optional)          F4  Browse K
        (From Subjects or Titles or Notes)               F5  Clear Scr
              AND                                         F6  Change S
Word/Phrase: _____ (Optional)             F7  Regular C
        (From Subjects or Titles or Notes)               F8  Select La
                                                          F9  Browse
     Status: Complete          19 Found                       Referenc
     Using: [X] Material Database                         F10 Select D
            [  ] Informational Database

  Enter Search      ■ ■  Move
```

```
Complete                    Computerized Catalog              19 Found
                          (Maya Art OR Maya History)

Material Title              Author          Location    Status
Ancient Maya Temples to M   Savage, Steph   East Rm     In
Origins of Maya Art: Monu   Parsons, Lee    East Rm     In
The Mystery of the Ancient  Meyer, Caroly   East Rm     In
The Ancient Maya            Morley, Silva   East Rm     In
The World of the Ancient    Henderson, Jo   West Rm     In
Ancient Maya Civilization   Hammond, Norm   East Rm     In
Ancient Cities & Modern T   Gann, Thomas    West Rm     In
Zacualpa, El Quiche, Guat   Wauchope, Rob   West Rm     In
A Guide to Ancient Maya R   Hunter, C. Br   West Rm     In
Hands of Time: The Sacred   Brennan, Mart   East Rm     In

 F1 Help   F9 Sort Results   F10 Print Bibliography
 Esc Exit  Enter Select  Del Delete  ■ ■ PgUp PgDn Home End Move
```

▶ HOW TO FIND PERIODICALS

Libraries have special sections for periodicals—newspapers and magazines. Periodicals are good sources for the latest information and for topics not covered in books. New issues of periodicals are usually displayed on a rack. Older issues are stored away, sometimes on film. Most libraries have an index or guide that lists magazine articles by subject. The most widely used guides are the *Children's Magazine Guide* and the *Readers' Guide to Periodical Literature*.

The entries in these guides are usually in alphabetical order by subject, author, or title. Abbreviations may be used for many parts of an entry, such as the name of the magazine and the date of the issue. Here is a sample entry for an article about prehistoric sculptures found in the country of Jordan.

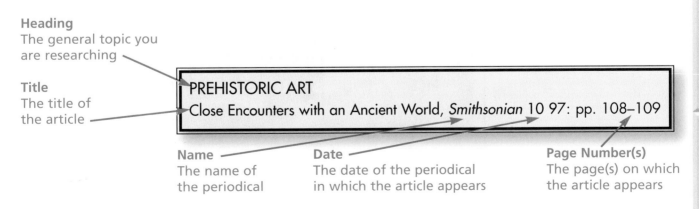

Heading
The general topic you are researching

Title
The title of the article

PREHISTORIC ART
Close Encounters with an Ancient World, *Smithsonian* 10 97: pp. 108–109

Name
The name of the periodical

Date
The date of the periodical in which the article appears

Page Number(s)
The page(s) on which the article appears

HOW TO FIND INTERNET RESOURCES

The World Wide Web, part of the Internet, is a rich resource for information. You can use the World Wide Web to read documents, see photographs and artworks, and examine other primary sources. You can also use it to listen to music, read electronic books, take a "tour" of a museum, or get the latest news.

Information on the World Wide Web changes all the time. What you find today may not be there tomorrow, and new information is always being added. Much of the information you find may be useful, but remember that some of it may not be accurate.

▶ PLAN YOUR SEARCH

1. Make a list of your research questions.
2. Think about possible sources for finding your answers.
3. Identify key words to describe your research topic.
4. Consider synonyms and variations of those terms.
5. Decide exactly how you will go about finding what you need.

▶ SEARCH BY SUBJECT

To search for topics, or subjects, choose a search engine. You can get a list of available search engines by clicking the SEARCH or NET SEARCH button at the top of your screen.

If you want to find Web sites for baseball, for example, enter "baseball" in the search engine field. Then click SEARCH or GO on the screen. You will see a list of sites all over the World Wide Web having to do with baseball. Because not all search engines list the same sites, you may need to use more than one search engine.

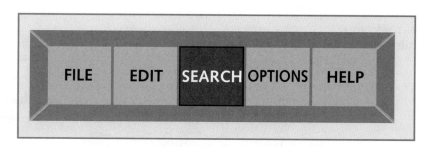

FILE   EDIT   SEARCH   OPTIONS   HELP

► SEARCH BY USING ADDRESSES

Each site on the World Wide Web has an address called a Uniform Resource Locator, or URL for short. A typical URL is shown in the box below.

To find URL listings, look in manuals, books, newspapers, magazines, and television and radio credits. To use a URL to go to a Web site, type the URL in the LOCATION/GO TO or NETSITE box in the upper left corner of the screen.

Go To   http://www.hbschool.com

► BOOKMARK YOUR RESOURCES

Once you have found a site that you think will be helpful, you can bookmark it. Bookmarking makes a copy of a URL and keeps a record of it so you can easily go back to the site later.

While you are at the site you want to bookmark, click BOOKMARKS at the top of your screen and choose ADD BOOKMARK. Your list of bookmarks might look like this:

BOOKMARKS

- Harcourt Brace School Publishers: The Learning Site

- Library of Congress Home Page

- The Smithsonian Institution Home Page

- National Archives Online Exhibit Hall

Knowing how to use the Internet can help you find a wide range of information on a subject quickly and easily.

Skills Handbook • **R7**

Interviewing can be a good way to gather firsthand information about a topic.

How to Conduct an Interview

Conducting interviews, or asking people questions, is a good way to get facts and points of view.

▶ Planning an Interview

1. Make a list of people to interview.
2. Call or write to each person to request an interview. Identify yourself, and let the person know what you want to talk about.
3. Ask the person you will interview to set a time and place to meet.

▶ Before the Interview

1. Read more about your topic and, if possible, about the person. That way, you will be better able to talk with the person about your topic.
2. Make a list of questions to ask.

▶ During the Interview

1. Listen carefully. Do not interrupt or argue with the person.
2. Take notes, and write down the person's exact words.
3. If you want to use a tape recorder, first ask the person if you may do so.

▶ After the Interview

1. Before you leave, thank the person you interviewed.
2. Follow up by writing a thank-you note.

How to Conduct a Survey

A good way to get information about the views of people in your community is to conduct a survey.

1. Identify your topic, and make a list of questions. Write them so that they can be answered with "yes" or "no" or with "for" or "against." You may also want to give a "no opinion" or "not sure" choice.
2. Make a tally sheet for recording the responses.
3. Decide how many people you will ask and where you will conduct your survey.
4. During the survey, record the responses carefully.
5. When you have finished your survey, count the responses and write a summary statement or conclusion that your survey supports.

HOW TO WRITE FOR INFORMATION

People in places far away can also give you information. You can write a letter to ask for it. When you write, be sure to do these things:

- Write neatly by hand or use a computer.
- Say who you are and why you are writing.
- Make your request specific and reasonable.
- Provide a self-addressed, stamped envelope for the answer.

HOW TO WRITE A REPORT

You may be asked to write a report on the information you have gathered. Most reports are 300 to 500 words long.

▶ GATHER AND ORGANIZE YOUR INFORMATION

Gather information about your topic from reference books, electronic references, or community resources. Then organize the information you have gathered.

- Take notes as you find information for your report.
- Review your notes to make sure that you have all the information you need.
- Outline your information.
- Make sure the information is in the right order.

▶ DRAFT YOUR REPORT

- Review your information. Decide whether you need more.
- Remember that the purpose of your report is to share information about your topic.
- Write a draft of your report. Put all your ideas on paper.

▶ REVISE

- Check that you have followed the order of your outline. Move sentences that seem out of place.
- Add any information that seems needed.
- Add quotations that show people's exact words if you can.
- Reword sentences if too many follow the same pattern.

▶ PROOFREAD AND PUBLISH

- Check for errors.
- Make sure nothing has been left out.
- Write a clean copy of your report by hand, or use a computer.

A good report is well-organized, informative, and error-free.

Almanac
FACTS ABOUT THE WORLD

Country Flag	Country	Capital	Population*	Area (sq. mi.)	Economy
Africa					
	Algeria	Algiers	29,830,000	918,497	oil, natural gas, light industry, food processing, grains, iron
	Angola	Luanda	10,624,000	481,351	textiles, coffee, sugarcane, bananas, iron, diamonds
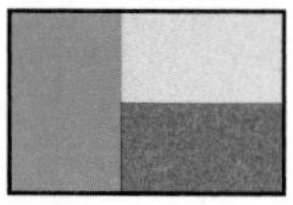	Benin	Porto-Novo	5,902,000	43,483	palm products, peanuts, cotton, corn, oil
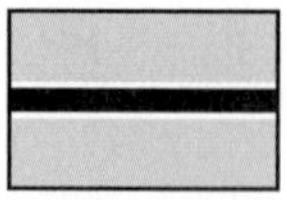	Botswana	Gaborone	1,501,000	219,916	livestock processing, corn, coal, copper, tourism
	Burkina Faso	Ouagadougou	10,891,000	105,869	agricultural processing, textiles, millet, sorghum, manganese
	Burundi	Bujumbura	6,053,000	10,759	food processing, coffee, cotton, tea, nickel
	Cameroon	Yaoundé	14,678,000	183,591	oil products, food processing, cocoa, coffee
	Cape Verde	Praia	394,000	1,557	bananas, coffee, sweet potatoes, salt
	Central African Republic	Bangui	3,342,000	240,376	textiles, cotton, coffee, diamonds

Country Flag	Country	Capital	Population*	Area (sq. mi.)	Economy
	Chad	N'Djamena	7,166,000	495,752	cotton, sorghum, millet, uranium
	Comoros	Moroni	590,000	863	perfume, textiles, vanilla, coconut oil, plants, fruits
	Congo Republic	Brazzaville	2,583,000	132,047	oil, wood products, cocoa, coffee, potash
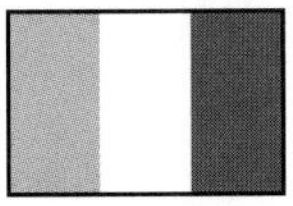	Côte d'Ivoire (Ivory Coast)	Yamoussoukro	14,986,000	124,503	food processing, coffee, cocoa, oil, diamonds
	Democratic Republic of the Congo	Kinshasa	47,440,000	905,356	mining, food processing, sugar, rice, cobalt
	Djibouti	Djibouti	434,000	8,880	mainly service activities
	Egypt	Cairo	64,792,000	386,900	textiles, tourism, chemicals, cotton, rice, beans, oil, gas
	Equatorial Guinea	Malabo	443,000	10,825	fish, cocoa, coffee, bananas, oil
	Eritrea	Asmara	3,590,000	45,405	food processing, cotton, coffee, tobacco, gold, potash
	Ethiopia	Addis Ababa	58,733,000	471,775	food processing, textiles, coffee, grains, platinum, gold
	Gabon	Libreville	1,190,000	102,317	textiles, cocoa, coffee, oil, manganese, uranium

*These population figures are from the most recent available statistics.

Country Flag	Country	Capital	Population*	Area (sq. mi.)	Economy
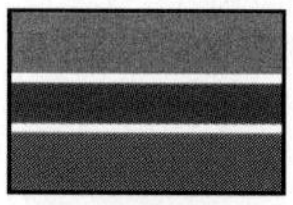	The Gambia	Banjul	1,248,000	4,003	tourism, peanuts, rice, fish
	Ghana	Accra	18,101,000	92,100	aluminum, cocoa, gold, manganese
	Guinea	Conakry	7,405,000	94,925	mining, bananas, pineapples, iron, bauxite, diamonds
	Guinea-Bissau	Bissau	1,179,000	13,948	peanuts, cashews, cotton, rice, bauxite
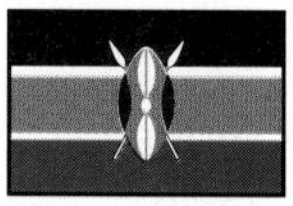	Kenya	Nairobi	28,803,000	224,960	tourism, oil refining, coffee, corn, gold, limestone
	Lesotho	Maseru	2,008,000	11,716	food processing, textiles, corn, grains, diamonds
	Liberia	Monrovia	2,602,000	43,000	mining, rice, cassava, coffee, iron, diamonds, gold, rubber, timber
	Libya	Tripoli	5,648,000	679,358	oil, food processing, dates, olives, gypsum
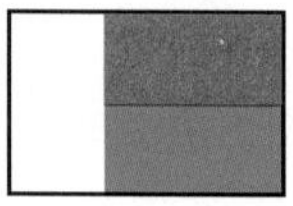	Madagascar	Antananarivo	14,062,000	226,657	textiles, meat processing, coffee, cloves, vanilla, chromite, graphite
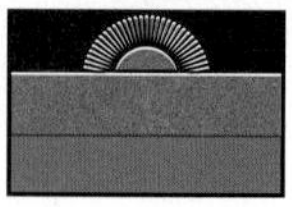	Malawi	Lilongwe	9,609,000	45,747	agricultural processing, sugar, tea, tobacco, coffee

Country Flag	Country	Capital	Population*	Area (sq. mi.)	Economy
	Mali	Bamako	9,945,000	478,652	millet, rice, peanuts, cotton, gold, phosphates
	Mauritania	Nouakchott	2,411,000	397,955	fish processing, dates, grains, iron ore, gypsum
	Mauritius	Port Louis	1,154,000	720	tourism, textiles, sugarcane, tea
	Morocco	Rabat	30,391,000	172,413	carpets, clothing, leather goods, grains, fruits, phosphates, iron ore
	Mozambique	Maputo	18,165,000	297,846	chemicals, petroleum products, cashews, cotton, sugar, coal, titanium
	Namibia	Windhoek	1,727,000	318,321	diamonds, copper, gold, fish
	Niger	Niamey	9,389,000	459,073	peanuts, cotton, uranium, coal, iron
	Nigeria	Abuja	107,129,000	356,669	oil, gas, textiles, cocoa, palm products
	Rwanda	Kigali	7,738,000	10,169	coffee, tea, tin
	São Tomé and Príncipe	São Tomé	148,000	372	cocoa, coconuts
	Senegal	Dakar	9,404,000	76,124	food processing, fishing, peanuts, millet, phosphates

*These population figures are from the most recent available statistics.

Almanac

Country Flag	Country	Capital	Population*	Area (sq. mi.)	Economy
	Seychelles	Victoria	78,000	107	food processing, tourism, coconut products, cinnamon, vanilla
	Sierra Leone	Freetown	4,892,000	27,699	mining, cocoa, coffee, diamonds, titanium
	Somalia	Mogadishu	9,940,000	246,154	sugar, bananas, iron, tin
	South Africa	Cape Town	42,327,000	471,445	steel, automobiles, corn, other grains, gold, diamonds, platinum
	Sudan	Khartoum	32,594,000	967,500	textiles, gum arabic, cotton, chromium, copper
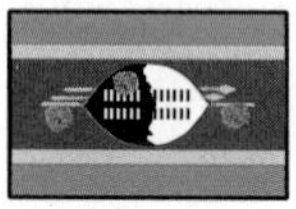	Swaziland	Mbabane	1,032,000	6,705	wood pulp, sugar, corn, cotton, asbestos, clay, coal
	Tanzania	Dar es Salaam	29,461,000	364,900	agricultural processing, cotton, tin, diamonds
	Togo	Lomé	4,736,000	21,853	textiles, coffee, cocoa, yams, phosphates
	Tunisia	Tunis	9,183,000	63,378	food processing, textiles, oil products, grains, olives, dates, phosphates
	Uganda	Kampala	20,605,000	91,134	textiles, cement, coffee, cotton, tea, copper, cobalt

Country Flag	Country	Capital	Population*	Area (sq. mi.)	Economy
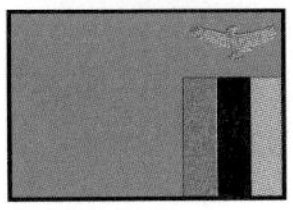	Zambia	Lusaka	9,350,000	290,585	corn, cassava, sugar, cobalt, copper, zinc, emeralds, gold, silver
	Zimbabwe	Harare	11,423,000	150,820	clothing, steel, chemicals, tobacco, sugar, chromium, gold, nickel

Asia

Country Flag	Country	Capital	Population*	Area (sq. mi.)	Economy
	Afghanistan	Kabul	23,738,000	250,775	textiles, furniture, wheat, fruits, copper, coal, wool
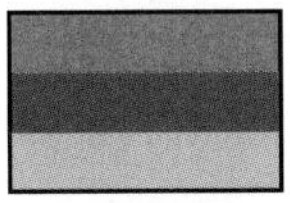	Armenia	Yerevan	3,466,000	11,506	vegetables, grapes, copper, gold
	Azerbaijan	Baku	7,736,000	33,436	oil, grains, cotton, iron, cattle
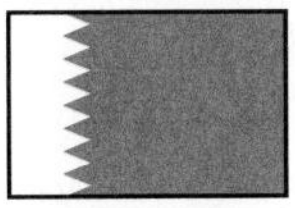	Bahrain	Manama	603,000	255	oil, gas, fruits, vegetables
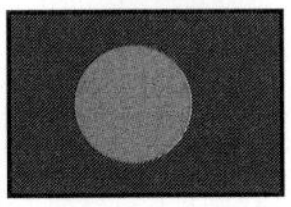	Bangladesh	Dhaka	125,340,000	55,126	jute, textiles, fertilizers, rice, tea
	Bhutan	Thimphu	1,865,000	16,000	rice, corn, timber
	Brunei	Bandar Seri Begawan	308,000	2,226	petroleum, rice, bananas, cassava
	Burma (Myanmar)	Rangoon (Yangôn)	46,822,000	261,789	textiles, petroleum, rice, sugarcane, lead, gemstones

*These population figures are from the most recent available statistics.

FACTS ABOUT THE WORLD

Country Flag	Country	Capital	Population*	Area (sq. mi.)	Economy
	Cambodia	Phnom Penh	11,164,000	69,898	rice, wood, rubber, corn, gemstones
	China	Beijing	1,221,600,000	3,700,000	iron, steel, textiles, tea, rice and other grains, cotton
	Cyprus	Nicosia	753,000	3,572	barley, grapes, olives, copper
	Georgia	Tbilisi	5,175,000	26,911	manganese, citrus fruits, potatoes, corn
	India	New Delhi	967,613,000	1,195,063	textiles, steel, rice and other grains, tea, spices, coal, iron
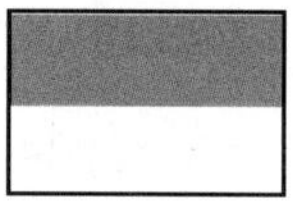	Indonesia	Jakarta	209,774,000	779,675	textiles, rice, cocoa, peanuts, nickel, tin, oil
	Iran	Tehran	67,540,000	635,932	sugar refining, carpets, rice and other grains, oil, gas
	Iraq	Baghdad	22,219,000	168,927	textiles, grains, dates, oil
	Israel	Jerusalem	5,535,000	7,992	diamond cutting, textiles, electronics, citrus fruits, copper, phosphates
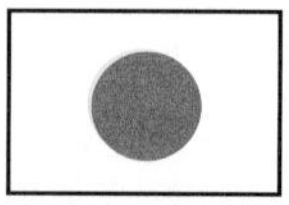	Japan	Tokyo	125,717,000	143,619	electronics, automobiles, fishing, rice, potatoes
	Jordan	Amman	4,325,000	34,575	oil refining, cement, grains, olives, phosphates

Almanac

Country Flag	Country	Capital	Population*	Area (sq. mi.)	Economy
	Kazakhstan	Aqmola	16,899,000	1,048,300	steel, grains, cotton
	Kuwait	Kuwait	2,077,000	6,880	oil, oil products, gas
	Kyrgyzstan	Bishkek	4,540,000	76,641	textiles, mining, tobacco, cotton, sugar beets, gold
	Laos	Vientiane	5,117,000	91,428	wood products, mining, sweet potatoes, corn, cotton, gypsum
	Lebanon	Beirut	3,859,000	3,949	banking, textiles, oil refining, fruits, olives, vegetables
	Malaysia	Kuala Lumpur	20,376,000	128,727	rubber goods, logging, steel, electronics, palm oil, tin, iron
	Maldives	Male	280,000	115	fish processing, tourism, coconuts, sweet potatoes, corn
	Mongolia	Ulaanbaatar	2,538,000	604,247	food processing, mining, grains, coal, oil
	Nepal	Kathmandu	22,641,000	54,362	sugar, jute, tourism, rice and other grains, quartz
	North Korea	P'yongyang	24,317,000	46,609	textiles, corn, potatoes, coal, lead
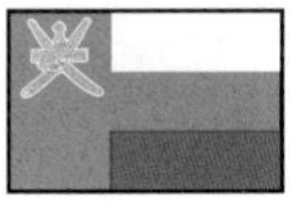	Oman	Muscat	2,265,000	82,000	dates, vegetables, limes, oil, gas

*These population figures are from the most recent available statistics.

FACTS ABOUT THE WORLD

Country Flag	Country	Capital	Population*	Area (sq. mi.)	Economy
	Pakistan	Islamabad	132,185,000	310,403	textiles, petroleum products, rice, wheat, natural gas, iron ore
	Palau	Koror	17,000	191	tourism, fish, coconuts, copra, cassava, sweet potatoes
	Philippines	Manila	76,104,000	115,651	textiles, clothing, wood products, sugar, cobalt, copper
	Qatar	Doha	665,000	4,400	oil, petroleum products
	Saudi Arabia	Riyadh	20,088,000	865,000	oil, oil products, gas, dates, wheat
	Singapore	Singapore	3,462,000	225	shipbuilding, oil refining, electronics, banking, tourism
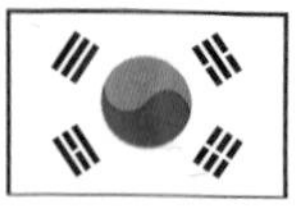	South Korea	Seoul	45,949,000	38,022	electronics, automobiles, textiles, clothing, rice, barley, tungsten
	Sri Lanka	Colombo	18,762,000	25,332	clothing, textiles, tea, coconuts, rice, graphite, limestone
	Syria	Damascus	16,138,000	71,498	oil products, textiles, cotton, grains, olives
	Taiwan	Taipei	21,656,000	13,887	textiles, clothing, electronics, rice, fruits, coal, marble

Country Flag	Country	Capital	Population*	Area (sq. mi.)	Economy
	Tajikistan	Dushanbe	6,014,000	55,251	aluminum, cement, barley, coal, lead
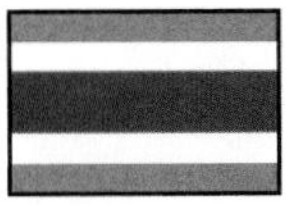	Thailand	Bangkok	59,451,000	198,455	textiles, tourism, rice, corn, tapioca, sugarcane
	Turkey	Ankara	63,528,000	301,380	steel, textiles, grains, mercury
	Turkmenistan	Ashgabat	4,225,000	188,455	oil, mining, textiles, grains, cotton, coal, sulfur, salt
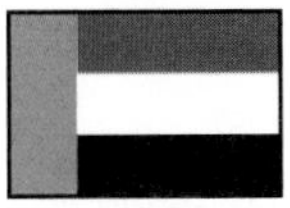	United Arab Emirates	Abu Dhabi	2,262,000	32,280	oil, vegetables, dates
	Uzbekistan	Tashkent	23,860,000	173,591	machinery, natural gas, vegetables, cotton
	Vietnam	Hanoi	75,124,000	130,468	food processing, textiles, rice, sugar, phosphates
	Yemen	Sanaa	13,972,000	203,849	oil, grains, fruits, salt

Australia and Oceania

Country Flag	Country	Capital	Population*	Area (sq. mi.)	Economy
	Australia	Canberra	18,439,000	2,967,909	iron, steel, textiles, electrical equipment, wheat, cotton, fruits, bauxite, coal
	Fiji	Suva	792,000	7,055	tourism, sugar, bananas, gold, timber

*These population figures are from the most recent available statistics.

Almanac

Country Flag	Country	Capital	Population*	Area (sq. mi.)	Economy
	Kiribati	Tarawa	82,000	277	fishing, coconut oil, breadfruit, sweet potatoes
	Marshall Islands	Majuro	61,000	70	agriculture, tourism
	Micronesia	Palikir	128,000	1,055	tourism, tropical fruits, vegetables, pepper
	Nauru	Yaren	10,000	8.5	phosphates
	New Zealand	Wellington	3,587,000	103,736	food processing, textiles, machinery, fish, forest products, grains, potatoes, gold, gas, iron, coal
	Papua New Guinea	Port Moresby	4,496,000	178,260	coffee, coconuts, cocoa, gold, copper, silver
	Samoa	Apia	220,000	1,100	timber, tourism, coconuts, yams, hardwoods, fish
	Solomon Islands	Honiara	427,000	11,500	fishing, coconuts, rice, gold, bauxite
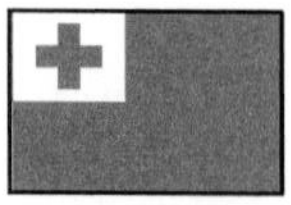	Tonga	Nuku'alofa	107,000	270	tourism, fishing, coconut products, bananas
	Tuvalu	Funafuti	10,000	9	coconut products, coconuts

Country Flag	Country	Capital	Population*	Area (sq. mi.)	Economy
	Vanuatu	Portvila	181,000	5,700	fish processing, meat canneries, tourism, coconut products, manganese

Europe

Country Flag	Country	Capital	Population*	Area (sq. mi.)	Economy
	Albania	Tiranë	3,293,000	11,100	cement, textiles, food processing, corn, wheat, chromium, coal
	Andorra	Andorra la Vella	75,000	180	tourism, sheep, tobacco products, iron, lead
	Austria	Vienna	8,054,000	32,375	steel, machinery, automobiles, grains, iron ore
	Belarus	Minsk	10,440,000	80,154	manufacturing, chemicals, grains, vegetables
	Belgium	Brussels	10,204,000	11,781	steel, glassware, diamond cutting, automobiles, wheat, coal
	Bosnia and Herzegovina	Sarajevo	2,608,000	19,904	steel, mining, textiles, timber, corn, wheat, berries, bauxite, iron
	Bulgaria	Sofia	8,653,000	42,823	chemicals, machinery, metals, textiles, grains, fruits, bauxite, copper, zinc
	Croatia	Zagreb	5,027,000	21,829	chemicals, plastics, steel, paper, olives, wheat, oil, bauxite

*These population figures are from the most recent available statistics.

Almanac

Country Flag	Country	Capital	Population*	Area (sq. mi.)	Economy
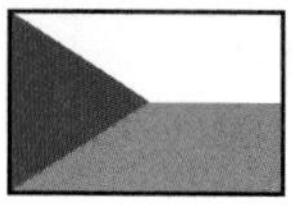	Czech Republic	Prague	10,319,000	30,450	machinery, oil products, glass, wheat, sugar beets, rye, coal, kaolin
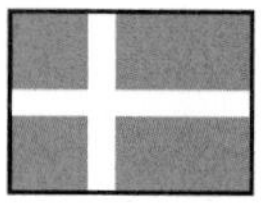	Denmark	Copenhagen	5,269,000	16,629	food processing, machinery, textiles, furniture, grains, potatoes, dairy products, oil, salt
	Estonia	Tallinn	1,445,000	17,413	shipbuilding, electric motors, potatoes, oil
	Finland	Helsinki	5,109,000	130,128	metal, wood products, grains, copper, iron
	France	Paris	58,470,000	210,918	steel, textiles, tourism, wine, perfume, grains, fruits, vegetables, bauxite, iron
	Germany	Berlin	84,068,000	137,735	shipbuilding, automobiles, grains, potatoes, coal, potash, steel
	Greece	Athens	10,583,000	50,944	textiles, tourism, chemicals, wine, grains, olives, grapes, citrus fruits, bauxite
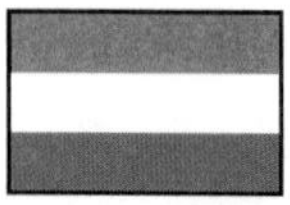	Hungary	Budapest	9,936,000	35,919	iron, steel, wheat, corn, sunflowers, bauxite, coal
	Iceland	Reykjavik	273,000	39,702	fish, aluminum, potatoes

Country Flag	Country	Capital	Population*	Area (sq. mi.)	Economy
	Ireland	Dublin	3,556,000	26,600	food processing, textiles, chemicals, tourism, potatoes, grains, zinc, lead
	Italy	Rome	57,534,000	116,313	tourism, steel, machinery, automobiles, textiles, shoes, grapes, olives and olive oil, mercury, potash, sulfur
	Latvia	Riga	2,438,000	24,595	machinery, train cars, grains, sugar beets
	Liechtenstein	Vaduz	31,461	62	electronics, textiles, ceramics, vegetables, wheat
	Lithuania	Vilnius	3,636,000	25,174	machinery, shipbuilding, grains, potatoes, vegetables
	Luxembourg	Luxembourg	422,474	999	steel, chemicals, food processing, grains, potatoes, grapes
	Macedonia	Skopje	2,114,000	9,928	mining, textiles, wheat, rice, chromium, lead
	Malta	Valletta	379,365	122	textiles, tourism, potatoes, tomatoes
	Moldova	Chisinau	4,475,000	13,012	canning, wine, textiles, grains, lignite, gypsum
	Monaco	Monaco	32,000	370 acres	tourism, chemicals, plastics

*These population figures are from the most recent available statistics.

Country Flag	Country	Capital	Population*	Area (sq. mi.)	Economy
	Netherlands	Amsterdam The Hague	15,653,000	16,033	metals, machinery, chemicals, grains, potatoes, flowers, oil, gas
	Norway	Oslo	4,404,000	154,790	paper, shipbuilding, grains, potatoes, copper
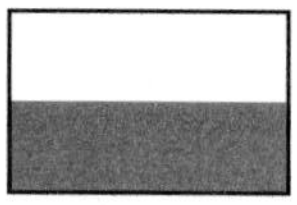	Poland	Warsaw	38,700,000	120,756	shipbuilding, chemicals, grains, potatoes, sugar beets, coal, copper, silver
	Portugal	Lisbon	9,868,000	35,383	textiles, footwear, cork, fish, grains, potatoes, tungsten, uranium, iron
	Romania	Bucharest	21,399,000	91,699	mining, machinery, oil, oil products, grains, grapes, gas, coal
	Russia**	Moscow	147,987,000	6,592,812	steel, machinery, motor vehicles, chemicals, textiles, grains, sugar beets, mercury, manganese, potash, bauxite, cobalt
	San Marino	San Marino	25,000	24	tourism, postage stamps, woolen goods, wheat, grapes
	Slovakia	Bratislava	5,393,000	18,923	iron, steel, glass, grains, potatoes
	Slovenia	Ljubljana	1,946,000	7,819	electronics, vehicles, coal, lead, zinc

**in both Asia and Europe

Almanac

Country Flag	Country	Capital	Population*	Area (sq. mi.)	Economy
	Spain	Madrid	39,244,000	194,881	machinery, textiles, grains, olives, grapes, lignite, uranium, lead
	Sweden	Stockholm	8,946,000	173,665	steel, machinery, vehicles, grains, potatoes, zinc, iron, lead
	Switzerland	Bern and Lausanne	7,249,000	15,941	machinery, chemicals, watches, cheese, chocolate products, tourism, salt
	Ukraine	Kiev	50,685,000	233,089	chemicals, machinery, grains, sugar beets, potatoes, iron, manganese
	United Kingdom	London	58,610,000	94,251	steel, vehicles, shipbuilding, banking, textiles, grains, sugar beets, coal, tin, oil, gas, limestone
	Vatican City	—	840	109 acres	tourism, postage stamps
	Yugoslavia	Belgrade	10,655,000	39,449	steel, machinery, corn and other grains, oil, gas, coal

North America

Country Flag	Country	Capital	Population*	Area (sq. mi.)	Economy
	Antigua and Barbuda	St. John's	66,000	171	manufacturing, tourism
	Bahamas	Nassau	262,000	5,386	tourism, rum, banking

*These population figures are from the most recent available statistics.

Almanac

Country Flag	Country	Capital	Population*	Area (sq. mi.)	Economy
	Barbados	Bridgetown	258,000	166	sugar, tourism
	Belize	Belmopan	225,000	8,867	sugar
	Canada	Ottawa	29,123,000	3,851,809	nickel, zinc, copper, gold, livestock, fish
	Costa Rica	San José	3,534,000	19,652	furniture, aluminum, textiles, fertilizers, coffee, gold
	Cuba	Havana	10,999,000	41,620	food processing, tobacco, sugar, rice, coffee, cobalt, nickel, iron, copper, salt
	Dominica	Roseau	83,226	289	tourism, bananas, citrus fruits, pumice
	Dominican Republic	Santo Domingo	8,228,000	18,657	cement, tourism, sugar, cocoa, coffee, nickel, bauxite
	El Salvador	San Salvador	5,662,000	8,260	food products, tobacco, coffee, corn, sugar
	Grenada	St. George's	96,000	120	textiles, spices, bananas, cocoa
	Guatemala	Guatemala City	11,558,000	42,042	furniture, rubber, textiles, coffee, sugar, bananas, oil
	Haiti	Port-au-Prince	6,611,000	10,714	textiles, coffee, sugar, bananas, bauxite

Country Flag	Country	Capital	Population*	Area (sq. mi.)	Economy
	Honduras	Tegucigalpa	5,751,000	43,277	textiles, wood products, bananas, sugar, gold, silver, copper, lead
	Jamaica	Kingston	2,616,000	4,471	tourism, sugar, coffee, bananas, potatoes, bauxite, limestone
	Mexico	Mexico City	97,563,000	759,530	steel, chemicals, textiles, rubber, petroleum, tourism, cotton, coffee, wheat, silver, lead, zinc, gold, oil, gas
	Nicaragua	Managua	4,386,000	49,579	food processing, chemicals, textiles, cotton, fruits, coffee, gold, silver, copper
	Panama	Panama City	2,693,000	33,659	oil refining, international banking, bananas, rice, copper, mahogany, shrimp
	Saint Kitts and Nevis	Basseterre	42,000	104	sugar, tourism
	Saint Lucia	Castries	160,000	238	clothing, tourism, bananas, coconuts, forests
	Trinidad and Tobago	Port-of-Spain	1,273,000	1,980	oil products, chemicals, tourism, sugar, cocoa, asphalt, oil, gas
	United States of America	Washington, D.C.	267,955,000	3,619,969	wheat, coal, lead, uranium, iron, copper, gold, computers, electronics, machinery

*These population figures are from the most recent available statistics.

South America

Country Flag	Country	Capital	Population*	Area (sq. mi.)	Economy
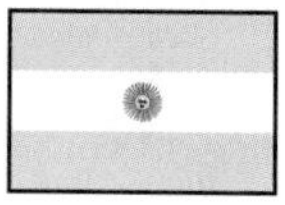	Argentina	Buenos Aires	35,798,000	1,072,156	food processing, automobiles, chemicals, grains, oil, lead
	Bolivia	La Paz/Sucre	7,670,000	424,162	mining, tobacco, coffee, sugar, potatoes, soybeans, tin, tungsten
	Brazil	Brasília	164,511,000	3,284,426	steel, automobiles, textiles, coffee, soybeans, sugar, iron, manganese
	Chile	Santiago	14,508,000	292,257	fish, wood, grains, grapes, beans, copper
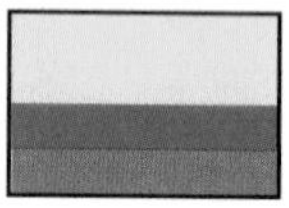	Colombia	Bogotá	37,418,000	439,735	textiles, food processing, coffee, rice, bananas, emeralds, oil, gas
	Ecuador	Quito	11,691,000	109,483	food processing, bananas, coffee, oil, gas, copper, zinc, silver, gold
	Guyana	Georgetown	706,000	83,000	mining, textiles, sugar, bauxite, diamonds, gold
	Paraguay	Asunción	5,652,000	157,043	food processing, textiles, cement, corn, cotton, iron, manganese, limestone
	Peru	Lima	24,950,000	496,222	fishing, mining, textiles, cotton, sugar, coffee, rice, copper, silver, gold, oil

Country Flag	Country	Capital	Population*	Area (sq. mi.)	Economy
	Saint Vincent and the Grenadines	Kingstown	119,000	150	tourism, bananas, arrowroot, coconuts
	Suriname	Paramaribo	443,000	63,251	aluminum, food processing, rice, sugar, fruits, bauxite, iron
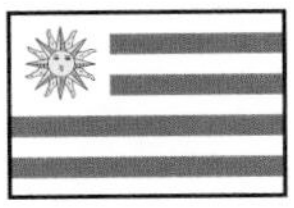	Uruguay	Montevideo	3,262,000	68,039	meat packing, textiles, wine, corn, wheat, oil refining
	Venezuela	Caracas	22,396,000	352,143	steel, textiles, coffee, rice, corn, oil, gas, iron

*These population figures are from the most recent available statistics.

Biographical Dictionary

The Biographical Dictionary lists many of the important people introduced in this book. The page number tells where the main discussion of each person starts. See the Index for other page references.

Abraham *c. 2000s B.C.* Earliest ancestor of the Israelites, according to the Bible. p. 84

Akbar (AK•ber) *1542–1605* Considered the greatest of Mogul emperors, he united nearly all of India and was responsible for many reforms. p. 479

Akhenaton (ahk•NAH•tuhn) *c. 1300s B.C.* Egyptian ruler who changed his name from Amenhotep IV. He and Nefertiti, his wife, urged the Egyptians to worship only one god, the Aton. p. 117

Alaric (AL•uh•rik) *c. 370–410* King of the Visigoths, who crossed the Alps and attacked the city of Rome in 410. p. 278

Alexander the Great *356 B.C.–323 B.C.* Son of Philip II. He was tutored by Aristotle and became king of Macedonia in 336 B.C. As ruler, Alexander built a huge empire. p. 247

Alexandra *1872–1918* Czarina of Russia and wife of Czar Nicholas II. She controlled the Russian government while Nicholas II led the World War I effort. p. 575

Alger, Horatio *1832–1899* American author of more than 100 popular books. p. 531

Allende, Salvador (ah•YEN•day) *1908–1973* Chilean politician; president from 1970 until 1973. p. 641

Amenemhet (AHM•uhn•em•HET) *1991 B.C.–1962 B.C.* Vizier who made Egypt an empire. Started the period called the Middle Kingdom, which lasted for 200 years. p. 115

Arafat, Yasir (AH•ruh•faht) *1929–* Palestinian political leader, chairperson of the Palestine Liberation Organization, and President representing the Palestinian people. p. 666

Archimedes (ar•kuh•MEE•deez) *c. 287 B.C.–212 B.C.* Greek teacher and inventor who used mathematics to build many useful machines. p. 251

Aristarchus (air•uh•STAR•kuhs) *c. 200s B.C.* Greek teacher who used mathematics to discover that the Earth moves in a path around the sun. p. 251

Aristophanes (air•uh•STAH•fuh•neez) *c. 450 B.C.–c. 388 B.C.* Ancient Greek writer of comedies, or humorous plays. p. 243

Aristotle (AIR•uh•staht•uhl) *384 B.C.–322 B.C.* Greek philosopher and tutor of Alexander the Great. He is considered one of the greatest thinkers of all time. p. 245

Ashoka (uh•SHOH•kuh) *c. 200s B.C.* Maurya emperor, remembered as "the greatest and noblest ruler India has known." p. 204

Atahuallpa (ah•tah•WAHL•puh) *c. 1502?–1533* Last Inca king to rule what is now Peru. He was killed in the Spanish conquest of the Incas. p. 456

Babur (BAH•ber) *1483–1530* A descendant of Genghis Khan, he was emperor of India, and founder of the Mogul dynasty. p. 479

Bakri, al- (al•BAHK•ree) *c. 1000s* Muslim geographer. p. 368

Bar Sauma, Rabban *c. 1220–1294* A Christian born in China, he traveled to Europe and brought back goods and tales of the West. p. 334

Batu *c. 1200s* Grandson of Genghis Khan and conqueror of what is now Russia, Poland, and Hungary in Europe and parts of Asia. p. 333

Begin, Menachem (BAY•gin, muh•NAH•kuhm) *1913–1992* Prime minister of Israel. He and Anwar as-Sadat signed the Camp David peace agreement which set the stage for peace between Egypt and Israel. p. 667

Belisarius (beh•luh•SAR•ee•uhs) *c. 505–c. 565* Byzantine general during the reign of Justinian I. He reclaimed much of the old Roman Empire. p. 300

Bhutto, Benazir (BOO•toh) *1953–* A prime minister of Pakistan. She was the first woman in modern times to lead a Muslim nation. p. 659

Bismarck, Otto von *1815–1898* Prussian statesperson and first chancellor of the German Empire. p. 537

Bolívar, Simón (boh•LEE•var, see•MOHN) *1783–1830* South American soldier, statesperson, and revolutionary leader. He freed Colombia, Venezuela, Ecuador, and Peru from Spanish rule. p. 510

Bonaparte, Joseph (BOH•nuh•part) *1768–1844* Napoleon Bonaparte's brother; ruled Spain from 1808 to 1814, after Napoleon conquered that country. p. 510

Bonaparte, Napoleon (BOH•nuh•part, nuh•POH•lee•uhn) *1769–1821* French military leader and emperor of France. p. 504

Bush, George *1924–* Forty-first President of the United States. p. 651

Cabot, John *c. 1450–c. 1499* Italian navigator and explorer. While seeking a western route to Asia, he reached North America and claimed it for England. p. 444

Cabral, Pedro (kah•BRAHL) *c. 1467–1520* Portuguese navigator who claimed Brazil for Portugal. p. 456

Caesar, Julius *100 B.C.–44 B.C.* Roman general and statesperson. He was dictator of Rome until he was murdered by a group of nobles. p. 260

Carter, Jimmy *1924–* Thirty-ninth President of the United States. He brought about a peace agreement between Israel and Egypt. p. 608

Cartier, Jacques (kar•TYAY, ZHAHK) *1491–1557* French sailor and explorer. His explorations gave France its claim to Canada. p. 457

Castro, Fidel *1926–* Cuban revolutionary leader, prime minister, and president. p. 605

Catherine the Great *1729–1796* Russian empress who supported learning and the arts but neglected the Russian peasant class. p. 574

Cavour, Camillo di (kah•VUR) *1810–1861* Italian statesperson who united much of northern Italy and encouraged Garibaldi to set up a kingdom of Italy. p. 537

Ceauşescu, Nicolae (chow•SHES•koo) *1918–1989* Romanian dictator from 1974 to 1989. He was overthrown and executed by the Romanian people during their revolt. p. 685

Chandragupta I (chuhn•druh•GUP•tuh) *c. 300s* Maurya emperor of India. He gave up his throne to his son Samudra Gupta. p. 205

Chandragupta II *c. 400s* Son of Samudra Gupta of India's Maurya dynasty. He encouraged learning during his reign, which lasted from about 380 to 415. p. 205

Chandragupta Maurya (chuhn•druh•GUP•tuh MOW•ree•uh) *?–c. 297 B.C.* Emperor who united India. He gave up the throne to his son in 297 B.C. p. 203

Charlemagne (SHAR•luh•mayn) *742–814* King of the Franks and emperor of the Romans. He strengthened Christianity, resulting in the start of the Holy Roman Empire. p. 309

Charles Martel *c. 688–741* Charlemagne's grandfather and the ruler who united Frankish lands. p. 310

Chiang Kai-shek (jee•AHNG KY•SHEK) *1887–1975* Chinese general and politician. He followed Sun Yat-sen as president of the Chinese Nationalist government. p. 625

Churchill, Winston *1874–1965* British statesperson, author, and prime minister of Britain from 1940 to 1945. p. 588

Cicero (SIH•suh•roh) *106 B.C.–43 B.C.* Roman orator, statesperson, and philosopher. He served as a consul of Rome. p. 260

Cleisthenes (KLYS•thuh•neez) *c. 570 B.C.–508 B.C.* Athenian leader who is regarded as the founder of democracy. p. 237

Cleopatra *69 B.C.–30 B.C.* Egyptian queen who, with Mark Antony, planned to set up an independent empire until the Roman leader Octavian defeated them. p. 261

Clinton, William *1946–* Forty-second President of the United States. p. 650

Columbus, Christopher *1451–1506* Italian–born Spanish explorer. In 1492 he sailed from Spain and thought he had reached Asia. Actually, he had reached islands near the Americas, lands that were unknown to the Europeans. p. 443

Confucius *551 B.C.–479 B.C.* Philosopher considered to be the most revered person in Chinese history. His philosophy, known as Confucianism, became a guide for the way people lived. p. 174

Constantine (KAHN•stuhn•teen) *c. 280–337* Roman general and emperor. The Edict of Milan, which was issued in 313 (during his reign), made Christianity an accepted religion within the Roman Empire. p. 277

Copernicus, Nicolaus (koh•PER•nih•kuhs, nik•uh•LAY•uhs) *1473–1543* Polish astronomer and philosopher. Against popular belief, he formed the theory that the Earth rotates on its axis and revolves around the sun. p. 434

Cortés, Hernando (kawr•TEZ, er•NAHN•doh) *1485–1547* Spanish conquistador who conquered the Aztec Empire. p. 455

Cyrus the Great *c. 585 B.C.–529 B.C.* Leader who built the Persian Empire and conquered Babylon. p. 208

Darius (duh•RY•uhs) *550 B.C.–486 B.C.* Persian ruler who brought order to the Persian Empire. He also built roads; established a postal system; and standardized weights, measures, and coinage. p. 209

David *c. 1010 B.C.–962 B.C.* Second king of Israel; led the defeat of the Philistines. p. 86

de Klerk, Frederik Willem *1936–* President of South Africa. Although an Afrikaner, he lifted the bans on the African National Congress and freed Nelson Mandela and other political prisoners. p. 676

Deng Xiaoping (DUHNG SHOW•PING) *1904–1997* Deputy premier and leader of the Chinese Communist party during the 1970s. His influence on economic changes helped make China an industrial power. p. 628

Dias, Bartholomeu (DEE•ahsh, bar•too•loo•MAY•oo) *1450–1500* Portuguese navigator who sailed around the tip of Africa and into the Indian Ocean. p. 442

Drake, Francis *c. 1540–1596* Admiral who was the first English navigator to circumnavigate the globe. p. 444

Dyer, Reginald H. *1864–1927* British general who ordered his troops to fire on the Indian protesters at Amritsar, India, in April, 1919. p. 656

Elizabeth I *1533–1603* Daughter of Henry VIII and Anne Boleyn. Known as Good Queen Bess, she made England a world power during her 45-year reign; gave the East India Company the right to control trade between India and England. p. 444

Equiano, Olaudah (ek•wee•AHN•oh, oh•LOW•duh) *c. 1750–1797* Nigerian who wrote of his life as a slave and helped in the movement to end slavery. p. 452

Euclid (YOO•kluhd) *c. 300s B.C.* Greek teacher who began the study of geometry. p. 250

Fatima *c. 616–633* Daughter of Muhammad and Khadija. p. 308

Faxian (FAH•SHYUHN) *c. 400s* Buddhist missionary from China who traveled in India and wrote about the scenes he observed. p. 206

Ferdinand *1452–1516* Spanish king who, with Queen Isabella, drove the Moors from Spain. He and Isabella paid for Columbus's expeditions to the Americas. p. 435

Ford, Gerald *1913–* Thirty-eighth President of the United States. p. 649

Francis Ferdinand *1863–1914* Archduke of Austria whose assassination in 1914 is considered the direct cause of World War I. p. 566

Frank, Anne *1929–1945* Young Jewish girl who hid with her family in order to escape the Nazi terror during the Holocaust. She is remembered for the diary she kept while in hiding. She met her death in a German concentration camp. p. 591

Galilei, Galileo (ga•luh•LAY•ee, ga•luh•LAY•oh) *1564–1642* Italian mathematician, astronomer, and physicist. He improved the telescope and used it to prove Nicolaus Copernicus's theory that the Earth revolves around the sun. p. 434

Gama, Vasco da *c. 1460–1524* Portuguese navigator who completed the first voyage from western Europe around Africa to the East. p. 442

Gandhi, Indira (GAHN•dee, in•DIR•uh) *1917–1984* Prime minister of India in the 1980s. p. 658

Gandhi, Mohandas (GAHN•dee, moh•HAHN•dahs) *1869–1948* Indian nationalist and spiritual leader. He was called Mahatma, or "Great Soul," by his followers and was considered the founder of independent India. p. 655

Gaozu (GOW•ZOO) *256 B.C.–195 B.C.* Ruler during the Han dynasty of China. He was a respected leader who combined ideas from Legalism and Confucianism. p. 182

Garibaldi, Giuseppe (joo•SEP•ay) *1807–1882* Italian military and nationalist leader who fought for freedom in southern Italy. p. 536

Gautama, Siddhartha (GOW•tuh•muh, sih•DAHR•tuh) *563 B.C.–c. 483 B.C.* Known as Buddha, or "Enlightened One," he gave up worldly goods to search for enlightenment and truth. He founded the religion of Buddhism in India. p. 194

Genghis Khan *c. 1162–1227* Mongol leader who built the Mongol Empire. p. 332

Gilgamesh *c. 2700s B.C.* King of the ancient Sumerian city-state of Uruk. He is the subject of one of the world's oldest stories. p. 76

Gorbachev, Mikhail (gawr•buh•CHAWF, mee•kah•EEL) *1931–* Secretary general of the Communist party of the Soviet Union from 1985 to 1991. He supported new ideas that included restructuring the government and making it more open to Soviet citizens. p. 684

Gouges, Olympe de (GOOZH, oh•LAMP duh) *1748–1793* Author of *The Rights of Woman*, which helped identify the roles of women in the French Revolution. p. 503

Gracchus, Gaius *153 B.C.–121 B.C.* Ancient Roman who, like his brother Tiberius, died while working to change Roman law to help the plebeian class. p. 259

Gracchus, Tiberius *163 B.C.–133 B.C.* Ancient Roman who, like his brother Gaius, died while working to change Roman law to help the plebeian class. p. 259

Gregory IX *1170–1241* Pope who set up the first Inquisition, in the 1230s. p. 438

Gutenberg, Johannes (GOO•tuhn•berg, yoh•HAHN•uhs) *c. 1400–1468* German who brought the idea of movable type to Europe. He printed Europe's first book, a 1,200-page Bible. p. 433

Hammurabi (hah•muh•RAH•bee) *c. 1792 B.C.–1750 B.C.* King of the city-state of Babylon. He compiled the set of laws known as the Code of Hammurabi. p. 80

Hannibal *247 B.C.–183 B.C.* Carthaginian general who attacked Rome during the Second Punic War. p. 258

Hargreaves, James *1720?–1778* English weaver who invented the spinning jenny. p. 516

Hatshepsut (hat•SHEP•soot) *c. 1503 B.C.–1482 B.C.* Female Egyptian pharaoh who expanded Egyptian trade routes. p. 117

Hawkins, John *1532–1595* English naval commander who led expeditions to the West Indies. p. 444

Henry VIII *1491–1547* King who began the English Reformation by separating from the Roman Catholic Church and becoming supreme head of the Church of England. p. 444

Biographical Dictionary

Henry the Navigator *1394–1460* Founder of a school of navigation, he made Portugal a world sea power. p. 442

Herodotus (hih•RAH•duh•tuhs) *c. 484 B.C.–c. 430 B.C.* Greek historian who traveled through most of the world known to the Greeks during his time. p. 209

Heyerdahl, Thor (HAY•er•dahl, THAWR) *1914–* Norwegian explorer who sailed a balsa-wood raft from Peru to Polynesia to prove that Native Americans could have made such a trip. p. 409

Hidalgo, Miguel (ee•DAHL•goh) *1753–1811* Mexican priest and revolutionary leader who campaigned for Mexican independence. p. 511

Hippocrates (hip•AHK•ruh•teez) *c. 460 B.C.–c. 377 B.C.* Greek physician known as the Father of Medicine. p. 243

Hirohito (hir•oh•HEE•toh) *1901–1989* Emperor of Japan. In 1951 the divine monarchy of Emperor Hirohito was transformed into a democratic government. p. 632

Hitler, Adolf *1889–1945* German politician and führer, or leader. As Nazi dictator of Germany, he planned to conquer the world, and claimed that the German people were superior to others. During his time of power he ordered 12 million people killed. p. 582

Ho Chi Minh (HOH CHEE MIN) *1890–1969* Vietnamese political leader and president of North Vietnam during the Vietnam War. p. 606

Homer *c. 700s B.C.* Greek poet and author of the *Iliad* and the *Odyssey*. Much of what we know of the Mycenaeans comes from his stories. p. 230

Hong Wu *1328–1398* Ruler who founded the Ming dynasty. He drove out the Mongols, ending the Yuan dynasty. Although he unified all of China, he proved to be a cruel leader. p. 471

Hoover, Herbert *1874–1964* Thirty-first President of the United States. p. 579

Horace *8 B.C.–A.D. 65* Roman poet. p. 264

Hussein, Saddam (hoo•SAYN, suh•DAHM) *1937–* Military ruler of Iraq and President since 1979. His invasion of Kuwait in 1990 led to the defeat of Iraq in the Persian Gulf War. p. 668

Ibn Battuta *c. 1304–c. 1377* Muslim geographer and traveler. p. 394

Ibn Rustah *c. 900s* Muslim geographer. p. 404

Idris Aloma (EE•drees AL•oh•muh) *c. 1500s* Ruler of Kanem-Bornu in Africa in the late 1500s, during its time of greatest growth. p. 449

Imhotep *c. 2600s B.C.* Royal architect of Egypt who built Pharaoh Zoser's step pyramid around 2650 B.C. p. 114

Irene *c. 700s* Byzantine empress who ruled the empire from 780 to 802. p. 301

Isaac *c. 2000s B.C.* Son of Abraham. p. 85

Isabella *1451–1504* Spanish queen who, along with King Ferdinand, drove the Moors from Spain. She and King Ferdinand paid for Columbus's expeditions to the Americas. p. 435

Ishmael *c. 2000s B.C.* Son of Abraham. p. 85

Jacob *c. 2000s B.C.* Early leader of the descendants of the Israelites. Later called Israel, he was the son of Isaac and grandson of Abraham. p. 85

Jefferson, Thomas *1743–1826* Third President of the United States and the main writer of the Declaration of Independence. p. 499

Jesus *c. 6 B.C.–c. A.D. 30* The person whose life and teachings are the basis of Christianity. Believing him to be the Son of God, his disciples proclaimed him the Messiah and savior of humankind. p. 273

Jiang Qing *1913–1991* Mao Zedong's widow. p. 628

Jiang, Zemin (JEE•ahng zuh•min) *1926–* President of China, who followed Deng Xiaoping as leader. p. 629

Jinnah, Muhammad Ali (JIH•nuh) *1876–1948* Indian politician and first governor general of Pakistan. He opposed Gandhi's methods and fought for separate Muslim statehood. p. 657

John *1167–1216* King of England who was made to sign the Magna Carta. p. 314

Johnson, Lyndon *1908–1973* Thirty-sixth President of the United States. p. 649

Jonson, Ben *1572–1637* English playwright and poet. p. 433

Justinian I *483–565* Byzantine emperor. His set of laws, known as the Justinian Code, is the basis of law in Europe today. p. 297

Kalidasa (kah•lih•DAH•suh) *c. 400s* An author during India's golden age, he is considered to be among India's greatest writers. p. 206

Kashta (KAHSH•tuh) *700s B.C.* King of ancient Kush; father of Piye. p. 127

Kennedy, John F. *1917–1963* Thirty-fifth President of the United States. p. 605

Kenyatta, Jomo (ken•YAH•tuh, JOH•moh) *1894–1978* First prime minister of independent Kenya. As leader of the Mau Mau terrorists, he freed Kenya from British rule. p. 674

Khadija (kah•DEE•juh) *c. 595–619* Wife of the prophet Muhammad. She provided encouragement to him and support for his mission. p. 304

Khomeini, Ayatollah (koh•MAY•nee, eye•uh•TOH•luh) *1900–1989* Leader of Shiite Muslims in Iran who supported the taking of American hostages. p. 668

Khrushchev, Nikita (KRUSH•chawf, nuh•KEE•tuh) *1894–1971* Soviet politician and premier. p. 605

Khufu *c. 2500s B.C.* Egyptian king who built the Great Pyramid at Giza, the most famous of Egypt's pyramids. p. 115

Khwarizmi, al- (al•KWAR•uhz•mee) *c. 780–c. 850* Arab mathematician. He was considered one of the greatest scientific minds of the Muslim Empire. p. 377

Kubitschek, Juscelino (KOO•buh•chek, zhoo•seh•LEE•noh) *1902–1976* President of Brazil during the 1950s. p. 642

Kublai Khan (KOO•bluh KAHN) *1215–1294* Grandson of Genghis Khan and founder of the Mongol dynasty in China. p. 333

Lenin (LEH•nuhn) *1870–1924* Russian leader of the Communist revolution of 1917 and first premier of the Soviet Union. p. 576

Leo *c. 680–741* Byzantine emperor who ordered all icons in the empire to be destroyed. p. 301

Leo Africanus (LEE•oh af•rih•KAY•nuhs) *c. 1485–c. 1554* Arab traveler and geographer. For a long time his writings were the only source of information about the geography of Sudan. p. 371

Leo X *1475–1521* Pope from 1513 to 1521. He was a patron of the arts but drained the papal treasury by his rich living; he excommunicated Martin Luther. p. 437

Leonardo da Vinci (lee•uh•NAR•doh duh VIN•chee) *1452–1519* Italian Renaissance painter, sculptor, architect, engineer, and scientist. The Mona Lisa is one of his best-known works. p. 432

Li Bo (LEE BOH) *c. 705–c. 762* Chinese poet and writer. His work describes China's progress during its Golden Age. p. 329

Li Si (LEE SUH) *c. 260 B.C.* Advisor for Emperor Shi Huangdi of the ancient Qin dynasty in China. p. 177

Livingstone, David *1813–1873* Scottish missionary and explorer who spent nearly 30 years exploring Africa. His writings influenced traders to become interested in Africa. p. 542

Locke, John *1632–1704* English writer and philosopher who was an important thinker during the Enlightenment. p. 500

Louis XI (LOO•ee) *1423–1483* King of France from 1461 to 1483. p. 435

Louis XVI *1754–1793* King of France. His efforts to raise taxes led to the French Revolution. p. 502

Lumumba, Patrice (luh•MUHM•buh) *1925–1961* First prime minister of the Democratic Republic of the Congo, formerly known as Zaire and earlier as the Belgian Congo. p. 675

Luther, Martin *1483–1546* German religious reformer whose ideas led to the Protestant Reformation. p. 438

MacArthur, Douglas *1880–1964* General of the United States Army and Commander-in-Chief of the Allied forces in the Pacific during World War II. p. 632

Magellan, Ferdinand (mah•JEH•lahn) *c. 1480–1521* Portuguese navigator who sailed through what is now known as the Strait of Magellan. One of his ships completed a circumnavigation of the globe. p. 444

Malintzin [Doña Marina] (mah•LINT•suhn) *c. 1500s* Aztec princess who was Cortés's interpreter and adviser. p. 457

Mandela, Nelson *1918–* South African leader of the African National Congress. He was imprisoned for 25 years for conspiracy to overthrow the South African government. In 1994 he became President of South Africa. p. 676

Mansa Musa *?–c. 1332* Emperor of Mali who is remembered for his pilgrimage to Mecca. During his rule Mali became known as a wealthy state and a center of learning. p. 369

Mao Zedong (MOW ZUH•DUNG) *1893–1976* Chinese soldier and statesperson. He was chairman of the Communist party and of the People's Republic of China. p. 626

Marie Antoinette (an•twuh•NET) *1755–1793* Wife of Louis XVI. Disliked for her extravagance and her influence on the king, she was tried for treason and executed. p. 503

Mark Antony *c. 82 B.C.–30 B.C.* Roman orator and general. He lost control of Roman lands when he was defeated by Octavian in 31 B.C. p. 261

Marquette, Jacques *1637–1675* French Jesuit missionary and explorer in North America. p. 458

Marx, Karl *1818–1883* German political philosopher. With Friedrich Engels, he wrote *The Communist Manifesto* and *Das Kapital*—books on social and political reform. p. 530

Mary *? B.C.–c. A.D. 63* Mother of Jesus. p. 273

Matsuo Basho (maht•SOO•oh BAH•shoh) *1644–1694* Japanese poet and master of haiku. p. 475

Mazzini, Giuseppe (maht•SEE•nee, joo•SEP•ay) *1805–1872* Italian patriot and founder of Young Italy, a group that worked to unite Italy under a republican form of government. p. 536

Meany, George *1894–1980* American labor leader. p. 649

Mehmed II (meh•MET) *1432–1481* Sultan of the Ottoman Empire who organized a well-run government and encouraged education. p. 476

Michelangelo Buonarroti (my•kuh•LAN•juh•loh bwaw•naw•RAW•tee) *1475–1564* Italian Renaissance sculptor, painter, architect, and poet. He is perhaps best remembered for his Sistine Chapel frescoes. p. 432

Mill, John Stuart *1806–1873* English philosopher and economist. He studied the conflict among social classes in Europe. p. 529

Minamoto Yoritomo (MEE•nah•MOH•toh YOH•rih•TOH•moh) *1147–1199* As shogun he created a system that ended in Japan's being divided by civil war. p. 341

Minos (MY•nuhs) *c. 2000s B.C.* According to legend, the ruler of ancient Crete during the years of its greatest success. p. 231

Mobutu Sese Seko (muh•BOO•too SAY•say SAY•koh) *1930–1997* President of the Republic of Zaire. He united Congo by allowing only one political party. p. 675

Mohammad Reza Pahlavi (rih•ZAH PA•luh•vee) *1919–1980* Shah, or emperor, of Iran from 1941 to 1979. p. 668

Moses *c. 1200s B.C.* Prophet and lawgiver who, according to the Bible, led the Israelites out of Egyptian captivity and received the Ten Commandments. p. 85

Motecuhzoma [Montezuma] (maw•tay•kwah•SOH•mah) *1466–1520* Ruler of the Aztecs; also known as Montezuma, when they were conquered by the Spanish. p. 455

Muhammad *c. 570–632* Prophet who brought the message of Islam to the world. p. 304

Murasaki Shikibu, Lady (MUR•ah•SAHK•ee SHEE•KEE•boo) *c. 978–1026* Japanese writer of *The Tale of Genji*. Her work is considered the first real novel in the world and is a classic of Japanese literature. p. 340

Mussolini, Benito (moo•suh•LEE•nee) *1883–1945* Italian dictator and Fascist prime minister of Italy. p. 587

Narmer *c. 2900s B.C.* Ruler who may have united the Two Lands of Egypt. p. 111

Nasser, Gamal Abdel *1918–1970* Egyptian soldier, politician, and president of Egypt during the 1950s. p. 664

Nefertiti (nef•er•TEET•ee) *c. 1300s B.C.* Wife of Akhenaton. p. 117

Nehru, Jawaharlal (NAIR•oo, juh•WAH•her•lahl) *1889–1964* Indian political leader and first prime minister of independent India. His work with Mohandas Gandhi helped bring about India's freedom. p. 656

Netanyahu, Benjamin (neh•tahn•YAH•hoo) *1947–* Israeli prime minister elected after the assassination of Yitzhak Rabin. p. 667

Newton, Isaac *1642–1727* British physicist and mathematician who explained the theory of gravity and used the scientific method. p. 434

Nicholas II *1868–1918* Russian czar when the Russian Revolution began. p. 574

Nixon, Richard *1913–1994* Thirty-seventh President of the United States. p. 649

Nkrumah, Kwame (en•KROO•muh, KWAH•mee) *1909–1972* First president of the Ghana republic. He was the leader in liberating the Gold Coast in Africa from British rule. p. 673

Nur Jahan (NOOR juh•HAHN) *?–c. 1645* Empress during the rule of Jahangir, she ruled the Mogul Empire on her husband's behalf. p. 480

Octavian (ahk•TAY•vee•uhn) *63 B.C.–A.D. 14* Julius Caesar's grandnephew, later known as Augustus. By defeating Mark Antony, he gained rule of all Roman lands. He was Rome's first true emperor. p. 261

Omar ibn Abi Rabi'a *644–c. 712* Muslim whose poetry is considered the greatest of early Arabic literature. p. 306

Owen, Robert *1771–1858* Welsh founder of a utopian community in Indiana during the late 1820s. p. 530

Pachacuti (pah•chah•KOO•tee) *?–1471* Inca ruler whose empire extended from Peru to Ecuador. p. 345

Paul *c. 5 B.C.–c. A.D. 62* Born a Jew, he converted to Christianity and became an apostle. He founded new churches and wrote many epistles, or letters, about Jesus to church members. p. 275

Pedro *1798–1834* Portuguese prince and emperor of Brazil who peacefully gained independence for Brazil from Portugal in 1825. p. 511

Peres, Shimon (PAIR•EZ, shee•MOHN) *1923–* Israeli prime minister; he was awarded the Nobel Peace Prize in 1994 while foreign minister of Israel. p. 667

Pericles (PAIR•uh•kleez) *c. 495 B.C.–429 B.C.* Leader who ruled Athens during its Golden Age. p. 241

Perry, Matthew *1794–1858* American naval officer who persuaded Japan to open its ports for trade with the United States and other countries. p. 538

Peter the Great *1672–1725* Russian czar from 1682 to 1725 who helped place Russia among the great European powers. p. 574

Philip II *382 B.C.–336 B.C.* King of Macedonia and father of Alexander the Great. A military genius, he controlled most of the Greek peninsula by 338 B.C. p. 247

Piye (PEE•yeh) *c. 751 B.C.–716 B.C.* King of Kush. and son of Kashta. He conquered Lower Egypt. Also known as Piankhi. p. 127

Pilate, Pontius *? B.C.–c. A.D. 36* Roman governor of Judaea. He was the judge at Jesus' trial and condemned him to death by crucifixion. p. 274

Pinochet, Augusto (pee•noh•CHET) *1915–* Chilean general and dictator. He seized control of the Chilean government from Allende and held control until 1990, when a freely elected government took charge. p. 641

Pizarro, Francisco (pee•ZAR•oh, fran•SIS•koh) *c. 1475–1541* Spanish conqueror of Peru. p. 455

Plato *c. 428 B.C.–c. 348 B.C.* Greek philosopher, student of Socrates and teacher of Aristotle. p. 244

Polo, Marco *1254–1324* Venetian traveler who was among the first European traders to visit China and record his experiences. p. 334

Pompey *106 B.C.–48 B.C.* Roman general and statesperson who became consul after Sulla. p. 260

Rabin, Yitzhak (rah•BEEN) *1922–1995* Prime minister of Israel who was assassinated. He signed a peace agreement with Palestinian leader Yasir Arafat. p. 667

Raleigh, Walter *1554–1618* English navigator, historian, and poet. In the service of Elizabeth I, he led many voyages of exploration. p. 444

Rasputin, Grigori (ras•PYOOT•uhn) *1872–1916* Russian peasant monk who greatly influenced the Czarina Alexandra. He was killed in 1916 by Russian nobles. p. 575

Reagan, Ronald *1911–* Fortieth President of the United States. p. 649

Richard III *1452–1485* Defeated by Henry Tudor, who then became king. His niece married Henry Tudor, thereby strengthening Henry's claim to the throne. p. 436

Roosevelt, Franklin D. *1882–1945* Twenty-sixth President of the United States. p. 581

Rousseau, Jean-Jacques (roo•SOH, ZHAHN•ZHAK) *1712–1778* French author and philosopher who was an important thinker during the time of the Enlightenment. p. 500

Roxelana (rahk•suh•LAHN•uh) *c. 1600s* Wife and adviser of Süleyman, who led the Ottoman Empire. p. 478

Sadat, Anwar as- (suh•DAT) *1918–1981* Egyptian soldier, statesperson, and president of Egypt after Nasser's death; signer of the Camp David peace agreement. p. 665

Samori Touré *c. 1830–1900* West African ruler who held off French invaders for 15 years before being captured. He died in exile. p. 544

Samudra Gupta (suh•MUH•druh) *c. 300* Son of Chandragupta I of India's Maurya dynasty. He extended the empire. p. 205

San Martín, José de (sahn mar•TEEN) *1778–1850* Argentinian soldier and statesperson; led the fight for independence from Spanish rule in southern South America. p. 510

Sarah *c. 2000s B.C.* Abraham's wife. p. 85

Sargon *c. 2334 B.C.–2279 B.C.* Warrior who founded the Akkadian Empire and so became the first ruler of an empire in the Fertile Crescent. p. 80

Saul *c. 1000s B.C.* First king of Israel. p. 86

Scipio (SIH•pee•oh) *c. 237 B.C.–183 B.C.* Roman general who defeated Hannibal of Carthage. p. 258

Shabaka (SHA•buh•kuh) *?–695 B.C.* Piye's brother and the pharaoh who firmly established the Kushite dynasty. p. 127

Shah Jahan (SHAH juh•HAHN) *1592–1666* During his reign Mogul power reached its highest point. He constructed the Taj Mahal, a beautiful tomb built in memory of his wife. p. 480

Shakespeare, William *1564–1616* British dramatist and poet. Considered among the greatest writers of all time. p. 433

Shi Huangdi (SHEE HWAHNG•DEE) *c. 259 B.C.–210 B.C.* Ruler of the Qin dynasty and unifier of China. p. 177

Sima Qian (SOO•MAH CHIH•YIN) *c. 100s B.C.* Scholar who recorded China's history during the Han dynasty. p. 184

Sinan (suh•NAHN) *1489–1588* Considered the greatest Ottoman architect. His ideas influenced nearly all later Turkish architecture. p. 478

Smith, Adam *1723–1790* Scottish economist and author. p. 527

Socrates (SAHK•ruh•teez) *c. 470 B.C.–c. 399 B.C.* Greek philosopher who taught by asking questions. p. 244

Solomon *c. 900s B.C.* David's son and king of Israel under whose rule Israel rose to the height of its greatness. p. 86

Solon *c. 630 B.C.–c. 560 B.C.* Poet and statesperson who helped bring democracy to Athens, Greece. p. 237

Sophocles (SAH•fuh•kleez) *c. 496 B.C.–c. 406 B.C.* Ancient Greek writer of tragedies, or serious plays. p. 243

Stalin, Joseph (STAH•luhn) *1879–1953* Soviet dictator after Lenin's death. During his rule the Soviet Union became a totalitarian state and a world power. p. 577

Süleyman I (SOO•lay•mahn) *c. 1494–1566* Sultan whose reign was considered a high point of the Ottoman Empire. He made Istanbul into a great capital and encouraged arts and sciences. p. 477

Sulla, Lucius *138 B.C.–78 B.C.* Roman general, politician, and dictator of Rome for three years. p. 260

Sun Yat-sen (SUN YAHT•SEN) *1866–1925* Chinese statesperson and revolutionary leader of the Guomindang, or People's Nationalist party. p. 625

Sundiata (sun•JAHT•ah) *?–1255* Founder and ruler of the ancient Mali Empire. p. 369

Theodora *c. 500–548* Empress and wife of Justinian I of the Byzantine Empire. Her influence helped women gain rights. p. 299

Thucydides (thoo•SIH•duh•deez) *471 B.C.–c. 400 B.C.* Greek teacher who is considered the greatest historian of ancient times. p. 237

Thutmose I *c. 1500s B.C.* Pharaoh who expanded Egypt's rule far into Nubia. p. 117

Thutmose II *c. 1500s B.C.* Son of Thutmose I. He continued to expand Egypt's land. p. 117

Thutmose III *c. 1500s B.C.* Son of Thutmose II. He continued Egypt's conquests after Pharaoh Hatshepsut. During his rule the Egyptian Empire grew to its largest size and was at its wealthiest. p. 117

Tokugawa Ieyasu (toh•ku•GAH•wah ee•uh•YAH•soo) *1543–1616* Japanese ruler who discouraged the Japanese from having contact with the West. p. 474

Tomyris (tuh•MY•ruhs) *c. 600s B.C.* Queen whose land was invaded by Cyrus the Great of Persia. Cyrus was killed during the battle with her armies. p. 208

Toussaint-Louverture (TOO•san LOO•vair•tyoor) *c. 1743–1803* Haitian general and liberator who established a free and independent country of Haiti. p. 509

Truman, Harry S. *1884–1972* Thirty-third President of the United States. p. 602

Tudor, Henry *1457–1509* Defeated Richard III at the Battle of Bosworth. He became King Henry VII and the first of the house of Tudor. p. 436

Tull, Jethro *1674–1741* English farmer who invented a machine drill for sowing seeds. p. 515

Tupac Amarú (too•PAHK ahm•ar•OO) *c. 1742–1781* Descendant of the last Inca ruler, he led an uprising in Peru to try to gain rights for the Inca people. p. 509

Tutankhamen (too•tahng•KAH•muhn) *c. 1370 B.C.–1352 B.C.* During his brief reign as pharaoh, his ministers restored the old religion of Egypt. He was buried in a solid-gold coffin. p. 118

Vargas, Getúlio (VAR•guhs, zheh•TOO•lyoo) *1883–1954* Brazilian politician and dictator. He encouraged Brazilians to expand into other industries besides coffee. p. 642

Vespucci, Amerigo (veh•SPOO•chee, uh•MAIR•ih•goh) *1454–1512* Italian navigator who explored the coast of what is now Brazil. The Americas are named after him. p. 444

Victor Emmanuel *1820–1878* King of Piedmont-Sardinia and first king of Italy. p. 537

Victoria *1819–1901* Queen of England who became empress of India after the Great Mutiny. p. 546

Virgil (VER•juhl) *70 B.C.–19 B.C.* Roman poet who wrote the epic *Aeneid,* which is about the founding of Rome. p. 265

Voltaire (vohl•TAIR) *1694–1778* French writer who was an important thinker during the Enlightenment. p. 500

Walesa, Lech (vah•LEHN•sah) *1943–* Leader of a workers' group called Solidarity, in Poland during the 1980s. He was elected president in Poland's first free election, in 1990. p. 685

Washington, George *1732–1799* Commander-in-chief of the Continental Army during the Revolutionary War and first President of the United States. p. 500

Watt, James *1736–1819* Scottish engineer and inventor who made many improvements to the steam engine. p. 516

Wilhelm I *1797–1888* King of Prussia and German emperor. p. 537

Wilson, Woodrow *1856–1924* Twenty-eighth President of the United States. p. 567

Wu *c. 1100s B.C.* Founder of the Zhou dynasty in China. p. 171

Wu Di (WOO DEE) *156 B.C.–87 B.C.* Han ruler who established a civil service administration to run the daily business of government in China. p. 183

Xerxes (ZERK•seez) *c. 519 B.C.–c. 465 B.C.* King of Persia and son of Darius I. p. 240

Xilingshi (SEE•LING•SHIR) *c. 2700s B.C.* Chinese ruler's wife who, according to a legend, discovered silk in 2700 B.C. p. 144

Yeltsin, Boris (YELT•suhn) *1931–* Russian political leader and first popularly elected president in Russia. p. 687

Yong Le (YUHNG LEH) *1360–1424* Hong Wu's son. The power of China's Ming dynasty reached its highest point during his reign. p. 471

You (YOO) *c. 1100s B.C.* Zhou dynasty king who reigned during the Warring Kingdoms Period. p. 173

Yu the Great *c. 2000s B.C.* King of the Huang He Valley in about 2000 B.C. According to legend, his family started the Xia dynasty. p. 140

Zarathustra (zar•uh•THOOS•trah) *c. 628 B.C.–c. 551 B.C.* Persian religious leader who founded a religion now known as Zoroastrianism. Its basic belief is that there are two gods—one good and one evil. p. 211

Zhang Qian (JAHNG CHIH•yin) *c. 100s B.C.* Ancient Chinese ambassador who introduced the outside world to the resources of China. p. 186

Zheng He (JUHNG HUH) *c. 1371–?* Chinese admiral and diplomat. During his travels he visited many ports and encouraged trade with China. p. 392

Zoser *c. 2600s B.C.* King of Egypt in the twenty-seventh century B.C. p. 114

Zuhri, al- (al•ZUKH•ree) *c. 1000s* Muslim scholar who wrote about Ghana's rise to power. p. 367

Gazetteer

The Gazetteer is a geographical dictionary that will help you locate places discussed in this book. The page number tells where each place appears on a map.

Aachen (AHK•uhn) A city near the western border of central Germany, former capital and cultural center of Charlemagne's empire. (51°N, 6°E) p. 310

Acre (AH•kruh) A city located on the west coast of Israel. (33°N, 35°E) p. 378

Adirondack Mountains A mountain group in northeastern New York. p. 459

Adriatic Sea An extension of the Mediterranean Sea; located east of Italy and west of the Balkan Peninsula. p. 230

Aegean Sea (ih•JEE•uhn) An arm of the Mediterranean Sea between Asia Minor and Greece. p. 223

Aegina (ih•JY•nuh) An ancient Greek city-state; a Greek island in the southwestern Aegean Sea. p. 235

Afghanistan A country in central Asia; located between Pakistan and Iran. p. 136

Africa One of the world's seven continents. p. 44

Agra The capital of the historic Mogul Empire located in northern central India on the Yamuna River. (27°N, 78°E) p. 479

Akhetaton [el-Amarna] The ancient Egyptian capital built by Akhenaton; located on the Nile River in central Egypt. (28°N, 31°E) p. 117

Albania A European country located on the Balkan Peninsula, on the Adriatic Sea. p. 567

Alberta A province of Canada; located between British Columbia and Saskatchewan. p. 647

Aleutian Islands A chain of volcanic islands extending southwest from the Alaska Peninsula; they separate the Bering Sea from the Pacific Ocean. p. 590

Alexandria (a•lig•ZAN•dree•uh) A port on the Mediterranean Sea; located on the northern coast of Egypt on the Nile delta; also the name of many other cities founded by Alexander the Great. (31°N, 30°E) p. 223

Algeria A country in northern Africa; located on the coast of the Mediterranean Sea. p. 493

Algiers The capital of Algeria; located in northern central Algeria on the Bay of Algiers. (37°N, 3°E) p. 478

Allegheny River A river in the northeastern United States; joins with the Monongahela at Pittsburgh, Pennsylvania. p. 459

Alps The largest group of mountains in Europe; located in France, Switzerland, Italy, Austria, Slovenia, Bosnia and Herzegovina, Yugoslavia, Albania, and Croatia. p. 44

Alsace-Lorraine An historic region in northeastern France. p. 538

Altai Mountains (al•TY) A mountain system in Asia where Russia, China, and Mongolia meet. p. 141

Al-Ubaid (oo•BAYD) An ancient settlement; located in present-day southeastern Iraq. (31°N, 46°E) p. 58

Amazon River The largest river in the world; flows across northern Brazil in South America and into the Atlantic Ocean. p. 102

Amman The capital of Jordan; located northeast of the Dead Sea. (32°N, 36°E) p. 665

Amsterdam The capital and the largest city of the Netherlands; located on the IJ River in the western central Netherlands. (52°N, 5°E) p. 504

Amur River A river in northeastern Asia; forms part of the border between Russia and China. p. 333

An Loc A city in southern Vietnam. (11°N, 106°E) p. 606

Andaman Sea A body of water in southeastern Asia; forms the eastern part of the Bay of Bengal. p. 147

Andes Mountains A mountain system in South America, extending along the western coast from Panama to Tierra del Fuego. p. 290

Angola A former part of the historic African kingdom of Kongo and a colony of Portugal; present-day country in southern Africa on the Atlantic coast. (12°S, 18°E) p. 493

Antarctica One of the world's seven continents. p. 52

Antioch A center of early Christianity; located in western Asia Minor near the town of Yalvac, Turkey. (36°N, 36°E) p. 223

Antwerp An agricultural and manufacturing province; located in northern Belgium. (51°N, 4°E) p. 520

Anyang (AHN•YAHNG) The last capital of the Shang dynasty of ancient China; located in present-day east central China. (36°N, 114°E) p. 142

Apennines (A•puh•nynz) A mountain range; runs north and south through the center of Italy. p. 222

Arabia The historic name for the lands now known as the Arabian Peninsula, the Sinai Peninsula, Syria, and Mesopotamia. p. 89

Arabian Peninsula A peninsula bordered by the Red Sea, the Persian Gulf, and the Arabian Sea in southwestern Asia; location of the countries of Saudi Arabia, Yemen, Oman, the United Arab Emirates, Qatar, and Kuwait. p. 89

Arabian Sea The sea located west of India and east of the Arabian Peninsula; forms the southern border of southwestern Asia. p. 136

Aragon (AIR•ah•gohn) A historic region and kingdom in northeastern Spain. p. 436

Aral Sea (AIR•uhl) A large inland body of water located in the countries of Kazakhstan and Uzbekistan in central Asia. p. 192

Archangel´sk A Russian port city in Europe. (65°N, 41°E) p. 577

Arctic Ocean One of the four oceans of the world. p. 52

Argentina A South American country on the Atlantic Coast. p. 509

Argos An ancient Greek city-state; a present-day town in the northeastern Peloponnesus. (38°N, 23°E) p. 235

Armenia A country in western Asia. p. 378

Asia One of the world's seven continents. p. 45

Asia Minor A peninsula at the western end of Asia; located between the Black Sea and the Mediterranean Sea; now occupied by Turkey. p. 74

Assisi A town in central Italy; home of St. Francis of Assisi during the Middle Ages. (43°N, 13°E) p. 430

Assur (AH•sur) [also called Assyria] An ancient Mesopotamian city on the Tigris River; included lands from the Mediterranean coast to Iraq. (36°N, 43°E) p. 82

Assyria (uh•SIR•ee•uh) An ancient empire in south-western Asia. p. 82

Asturias (uh•STOOR•ee•uhs) An historic region and former kingdom in northwestern Spain. p. 436

Aswan Ancient trade center; present-day city located in southeastern Egypt on the Nile River, near Lake Nasser and the Aswan Dam. (24°N, 33°E) p. A6

Athens An ancient Greece city-state; the capital of present-day Greece; located near the southeastern coast of Greece. (38°N, 24°E) p. 223

Atlantic Ocean One of the world's four oceans. p. 44

Atlas Mountains A mountain system in northern Africa. p. 44

Attica (AT•ih•kuh) An ancient region in the southeastern part of the Greek mainland; home of the ancient Greek city-state of Athens. p. 235

Australia One of the world's seven continents; a present-day country filling the continent of Australia. p. 52

Austria A country in central Europe. p. 439

Azerbaijan (a•zer•by•JAHN) A country in southeastern Europe; located west of the Caspian Sea; formerly part of the Soviet Union. p. 621

Babylon The capital of ancient Babylonia; located on the Euphrates River in central Iraq. (33°N, 44°E) p. 82

Babylonia (ba•buh•LOH•nyuh) An ancient kingdom in the lower Tigris-Euphrates river valley in southwestern Asia. p. 82

Bactria An ancient country of southwestern Asia. p. 209

Baghdad The capital of Iraq; located on both sides of the Tigris River in the eastern part of the country. (33°N, 44°E) p. 305

Baja California Norte The northern part of a peninsula extending between the Pacific Ocean and the Gulf of California. p. 648

Baja California Sur The southern part of a peninsula extending between the Pacific Ocean and the Gulf of California. p. 648

Balearic Islands (ba•lee•AIR•ik) An island group in the western Mediterranean Sea; off the eastern coast of Spain; forms the Spanish province of Baleares. p. 310

Balkan Peninsula A peninsula extending from mainland Europe into the Mediterranean Sea; occupied by Greece, Albania, Slovenia, Croatia, Bosnia and Herzegovina, Yugoslavia, Romania, Bulgaria, and Turkey. p. 230

Baltic Sea The sea located on the southeastern side of the Scandinavian Peninsula. p. 298

Bangalore (BANG•uh•lohr) A city in southern India. (13°N, 78°E) p. 660

Bangkok The capital of Thailand; located on the southern end of the Chao Phraya River on the Gulf of Thailand. (14°N, 100°E) p. 147

Bangladesh (bahn•gluh•DESH) A country in southern Asia on the coast of the Bay of Bengal. p. 136

Barcelona A province and city of Spain; located southeast of Madrid. (41°N, 2°E) p. 520

Barents Sea A sea comprising the part of the Arctic Ocean between Spitsbergen and Novaya Zemlya. p. 577

Bataan A peninsula located in the Philippines on Manila Bay. p. 590

Bavaria A historic and modern state in southeastern Germany. p. 403

Bay of Bengal An inlet of the Indian Ocean that runs alongside eastern India. p. 45

Beersheba (bir•SHEE•buh) A city in southern Israel; a part of the Negev region; the ancient town in which Abraham settled. (31°N, 35°E) p. 86

Beijing (BAY•JING) The capital of China; located in northeastern China; present-day name for Kublai Khan's historic capital of Khanbalik. (40°N, 116°E) p. 165

Belarus (byeh•luh•ROOS) A country in Asia; located north of Ukraine, west of Russia, and east of Poland; formerly part of the Soviet Union. p. 686

Belgium A country in Europe; located on the coast of the North Sea. p. 538

Belgrade The capital of Serbia; located at the junction of the Sava and Danube rivers. (45°N, 21°E) p. 478

Belize (buh•LEEZ) A country in Central America. p. 151

Benin (buh•NIN) A former kingdom of western Africa; present-day country in Africa. (10°N, 2°E) p. 450

Berlin The capital of Germany; located in the northeastern part of Germany. (53°N, 12°E) p. 592

Bern The capital of Switzerland. (47°N, 7°E) p. 570

Bethlehem An ancient and present-day city in southwestern Asia; birthplace of Jesus, according to the Bible. (32°N, 35°E) p. 665

Bhutan (boo•TAN) A country in Asia; located south of China and north of India. p. 136

Birmingham A city located northwest of London, England. (52°N, 2°W) p. 521

Black Sea A sea between Europe and Asia; surrounded by Bulgaria, Romania, Moldova, Ukraine, Russia, Georgia, and Turkey. p. 44

Bohemia A historic region and kingdom in central Europe; located in present-day Czech Republic. p. 439

Bolan Pass A mountain pass located in Pakistan. (30°N, 67°E) p. 192

Bolivia A country in South America. p. 461

Bologna A historic and present-day city in northern central Italy. (45°N, 11°E) p. 430

Bombay A city on the western coast of central India, also known as Mumbai. (19°N, 73°E) p. 479

Bordeaux (bawr•DOH) A city in southwestern France on the Garonne River. (45°N, 1°W) p. 403

Borneo An island on the Malay Archipelago. (1°N, 115°E) p. 378

Bosnia and Herzegovina (BAHZ•nee•uh hairt•suh•goh•VEE•nuh) A country in Europe; formerly part of Yugoslavia. p. 567

Botswana A country in southern Africa. p. 675

Brahmaputra River A river in southern Asia; flows through China, India, and Bangladesh into the Bay of Bengal. p. 479

Brazil A country in eastern South America. p. 461

Bristol A city on the Avon River, in southwestern England. (51°N, 3°W) p. 520

British Honduras The colonial name of Belize, a Central American country on the Caribbean Sea. p. 509

British Isles The islands of Ireland and Great Britain; located off the northwestern coast of mainland Europe. p. 298

British Somaliland The now independent country of Somalia in northeastern Africa; once controlled by Italy and the British Empire. p. 544

Brittany A region in northwestern France. p. 403

Bruges (BROOZH) A historic city near the North Sea, in northwestern Belgium. (51°N, 3°E) p. 360

Brunei A country in southeastern Asia. p. 621

Brunswick A former German province; part of the German state of Lower Saxony. p. 538

Brussels The capital city of Belgium in Europe. (51°N, 4°E) p. 520

Bucharest The capital city of Romania. (44°N, 26°E) p. 521

Budapest The capital city of Hungary; includes the former towns of Buda and Pest. (47°N, 19°E) p. 521

Buenos Aires (BWAY•nohs EYE•rays) A port city and capital of Argentina, in South America. (34°S, 58°W) p. 492

Bulgaria A country in southeastern Europe; located on the Balkan Peninsula. p. 567

Burkina Faso A country in western Africa. p. 675

Burma [Myanmar] A country on the Indochina peninsula in southeastern Asia. p. 136

Burundi A country in central Africa. p. 621

Byzantium (buh•ZAN•tee•uhm) See Constantinople. p. 223

Cádiz (KAYD•iz) A port in southwestern Spain on the Gulf of Cádiz, an inlet of the Atlantic Ocean. p. 436

Cahokia (kuh•HOH•kee•uh) An ancient settlement of the Mound Builders of the Mississippian culture; located near present-day East St. Louis, Illinois. p. 290

Cairo The capital of Egypt; located in northeastern Egypt on the Nile River. (30°N, 31°E) p. 115

Calcutta A port in northeastern India, near the Bay of Bengal. (23°N, 88°E) p. 479

Calicut A city in southwestern India, on the coast of the Arabian Sea. p. 423

Cambodia A country in southeastern Asia; located on the Indochina Peninsula. p. 147

Cameroon (ka•muh•ROON) A former French and British colony; now an independent country in western Africa. p. 544

Can Tho A town in southern Vietnam; located on the Mekong delta. (10°N, 106°E) p. 606

Canaan An ancient region in southwestern Asia that is located between the Jordan River and the Mediterranean Sea. p. 90

Canada A country in the northern part of North America. p. 461

Canary Islands An island group in the Atlantic Ocean; located off the northwestern coast of Africa. p. 544

Cape Horn The southernmost point of South America. p. 639

Cape of Good Hope The southernmost point of Africa. p. 680

Cape Town A seaport city of Cape Province and the capital of the country of South Africa. (34°S, 18°E) p. 493

Cape Verde An island country in the Atlantic Ocean, located off the coast of western Africa. (17°N, 25°W) p. 675

Caracas (kah•RAH•kahs) The capital city of Venezuela, South America; located near the coast of the Caribbean Sea. (11°N, 67°W) p. 573

Caribbean Sea The sea bordered by Central America, South America, and the West Indies. p. 151

Cartagena (kar•tah•HEN•nah) An ancient and present-day city in southeastern Spain; also called New Carthage. (38°N, 1°W) p. 436

Carthage (KAR•thij) An ancient Phoenician city-state; located on the northern coast of present-day Tunisia. (37°N, 10°E) p. 222

Caspian Sea A salt lake between Europe and Asia, east of the Black Sea. p. 44

Castile (ka•STEEL) A region and ancient kingdom of central Spain. p. 436

Çatal Hüyük (CHA•tahl HOO•yook) One of the earliest human agricultural settlements discovered; dating from c. 7000 B.C. to 5600 B.C.; located in central Turkey. (38°N, 33°E) p. 58

Caucasus Mountains (KAW•kuh•suhs) A mountain range between the Black and Caspian seas; borders Russia, Georgia, and Azerbaijan. p. 44

Celebes (SEL•uh•beez) An Indonesian island; located in southeastern Asia in the Malay Archipelago. (2°S, 120°E) p. 546

Central African Republic A country in central Africa. p. 621

Ceylon See Sri Lanka. p. 378

Chad A country in northern Africa. p. 621

Chang Jiang (CHAHNG JYAHNG) A river in eastern China; flows from the Plateau of Tibet to the East China Sea. p. 45

Chang'an (CHAHNG•AHN) An ancient capital of the Han dynasty of China; now known as Xian, or Sian; located in central China on the Wei River. (34°N, 109°E) p. 165

Chao Phraya (CHOW PRY•uh) A river in Thailand. p. 147

Chapultepec (chuh•POOL•tah•pek) A Mexican fort; located southwest of Mexico City. (19°N, 99°W) p. 349

Chatham Islands An island group; located in the southern Pacific Ocean, east of New Zealand. p. 410

Chattahoochee River A river in the United States that begins in northeastern Georgia and flows southwest and south along the Alabama-Georgia border into Lake Seminole. p. 293

Chiapas (chee•AH•pahs) A Mexican state; located in southeastern Mexico. p. 648

Chile (CHEE•lay) A country on the southwestern coast of South America. p. 461

China An ancient empire and present-day country in eastern Asia; currently the world's most heavily populated country. p. 141

Cologne (kah•LOHN) A city in northwestern Germany on the Rhine River. (51°N, 7°E) p. 360

Colombia A country in northwestern South America. p. 461

Constantinople (kahn•stan•tuh•OH•puhl) Formerly the ancient city of Byzantium; rebuilt, renamed, and made the capital of the Byzantine Empire by Constantine I in A.D. 330; now known as Istanbul, Turkey. (41°N, 29°E) p. 378

Copenhagen The capital city and a port of Denmark. (56°N, 13°E) p. 520

Coral Sea A sea located north of Queensland, Australia, and south of Papua New Guinea. p. 590

Córdoba The historic capital of Andalusia; located in southern Spain on the Guadalquivir River. (38°N, 5°W) p. 307

Corinth An ancient city-state and a present-day city; located on the isthmus between the Peloponnesus and the Greek mainland. (38°N, 23°E) p. 235

Corsica A French island in the Mediterranean Sea; located west of Italy. (42°N, 9°E) p. 310

Costa Rica A country in Central America; located west of Panama; bordered by the Caribbean Sea and Pacific Ocean. p. 461

Côte d'Ivoire (koht dee•VWAHR) A country in western Africa; the Ivory Coast. p. 675

Crete A large Greek island; located southeast of the Balkan Peninsula; separates the Mediterranean and Aegean seas. p. 223

Croatia (kroh•AY•shuh) A country in southeastern Europe; part of the former Yugoslavia. p. 567

Cuba An island country; located south of the United States in the Greater Antilles of the West Indies. p. 422

Cuzco (KOO•skoh) The capital of the ancient Inca Empire and a present-day city in southern Peru. (14°S, 72°W) p. 290

Cyprus An island country in the eastern Mediterranean Sea. p. 74

Cyrene (sy•REE•nee) An ancient city in northern Africa; located in Libya on the Mediterranean Sea. (33°N, 22°E) p. 223

Czech Republic (CHEK) A country in central Europe; formerly part of Czechoslovakia. p. 621

Czechoslovakia (che•kuh•sloh•VAH•kee•uh) A former country in central Europe; where the Czech Republic and Slovakia are today. p. 591

Dahomey (duh•HOH•mee) The early name for the land that today makes up the country of Benin in Africa. p. 450

Damascus (duh•MAS•kuhs) The capital of Syria, in southwestern Asia. (33°N, 36°E) p. 74

Danube River (DAN•yoob) A river in central Europe; flows from southwestern Germany to the Black Sea. p. 44

Danzig A port in central northern Poland, on the Gulf of Gdansk, an inlet of the Baltic Sea; now known as Gdansk. (54°N, 19°E) p. 360

Dead Sea A salt lake in Israel and Jordan; the world's lowest place at 1,302 feet (397 m) below sea level. p. 86

Deccan Plateau (DEH•kuhn) A triangle-shaped plateau in central India, between the Western and Eastern Ghats. p. 192

Delhi (DEH•lee) A city in northern India. (29°N, 77°E) p. 165

Delphi (DEL•fy) A sacred place to the ancient Greeks; located in central Greece, near the Gulf of Corinth. (38°N, 23°E) p. 235

Denmark A country in central Europe; occupies the northern part of the Jutland Peninsula. p. 403

Djibouti (juh•BOO•tee) A country in eastern Africa. p. 621

Dnieper River (NEE•per) A river in eastern Europe; flows from west of Moscow, Russia, to the Black Sea. p. 403

Dresden A German industrial city and the capital of Dresden district; located southeast of Leipzig. (51°N, 14°E) p. 521

Dublin The capital of the Republic of Ireland; located on the River Liffey, near Dublin Bay. (53°N, 6°W) p. 403

Duero River (DWAIR•oh) A river on the Iberian Peninsula; begins in Spain, flows across Portugal and into the Atlantic Ocean. p. 436

Dunhuang A city in eastern Asia; located in western China. (40°N, 95°E) p. 384

Dutch East Indies A southeastern Asia republic; an archipelago extending from 95°E to 141°E. p. 493

East China Sea The part of the China Sea north of Taiwan. p. 45

Easter Island An island off the western coast of South America, in the Pacific Ocean. p. 410

Eastern Ghats (GAWTS) A chain of mountains in southeastern India. p. 136

Ecuador (EH•kwah•dohr) A country in northwestern South America; located on the Pacific coast. p. 461

Edessa (ih•DES•uh) The ancient capital of Macedonia and a present-day city in central Greece. (41°N, 22°E) p. 277

Edinburgh The capital of Scotland; located in southeastern Scotland, on the North Sea coast. (56°N, 3°W) p. 518

Edo The historic name for Tokyo, the capital of Japan; located on the coast of the island of Honshu, on Tokyo Bay. (36°N, 140°E) p. 474

Egypt An ancient land and present-day country in northern Africa, on the coast of the Mediterranean and Red seas. p. 160

El Salvador A Central American republic; located south of Guatemala, on the Pacific Ocean. p. 461

Elba An Italian island in the Tyrrhenian Sea off the northern coast of Italy. p. 430

Elbe River A river in northern Europe; flows from the Czech Republic, across Germany, and into the North Sea. p. 405

England One of the four divisions of the United Kingdom; occupies most of the southern part of Great Britain. p. 403

English Channel An extension and connection of the Atlantic Ocean and the North Sea; south of the British Isles and north of France. p. 518

Equatorial Guinea A country in western Africa. p. 621

Eridu (AIR•uh•doo) The earliest known Sumerian city; located in Mesopotamia on the Euphrates River in present-day southeastern Iraq. (31°N, 46°E) p. 58

Eritrea (air•ih•TREE•uh) A country on the Red Sea in northern Africa; located north of Ethiopia. p. 544

Eshnunna A locality in Iraq; located northeast of Baghdad. (33°N, 45°E) p. 98

Estonia A country in northeastern Europe; formerly part of the Soviet Union. p. 570

Ethiopia A country in northern Africa. p. 591

Etowah An ancient settlement of the Mound Builders of the Mississippian culture in what is now northwestern Georgia in the United States. (34°N, 85°W) p. 293

Euphrates River (yoo•FRAY•teez) A river that begins in Turkey, flows through Syria and Iraq, and empties into the Persian Gulf. p. 44

Europe One of the world's seven continents. p. 44

Ezion-geber (ee•zee•uhn•GEE•ber) An ancient town and present-day archaeological site; located near Aqaba, in southwestern Jordan. (29°N, 35°E) p. 90

Ferghana A city in northwestern China, near the border of Kyrgyzstan. (40°N, 70°E) p. 384

Fez A sacred Muslim city in northern Morocco, near the Middle Atlas Mountains. (34°N, 5°W) p. 370

Fiji An island country in Melanesia, Oceania, in the southern Pacific Ocean. p. 410

Finland A country in northern Europe; located north of Estonia and east of the Gulf of Bothnia and Sweden. p. 603

Florence A city on the Arno River in central Italy. (44°N, 11°E) p. 360

Formosa See Taiwan. p. 546

France A country in western Europe. p. 504

Frankfurt A city and district of Germany. p. 521

French Equatorial Africa The colonial name of former French territories in northern Africa: Chad, Ubangi-Shari, Gabon, and Middle Congo. p. 544

French Guiana An overseas department of France; located on the northern Atlantic coast of South America. p. 461

French Indochina The colonial name of former French territories in southeastern Asia; located where Cambodia, Laos, and Vietnam are now. p. 546

Gazetteer

Gabon A country in western Africa. p. 493

Ganges River (GAN•jeez) A holy river in India; flows from the Himalaya Mountains into the Bay of Bengal. p. 45

Gao (GOW) A trading center of the ancient Songhay Empire of West Africa; located on the Niger River in central Mali. (15°N, 4°W) p. 363

Gaul An ancient land that included most of the present-day countries of France and Belgium; once part of the Roman Empire. p. 222

Gaza (GAH•zuh) A city in southwestern Asia; located near the Mediterranean Sea. (32°N, 34°E) p. 86

Genoa A historic city-state trading center and present-day seaport on the Ligurian Sea, on the coast of northwestern Italy. (44°N, 9°E) p. 360

Georgia A country on the Black Sea in southeastern Europe; formerly part of the Soviet Union. p. 621

Germany A European country; located in northern central Europe. p. 538

Ghana (GAH•nuh) A country on the western coast of Africa; called the Gold Coast by Portuguese and Dutch colonizers. p. 621

Ghent Belgian city and capital of East Flanders province; located in northwestern Belgium. (51°N, 4°E) p. 520

Giza (GEE•zuh) An ancient and present-day city in northeastern Egypt; located on the Nile River, across from Cairo. (30°N, 31°E) p. 115

Glasgow A port near the Atlantic coast of southwestern Scotland. (56°N, 4°W) p. 518

Goa A state in India; located on the Malabar coast. (16°N, 74°E) p. 479

Gobi (Desert) A desert in eastern Asia; located in Mongolia and China. p. 141

Golan Heights A region in southwestern Asia under the control of Israel. (33°N, 36°E) p. 665

Gold Coast See Ghana. p. 544

Granada A country in the Sierra Nevada, in southern Spain. (37°N, 4°W) p. 277

Great Britain A western European kingdom; includes England, Scotland, and Wales. p. 591

Great Zimbabwe An ancient African settlement; located in what is present-day Zimbabwe. p. 393

Greece An ancient land and present-day country in Europe; located on the southern end of the Balkan Peninsula. p. 223

Greenland The largest island in the world; located off northeastern North America; a territory of Denmark. p. 372

Guadalajara (gwah•duh•luh•HAR•uh) The capital of Jalisco state; located in central Mexico. (21°N, 103°W) p. 648

Guadalcanal An island of the Solomon Islands in the western Pacific Ocean. p. 590

Guam An unincorporated United States territory; largest and southernmost of the Mariana Islands; located in the western Pacific Ocean. p. 590

Guangzhou (GWAHNG•JOH) A Chinese port city located on the Zhu River in southeastern China; formerly Canton. (23°N, 113°E) p. 165

Guatemala A country in Central America; former part of the region controlled by the Mayas and later a colony of Spain. p. 151

Guinea (GIH•nee) A country in western Africa. p. 561

Guinea-Bissau (GIH•nee bih•SOW) A former Portuguese province; now an independent country in western Africa. p. 621

Gulf of Aqaba (AH•kah•buh) An inlet of the Red Sea; located between Saudi Arabia and the Sinai Peninsula. p. 90

Gulf of Bothnia An inlet of the Baltic Sea, between Sweden and Finland. p. 405

Gulf of Guinea A gulf located on the western coast of Africa. p. 363

Gulf of Mexico A gulf located south of the United States, east of Mexico, and west of Cuba. p. 151

Gulf of Suez An inlet of the Red Sea, between Egypt and the Sinai Peninsula. p. 90

Gulf of Thailand An inlet of the South China Sea; located between Malaysia and Thailand. p. 147

Gulf of Tonkin An inlet of the South China Sea; located between Vietnam and China. p. 147

Guyana (gy•AH•nuh) A country in the northern part of South America. p. 461

Hainan An island in the South China Sea; located in southeastern China. (19°N, 110°E) p. 606

Haiti A country in the Caribbean, southeast of Cuba. p. 461

Hamburg A city in northern Germany; located near the Elbe River and the North Sea. (54°N, 10°E) p. 360

Hangzhou (HAHNG•JOH) An ancient and present-day city located on the eastern coast of central China. (30°N, 120°E) p. 165

Hanoi (ha•NOY) The capital of Vietnam; located on the northern Red River. (21°N, 106°E) p. 147

Hanover A former German state; now part of the German state of Lower Saxony; also spelled Hannover. p. 538

Hao (HOW) The ancient Zhou dynasty capital city; located near the Chang Jiang in eastern present-day China. p. 173

Harappa (huh•RA•puh) An ancient center of Indus civilization; located in the Indus Valley, in present-day Pakistan. (31°N, 71°E) p. 137

Harbin The capital of Heilungkiang province; located in northeastern China. p. 218

Gazetteer

Hawaii A state of the United States; the Hawaiian Islands are a chain of volcanic and coral islands in the northern central Pacific Ocean. p. 410

Hebron (HEE•bruhn) An ancient city of Judaea; located southwest of Jerusalem on the West Bank. (32°N, 35°E) p. 86

Helsinki The capital city and port of Finland, in Europe. (60°N, 25°E) p. 570

Heracleopolis Magna (hair•uh•klee•AHP•uh•luhs) The capital of the ninth and tenth dynasties of ancient Egypt; located on the Nile River, in central Egypt. (41°N, 31°E) p. 117

Herat The present-day name of an ancient city located in what is today northwestern Afghanistan. (34°N, 62°E) p. 384

Himalayas (hih•muh•LAY•uhz) A mountain system on the northern edge of southern Asia; runs through Nepal, Bhutan, southern Tibet, and northern India. p. 45

Hindu Kush A mountain system that extends southwest from the Pamirs in eastern Tajikistan, through northwestern Afghanistan. p. 136

Hiroshima (hir•uh•SHEE•muh) An industrial city located on the island of Honshu, Japan. (34°N, 133°E) p. 590

Hispaniola An island in the Greater Antilles of the West Indies in the Caribbean; occupied by the countries of Haiti and the Dominican Republic. p. 422

Hokkaido (hah•KYD•oh) The northernmost of the four main islands of Japan. p. 474

Honduras A country in Central America. p. 461

Hong Kong A large city in southeastern China; formerly a British colony. (22°N, 114°E) p. 635

Honshu The largest of the four main islands of Japan. p. 474

Huang He (HWAHNG HUH) A river in China that flows east from the Plateau of Tibet. p. 45

Hudson Bay A large bay located in northern Canada; borders the Northwest Territories, Manitoba, Ontario, and Quebec. p. 460

Hudson River A river in the northeastern United States; begins in upper New York and flows into the Atlantic Ocean. p. 459

Hungary A country in central Europe. p. 439

Hyderabad (HY•duh•ruh•bad) A city in central India. p. 660

Iberian Peninsula A peninsula forming southwestern Europe; extends into the Atlantic Ocean and the Mediterranean Sea; occupied by the countries of Portugal and Spain. p. 230

Iceland A European island country in the northern Atlantic Ocean; located southeast of Greenland. p. 403

Illinois River Located in Arkansas and Oklahoma; flows west, joins the Arkansas River in Oklahoma. p. 293

India A country in southern Asia; occupies much of a large peninsula extending from central Asia into the Indian Ocean; the name given to the ancient land that is present-day Pakistan and India. p. 136

Indian Ocean One of the world's oceans. p. 45

Indonesia A country of islands in southeastern Asia. p. 361

Indus River A river in southern Asia; flows from Tibet, through northern India and Pakistan, and into the Arabian Sea. p. 45

Ionian Sea The sea located east of Italy and west of Greece. p. 230

Iran A country in southwestern Asia; formerly known as Persia; located on the Persian Gulf. p. 74

Iraq A country in southwestern Asia; includes former lands of the Mesopotamians, Babylonians, Sumerians, and Assyrians. p. 74

Ireland A country of Europe; located in the British Isles. p. 403

Irrawaddy River A river in southern central Burma (Myanmar). p. 147

Islamabad (is•LAH•muh•bahd) The capital of Pakistan. (34°N, 73°E) p. 196

Isonzo River A river in Slovenia and northeast Italy; area of heavy fighting during World War I. p. 568

Israel An ancient kingdom and present-day country; a holy land for Jews, Christians, and Muslims; located on the eastern coast of the Mediterranean Sea. p. 86

Isthmus of Panama (IHS•muhs) A narrow land bridge containing the country of Panama; located between the Caribbean Sea and the Pacific Ocean; connects Central and South America. p. 509

Italian Peninsula A boot-shaped peninsula that extends from southern central Europe into the Mediterranean Sea. p. 230

Italy An ancient land and a present-day European country; located on the Italian Peninsula. p. 298

Ithotwe A city located in Egypt on the Nile River. (31°N, 30°E) p. 675

Ivory Coast See Côte d'Ivoire. p. 675

Iwo Jima (EE•woh•JEE•muh) Center island of the Volcano Islands, Japan; located south of Tokyo. p. 590

Jamaica An island country in the Greater Antilles of the West Indies. p. 422

Jammu and Kashmir A former princely state; now divided into Indian states and Pakistan territory. p. 657

Japan An island country in eastern Asia, off the Pacific coasts of China and Russia. p. 474

Jarmo Site of the ancient Kurdish village of Qallat Jarmo; located in northern Iraq. (36°N, 45°E) p. 58

Java The most populated island of Indonesia; located in southern Indonesia. p. 361

Java Sea Part of the Pacific Ocean north of Java, south of Borneo, and east of Sumatra. p. 590

Jenné (jeh•NAY) A city of the ancient Songhay Empire of western Africa; located on the Niger River in central Mali. (14°N, 4°W) p. 363

Jericho The oldest known city in the world; located north of the Dead Sea, in present-day Jordan. (32°N, 35°E) p. 58

Jerusalem The capital of Israel; a holy city for Jews, Christians, and Muslims. (32°N, 35°E) p. 82

Johannesburg A city located in the country of South Africa. (26°S, 28°E) p. 680

Joppa An ancient city in Israel, now known as Jaffa; located northwest of Jerusalem. (32°N, 35°E) p. 86

Jordan A country in southwestern Asia. p. 74

Jordan River A river that flows from the mountains of Syria in southwestern Asia into the Dead Sea. p. 86

Jutland A peninsula occupied by the mainland of Denmark. p. 568

Kalahari Desert A desert in southern Africa; located in Botswana, Namibia, and South Africa. p. 367

Kamchatka Peninsula (kuhm•CHAHT•kuh) A peninsula in northeastern Russia; surrounded by the Sea of Okhotsk and the Bering Sea. p. 577

Kanem-Bornu (KAHN•em BAWR•noo) An ancient African kingdom, later part of French Equatorial Africa, northeast of Lake Chad. p. 450

Karakorum (kar•uh•KOHR•uhm) The capital of Mongolia under Genghis Khan; located in the Gobi on the southern end of the Orhon River. (47°N, 103°E) p. 333

Kashgar A city in the Takla Makan Desert in north-western China near the border with Kyrgyzstan. (39°N, 76°E) p. 384

Kathmandu The capital of Nepal on the Indian subcontinent; located in a valley of the Himalayas. (27°N, 85°E) p. 196

Kazakhstan (ka•zak•STAHN) A country in central Asia; formerly part of the Soviet Union. p. 141

Kenya A country in eastern Africa. p. 621

Kerma A capital of the ancient kingdom of Kush; located on the Nile River in Sudan. (20°N, 30°E) p. 108

Khanbalik (kahn•buh•LEEK) See Beijing. p. 333

Khyber Pass (KY•ber) A narrow pass through the Hindu Kush Mountains on the border between Afghanistan and Pakistan in Asia. p. 192

Kiev (KEE•ef) The capital of Ukraine; located on the Dnieper River, in central Ukraine. (50°S, 31°E) p. 333

Kilwa (KIL•wah) An ancient Swahili trading city on a small island near what is today the country of Tanzania in eastern Africa. (9°S, 40°E) p. 360

King's Lynn A town in England located in Norfolk on the Ouse River. (53°N, 0°) p. 405

Kish An ancient Sumerian city-state on the Euphrates River, located in present-day Iraq. (33°N, 45°E) p. 74

Knossos (NAHS•uhs) The capital of the ancient Minoan civilization; located on the island of Crete off the coast of present-day Greece. (35°N, 25°E) p. 230

Kobe (KOH•bee) A Japanese seaport and commercial city; located on the southern coast of Honshu. (35°N, 137°E) p. 634

Kongo (Congo) An historic kingdom in southern Africa; located within the present-day countries of Angola and the Democratic Republic of the Congo. p. 450

Königsberg (KAY•nigz•berg) A port city in western Russia and former capital of East Prussia, also known as Kaliningrad. (55°N, 21°E) p. 520

Korea A peninsula off the coast of China, now divided between two countries—North Korea and South Korea. p. 360

Kowloon A town on western Kowloon Peninsula; located in southeastern China. (22°N, 114°E) p. 635

Kowloon Peninsula A peninsula opposite Hong Kong Island. p. 635

Kumbi-Saleh (KOOM•bee SAH•lay) The ancient capital of the empire of Ghana in western Africa; located in the southwestern corner of what is today Mauritania. (16°N, 15°W) p. 360

Kunlun Shan (KOON•LOON SHAN) A mountain range in western China. p. 141

Kush An ancient Nubian kingdom; located in the Nile Valley in northern part of present-day Sudan. p. 127

Kuwait (ku•WAYT) An independent state on the northwestern Persian Gulf; located between Iraq and Saudi Arabia. p. 74

Kyoto (kee•OH•toh) Formerly Heian-Yo, the imperial capital of Japan for more than a thousand years; now a leading cultural center of Japan; located in south-central Honshu. (35°N, 136°E) p. 291

Kyrgyzstan (kir•gih•STAN) A country in central Asia; formerly part of the Soviet Union. p. 141

Kyushu (kee•OO•shoo) The southernmost of the four main islands of Japan. p. 474

Lagash (LAY•gash) A city of ancient Sumer and a city-state in ancient Babylonia; located near the coast of the Persian Gulf, in southeastern Iraq. (32°N, 47°E) p. 74

Lake Chad A lake in northern Africa on the border of Chad, Cameroon, Nigeria, and Niger. p. 370

Lake Erie The fourth-largest of the Great Lakes; borders Canada and the United States. p. 459

Lake Huron The second-largest of the Great Lakes; borders Canada and the United States. p. 501

Lake Malawi A large lake along the eastern border of Malawi in southern Africa; also called Lake Nyasa. p. 393

Lake Michigan The third-largest of the Great Lakes, the only one entirely within the United States. p. 501

Lake Ontario The smallest of the Great Lakes; borders Canada and the United States. p. 459

Lake Superior The largest of the Great Lakes; borders Canada and the United States. p. 501

Lake Tanganyika (tang•uhn•YEE•kuh) A lake in Tanzania and Zaire, in the Great Rift Valley of southern Africa. p. 393

Lake Texcoco (tays•KOH•koh) A dry lake near Mexico City; an island in the lake was the site of the Aztec capital Tenochtitlán. p. 346

Lake Tiberias See Sea of Galilee. p. 665

Lake Victoria A lake in Tanzania, Kenya, and Uganda in southeastern Africa. p. 44

Lake Xaltocan (hahl•tuh•KAHN) A lake in the Valley of Mexico located northeast of Mexico City. p. 349

Lake Xochimilco (soh•chih•MEEL•koh) A lake in central Mexico in North America; located southeast of Mexico City. p. 346

Laos A country located on the Indochina Peninsula in southeastern Asia; once part of former French Indochina. p. 147

Larsa A city in ancient Babylonia, near the Euphrates River, in what is today southeastern Iraq. (31°N, 46°E) p. 74

Latvia A country in eastern Europe; formerly part of the Soviet Union. p. 570

Lebanon The land of the ancient Phoenicians and present-day country on the eastern shore of the Mediterranean Sea in southwestern Asia. p. 74

Leeds An inland port in central England, on the River Aire. (54°N, 2°W) p. 518

Leningrad See St. Petersburg. p. 591

León (Mexico) A city in central Mexico; located northwest of Guanajuato. (21°N, 102°W) p. 648

León (Spain) A historic region and former kingdom in northwestern Spain. p. 436

Lesotho An independent country located within the borders of the country of South Africa in Africa. (30°S, 28°E) p. 621

Liberia A country in western Africa; originally a republic for freed slaves from the United States; located on the Atlantic coast of West Africa. p. 544

Libya A country in northern Africa; located on the Mediterranean Sea. p. 544

Libyan Desert A desert in northern Africa; located in Libya, Egypt, and Sudan. p. 108

Lisbon The capital of Portugal; located on the Atlantic coast of Europe. (39°N, 9°W) p. 403

Lithuania A country in eastern Europe; formerly part of the Soviet Union. p. 570

Liverpool A port on the English coast of the northwestern British Isles. (53°N, 3°W) p. 518

Lodz A province of central Poland. p. 568

Loire River (luh•WAR) The longest river in France; located in southeastern France. p. 222

Lombardy A region in northern Italy. p. 536

London The capital of the United Kingdom; located on the Thames River, in southeastern England. (51°N, 0°) p. 313

Lothal An ancient settlement in northern India. (22°N, 72°E) p. 137

Luoyang (luh•WOH•yahng) The former capital of the Zhou dynasty in ancient China; located in what is present-day central China, on the Huang He River. (35°N, 113°E) p. 183

Luxembourg A country in western Europe. p. 568

Lydia A region and ancient kingdom in Asia Minor, on the Aegean Sea. p. 89

Lyons A manufacturing and commercial city in central France; capital of Rhône department. (46°N, 5°E) p. 520

Macao (muh•KOW) A Portuguese colony in southern China, on the South China Sea. (22°N, 114°E) p. 473

Macedonia A present-day country in Europe; an ancient kingdom near the Aegean Sea; located on lands that are part of present-day Greece and Turkey. p. 209

Machu Picchu (mah•choo PEEK•choo) The ruins of an ancient Inca city; located in the Andes mountains in what is now central Peru in South America. (13°S, 73°W) p. 290

Madagascar An island country located in the Indian Ocean, off the eastern coast of southern Africa. p. 367

Madras The capital of Tamil Nadu state, India. (13°N, 80°E) p. 657

Madrid A city located in central Spain, in Europe, on the Manzanares River. (40°N, 4°W) p. 436

Majorca (mah•YOR•kah) The largest island of the Balearic group, in Spain. p. 398

Malawi (muh•LAH•wee) A country in southeastern Africa. p. 675

Malay Peninsula A peninsula in southeastern Asia, divided between Thailand and Malaysia. p. 378

Malaysia (muh•LAY•zhuh) An independent federation; located in southeastern Asia. p. 361

Mali A former West African empire and a present-day country. p. 363

Manchester A manufacturing port city on the Irwell River in England. (54°N, 2°W) p. 518

Manchuria A large region on the northeastern end of China. p. 473

Manitoba A province in central Canada. p. 647

Marathon An ancient Greek town in eastern Attica; the site of a Greek victory during the Persian Wars. (38°N, 24°E) p. 241

Mariana Islands An island group in Micronesia, Oceania; includes the unincorporated United States territory of Guam. p. 410

Marne A river in northeastern France; flows west into the Seine River. p. 568

Marrakesh A city near the Grand Atlas Mountains, in Morocco. (32°N, 8°W) p. 370

Marseilles (mar•SAY) A seaport located in southeast France; on the Gulf of Lion. (43°N, 5°E) p. 520

Marshall Islands A group of 32 islands and more than 867 reefs; located in the western Pacific Ocean. p. 410

Mauritania (maw•ruh•TAY•nee•uh) A country in western Africa. p. 675

Mauritius (maw•RIH•shuhs) An island country of the Mascarene Islands; located in the Indian Ocean. p. 675

Mecca (MEH•kuh) A city in Saudi Arabia near the Red Sea; a holy city for Muslims. (22°N, 40°E) p. 291

Media The ancient country of the Medes; located in present-day northwestern Iran. p. 209

Medina A city in western Saudi Arabia. (25°N, 40°E) p. 291

Mediterranean Sea The sea south of Europe, north of Africa, and west of Asia; connects to the Atlantic Ocean, the Red Sea, and the Black Sea. p. 44

Mekong Delta The fertile region across which flow the several mouths of the Mekong River; near Ho Chi Minh City, Vietnam. p. 606

Mekong River A river in southeastern Asia; flows from the mountains of Tibet into the South China Sea. p. 384

Melanesia (meh•luh•NEE•zhuh) The name given to a group of the southwestern Pacific Islands; located northeast of Australia and south of the equator. p. 410

Memphis An ancient Egyptian capital; located along the Nile River in northern Egypt. (30°N, 31°E) p. 90

Meroë (MAIR•oh•wee) A capital of the ancient kingdom of Kush; located on the eastern bank of the Nile River in northern Sudan. (17°N, 34°E) p. 108

Mesopotamia (meh•suh•puh•TAY•mee•uh) An ancient land in southwestern Asia; located between the Tigris and Euphrates rivers. p. 74

Messina An ancient seaport and modern province of Sicily, Italy. (38°N, 16°E) p. 520

Mexico A country in southern North America; located between the United States and Central America. p. 151

Mexico City The capital of Mexico; located in central Mexico. (19°N, 99°W) p. 492

Micronesia (my•kruh•NEE•zhuh) The name of a group of western Pacific Islands, east of the Philippines and north of the equator. p. 410

Middle America A world region; includes Mexico, the countries of Central America, and sometimes the islands of the Caribbean Sea. p. 151

Midway Composed of Eastern and Sand islands, parts of a coral atoll; located in the central Pacific Ocean. p. 590

Milan A city in northern Italy. p. 360

Mississippi River The largest river in the United States; flows from Minnesota to the Gulf of Mexico. p. 102

Missouri River A tributary of the Mississippi River; flows from Montana to St. Louis, Missouri. p. 460

Mogadishu (mah•guh•DIH•shoo) A port on the Indian Ocean in southern Somalia in Africa. (2°N, 45°E) p. 360

Mohenjo-Daro (moh•HEN•joh DAR•oh) An important center of ancient Indus civilization, on the western bank of the Indus River, in present-day Pakistan. (27°N, 68°E) p. 137

Moldova A country in eastern Europe; formerly part of the Soviet Union. p. 621

Mombasa An island port on the coast of the Indian Ocean, in southern Kenya in Africa. (4°S, 40°E) p. 360

Mongolia A country in eastern Asia. p. 141

Montenegro A part of Yugoslavia. p. 567

Monterrey The capital of Nuevo León state; located in northeastern Mexico. (26°N, 100°W) p. 648

Montreal Canada's largest city and chief port of entry. (46°N, 74°W) p. 492

Morocco (muh•RAH•koh) A country in northern Africa; bordered by the Mediterranean Sea and the Atlantic Ocean. p. 493

Moscow The capital of Russia; located on the Moscow River. (56°N, 38°E) p. 333

Moundville An ancient settlement of the Mound Builders of the Mississippian culture; located in central Alabama. (33°N, 87°W) p. 290

Mount Olympus A mountain believed to be the home of the gods and goddesses of ancient Greek mythology; located on the eastern coast of Greece. (40°N, 23°E) p. 230

Mount Sinai A mountain peak located on the Sinai Peninsula. p. 90

Mozambique (moh•zuhm•BEEK) A country in southern Africa; formerly Portuguese East Africa. p. 450

Mureybit A village in ancient Mesopotamia; located in present-day Turkey. (37°N, 38°E) p. 58

My Lai A Vietnamese village located south of Chu Lai. (15°N, 109°E) p. 606

Mycenae (my•SEE•nee) An ancient city-state and empire in ancient Greece; located on the eastern side of the Peloponnesus. (38°N, 23°E) p. 230

Nagasaki (nah•guh•SAH•kee) A Japanese city on the coast of Kyushu in southern Japan. (33°N, 130°E) p. 474

Namibia A country in southwestern Africa. p. 621

Napata (NA•puh•tuh) A capital of the ancient kingdom of Kush; located on the Nile River, in northern Sudan in Africa. (19°N, 32°E) p. 108

Naples (NAY•puhlz) An Italian port on the Tyrrhenian Sea; located on the western coast of southern Italy. (41°N, 14°E) p. 256

Nara A former capital of Japan; a Buddhist center located in southwestern Honshu. (35°N, 136°E) p. 291

Narmada River (ner•MUH•duh) A sacred Hindu river; begins in eastern India and empties into the Gulf of Cambay. p. 137

Nazareth (NA•zuh•ruhth) A city in northern Israel. (33°N, 35°E) p. 86

Negev (NEH•gev) A desert located in southern Israel. p. 665

Nepal (NAY•pawl) A country located in southern Asia, north of India. p. 136

Netherlands A country on the northern coast of central Europe, on the North Sea. p. 439

New Carthage See Cartagena. p. 222

New Delhi The capital of India; located in northern India. (29°N, 77°E) p. 196

New Guinea An island in the Malay Archipelago; located north of eastern Australia; occupied by Papua New Guinea and part of Indonesia. p. 410

New Zealand An island-group country in the southwestern Pacific Ocean, southeast of Australia. p. 410

Newcastle upon Tyne A city in northern England on the Tyne River. (55°N, 2°W) p. 518

Newfoundland A province of Canada; an island in the Atlantic Ocean east of Canada. p. 647

Niani An ancient Songhay trading center and present-day city; located in the country of Mali on the Niger River. (12°N, 8°W) p. 363

Nicaragua A country in Central America. p. 461

Niger (NY•jer) A country in western Africa. p. 621

Niger River A river in western Africa; flows from Guinea through Mali, Niger, and Nigeria into the Gulf of Guinea. p. 363

Nigeria (ny•JIR•ee•uh) A country on the Gulf of Guinea, in western Africa. p. 544

Nile River A river in northeastern Africa; flows from Lake Victoria to the Mediterranean Sea at the northeastern coast of Egypt. p. 44

Nineveh (NIN•uh•vah) The capital of the ancient Assyrian Empire; ruins located on the Tigris River, in northern Iraq. (36°N, 43°E) p. 58

Nippur (ni•PUR) An ancient Sumerian and Babylonian city in what is today called Southwest Asia, in present-day central Iraq. (32°N, 45°E) p. 74

Normandy A historical region of northwestern France; site of Allied D-day invasion during World War II. p. 591

North America One of the world's seven continents. p. 52

North Borneo The British colonial name of Sabah; a state of Malaysia; located in northeastern Borneo. p. 546

North Korea See Korea. p. 604

North Sea The sea located east of Great Britain and west of Denmark. p. 298

North Vietnam A former country located in southeastern Asia; now part of Vietnam. p. 606

Norway A European country; located on the northwestern Scandinavian Peninsula. p. 403

Nova Scotia A province of Canada; located on the eastern coast of Canada. p. 647

Novgorod (NAHV•guh•rahd) A medieval principality in eastern Europe in what is present-day Russia. p. 403

Nubia (NOO•bee•uh) An ancient land in Africa that extended along the Nile River from Egypt's southern border to close to present-day Khartoum, Sudan. p. 108

Nubian Desert A desert region in Sudan, Africa; east of the Nile River. p. 108

Ocmulgee An ancient settlement of the Mound Builders of the Mississippian culture in present-day United States; located in central Georgia. (33°N, 83°W) p. 293

Oder River A large river in central Europe; flows from northeastern Czech Republic to the Baltic Sea. p. 405

Ohio River A tributary of the Mississippi River; begins in Pittsburgh, Pennsylvania, and ends in Cairo, Illinois. p. 293

Okinawa (oh•kee•NAH•wah) An island group; center of Ryukyu Islands between the East China Sea and the Pacific Ocean. p. 590

Olympia A plain in the northwestern Peloponnesus; an ancient Greek religious center and site of the early Olympic Games. (40°N, 22°E) p. 235

Oman A country in southwestern Asia; located on the Arabian Peninsula. p. 136

Ontario A Canadian province; located between the provinces of Quebec and Manitoba. p. 647

Orkney Islands A Scottish archipelago; located off the northeastern coast of Scotland. p. 64

Osaka (oh•SAH•kuh) A Japanese port in southern Honshu where the Yodo River meets Osaka Bay. (35°N, 136°E) p. 474

Oslo The capital of Norway; located in southeastern Norway at the northern end of the Oslo Fjord. (60°N, 11°E) p. 570

Ottawa The capital of Canada; located in the province of Ontario. (45°N, 76°W) p. 620

Oxus River A river in Asia flowing from Pamir Plateau into the Aral Sea; also known as Amu Darya. p. 384

Oyo (oh•YOH) A town and state in southwestern Nigeria. (8°N, 4°E) p. 450

Pacific Ocean The largest of the world's four oceans. p. 45

Pagan The ruins and capital of a powerful dynasty; located in central Burma (Myanmar). (21°N, 95°E) p. 378

Pakistan A country in southern Asia. p. 136

Palermo The capital of Sicily, Italy; located on the Bay of Palermo, southeast of Rome. (38°N, 13°E) p. 520

Pamirs A mountainous region in central Asia in Tajikistan. p. 384

Pamplona (pam•PLOH•nah) A city in northern Spain. (43°N, 2°W) p. 436

Panama A country in Central America. p. 422

Papal States The home and kingdom of the Roman Catholic Church from 754–1870; located in central Italy. p. 430

Paraguay (pah•rah•GWY) A country in central South America. p. 461

Paris The capital of France; located on the Seine River. (49°N, 2°E) p. 502

Parthia (PAR•thee•uh) A land that was part of the ancient Assyrian and Persian empires; located in what is now Iran. p. 209

Pearl Harbor An inlet on the southern coast of Oahu island, Hawaii; site of the Japanese bombing attack that brought the United States into World War II. p. 590

Peloponnesus (pehl•uh•puh•NEE•suhs) A wide peninsula on the southern end of Greece; home of the ancient city-states of Sparta and Corinth. p. 230

Persepolis (per•SEH•puh•luhs) The capital of the ancient Persian Empire; located near Shiraz in present-day Iran. (30°N, 53°E) p. 164

Persia An ancient empire that included the lands of Persia, Egypt, Syria, Assyria, Mesopotamia, and Babylonia. p. 209

Persian Gulf A gulf in southwestern Asia; connected to the Gulf of Oman and the Arabian Sea. p. 74

Peru A country on the Pacific coast of South America; the former center of the Inca Empire. p. 461

Perugia An ancient city of the Etruscans and a city in central Italy on the Tiber River. (43°N, 12°E) p. 256

Philippine Sea A part of the western Pacific Ocean east of the Philippines. p. 590

Philippines An archipelago of southeastern Asia; located east of the Indochina Peninsula. p. 361

Philistia (fuh•LIS•tee•uh) An ancient land in southwestern Asia. p. 86

Phnom Penh (NAHM PEN) The capital of Cambodia. (12°N, 105°E) p. 147

Phoenicia (fih•NIH•shuh) An ancient land; located in present-day Syria and Lebanon. p. 86

Pisa (PEE•zuh) A city on the Arno River in northern Italy. (44°N, 10°E) p. 398

Plataea (pluh•TEE•uh) The site of an ancient Greek land victory that led to the end of the Persian Wars; located in what is today southeastern Greece, near Thebes. (38°N, 23°E) p. 241

Po River A river in northern Italy; flows from Mount Viso into the northern Adriatic Sea. p. 222

Polynesia (pah•luh•NEE•zhuh) The name of a group of central Pacific Islands; includes New Zealand, Samoa, Tahiti, and the Hawaiian Islands. p. 410

Portugal A country in Europe. p. 422

Portuguese Guinea A former Portuguese colony on the West African coast; the present-day country of Guinea-Bissau. p. 544

Potsdam A German industrial city; located southwest of Berlin. (52°N, 13°E) p. 592

Prague The capital of the Czech Republic; located on both sides of the Vltava River. (50°N, 14°E) p. 520

Pretoria The administrative capital of the Republic of South Africa. (26°S, 28°E) p. 621

Prince Edward Island A Canadian province; located in the Gulf of St. Lawrence. p. 647

Prussia A former kingdom in northern Europe; located in what is present-day Germany. p. 439

Puerto Rico An island and a self-governing commonwealth of the United States; located in the Greater Antilles of the West Indies. p. 461

P'yongyang (pee•AWNG•yahng) The capital of North Korea; located on the Taedong River. (39°N, 126°E) p. 339

Pyrenees Mountains (PIR•uh•neez) The mountain range that separates the Iberian Peninsula from Europe; forms the border between Spain and France. p. 44

Quebec A province in eastern Canada. p. 647

R

Ramses An ancient Egyptian city; located in Goshen, near Tanis. p. 90

Rangoon [Yangon] The capital of Burma (Myanmar). (17°N, 96°E) p. 147

Red Sea The sea between northeastern Africa and the Arabian Peninsula; connected to the Mediterranean Sea by the Suez Canal and to the Arabian Sea by the Gulf of Aden. p. 58

Reunion One of the Mascarene Islands; located in the Indian Ocean. p. 621

Reval The former name of the capital of Estonia; now known as Tallinn. (60°N, 25°E) p. 360

Rhine River A river in western Europe; flows across Switzerland, western Germany, and the Netherlands to the North Sea. p. 44

Rhodes A Greek island in the southeast Aegean Sea. p. 478

Rhone River A river in Switzerland and France, rising in the Alps and flowing into the Gulf of Lion. p. 568

Riga The capital of Latvia in eastern Europe. (57°N, 24°E) p. 360

Romania A country in southeastern Europe, bordering the Black Sea. p. 568

Rome The capital of the ancient Roman Empire and of present-day Italy; located on the Tiber River. (42°N, 13°E) p. 222

Russia A historic empire and the largest republic of the former Soviet Union; a country in northeastern Europe and northern Asia. p. 141

Rwanda A country in eastern Africa. p. 621

S

Sahara A desert covering the northern third of Africa. p. 108

Saigon The city that was the capital of South Vietnam; renamed Ho Chi Minh City; now part of Vietnam. (11°N, 107°E) p. 606

Salamis (SAL•uh•muhs) A Greek island in the Aegean Sea; the site of an ancient Greek sea victory leading to the end of the Persian Wars. p. 241

Samaria An ancient area of southwestern Asia; located between Judaea and Galilee. p. 86

Samarkand A city in eastern Uzbekistan. (40°N, 67°E) p. 333

Samoa A group of Pacific islands in southwestern Polynesia. p. 410

San Marino A small country on Mount Titano within northern Italy. p. 536

San Salvador One of the Bahama Islands; where Christopher Columbus first landed in the Americas on October 12, 1492. p. 443

São Tomé and Príncipe (SOW tuh•MAY PRIN•suh•puh) Equatorial islands; located off western Africa, in the Gulf of Guinea. p. 621

Sapporo A Japanese city. (43°N, 141°E) p. 634

Saragossa A Spanish city; located in western Aragon. p. 521

Sarajevo (sair•uh•YAY•voh) A city in central Bosnia and Herzegovina. (44°N, 18°E) p. 561

Sardinia An island in the Mediterranean Sea; located west of mainland Italy. p. 222

Sardis The capital of ancient Lydia; located in western central Turkey. (38°N, 28°E) p. 89

Saskatchewan A Canadian province; located in western Canada. p. 647

Saudi Arabia A country that occupies most of the Arabian Peninsula in southwestern Asia. p. 74

Savannah River A river forming the boundary between Georgia and South Carolina in the United States; flows into the Atlantic Ocean. p. 293

Saxony A historic region of Germany; now part of the German state of Lower Saxony. p. 403

Scotland One of four kingdoms in the United Kingdom; occupies the northern part of the isle of Great Britain. p. 403

Sea of Galilee A freshwater lake in northern Israel; also known as Lake Tiberias. p. 86

Sea of Japan The sea located west of Japan and east of Russia, North Korea, and South Korea. p. 45

Sea of Marmara A small sea in northwestern Turkey; connects the Black and Aegean seas. p. 230

Sea of Okhotsk (oh•KAHTSK) A sea off the eastern coast of Russia. p. 45

Seine River (SAYN) A river in northern France; flows northwest into the Bay of Seine. p. 502

Senegal A country located in western Africa. p. 675

Senegal River A river in western Africa; flows from the highlands of Guinea into the Atlantic Ocean at Senegal. p. 370

Seoul The capital of South Korea; located on the Han River. (38°N, 127°E) p. 339

Serbia A part of the present-day country of Yugoslavia. p. 567

Seville A city on the Guadalquivir River in southwestern Spain. (37°N, 6°W) p. 403

Seychelles An island group and republic; located in the Indian Ocean. p. 621

Shanghai (SHANG•HY) A Chinese port on the East China Sea; located near the mouth of the Chang Jiang. (31°N, 121°E) p. 180

Shechem (SHEK•uhm) An ancient town located north of Jerusalem, Israel. (32°N, 35°E) p. 90

Shikoku The smallest of the four main islands of Japan; located south of Honshu. p. 474

Siam See Thailand. p. 546

Gazetteer

Sicily An Italian island off the southwestern tip of the Italian peninsula. p. 222

Sierra Leone A country on the Atlantic coast of western Africa; a former slave colony. p. 544

Sierra Madre del Sur A mountain range that runs along the Pacific coast. p. 151

Sierra Madre Occidental A mountain range in northwestern Mexico that runs along the Pacific coast. p. A13

Sierra Madre Oriental A mountain range in eastern Mexico that runs along the coast of the Gulf of Mexico. p. A13

Sikkim A state in northeastern India. p. 627

Sinai Peninsula The peninsula between northeastern Africa and southwestern Asia; part of the country of Egypt. p. 89

Singapore A small island country off the southern tip of the Malay Peninsula; in southeastern Asia. p. 361

Skara Brae A Neolithic settlement located on the western coast of Mainland Island in the Orkneys, Scotland. p. 64

Slovenia (sloh•VEE•nee•uh) A country in eastern Europe. p. 567

Sofia The capital of Bulgaria. (43°N, 23°E) p. 568

Somalia A country in eastern Africa. p. 621

South Africa A country located on the southern tip of Africa, between the Atlantic and Indian oceans. p. 621

South America One of the world's seven continents. p. 52

South China Sea The part of the China Sea south of Taiwan. p. 45

South Korea See Korea. p. 604

South Vietnam A former independent country; located east of the South China sea; now part of Vietnam. p. 606

Soweto An area west of Johannesburg, South Africa. p. 680

Spain A country in southwestern Europe; on the Iberian Peninsula. p. 222

Sparta An ancient Greek city-state and rival of Athens; located on the southern end of the Peloponnesus. (37°N, 22°E) p. 223

Sri Lanka An island country in southern Asia; formerly Ceylon; located off the west coast of India. p. 136

St. John's The capital of Newfoundland, Canada. (48°N, 53°W) p. 647

St. Lawrence River A river located in northeastern North America; forms part of the border between the United States and Canada. p. A13

St. Petersburg A city formerly known as Leningrad when it served as the capital of the Russian empire; located on the Neva River on the Gulf of Finland. (60°N, 30°E) p. 520

Stalingrad The former name of Volgograd; located on the Volga River. (49°N, 44°E) p. 591

Stockholm The largest city and capital of Sweden; located on the Baltic Sea. (59°N, 18°E) p. 360

Strasbourg A city located in northeastern France. (48°N, 8°E) p. 520

Sudan A country on the eastern coast of northern Africa. p. 544

Suez Canal A canal linking the Mediterranean Sea and the Gulf of Suez; located in northeastern Egypt. p. 544

Sumatra (su•MAH•truh) The westernmost island of Indonesia; located off the Malay Peninsula in southeastern Asia. p. 378

Sumer An ancient region in southern Mesopotamia; located on the Persian Gulf, in what is today southeastern Iraq. p. 74

Suriname A country in South America. p. 461

Swaziland A country in southern Africa. p. 621

Sweden A European country on the southeastern part of the Scandinavian Peninsula. p. 403

Switzerland A country in central Europe. p. 504

Syracuse A seaport city in Sicily, Italy; located on the Ionian Sea. (37°N, 15°E) p. 360

Syria A country located on the eastern end of the Mediterranean Sea. p. 74

Syrian Desert A desert in southwestern Asia covering southern Syria, northeastern Jordan, western Iraq, and northern Saudi Arabia. p. 58

Tabriz (tuh•BREEZ) A city in northwestern Iran, on a small river near Lake Urmia. (38°N, 46°E) p. 333

Tagus River (TAY•gahs) A river running through the center of the Iberian Peninsula; flows from Spain through Portugal. p. 222

Taiwan (TY•WAHN) An island country; located off the southeastern coast of China. p. 141

Tajikistan (tah•jihk•ih•STAN) A country in western Asia; formerly part of the Soviet Union. p. 621

Takla Makan A desert in northwestern China. p. 141

Tanzania A country in eastern Africa. p. 621

Tashkent The capital of Uzbekistan; located in western Asia. (41°N, 69°E) p. 384

Taurus Mountains A mountain range in southern Turkey; runs parallel to the southern Mediterranean coast and the border between Turkey and Syria. p. 58

Tel Aviv A city in and former capital of Israel. (32°N, 35°E) p. 665

Tennessee River A tributary of the Ohio River; begins in eastern Tennessee and flows into the Ohio River. p. 293

Tenochtitlán (tay•nohch•teet•LAHN) The capital of the ancient Aztec Empire; present-day Mexico City has been built on the ruins of Tenochtitlán. (19°N, 99°W) p. 290

Teotihuacán (tay•oh•tee•wah•KAHN) A city in central Mexico. (20°N, 99°W) p. 349

Texcoco (tes•KOH•koh) A city in central Mexico; east of Lake Texcoco. (19°N, 99°W) p. 349

Thailand A country formerly known as Siam; located in southeastern Asia on the Indochina and Malay peninsulas. p. 136

Thar Desert Also called the Great Indian Desert; located in India and Pakistan. p. 137

Thebes The capital of ancient Egypt during the Middle Kingdom; located in southern Egypt. (26°N, 33°E) p. 108

Thermopylae (ther•MAHP•uh•lee) The site of an ancient Greek defeat during the Persian Wars; a mountain pass in southern Greece. (39°N, 23°E) p. 241

Thessaly (THES•uh•lee) An ancient and present-day region in Greece; located on the eastern Balkan Peninsula. p. 241

Thimphu (thim•POO) The capital of Bhutan; located north of western India. (28°N, 90°E) p. 196

Thrace An ancient land; located in what are the countries of Turkey, Bulgaria, Macedonia, and much of northwestern Greece. p. 209

Tian Shan A mountain system in central Asia; extends northeast from the Pamirs into Xinjiang Uygur. p. 141

Tiber River A river in central Italy; flows from the Apennine Mountains, through Rome, and into the Tyrrhenian Sea. p. 256

Tibet A region covering most of southwestern China. p. 378

Tigris River A river in southwestern Asia; begins in eastern Turkey and joins the Euphrates River. p. 44

Tijuana (tee•WAH•nah) A town in Baja California in Mexico. (33°N, 117°W) p. 648

Timbuktu (tim•buhk•TOO) An ancient Songhay trading center and present-day city; located in Mali in the Sahara, north of the Niger River. (17°N, 3°W) p. 360

Timor An island in eastern Indonesia. p. 546

Tiranë The capital of Albania. (41°N, 20°E) p. 570

Tlacopán (tlah•koh•PAHN) An ancient Aztec city. (20°N, 100°W) p. 349

Tokyo The capital of Japan. (36°N, 140°E) p. 634

Toledo A Moorish capital during the Middle Ages and a present-day city; located in central Spain, on the Tagus River. (40°N, 4°W) p. 436

Toronto The capital of Ontario, Canada. (44°N, 79°W) p. 647

Toulouse (tu•LOOZ) The capital of Haute-Garonne department; located in southern France. (44°N, 1°E) p. 520

Tours A French city; located southwest of Paris. (47°N, 1°E) p. 291

Transoxiana A region in western Asia. p. 384

Transylvania A former region in southeastern Europe; now part of Romania; located in northwestern Romania. p. 439

Tres Zapotes (trays suh•POHT•uhs) A village located in eastern Mexico. (19°N, 95°W) p. 349

Tripoli The ancient Phoenician city of Oea and present-day capital of Libya. (33°N, 13°E) p. 370

Troy An ancient city in northwestern Asia Minor. (40°N, 26°E) p. 230

Tunis Capital of Tunisia. (37°N, 10°E) p. 360

Tunisia A country in northern Africa. p. 561

Turin An ancient and modern city; located in northwestern Italy. (45°N, 8°E) p. A8

Turkey A country located in southeastern Europe and southwestern Asia. p. 74

Turkmenistan (terk•mehn•uh•STAN) A country in western Asia; formerly part of the Soviet Union. p. 621

Tuscany A region on the western coast of Italy. p. 504

Tyre (TYR) The capital of ancient Phoenicia and present-day town in southern Lebanon. (33°N, 35°E) p. 89

Tyrrhenian Sea (tuh•REE•nee•uhn) The sea located west of the Italian peninsula, north of Sicily, and east of Sardinia and Corsica. p. 230

Uganda A country in eastern Africa. p. 544

Ukraine (yoo•KRAYN) A country in eastern Europe; formerly part of the Soviet Union. p. 621

Union of South Africa The country now called South Africa; created from former British and Portuguese territories. p. 544

Union of Soviet Socialist Republics Another name for the Soviet Union, which ended in 1991. p. 590

United Arab Emirates A country on the eastern Arabian Peninsula. p. 621

United Kingdom A European kingdom in the British Isles made up of England, Scotland, Wales, and Northern Ireland. p. 64

United States A country in North America; a federal republic of 50 states. p. 461

Ur (UR) A city in ancient Sumer; located on the Euphrates River, near present-day southeastern Iraq. (31°N, 46°E) p. 74

Ural Mountains (YUR•uhl) A mountain range in Russia and Kazakhstan; extends south from the coast of the Arctic Ocean; boundary between Europe and Asia. p. 333

Ural River A river in Russia and Kazakhstan. p. 637

Uruguay (YUR•uh•gway) A country on the Atlantic coast of South America. p. 461

Uruk An ancient Sumerian city in southwestern Asia; located near the eastern bank of the Euphrates River, in present-day southeastern Iraq. (31°N, 46°E) p. 74

Uzbekistan (uz•behk•ih•STAN) A country in western Asia; formerly part of the Soviet Union. p. 621

Gazetteer

Valencia The city on the Turia River, near the eastern coast of Spain. (39°N, 0°) p. 436

Valley of Mexico A large valley in central Mexico; site of the ancient Aztec Empire capital, Tenochtitlán; location of present-day Mexico City. p. 151

Vancouver A city in southwestern Canada; located in British Columbia. (49°N, 123°W) p. 620

Venezuela A country in northern South America. p. 461

Venice A city of 118 islands in northeastern Italy on the Adriatic Sea. (45°N, 12°E) p. 360

Veracruz A seaport in eastern Mexico, on the Gulf of Mexico. (19°N, 96°W) p. 456

Victoria A port city of Hong Kong. (22°N, 114°E) p. 635

Victoria Falls The Zambezi River waterfall; located between Zimbabwe and Zambia, in Central Africa. (18°S, 26°E) p. 367

Vienna The capital city of Austria in Europe; located in northeastern Austria, on the Danube River. (48°N, 16°E) p. 478

Vientiane (vyen•TYAHN) An administrative capital of Laos. (18°N, 103°E) p. 147

Vietnam A country in southeastern Asia; located on the Indochina Peninsula. p. 147

Vindhya Range (VIN•dyuh) A mountain range in central India. p. 136

Vistula River A river in Poland in eastern Europe; flows from the Carpathian Mountains into the Baltic Sea. p. 538

Volga River The longest river in Europe; runs from Russia to the Caspian Sea. p. 103

Wabash River Located in Indiana and Illinois; empties into the Ohio River in southwestern Indiana. p. 293

Warsaw The capital of Poland. (52°N, 21°E) p. 504

Waterloo A small city located in central Belgium, near Brussels. (51°N, 4°E) p. 504

West Indies A group of islands between North and South America in the Caribbean Sea. p. 453

Western Ghats (GAWTS) A chain of mountains in southwestern India. p. 136

White Nile River Part of the Nile River in Africa. p. 108

Württemberg (WUHR•tuhm•berg) A former German monarchy and state; now part of the German state of Baden-Württemberg. p. 538

Xi'an (SHEE•AHN) A city in eastern China; also known as Sian; formerly Chang'an. (34°N, 109°E) p. 180

Yalta A city in Ukraine. (45°N, 34°E) p. 591

Yellow Sea The sea west of the Korean Peninsula and east of China. p. 141

Yellowknife The capital of the Northwest Territories in Canada. (63°N, 114°W) p. 647

Yucatán A state in southeastern Mexico; located on the northern Yucatán Peninsula. p. 648

Yucatán Peninsula A peninsula extending from the eastern coast of Central America; occupied by the countries of Mexico, Belize, and Guatemala. p. 151

Yugoslavia (yoo•goh•SLAH•vee•uh) A country in eastern Europe that broke up into several independent republics; today only Serbia and Montenegro remain part of Yugoslavia. p. 567

Yukon Territory A territory in northwestern Canada. p. 647

Zagros Mountains (ZAH•gruhs) A mountain range located in western and southern Iran. p. 58

Zama The site of Hannibal and Carthage's final defeat in the Second Punic War; located in northern Tunisia. (35°N, 9°E) p. 259

Zambezi River A river in southern Africa; flows from northwestern Zambia to the Indian Ocean. p. 367

Zambia A country in southern Africa. p. 621

Zaragoza (za•ruh•GOH•zuh) A city along the Ebro River in northeastern Spain. (42°N, 1°W) p. 436

Zimbabwe (zim•BAH•bway) A country in southern Africa. p. 621

Gazetteer

Glossary

The Glossary contains important social studies terms and their definitions. Each word is respelled as it would be in a dictionary. When you see the stress mark (´) after a syllable, pronounce that syllable with more force than the other syllables. The page number at the end of the definition tells where to find the word in your book.

add, āce, câre, pälm; end, ēqual; it, īce; odd, ōpen, ôrder; tŏŏk, pōōl; up, bûrn; yōō as *u* in *fuse*; oil; pout; ə as *a* in *above*, *e* in *sicken*, *i* in *possible*, *o* in *melon*, *u* in *circus*; check; ring; thin; this; zh as in *vision*

absolute location (ab´sə•lŏŏt lō•kā´shən) Exact location on Earth. p. 35

acid rain (as´id rān) Rain water mixed with gases from burning fossil fuels, such as coal and oil. p. 264

acropolis (ə•kro´pə•ləs) A fortress built on a hill. p. 234

A.D. (ā•dē) Stands for *anno Domini*, a Latin phrase meaning "in the year of the Lord." This abbreviation identifies approximately how many years have passed since the birth of Jesus Christ. p. 61

Afrikaans (a•fri•känz) The language spoken by the Boers in South Africa. p. 676

agora (a´gə•rə) An open-air market and gathering place in many ancient Greek city-states. p. 234

agriculture (a´gri•kul•chər) The raising of domesticated plants and animals; farming. p. 57

alliance (ə•lī´əns) An agreement to cooperate. p. 247

ambassador (am•ba´sə•dər) A representative of a government. p. 183

analyze (a´nəl•īz) To break something down into its parts to see how those parts connect with each other. p. 33

ancestor (an´ses•tər) A deceased relative who lived longer ago than a grandparent. p. 143

annex (ə•neks´) To take over. p. 126

apartheid (ə•pär•tāt) The government policy of South Africa that stressed the separation, or "apartness," of races. p. 676

apostle (ə•pä´səl) A person sent on a mission. p. 275

appeasement (ə•pēz´mənt) The policy of not opposing fascism. p. 588

aqueduct (a´kwə•dəkt) A system of bridges and canals that carries water from place to place. p. 264

Arabic numerals (ar´ə•bik nüm´rəlz) The base-ten number system: 1 through 9 and the zero; used in India as early as A.D. 595. p. 207

archipelago (är•kə•pe´lə•gō) A chain of islands. p. 411

aristocracy (ar´ə•stä•krə•sē) A wealthy ruling class. p. 234

Armada (är•mä´də) A fleet of warships. p. 445

armistice (är´mə•stəs) An agreement to stop fighting. p. 570

arms race (ärmz rās) A competition among nations to have the most weapons. p. 566

artifact (är´tə•fakt) A humanmade object, especially from long ago. p. 54

Aryans (ar´ē•ənz) Warriors and herders from eastern Europe and western Asia who migrated to India beginning about 3,000 years ago. p. 191

assassination (ə•sas•ən•ā´shən) Murder for a political reason. p. 203

assembly (ə•sem´blē) A lawmaking group. p. 234

astrolabe (as´trə•lāb) An instrument that helped sailors navigate using the positions of the stars. p. 307

atoll (a´tôl) An island formed from a coral reef. p. 407

authority (ə•thôr´ə•tē) The right to command or influence. p. 76

autocrat (ô´tə•krat) A leader with unlimited authority. p. 574

autonomy (o•tä´nə•mē) The right of a state to rule itself. p. 667

balance of trade (ba´ləns uv trād) The comparison of a country's exports with its imports. p. 633

Balfour Declaration (bal´fər de•klə•rā´shən) A British document that called for a national home for the Jewish people. p. 663

band (band) A small group of people. p. 51

Bantustan (ban•tōō•stan´) An all-black area in South Africa. p. 676

bar graph (bär graf) A graph that uses horizontal or vertical bars to show and compare information. p. 400

barter (bär´tər) The exchange of one good or service for another. p. 88

basilica (bə•si´li•kə) A huge marble government building in ancient Rome. p. 263

B.C. (bē•sē) Stands for "before Christ." p. 61

B.C.E. (bē•sē•ē) Stands for "before the Common Era." p. 61

bias (bī´əs) A leaning toward or against someone or something. p. 541

bilingual (bī•ling´gwəl) Having two official languages, as Canada has. p. 647

Bill of Rights (bil uv rīts) The first ten amendments that were added to the Constitution of the United States of America to protect the rights of individuals. p. 501

Glossary

bloc (blok) A group of countries with the same interests. p. 651

boycott (boi´kot) To refuse to buy or use goods. p. 656

bubonic plague (byōō•bä´nik plāg) A deadly sickness spread throughout Europe in the 1340s by fleas on rats; also called the Black Death. p. 314

Buddhism (bōō´diz•əm) An Asian religion based on the teachings of Buddha. p. 195

bureaucracy (byŏŏ•rok´rə•sē) A network of appointed government officials. p. 181

Bushido (bŏŏ´shi•dō) The Japanese samurai code. p. 474

C.E. (sē•ē) Stands for "Common Era." p. 61

caliph (kā•ləf) A "successor" to Muhammad. p. 305

calligraphy (kə•li´grə•fē) The art of beautiful handwriting. p. 472

capitalism (kap´ə•təl•iz•əm) An economic system in which individuals invest money, or capital, in businesses. p. 527

caravan (kar´ə•van) A group of traders. p. 186

caravansary (kar•ə•van´sə•rē) An inn where desert travelers could find food and shelter. p. 376

caravel (kar´ə•vəl) A type of ship that used either square or lateen sails to travel long distances. p. 442

cardinal directions (kär´də•nəl də•rek´shənz) The main directions—north, south, east, and west. p. 39

cartogram (kär´tə•gram) A map that gives information about places by the size shown for each place. p. 630

cartographer (kär•tä´grə•fər) A mapmaker. p. 377

cash crop (kash krop) A crop that is raised to sell to others rather than to use at home. p. 543

caste (kast) A group within a social class. p. 193

cataract (ka´tə•rakt) A waterfall or a spot where water runs fast over rocks. p. 110

Catholic (kath´lik) All-embracing. p. 301

cavalry (ka´vəl•rē) Soldiers who ride horses or other animals to make swift attacks. p. 208

census (sen´səs) A count of a country's people. p. 262

chinampa (chē•näm´pä) An island made from platforms of woven reeds. p. 343

Christendom (kri´sən•dəm) The community of Christians from all kingdoms and nations. p. 312

Christianity (kris•chē•an´ə•tē) The religion based on the life and teachings of Jesus Christ. p. 275

chronology (krə•nä´lə•jē) A record of events in the order in which they happened. p. 33

circle graph (sûr´kəl graf) A graph that shows information by means of a circle divided into parts; also called a pie chart. p. 400

circumnavigation (sər•kəm•nav•ə•gā´shən) A journey around the world by ship. p. 444

citizen (sit´ə•zən) A member of a town, state, or country. p. 23

city-state (sit´ē•stāt) A city and its surrounding farmlands, with its own leaders and government. p. 75

civil service (siv´əl sûr´vəs) The part of a bureaucracy that oversees the day-to-day business of running a government. p. 184

civil war (siv´əl wôr) A war in which groups of people from the same place or country fight one another. p. 181

civilization (siv•ə•lə•zā´shən) A centralized society with developed forms of religion, ways of governing, and learning. p. 73

classified (kla´sə•fīd) Sorted. p. 187

clergy (klûr´jē) Ordained church officers. p. 437

climograph (klī´mə•graf) A graph that shows both the average monthly temperature and the average monthly precipitation for a place. p. 637

Code of Hammurabi (kōd uv ha•mə•rä´bē) The collection of laws organized by Hammurabi for the people of Babylon to follow. p. 81

Cold War (kōld wôr) A conflict of words and ideas between nations rather than armies. p. 602

collective (kə•lek´tiv) A large farm on which people work together as a group. p. 577

colony (kol´ə•nē) A settlement separated from, but under the control of, a home country. p. 87

Columbian exchange (kə•lum´bē•an iks•chänj´) The movement of people, animals, plants, diseases, and ideas between Europe and the Americas in the 1400s and 1500s. p. 457

comedy (kom´ə•dē) A humorous play. p. 243

command economy (kə•mand´ i•kon´ə•mē) An economy in which the government owns almost all the land and natural resources. p. 526

common market (kom´ən mär´kit) A union formed to improve trade and encourage the economic growth of member nations. p. 689

commune (kom´yōōn) In China, a government-run farming community in which people share housing, food, and work. p. 627

communism (kom´yə•niz•əm) A system in which all property and all means of production belong to the people as a group. p. 575

compass rose (kum´pəs rōz) A direction marker on a map. p. 39

compromise (kom´prə•mīz) To give up some of what you want in order to reach an agreement. p. 691

concentration camp (kon•sən•trā´shən kamp) A type of prison. p. 590

confederation (kən•fed•ə•rā´shən) A loose group of governments. p. 501

conformal projection (kən•fôr´məl prə•jek´shən) A map projection that shows directions correctly but distorts sizes, especially of places near the poles. p. 373

Confucianism (kən•fyōō´shə•ni•zəm) The ideas of the Chinese philosopher Confucius, which became a guide for the way people live. p. 175

conquer (kän´kər) To take over. p. 79

conquistador (kän•kēs´tä•dôr) A Spanish adventurer who came to the Americas in search of gold. p. 455

conscription (kən•skrip´shən) The drafting of citizens to serve in the armed forces for a set number of years. p. 566

consequence (kän´sə•kwens) An effect. p. 51

Constitution of the United States of America
(kon•stə•tōō´shən uv the yōō•nī´təd stāts uv
ə•mer´ə•kə) The document describing the plan for governing the United States. It was accepted in 1787 and is still the supreme law of the United States. p. 501

consul (kon´səl) One of two chief officials who held office in the ancient Roman Republic. p. 257

containment (kən•tān´mənt) The policy of preventing a country from gaining control of another country. p. 602

contour line (kän´tûr līn) On an elevation map, a line that connects all points of equal elevation. p. 146

contract (kän´trakt) A written agreement. p. 312

cottage industry (kä´tij in´dəs•trē) A business in which family members work in their homes to prepare products for a merchant. p. 516

coureurs de bois (kōō•rûr´ də bwä´) A term that means "runners of the woods," referring to French trappers who traded with the Native Americans. p. 458

courier (kŏŏr´ē•ər) A person who delivers messages. p. 210

covenant (kəv´ə•nənt) An agreement. p. 85

Creole (krē´ōl) A person of Spanish or Portuguese descent who was born in the Americas. Creoles belonged to the middle class of people in colonial Latin America. p. 507

crop rotation (krop rō•tā´shən) A farming method in which the kinds of crops planted in a field are alternated every year to help the soil remain fertile. p. 515

crucifixion (krōō•sə•fik´shən) A type of execution in which a person is nailed to a cross and left to die. p. 274

crusader (krōō•sā´dər) A Christian soldier who fought to free the Holy Land from Muslim Turks in the Middle Ages. p. 313

cultural borrowing (kəlch´rəl bär´ə•wing) Adapting customs from one culture for use in another. p. 231

cultural diffusion (kəlch´rəl di•fyōō´zhən) The spread of ideas from one place to others. p. 88

cultural identity (kəlch´rəl ī•den´tə•tē) A connection people feel with one another. p. 238

Cultural Revolution (kəlch´rəl rev•ə•lōō´shən) Mao Zedong's unsuccessful attempt from 1966 to 1968 to cut the Chinese people's ties to the past. p. 627

culture (kəl´chər) A unique way of life that sets a group of people apart from others. p. 54

currency (kər´ən•sē) Money. p. 329

czar (zär) A Russian title meaning "caesar," or ruler. p. 574

daimyo (dī´mē•ō) A local noble in feudal Japan. p. 340

Daoism (dou´i•zəm) A religion and philosophy that teaches that the key to long life and happiness is to accept life as it is. p. 184

Declaration of Independence (dek•lə•rā´shən uv in•di•pen´dəns) The document that proclaimed the American colonies' freedom from Britain. p. 499

Declaration of the Rights of Man and of the Citizen (dek•lə•rā´shən uv the rīts uv man ənd uv the

si´tə•zən) A document, issued during the French Revolution, that guaranteed certain human rights and other freedoms. p. 503

deforestation (dē•fôr•ə•stā´shən) The clearing of forests. p. 642

delta (del´tə) A triangle-shaped area of islands and marshes at the mouth of a river. p. 107

demagogue (de´mə•gog) A bad leader. p. 244

demand (di•mand´) In economics, the amount of a good or service that people want to buy. p. 527

democracy (di•mok´rə•sē) Rule by the people. p. 237

desertification (di•zər•tə•fə•kā´shən) Any change of fertile land into desert. p. 107

détente (dā•tänt´) An easing of tensions. p. 607

developing country (di•ve´lə•ping kən´trē) A country with a fast-growing population, few resources, and an economy based on agriculture. p. 639

dhow (dou) An Arab ship. p. 391

dictator (dik´tā•tər) A ruler with absolute authority. p. 257

diplomat (di´plə•mat) A person skilled in developing treaties between nations. p. 393

direct rule (di•rekt´ rōōl) A type of colonial government in which Europeans chose all government officials. p. 543

disciple (di´sī•pəl) Follower of a religion. p. 274

discriminate (dis•kri´mə•nāt) To treat unfairly because of race or for other reasons. p. 656

dissident (di´sə•dənt) A person who speaks out against his or her government. p. 685

distortion (di•stôr´shən) An area that is not accurate on a map projection. p. 372

division of labor (də•vi´zhən uv lā´bər) A system in which the members of a group do different tasks according to their abilities and the group's needs. p. 55

doge (dōj) A leader in the Italian city-states. p. 399

domesticate (də•mes´tə•kāt) To tame plants and animals for people's use. p. 56

double-bar graph (də´bəl bär graf) A bar graph that shows two sets of statistics, or facts shown with numbers. p. 594

draft (draft) A system for choosing citizens to serve in an army. p. 328

dynasty (dī´nəs•tē) A series of rulers from the same family. p. 112

economic system (ek•ə•nom´ik sis´təm) The way a country produces and uses goods and services. p. 526

economy (i•kon´ə•mē) The way people use resources to meet their needs. p. 56

edict (ē´dikt) A command. p. 112

elevation (el•ə•vā´shən) The height of land. p. 146

embargo (im•bär´gō) A ban on trade. p. 405

emperor (em´pər•ər) The ruler of an empire. p. 80

empire (em´pīr) A conquered land of many people and places governed by one ruler. p. 80

Glossary

encomienda (en•kō•mē•en´dä) A system in which Native Americans had to work for European colonists and accept their religion. p. 457

English Bill of Rights (in´glish bil uv rīts) A British document, written in 1689, that granted individual rights. p. 499

Enlightenment (in•līt´ən•mənt) A movement that began in France in the 1700s and focused on ways to create a government for protecting the rights of individuals. p. 500

entrepreneur (än•trə•prə•nür´) A person who takes a financial risk by providing money to start a business venture. p. 517

environment (en•vī´rən•mənt) Surroundings. p. 58

epic (e´pik) A long story-poem. p. 232

equal justice (ē´kwəl jus´təs) Fair treatment under the law. p. 81

equal-area projection (ē´kwəl âr´ē•ə prə•jek´shən) A map projection that shows the sizes of regions in correct relation to one another but distorts shapes. p. 372

equidistant projection (ē•kwə•dis´tənt prə•jek´shən) A map projection that shows accurate distances from a central point. p. 373

evaluate (i•val´yə•wāt) To decide whether information can be trusted. p. 540

evidence (e´və•dəns) Proof. p. 61

export (ek•spōrt´) To send out goods for sale to other places. p. 185

fact (fakt) A statement that can be proved to be true. p. 540

factory (fak´tə•rē) A large building where goods are made. p. 516

fascism (fa´shi•zəm) Political ideas that stress strong government control, military strength, and intense nationalism. p. 587

favela (fə•ve´lə) A slum outside a city in Brazil. p. 642

feudal system (fyōōd´əl sis´təm) A system of trading loyalties for protection in the Middle Ages. p. 312

filial piety (fi´lē•əl pī´ə•tē) Kind treatment of parents; translation of the Chinese word *xiao*. p. 175

forum (fōr´əm) A public square in ancient Rome. p. 261

free enterprise (frē en´tər•prīz) A system in which people choose how they make and spend their money. p. 528

free port (frē pôrt) A place that does not charge tariffs on imports or exports. p. 635

generalization (je´nə•rəl•i•zā´shən) A summary statement made about a group of related ideas. p. 69

genocide (je´nə•sīd) The killing of an entire group of people. p. 591

gladiator (glad´ē•ā•tər) In ancient Rome, a slave or prisoner forced to fight, often to the death. p. 264

glasnost (glaz´nōst) The "openness," or new freedom, that allowed Soviet citizens to speak out without fear of punishment. p. 684

Gospels (gäs´pəlz) The first four books of the New Testament which describe Jesus Christ's life and actions. p. 276

government (guv´ərn•mənt) An organized system that groups use to make laws and decisions. p. 75

grand vizier (grand və•zir´) The chief minister in the Ottoman Empire. p. 478

graph (graf) A diagram for showing relations between numbers. p. 400

gravity (gra´və•tē) The force that holds objects to the Earth and keeps the planets circling around the sun. p. 434

great circle (grāt sûr´kəl) Any imaginary circle that divides the Earth into equal parts. p. 374

Great Depression (grāt di•pre´shən) The economic decline during the 1930s that was the worst in the world's history. p. 580

Great Mutiny (grāt myōō´tən•ē *or* myōōt´nē) The rebellion in which Indians and sepoys mutinied against the East India Company's rule. p. 546

Great Society (grāt sə•sī´ə•tē) A goal proposed by United States President Lyndon Johnson according to which every American would have the chance for a good life. p. 649

Greek fire (grēk fīr) A chemical mixture, used by the Byzantine navy, that caught fire when water hit it. p. 396

grid (grid) The north-south and east-west lines on a map that cross each other to form a pattern of squares. p. 40

gross domestic product (grōs də•mes´tik prä´dəkt) (GDP) The total value of the goods and services produced in a country. p. 633

hacienda (ä•sē•en´dä) A huge farm or plantation in colonial Latin America. p. 507

haiku (hī´kōō) A 17-syllable Japanese poem that is often about nature. p. 475

Hansa (han´sə *or* hän´zä) A group of northern European merchants who worked together to protect themselves. p. 405

harijan (här•i•jän´) The name that Mohandas Gandhi gave to the untouchables of India. It means "child of God." p. 656

Hellenistic (he•lə•nis´tik) "Greek-like." p. 249

helot (he´lət) In ancient Sparta, a slave owned by the state. p. 236

heraldry (her´əl•drē) The system of colors, patterns, and picture symbols that knights used during the Middle Ages in Europe. p. 316

heresy (her´ə•sē) The denial of the beliefs of a church. p. 438

heritage (her´ə•tij) A set of ideas that have been passed down from one generation to another. p. 171

hieroglyphics (hī•rə•gli´fiks) A writing system in which pictures or symbols stand for sounds, whole words, or ideas. p. 113

Hinduism (hin´dōō•iz•əm) A religion native to India, featuring belief in many gods and reincarnation. p. 192

historical empathy (hi•stôr•i•kəl em´pə•thē) Understanding the actions and feelings of people from other times and other places. p. 32

historical map (hi•stôr•i•kəl map) A map that provides information about the past. Historical maps may show where events took place or how the world looked at a certain time in the past. p. 266

Holocaust (hōl´ə•kôst) The mass killing of millions of Jewish people during World War II. p. 592

hostage (hos´tij) Someone who is taken prisoner and held until demands are met. p. 668

human features (hyōo´mən fē´chərz) Buildings, bridges, farms, roads, and people themselves. p. 36

hydroelectric power (hī•drō•i•lek´trik pou´ər) Electricity produced by water power. p. 638

Ice Age (īs āj) A long cold-weather period when huge sheets of ice covered part of the Earth's surface. p. 53

icon (ī´kän) A holy picture of Jesus Christ or the saints. p. 300

immunity (i•myōo´nə•tē) Resistance to disease. p. 457

imperialism (im•pir´ē•əl•iz•əm) The practice by a country of adding more lands, establishing colonies, and controlling the colonies. p. 543

import (im•pōrt´) To bring in goods for sale from other places. p. 185

independence (in•di•pen´dəns) Complete freedom. p. 126

indirect rule (in•də•rekt´ rōol) A type of colonial government that allowed some participation by local officials. p. 543

indulgence (in•dul´jəns) A pardon for sins. p. 438

Industrial Revolution (in•dus´trē•əl rev•ə•lōo´shən) The period of technological advances, beginning in the 1700s, that forever changed the way people live and work. p. 515

inflation (in•flā´shən) A continuing increase in the price of goods and services. p. 582

innovation (i•nə•vā´shən) A new way of doing things. p. 78

inoculation (i•nä•kyə•lā´shən) Giving a person a mild form of a disease so that he or she will not get sick with a more serious form. p. 207

inscription (in•skrip´shən) A written message etched into a long-lasting surface. p. 138

inset map (in´set map) A small map within a larger map. p. 39

intercropping (in•tər•krä´ping) Planting different crops together. p. 148

intifada (in•tē•fä´də) The Palestinian uprising against Israeli occupation of the West Bank and the Gaza Strip. p. 666

Islam (is•läm´) The religion of Muslims, based on belief in one God, or Allah. p. 304

isolation (ī•sə•lā´shən) Separation from others. p. 472

isthmus (is´məs) A small strip of land, with water on both sides, that connects two larger areas of land. p. 229

Janissary (ja´nə•sâr•ē) A member of a well-trained group of soldiers who served in the Ottoman army. p. 477

Judaism (jōo´dē•iz•əm) The religion of the Jewish people. p. 86

junk (jungk) A Chinese wooden boat with four-sided sails. p. 392

junta (hōon´tə) In Latin America, an independent governing council. p. 510

Justinian Code (jus•tin´ē•ən kōd) A set of laws, written by the Byzantine emperor Justinian, that served the Byzantine Empire for hundreds of years. p. 298

kaiser (kī´zər) The German word for *emperor*. p. 538

kami (kä´mē) In the Shinto religion, spirits that live in all natural things. p. 338

khan (kän) The title given to strong Mongol leaders who sometimes brought rival clans together and created almost unstoppable fighting forces. p. 332

labor union (lā´bər yōon´yən) An organized workers' group whose goal is to ensure good working conditions and fair treatment by employers. p. 529

lagoon (lə•gōon´) A small body of water found in the center of an atoll. p. 407

laissez-faire (le•sā•far´) A government policy of letting an economy continue without interference. p. 527

lateen sail (lə•tēn´ sāl´) A triangle-shaped sail that allows a ship to travel into the wind. p. 391

league (lēg) A group of allies. p. 241

Legalism (lē´gə•li•zəm) Chinese teachings that express a belief in the strict following of laws. p. 178

legend (le´jənd) A story handed down from earlier times to explain the past. p. 140

legion (lē´jən) A unit of soldiers in the ancient Roman army. p. 263

limited war (li´mət•əd wôr) A war in which total victory is not the goal. Such limitations make it less likely that nuclear weapons will be used. p. 604

line graph (līn graf) A graph that shows change over time by using one or more lines. The lines connect dots that stand for specific information. p. 400

livestock (līv´stok) Domesticated animals such as cattle, sheep, and pigs. p. 57

logical conclusion (lä´ji•kəl kən•klōo´zhən) A decision or idea reached by thoughtful study of all the known facts. p. 406

Long March (lông märch) Mao Zedong and his followers' 6,000-mile (9,656 km) journey across China to escape Nationalist forces. p. 626

Glossary

Magna Carta (mag´nə kär´tə) The document that English nobles forced King John to approve in 1215, limiting the king's power and protecting the rights of the people. p. 315

Mahatma (mə•hät´mə) A word meaning "Great Soul." Indians referred to Mohandas Gandhi as *Mahatma* because they considered him a holy man. p. 656

maize (māz) Corn. p. 59

majority rule (mə•jôr´ə•tē rōol) A system in which the ideas and decisions supported by the most people are followed. p. 237

Mandate of Heaven (man´dāt uv hev´ən) The right to rule; the Chinese believed heaven gave it to their emperors. When an emperor was weak or disasters occurred, the emperor was thought to have lost the Mandate of Heaven. p. 171

manor (ma´nər) A large block of land made up of forests, meadows, farmland, a village, a church, and the house or castle of the noble who owned it all. p. 311

mansa (män´sə) The title for a ruler in West Africa. p. 369

map key (map kē) The part of a map that explains what the symbols on the map stand for; sometimes called a map legend. p. 39

map scale (map skāl) The part of a map that gives a comparison of distance on the map itself with distance in the real world. p. 39

map title (map tī´təl) The words on a map that describe the subject of the map. p. 39

market economy (mär´kit i•kon´ə•mē) An economy in which people, not the government, decide which goods and services they will buy. p. 527

martyr (mär´tər) A person who willingly suffers or dies for his or her beliefs. p. 275

megalopolis (meg•ə•lop´ə•lis) A large, heavily populated area where cities have grown together. p. 634

merchant (mûr´chənt) A person who buys and sells goods to make a living. p. 76

mesa (mā´sä) A flat-topped hill with steep slopes. p. 347

messiah (mə•sī´ə) A wise leader who would establish the kingdom of God on Earth, according to Judaism. p. 274

mestizo (me•stē´zō) A person of European and American Indian descent, living in the Spanish colonies. p. 508

Middle Ages (mi´dəl ā´jəz) The period of European history that lasted from about A.D. 500 to 1500. p. 309

Middle America (mi´dəl ə•mer´ə•kə) The region of North America where southern Mexico, Belize, Guatemala, Honduras, El Salvador, Nicaragua, Costa Rica, and Panama are located. p. 148

Middle Passage (mi´dəl pa´sij) In the triangle trade system, the part in which enslaved peoples were shipped across the Atlantic from Africa to the Americas. p. 452

migration (mī•grā´shən) Movement of groups of people from one place to another. p. 52

militarism (mi´lə•tə•ri•zəm) A nation's interest in armed power. p. 566

minaret (min•ə•ret´) A tower on top of a mosque, from which the faithful are called to prayer. p. 306

minority rights (mə•nor´ə•tē rīts) Freedoms that are given to groups of people who make up a small part of a population. p. 657

missionary (mi´shə•ner•ē) A person sent out to teach about a religion. p. 205

monarchy (mon´ər•kē) The system of government in which a king or a queen rules. p. 76

money economy (mu´nē i•kon´ə•mē) An economic system based on money rather than on barter. p. 88

monopoly (mə•nä´pə•lē) Complete control or ownership. p. 298

monotheism (mä´nə•thē•i•zəm) A belief in one God. p. 84

monsoon (mon•sōon´) Strong seasonal winds in the Indian Ocean. p. 391

mosaic (mō•zā´ik) A picture made from bits of colored stone or glass. p. 298

mosque (mosk) An Islamic house of worship. p. 306

Mound Builders (mound bil´dərz) People who lived in the Eastern Woodlands region of North America. They got their name from the mounds of earth they used to bury their dead and to build temples on. p. 347

movable type (mōō´və•bəl tīp) Letters and numbers made from individual pieces of metal that can be positioned to form rows of words. p. 433

mulatto (mə•lä´tō) A person of African and European background. p. 508

multicultural (məl•tē•kəlch´rəl) Relating to many cultures. p. 249

mummy (mum´ē) A preserved body. p. 114

Muslim (məz´ləm) A follower of Islam. p. 304

myth (mith) A story that is passed down from generation to generation and usually tells about an ancient god or hero. p. 238

Napoleonic Code (nə•pō•lē•on´ik kōd) A set of laws made in 1804 that guaranteed certain freedoms for the people of France. French law is still based on this code. p. 505

national debt (nash´nəl *or* na´shə•nəl det) The amount of money a government owes. p. 650

nationalism (nash´nə•li•zəm *or* na´shə•nəl•i•zəm) A strong feeling of loyalty to one's nation, or country. p. 535

nationalize (nash´nə•līz *or* na´shə•nəl•īz) To put under government control. p. 640

nation-state (nā´shən•stāt) A country with a strong central government and a single ruler and usually a common history and culture. p. 314

New Testament (nōō tes´tə•mənt) The second part of the Christian Bible. It tells about the life and teachings of Jesus Christ and his followers. p. 276

nomad (nō´mad) A person with no settled home. p. 57

oasis (ō•ā´səs) A water hole in the desert. p. 376

obelisk (ō´bə•lisk) An ancient stone monument. p. 125

Old Testament (ōld tes´tə•mənt) The Christian Bible's first part, which contains the same books as the Jewish Bible. p. 276

oligarchy (ä´lə•gär•kē) A system in which a small group controls the government. p. 236

Open Door policy (ō´pən dōr pä´lə•sē) A policy whereby all countries have an equal opportunity to trade freely in a certain place. p. 547

opinion (ō•pin´yən) A statement of belief or judgment. p. 540

opportunity cost (ä•pər•tü´nə•tē kôst) The cost of giving up something when choosing something else instead. p. 644

oracle (ôr´ə•kəl) A person who gives wise advice. p. 144

orthodox (ôr´thə•däks) In religion, supported and accepted by tradition. p. 300

outrigger (out´ri•gər) A wooden frame placed on the side of a boat or canoe to keep the craft steady in rough seas. p. 410

papyrus (pə•pī´rəs) A paperlike material ancient Egyptians used to write on; made from reeds that grow in the Nile River. p. 113

parable (par´ə•bəl) A story that teaches a religious idea. p. 273

parallel time line (par´ə•lel tīm līn) A grouping of time lines that display different types of information for the same period of time. p. 60

partition (pär•ti´shən) To divide. p. 664

passive resistance (pa´siv ri•zis´təns) The use of peaceful means instead of violence to bring about change. p. 655

patent (pa´tənt) A document giving the inventor of a new idea or product the exclusive right to make or sell it for a limited period of time. p. 517

patriarch (pā´trē•ärk) A church leader. p. 301

patrician (pə•tri´shən) A descendant of Rome's earliest settlers. p. 257

patron (pā´trən) A wealthy person who pays artists and writers to produce their work. p. 430

peasant (pe´zənt) A poor person who lives on and farms the land. p. 116

peninsular (pe•nin´sû•lâr) A person born in Spain or Portugal and belonging to the highest social class of people in colonial Latin America. p. 507

perestroika (pâr•ə•stroi´kə) A "restructuring," or rebuilding, of the Soviet political and economic systems. p. 684

persecute (pûr´si•kyōōt) To punish people for their religious beliefs. p. 275

perspective (pər•spek´tiv) A painting technique that shows the differences between things that are close and things that are far away. p. 431

pharaoh (fer´ō) A ruler of ancient Egypt. p. 112

philosopher (fi•los´ə•fər) A person who studies the meaning of life. p. 174

physical features (fiz´i•kəl fē´chərz) Landforms, bodies of water, climate, soil, plant and animal life, and other natural resources. p. 36

pictograph (pik´tə•graf) A drawing or symbol used to represent a word in the Chinese language. p. 144

plantation (plan•tā´shən) A huge farm. p. 451

plateau (pla•tō´) A high, flat area of land. p. 208

plebeian (pli•bē´ən) A farmer, worker, merchant, or craftworker whose family came to ancient Rome later than the families of patricians. p. 257

plunder (plun´dər) To take goods by force. p. 333

polar projection (po´lər prə•jek´shən) An equidistant map projection that has one of the poles as its central point. p. 373

policy (pä´lə•sē) A plan. p. 261

polis (pä´ləs) In ancient Greece, a city-state consisting of a town and the farms and villages that surround it. p. 234

political cartoon (pə´li•ti•kəl kär•tōōn´) A cartoon that presents the artist's point of view about people and current events in politics and government. p. 506

pope (pōp) The leader of the Roman Catholic Church. p. 310

population density (pop•yə•lā´shən den´sə•tē) The average number of people living on a square unit of land. p. 661

population distribution (pop•yə•lā´shən dis•trib•yōō´shən) The number of people who live in different places in a given part of the world. p. 660

population pyramid (pop•yə•lā´shən pir´ə•mid) A graph that shows how a country's population is divided by age. p. 481

porcelain (pôr´sə•lin) A kind of clay pottery so thin it looks almost clear. p. 329

predict (pri•dikt´) To tell ahead of time what will happen. p. 109

primary source (prī´mār•ē sôrs) A record made by people who saw or took part in an event. p. 540

profit (prä´fət) Money gained. p. 186

projection (prə•jek´shən) A representation of the Earth on a map; a view of the round Earth on a flat surface. p. 372

propaganda (prä•pə•gan´də) The spreading of information, ideas, or rumors to help or hurt a cause. p. 583

prophet (prä´fət) A person who others believe speaks or writes a divine message. p. 211

protectionism (prə•tek´shə•ni•zəm) A government policy that calls for some type of action, such as raising tariffs, to protect a market from imports. p. 635

protein (prō´tēn) A substance in food that helps build the body and keeps it healthy. p. 148

Protestant (prä´təs•tənt) Name of the churches that were formed as a result of protests against the Roman Catholic Church. p. 439

province (prä´vins) A self-governing region. p. 259

public works (pu´blik wûrks) Structures built by the government for use by everyone. p. 172

pueblo (pwe´blō) An apartment-like shelter built on a cliff ledge or on a mesa in what is now the southwestern part of the United States. p. 347

purge (pərj) A government order to kill or imprison citizens who oppose the government. p. 578

pyramid (pir´ə•mid) A burial place for the dead, often for a dead ruler. p. 114

quota (kwō´tə) A required amount of particular goods to be produced. p. 628

Qur'an (kə•ran´ *or* kə•rän) The holy book of Islam. p. 304

racism (rā´siz•əm) The belief that one person is better than another because of color or race. p. 454

rajah (rä´jə) An Indian prince. p. 203

ratify (rat´ə•fī) To approve an agreement. p. 647

raw material (rô mə•tir´ē•əl) A natural resource, such as cotton, lumber, or wool, that can be made into a useful product. p. 517

reclaimed (ri•klāmd´) In archaeology, taken back by the surrounding environment, as humanmade structures can be. p. 151

Reconquista (rā•kôn•kēs´tä) A plan to make Spain all Catholic; also called the Reconquest. p. 435

Red Guard (red gärd) People who supported Mao Zedong and tried to carry out the Cultural Revolution. p. 628

Reformation (re•fər•mā´shən) A religious movement that began in sixteenth-century Europe as an attempt to reform the Roman Catholic Church; resulted in the founding of Protestantism. p. 439

refugee (re´fyoŏ•jē) A person who leaves his or her home to find shelter and safety elsewhere. p. 592

regent (rē´jənt) A person who governs in place of a ruler. p. 340

region (rē´jən) An area on Earth whose features make it different from other areas. p. 37

Reign of Terror (rān uv ter´ər) A period of rule by fear during the French Revolution; thousands of people were executed. p. 503

reincarnation (rē•in•kär•nā´shən) The belief that the soul lives on after death and returns to life in a new body. p. 193

relative location (re´lə•tiv lō•kā´shən) What a place is near or what is around it. p. 35

Renaissance (re´nə•säns) The time from about 1400 to 1600 in which Europeans entered an age of thought, learning, art, and science; a French word meaning "rebirth." p. 429

republic (ri•pu´blik) A form of government in which the citizens elect representatives to make all government decisions. p. 256

responsibility (ri•spän•sə•bi´lə•tē) A duty. p. 174

role (rōl) The part a person plays in society. p. 55

saga (sä´gə) An adventure story about the brave deeds of people. p. 402

samurai (sa´mə•rī) A Japanese warrior. p. 340

Sanskrit (san´skrit) A language of India, first spoken by the ancient Aryans. p. 192

satyagraha (sə•tyä´grə•hə) A term that Mohandas Gandhi used, meaning "soul force." It refers to a way for people to gain rights through peaceful methods. p. 655

savanna (sə•va´nə) A grassy plain. p. 365

scientific method (sī•ən•ti´fik me´thəd) A system of observing and experimenting to determine whether an idea should be accepted as true. p. 434

scribe (skrīb) A person who writes. p. 77

secede (si•sēd´) To separate from. p. 647

secondary source (sek´ən•dâr•ē sôrs) A record of an event, written by someone not there at the time. p. 540

senate (se´nət) A council of representatives. p. 257

sepoy (sē´poi) An Indian soldier led by British officers. p. 545

serf (sûrf) A peasant who worked on a manor. p. 311

Shiite (shē´īt) A group of Muslims who stayed loyal to the descendants of the fourth caliph, Ali, during the eighth century. p. 308

Shinto (shin´tō) A religion of Japan. The word means "the way of the gods." p. 338

shogun (shō´gən) In Japan, a "leading general" who held all the authority. p. 341

Silk Road (silk rōd) A trade route that stretched from China to the Mediterranean Sea. p. 186

silt (silt) Fine bits of rock and soil carried or deposited by water. p. 108

social class (sō´shəl klas) A group that has a particular amount of importance in a society. p. 77

socialism (sō´shə•li•zəm) An economic system in which a government owns and runs all industries. p. 529

society (sə•sī´ə•tē) An organized group of people living and working under a set of rules and traditions. p. 55

soviet (sō´vē•et) A workers' group that formed in Russia to plan and carry out the revolution. p. 577

standard of living (stan´dərd uv liv´ing) A measure of how well people in a country live. p. 633

standardization (stan•dər•də•zā´shən) The practice of making all things of a certain type alike. p. 180

star path (stär path) The way stars seem to move because of the Earth's rotation. p. 410

statistics (stə•tis´tiks) Facts shown with numbers. p. 594

steppe (step) Semi-dry plain that produces some grasses and thorny plants. p. 303

Glossary

strike (strīk) The action of refusing to work until certain requirements are met. p. 529

subcontinent (sub•kon´tə•nənt) A large land area isolated from the rest of a continent. p. 135

subsist (səb•sist´) To survive. p. 59

subsistence farming (səb•sis´təns färm´ing) Farming in which people raise only enough food for their families. p. 639

sultan (sul´tən) A Muslim ruler in India. p. 479

Sunni (soo´nē) A group of Muslims who accepted the changing dynasties of the Muslim Empire during the eighth century. p. 308

superpower (soo´pər•pou´ər) A nation that is one of the world's most powerful. p. 602

supply (sə•plī) The amount of a product or service offered for sale. p. 527

surplus (sûr´plus) An extra supply. p. 76

Swahili (swä•hē´lē) A people and a language of East Africa. p. 393

table (tā´bəl) A chart that lists information in categories. p. 187

tariff (tar´if) A tax on goods or services. p. 368

taxation (tak•sā´shən) The practice of requiring people to pay taxes to support a government. p. 81

technology (tek•nol´ə•jē) The skills and knowledge to make products or meet goals. p. 74

telescope (tel´ə•skōp) An instrument that can make faraway objects look close. p. 434

telescoping time line (tel´ə•skōp•ing tīm līn) A time line that includes a second time line that gives a closer view of one time period. p. 279

Ten Commandments (ten kə•mand´mənts) A set of laws for responsible behavior, which, according to the Bible, were given to Moses by God. p. 85

tenant (te´nənt) Someone who pays rent to a landowner. p. 311

territorial expansion (ter•ə•tôr´ē•əl ik•span´shən) The adding of new lands. p. 403

terrorism (ter´ər•i•zəm) The use of violent acts to further a cause. p. 664

textile (teks´tīl) Cloth. p. 516

time zone (tīm zōn) A division of the Earth in which all places have the same time; the time is different from that in other zones. p. 572

Torah (tōr´ə) Jewish scriptures; the first five books of the Bible. p. 86

totalitarian (tō•ta•lə•târ´ē•ən) Having complete control over people's lives. p. 578

trade surplus (trād sûr´plus) A balance of trade in which a country exports more goods than it imports. p. 634

trade-off (trād•of) Giving up the use of resources in one way in order to use them in another way. p. 644

trading network (trād´ing net´wərk) A group of buyers and sellers. p. 128

traditional economy (trə•dish´ən•əl i•kon´ə•mē) An economy that does not change much over time. p. 526

tragedy (traj´ə•dē) A serious play in which the main character comes to an unhappy end. p. 243

trend (trend) The way something changes over time. p. 401

triangular trade (trī´ang•yə•lər trād) A system in which traders exchanged goods for slaves, sold the slaves for products from plantations, and then sold the products in Europe. p. 452

tribune (tri´byoon) A plebeian official who could attend meetings of the senate in ancient Rome. p. 257

tributary (tri´byə•ter•ē) A smaller river that feeds into a larger river. p. 135

tribute (tri´byoot) Yearly payments. p. 209

tropical rain forest (trä´pi•kəl rān fôr´əst) A hot, wet land with tall trees that block the sunlight. p. 365

tundra (tun´drə) A cold, treeless plain whose subsoil is permanently frozen. p. 54

turning point (tərn´ing point) A time of important change. p. 204

typhoon (tī•foon´) A type of fierce storm. p. 338

tyrant (tī´rənt) Someone who takes control of a government by force and rules alone. p. 234

untouchables (un•tuch´ə•bəlz) In India, people below all castes. The name came from the idea that others would be made impure from their touch. p. 193

utopian (yoo•tō´pē•ən) A person who believes in and wants to create a perfect society. p. 530

vassal (va´səl) In the Middle Ages, a noble who agreed to perform services for the king in return for being given the use of land. p. 311

Vedas (vā´dəz) Ancient books of sacred Hindu writings. p. 192

veto (vē´tō) To stop passage of a law; from a Latin word meaning "I forbid." p. 257

virtue (vər´choo) A good quality. p. 171

warlord (wôr´lôrd) In China, a person who commanded his own small army. p. 625

ziggurat (zi´gə•rat) A huge mud-brick temple built by the ancient Sumerians. p. 74

Zionism (zī´ə•ni•zəm) The movement to build a modern Jewish state. p. 663

Zoroastrianism (zōr•ə•was´trē•ə•ni•zəm) A religion started by Zarathustra that teaches the belief in two gods—one good and one evil. p. 211

Index

Page references for illustrations are set in italic type. An italic *m* indicates a map. Page references set in boldface type indicate the pages on which vocabulary terms are defined.

Index

Index

Index

For permission to reprint copyrighted material, grateful acknowledgment is made to the following sources:

Atheneum Books for Young Readers, an imprint of Simon & Schuster Children's Publishing Division: Cover illustration from *Gandhi* by Leonard Everett Fisher. Copyright © 1995 by Leonard Everett Fisher. From *The Avenger* by Margaret Hodges. Text copyright © 1982 by Margaret Hodges. Cover illustration from *Tomatoes, Potatoes, Corn and Beans: How the Foods of the Americas Changed Eating Around the World* by Sylvia A. Johnson. Copyright © 1997 by Sylvia A. Johnson.

Cashmir Inc.: Cover illustration from *Come With Me To India* by Sudha Koul. Copyright © 1997.

Chelsea House Publishers, a division of Main Line Book Co.: Cover illustration from *Ancient Ghana: The Land of Gold* by Philip Koslow. Copyright © 1995 by Chelsea House Publishers, a division of Main Line Book Co.

Cobblestone Publishing Company, 30 Grove Street, Suite C, Peterborough, NH 03458: "Discovery and Excavation of Shi-Huangdi's Tomb" by Helen Weiman Bledsoe from *Calliope Magazine*, October 1997. Text © 1997 by Cobblestone Publishing Company.

Delacorte Press, a division of Bantam Doubleday Dell Publishing group, Inc.: From *The Clock* by James Lincoln Collier and Christopher Collier. Text copyright © 1992 by James Lincoln Collier and Christopher Collier.

Dial Books for Young Readers, a division of Penguin Putnam Inc.: Cover illustration by Herbert Tauss from *My Palace of Leaves in Sarajevo* by Marybeth Lorbiecki. Illustration copyright © 1997 by Herbert Tauss.

Dillon Press, a division of Simon & Schuster: Cover photographs from *Clothes & Crafts In the Middle Ages* by Imogen Dawson. Copyright © 1997 by Zoë Books Limited.

Dutton Children's Books, a division of Penguin Books USA Inc.: From *Sir Dana: A Knight, as told by his trusty armor* by Dana Fradon. Copyright © 1988 by Dana Fradon.

Farrar, Straus & Giroux, Inc.: From *I, Juan de Paraja* by Elizabeth Borton de Treviño. Text copyright © 1965, renewed 1993 by Elizabeth Borton de Treviño; cover illustration © 1965 by Enrico Arno. Cover illustration by Juan Ramón Alonso from *The Apprentice* by Pilar Molina Llorente. Illustration copyright © 1989 by Juan Ramón Alonso.

Grove/Atlantic Inc. From poem #130 in *The Book of Songs*, translated from the Chinese by Arthur Waley. Text copyright 1937 by Arthur Waley.

HarperCollins Publishers: From *The Rights of Man, The Reign of Terror: The Story of the French Revolution* by Susan Banfield. Text copyright © 1989 by Susan Banfield. Cover

painting courtesy of Giraudon/Art Resource. From *His Majesty, Queen Hatshepsut* by Dorothy Sharp Carter, cover illustration by Michele Chessare. Text copyright © 1987 by Dorothy Sharp Carter; cover illustration copyright © 1987 by Michele Chessare. Cover from *Red Scarf Girl: A Memoir of the Cultural Revolution* by Ji-li Jiang, copyright © 1997 by HarperCollins Publishers. From *The Silk Route: 7,000 Miles of History* by John S. Major, illustrated by Stephen Fieser. Text copyright © 1995 by John S. Major; illustrations copyright © 1995 by Stephen Fieser. From *Journey to Jo'Burg: A South African Story* by Beverley Naidoo. Text copyright © 1986 by Beverley Naidoo/British Defence and Aid Fund for South Africa; illustration copyright © 1986 by Eric Velasquez. Cover illustration by Vo-Dinh Mai from *The Land I Lost: Adventures of a Boy in Vietnam* by Huynh Quang Nhuong. Illustration copyright © 1982 by Vo-Dinh Mai.

Holiday House, Inc: From *Skara Brae: The Story of a Prehistoric Village* by Olivier Dunrea. Copyright © 1985 by Olivier Dunrea.

Henry Holt and Company, Inc.: "The Great Hajj" from *The Royal Kingdoms of Ghana, Mali, and Songhay* by Patricia and Fredrick McKissack. Text copyright © 1994 by Patricia and Fredrick McKissack.

Houghton Mifflin Company: From "Friends and Neighbors" and "The Wonders of Palace Life" in *Jataka Tales*, edited by Nancy DeRoin. Text copyright © 1975 by Nancy DeRoin. From *Number the Stars* by Lois Lowry. Text copyright © 1989 by Lois Lowry. Cover illustration from *The Boy and the Samurai* by Erik Christian Haugaard. Copyright *Holiday House, Inc.:* From *Skara Brae: The Story of a Prehistoric Village* by Olivier Dunrea. Copyright © 1985 by Olivier Dunrea. Cover illustration from *The Boy and the Samurai* by Erik Christian Haugaard. Copyright © 1991 by Erik Christian Haugaard.

Hyperion Books for Children: From *Morning Girl* by Michael Dorris. Text copyright © 1992 by Michael Dorris; cover illustration copyright © 1994 by Ellen Thompson.

Little, Brown and Company: From "The Mounds of Cahokia" in *US Kids History: Book of the American Indians* by Marlene Smith-Baranzini and Howard Egger-Bovet. Text copyright © 1994 by Yolla Bolly Press.

Lodestar Books, an affiliate of Dutton Childrens Books, a division of Penguin Putnam Inc.: Cover illustration from *Lyddie* by Katherine Paterson. Copyright © 1991 by Katherine Paterson.

Lothrop, Lee & Shepard Books, a division of William Morrow & Company, Inc.: Cover illustration from *Commodore Perry in the Land of the Shogun* by Rhoda Blumberg. Copyright © 1985 by Rhoda Blumberg.

Cover illustration by Fiona French from *Pepi and the Secret Names* by Jill Paton Walsh. Illustration copyright © 1994 by Fiona French.

Viqui Maggio: Cover illustration by Viqui Maggio from *The Royal Kingdoms of Ghana, Mali, and Songhay* by Patricia and Fredrick McKissack. Illustration copyright © 1994 by Viqui Maggio.

Mikaya Press Inc.: Cover illustration by Alan Witschonke from *The Great Wall* by Elizabeth Mann. Original illustration copyright © 1997 by Mikaya Press Inc.

The Millbrook Press, Inc.: From *The Berlin Wall: How It Rose and Why It Fell* by Doris M. Epler. Text copyright © 1992 by Doris M. Epler.

W.W. Norton & Company: From "The Charms of Nian-nu" by Su Shi in *An Anthology of Chinese Literature*, edited and translated by Stephen Owen. Text copyright © 1996 by Stephen Owen and The Council for Cultural Planning and Development of the Executive Yuan of the Republic of China.

Oxford University Press: From *The Footsoldier* by Martin Windrow and Richard Hook. © by Oxford University Press.

Philomel Books, a division of Penguin Putnam Inc.: From *Boy of the Painted Cave* by Justin Denzel. Text copyright © 1988 by Justin Denzel.

Marian Reiner: Japanese haiku from *More Cricket Songs*, translated by Harry Behn. Text copyright © 1971 by Harry Behn.

Scholastic Press, a division of Scholastic Inc.: Cover from *Out of the Dust* by Karen Hesse. Cover illustration copyright © 1997 by Scholastic Inc. Cover photograph courtesy of Library of Congress Prints and Photographs division, Farm Security Administration collection.

Simon & Schuster Books for Young Readers, an imprint of Simon and Schuster Children's Publishing Division: Cover illustration by Michael Welply from *If You Were There: Aztec Times* by Antony Mason. Illustration copyright © 1997 by Marshall Editions Developments Ltd.

Steck-Vaughn Company: Cover illustration from *Technology in the Time of the Vikings* by Peter Hicks. Copyright © 1998 by Steck-Vaughn Company. From *Egyptian Stories*, retold by Robert Hull. Text copyright © 1993 by Wayland (Publishers) Ltd; U.S. version text copyright © 1994 by Thomson Learning. Originally published in the United States by Thomson Learning.

Stormking Music, Inc.: From "I don't want your millions, mister" by Jim Garland. Lyrics © 1947 by Stormking Music, Inc.

Tundra Books: Cover illustration from *Gilgamesh the King*, retold and illustrated by Ludmila Zeman. © 1992 by Ludmila Zeman.

Viking Penguin, a division of Penguin Putnam Inc.: Cover illustration by Bill Le Fever from *Ancient Rome* by Simon James. Copyright © 1992 by Reed International Books Ltd. Cover illustration by James Field from *Ancient China* by Brian Williams. Copyright © 1996 by Reed Educational and Professional Publishing, Ltd.

Franklin Watts: Cover photograph from *The American Revolution* by Alden R. Carter. Photograph copyright © by The Historical Society of Pennsylvania. Cover illustration by S.D. Schindler from *Digging Up the Past: The Story of An Archaeological Adventure* by Carollynn James. Illustration copyright © 1990 by S.D. Schindler.

Honi Werner: Cover illustration by Honi Werner from *The Avenger* by Margaret Hodges. Published by Charles Scribner's Sons.

Zondervan Publishing House: Scriptures from the *Holy Bible, New International Version.* Text copyright © 1973, 1978, 1984 by International Bible Society.

Every effort has been made to locate the copyright holders for the selections in this work. The publisher would be pleased to receive information that would allow the correction of any omissions in future printings.

ILLUSTRATION CREDITS:

Page 69 Navin Patel; 96–97 Jeffrey Terreson; 116 Navin Patel; 119 Lonnie Knabel; 158–159, 216–217 Jeffrey Terreson; 284–285 David Beck; 354–355 Jeffrey Terreson; 416–417 Don Stewart; 486–487 Jeffrey Barson; 554–555 James Steward; 614–615 Jeffrey Terreson; 696–697 Sergio Giovine.

COVER CREDITS:

Collage by Miriello Grafico, Inc.

Photography by Ken West Photography

All maps by GeoSystems

PHOTO CREDITS:

Page Placement Key: (t)-top (c)-center (b)-bottom (l)-left (r)-right (fg)-foreground (bg)-background

COVER:

(by object); Egyptian sculpture, Boltin Picture Library; astrolabe, The Granger Collection, New York; all others, Ken West Photography/Miriello Grafico, Inc.

Harcourt Brace & Company Photos:

Page number iii, 24, 25 (b), 25 (t), 28, 33, 35, 99, 219, 484–485 (bg), R7, Weronica Ankarorn 22 (fg), 25 (all), 31 (br), 34, 485 (inset) P & F Communications; 32 (bg), 414–415 (b) Victoria Bowen; 282–283 (c) (coins), 357, 419, 462, 528 Harcourt Brace & Company; 99, 161, 219, 287, 521, RX Ron Kunzman.

Contents

Page x Rob Crandall/Stock, Boston; faces: (by chapter number) Chapter 1 Sisse Brimberg/National Geographic Society; 2 Ancient Art & Architecture Collection; 3 Erich Lessing/Art Resource, NY; 4 Boltin Picture Library; 5 170 Ancient Art and Architecture Collection; 6 Burt Glinn/Magnum Photos; 7 Delphi Museum of Archaeology/Nimatallah/Art Resource, NY; 8 Napoli, Museo Nazionale/Scala/Art Resource, NY; 9 Scala/Art Resource, NY; 10 Ancient Art & Architecture Collection; 11 Richard Nowitz; 12 Oslo, Historical Museum/Knudsens-Giraudon/Art Resource, NY; 13 Scala/Art Resource, NY; 14 Musee des Arts Africaines et Oceaniens, Paris; 15; The Granger Collection; 16 Museum of National History, Buenos Aires, Argentina/G. Dagli Orti; 17 Hulton Duetsch Collection/Woodfin Camp & Associates; 18 The Granger Collection; 19 Detail, photo by Dorothea Lange, The Bettman Archive; 20 Detail, photo by Philip Jones Griffiths/Magnum Photos; 21 Mireille Vautier/Woodfin Camp & Associates; 22 Francios Perri/Cosmos/Woodfin Camp & Associates; 23 Jeremy Hartley/Panos Pictures.

Introduction

Page 22 (bg) British Library, London/ Bridgman Art Library, London/ Superstock; 23 The Granger Collection; 30 (t) Maritime Museum/Michael Holford Photographs; 30 (c) Erich Lessing/Art Resource, NY; 30 (b) Borromeo/Art Resource, NY; 31 (t) Kenneith Garrett/Woodfin Camp & Associates; 31 (bl) National Museum of American Art/ Art Resource, NY; 332 (insets left to right) Rijsmuseum van Oudheden-Egyptian Collection, Leiden, Netherlands/Erich Lessing/Art Resource, NY; 36 (t) Joachim Messerschmidt/The Stock Market; 36 (c) Nacchietto Della Rossa/Gamma Liaison; 36 (b) Joe Sohm/ChromoSohm/The Stock Market; 41 (t) Epix/Sygma Photo News; 41 (c) Jean Pragen/Tony Stone Images; 41 (b) Cheryl Sheridan/Odyssey Productions.

Unit 1

42–43 (t) Jack Unruh/© National Geographic Society; 42 (bl) Michael Holford Photographs; 42 (br) Ancient Art & Architecture Collection; 42–43 (b)(bg) Philip & Karen Smith/Tony Stone Images; 43 (bl) The British Museum; 43 (bcl) Erich Lessing/Art Resource, NY; 43 (bcr) Erich Lessing/Art Resource, NY; 43 (br) Ancient Art & Architecture Collection; 46–49 (bg) Philip & Karen Smith/Tony Stone Images; 46 F. Gohier/Photo Researchers; 47 Sisse Brimberg /National Geographic Society; 48 (t) Art Resource, NY; 48 (b) Philip & Karen Smith/Tony Stone Images; 49 Superstock; 50 Sisse Brimberg/National

Geographic Society; 51 (l) T. Anderson/Explorer; 52 (cr) Dr. Ralph Solecki/Texas A & M University; 54 (t) C M Dixon; 54 (c) Alexander Marshack; 54 (b) Boltin Picture Library; 56 C M Dixon/Photo Resources; 59 Erich Lessing/Art Resource, ny; 64 (t) C M Dixon; 67 C M Dixon; 68 C M Dixon; 72 Ancient Art & Architecture Collection; 73 British Museum/Michael Holford Photographs; 75 (t) Superstock; 76 British Museum/Michael Holford Photographs; 77 (l) Erich Lessing/Art Resource, NY; 77 (r) Erich Lessing/Art Rsource, NY; 78 Scala/Art Resource, NY; 79 British Museum/Michael Holford Photographs; 80 (t) British Museum/Michael Holford Photographs; 80 (l) Scala/Art Resource, NY; 81 Erich Lessing/Art Resource, NY; 83 Aleppo Museum, Syria/E.T. Archive; 84 Bill Aron/PhotoEdit; 85 Jewish Museum/Art Resource, NY; 86 Scala/Art Resource, NY; 88 (b) E.T. Archive; 88 (t) Ancient Art & Architecture Collection; 94–95 (bg) David W. Hamilton/The Image Bank; 94 (l) (inset) Kevin Horan/Tony Stone Images; 94 (r) (inset) Charles Gupton/Stock, Boston; 95 (l) (inset) Tony Stone Images; 95 (r) (inset) Cary Wolinsky/Stock, Boston.

Unit 2

100–101 Geoffrey Clifford/Woodfin Camp & Associates; 105 Robert Harding Picture Library; 106 Erich Lessing/Art Resource, NY; 107 Michele Burgess/The Stock Market; 108 Michael Holford Photographs; 109 The British Museum/Michael Holford Photographs; 110 (t) The British Museum/Michael Holford Photographs; 110 (b) The British Museum/Michael Holford Photographs; 112 Erich Lessing/Art Resource, NY; 113 (bg) Scala/Art Resource, NY; 99 (fg) The Louvre/Reunion des Musées Nationaux; 114 Robert Hashimoto/The Art Institute of Chicago; 115 Robert Frerck/Woodfin Camp & Associates; 117 Erich Lessing/Art Resource, NY; 118 Adam Woolfitt/Robert Harding Picture Library; 121 The Louvre/Reunion des Musées Nationaux; 122 Superstock; 123 Scala/Art Resource, NY; 124 The Metropolitan Museum of Art, Rogers Fund, 1931. (31.3.166)" copyright, 1995"; 125 Museum Expedition/Museum of Fine Arts, Boston; 126 Copyright 1978 Egyptian Expedition of the Metropolitan Museum of Art, Rogers Fund, 1930 (detail) No. 30.4.21; 127 Borromeo/Art Resource, NY; 128 Museum Expedition/Museum of Fine Arts, Boston, detail, fig. of Frederick Chase; 129 Museum Expedition/Museum of Fine Arts, Boston; 130 Oriental Institute Museum of the University of Chicago; 130–131 Rober Caputo/Aurora; 134 Boltin Picture Library; 135 Jehangir Gazdar/Woodfin Camp & Associates; 137 Borromeo/Art Resource, NY; 138 (l) Jehangir Gazdar/Woodfin

Camp & Associates; 138 (r) Jehangir Gazdar/Woodfin Camp & Associates; 139 (l) Harappa Museum/Robert Harding Picture Library; 139 (r) Karachi Museum/Robert Harding Library; 140 Art Resource; NY; 142 E.T. Archive; 143 (t) Tim Megarry/Robert Harding Picture Library; 143 (b) Werner Forman/Art Resource, NY; 144 Hermitage Museum, Leningrad/C M Dixon; 148 John Elk III/Bruce Coleman, Inc.; 149 (r) Boltin Picture Library; 149 (l) Andrew Rakoczy/Bruce Coleman, Inc.; 150 (b) D. Newman/Superstock; 150 (inset) Robert Frerck/Odyssey Productions, Chicago; 152 Jurgen Liepe; 153 (l) Boltin Picture Library; 153 (r) Department of Asian Art, Metropolitan Museum of Art, NY, on behalf of the Cultural Relics Bureau, Beijing, China; 156–157 (bg) Paul Solomon/Woodfin Camp & Associates; 157 (t)(inset) Elie S. Rogers/National Geographic Society; 157 (b)(inset) Mike Yamashita/Woodfin Camp & Associates.

Unit 3

162–163 Bibliotheque Nationale, Paris, France/Giraudon/Art Resource, NY; 170 Ancient Art and Architecture Collection; 171 The Nelson Atkins Museum of Art, Kansas City, Missouri (Purchase: Nelson Trust) 33–81; 172 Maria Antoinette Evans Fund/Museum of Fine Arts, Boston; 173 (l) British Museum/Michael Holford Photographs; 173 (r) Robert Harding Picture Library; 174 (l) The Granger Collection; 174 (r) Ancient Art & Architecture Collection; 177 Ancient Art and Architecture Collection; 178 Bibliotheque Nationale, Paris/E.T. Archive; 179 James Montgomery/Bruce Coleman, Inc.; 180 Ancient Art & Architecture Collection; 181 Wang Lu/ChinaStock Photo Library; 182 Boston Museum of Fine Art/Scala/Art Resource, NY; 185 (t) ChinaStock Photo Library; 185 (b) The Nelson Atkins Museum of Art, Kansas City, Missouri (Purchase: Nelson Trust) 33–521; 186 China Pictorial; 190 Burt Glinn/Magnum Photos; 191 Boltin Picture Library; 193 (t) Giraudon/Art Resource, NY; 177 (bl) Ravi Shekhar/Dinodia Picture Agency; 177 (br) Museo Nazionale d'Arte Orientale, Rome, Italy/Scala/Art Resource, NY; 194 (l) Borromeo/Art Resource, NY; 194 (r) G.C. Patel/Dinodia Picture Agency; 197 Robert Frerck/Odyssey Productions, Chicago; 203 Ancient Art & Architecture Collection; 204 (t) Adam Woolfitt/Woodfin Camp & Associates; 204 (b) Adam Woolfitt/Woodfin Camp & Associates; 205 Calcutta Indian Museum/Scala/Art Resource, NY; 206 (bg) Dinodia Picture Agency; 206 (inset) Ancient Art & Architecture Collection; 207 Viren Desai/Dinodia Picture Agency; 208 Louvre, Dept. des Antiquites Orientales, Paris France/Erich Lessing/Art Resource, NY; 210 (bg) Giraudon/Art Resource, NY; 210 (inset) SEF/Art Resource, NY; 211 (l)

British Museum/C M Dixon; 211 (r) Ancient Art & Architecture Collection; 214–215 (t) Francene Keery/Stock, Boston; 214–215 (c) Tim Barnwell/Stock, Boston; 214–215 (b) Phyllis Picardi/Stock, Boston; 214 (inset) Robert Brenner/PhotoEdit; 215 (tl) Mark C. Burnet/Stock, Boston; 215 (tr) Jeff Greenberg/Photo Researchers; 215 Don Farber/Woodfin /Camp & Associates.

Unit 4

220–221 Archaeological Museum, Herakleion, Crete/Scala/Art Resource, NY; 228 Delphi Museum of Archaeology/ Nimatallah/Art Resource, NY; 229 Robert Frerck/The Stock Market; 230 Heraklion Museum/Robert Harding Picture Library; 231 (t) Michael Holford Photographs; 231 (b) S. Vidler/Superstock; 232 (t) C M Dixon; 232 (c) The British Museum/Michael Holford Photographs; 232 (b) The British Museum/Michael Holford Photographs; 233 Athens National Museum/Nimatallah/Art Resource, NY; 234 Louvre, Dept. des Antiquites Grecques et Romaines, Paris, France/Erich Lessing/ Art Resource, NY; 235 The British Museum/Michael Holford Photographs; 236 Jose Fuste Raga/The Stock Market; 237 National Museum, Warsaw, Poland/ Erich Lessing/Art Resource, NY; 238 (t) The British Museum/Michael Holford Photographs; 238 (b) Archaeological Museum Ferrara/E.T. Archive; 239 Louvre, Paris/Giraudon/Art Resource, NY; 240 The British Museum/Michael Holford Photographs; 242 Richard Steedman/the Stock Market; 243 Superstock; 244 Museo Capitolino, Rome/Superstock; 245 (t) Louvre, Dept. des Antiquites Grecques/ Romaines, Paris, France/Erich Lessing/ Art Resource, NY; 247 Louvre, Dept. des Antiquities Grecques/Romaines, Paris, France/Erich Lessing/Art Resource, NY; 248 (bg) Scala/Art Resource, NY; 248 (inset) Thessalonike Museum/Art Resource, NY; 249 Copyright British Museum; 250 (t) Istanbul Museum of Archaeology/Scala/Art Resource, NY; 250 (b) Victoria and Albert Museum/C M Dixon; 251 Robert Frerck/Odyssey Productions, Chicago; 254 Napoli, Museo Nazionale/Scala/Art Resource, NY; 255 Museo Nazionale/Scala/Art Resource, NY; 259 Louvre, Dept. des Antiquites Grecques/Romaines, Paris, France/Erich Lessing/Art Resource, NY; 258 Ronald Sheridan/Ancient Art & Architecture Collection; 259 British Museum/Michael Holford Photographs; 260 Vatican Museum-Lazio/John G. Ross/Robert Harding Picture Library; 261 Scala/Art Resource; 263 (l) Erich Lessing/Art Resource, NY; 263 (r) Erich Lessing/Art Resource, NY; 264 (r) Mike Yamashita/ Woodfin Camp & Associates; 264 (tl) Michael Holford Photographs; 264 (bl) Dan Budnik/Woodfin Camp & Associates; 265

(t) Adam Woolfitt/Woodfin Camp & Associates; 265 (b) National Museum, Athens/Robert Harding Picture Library; 268 (inset), 269 (t), 269 (b), 271, Harcourt Brace & Company/John Gibbons Studio, object courtesy the Ermine Street Guard; 272 British Museum/Michael Holford Photographs; 273 Museo Rio Christiano, Vatican/Scala/Art Resource, NY; 275 (bg) Galleria Centrale al l'piano, Roma/Scala/Art Resource, NY; 275 (t)(inset) Scala/Art Resource, NY; 275 (b)(inset) Vatican Museum/C M Dixon/Photo Resources; 276 (t) The Terry Wild Studio; 276 (b) Betty Press/Woodfin Camp & Associates; 282–283 (t) James Blank/The Stock Market; 282–283 (b) Duomo Photography; 283 (b) Duomo Photography; 283 (b) Catherine Ursillo/Photo Researchers.

Unit 5

288–289 (t) Robert Frerck/Odyssey Productions, Chicago; 288 (bl) Erich Lessing/Art Resource, NY; 288 (bc) Superstock; 288 (br) Victoria and Albert Museum/Michael Holford Photographs; 289 (bl) The Granger Collection; 289 (br) Robert Frerck/Odyssey Productions, Chicago; 293 (t) Cahokia Mounds, Illinois State Historic Site; 293 (b) Cahokia Mounds, Illinois State Historic Site; 295 Illinois Transportation Archaeological Research Program, University of Illinois, Urbana; 296 Scala/Art Resource, NY; 297 Werner Forman Archive/Thessalonicki Archaeological Museum/Art Resource, NY; 299 (t) Scala/Art Resource, NY; 299 (b) Robert Frerck/Odyssey Productions, Chicago; 299 (inset) Roland & Sabrina Michaud/Woodfin Camp & Associates; 300 Erich Lessing/Art Resource, NY; 301 E.T. Archive; 302 Hungarian National Museum, Budapest, Hungary/Scala/Art Resource, NY; 303 Robert Azzi/Woodfin Camp & Associates; 304 (l) The British Museum/Michael Holford Photographs; 304 (r) E.T. Archive; 306 (r) Superstock; 306 (l) Robert Frerck/Woodfin Camp & Associates; 307 Michael Pasdzior/The Image Bank; 308 C M Dixon; 309 E.T. Archive; 310 Scala/Art Resource, NY; 311 (tl) Scala/Art Resource, NY; 311 (tr) Scala/Art Resource, NY; 312 (t) Michael Howell/Superstock; 312 (b) Sonia Halliday Photographs; 312 (inset) The British Museum/E.T. Archive; 315 The Granger Collection; 317 The World Almanac and Book of Facts 1996, copyright 1995 Funk & Wagnalls Corporation. All rights reserved; 318 The Granger Collection; 323 (t) Museum del'Armee/Robert Harding Picture Library; 323 (b) Robert Harding Picture Library; 326 Ancient Art & Architecture Collection; 327 E.T. Archive; 328 Wang Lu/ChinaStock Photo Library; 329 (tl) Wolfgang Kaehler Photography; 329 (tr) Art Resource, NY; 330 National

Palace Museum, Taiwan/E.T. Archive; 331 Rob Kendrick; 332 Werner Forman Archive/Imperial Library, Tehran/Art Resource, NY; 334 (l) E.T. Archive; 334 (r) Giraudon/Art Resource, NY; 335 Ancient Art & Architecture Collection; 336 E.T. Archive; 337 E.T. Archive; 338 Ancient Art & Architecture Collection; 340 Victoria and Albert Museum/Michael Holford Photographs; 341 Michael Holford Photographs; 342 National Museum of Anthropology, Mexico City, Mexico/Michael Zabe/Art Resource, NY; 343 (l) Robert Frerck/Woodfin Camp & Associates; 343 (r) Lenars, Explorer/Mary Evans Picture Library; 344 National Geographic painting by Felipe Davalos/National Geographic Society; 345 (t) Martin Rogers/Woodfin Camp & Associates; 345 (c) Michael Holford Photographs; 345 (b) Robert Frerck/ Odyssey Productions, Chicago; 346 Dumbarton Oaks Research Library Collections, Washington, D.C.; 347 David Muench; 352–353 (fg) John Chaisson/Gamma Liaison; 352 (t) "World Peace" by Samrat Chatterjee, age 12, India, courtesy of the International Children's Art Museum/Paintbrush Diplomacy; 352 (b) Robert Wallis/SABA Press; 353 (t) Mending the World, Anna Akeenoba, 16, Russia, Courtesy of the International Children's Art Museum; 353 (b) David Silverman/Reuters/Corbis-Bettman.

Unit 6

358–359 (t) ChinaStock Photo Library; 358 (bl) Historical Museum, Stockholm, Giraudon/Art Resource, NY; 358 (br) C M Dixon; 359 (bl) Collection Musée d l'Homme, Paris; 359 (bc) Giraudon/Art Resource, NY 359 (br) ChinaStock Photo Library; 362 Bibliotheque Nationale, Paris (detail); 364 Richard Nowitz; 365 Museum of Mankind (British Museum)/Michael Holford Photographs; 366 (l) Geoff Renner/Robert Harding Picture Library; 366 (c) Michael Fogden/DRK; 366 (r) T.A. Wiewandt/DRK; 368 (l) Collection Musée de 'Homme, Paris; 368 (r) Collection Musée de 'Homme, Paris; 369 Bibliotheque Nationale, Paris; 370 Photograph copyright The Detroit Institute of Arts, 1995 Founders Society Purchase, Eleanor Clay Ford Fund for African Art; 371 (l) Ronald Sheridan/ Ancient Art & Architecture Collection; 371 (r) Werner Forman Archive/Art Resource, NY; 375 Michael Holford Photographs; 377 (l) Jean-Loup CHARMET; 377 (tr) Arabic ms. of De Materia Medica Baghdad/The Granger Collection; 377 (b) The Granger Collection; 379 (l) Ancient Art & Architecture Collection; 379 (r) Ancient Art & Architecture Collection; 380 (l) Sonia Halliday Photographs; 380 (r) Ronald Sheridan/Ancient Art & Architecture Collection; 390 Oslo, Historical Museum/ Knudsens-Giraudon/Art Resource, NY; 391

Sonia Halliday Photographs; 392 (t) Wendy Stone/Odyssey, Chicago; 392 (b) Ronald Sheridan/Ancient Art & Architecture Collection; 392 (r)(inset) ChinaStock Photo Library; 393 ChinaStock Photo Library; 394 Philadelphia Museum of Art: Given by John T. Dorrance; 395 (inset) Naomi Peck/Robert Harding Picture Library; 395 M.P. Kahl/DRK; 396 (l) British Museum/Werner Forman Archive/Art Resource, NY; 396 (r) Diozescanmuseum Trier/E.T. Archive; 398 (l) Museo degli Argenti, Palazzo Pitti, Florence, Italy/Art Resource, NY; 398 (r) Correr Museum, Venice/E.T. Archive; 402 Historical Museum, Stockholm/Giraudon/Art Resource, NY; 403 (l) Richard Nowitz; 403 (r) C M Dixon; 404 The Granger Collection; 406 (t) Helge Ingstad; 406 (b) Helge Ingstad; 407 Guido Alberto Rossi/The Image Bank; 408 ChinaStock Photo Library; 409 Tom Till/DRK; 411 (l) Ron Testa/The Field Museum, Chicago, Neg. #A107959C; 411 (r) Wolfgang Kaehler Photography; 414–415 (bg) Corel; 414 Bob Daimmrich Photography/Stock, Boston; 415 (t) Will & Deni McIntyre/Photo Researchers.

Unit 7

420–421 (t) Scala/Art Resource, NY; 420 (bl) E.T. Archive; 420 (br) The Granger Collection; 421 (bl) Boltin Picture Library; 421 (br) C M Dixon; 424 Scala/Art Resource, NY; 425 Copyright, 1989, Malcolm Varon, NYC/The Metropolitan Museum of Art, Fletcher Fund, and Bequest of Miss Adelaide Milton de Groot (1867–1967), by exchange, supplemented by gifts from friends of the Museum, 1971 (1971.86); 426 Prado, Madrid/E.T. Archive; 427 Museo del Prado, Madrid, Spain/Erich Lessing/Art Resource, NY; 428 Scala/Art Resource, NY; 429 Musee Rheinisches Landesmuseum/Giraudon/Art Resource, NY; 430 Basel Museum of Fine Arts/ SEF/Art Resource, NY; 431 Vatican Museum & Galleries, Rome/Scala/ Superstock; 432 (tr) Giraudon/Art Resource, NY; 432 (b) Scala/Art Resource, NY; 433 (l) The Granger Collection; 432 (r) Jean-Loup CHARMET; 434 (t) Erich Lessing/Art Resource, NY; 434 (b) E.T. Archive; 435 E.T. Archive; 436 The Granger Collection; 437 Bridgeman/Art Resource, NY; 438 (t) Alinari/Art Resource, NY; 438 (b) Foto Marburg/Art Resource, NY; 440 The Bettmann Archive; 441 Sonia Halliday Photographs; 442 (l) Jean-Loup CHARMET; 442 (r) Michael Holford Photographs; 443 The Granger Collection; 444 (t) Museo Navale dei Pegli Genova/Scala/Art Resource, NY; 444 (b) The Granger Collection; 445 (l) Michael Holford Photographs; 445 (r) C M Dixon; 448 Musee des Arts Africaines et Oceaniens, Paris; 449 Boltin Picture Library; 450 (t) The British Museum/Michael Holford

Photographs; 450 (b) Boltin Picture Library; 451 (t) The British Museum/J.R. Freeman/Robert Harding Picture Library; 451 (b) The Granger Collection; 452 The Granger Collection; 455 Werner Forman Archive/Art Resource, NY; 456 Boltin Picture Library; 457 E.T. Archive; 466 (t) Antonio Mercado/Art Resource, NY; 457 (b) National Collection of Fine Arts, Smithsonian Institution/Robert Harding Picture Library; 470 The Granger Collection; 471 British Museum/C M Dixon; 472 (l) E.T. Archive; 472 (r) Musée Guimet, Paris/G. Dagli Orti; 474 Ueno, Ninja Museum/Werner Forman/Art Resource, NY; 475 Paris Collection, Paris/G. Dagli Orti; 46 Topkapi Palace Museum, Istanbul/Sonia Halliday Photographs; 477 (l) G. Dagli Orti; 477 (r) Giraudon/Art Resource, NY; 479 (t) Michael Holford Photographs; 479 (b) Boltin Picture Library; 480 Chris Haigh/Tony Stone Images.

Unit 8

490–491 (t) The Granger Collection; 490 (b) The Granger Collection; 491 (bl) Mus. Nat. de la Legion d'Honneur/Lauros-Giraudon/Art Resource, NY; 491 (br) The Granger Collection; 495 Clich'e Museum, Paris/Jean-Loup CHARMET; 497 Musée de Louvre, Paris/AKG, Berlin/Superstock; 498 Museum of National History, Buenos Aires, Argentina/G. Dagli Orti; 499 The Granger Collection; 500 The Granger Collection; 500 Ed Wheeler/The Stock Market; 500 Giraudon/Art Resource, NY; 501 The Granger Collection; 502 Musée de Carnavalet, Paris/G. Dagli Orti; 503 G. Dagli Orti; 503 (inset) The Granger Collection; 503 (inset) Erich Lessing/Musee Carnavalet, Paris, France; 505 (l) E.T. Archive; 505 (r) Musée Malmaison/E.T. Archive; 505 (inset) E.T. Archive; 506 (t) Courtesy, Museum of Fine Arts, Boston, Babcock Bequest; 506 (b) The Granger Collection; 507 The Granger Collection; 508 (t) Museo de America, Madrid/E.T. Archive; 508 (b) Robert Frerck/Odyssey Productions, Chicago; 508 (b)(inset) Robert Frerck/Odyssey Productions, Chicago; 509 E.T. Archive; 510 (l)(inset) E.T. Archive; 510 (r) Museu Nacional de Historia, Peru/E.T. Archive; 511 The Granger Collection; 514 Hulton Deutsch Collection/Woodfin Camp & Associates; 515 Mary Evans Picture Library; 516 (l) The Granger Collection; 516 (r)(inset) The Mansell Collection Limited; 517 Jean-Loup CHARMET; 519 (l) Mary Evans Picture Library; 519 (r)(inset) Hulton Deutsch Collection Limited/Woodfin Camp & Associates; 522 The Granger Collection; 522–523 The Granger Collection; 524–525 The Granger Collection; 526 British Museum/Michael Holford Photographs; 527 Mary Evans Picture Library; 528 Victoria & Albert Museum,

London/Art Resource, NY; 528 (inset) Aldo Tutino/Art Resource, NY; 529 (l) The Granger Collection; 529 (r) The Granger Collection; 530 (b) The Mansell Collection Limited; 530 (tl) The Granger Collection; 530 (tr) The Bettmann Archive; 531 (l) The Granger Collection; 531 (r) Archive Photos; 534 The Granger Collection; 535 The Granger Collection; 536 Jean-Loup CHARMET; 537 Risorgimento Museum, Milan/Scala/Art Resource, NY; 538 Mary Evans Picture Library; 539 (l) The British Museum/E.T. Archive; 539 (r) Christie's Images; 540 Courtesy of The Mariner's Museum, Newport News, Virginia; 541 Franklin D. Roosevelt Library; 542 City Museum, Copenhagen/E.T. Archive; 543 E.T. Archive; 544 (t) The Granger Collection; 544 (b) The Granger Collection; 545 Jean-Loup CHARMET; 547 E.T. Archive; 549 (t) E.T. Archive; 549 (b) The Granger Collection; 552–553 (bg) Telegraph Colour Library/FPG International; 552 (bl) NASA; 552 (tl) Ted Soqui/Sygma Photo News; 553 (tl) M. Tcherevkoff/The Image Bank; 553 (c) UPI/Corbis-Bettmann; 553 (br) IBM Zurich Research Laboratory.

Unit 9

558–559 (t) P.J. Griffiths/Magnum Photos; 558 (bl) The Granger Collection; 558 (br) The Granger Collection; 559 (b) Peter Marlow/Magnum Photos; 562 Musée d'Orsay, Paris, France/Erich Lessing/Art Resource, NY; 563 Musée d'Orsay, Paris, France/Erich Lessing/Art Resource, NY; 564 Detail, photo by Dorothea Lange, The Bettman Archive; 565 Erich Lessing/Art Resource, NY; 566 The Bettmann Archive; 567 (l) Scala/Art Resource, NY; 567 (r) The Granger Collection; 568 (l) The Bettmann Archive; 568 (r)(inset) Culver Pictures; 569 (l) The Bettmann Archive, 569 (r) The Bettmann Archive; 571 The Bettmann Archive; 574 Christies, London/Superstock; 575 (tl) Giraudon/Art Resource, NY; 575 (tr) Giraudon/Art Resource, NY; 575 (b) Itar-Tass/Sovfoto; 576 (tl) The Granger Collection; 576 (tr) Scala/Art Resource, NY; 576 (b) Museo Statale Russo/Scala/Art Resource, NY; 578 Ria Novosti/Sovfoto; 578 (inset) Pierre Vauthey/Sygma Photos News; 579 The Bettmann Archive; 580 The Bettmann Archive; 581 The Bettmann Archive; 582 (t) The Granger Collection; 582 (b) The Bettmann Archive; 583 The Bettmann Archive; 586 Detail, photo by Philip Jones Griffiths/Magnum Photos; 587 The Bettmann Archive; 588 Hulton Deutsch/

Woodfin Camp & Associates; 588 (inset) Corbis Bettmann; 589 (l) Reuters/The Bettmann Archvie; 589 (c) Robert Capa/Magnum Photos; 589 (r) The Granger Collection; 591 (t) The Bettmann Archive; 591 (b) The Bettmann Archive; News; 594 The Bettmann Archive; 602 Library of Congress; 604 Ed Hoffman, Acme, UPI/Bettmann; 605 (t) Keystone/Hulton Deutsch/Woodfin Camp & Associates; 605 (b) Dan Budnik/Woodfin Camp & Associates; 606 Kyoicki Sawada/UPI/The Bettmann Archive; 607 (t) Kyoicki Sawada, UPI/The Bettmann Archive; 607 (c) P. Jones Griffith/Magnum Photos; 607 (b) Sara Matthews/Swathmore College Peace Collection; 608 Peter Marlow/Magnum Photos; 608 (inset) Tommy Thompson/Black Star; 609 (l) Yousuf Karsh/Woodfin Camp & Associates; 609 (r) Erich Lessing/Magnum Photos; 612–613 (b)(fg) Mike Goldwater-Network-Matrix; 612 (fg) Steve McCurry/Magnum Photos; 612 (l) R. Maiman/Sygma Photo News; 612 (r) Sandra Baker/Liaison International; 613 (l) Sandra Baker/Liaison International; 613 (c) Everett C. Johnson/Folio; 613 (r) Sandra Baker/Liaison International.

Unit 10

618–619 (t) Ed Nachtrieb/The Bettmann Archive; 518 (bl) Susan Mcelhinney/Woodfin Camp & Associates; 618 (br) A. Nogues/Sygma; 619 (bl) J. Langevin/Sygma Photo News; 619 (br) Wide World Photos; 622 (t) Alexandra Avakian/Woodfin Camp & Associates; 622 (b) Patrick Piel/Gamma Liaison; 623 (inset) Chip Hires/Gamma Liaison; 623 Eric Bouvet/Gamma Liaison; 624 Mireille Vautier/Woodfin Camp & Associates; 625 Bettmann/Hulton/Woodfin Camp & Associates; 626 (l) Sovfoto; 626 (r) New China Pictures/Eastfoto; 629 Chris Stowers/Panos Pictures; 632 Tony Stone Images, 633 Tom Wagner/Odyssey Productions, Chicago; 634 Kim Newton/Woodfin Camp & Associates; 636 Tom Wagner/SABA; 636 (inset) Wide World Photos; 638 D. Donne Bryant; 640 Alain Keler/Sygma; 641 Susan Meiselas/Magnum Photos; 642 (l) Luiz C. Marigo/Peter Arnold, Inc.; 642 (r) David R. Frazier/Tony Stone Images; 643 (t) Mireille Vautier/Woodfin Camp & Associates; 643 (b) Will & Deni Mcintyre/Photo Researchers; 644 (t) Wolfgang Kaehler Photography; 644 (b) Mireille Vautier/Woodfin Camps & Associates; 645 (l) Wolfgang Kaehler Photography;

645 (r) Mireille Vautier/Woodfin Camp & Associates; 646 The Bettmann Archive; 647 (t) Robert Mackinlay/Peter Arnold, Inc.; 647 (b) Tibor Bognar/The Stock Market; 649 (l) Robert Frerck/Odyssey/The Stock Market; 649 (r) Bob Daemmrich/Uniphoto; 650 Al Stephens/Woodfin Camp & Associates; 651 (t) David Sams/Sipa Press; 651 (b) Al Stephens/Woodfin Camp & Associates; 654 Francios Perri/Cosmos/ Woodfin Camp & Associates; 655 Brown Brothers; 656 The Bettmann Archive; 657 Wide World Photos; 658 (l) Baldev/Sygma; 658 (r) Jehangir Gazdar/Woodfin Camp & Associates; 659 Victoria Brynner/Gamma Liaison; 659 Baldev/Sygma Photo News; 662 Jeff Dunn/Stock, Boston; 664 (ACME)/The Bettmann Archive; 665 The Bettmann Archive; 667 Ron Edmonds/Wide World Photos; 668 (l) M. Philippot/Sygma; 668 (r)(inset) Olivier Rebbot/Woodfin Camp & Associates; 669 (tl) Eric Bouvet/Gamma Liaison; 669 (b)(inset) B. Markel/Gamma Liaison; 669 (t)(inset) CNN International/Gamma Liaison; 672 Jeremy Hartley/Panos Pictures; 673 Hulton Deutsch Collection/Woodfin 674 (l) Betty Press/Woodfin Camp & Associates; 674 (r) Betty Press/Woodfin Camp & Associates; 676 Alon Reininger/Woodfin Camp & Associates; 677 (t) Brooks Kraft/Sygma; 677 (bl) Broods Kraft/Sygma; 677 (br) Jon Jones/Sygma; 678 Charles Platiau Reuter/The Bettmann Archive; 684 Chuck Nacke/Woodfin Camp & Associates; 685 Fabrizio Bensch/Archive Photos; 686 (t) Michael Springer/Gamma Liaison; 686 (b) Klaus Reisinger/Black Star; 687 Jeremy Nicholl/Matrix Int'l.; 688 (l) S. Morgan-Spooner/Gamma Liaison; 688 (t) Enrico Dagino/Woodfin Camp & Associates; 688 (b) Ar Zamur/Gamma Liaison; 690 NASA Electronic Image/Wide World Photos; 690 Jacques Langevin/Sygma Photos; 691 Wide World Photos; 694–695 (bg) Douglas Struthers/ Tony Stone Images; 695 (t) AP/Wide World Photos; 695 (c) Romeo Ranoco/Reuters/Archive Photos; 695 (b) Jim Hollander/Reuters/Archive Photos.

Reference

Reference content Pages; Michael Holford Photographs; R1 (t) Science Museum, London/Michael Holford Photographs; R1 (bl) John M. Roberts/The Stock Market; R1 (br) Pierre Boulat/COS/Woodfin Camp & Associates; R8 Bob Daemmrich.